KU-308-121

KARL MARX
FREDERICK ENGELS

COLLECTED WORKS

VOLUME

11

KARL MARX
FREDERICK ENGELS

COLLECTED
WORKS

LAWRENCE & WISHART

LONDON

KARL MARX
FREDERICK ENGELS

Volume
11

MARX AND ENGELS: 1851-53

POLYTECHNIC LIBRARY
WOLVERHAMPTON

ACC. No. 553440 | CLASS

CONTROL | 335·4 MAR

DATE 19 APR 1982 | SITE RS

1979

LAWRENCE & WISHART

LONDON

This volume has been prepared jointly by Lawrence & Wishart Ltd., London, International Publishers Co. Inc., New York, and Progress Publishers, Moscow, in collaboration with the Institute of Marxism-Leninism, Moscow.

Editorial commissions:

GREAT BRITAIN: Jack Cohen, Maurice Cornforth, E. J. Hobsbawm, Nicholas Jacobs, Martin Milligan, Ernst Wangermann.
USA: James S. Allen, Louis Diskin, Philip S. Foner, Dirk J. Struik, William W. Weinstone.
USSR: for Progress Publishers—N. P. Karmanova, V. I. Neznanov, V. N. Sedikh, M. K. Shcheglova; for the Institute of Marxism-Leninism— P. N. Fedoseyev, L. I. Golman, A. I. Malysh, M. P. Mchedlov, A. G. Yegorov.

Copyright © Progress Publishers, Moscow, 1979

All rights reserved. Apart from any fair dealing for the purpose of private study research, criticism, or review, no part of this publication may be reproduced, stored in a retrieval system, or transmitted, in any form or by any means, electronic, electrical, chemical, mechanical, optical, photocopying, recording or otherwise, without the prior permission of the copyright owner.

ISBN 0 85315 356 6

Printed in the Union of Soviet Socialist Republics in 1978

Contents

KARL MARX AND FREDERICK ENGELS
WORKS

August 1851-March 1853

Contents VII

ILLUSTRATIONS

TRANSLATORS:

CLEMENS DUTT: Articles 2, 8; From the Preparatory
   Materials 38; Appendices 41

RODNEY LIVINGSTONE: Articles 9, 24

CHRISTOPHER UPWARD: Articles 4, 7; Appendices
   43, 44

Preface

Volume 11 of the *Collected Works* of Marx and Engels covers the period from August 1851 to March 1853, when the forces of reaction were consolidating their hold throughout Europe. The revolution in Germany and Italy had already been defeated in 1849. Louis Napoleon's coup d'état of December 2, 1851 came as a climax to the development of the counter-revolution in France, putting an end to the Second Republic, which had still retained at least some democratic institutions, and creating the Bonapartist monarchy, another bulwark of reaction in Europe and a hotbed of international conflict and military escapades. There was little prospect of a fresh revolutionary outbreak, such as had been possible during the first few months after the defeat of the German, Hungarian and Italian revolutionary movements. The counter-revolutionary order had now, at least for a time, become established.

Under these conditions, Marx and Engels found it essential to continue the theoretical generalisation of the experience of the 1848 revolution, which they had begun immediately after its rearguard battles. In particular, they set out to examine the reasons for the temporary triumph of the counter-revolutionary forces and to analyse the historical developments over the last few years.

Marxist thinking rose to new heights in this analytical and generalising work, exemplified by many of the writings included in this volume, above all by such masterpieces as *The Eighteenth Brumaire of Louis Bonaparte* by Marx and *Revolution and Counter-Revolution in Germany* by Engels.

Marx also intensified his economic researches, interrupted by the revolution of 1848-49. The present volume includes conclusions he drew in the course of these researches in his journalistic writings for the working-class and progressive bourgeois press. Engels, for his part, realising the importance of armed struggle in the forthcoming revolutionary battles, immersed himself in studying the art of war. Several pieces indicative of his military studies are included in this volume.

Particularly important among the practical activities of Marx and Engels were their efforts to preserve, and to educate and rally the proletarian revolutionary cadres, and to protect those among them who had become victims of police persecution. The Cologne trial of Communist League members in Germany was a very severe test for the Communists.

The volume opens with Engels' *Revolution and Counter-Revolution in Germany*, which deals with the causes, nature and motive forces of the 1848-49 revolution in Germany and reaches a whole series of important political conclusions. Drawing on the assessments already arrived at by Marx and himself in the *Neue Rheinische Zeitung*, Engels developed them into a self-consistent account of the successive features characteristic of the key stages of the revolutionary process in the German states. He threw fresh light on the international significance of the revolution in Germany by disclosing its ties with events in other European countries, especially France, at the same time explaining the influence of the June 1848 uprising of the Paris proletariat on the situation in Germany. This laid the foundation for every subsequent Marxist analysis of the history of the German bourgeois-democratic revolution.

Engels examines the economic basis for the political events. He gives a vivid and accurate analysis of the level of Germany's economic and social development at that time, the class relations and the deployment of political forces. He stresses the role of the class struggle in historical development, demonstrates the inevitability of revolutions and describes them as "a powerful agent of social and political progress" (see this volume, p. 32).

Engels shows that the German revolution was defeated because the liberal bourgeoisie, alarmed by the scale of the revolutionary movement, betrayed the people and the cause of democracy and rushed into a compromise with the forces of feudal-Junker reaction. The petty bourgeoisie, who then found themselves at the head of the revolutionary masses, fell prey to vacillation and indecision at crucial moments. Blindly trusting the power of parliamentary institutions, they were afraid to rely, instead, on the people and unleash its revolutionary energies. At this stage, the proletariat was not yet sufficiently developed and organised to take its place at the head of the movement. Nevertheless, in the course of the revolution, it "represented the real and well-understood interest of the nation at large" (p. 88).

Engels concludes that bold and resolute action is essential for the victory of revolution. "In revolution, as in war," he wrote, "it is always necessary to show a strong front, and he who attacks is in the advantage; and in revolution, as in war, it is of the highest necessity to stake everything on the decisive moment, whatever the odds may be. There is not a single successful revolution in history that does not prove the truth of these axioms" (p. 68).

This work lays down basic principles of Marxist teaching on armed insurrection. Engels formulates for the first time the idea that "insurrection is an art quite as much as war" (p. 85). He gives a list of the basic rules by which insurgents should be guided. As Lenin was to stress, this text "summed up the lessons of all revolutions with respect to armed uprising" (*Collected Works*, Vol. 26, p. 180).

A substantial part of the work is devoted to the national question, which Engels examines from a revolutionary and internationalist standpoint. He denounces the policy of national oppression pursued by the Hohenzollerns and the Habsburgs, and declares that to grant independence to the oppressed peoples—the Poles, the Hungarians, the Italians, and others—is one of the most important tasks of the bourgeois-democratic revolution.

In this work, as in a series of articles published during the revolutionary period in the *Neue Rheinische Zeitung* (see present edition, Vols. 7-9), Engels examines the question of the national movement of the Slavs in the Austrian Empire. In the first stage of the 1848-49 revolution, when revolutionary-democratic trends were active in the national movement of the Czechs and other Slav peoples under the Habsburgs (the Prague uprising in June 1848, mass anti-feudal demonstrations in the countryside), Marx and Engels expressed great sympathy for the struggle of these peoples, since it coincided with the interests of the entire European revolutionary movement. In the movement of the Czechs and a number of South-Slav peoples, however, the upper hand was later gained by Right-wing bourgeois and feudal-clerical elements who entered into a compact with the ruling circles of the Habsburg monarchy, and this enabled the latter to use the military formations of the South Slavs against the Hungarian revolution and the revolutionary movement in Austria and Italy. The Czech and South-Slav deputies of the Austrian Imperial Diet came out in support of the Habsburg monarchy against revolutionary Hungary and the Vienna October uprising, and also against the abolition of feudal exactions without compensation. As a result of this, Marx and Engels, who had always seen the national question from the viewpoint of the interests of the revolution as a whole, changed their attitude to these national movements. "It was for this reason, and exclusively for this reason," as Lenin later explained, "that Marx and Engels were opposed to the national movement of the Czechs and South Slavs" (*Collected Works*, Vol. 22, p. 340).

But if this general assessment of the Slav national movements in the specific conditions of 1848-49 was justified, *Revolution and Counter-Revolution in Germany* also contains certain inaccurate forecasts. Engels thought that some of the Slav peoples had lost their capacity for independent national existence and would inevitably be absorbed by their more powerful neighbours. And this idea was tied up with his general views on the role of small nations in history. Engels considered that the creation of large states, the main tendency under capitalism, leads to the absorption of small nations by big nations. He did not, however, make due allowance—and, indeed, the historical experience was still inadequate—for another fact: the irrepressible struggle of small nations against national oppression and for independence, their strivings to create their own states. It is this which led to the final result that, in the course of their independent development, the Slav peoples of the former Austrian Empire created their own independent states and then entered the front ranks in the fight for socialism.

This volume includes one of Marx's most outstanding works, *The Eighteenth Brumaire of Louis Bonaparte*. A profound analysis of the historical events and far-reaching theoretical conclusions are cast in unsurpassed literary form which, in the words of Wilhelm Lieb-knecht, "combines the indignant severity of a Tacitus with the deadly satire of a Juvenal and the holy wrath of a Dante" (*Reminiscences of Marx and Engels*, Moscow, 1957, p. 103).

In subject-matter and in conclusions alike, *The Eighteenth Brumaire of Louis Bonaparte* is a direct sequel to *The Class Struggles in France, 1848 to 1850*. It would however be wrong to assume that *The Eighteenth Brumaire of Louis Bonaparte* is merely a continuation of the narrative part of that work which takes up the analysis of events from November 1850 to December 1851. Those events, as Marx shows, were the climax to a whole period of French history, and they enabled him to characterise it in full and draw important conclusions about the results and prospects of the French revolutionary movement.

Although Marx's contemporaries, and later historians too, wrote many articles and volumes about the coup d'état of Louis Bonaparte, its true causes remained a closed book for all of them. They were content, for the most part, to attribute it simply and solely to the mistakes or evil intentions of various historical personages. Only Marx was able to understand what had happened in France, to uncover the real social relations in the historical facts, and to disclose the actual trends of social development manifest in them. He succeeded in doing so because, as Engels wrote in the Preface to the third German edition (1885): "It was precisely Marx who had first discovered the great law of motion of history, the law according to which all historical struggles, whether they proceed in the political, religious, philosophical or some other ideological domain, are in fact only the more or less clear expression of struggles of social classes, and that the existence and thereby the collisions, too, between these classes are in turn conditioned by the degree of development of their economic position, by the mode of their production and of their exchange determined by it" (see present edition, Vol. 27).

In its brilliant analysis of what was then contemporary history, *The Eighteenth Brumaire of Louis Bonaparte* provides one of the classic expositions of the mature theory of historical materialism and of the dialectic of history. Marx made clear the whole complex interaction between the social-economic basis and the political superstructure, further developed the theory of the state in relation to its forms and executive organs, and demonstrated the role of political parties, the relationship between parties and classes, and the real link between classes and their ideological and political representatives.

Marx maintained that "in historical struggles one must ... distinguish the language and the imaginary aspirations of parties from their real organism and their real interests, their conception of themselves from their reality" (p. 128), and he showed that every party struggle is an expression of concealed class interests. He stressed the difference between objective social and political processes and relations and the subjective motives and impulses of the actual participants in events, and showed how the real relationships are reflected, though often in a distorted fashion, in their minds.

Marx attacks the simplistic view that ideologists, as the political and literary representatives of this or that class, must always occupy the same social position and lead the same manner of life as the rest of the class. Marx points out that a politician or writer becomes the ideologist of a certain class when he arrives, in a theoretical way, at the formulation of tasks and goals which the rank-and-file representatives of the class reach, in a practical way, under the influence of direct material needs and interests.

Marx explains the specific features of the 1848 revolution in France and thus rounds off the analysis he began in *The Class Struggles in France.* He stresses that, as distinct from its historical antecedent at the close of the eighteenth century, the 1848 revolution moved "in a descending line". The cause of this was the counter-revolutionary resurgence of the French bourgeoisie as a result of the growing class antagonisms in capitalist society. Alarmed by the upsurge of the proletariat, the bourgeoisie was ready in part or wholly to renounce the democratic institutions and representative bodies for which, in its time, it had led the struggle against the reactionary forces of feudal society. To secure and consolidate the inviolability of its material and economic position and obstruct the deepening of the revolution, the French bourgeoisie sacrificed even the bourgeois republic itself, and helped to establish the reactionary Bonapartist regime in which power was transferred to a clique of political adventurers.

Marx saw the Bonapartist coup as the predictable result of the retrograde development of the revolutionary process in France, of the transfer of power at each new stage to increasingly Right-wing elements who were trying on an ever growing scale to eliminate the gains of the revolution, and of the relapse of wider and wider strata of the French bourgeoisie into overtly counter-revolutionary positions. Marx demonstrated that autocratic dictatorships like that of Louis Bonaparte emerge primarily as a result of the counter-revolutionary nature of the exploiting classes, that they are established when the balance of class forces is such that the bourgeoisie is no longer able, and is afraid, to rule by parliamentary methods, while the working class is not yet strong enough to put up a successful resistance.

Marx described Bonapartism as the dictatorship of the most counter-revolutionary elements of the bourgeoisie. Its distinguishing features were: a policy of manoeuvring between classes to create a state power seen to be ruling over all alike; crude demagogy camouflaging the defence of the interests of the exploiters, combined with political terrorism; the omnipotence of the military machine; venality and corruption; the employment of criminals, and the widespread use of blackmail and bribery. Marx showed up the profound inner contradictions of Bonapartism at the very outset of its existence and prophetically foretold its inevitable downfall.

Marx devotes much attention to the French peasantry and its attitude to the Bonapartist coup. He notes that to establish their dictatorship Louis Bonaparte and his clique made adroit use of the political backwardness of the downtrodden French peasantry, and of its remoteness from the social and political life of the cities. The bourgeois governments of the Second Republic, which treated the peasants merely as an object of taxation, had discredited the revolution in their eyes, and this stimulated their support for Bonaparte. Added to this motive was the attachment of the property-owning peasants to their smallholdings and the fact that they had always looked up to the representative of the Napoleonic dynasty as their own traditional patron. In this way, Bonaparte exploited the conservatism of the property-owning peasants. Marx, however, did not regard conservatism as the only and overriding feature of the peasantry. He stressed that there were peasant traditions of liberation struggle too, that the oppression and exploitation of the peasantry could not but foster a contrary tendency among them—a revolutionary one which, as the result of the further ruin of the small-holding economy, would drive them into irreconcilable contradiction with the bourgeoisie and a close alliance with the working class. "Hence the peasants find their natural ally and leader in the *urban proletariat,* whose task is the overthrow of the bourgeois order" (p. 191).

The proletarian revolution itself, he concluded, could only triumph provided that the working class was supported by the broad non-proletarian masses of working people, above all by the peasantry. It would obtain in the peasants "*that chorus without which its solo becomes a swan song in all peasant countries*" (p. 193).

In *The Eighteenth Brumaire of Louis Bonaparte,* Marx made clear the fundamental difference between bourgeois and proletarian revolutions. Proletarian revolutions differ from bourgeois not only in their class aims, but, as Marx pointed out, in the permanence of their achievements, the considerably greater scope and volume of the transformations they bring about, and their greater force of impact on social development. As distinct from bourgeois revolutions, they effect a thoroughgoing break-up of the existing order, with revolutionary changes in all social relations. If bourgeois revolutions are short-lived and comparatively superficial, proletarian revolutions are characterised by depth, thoroughness, a critical approach to their own actions and the results achieved, and an urgent desire to surpass them by moving further ahead.

Of particular theoretical and practical importance is Marx's development in this work of his teaching on the state and, in particular, on the attitude of the proletarian revolution to the bourgeois state. Investigating the history of the development of executive power in France and its essential element, the state machine, Marx comes to the conclusion that all previous revolutions had only perfected that machine with the aim of exploiting and suppressing the masses. But the proletarian revolution must "concentrate all its forces of destruction against it" (p. 185). Marx draws a brief but extremely important conclusion: "All revolutions perfected this machine instead of breaking it" (p. 186).

"In this remarkable argument," Lenin wrote, "Marxism takes a tremendous step forward compared with the *Communist Manifesto*. In the latter, the question of the state is still treated in an extremely abstract manner, in the most general terms and expressions. In the above-quoted passage, the question is treated in a concrete manner, and the conclusion is extremely precise, definite, practical and palpable: all previous revolutions perfected the state machine, whereas it must be broken, smashed.

"This conclusion is the chief and fundamental point in the Marxist theory of the state" (*Collected Works,* Vol. 25, p. 406).

A short series of articles by Engels, "Real Causes Why the French Proletarians Remained Comparatively Inactive in December Last", is close in content to Marx's *The Eighteenth Brumaire of Louis Bonaparte.* Engels shows how unfounded and dishonest were the attempts of the bourgeois writers and the press to lay the responsibility for the Bonapartist coup d'état on the French proletariat. Engels draws on irrefutable facts to show that it was, in fact, the French bourgeoisie, hypocritically reproaching the workers for not defending the bourgeois parliamentary republic from Louis Bonaparte's attempts to destroy it, who with its counter-revolutionary policy prepared the ground for the establishment of the Bonapartist dictatorship. Published between February and April 1852 in the newspaper *Notes to the People,* this series for the first time acquainted the English reader with the Marxist evaluation of the events in France.

This volume includes a joint work by Marx and Engels, the pamphlet *The Great Men of the Exile,* aimed against the leaders of petty-bourgeois democracy. It was written to defend and promote the political, organisational and ideological independence of the working-class movement.

Marx and Engels considered it essential to criticise the adventurist activities of many of the émigré groupings. For these people ignored the real situation and conditions of revolutionary struggle, behaved as though they could at will create a revolution, and all the time did no more than engage in catch-phrases, careerism, ambition, internal feuds and unprincipled squabbles. In satirical sketches of a whole gallery of the leaders of the petty-bourgeois emigration—the heads of various ephemeral émigré organisations, members of fictitious provisional governments and committees, would-be revolutionary dictators and so on—Marx and Engels showed up the primitiveness of their philosophical views and political standpoints. They once again demonstrated how pernicious were the effects of playing at revolution, and how ludicrous the claims of mere petty-bourgeois windbags to the leadership of the working class and the revolutionary struggle.

The clumsy activities of the émigrés were used by the police as a pretext to clamp down upon the real revolutionaries. In May and June 1851, the Prussian Government arrested a number of prominent members of the Communist League in Germany. Forgeries and falsifications readily provided "material for the prosecution" and, on the basis of this, the trial of eleven Communists was staged in Cologne, starting on October 4, 1852.

As soon as the arrests began, Marx and Engels did everything in their power to help the accused, denouncing the unprincipled methods resorted to by the Prussian Government and the police. Describing the atmosphere in which Marx, Engels and their associates were struggling against police arbitrariness, Jenny Marx wrote on October 28, 1852 to Adolf Cluss, a member of the Communist League who had emigrated to the USA: "As you can imagine, the 'Marx party' is busy day and night and is having to throw itself into the work body and soul.... A complete office has now been set up in our house. Two or three people writing, others running errands, others scraping pennies together so that writers may continue to exist and provide proof of the most outrageous scandals ever perpetrated by the old world of officialdom" (see present edition, Vol. 39).

How much Marx and Engels helped the accused Communists is shown by the number of statements they sent to the editors of English newspapers and appeals to the American workers. The trial was covered in Engels' article "The Late Trial at Cologne", published in the *New-York Daily Tribune*.

The whole machinery of Prussian police-Junker justice was exposed by Marx in his pamphlet *Revelations Concerning the Communist Trial in Cologne*. He not only proved that the charges preferred at the trial were groundless, but denounced the Prussian police-bureaucratic order and the class bias of the bourgeois jury, and exposed the whole string of provocations, espionage and perjury on which the organisers of the Cologne trial relied. This work is a passionate defence of the Communists not only from police persecution, but from attempts to slander them in the eyes of the public by portraying them as organisers of sinister putsches and conspiracies. Marx exposed the fabricated police charge of conspiracy, which was the trump card of the prosecution at the Cologne trial.

At the same time, Marx publicly dissociated himself from the sectarian and adventurist elements in the communist movement of that time. He proved that the split in the Communist League was provoked by the attempts of the Willich-Schapper group to push the League into adventurist acts on the pretext that these would unleash revolution in Germany. Such tactics, he said, do nothing but harm to the working-class movement, lead to isolation from the masses and play into the hands of the police.

Although the pamphlet was mainly devoted to the issues at stake in the trial, Marx, in this work too, dwelt upon some of the vital questions of the theory of scientific communism. He emphasised the Communist League's disagreements with the Willich-Schapper group and attacked its simplistic voluntarist ideas about revolution and the possibility of leaping straight into communism even in countries where the tasks of the bourgeois-democratic revolution were not yet solved. The real revolutionary process, Marx declared, must go through a complex and comparatively lengthy span of revolutionary development. There must inevitably be a series of stages, and the transformation of the people themselves as well as of circumstances (p. 403). He thus made clear the essential point of the theory of permanent or uninterrupted revolution which he and Engels had put forward earlier (see present edition, Vol. 10, pp. 281-86).

The result of the arrest and imprisonment of the Communist League members was the virtual disintegration of the organisation in Germany. The position was much the same in other European countries. In conditions of steadily growing reaction, Marx and Engels concluded that the Communist League—a secret and relatively narrow organisation—had exhausted its possibilities and that it would be useless for its activities to continue any further.

The Communist League in fact proved to have been the historical prototype of an international proletarian party, a precursor of the First International. After its dissolution the struggle by Marx and Engels for a proletarian party did not cease, but continued in other forms corresponding to the new situation. They worked might and main to preserve the cadres of revolutionary fighters. They never ceased to propagate scientific communism and, in particular, used the progressive bourgeois press for these purposes.

In this volume there also begins the publication of articles written by Marx for the *New-York Daily Tribune* and partly reprinted in the Chartist *People's Paper*.

The *New-York Daily Tribune* had, on the whole, a progressive political orientation in those years. This offered Marx and Engels opportunities, however limited, for legal expression of a revolutionary political line. Their reports and articles are, indeed, models of how to utilise such opportunities. They were able to develop an extensive critique of the capitalist social system, which made clear to their readers its main contradictions. They were able to denounce in very forthright terms the anti-popular regimes in Europe, and both the home and foreign policies of the European ruling classes. And they set forth the positions of the working class and revolutionary democracy on the major issues of the day.

Marx, in particular, supplied an all-round critical analysis of economic, political and social life in England. Thus in his articles "The Elections in England.—Tories and Whigs", "Political Parties and Prospects" and others, he examined the bourgeois-aristocratic political system of England, under which the two most powerful parties of the ruling classes, the Tories and the Whigs, enjoyed power alternately, creating the semblance of a great battle between opposed political forces. He showed up the anti-democratic nature of the English electoral system which denied to the majority the right to vote, and drew a vivid picture of the bribery and intimidation which flourished at the elections (this is the subject of the articles "Corruption at Elections", "Result of the Elections" and others).

Marx devoted considerable attention to the English workers' struggle. Particularly interesting is his article "The Chartists", in which he made clear the real opportunities in England, unlike other European countries at that time, for a peaceful transfer of power into the hands of the working class. In England, he explained, there was no highly developed military-bureaucratic machine, and the proletariat formed the large majority of the population. What was above all essential was to introduce universal suffrage and to meet the other demands of the Chartist programme—the People's Charter. In English conditions, this could open up the way to the radical transformation of the existing parliamentary system and the democratisation of the entire political structure. Consequently, wrote Marx, universal suffrage in England "would be a far more socialistic measure" than on the Continent. For there it did not go beyond the framework of a bourgeois-democratic programme, and was sometimes even used demagogically by reaction, as, for example, in Bonapartist France. The English working class could achieve its demands, Marx considered, by uniting its forces, strengthening its organisations and intensifying its political campaigning. This is why he attached such importance to the Chartists' activities and in every way assisted and supported their efforts to revive the greatness of the Chartist movement after its setback in 1848.

In a series of articles, Marx was able to dispel the myth of "permanent prosperity" under capitalism. He demonstrated how false were the claims of bourgeois apologists that any swing from slump to boom brings prosperity to all the working people. On the contrary, no boom in industry and commerce in the capitalist countries had ever yet halted the impoverishment of the toiling masses or the growth of unemployment.

At that time, the "population problem" was becoming particularly acute. In his article "Forced Emigration", Marx indicated that under capitalism "it is the increase of productive power which demands a diminution of population, and drives away the surplus by famine or emigration" (p. 531). To put an end to this situation, the workers must take over the productive forces and place them at the service of society.

During this period Marx was already directing his attention towards primitive accumulation as the most important feature of the genesis of capitalist society. His article "Elections.— Financial Clouds.— The Duchess of Sutherland and Slavery" contains the first outline of his analysis. The material it contains on the merciless expropriation of the crofters, their eviction from their ancestral lands and the history of the enrichment of the Sutherland family, was to be used later in *Capital.*

Castigating the evils of capitalist society, Marx also examined the problem of crime. He showed (in his article "Capital Punishment") that the growth of criminality was conditioned by social causes and that crime could only be eradicated after liquidating bourgeois society, itself the nutrient of crime.

The section "From the Preparatory Materials" contains Engels' "Critical Review of Proudhon's Book *Idée générale de la Révolution au XIX-e siècle*". It was Marx who suggested a critique of Proudhon's book, having conceived but not written this work under the title "The Latest Discoveries of Socialism, or 'The General Idea of Revolution in the 19th Century' by P.-J. Proudhon".

Proudhon claimed to have created his own political economy and science of social revolution. Using Marx's preliminary comments in his letters of August 8 and 14, 1851, Engels subjects Proudhon's anarchistic views to a searching political analysis—his idea of "social liquidation", and his plans for the peaceful institution of an "economic system" in which the political or, to use his term, governmental system was supposed to disappear. Engels disclosed the utopian character of Proudhon's idea of "social liquidation", calling his projects to pay off the national debt, abolish interest, buy up privately-owned land, etc., "colossal nonsense" (p. 563). He showed that Proudhon's social ideal meant nothing—above all because he did not propose to touch private ownership of the means of production. Proudhon's social utopia, as Engels emphasised, amounted to preserving capitalism, but without, as Proudhon fondly hoped, its "bad sides" and its grievous consequences for the petty-bourgeois producer.

Engels showed that Proudhon's so-called anti-government ideas were not aimed at abolishing the bourgeois state, and amounted to no more than utopian and essentially reactionary projects for the decentralisation of political power. Engels made clear the kinship between Proudhon's milk and water anarchism and Stirner's extreme individualism. He made clear, too, the thoroughly retrograde character of Proudhon's attacks on the representatives of utopian socialism and communism, and of his polemics against the progressive democratic ideas of the Enlightenment and the French Revolution.

The task of fighting Proudhonism—a petty-bourgeois reformist trend which was becoming an obstacle to the formation of class consciousness among the proletariat, especially in France, Italy and Spain—became even more urgent in the next few years, and this prompted Marx and Engels to turn many times to critical analysis of the works of Proudhon and like-minded theoreticians.

In the "Appendices" are included, for the first time in any collection of the works of Marx and Engels, articles by Ernest Jones and Johann Georg Eccarius written with Marx's collaboration. Marx's role as the virtual co-author or editor of these articles was established in research carried out at the Moscow Institute of Marxism-Leninism in preparing this volume. The articles on the co-operative movement by Ernest Jones, Chartist and editor of the weekly *Notes to the People*, contain ideas which Marx was to elaborate further in the "Inaugural Address of the International Working Men's Association" and other documents. In these articles, criticism is levelled against the theory and practice of the bourgeois co-operators, "Christian socialists" and others who were attempting to distract the workers from class struggle and convince them that it was possible to abolish social evils and exploitation by creating workers' co-operative societies. Jones contended that co-operation could never serve as a lever for social transformation so long as it was practised only in the form of scattered, local and isolated societies acting in the conditions, and on the basis, of the capitalist system. On the other hand, co-operative production and trade would be one of the main economic measures of the working class after it had won state power on a nation-wide scale. Co-operation must needs be nation-wide, and its success must depend on who commands political power. Political power was needed "to reconstruct the bases of society". "Under the present system," Jones wrote, addressing the co-op members, "... all your efforts must prove vain—have proved vain—towards the production of a *national* result" (p. 577).

Marx's direct participation in these articles by Jones bears witness to the close association of the founders of Marxism and the representatives of the revolutionary wing of the Chartist movement, and also to the extent of the influence of Marxist ideas on the Left-wing Chartists.

Written by Marx's colleague Georg Eccarius and published in the Chartist *People's Paper,* "A Review of the Literature on the *Coup d'Etat*" is also an item of propaganda for the ideas of scientific communism in the English working-class press. Following Marx's advice, Eccarius reviewed the books of Xavier Durrieu, Victor Hugo and Pierre Joseph Proudhon on the coup d'état. "All these publications," he wrote, "pretend, more or less, to be the expressions and sentiments of the parties or classes to which their authors respectively belong" (p. 592). Not one of them could properly explain the causes and nature of the Bonapartist coup. The only account of it that met the requirements of science, Eccarius declared, was that written by Marx, who had approached these events from the standpoint of the most revolutionary and progressive class and was guided by the revolutionary theory which he had created, the effectiveness and force of which he clearly demonstrated. Eccarius' review contains copious excerpts from the first chapter of Marx's *The Eighteenth Brumaire of Louis Bonaparte.*

Other documents published in the Appendices illustrate the practical revolutionary activities of Marx and Engels in the period covered.

* * *

In this volume, eight works by Marx and Engels are published in English for the first time. They include Engels' article "England", his "Critical Review of Proudhon's Book *Idée générale de la Révolution au*

XIX-e siècle", letters to newspaper editors and appeals for aid for the accused in the Cologne trial (in the Appendices). This volume also includes 15 articles by Marx and Engels published in American and English newspapers, but never subsequently reprinted in English. Marx's work *The Eighteenth Brumaire of Louis Bonaparte* is published for the first time in English with the variants in the different editions that appeared in his lifetime. Articles printed in both the *New-York Daily Tribune* and *The People's Paper* are reproduced in the different readings in the texts of these two periodicals.

Works of Marx and Engels written in German and previously published in English are given in verified and improved translations. Details of the first English publication of these works are supplied in the notes. A description is also supplied of the layout of the text of individual works, especially the manuscripts.

Texts originally written in English are reproduced from the sources indicated at the end. Obvious misprints, misspellings of proper and geographical names, inaccurate statistics, etc., particularly frequent in articles by Marx and Engels in the *New-York Daily Tribune*, have been corrected without comment. Errors in quotations have been corrected from the originals, but the authors' form of quoting has been preserved.

The volume was compiled, the text prepared, and the Preface and Notes written by Lev Churbanov and edited by Lev Golman (CC CPSU Institute of Marxism-Leninism). The Name Index, the Index of Quoted and Mentioned Literature and the Index of Periodicals were prepared by Nina Loiko and the Subject Index by Marlen Arzumanov (both of the Institute of Marxism-Leninism).

The English translations were made by Clemens Dutt, Rodney Livingstone and Christopher Upward and edited by Maurice Cornforth, E. J. Hobsbawm, Nicholas Jacobs and Margaret Mynatt (Lawrence & Wishart), Salo Ryazanskaya, Lydia Belyakova and Victor Schnittke (Progress Publishers), and Norire Ter-Akopyan, scientific editor (Institute of Marxism-Leninism).

The volume was prepared for the press by Yelena Kalinina, Nadezhda Rudenko and Alla Varavitskaya (Progress Publishers).

KARL MARX
and
FREDERICK ENGELS

WORKS

August 1851-March 1853

Frederick Engels

REVOLUTION AND COUNTER-REVOLUTION
IN GERMANY[1]

Written in August 1851-September 1852

First published in the *New-York Daily Tribune* on October 25 and 28, November 6, 7, 12 and 28, 1851; February 27, March 5, 15, 18 and 19, April 9, 17 and 24, July 27, August 19, September 18, and October 2 and 23, 1852

Signed: *Karl Marx*

Reproduced from the newspaper

I

GERMANY AT THE OUTBREAK OF THE REVOLUTION

[*New-York Daily Tribune*, №.3282, October 25, 1851]

The first act of the revolutionary drama on the Continent of Europe has closed. The "powers that were" before the hurricane of 1848, are again "the powers that be," and the more or less popular rulers of a day, provisional governors, triumvirs, dictators, with their tail of representatives, civil commissioners, military commissioners, prefects, judges, generals, officers and soldiers, are thrown upon foreign shores, and "transported beyond the seas" to England or America, there to form new governments "*in partibus infidelium,*"[a] European committees, central committees, national committees, and to announce their advent with proclamations quite as solemn as those of any less imaginary potentates.

A more signal defeat than that undergone by the continental revolutionary party—or rather parties—upon all points of the line of battle, cannot be imagined. But what of that? Has not the struggle of the British middle classes for their social and political supremacy embraced forty-eight, that of the French middle classes forty years of unexampled struggles? And was their triumph ever nearer than at the very moment when restored monarchy thought itself more firmly settled than ever? The times of that superstition which attributed revolutions to the ill-will of a few agitators, have long passed away. Everyone knows nowadays, that wherever there is a revolutionary convulsion, there must be some social want in the background, which is prevented by outworn institutions from satisfying itself. The want may not yet be felt as strongly, as

---

[a] *In partibus infidelium*—literally: in parts inhabited by infidels. The words are added to the title of Roman Catholic bishops appointed to purely nominal dioceses in non-Christian countries. In the figurative sense, they mean "not really existing".— *Ed.*

generally, as might insure immediate success, but every attempt at forcible repression will only bring it forth stronger and stronger, until it bursts its fetters. If, then, we have been beaten, we have nothing else to do but to begin again from the beginning. And, fortunately, the probably very short interval of rest which is allowed us between the close of the first and the beginning of the second act of the movement, gives us time for a very necessary piece of work: the study of the causes that necessitated both the late outbreak, and its defeat; causes that are not to be sought for in the accidental efforts, talents, faults, errors or treacheries of some of the leaders, but in the general social state and conditions of existence of each of the convulsed nations. That the sudden movements of February and March, 1848, were not the work of single individuals, but spontaneous, irresistible manifestations of national wants and necessities, more or less clearly understood, but very distinctly felt by numerous classes in every country, is a fact recognised everywhere; but when you inquire into the causes of the counter-revolutionary successes, there you are met on every hand with the ready reply that it was Mr. This or Citizen That, who "betrayed" the people. Which reply may be very true, or not, according to circumstances, but under no circumstances does it explain anything—not even show how it came to pass that the "people" allowed themselves to be thus betrayed. And what a poor chance stands a political party whose entire stock-in-trade consists in a knowledge of the solitary fact, that Citizen So-and-so is not to be trusted.

The inquiry into, and the exposition of, the causes both of the revolutionary convulsion and its suppression, are, besides, of paramount importance in a historical point of view. All these petty personal quarrels and recriminations—all these contradictory assertions, that it was Marrast, or Ledru-Rollin, or Louis Blanc, or any other member of the Provisional Government, or the whole of them, that steered the revolution amidst the rocks upon which it foundered—of what interest can they be, what light can they afford to the American or Englishman, who observed all these various movements from a distance too great to allow of his distinguishing any of the details of operations? No man in his senses will ever believe that eleven men,[a] mostly of very indifferent capacity, either for good or evil, were able in three months to ruin a nation of thirty-six millions, unless those thirty-six millions saw as little of their way before them as the eleven did. But how it came to pass, that these thirty-six millions were at once called upon to decide for themselves

---

[a] Members of the French Provisional Government.— *Ed.*

which way to go, although partly groping in dim twilight, and how then they got lost and their old leaders were for a moment allowed to return to their leadership, that is just the question.

If then, we try to lay before the readers of *The Tribune*[2] the causes which, while they necessitated the German Revolution of 1848, led quite as inevitably to its momentary repression in 1849 and '50, we shall not be expected to give a complete history of the events as they passed in that country. Later events, and the judgment of coming generations, will decide what portion of that confused mass of seemingly accidental, incoherent and incongruous facts is to form a part of the world's history. The time for such a task has not yet arrived; we must confine ourselves to the limits of the possible, and be satisfied, if we can find rational causes, based upon undeniable facts, to explain the chief events, the principal vicissitudes of that movement, and to give us a clue as to the direction which the next and perhaps not very distant outbreak will impart to the German people.

And firstly, what was the state of Germany at the outbreak of the revolution?

The composition of the different classes of the people which form the groundwork of every political organization was, in Germany, more complicated than in any other country. While in England and France feudalism was entirely destroyed, or at least reduced, as in the former country, to a few insignificant forms, by a powerful and wealthy middle class, concentrated in large towns, and particularly in the Capital, the feudal nobility in Germany had retained a great portion of their ancient privileges. The feudal system of tenure was prevalent almost everywhere. The Lords of the Land had even retained the jurisdiction over their tenants. Deprived of their political privileges, of the right to control the Princes, they had preserved almost all their medieval supremacy over the peasantry of their demesnes, as well as their exemption from taxes. Feudalism was more flourishing in some localities than in others, but nowhere except on the left bank of the Rhine was it entirely destroyed.[3] This feudal nobility, then extremely numerous and partly very wealthy, was considered, officially, the first "Order" in the country. It furnished the higher Government officials, it almost exclusively officered the army.

The bourgeoisie of Germany was by far not as wealthy and concentrated as that of France or England. The ancient manufactures of Germany had been destroyed by the introduction of steam, and by the rapidly extending supremacy of English manufactures; the more modern manufactures, started under the Napoleonic continental system,[4] established in other parts of the country, did not compensate for the loss of the old ones, nor suffice to create a manufacturing interest strong enough to force its wants upon the notice of Governments jealous of every extension of non-noble wealth and power. If France carried her silk manufactures victorious through fifty years of revolutions and wars, Germany, during the same time, all but lost her ancient linen trade. The manufacturing districts, besides, were few and far between; situated far inland, and using, mostly, foreign, Dutch or Belgian, ports for their imports and exports, they had little or no interest in common with the large seaport towns on the North Sea and the Baltic; they were, above all, unable to create large manufacturing and trading centers, such as Paris and Lyons, London and Manchester. The causes of this backwardness of German manufactures were manifold, but, two will suffice to account for it: the unfavorable geographical situation of the country, at a distance from the Atlantic, which had become the great highway for the world's trade, and the continuous wars in which Germany was involved, and which were fought on her soil, from the sixteenth century to the present day. It was this want of numbers, and particularly of anything like concentrated numbers, which prevented the German Middle Classes from attaining that political supremacy which the English bourgeois has enjoyed ever since 1688, and which the French conquered in 1789. And yet, ever since 1815, the wealth, and with the wealth, the political importance of the middle class in Germany, was continually growing. Governments were, although reluctantly, compelled to bow at least to its more immediate material interests. It may even be truly said, that from 1815 to 1830, and from 1832 to 1840, every particle of political influence, which, having been allowed to the middle class in the Constitutions of the smaller States, was again wrested from them during the above two periods of political reaction—that every such particle was compensated for by some more practical advantage allowed to them. Every political defeat of the middle class drew after it a victory on the field of commercial legislation. And, certainly, the Prussian Protective Tariff of 1818, and the formation of the Zollverein,[5] were worth a good deal more to the traders and manufacturers of Germany than the equivocal right of expressing, in the chambers of some diminutive dukedom, their want of confidence in ministers who laughed at their votes. Thus, with growing wealth and extending trade, the bourgeoisie soon arrived at a stage where it found the development of its most important interests checked by the political constitution of the country—by its random division among thirty-six princes with conflicting tendencies and caprices; by the feudal fetters upon agriculture and the trade connected with it; by the prying superintendence to which an ignorant and presumptuous bureaucracy subjected all its transactions. At the same time, the extension and consolidation of the *Zollverein*, the general introduction of steam communication, the growing competition in the home trade, brought the commercial classes of the different States and Provinces closer together, equalized their interests, centralized their strength. The natural consequence was the passing of the whole mass of them into the camp of the Liberal Opposition, and the gaining of the first serious struggle of the German middle class for political power. This change may be dated from 1840, from the moment when the bourgeoisie of Prussia assumed the lead of the middle-class movement of Germany. We shall hereafter revert to this Liberal Opposition movement of 1840-47.

The great mass of the nation, which neither belonged to the nobility nor to the bourgeoisie, consisted, in the towns, of the small trading and shopkeeping class and the working people, and in the country, of the peasantry.

The small trading and shopkeeping class is exceedingly numerous in Germany, in consequence of the stunted development which the large capitalists and manufacturers, as a class, have had in that country. In the larger towns it forms almost the majority of the inhabitants; in the smaller ones it entirely predominates, from the absence of wealthier competitors for influence. This class, a most important one in every modern body politic, and in all modern revolutions, is still more important in Germany, where during the recent struggles it generally played the decisive part. Its intermediate position between the class of larger capitalists, traders and manufacturers, the bourgeoisie, properly so called, and the proletarian or industrial class, determines its character. Aspiring to the position of the first, the least adverse turn of fortune hurls the individuals of this class down into the ranks of the second. In monarchical and feudal countries the custom of the court and aristocracy becomes necessary to its existence; the loss of this custom might ruin a great part of it. In the smaller towns, a military garrison, a county government, a court of law with its followers, form very often the base of its prosperity; withdraw these and down go the shopkeepers, the tailors, the shoemakers, the joiners. Thus, eternally tossed about between the hope of entering the ranks of the wealthier class, and the fear of being reduced to the state of proletarians or even paupers; between the hope of promoting their interests by conquering a share in the direction of public affairs, and the dread of rousing, by ill-timed opposition, the ire of a Government which disposes of their very existence, because it has the power of removing their best customers; possessed of small means, the insecurity of the possession of which is in the inverse ratio of the amount; this class is extremely vacillating in its views. Humble and crouchingly submissive under a powerful feudal or monarchical government, it turns to the side of Liberalism when the middle class is in the ascendent; it becomes seized with violent Democratic fits as soon as the middle class has secured its own supremacy, but falls back into the abject despondency of fear as soon as the class below itself, the proletarians, attempt an independent movement. We shall, by and by, see this class, in Germany, pass alternately from one of these stages to the other.

The working class in Germany is, in its social and political development, as far behind that of England and France as the German bourgeoisie is behind the bourgeoisie of those countries. Like master, like man. The evolution of the conditions of existence for a numerous, strong, concentrated and intelligent proletarian class, goes hand in hand with the development of the conditions of existence for a numerous, wealthy, concentrated and powerful middle class. The working-class movement itself never is independent, never is of an exclusively proletarian character, until all the different factions of the middle class, and particularly its most progressive faction, the large manufacturers, have conquered political power and remodelled the State according to their wants. It is then that the inevitable conflict between the employer and the employed becomes imminent and cannot be adjourned any longer; that the working class can no longer be put off with delusive hopes and promises never to be realized; that the great problem of the nineteenth century, the abolition of the proletariat, is at last brought forward fairly and in its proper light. Now, in Germany, the mass of the working class were employed, not by those modern manufacturing lords of which Great Britain furnishes such splendid specimens, but by small tradesmen whose entire manufacturing system is a mere relic of the Middle Ages. And as there is an enormous difference between the great cotton lord and the petty cobbler or master tailor, so there is a corresponding distance from the wide-awake factory operative of modern manufacturing Babylons to the bashful journeyman tailor or cabinet-maker of a small country town, who lives in circumstances and works after a plan very little different from those of the like sort of men some five hundred years ago. This general absence of modern conditions of life, of modern modes of industrial production, of course was accompanied by a pretty equally general absence of modern ideas, and it is therefore not to be wondered at if, at the outbreak of the revolution, a large part of the working classes should cry out for the immediate re-establishment of guilds and medieval privileged trades' corporations. Yet, from the manufacturing districts, where the modern system of production predominated, and in consequence of the facilities of intercommunication and mental development afforded by the migratory life of a large number of the working men, a strong nucleus formed itself whose ideas about the emancipation of their class were far clearer and more in accordance with existing facts and historical necessities; but they were a mere minority. If the active movement of the middle classes may be dated from 1840, that of the working class commences its advent by the insurrections of the Silesian and Bohemian[a] factory operatives in 1844,[6] and we shall soon have occasion to pass in review the different stages through which this movement passed.

Lastly, there was the great class of the small farmers, the peasantry, which, with its appendix of farm-laborers, constitutes a considerable majority of the entire nation. But this class again subdivided itself into different fractions. There were, firstly, the more wealthy farmers, what is called in Germany *Gross-* and *Mittel-Bauern*, proprietors of more or less extensive farms, and each of them commanding the services of several agricultural laborers. This class, placed between the large untaxed feudal landowners and the smaller peasantry and farm-laborers, for obvious reasons found in an alliance with the anti-feudal middle class of the towns its most natural political course. Then there were, secondly, the small freeholders, predominating in the Rhine country, where feudalism had succumbed before the mighty strokes of the great French Revolution. Similar independent small freeholders also existed here and there in other provinces, where they had succeeded in buying off the feudal charges formerly due upon their lands. This class, however, was a class of freeholders by name only, their property being generally mortgaged to such an extent, and under such onerous conditions, that not the peasant, but the usurer who had advanced the money, was the real landowner. Thirdly, the feudal tenants, who could not be easily turned out of their holdings, but who had to pay a perpetual rent, or to perform in perpetuity a certain amount of labor in favor of the lord of the manor. Lastly, the agricultural laborers, whose condition, in many large farming concerns, was exactly that of the same class in England, and who, in all cases, lived and died poor, ill-fed, and the slaves of their employers. These three latter classes of the agricultural population,

---

[a] Czech.— *Ed.*

the small freeholders, the feudal tenants, and the agricultural laborers, never troubled their heads much about politics before the revolution, but it is evident that this event must have opened to them a new career, full of brilliant prospects. To every one of them the revolution offered advantages, and the movement once fairly engaged in, it was to be expected that, each in their turn, they would join it. But at the same time it is quite as evident, and equally borne out by the history of all modern countries, that the agricultural population, in consequence of its dispersion over a great space, and of the difficulty of bringing about an agreement among any considerable portion of it, never can attempt a successful independent movement; they require the initiatory impulse of the more concentrated, more enlightened, more easily moved people of the towns.

The preceding short sketch of the most important of the classes, which in their aggregate formed the German nation at the outbreak of the recent movements, will already be sufficient to explain a great part of the incoherence, incongruence and apparent contradiction which prevailed in that movement. When interests so varied, so conflicting, so strangely crossing each other, are brought into violent collision; when these contending interests in every district, every province are mixed in different proportions; when, above all, there is no great center in the country, no London, no Paris, the decisions of which, by their weight, may supersede the necessity of fighting out the same quarrel over and over again in every single locality; what else is to be expected but that the contest will dissolve itself into a mass of unconnected struggles, in which an enormous quantity of blood, energy and capital is spent, but which for all that remain without any decisive results?

The political dismemberment of Germany into three dozen of more or less important principalities is equally explained by this confusion and multiplicity of the elements which compose the nation, and which again vary in every locality. Where there are no common interests there can be no unity of purpose, much less of action. The German Confederation, it is true, was declared everlastingly indissoluble; yet the Confederation and its organ, the Diet, never represented German unity.[7] The very highest pitch to which centralization was ever carried in Germany was the establishment of the Zollverein; by this the States on the North Sea were also forced into a Customs Union of their own,[8] Austria remaining wrapped up in her separate prohibitive tariff. Germany had the satisfaction to be, for all practical purposes, divided between three independent powers only, instead of between thirty-six. Of course, the paramount supremacy of the Russian Czar, as established in 1814, underwent no change on this account.

Having drawn these preliminary conclusions from our premises, we shall see, in our next, how the aforesaid various classes of the German people were set into movement one after the other, and what character this movement assumed on the outbreak of the French Revolution of 1848.

London, September, 1851

II
THE PRUSSIAN STATE

[*New-York Daily Tribune*, No. 3284, October 28, 1851]

The political movement of the middle class, or bourgeoisie, in Germany, may be dated from 1840. It had been preceded by symptoms showing that the moneyed and industrial class of that country was ripening into a state which would no longer allow it to continue apathetic and passive under the pressure of a half-feudal, half-bureaucratic monarchism. The smaller Princes of Germany, partly to insure to themselves a greater independence against the supremacy of Austria and Prussia, or against the influence of the nobility in their own States, partly in order to consolidate into a whole the disconnected provinces united under their rule by the Congress of Vienna,[9] one after the other granted constitutions of a more or less liberal character. They could do so without any danger to themselves; for if the Diet of the Confederation, this mere puppet of Austria and Prussia, was to encroach upon their independence as sovereigns, they knew that in resisting its dictates they would be backed by public opinion and the Chambers; and if, on the contrary, these Chambers grew too strong, they could readily command the power of the Diet to break down all opposition. The Bavarian, Württemberg, Baden, or Hanoverian constitutional institutions could not, under such circumstances, give rise to any serious struggle for political power, and therefore the great bulk of the German middle class kept very generally aloof from the petty squabbles raised in the legislatures of the small States, well knowing that without a fundamental change in the policy and constitution of the two great powers of Germany, no secondary efforts and victories would be of any avail. But, at the same time, a race of liberal lawyers, professional oppositionists, sprung up in these small assemblies: the Rottecks, the Welckers, the Roemers, the Jordans, the Stüves, the

Eisenmanns, those great "popular men" (*Volksmänner*), who after a more or less noisy, but always unsuccessful, opposition of twenty years, were carried to the summit of power by the revolutionary spring tide of 1848, and who, after having there shown their utter impotency and insignificance, were hurled down again in a moment. These first specimens, upon German soil, of the trader in politics and opposition, by their speeches and writings made familiar to the German ear the language of constitutionalism, and by their very existence, foreboded the approach of a time when the middle class would seize upon and restore to their proper meaning the political phrases which these talkative attorneys and professors were in the habit of using without knowing much about the sense originally attached to them.

German literature, too, labored under the influence of the political excitement into which all Europe had been thrown by the events of 1830.[10] A crude constitutionalism, or a still cruder republicanism, were preached by almost all writers of the time. It became more and more the habit, particularly of the inferior sorts of *literati*, to make up for the want of cleverness in their productions by political allusions which were sure to attract attention. Poetry, novels, reviews, the drama, every literary production teemed with what was called "tendency," that is, with more or less timid exhibitions of an anti-governmental spirit. In order to complete the confusion of ideas reigning after 1830 in Germany, with these elements of political opposition there were mixed up ill-digested university-recollections of German philosophy, and misunderstood gleanings from French socialism, particularly Saint-Simonism; and the clique of writers who expatiated upon this heterogeneous conglomerate of ideas, pre-sumptuously called themselves "Young Germany," or "the Modern School."[11] They have since repented their youthful sins, but not improved their style of writing.

Lastly, German philosophy, that most complicated, but at the same time most sure thermometer of the development of the German mind, had declared for the middle class, when Hegel pronounced, in his *Philosophy of Law*,[a] Constitutional Monarchy to be the final and most perfect form of Government. In other words, he proclaimed the approaching advent of the middle classes of the country to political power. His school, after his death, did not stop here. While the more advanced section of his followers, on one hand, subjected every religious belief to the ordeal of a rigorous criticism, and shook to its foundation the ancient fabric of Christianity, they at the same

---

[a] G.W.F. Hegel. *Grundlinien der Philosophie des Rechts*, § 273.— *Ed.*

time brought forward bolder political principles than hitherto it had been the fate of German ears to hear expounded, and attempted to restore to glory the memory of the heroes of the first French Revolution. The abstruse philosophical language in which these ideas were clothed, if it obscured the mind of both the writer and the reader, equally blinded the eyes of the censor, and thus it was that the "Young Hegelian" writers enjoyed a liberty of the press unknown in every other branch of literature.

Thus it was evident that public opinion was undergoing a great change in Germany. By degrees, the vast majority of those classes whose education or position in life enabled them, under an absolute monarchy, to gain some political information, and to form anything like an independent political opinion, united into one mighty phalanx of opposition against the existing system. And in passing judgment upon the slowness of political development in Germany, no one ought to omit taking into account the difficulty of obtaining correct information upon any subject in a country, where all sources of information were under control of the Government; where from the Ragged School and Sunday School, to the Newspaper and the University, nothing was said, taught, printed or published, but what had previously obtained its approbation. Look at Vienna, for instance. The people of Vienna, in industry and manufactures, second perhaps to none in Germany, in spirit, courage, and revolutionary energy, proving themselves far superior to all, were yet more ignorant as to their real interests, and committed more blunders during the revolution than any others, and this was due, in a very great measure, to the almost absolute ignorance with regard to the very commonest political subjects in which Metternich's Government had succeeded in keeping them.

It needs no further explanation why, under such a system, political information was an almost exclusive monopoly of such classes of society as could afford to pay for its being smuggled into the country, and more particularly of those whose interests were most seriously attacked by the existing state of things—namely, the manufacturing and commercial classes. They, therefore, were the first to unite in a mass against the continuance of a more or less disguised absolutism, and from their passing into the ranks of the opposition must be dated the beginning of the real revolutionary movement in Germany.

The oppositional pronunciamento of the German bourgeoisie may be dated from 1840, from the death of the late King of Prussia,[a] the

---

[a] Frederick William III.—*Ed.*

last surviving founder of the Holy Alliance of 1815.[12] The new King was known to be no supporter of the predominantly bureaucratic and military monarchy of his father. What the French middle classes had expected from the advent of Louis XVI, the German bourgeoisie hoped, in some measure, from Frederick William IV of Prussia. It was agreed upon all hands that the old system was exploded, worn out, and must be given up; and what had been borne in silence under the old King, now was loudly proclaimed to be intolerable.

But if Louis XVI, "Louis-le-Désiré," had been a plain, unpretending simpleton, half-conscious of his own nullity, without any fixed opinions, ruled principally by the habits contracted during his education, "Frederick William-le-Désiré" was something quite different. While he certainly surpassed his French original in weakness of character, he was neither without pretensions nor without opinions. He had made himself acquainted, in an amateur sort of way, with the rudiments of most sciences, and thought himself, therefore, learned enough to consider final his judgment upon every subject. He made sure he was a first-rate orator, and there was certainly no commercial traveller in Berlin who could beat him either in prolixity of pretended wit or in fluency of elocution. And above all, he had his opinions. He hated and despised the bureaucratic element of the Prussian Monarchy, but only because all his sympathies were with the feudal element. Himself one of the founders of and chief contributors to the "Berlin political weekly paper,"[a] the so-called Historical School (a school living upon the ideas of Bonald, De Maistre, and other writers of the first generation of French Legitimists),[13] he aimed at a restoration, as complete as possible, of the predominant social position of the nobility. The King, first nobleman of his realm, surrounded in the first instance by a splendid court of mighty vassals, princes, dukes and counts; in the second instance, by a numerous and wealthy lower nobility; ruling according to his discretion over his loyal burgesses and peasants, and thus being himself the chief of a complete hierarchy of social ranks or castes, each of which was to enjoy its particular privileges, and to be separated from the others by the almost insurmountable barrier of birth or of a fixed, inalterable social position; the whole of these castes or "estates of the realm" balancing each other, at the same time, so nicely in power and influence, that a complete independence of action should remain to the King—such was the *beau idéal* which

---

[a] *Berliner politisches Wochenblatt.— Ed.*

Frederick William IV undertook to realize, and which he is again trying to realize at the present moment.

It took some time before the Prussian bourgeoisie, not very well versed in theoretical questions, found out the real purport of their King's tendency. But what they very soon found out, was the fact that he was bent upon things quite the reverse of what they wanted. Hardly did the new King find his "gift of the gab" unfettered by his father's death when he set about proclaiming his intentions in speeches without number; and every speech, every act of his went far to estrange from him the sympathies of the middle class. He would not have cared much for that, if it had not been for some stern and startling realities which interrupted his poetic dreams. Alas, that romanticism is not very quick at accounts, and that feudalism, ever since Don Quixote, reckons without its host! Frederick William IV partook too much of that contempt for ready cash whichever has been the noblest inheritance of the sons of the Crusaders. He found, at his accession, a costly, although parsimoniously arranged system of Government, and a moderately filled State Treasury. In two years every trace of a surplus was spent in court festivals, royal progresses, largesses, subventions to needy, seedy and greedy noblemen, &c., and the regular taxes were no longer sufficient for the exigencies of either court or government. And thus, his Majesty found himself very soon placed between a glaring deficit on one side, and a law of 1820 on the other, by which any new loan, or any increase of the then existing taxation, was made illegal without the assent of "the future Representation of the People." [a] This representation did not exist; the new King was less inclined than even his father to create it; and if he had been, he knew that public opinion had wonderfully changed since his accession.

Indeed the middle classes, who had partly expected that the new King would at once grant a Constitution, proclaim the Liberty of the Press, Trial by Jury, &c., &c.—in short, himself take the lead of that peaceful revolution which they wanted in order to obtain political supremacy —the middle classes had found out their error and had turned ferociously against the King. In the Rhine Province, and more or less generally, all over Prussia, they were so exasperated that they, being short themselves of men able to represent them in the Press, went to the length of an alliance with the extreme philosophical party, of which we have spoken above. The fruit of this

---

[a] A reference to the law of January 17, 1820: "Verordnung wegen der künftigen Behandlung des gesammten Staatsschulden-Wesens".— Ed.

alliance was the *Rhenish Gazette*,[a] of Cologne, a paper which was suppressed after fifteen months' existence, but from which may be dated the existence of the Newspaper Press in Germany. This was in 1842.

The poor King, whose commercial difficulties were the keenest satire upon his medieval propensities, very soon found out that he could not continue to reign without making some slight concession to the popular outcry for that "Representation of the People," which, as the last remnant of the long-forgotten promises of 1813 and 1815, had been embodied in the law of 1820.[14] He found the least objectionable mode of satisfying this untoward law in calling together the Standing Committees of the Provincial Diets.[15] The Provincial Diets had been instituted in 1823. They consisted, for every one of the eight provinces of the kingdom, of: 1. The higher nobility, the formerly sovereign families of the German Empire, the heads of which were members of the Diet by birthright. 2. Of the representatives of the knights or lower nobility. 3. Of representatives of towns; and 4. Of deputies of the peasantry or small farming class. The whole was arranged in such a manner that in every province the two sections of the nobility always had a majority of the Diet. Every one of these eight Provincial Diets elected a Committee, and these eight Committees were now called to Berlin, in order to form a Representative Assembly for the purpose of voting the much-desired loan. It was stated that the Treasury was full, and that the loan was required, not for current wants, but for the construction of a State Railway. But the united Committees gave the King a flat refusal, declaring themselves incompetent to act as the Representatives of the People, and called upon his majesty to fulfill the promise of a Representative Constitution which his father had given when he wanted the aid of the people against Napoleon.

The sitting of the united Committees proved that the spirit of opposition was no longer confined to the bourgeoisie. A part of the peasantry had joined them, and many nobles, being themselves large farmers on their own property, and dealers in corn, wool, spirits and flax, requiring the same guaranties against absolutism, bureaucracy and feudal restoration, had equally pronounced against the Government and for a Representative Constitution. The King's plan had signally failed; he had got no money, and had increased the power of the opposition. The subsequent sitting of the Provincial Diets themselves was still more unfortunate for the King. All of them asked for reforms, for the fulfillment of the promises of 1813 and

---

[a] *Rheinische Zeitung.*—*Ed.*

'15, for a Constitution and a Free Press; the resolutions, to this effect, of some of them, were rather disrespectfully worded, and the ill-humored replies of the exasperated King made the evil still greater.

In the meantime the financial difficulties of the Government went on increasing. For a time abatements made upon the moneys appropriated for the different public services, fraudulent transactions with the "Seehandlung," [16] a commercial establishment speculating and trading for account and risk of the State, and long since acting as its money-broker, had sufficed to keep up appearances; increased issues of State paper money had furnished some resources; and the secret, upon the whole, had been pretty well kept. But all these contrivances were soon exhausted. There was another plan tried: the establishment of a Bank, the capital of which was to be furnished partly by the State and partly by private shareholders; the chief direction to belong to the State, in such a manner as to enable the Government to draw upon the funds of this Bank to a large amount, and thus to repeat the same fraudulent transactions that would no longer do with the "Seehandlung." But, as a matter of course, there were no capitalists to be found who would hand over their money upon such conditions; the statutes of the Bank had to be altered, and the property of the shareholders guarantied from the encroachments of the Treasury, before any shares were subscribed for. Thus, this plan having failed, there remained nothing but to try a loan—if capitalists could be found who would lend their cash without requiring the permission and guarantee of that mysterious "future Representation of the People." Rothschild was applied to, and he declared that if the loan was to be guarantied by this "Representation of the People," he would undertake the thing at a moment's notice—if not, he could not have anything to do with the transaction.

Thus every hope of obtaining money had vanished, and there was no possibility of escaping the fatal "Representation of the People." Rothschild's refusal was known in Autumn, 1846, and in February of the next year the King called together all the eight Provincial Diets to Berlin, forming them into one "United Diet." [17] This Diet was to do the work required, in case of need, by the law of 1820; it was to vote loans and increased taxes, but beyond that it was to have no rights. Its voice upon general legislation was to be merely consultative; it was to assemble, not at fixed periods, but whenever it pleased the King; it was to discuss nothing but what the Government pleased to lay before it. Of course, the members were very little satisfied with the part they were expected to perform. They repeated the wishes they

had enounced when they met in the provincial assemblies; the
relations between them and the Government soon became acrimonious, and when the loan, which was again stated to be required for
railway constructions, was demanded from them, they again refused
to grant it.

This vote very soon brought their sitting to a close. The King,
more and more exasperated, dismissed them with a reprimand, but
still remained without money. And, indeed, he had every reason to
be alarmed at his position, seeing that the Liberal league, headed by
the middle classes, comprising a large part of the lower nobility and
all the manifold discontents that had been accumulated in the
different sections of the lower orders—that this Liberal league was
determined to have what it wanted. In vain the King had declared, in
the opening speech, that he would never, never grant a Constitution
in the modern sense of the word [18]; the Liberal league insisted upon
such a modern, anti-feudal, Representative Constitution, with all its
sequels, liberty of the press, trial by jury, &c.; and before they got it,
not a farthing of money would they grant. There was one thing
evident: that things could not go on long in this manner, and that
either one of the parties must give way, or that a rupture, a bloody
struggle, must ensue. And the middle classes knew that they were on
the eve of a revolution, and they prepared themselves for it. They
sought to obtain, by every possible means, the support of the
working class of the towns, and of the peasantry in the agricultural
districts, and it is well known that there was, in the latter end of 1847,
hardly a single prominent political character among the bourgeoisie
who did not proclaim himself a "Socialist," in order to insure to
himself the sympathy of the proletarian class. We shall see these
"Socialists" at work by and by.

This eagerness of the leading bourgeoisie to adopt at least the
outward show of Socialism, was caused by a great change that had
come over the working classes of Germany. There had been, ever
since 1840, a fraction of German workmen who, travelling in France
and Switzerland, had more or less imbibed the crude Socialist and
Communist notions then current among the French workmen. The
increasing attention paid to similar ideas in France, ever since 1840,
made Socialism and Communism fashionable in Germany also, and
as far back as 1843, all newspapers teemed with discussions of social
questions. A school of Socialists very soon formed itself in Germany,
distinguished more for the obscurity than for the novelty of its
ideas; its principal efforts consisted in the translation of French
Fourierist, Saint-Simonian and other doctrines into the abstruse
language of German philosophy.[19] The German Communist

School, entirely different from this sect, was formed about the same time.

In 1844 there occurred the Silesian weavers' riots, followed by the insurrection of the calico printers in Prague. These riots, cruelly suppressed, riots of working men, not against the Government, but against their employers, created a deep sensation, and gave a new stimulus to Socialist and Communist propaganda amongst the working people. So did the bread riots during the year of famine, 1847.[20] In short, in the same manner as Constitutional opposition rallied around its banner the great bulk of the propertied classes (with the exception of the large feudal land-holders), so the working classes of the larger towns looked for their emancipation to the Socialist and Communist doctrines, although, under the then existing press laws, they could be made to know only very little about them. They could not be expected to have any very definite ideas as to what they wanted—they only knew that the programme of the Constitutional bourgeoisie did not contain all they wanted, and that their wants were in no wise contained in the Constitutional circle of ideas.

There was then no separate republican party in Germany. People were either Constitutional monarchists, or more or less clearly defined Socialists or Communists.

With such elements, the slightest collision must have brought about a great revolution. While the higher nobility, and the older civil and military officers, were the only safe supports of the existing system; while the lower nobility, the trading middle classes, the universities, the school-masters of every degree, and even part of the lower ranks of the bureaucracy and military officers, were all leagued against the Government; while, behind these, there stood the dissatisfied masses of the peasantry, and of the proletarians of the large towns, supporting, for the time being, the liberal opposition, but already muttering strange words about taking things into their own hands; while the Bourgeoisie was ready to hurl down the Government, and the Proletarians were preparing to hurl down the Bourgeoisic in its turn;—this Government went on obstinately in a course which must bring about a collision. Germany was, in the beginning of 1848, on the eve of a revolution, and this revolution was sure to come, even had the French revolution of February not hastened it.

What the effects of this Parisian Revolution were upon Germany, we shall see in our next.

London, September, 1851

III
THE OTHER GERMAN STATES

[*New-York Daily Tribune*, No. 3292, November 6, 1851]

In our last we confined ourselves almost exclusively to that State which, during the years 1840 to 1848, was by far the most important in the German movement; namely, to Prussia. It is, however, time to pass a rapid glance over the other States of Germany during the same period.

As to the petty States, they had, ever since the revolutionary movements of 1830, completely passed under the dictatorship of the Diet, that is, of Austria and Prussia. The several constitutions, established as much as a means of defense against the dictates of the larger States, as to insure popularity to their princely authors and unity to heterogeneous assemblies of provinces, formed by the Congress of Vienna, without any leading principle whatever—these constitutions, illusory as they were, had yet proved dangerous to the authority of the petty princes themselves during the excited times of 1830 and 1831. They were all but destroyed; whatever of them was allowed to remain, was less than a shadow, and it required the loquacious self-complacency of a Welcker, a Rotteck, a Dahlmann, to imagine that any results could possibly flow from the humble opposition, mingled with degrading flattery, which they were allowed to show off in the impotent chambers of these petty States.

The more energetic portion of the middle class in these smaller States, very soon after 1840, abandoned all the hopes they had formerly based upon the development of Parliamentary government in these dependencies of Austria and Prussia. No sooner had the Prussian bourgeoisie, and the classes allied to it, shown a serious resolution to struggle for Parliamentary government in Prussia, than they were allowed to take the lead of the Constitutional movement over all non-Austrian Germany. It is a fact which now will not be any longer contested, that the nucleus of those Constitutionalists of Central Germany, who afterwards seceded from the Frankfort National Assembly, and who, from the place of their separate meetings, were called the Gotha party,[21] long before 1848 contemplated a plan which, with little modification, they in 1849 proposed to the representatives of all Germany. They intended a complete exclusion of Austria from the German Confederation, the establishment of a new Confederation with a new fundamental law and with a federal Parliament, under the protection of Prussia, and the incorporation of the more insignificant States into the larger ones. All this was to be carried out the moment Prussia entered into the ranks of constitutional monarchy, established the liberty of the press, assumed a policy independent from that of Russia and Austria, and thus enabled the Constitutionalists of the lesser States to obtain a real control over their respective Governments. The inventor of this scheme was Professor Gervinus, of Heidelberg (Baden). Thus the emancipation of the Prussian bourgeoisie was to be the signal for that of the middle classes of Germany generally, and for an alliance, offensive and defensive, of both against Russia and Austria; for Austria was, as we shall see presently, considered as an entirely barbarian country, of which very little was known, and that little not to the credit of its population; Austria, therefore, was not considered as an essential part of Germany.

As to the other classes of society, in the smaller States, they followed, more or less rapidly, in the wake of their equals in Prussia. The shopkeeping class got more and more dissatisfied with their respective Governments, with the increase of taxation, with the curtailments of those political sham-privileges of which they used to boast when comparing themselves to the "slaves of despotism" in Austria and Prussia; but as yet they had nothing definite in their opposition which might stamp them as an independent party, distinct from the Constitutionalism of the higher bourgeoisie. The dissatisfaction among the peasantry was equally growing, but it is well known that this section of the people, in quiet and peaceful times, will never assert its interests and assume its position as an independent class, except in countries where universal suffrage is established. The working classes in the trades and manufactures of the towns commenced to be infected with the "poison" of Socialism and Communism, but there being few towns of any importance out of Prussia, and still fewer manufacturing districts, the movement of this class, owing to the want of centers of action and propaganda, was extremely slow in the smaller States.

Both in Prussia and in the smaller States, the difficulty of giving vent to political opposition created a sort of religious opposition in the parallel movements of German Catholicism and Free Congregationalism.[22] History affords us numerous examples where, in countries which enjoy the blessings of a State Church, and where political discussion is fettered, the profane and dangerous opposition against the worldly power is hid under the more sanctified and apparently more disinterested struggle against spiritual despotism. Many a government that will not allow of any of its acts being discussed, will hesitate before it creates martyrs and excites the religious fanaticism of the masses. Thus in Germany, in 1845, in every State, either the Roman Catholic or the Protestant religion, or both, were considered part and parcel of the law of the land. In every State, too, the clergy of either of those denominations, or of both, formed an essential part of the bureaucratic establishment of the Government. To attack Protestant or Catholic orthodoxy, to attack priestcraft, was, then, to make an underhand attack upon the Government itself. As to the German Catholics, their very existence was an attack upon the Catholic Governments of Germany, particularly Austria and Bavaria; and as such it was taken by those Governments. The Free Congregationalists, Protestant Dissenters, somewhat resembling the English and American Unitarians,[23] openly professed their opposition to the clerical and rigidly orthodox tendency of the King of Prussia and his favorite Minister for the Educational and Clerical Department, Mr. Eichhorn. The two new sects, rapidly extending for a moment, the first in Catholic, the second in Protestant countries, had no other distinction but their different origin; as to their tenets, they perfectly agreed upon this most important point—that all definite dogmas were nugatory. This want of any definition was their very essence; they pretended to build that great temple under the roof of which all Germans might unite; they thus represented, in a religious form, another political idea of the day—that of German Unity; and yet, they could never agree among themselves.

The idea of German Unity, which the above-mentioned sects sought to realize at least upon religious ground, by inventing a common religion for all Germans, manufactured expressly for their use, habits, and taste—this idea was indeed very widely spread, particularly in the smaller States. Ever since the dissolution of the German Empire, by Napoleon,[24] the cry for a union of all the *disjecta membra*ᵃ of the German body had been the most general expression of discontent with the established order of things, and most so in the smaller States, where the costliness of a court, an administration, an army, in short, the dead weight of taxation, increased in a direct ratio with the smallness and impotency of the State. But what this German Unity was to be when carried out, was a question upon which parties disagreed. The bourgeoisie, which wanted no serious revolutionary convulsions, were satisfied with what we have seen they considered "practicable," namely, a union of all Germany, exclusive of Austria, under the supremacy of a constitutional government of Prussia; and surely, without conjuring dangerous storms, nothing more could, at that time, be done. The shopkeeping class and the peasantry, as far as these latter troubled themselves about such things, never arrived

---

ᵃ Scattered members.—*Ed.*

at any definition of that German Unity they so loudly clamored after; a few dreamers, mostly feudalist reactionists, hoped for the re-establishment of the German Empire; some few ignorant, *soi-disant* radicals, admiring Swiss institutions, of which they had not yet made that practical experience which afterward most ludicrously undeceived them, pronounced for a federated republic; and it was only the most extreme party which, at that time, dared pronounce for a German Republic,[25] one and indivisible. Thus, German Unity was in itself a question big with disunion, discord, and, in the case of certain eventualities, even civil war.

To resume, then; this was the state of Prussia and the smaller States of Germany, at the end of 1847. The middle class, feeling its power, and resolved not to endure much longer the fetters with which a feudal and bureaucratic despotism enchained their commercial transactions, their industrial productivity, their common action as a class; a portion of the landed nobility so far changed into producers of mere marketable commodities as to have the same interests and to make common cause with the middle class; the smaller trading class, dissatisfied, grumbling at the taxes, at the impediments thrown in the way of their business, but without any definite plan for such reforms as should secure their position in the social and political body; the peasantry, oppressed here by feudal exactions, there by money-lenders, usurers, and lawyers; the working people of the towns, infected with the general discontent, equally hating the Government and the large industrial capitalists, and catching the contagion of Socialist and Communist ideas; in short, a heterogeneous mass of opposition, springing from various interests, but more or less led on by the bourgeoisie, in the first ranks of which again marched the bourgeoisie of Prussia and particularly of the Rhine Province. On the other hand, governments disagreeing upon many points, distrustful of each other, and particularly of that of Prussia, upon which yet they had to rely for protection; in Prussia, a government forsaken by public opinion, forsaken by even a portion of the nobility, leaning upon an army and a bureaucracy which every day got more infected by the ideas and subjected to the influence of the oppositional bourgeoisie—a government, besides all this, penniless in the most literal meaning of the word, and which could not procure a single cent to cover its increasing deficit, but by surrendering at discretion to the opposition of the bourgeoisie. Was there ever a more splendid position for the middle class of any country, while it struggled for power against the established government?

London, September, 1851

IV

AUSTRIA

[*New-York Daily Tribune*, No. 3293, November 7, 1851]

We have now to consider Austria, that country which up to March, 1848, was sealed up to the eyes of foreign nations almost as much as China before the late war with England.[26]

As a matter of course, we can here take into consideration nothing but German Austria. The affairs of the Polish, Hungarian or Italian Austrians do not belong to our subject, and as far as they, since 1848, have influenced the fate of the German Austrians, they will have to be taken into account hereafter.

The Government of Prince Metternich turned upon two hinges: firstly, to keep every one of the different nations, subjected to the Austrian rule, in check by all other nations similarly conditioned; secondly, and this always has been the fundamental principle of absolute monarchies, to rely for support upon two classes, the feudal landlords and the large stockjobbing capitalists; and to balance, at the same time, the influence and power of either of these classes by that of the other, so as to leave full independence of action to the Government. The landed nobility, whose entire income consisted in feudal revenues of all sorts, could not but support a government which proved their only protection against that downtrodden class of serfs upon whose spoils they lived; and whenever the less wealthy portion of them, as in Galicia, in 1846, rose in opposition against the Government, Metternich, in an instant, let loose upon them these very serfs, who at any rate profited by the occasion to wreak a terrible vengeance upon their more immediate oppressors.[27] On the other hand, the large capitalists of the Exchange were chained to Metternich's Government by the vast share they had in the public funds of the country. Austria, restored to her full power in 1815, restoring and maintaining in Italy absolute monarchy ever since 1820, freed of part of her liabilities by the bankruptcy of 1810,[a] had after the peace very soon re-established her credit in the great European money markets, and in proportion as her credit grew, she had drawn against it. Thus all the large European money-dealers had engaged considerable portions of their capital in the Austrian funds; they all of them were interested in upholding the credit of that country, and as Austrian public credit, in order to be upheld, ever required new loans, they were obliged from time to time to

---

[a] More accurately: 1811.— *Ed.*

advance new capital in order to keep up the credit of the securities for that which they already had advanced. The long peace after 1815, and the apparent impossibility of a thousand years old empire, like Austria, being upset, increased the credit of Metternich's Government in a wonderful ratio, and made it even independent of the good will of the Vienna bankers and stockjobbers; for as long as Metternich could obtain plenty of money at Frankfort and Amsterdam, he had, of course, the satisfaction of seeing the Austrian capitalists at his feet. They were, besides, in every other respect at his mercy; the large profits which bankers, stockjobbers and government contractors always contrive to draw out of an absolute monarchy, were compensated for by the almost unlimited power which the Government possessed over their persons and fortunes; and not the smallest shadow of an opposition was, therefore, to be expected from this quarter. Thus, Metternich was sure of the support of the two most powerful and influential classes of the empire, and he possessed, besides, an army and a bureaucracy which, for all purposes of absolutism, could not be better constituted. The civil and military officers in the Austrian service form a race of their own; their fathers have been in the service of the *Kaiser*, and so will their sons be; they belong to none of the multifarious nationalities congregated under the wing of the double-headed eagle; they are, and ever have been, removed from one end of the empire to the other, from Poland to Italy, from Germany to Transylvania; Hungarian, Pole, German, Rumanian, Italian, Croat, every individual not stamped with "imperial and royal" authority, &c., bearing a separate national character, is equally despised by them; they have no nationality, or rather they alone make up the really Austrian nation. It is evident what a pliable and at the same time powerful instrument, in the hands of an intelligent and energetic chief, such a civil and military hierarchy must be.

As to the other classes of the population, Metternich, in the true spirit of a statesman of the *ancien régime*, cared little for their support. He had, with regard to them, but one policy: to draw as much as possible out of them in the shape of taxation, and at the same time, to keep them quiet. The trading and manufacturing middle class was but of slow growth in Austria. The trade of the Danube was comparatively unimportant; the country possessed but one port, Trieste, and the trade of this port was very limited. As to the manufacturers, they enjoyed considerable protection, amounting even in most cases to the complete exclusion of all foreign competition; but this advantage had been granted to them principally with a view to increase their tax-paying capabilities, and was in a high degree counterpoised by internal restrictions on manufactures, privileges of guilds and other feudal corporations, which were scrupulously upheld as long as they did not impede the purposes and views of the Government. The petty tradesmen were encased in the narrow bounds of these medieval guilds, which kept the different trades in a perpetual war of privilege against each other, and at the same time, by all but excluding individuals of the working class from the possibility of raising themselves in the social scale, gave a sort of hereditary stability to the members of those involuntary associations. Lastly, the peasant and the working man were treated as mere taxable matter, and the only care that was taken of them, was to keep them as much as possible in the same conditions of life in which they then existed, and in which their fathers had existed before them. For this purpose, every old established hereditary authority was upheld in the same manner as that of the State; the authority of the landlord over the petty tenant-farmer, that of the manufacturer over the operative, of the small master over the journeyman and apprentice, of the father over the son, was everywhere rigidly maintained by the Government, and every branch of disobedience punished, the same as a transgression of the law, by that universal instrument of Austrian justice—the stick.

Finally, to wind up into one comprehensive system all these attempts at creating an artificial stability, the intellectual food allowed to the nation was selected with the minutest caution, and dealt out as sparingly as possible. Education was everywhere in the hands of the Catholic priesthood, whose chiefs, in the same manner as the large feudal landowners, were deeply interested in the conservation of the existing system. The universities were organized in a manner which allowed them to produce nothing but special men, that might or might not obtain great proficiency in sundry particular branches of knowledge, but which, at all events, excluded that universal liberal education which other universities are expected to impart. There was absolutely no newspaper press, except in Hungary, and the Hungarian papers were prohibited in all other parts of the monarchy. As to general literature, its range had not widened for a century; it had been narrowed again after the death of Joseph II. And all around the frontier, wherever the Austrian States touched upon a civilized country, a *cordon* of literary censors was established in connection with the *cordon* of custom-house officials, preventing any foreign book or newspaper from passing into Austria before its contents had been twice or three times thoroughly sifted, and found pure of even the slightest contamination of the malignant spirit of the age.

For about thirty years after 1815, this system worked with wonderful success. Austria remained almost unknown to Europe, and Europe was quite as little known in Austria. The social state of every class of the population, and of the population as a whole, appeared not to have undergone the slightest change. Whatever rancor there might exist from class to class—and the existence of this rancor was, for Metternich, a principal condition of government, which he even fostered by making the higher classes the instruments of all government exactions, and thus throwing the odium upon them—whatever hatred the people might bear to the inferior officials of the State, there existed, upon the whole, little or no dissatisfaction with the Central Government. The Emperor was adored, and old Francis the First seemed to be borne out by facts, when, doubting of the durability of this system, he complacently added: "and yet it will hold while I live, and Metternich."

But there was a slow underground movement going on which baffled all Metternich's efforts. The wealth and influence of the manufacturing and trading middle class increased. The introduction of machinery and steam power in manufactures upset in Austria, as it had done everywhere else, the old relations and vital conditions of whole classes of society; it changed serfs into free men, small farmers into manufacturing operatives; it undermined the old feudal trades-corporations and destroyed the means of existence of many of them. The new commercial and manufacturing population came everywhere into collision with the old feudal institutions. The middle classes, more and more induced by their business to travel abroad, introduced some mythical knowledge of the civilized countries situated beyond the imperial line of customs; the introduction of railways, finally, accelerated both the industrial and intellectual movement. There was, too, a dangerous part in the Austrian State establishment, viz.: the Hungarian feudal Constitution, with its parliamentary proceedings and its struggles of the impoverished and oppositional mass of the nobility against the Government and its allies, the magnates. Pressburg,[a] the seat of the Diet, was at the very gates of Vienna. All the elements contributed to create among the middle classes, of the towns, a spirit, not exactly of opposition, for opposition was as yet impossible, but of discontent; a general wish for reforms, more of an administrative than of a constitutional nature. And in the same manner as in Prussia, a portion of the bureaucracy joined the bourgeoisie. Among this hereditary caste of officials the traditions of Joseph II were not forgotten; the more educated

---

[a] The Slovak name: Bratislava.— Ed.

functionaries of the Government, who themselves sometimes
meddled with imaginary possible reforms, by far preferred the
progressive and intellectual despotism of that Emperor to the
"paternal" despotism of Metternich. A portion of the poorer nobility
equally sided with the middle class, and as to the lower classes of the
population, who always had found plenty of grounds to complain of
their superiors, if not of the Government, they in most cases could
not but adhere to the reformatory wishes of the bourgeoisie.

It was about this time, say 1843 or 1844, that a particular branch of
literature, agreeably to this change, was established in Germany. A
few Austrian writers, novelists, literary critics, bad poets, the whole
of them of very indifferent ability, but gifted with that peculiar
industrialism proper to the Jewish race, established themselves in
Leipsic and other German towns out of Austria, and there, out of the
reach of Metternich, published a number of books and pamphlets on
Austrian affairs. They and their publishers made "a roaring trade"
of it. All Germany was eager to become initiated into the secrets of
the policy of European China; and the Austrians themselves, who
obtained these publications by the wholesale smuggling carried on
upon the Bohemian ᵃ frontier, were still more curious. Of course, the
secrets let out in these publications were of no great importance, and
the reform plans schemed out by their well-wishing authors bore the
stamp of an innocuousness almost amounting to political virginity. A
constitution and a free press for Austria were things considered
unattainable; administrative reforms, extension of the rights of the
provincial diets, admission of foreign books and newspapers, and a
less severe censorship—the loyal and humble desires of these good
Austrians did hardly go any further.

At all events, the growing impossibility of preventing the literary
intercourse of Austria with the rest of Germany, and through
Germany with the world, contributed much toward the formation
of an anti-governmental public opinion, and brought at least some
little political information within the reach of part of the Austrian
population. Thus, by the end of 1847, Austria was seized,
although in an inferior degree, by that political and politico-
religious agitation which then prevailed in all Germany; and if its
progress in Austria was more silent, it did nevertheless find
revolutionary elements enough to work upon. There was the
peasant, serf or feudal tenant, ground down into the dust by
lordly or government exactions; then the factory operative, forced,

---

ᵃ Czech.— *Ed.*

by the stick of the policeman, to work upon any terms the manufacturer chose to grant; then the journeyman, debarred by the corporative laws from any chance of gaining an independence in his trade; then the merchant, stumbling, at every step in business, over absurd regulations; then the manufacturer, in uninterrupted conflict with trades-guilds jealous of their privileges, or with greedy and meddling officials; then the schoolmaster, the *savant,* the better educated functionary, vainly struggling against an ignorant and presumptuous clergy, or a stupid and dictating superior. In short, there was not a single class satisfied, for the small concessions Government was obliged now and then to make were made not at its own expense, for the Treasury could not afford that, but at the expense of the high aristocracy and clergy; and, as to the great bankers and fund-holders, the late events in Italy, the increasing opposition of the Hungarian Diet, and the unwonted spirit of discontent and cry for reform manifesting themselves all over the Empire, were not of a nature to strengthen their faith in the solidity and solvency of the Austrian Empire.

Thus Austria, too, was marching, slowly but surely, toward a mighty change, when of a sudden an event broke out in France which at once brought down the impending storm, and gave the lie to old Francis's assertion, that the building would hold out both during his and Metternich's lifetime.

London, September, 1851

V

THE VIENNA INSURRECTION

[*New-York Daily Tribune,* No. 3297, November 12, 1851]

On the 24th of February, 1848, Louis Philippe was driven out of Paris and the French Republic was proclaimed. On the 13th of March following, the people of Vienna broke the power of Prince Metternich and made him flee shamefully out of the country. On the 18th of March the people of Berlin rose in arms, and, after an obstinate struggle of eighteen hours, had the satisfaction of seeing the King[a] surrender himself over to their hands. Simultaneous outbreaks of a more or less violent nature, but all with the same

---

[a] Frederick .William IV.— *Ed.*

success, occurred in the capitals of the smaller States of Germany. The German people, if they had not accomplished their first revolution, were at least fairly launched into the revolutionary career.

As to the incidents of these various insurrections, we cannot enter here into the details of them: what we have to explain is their character, and the position which the different classes of the population took up with regard to them.

The revolution of Vienna may be said to have been made by an almost unanimous population. The bourgeoisie, with the exception of the bankers and stockjobbers, the petty trading class, the working people, one and all, arose at once against a government detested by all, a government so universally hated, that the small minority of nobles and money-lords which had supported it, made itself invisible on the very first attack. The middle classes had been kept in such a degree of political ignorance by Metternich, that to them the news from Paris about the reign of Anarchy, Socialism and Terror, and about impending struggles between the class of capitalists and the class of laborers, proved quite unintelligible. They, in their political innocence, either could attach no meaning to these news, or they believed them to be fiendish inventions of Metternich, to frighten them into obedience. They, besides, had never seen working men act as a class, or stand up for their own distinct class interests. They had, from their past experience, no idea of the possibility of any differences springing up between classes that now were so heartily united in upsetting a government hated by all. They saw the working people agree with themselves upon all points: a constitution, trial by jury, liberty of the press, &c. Thus, they were, in March, 1848, at least, heart and soul with the movement, and the movement, on the other hand, at once constituted them the (at least in theory) predominant class of the State.

But it is the fate of all revolutions that this union of different classes, which in some degree is always the necessary condition of any revolution, cannot subsist long. No sooner is the victory gained against the common enemy, than the victors become divided among themselves into different camps and turn their weapons against each other. It is this rapid and passionate development of class antagonism which, in old and complicated social organisms, makes a revolution such a powerful agent of social and political progress; it is this incessantly quick upshooting of new parties succeeding each other in power which, during those violent commotions, makes a nation pass in five years over more ground than it would have done in a century under ordinary circumstances.

The revolution, in Vienna, made the middle class the theoretically predominant class; that is to say, the concessions wrung from the Government were such as, once carried out practically and adhered to for a time, would inevitably have secured the supremacy of the middle class. But, practically, the supremacy of that class was far from being established. It is true that by the establishment of a National Guard, which gave arms to the bourgeoisie, and petty tradesmen, that class obtained both force and importance; it is true, that by the installation of a "Committee of Safety," a sort of revolutionary, irresponsible government, in which the bourgeoisie predominated, it was placed at the head of power. But at the same time, the working classes were partially armed too; they and the students had borne the brunt of the fight, as far as fight there had been; and the students, about 4,000 strong, well armed and far better disciplined than the National Guard, formed the nucleus, the real strength of the revolutionary force, and were noways willing to act as a mere instrument in the hands of the Committee of Safety. Though they recognized it and even were its most enthusiastic supporters, they yet formed a sort of independent and rather turbulent body,[28] deliberating for themselves in the "Aula," keeping an intermediate position between the bourgeoisie and the working classes, preventing, by constant agitation, things to settle down to the old everyday tranquillity, and very often forcing their resolutions upon the Committee of Safety. The working men, on the other hand, almost entirely thrown out of employment, had to be employed in public works at the expense of the State, and the money for this purpose had of course to be taken out of the purse of the tax-payers or out of the chest of the city of Vienna. All this could not but become very unpleasant to the tradesmen of Vienna. The manufactures of the city, calculated for the consumption of the rich and aristocratic courts of a large country, were as a matter of course entirely stopped by the revolution, by the flight of the aristocracy and court; trade was at a standstill, and the continuous agitation and excitement kept up by the students and working people was certainly not the means to "restore confidence," as the phrase went. Thus, a certain coolness very soon sprung up between the middle classes on the one side, and the turbulent students and working people on the other; and if, for a long time, this coolness was not ripened into open hostility, it was because the Ministry, and particularly the Court, in their impatience to restore the old order of things, constantly justified the suspicions and the turbulent activity of the more revolutionary parties, and constantly made arise, even before the eyes of the middle classes, the spectre of old Metternichian despotism. Thus on the 15th of May, and again on the 26th, there were fresh risings of all classes in Vienna,[a] on account of the Government having tried to attack or to undermine some of the newly conquered liberties, and on each occasion, the alliance between the National Guard or armed middle class, the students, and the working men, was again cemented for a time.

As to the other classes of the population, the aristocracy and the money-lords had disappeared, and the peasantry were busily engaged everywhere in the removing, down to the very last vestiges, of feudalism. Thanks to the war in Italy,[29] and the occupation which Vienna and Hungary gave to the Court, they were left at full liberty, and succeeded in their work of liberation, in Austria, better than in any other part of Germany. The Austrian Diet very shortly after had only to confirm the steps[30] already practically taken by the peasantry, and whatever else the Government of Prince Schwarzenberg may be enabled to restore, it will never have the power of re-establishing the feudal servitude of the peasantry. And if Austria at the present moment is again comparatively tranquil, and even strong, it is principally because the great majority of the people, the peasants, have been real gainers by the revolution, and because whatever else has been attacked by the restored Government, these palpable, substantial advantages, conquered by the peasantry, are as yet untouched.

London, October, 1851

VI

THE BERLIN INSURRECTION

[New-York Daily Tribune, No. 3311, November 28, 1851]

The second center of revolutionary action was Berlin. And from what has been stated in the foregoing papers, it may be guessed that there this action was far from having that unanimous support of almost all classes by which it was accompanied in Vienna. In Prussia the bourgeoisie had been already involved in actual

---

[a] See this volume, pp. 54-55.— Ed.

struggles with the Government; a rupture had been the result of the "United Diet"; a bourgeois revolution was impending, and that revolution might have been, in its first outbreak, quite as unanimous as that of Vienna, had it not been for the Paris revolution of February. That event precipitated everything, while, at the same time, it was carried out under a banner totally different from that under which the Prussian bourgeoisie was preparing to defy its Government. The revolution of February upset, in France, the very same sort of government which the Prussian bourgeoisie were going to set up in their own country. The revolution of February announced itself as a revolution of the working classes against the middle classes; it proclaimed the downfall of middle-class government and the emancipation of the working man. Now the Prussian bourgeoisie had of late had quite enough of working-class agitation in their own country. After the first terror of the Silesian riots had passed away, they had even tried to give this agitation a turn in their own favor; but they always had retained a salutary horror of revolutionary Socialism and Communism; and, therefore, when they saw men at the head of the Government in Paris whom they considered as the most dangerous enemies of property, order, religion, family, and of the other *penates*[31] of the modern bourgeois, they at once experienced a considerable cooling down of their own revolutionary ardor. They knew that the moment must be seized, and that without the aid of the working masses they would be defeated; and yet their courage failed them. Thus they sided with the Government in the first partial and provincial outbreaks, tried to keep the people quiet in Berlin, who during five days met in crowds before the royal palace to discuss the news and ask for changes in the Government; and when at last, after the news of the downfall of Metternich, the King made some slight concessions, the bourgeoisie considered the revolution as completed, and went to thank his Majesty for having fulfilled all the wishes of his people. But then followed the attack of the military on the crowd, the barricades, the struggle, and the defeat of Royalty. Then everything was changed; the very working classes, which it had been the tendency of the bourgeoisie to keep in the background, had been pushed forward, had fought and conquered, and all at once were conscious of their strength. Restrictions of suffrage, of the liberty of the press, of the right to sit on juries, of the right of meeting—restrictions that would have been very agreeable to the bourgeoisie, because they would have touched upon such classes only as were beneath it—now were no longer possible. The danger of a repetition of the Parisian scenes of "anarchy" was imminent. Before this danger all former differences disappeared. Against the victorious working man, although he had not yet uttered any specific demands for himself, the friends and the foes of many years united, and the alliance between the bourgeoisie and the supporters of the overturned system was concluded upon the very barricades of Berlin. The necessary concessions, but no more than was unavoidable, were to be made; a ministry of the opposition leaders of the United Diet was to be formed, and in return for its services in saving the Crown, it was to have the support of all the props of the old Government, the feudal aristocracy, the bureaucracy, the army. These were the conditions upon which Messrs. Camphausen and Hansemann undertook the formation of a Cabinet.

Such was the dread evinced, by the new ministers, of the aroused masses, that in their eyes every means was good if it only tended to strengthen the shaken foundations of authority. They, poor deluded wretches, thought every danger of a restoration of the old system had passed away; and thus they made use of the whole of the old state machinery for the purpose of restoring "order." Not a single bureaucrat or military officer was dismissed; not the slightest change was made in the old bureaucratic system of administration. These precious constitutional and responsible ministers even restored to their posts those functionaries whom the people, in the first heat of revolutionary ardor, had driven away on account of their former acts of bureaucratic overbearing. There was nothing altered, in Prussia, but the persons of the ministers; even the ministerial staffs in the different departments were not touched upon, and all the constitutional place-hunters, who had formed the chorus of the newly-elevated rulers, and who had expected their share of power and office, were told to wait until restored stability allowed changes to be operated in the bureaucratic personnel which now were not without danger.

The King, chap-fallen in the highest degree after the insurrection of the 18th of March, very soon found out that he was quite as necessary to these "liberal" ministers as they were to him. The throne had been spared by the insurrection; the throne was the last existing obstacle to "anarchy," the liberal middle class and its leaders, now in the ministry, had therefore every interest to keep on excellent terms with the Crown. The King, and the reactionary camarilla that surrounded him, were not slow in discovering this, and profited by the circumstance in order to fetter the march of the ministry even in those petty reforms that were from time to time intended.

The first care of the ministry was to give a sort of legal appearance to the recent violent changes. The United Diet was convoked, in spite of all popular opposition, in order to vote, as the legal and constitutional organ of the people, a new electoral law for the election of an assembly, which was to agree with the Crown upon a new Constitution.[32] The elections were to be indirect, the mass of voters electing a number of electors, who then were to choose the representative. In spite of all opposition, this system of double elections passed. The United Diet was then asked for a loan of twenty-five millions of dollars, opposed by the popular party, but equally agreed to.

These acts of the ministry gave a most rapid development to the popular, or as it now called itself, the democratic party. This party, headed by the petty trading and shopkeeping class, and uniting under its banner, in the beginning of the revolution, the large majority of the working people, demanded direct and universal suffrage, the same as established in France, a single Legislative Assembly, and full and open recognition of the revolution of the 18th of March, as the base of the new governmental system. The more moderate faction would be satisfied with a thus "democratized" monarchy, the more advanced demanded the ultimate establishment of the Republic. Both factions agreed in recognizing the German National Assembly at Frankfort as the supreme authority of the country, while the Constitutionalists and Reactionists affected a great horror of the sovereignty of this body, which they professed to consider as utterly revolutionary.

The independent movement of the working classes had, by the revolution, been broken up for a time. The immediate wants and circumstances of the movement were such as not to allow of any of the specific demands of the Proletarian party to be put in the foreground. In fact, as long as the ground was not cleared for the independent action of the working men, as long as direct and universal suffrage was not yet established, as long as the 36 larger and smaller States continued to cut up Germany into numberless morsels, what else could the Proletarian party do but watch the—for them all-important—movement of Paris, and struggle in common with the petty shopkeepers for the attainment of those rights which would allow them to fight, afterward, their own battle?

There were only three points, then, by which the Proletarian party in its political action essentially distinguished itself from the petty trading class, or properly so-called democratic party: firstly, in judging differently the French movement, with regard to which the democrats attacked, and the Proletarian Revolutionists defended the extreme party in Paris; secondly, in proclaiming the necessity of establishing a German Republic, one and indivisible, while the very extremest ultras among the democrats only dared to sigh for a Federative Republic; and thirdly, in showing upon every occasion, that revolutionary boldness and readiness for action, in which any party, headed by and composed principally, of petty tradesmen, will always be deficient.

The Proletarian, or really revolutionary party, succeeded only very gradually in withdrawing the mass of the working people from the influence of the democrats, whose tail they formed in the beginning of the revolution. But in due time the indecision, weakness and cowardice of the democratic leaders did the rest, and it may now be said to be one of the principal results of the last years' convulsions, that wherever the working class is concentrated in anything like considerable masses, they are entirely freed from that democratic influence which led them into an endless series of blunders and misfortunes during 1848 and 1849. But we had better not anticipate; the events of these two years will give us plenty of opportunities to show the democratic gentlemen at work.

The peasantry in Prussia, the same as in Austria, but with less energy, feudalism pressing, upon the whole, not quite so hard upon them here, had profited by the revolution to free themselves at once from all feudal shackles. But here, from the reasons stated before, the middle classes at once turned against them, their oldest, their most indispensable allies; the democrats, equally frightened with the bourgeois by what was called attacks upon private property, failed equally to support them; and thus, after three months' emancipation, after bloody struggles and military executions, particularly in Silesia, feudalism was restored by the hands of the, until yesterday, anti-feudal bourgeoisie. There is not a more damning fact to be brought against them than this. Similar treason against its best allies, against itself, never was committed by any party in history, and, whatever humiliation and chastisement may be in store for this middle-class party, it has deserved by this one act every morsel of it.

London, October, 1851

VII
THE FRANKFORT NATIONAL ASSEMBLY

[*New-York Daily Tribune*, No. 3389, February 27, 1852]

It will perhaps be in the recollection of our readers that in the six preceding papers we followed up the revolutionary movement of Germany to the two great popular victories of March 13, in Vienna, and March 18, in Berlin. We saw, both in Austria and Prussia, the establishment of Constitutional Governments and the proclamation, as leading rules for all future policy, of liberal or middle-class principles; and the only difference observable between the two great centers of action was this, that in Prussia the liberal bourgeoisie in the persons of two wealthy merchants, Messrs. Camphausen and Hansemann, directly seized upon the reins of power; while in Austria, where the bourgeoisie was, politically, far less educated, the liberal *Bureaucratie* walked into office and professed to hold power in trust for them. We have further seen, how the parties and classes of society, that were heretofore all united in their opposition to the old Government, got divided among themselves after the victory or even during the struggle; and how that same liberal bourgeoisie that alone profited from the victory turned round immediately upon its allies of yesterday, assumed a hostile attitude against every class or party of a more advanced character, and concluded an alliance with the conquered feudal and bureaucratic interests. It was in fact evident, even from the beginning of the revolutionary drama, that the liberal bourgeoisie could not hold its ground against the vanquished, but not destroyed, feudal and bureaucratic parties except by relying upon the assistance of the popular and more advanced parties; and that it equally required, against the torrent of these more advanced masses, the assistance of the feudal nobility and of the bureaucracy. Thus, it was clear enough, that the bourgeoisie, in Austria and Prussia, did not possess sufficient strength to maintain their power and to adapt the institutions of the country to their own wants and ideas. The liberal Bourgeois Ministry was only a halting place from which, according to the turn circumstances might take, the country would either have to go on to the more advanced stage of Unitarian Republicanism, or to relapse into the old clerico-feudal and bureaucratic *régime*. At all events, the real, decisive struggle was yet to come; the events of March had only engaged the combat.

Austria and Prussia being the two ruling States of Germany, every decisive revolutionary victory in Vienna or Berlin would have been decisive for all Germany. And as far as they went, the events of March, 1848, in these two cities, decided the turn of German affairs.

3*

It would, then, be superfluous to recur to the movements that occurred in the minor States; and we might, indeed, confine ourselves to the consideration of Austrian and Prussian affairs exclusively, if the existence of these minor States had not given rise to a body which was, by its very existence, a most striking proof of the abnormal situation of Germany and of the incompleteness of the late revolution; a body so abnormal, so ludicrous by its very position, and yet so full of its own importance, that history will, most likely, never afford a pendant to it. This body was the so-called *German National Assembly* at Frankfort-on-the-Main.

After the popular victories of Vienna and Berlin, it was a matter of course that there should be a Representative Assembly for all Germany. This body was consequently elected, and met at Frankfort, by the side of the old Federative Diet. The German National Assembly was expected, by the people, to settle every matter in dispute, and to act as the highest legislative authority for the whole of the German Confederation. But at the same time the Diet which had convoked it had in no way fixed its attributions. No one knew whether its decrees were to have force of law, or whether they were to be subject to the sanction of the Diet or of the individual Governments. In this perplexity, if the Assembly had been possessed of the least energy, it would have immediately dissolved and sent home the Diet—than which no corporate body was more unpopular in Germany—and replaced it by a Federal Government chosen from among its own members. It would have declared itself the only legal expression of the sovereign will of the German people, and thus attached legal validity to every one of its decrees. It would, above all, have secured to itself an organized and armed force in the country sufficient to put down any opposition on the part of the Governments. And all this was easy, very easy at that early period of the revolution. But that would have been expecting a great deal too much from an Assembly composed in its majority of liberal attorneys and *doctrinaire* professors, an Assembly which, while it pretended to embody the very essence of German intellect and science, was in reality nothing but a stage where old and worn-out political characters exhibited their involuntary ludicrousness and their impotence of thought, as well as action, before the eyes of all Germany. This Assembly of old women was, from the first day of its existence, more frightened of the least popular movement than of all the reactionary plots of all the German Governments put together. It deliberated under the eyes of the Diet, nay, it almost craved the Diet's sanction to its decrees, for its first resolutions had to be promulgated by that odious body. Instead of asserting its own sovereignty, it studiously avoided the discussion of any such dangerous questions. Instead of surrounding itself by a popular force, it passed to the order of the day over all the violent encroachments of the Governments; Mayence, under its very eyes, was placed in a state of siege and the people there disarmed, and the National Assembly did not stir.[33] Later on it elected Archduke John of Austria Regent of Germany, and declared that all its resolutions were to have the force of law[34]; but then, Archduke John was only instituted in his new dignity after the consent of all the Governments had been obtained, and he was instituted not by the Assembly, but by the Diet; and as to the legal force of the decrees of the Assembly, that point was never recognized by the larger Governments, nor enforced by the Assembly itself; it therefore remained in suspense. Thus we had the strange spectacle of an Assembly pretending to be the only legal representative of a great and sovereign nation, and yet never possessing either the will or the force to make its claims recognized. The debates of this body, without any practical result, were not even of any theoretical value, reproducing, as they did, nothing but the most hackneyed commonplace themes of superannuated philosophical and juridical schools; every sentence that was said or rather stammered forth in that Assembly having been printed a thousand times over and a thousand times better long before.

Thus, the pretended new central authority of Germany left every thing as it had found it. So, far from realizing the long-demanded unity of Germany, it did not dispossess the most insignificant of the princes who ruled her; it did not draw closer the bonds of union between her separated provinces; it never moved a single step to break down the custom-house barriers that separated Hanover from Prussia and Prussia from Austria; it did not even make the slightest attempt to remove the obnoxious dues that everywhere obstruct river navigation in Prussia. But the less this Assembly did, the more it blustered. It created a German Fleet—upon paper; it annexed Poland and Schleswig; it allowed German Austria to carry on war against Italy, and yet prohibited the Italians from following up the Austrians into their safe retreat in Germany; it gave three cheers and one cheer more for the French Republic and it received Hungarian Embassies, which certainly went home with far more confused ideas about Germany than what they had come with.

This Assembly had been, in the beginning of the Revolution, the bugbear of all German Governments. They had counted upon a very dictatorial and revolutionary action on its part—an account of the very want of definiteness in which it had been found necessary to leave its competency. These Governments, therefore, got up a most

comprehensive system of intrigues in order to weaken the influence
of this dreaded body; but they proved to have more luck than wits,
for this Assembly did the work of the Governments better than they
themselves could have done. The chief feature among these
intrigues was the convocation of local Legislative Assemblies, and in
consequence, not only the lesser States convoked their Legislatures,
but Prussia and Austria also called Constituent Assemblies. In these,
as in the Frankfort House of Representatives, the liberal middle
class, or its allies, liberal lawyers and bureaucrats, had the majority,
and the turn affairs took in each of them was nearly the same. The
only difference is this, that the German National Assembly was the
parliament of an imaginary country, as it had declined the task of
forming what nevertheless was its own first condition of existence,
viz.: a United Germany; that it discussed the imaginary and
never-to-be-carried-out measures of an imaginary Government of its
own creation, and that it passed imaginary resolutions for which
nobody cared; while in Austria and Prussia the constituent bodies
were at least real parliaments, upsetting and creating real ministries,
and forcing, for a time at least, their resolutions upon the Princes
with whom they had to contend. They, too, were cowardly, and
lacked enlarged views of revolutionary resolution; they, too,
betrayed the people, and restored power to the hands of feudal,
bureaucratic and military despotism. But then, they were at least
obliged to discuss practical questions of immediate interest, and to
live upon earth with other people, while the Frankfort humbugs
were never happier than when they could roam in "the airy realms
of dream," im Luftreich des Traums.[a] Thus the proceedings of the
Berlin and Vienna Constituents form an important part of German
revolutionary history, while the lucubrations of the Frankfort
collective tomfoolery merely interest the collector of literary and
antiquarian curiosities.

The people of Germany, deeply feeling the necessity of doing
away with the obnoxious territorial division that scattered and
annihilated the collective force of the nation, for some time expected
to find in the Frankfort National Assembly at least the beginning of a
new era. But the childish conduct of that set of wiseacres soon
disenchanted the national enthusiasm. The disgraceful proceedings
occasioned by the armistice of Malmoe (September, 1848),[35] made
the popular indignation burst out against a body, which, it had been
hoped, would give the nation a fair field for action, and which

---

[a] Heinrich Heine, Deutschland, ein Wintermärchen, Chapter VII.— Ed.

instead, carried away by unequalled cowardice, only restored to their former solidity the foundations upon which the present counter-revolutionary system is built.

London, January, 1852

VIII

POLES, TSCHECHS AND GERMANS[36]

[*New-York Daily Tribune,* No. 3395, March 5, 1852]

From what has been stated in the foregoing articles, it is already evident that unless a fresh revolution was to follow that of March, 1848, things would inevitably return, in Germany, to what they were before this event. But such is the complicated nature of the historical theme upon which we are trying to throw some light, that subsequent events cannot be clearly understood without taking into account what may be called the foreign relations of the German Revolution. And these foreign relations were of the same intricate nature as the home affairs.

The whole of the eastern half of Germany, as far as the Elbe, Saale and Bohemian Forest,[a] has, it is well known, been reconquered during the last thousand years, from invaders of Slavonic origin. The greater part of these territories have been Germanized, to the perfect extinction of all Slavonic nationality and language, for several centuries past; and if we except a few totally isolated remnants, amounting in the aggregate to less than a hundred thousand souls (Kassubians in Pomerania, Wends or Sorbians in Lusatia), their inhabitants are, to all intents and purposes, Germans. But the case is different along the whole of the frontier of ancient Poland, and in the countries of the Tschechian tongue, in Bohemia and Moravia. Here the two nationalities are mixed up in every district, the towns being generally more or less German, while the Slavonic element prevails in the rural villages, where, however, it is also gradually disintegrated and forced back by the steady advance of German influence.

The reason of this state of things is this. Ever since the time of Charlemagne the Germans have directed their most constant and persevering efforts to the conquest, colonization, or, at least, civilization of the East of Europe. The conquests of the feudal

---

[a] Czech Forest.— *Ed.*

nobility, between the Elbe and the Oder, and the feudal colonies of
the military orders of knights in Prussia and Livonia only laid the
ground for a far more extensive and effective system of Germanization by the trading and manufacturing middle classes, which in
Germany, as in the rest of Western Europe, rose into social and
political importance since the fifteenth century. The Slavonians, and
particularly the Western Slavonians (Poles and Tschechs), are
essentially an agricultural race; trade and manufactures never were
in great favor with them. The consequence was, that with the
increase of population and the origin of cities, in these regions, the
production of all articles of manufacture fell into the hands of
German immigrants, and the exchange of these commodities against
agricultural produce became the exclusive monopoly of the Jews,
who, if they belong to any nationality, are in these countries certainly
rather Germans than Slavonians. This has been, though in a less
degree, the case in all the East of Europe. The handicraftsman, the
small shopkeeper, the petty manufacturer is a German up to this day
in Petersburg, Pesht, Jassy and even Constantinople; while the
money-lender, the publican, the hawker—a very important man in
these thinly populated countries—is very generally a Jew, whose
native tongue is a horribly corrupted German. The importance of
the German element in the Slavonic frontier localities, thus rising
with the growth of towns, trade and manufactures, was still increased
when it was found necessary to import almost every element of
mental culture from Germany; after the German merchant, and
handicraftsman, the German clergyman, the German schoolmaster,
the German *savant* came to establish himself upon Slavonic soil. And
lastly, the iron tread of conquering armies, or the cautious,
well-premeditated grasp of diplomacy not only followed, but many
times went ahead of the slow but sure advance of denationalization
by social developments. Thus, great parts of Western Prussia and
Posen have been Germanized since the first partition of Poland,[37] by
sales and grants of public domains to German colonists, by
encouragements given to German capitalists for the establishment of
manufactories, &c., in those neighborhoods, and very often, too, by
excessively despotic measures against the Polish inhabitants of the
country.

In this manner, the last seventy years had entirely changed the line
of demarcation between the German and Polish nationalities. The
revolution of 1848 calling forth, at once, the claim of all oppressed
nations to an independent existence, and to the right of settling their
own affairs for themselves, it was quite natural that the Poles should
at once demand the restoration of their country within the frontiers

of the old Polish Republic before 1772. It is true, this frontier, even at that time, had become obsolete, if taken as the delimitation of German and Polish nationality; it had become more so every year since by the progress of Germanization; but then, the Germans had proclaimed such an enthusiasm for the restoration of Poland, that they must expect to be asked, as a first proof of the reality of their sympathies, to give up *their* share of the plunder. On the other hand, should whole tracts of land, inhabited chiefly by Germans, should large towns, entirely German, be given up to a people that as yet had never given any proofs of its capability of progressing beyond a state of feudalism based upon agricultural serfdom? The question was intricate enough. The only possible solution was in a war with Russia; the question of delimitation between the different revolutionized nations would have been made a secondary one to that of first establishing a safe frontier against the common enemy; the Poles, by receiving extended territories in the east, would have become more tractable and reasonable in the west; and Riga and Mitau[a] would have been deemed, after all, quite as important to them as Danzig and Elbing.[b] Thus the advanced party in Germany, deeming a war with Russia necessary to keep up the Continental movement, and considering that the national re-establishment even of a part of Poland would inevitably lead to such a war, supported the Poles; while the reigning liberal middle-class party clearly foresaw its downfall from any national war against Russia, which would have called more active and energetic men to the helm, and therefore, with a feigned enthusiasm for the extension of German nationality, they declared Prussian Poland, the chief seat of Polish revolutionary agitation, to be part and parcel of the German Empire that was to be. The promises given to the Poles in the first days of excitement were shamefully broken; Polish armaments, got up with the sanction of the Government, were dispersed and massacred by Prussian artillery; and as soon as the month of April, 1848, within six weeks of the Berlin Revolution, the Polish movement was crushed, and the old national hostility revived between Poles and Germans.[38] This immense and incalculable service to the Russian Autocrat was performed by the liberal merchant-ministers, Camphausen and Hansemann. It must be added, that this Polish campaign was the first means of reorganising and reassuring that same Prussian army, which afterward turned out the Liberal party and crushed the movement which Messrs. Camphausen and Hansemann had taken

---

[a] Lettish name: Jelgava.— *Ed.*
[b] Polish names: Gdansk and Elblong.— *Ed.*

such pains to bring about. "Whereby they sinned, thereby are they punished."[a] Such has been the fate of all the upstarts of 1848 and '49, from Ledru-Rollin to Changarnier, and from Camphausen down to Haynau.

The question of nationality gave rise to another struggle in Bohemia. This country, inhabited by two millions of Germans, and three millions of Slavonians of the Tschechian tongue, had great historical recollections, almost all connected with the former supremacy of the Tschechs. But then the force of this branch of the Slavonic family had been broken ever since the wars of the Hussites in the fifteenth century[39]; the provinces speaking the Tschechian language were divided, one part forming the kingdom of Bohemia, another the principality of Moravia, a third, the Carpathian hill-country of the Slovaks, being part of Hungary. The Moravians and Slovaks had long since lost every vestige of national feeling and vitality, although mostly preserving their language. Bohemia was surrounded by thoroughly German countries on three sides out of four. The German element had made great progress on her own territory; even in the capital, in Prague, the two nationalities were pretty equally matched; and everywhere capital, trade, industry, and mental culture were in the hands of the Germans. The chief champion of the Tschechian nationality, Professor Palacký, is himself nothing but a learned German run mad, who even now cannot speak the Tschechian language correctly and without foreign accent. But as it often happens, dying Tschechian nationality—dying according to every fact known in history for the last four hundred years—made in 1848 a last effort to regain its former vitality—an effort whose failure, independently of all revolutionary considerations, was to prove that Bohemia could only exist, henceforth, as a portion of Germany, although part of her inhabitants might yet, for some centuries, continue to speak a non-German language.

London, February, 1852

IX

PANSLAVISM. THE SCHLESWIG-HOLSTEIN WAR

[New-York Daily Tribune, No. 3403, March 15, 1852]

Bohemia and Croatia (another disjected member of the Slavonic family, acted upon by the Hungarian as Bohemia by the German)

---

[a] The Wisdom of Solomon 11:16.—Ed.

were the homes of what is called on the European Continent "*Panslavism.*" Neither Bohemia nor Croatia was strong enough to exist as a nation by herself. Their respective nationalities, gradually undermined by the action of historical causes that inevitably absorbs them into a more energetic stock, could only hope to be restored to something like independence by an alliance with other Slavonic nations. There were twenty-two millions of Poles, forty-five millions of Russians, eight millions of Serbians and Bulgarians—why not form a mighty Confederation of the whole eighty millions of Slavonians, and drive back or exterminate the intruder upon the holy Slavonic soil, the Turk, the Hungarian, and, above all, the hated, but indispensable *Niemetz*, the German? Thus, in the studies of a few Slavonian *dilettanti* of historical science was this ludicrous, this anti-historical movement got up, a movement which intended nothing less than to subjugate the civilized West under the barbarian East, the town under the country, trade, manufactures, intelligence, under the primitive agriculture of Slavonian serfs. But behind this ludicrous theory stood the terrible reality of the *Russian Empire*, that empire which by every movement proclaims the pretension of considering all Europe as the domain of the Slavonic race and especially of the only energetic part of this race, of the Russians; that empire which, with two capitals such as St. Petersburg and Moscow, has not yet found its center of gravity, as long as the "*City of the Czar*" (Constantinople, called in Russian Tzarigrad, the Czar's city), considered by every Russian peasant as the true metropolis of his religion and his nation, is not actually the residence of its Emperor; that empire which, for the last 150 years, has never lost, but always gained territory by every war it has commenced. And well known in Central Europe are the intrigues by which Russian policy supported the new-fangled system of Panslavism, a system than which none better could be invented to suit its purposes. Thus, the Bohemian and Croatian Panslavists, some intentionally, some without knowing it, worked in the direct interest of Russia; they betrayed the revolutionary cause for the shadow of a nationality which, in the best of cases, would have shared the fate of the Polish nationality under Russian sway. It must, however, be said for the honor of the Poles, that they never got to be seriously entangled in these Panslavistic traps; and if a few of the aristocracy turned furious Panslavists, they knew that by Russian subjugation they had less to lose than by a revolt of their own peasant serfs.

The Bohemians and Croatians called, then, a general Slavonic Congress at Prague, for the preparation of the universal Slavonian alliance.[40] This Congress would have proved a decided failure even

without the interference of the Austrian military. The several
Slavonic languages differ quite as much as the English, the German
and the Swedish, and when the proceedings opened, there was no
common Slavonic tongue by which the speakers could make
themselves understood. French was tried, but was equally unintelligible to the majority, and the poor Slavonic enthusiasts, whose only
common feeling was a common hatred against the Germans, were at
last obliged to express themselves in the hated German language, as
the only one that was generally understood! But just then, another
Slavonic Congress was assembling in Prague, in the shape of Galician
lancers, Croatian and Slovak grenadiers, and Bohemian gunners and
cuirassiers; and this real, armed Slavonic Congress, under the
command of Windischgrätz, in less than twenty-four hours drove the
founders of an imaginary Slavonian supremacy out of the town and
dispersed them to the winds.

The Bohemian, Moravian, Dalmatian, and part of the Polish
Deputies (the aristocracy) to the Austrian Constituent Diet, made in
that Assembly a systematic war upon the German element. The
Germans and part of the Poles (the impoverished nobility) were in
this Assembly the chief supporters of revolutionary progress; the
mass of the Slavonic Deputies, in opposing them, were not satisfied
with thus showing clearly the reactionary tendencies of their entire
movement, but they were degraded enough to tamper and conspire
with the very same Austrian Government which had dispersed their
meeting at Prague. They, too, were paid for this infamous conduct;
after supporting the Government during the insurrection of
October, 1848, an event which finally secured to them the majority
in the Diet, this now almost exclusively Slavonic Diet was dispersed
by Austrian soldiers,[a] the same as the Prague Congress, and the
Panslavists threatened with imprisonment if they should stir again.
And they have only obtained this, that Slavonic nationality is
now being everywhere undermined by Austrian centralization, a
result for which they may thank their own fanaticism and blind-
ness.

If the frontiers of Hungary and Germany had admitted of any
doubt, there would certainly have been another quarrel there. But,
fortunately, there was no pretext, and the interests of both nations
being intimately related, they struggled against the same enemies,
viz., the Austrian Government and the Panslavistic fanaticism. The

---

[a] See below, p. 70.— Ed.

good understanding was not for a moment disturbed. But the Italian revolution entangled a part at least of Germany in an internecine war; and it must be stated here, as a proof how far the Metternichian system had succeeded in keeping back the development of the public mind, that during the first six months of 1848 the same men that had in Vienna mounted the barricades, went, full of enthusiasm, to join the army that fought against the Italian patriots. This deplorable confusion of ideas did not, however, last long.

Lastly, there was the war with Denmark about Schleswig and Holstein. These countries, unquestionably German by nationality, language, and predilection, are also, from military, naval and commercial grounds, necessary to Germany. Their inhabitants have, for the last three years, struggled hard against Danish intrusion. The right of treaties, besides, was for them. The revolution of March brought them into open collision with the Danes, and Germany supported them. But while in Poland, in Italy, in Bohemia, and later on, in Hungary, military operations were pushed with the utmost vigor, in this, the only popular, the only, at least partially, revolutionary war, a system of resultless marches and counter-marches was adopted, and an interference of foreign diplomacy was submitted to, which led, after many an heroic engagement, to a most miserable end. The German Governments betrayed, during this war, the Schleswig-Holstein revolutionary army on every occasion, and allowed it purposely to be cut up, when dispersed or divided, by the Danes. The German corps of volunteers were treated the same.

But while thus the German name earned nothing but hatred on every side, the German constitutional and liberal Governments rubbed their hands for joy. They had succeeded in crushing the Polish and Bohemian[a] movements. They had everywhere revived the old national animosities, which heretofore had prevented any common understanding and action between the German, the Pole, the Italian. They had accustomed the people to scenes of civil war and repression by the military. The Prussian army had regained its confidence in Poland, the Austrian army in Prague; and while the superabundant patriotism ("*die patriotische Überkraft*", as Heine has it[b]) of revolutionary, but short-sighted youth was led, in Schleswig and Lombardy, to be crushed by the grape-shot of the enemy, the

---

[a] Czech.— *Ed.*
[b] Heinrich Heine, "Bei des Nachtwächters Ankunft zu Paris" (from the cycle *Zeitgedichte*).— *Ed.*

regular army, the real instrument of action, both of Prussia and Austria, was placed in a position to regain public favor by victories over the foreigner. But we repeat: these armies, strengthened by the Liberals as a means of action against the more advanced party, no sooner had recovered their self-confidence and their discipline in some degree, than they turned themselves against the Liberals, and restored to power the men of the old system. When Radetzky, in his camp behind the Adige, received the first orders from the "responsible Ministers" at Vienna, he exclaimed: "Who are these Ministers? They are not the Government of Austria! Austria is, now, nowhere, but in my camp; I and my Army, we are Austria; and when we shall have beaten the Italians we shall reconquer the Empire for the Emperor[a]!" And old Radetzky was right—but the imbecile, "responsible" Ministers at Vienna heeded him not.

London, February, 1852

X

THE PARIS RISING. THE FRANKFORT ASSEMBLY

[New-York Daily Tribune, No. 3406, March 18, 1852]

As early as the beginning of April, 1848, the revolutionary torrent had found itself stemmed all over the Continent of Europe by the league which those classes of Society that had profited by the first victory immediately formed with the vanquished. In France, the petty trading class and the republican fraction of the bourgeoisie had combined with the monarchist bourgeoisie against the proletarians; in Germany and Italy, the victorious bourgeoisie had eagerly courted the support of the feudal nobility, the official bureaucracy and the army, against the mass of the people and the petty traders. Very soon the united Conservative and Counter-Revolutionary parties again regained the ascendant. In England, an untimely and ill-prepared popular demonstration (April 10) turned out in a complete and decisive defeat of the movement party.[41] In France, two similar movements (16th April and 15th May) were equally defeated.[42] In Italy, King Bomba[b] regained his authority by a single stroke on the 15th of May.[43] In Germany, the different new bourgeoisie governments and their respective constituent assemblies consolidated

---

[a] Ferdinand I.— Ed.
[b] Ferdinand II.— Ed.

themselves, and if the eventful 15th of May gave rise, in Vienna, to a popular victory, this was an event of merely secondary importance, and may be considered the last successful flash of popular energy. In Hungary, the movement appeared to turn into the quiet channel of perfect legality, and the Polish movement, as we have seen in our last, was stifled in the bud by Prussian bayonets. But as yet nothing was decided as to the eventual turn which things would take, and every inch of ground lost by the revolutionary parties in the different countries only tended to close their ranks more and more for the decisive action.

The decisive action drew near. It could be fought in France only; for France, as long as England took no part in the revolutionary strife, or as Germany remained divided, was, by its national independence, civilization and centralization, the only country to impart the impulse of a mighty convulsion to the surrounding countries. Accordingly, when, on the 23d of June, 1848, the bloody struggle began in Paris, when every succeeding telegraph or mail more clearly exposed the fact to the eyes of Europe, that this struggle was carried on between the mass of the working people on the one hand, and all the other classes of the Parisian population, supported by the army, on the other; when the fighting went on for several days with an exasperation unequalled in the history of modern civil warfare, but without any apparent advantage for either side—then it became evident to every one that this was the great decisive battle which would, if the insurrection were victorious, deluge the whole continent with renewed revolutions, or, if it was suppressed, bring about an, at least momentary, restoration of counter-revolutionary rule.

The proletarians of Paris were defeated, decimated, crushed with such an effect that even now they have not yet recovered from the blow. And immediately, all over Europe, the new and old conservatives and counter-revolutionists raised their heads with an effrontery that showed how well they understood the importance of the event. The press was everywhere attacked, the rights of meeting and association were interfered with, every little event in every small provincial town was taken profit of to disarm the people, to declare a state of siege, to drill the troops in the new maneuvers and artifices that Cavaignac had taught them. Besides, for the first time since February, the invincibility of a popular insurrection in a large town had been proved to be a delusion; the honor of the armies had been restored; the troops, hitherto always defeated in street battles of importance, regained confidence in their efficiency even in this kind of struggle.

From this defeat of the *ouvriers* of Paris may be dated the first positive steps and definite plans of the old feudal-bureaucratic party in Germany, to get rid even of their momentary allies, the middle classes, and to restore Germany to the state she was in before the events of March. The army again was the decisive power in the State, and the army belonged not to the middle classes, but to themselves. Even in Prussia, where before 1848 a considerable leaning of part of the lower grades of officers towards a constitutional government had been observed, the disorder introduced into the army by the revolution had brought back those reasoning young men to their allegiance; as soon as the private soldier took a few liberties with regard to the officers, the necessity of discipline and passive obedience became at once strikingly evident to them. The vanquished nobles and bureaucrats now began to see their way before them; the army, more united than ever, flushed with victory in minor insurrections and in foreign warfare, jealous of the great success the French soldiers had just attained—this army had only to be kept in constant petty conflicts with the people, and, the decisive moment once at hand, it could with one great blow crush the revolutionists and set aside the presumptions of the middle-class parliamentarians. And the proper moment for such a decisive blow arrived soon enough.

We pass over the sometimes curious, but mostly tedious, parliamentary proceedings and local struggles that occupied, in Germany, the different parties during the summer. Suffice it to say that the supporters of the middle-class interest, in spite of numerous parliamentary triumphs, not one of which led to any practical result, very generally felt that their position between the extreme parties became daily more untenable, and that, therefore, they were obliged now to seek the alliance of the reactionists, and the next day, to court the favor of the more popular fractions. This constant vacillation gave the finishing stroke to their character in public opinion, and according to the turn events were taking, the contempt, into which they had sunk, profited for the moment principally the bureaucrats and feudalists.

By the beginning of autumn the relative position of the different parties had become exasperated and critical enough to make a decisive battle inevitable. The first engagements in this war between the democratic and revolutionary masses and the army took place at Frankfort. Though a mere secondary engagement, it was the first advantage of any note the troops acquired over insurrection, and had a great moral effect. The fancy government established by the Frankfort National Assembly had been allowed by Prussia, for very obvious reasons, to conclude an armistice with Denmark which not only surrendered to Danish vengeance the Germans of Schleswig, but which also entirely disclaimed the more or less revolutionary principles which were generally supposed in the Danish war.[44] This armistice was, by a majority of two or three, rejected in the Frankfort Assembly. A sham Ministerial crisis followed this vote, but three days later the Assembly reconsidered their vote, and were actually induced to cancel it and acknowledge the armistice. This disgraceful proceeding roused the indignation of the people. Barricades were erected, but already sufficient troops had been drawn to Frankfort, and, after six hours fighting, the insurrection was suppressed. Similar but less important movements connected with this event took place in other parts of Germany (Baden, Cologne), but were equally defeated.

This preliminary engagement gave to the counter-revolutionary party the one great advantage, that now the only Government which had entirely—at least in semblance—originated with popular election, the Imperial Government of Frankfort, as well as the National Assembly, was ruined in the eyes of the people. This Government and this Assembly had been obliged to appeal to the bayonets of the troops against the manifestation of the popular will. They were compromised, and what little regard they might have been hitherto enabled to claim, this repudiation of their origin, the dependency upon the anti-popular Governments and their troops, made both the Lieutenant of the Empire, his Ministers and his Deputies, to be henceforth complete nullities. We shall soon see how first Austria, then Prussia, and later on the smaller States too, treated with contempt every order, every request, every deputation they received from this body of impotent dreamers.

We now come to the great counter-stroke, in Germany, of the French battle of June, to that event which was as decisive for Germany as the proletarian struggle of Paris had been for France; we mean the revolution and subsequent storming of Vienna, in October, 1848. But the importance of this battle is such, and the explanation of the different circumstances that more immediately contributed to its issue will take up such a portion of *The Tribune*'s columns, as to necessitate its being treated in a separate letter.

London, February, 1852

XI

THE VIENNA INSURRECTION

[*New-York Daily Tribune*, No. 3407, March 19, 1852]

We now come to the decisive event which formed the revolutionary counterpart in Germany to the Parisian insurrection of June, and which, by a single blow, turned the scale in favor of the counter-revolutionary party—the insurrection of October, 1848, in Vienna.

We have seen what the position of the different classes was, in Vienna, after the victory of the 13th of March. We have also seen how the movement of German Austria was entangled with and impeded by the events in the non-German provinces of Austria. It only remains for us, then, briefly to survey the causes which led to this last and most formidable rising of German Austria.

The high aristocracy and the stockjobbing bourgeoisie, which had formed the principal non-official supports of the Metternichian Government, were enabled, even after the events of March, to maintain a predominating influence with the Government, not only by the court, the army and the bureaucracy, but still more by the horror of "anarchy," which rapidly spread among the middle classes. They very soon ventured a few feelers in the shape of a Press Law, a nondescript Aristocratic Constitution and an Electoral Law based upon the old division of "Estates."[45] The so-called constitutional ministry, consisting of half Liberal, timid, incapable bureaucrats, on the 14th of May, even ventured a direct attack upon the revolutionary organisations of the masses by dissolving the Central Committee of Delegates of the National Guard and Academic Legion, a body formed for the express purpose of controlling the Government and calling out against it, in case of need, the popular forces. But this act only provoked the insurrection of the 15th of May, by which the Government was forced to acknowledge the Committee, to repeal the Constitution and the Electoral Law, and to grant the power of framing a new fundamental law to a Constitutional Diet, elected by universal suffrage. All this was confirmed on the following day by an Imperial proclamation. But the reactionary party, which also had its representatives in the ministry, soon got their "Liberal" colleagues to undertake a new attack upon the popular conquests. The Academic Legion, the stronghold of the movement party, the center of continuous agitation, had, on this very account, become obnoxious to the more moderate burghers of Vienna; on the 26th a ministerial decree dissolved it. Perhaps this blow might have succeeded, if it had been carried out by a part of the National Guard only; but the Government, not trusting them either, brought the military forward, and at once the National Guard turned round, united with the Academic Legion, and thus frustrated the ministerial project.

In the meantime, however, the Emperor and his court had, on the 16th of May, left Vienna and fled to Innspruck.[a] Here, surrounded by the bigoted Tyroleans, whose loyalty was roused again by the danger of an invasion of their country by the Sardo-Lombardian army, supported by the vicinity of Radetzky's troops, within shell-range of whom Innspruck lay, here the counter-revolutionary party found an asylum, from whence, uncontrolled, unobserved and safe, it might rally its scattered forces, repair and spread again all over the country the network of its plots. Communications were re-opened with Radetzky, with Jellachich, and with Windischgrätz, as well as with the reliable men in the administrative hierarchy of the different provinces; intrigues were set on foot with the Slavonic chiefs; and thus a real force at the disposal of the counter-revolutionary camarilla was formed, while the impotent Ministers in Vienna were allowed to wear their short and feeble popularity out in continual bickerings with the revolutionary masses, and in the debates of the forthcoming Constituent Assembly. Thus, the policy of leaving the movement of the capital to itself for a time, a policy which must have led to the omnipotence of the movement party in a centralized and homogeneous country like France, here, in Austria, in a heterogeneous political conglomerate, was one of the safest means of reorganizing the strength of the reactionists.

In Vienna, the middle class, persuaded that after three successive defeats, and in the face of a Constituent Assembly based upon universal suffrage, the Court party was no longer an opponent to be dreaded, fell more and more into that weariness and apathy, and that eternal outcry for order and tranquillity, which has everywhere seized this class after violent commotions and consequent derangement of trade. The manufacturers of the Austrian Capital are almost exclusively limited to articles of luxury, for which, since the revolution and the flight of the Court, there had necessarily been very little demand. The shout for a return to a regular system of Government, and for a return of the Court, both of which were expected to bring about a revival of

---

[a] Innsbruck.— Ed.

commercial prosperity—this shout became now general among the middle classes. The meeting of the Constituent Assembly, in July, was hailed with delight as the end of the revolutionary era; so was the return of the Court, which, after the victories of Radetzky in Italy, and after the advent of the reactionary Ministry of Doblhoff, considered itself strong enough to brave the popular torrent, and which, at the same time, was wanted in Vienna in order to complete its intrigues with the Slavonic majority of the Diet. While the Constituent Diet discussed the laws on the emancipation of the peasantry from feudal bondage and forced labor for the nobility, the Court completed a master-stroke. On the 19th of August, the Emperor was made to review the National Guard; the imperial family, the courtiers, the general officers, outbid each other in flatteries to the armed burghers, who were already intoxicated with pride at thus seeing themselves publicly acknowledged as one of the important bodies of the State; and immediately afterward a decree, signed by M. Schwarzer, the only popular Minister in the Cabinet, was published, withdrawing the Government aid given hitherto to the workmen out of employ. The trick succeeded; the working classes got up a demonstration; the middle-class National Guards declared for the decree of their Minister; they were launched upon the "Anarchists," fell like tigers on the unarmed and unresisting workpeople, and massacred a great number of them on the 23d of August. Thus the unity and strength of the revolutionary force was broken; the class struggle between Bourgeois and Proletarian had come, in Vienna too, to a bloody outbreak, and the counter-revolutionary camarilla saw the day approaching on which it might strike its grand blow.

The Hungarian affairs very soon offered an opportunity to proclaim openly the principles upon which it intended to act. On the 5th of October an imperial decree in the Vienna official *Gazette*[a]—a decree countersigned by none of the responsible ministers for Hungary—declared the Hungarian Diet dissolved, and named the Ban Jellachich, of Croatia, civil and military governor of that country—Jellachich, the leader of South-Slavonian reaction, a man who was actually at war with the lawful authorities of Hungary. At the same time orders were given to the troops in Vienna to march out and form part of the army which was to enforce Jellachich's authority. This, however, was showing the cloven foot too openly; every man in Vienna felt that war

---

[a] A reference to the "Königliches Rescript" of October 3, published in the *Wiener Zeitung* on October 5, 1848.— *Ed.*

upon Hungary was war upon the principle of constitutional government, which principle was in the very decree trampled upon by the attempt of the Emperor to make decrees with legal force, without the countersign of a responsible minister. The people, the Academic Legion, the National Guard of Vienna, on the 6th of October, rose in mass and resisted the departure of the troops; some grenadiers passed over to the people; a short struggle took place between the popular forces and the troops; the Minister of War, Latour, was massacred by the people, and in the evening the latter were victors. In the meantime, Ban Jellachich, beaten at Stuhlweissenburg[a] by Perczel, had taken refuge near Vienna on German-Austrian territory[46]; the Viennese troops that were to march to his support now took up an ostensibly hostile and defensive position against him; and the Emperor and Court had again fled to Olmütz,[b] on semi-Slavonic territory.

But at Olmütz, the Court found itself in very different circumstances to what it had been at Innspruck. It was now in a position to open immediately the campaign against the revolution. It was surrounded by the Slavonian deputies of the Constituent, who flocked in masses to Olmütz, and by the Slavonian enthusiasts from all parts of the monarchy. The campaign, in their eyes, was to be a war of Slavonian restoration and of extermination against the two intruders upon what was considered Slavonian soil, against the German and the Magyar. Windischgrätz, the conqueror of Prague, now commander of the army that was concentrated around Vienna, became at once the hero of Slavonian nationality. And his army concentrated rapidly from all sides. From Bohemia, Moravia, Styria, Upper Austria and Italy, marched regiment after regiment on routes that converged at Vienna, to join the troops of Jellachich and the ex-garrison of the capital. Above sixty thousand men were thus united toward the end of October, and soon they commenced hemming in the imperial city on all sides, until, on the 30th of October, they were far enough advanced to venture upon the decisive attack.

In Vienna, in the meantime, confusion and helplessness was prevalent. The middle class, as soon as the victory was gained, became again possessed of their old distrust against the "anarchic" working classes; the working men, mindful of the treatment they had received, six weeks before, at the hands of the armed tradesmen, and of the unsteady, wavering policy of the middle

---

[a] Hungarian name: Székesfehérvár.— Ed.
[b] Czech name: Olomouc.— Ed.

class at large, would not trust to them the defense of the city, and
demanded arms and military organization for themselves. The
Academic Legion, full of zeal for the struggle against imperial
despotism, were entirely incapable of understanding the nature of
the estrangement of the two classes, or of otherwise comprehending the necessities of the situation. There was confusion in the
public mind, confusion in the ruling councils. The remnant of the
Diet, German deputies, and a few Slavonians, acting the part of
spies for their friends at Olmütz, besides a few of the more
revolutionary Polish deputies, sat in permanency, but instead of
taking part resolutely, they lost all their time in idle debates upon
the possibility of resisting the imperial army without overstepping
the bounds of Constitutional conventionalities. The Committee of
Safety composed of deputies of almost all the popular bodies of
Vienna, although resolved to resist, was yet dominated by a
majority of burghers and petty tradesmen, who never allowed it to
follow up any determined, energetic line of action. The council of
the Academic Legion passed heroic resolutions, but was noways
able to take the lead. The working classes, distrusted, disarmed,
disorganized, hardly emerging from the intellectual bondage of
the old *régime*, hardly awaking not to a knowledge, but to a mere
instinct of their social position and proper political line of action,
could only make themselves heard by loud demonstrations, and
could not be expected to be up to the difficulties of the moment.
But they were ready—as ever they were in Germany during the
Revolution—to fight to the last, as soon as they obtained arms.

That was the state of things in Vienna. Outside, the reorganized
Austrian army, flushed with the victories of Radetzky in Italy;
sixty or seventy thousand men, well armed, well organized, and if
not well commanded, at least possessing commanders. Inside,
confusion, class division, disorganization; a national guard of
which part was resolved not to fight at all; part irresolute, and
only the smallest part ready to act; a proletarian mass, powerful by
numbers, but without leaders, without any political education,
subject to panic as well as to fits of fury almost without cause, a
prey to every false rumor spread about, quite ready to fight, but
unarmed, at least in the beginning, and incompletely armed and
barely organized when at last they were led to the battle; a helpless
Diet, discussing theoretical quibbles while the roof over their heads
was almost burning; a leading committee without impulse or
energy. Everything was changed from the days of March and May,
when, in the counter-revolutionary camp, all was confusion, and
when the only organized force was that created by the revolution.

There could hardly be a doubt about the issue of such a struggle, and whatever doubt there might be, was settled by the events of the 30th and 31st October and 1st November.

London, March, 1852

XII

THE STORMING OF VIENNA. THE BETRAYAL OF VIENNA

[*New-York Daily Tribune*, No. 3425, April 9, 1852]

When at last the concentrated army of Windischgrätz commenced the attack upon Vienna, the forces that could be brought forward in defense were exceedingly insufficient for the purpose. Of the National Guard, only a portion was to be brought to the entrenchments. A Proletarian Guard, it is true, had at last been hastily formed, but owing to the lateness of the attempt to thus make available the most numerous, most daring and most energetic part of the population it was too little inured to the use of arms and to the very first rudiments of discipline, to offer a successful resistance. Thus the Academic Legion, three to four thousand strong, well exercised and disciplined to a certain degree, brave and enthusiastic, was, militarily speaking, the only force which was in a state to do its work successfully. But what were they, together with the few reliable National Guards, and with the confused mass of the armed proletarians, in opposition to the far more numerous regulars of Windischgrätz, not counting even the brigand hordes of Jellachich, hordes that were, by the very nature of their habits, very useful in a war from house to house, from lane to lane? And what, but a few old, outworn, ill-mounted and ill-served pieces of ordnance had the insurgents to oppose to that numerous and perfectly appointed artillery, of which Windischgrätz made such an unscrupulous use?

The nearer the danger drew, the more grew the confusion in Vienna. The Diet, up to the last moment, could not collect sufficient energy to call in for aid the Hungarian army of Perczel, encamped a few leagues below the capital. The Committee [a] passed contradictory resolutions, they themselves being, like the popular armed masses, floated up and down with the rising and alternately receding tide of rumors and counter-rumors. There was only one

---

[a] The Committee of Safety.— *Ed.*

thing upon which all agreed—to respect property; and this was done in a degree almost ludicrous for such times. As to the final arrangement of a plan of defense, very little was done. Bem, the only man present who could have saved Vienna, if any could, then in Vienna an almost unknown foreigner, a Slavonian by birth, gave up the task, overwhelmed as he was by universal distrust. Had he persevered, he might have been lynched as a traitor. Messenhauser, the commander of the insurgent forces, more of a novel writer than even of a subaltern officer, was totally inadequate to the task; and yet, after eight months of revolutionary struggles, the popular party had not produced or acquired a military man of more ability than he. Thus the contest began. The Viennese, considering their utterly inadequate means of defense, considering their utter absence of military skill and organization in the ranks, offered a most heroic resistance. In many places the order given by Bem, when he was in command, "to defend that post to the last man," was carried out to the letter. But force prevailed. Barricade after barricade was swept away by the imperial artillery in the long and wide avenues which form the main streets of the suburbs; and on the evening of the second day's fighting the Croats occupied the range of houses facing the glacis of the Old Town. A feeble and disorderly attack of the Hungarian army had been utterly defeated; and during an armistice, while some parties in the Old Town capitulated, while others hesitated and spread confusion, while the remnants of the Academic Legion prepared fresh entrenchments, an entrance was made by the Imperialists, and in the midst of this general disorder the Old Town was carried.

The immediate consequences of this victory, the brutalities and executions by martial law, the unheard-of cruelties and infamies committed by the Slavonian hordes let loose upon Vienna, are too well known to be detailed here. The ulterior consequences, the entire new turn given to German affairs by the defeat of the revolution in Vienna, we shall have reason to notice hereafter. There remain two points to be considered in connection with the storming of Vienna. The people of that capital had two allies: the Hungarians and the German people. Where were they in the hour of trial?

We have seen that the Viennese, with all the generosity of a newly-freed people, had risen for a cause which, though ultimately their own, was, in the first instance and above all, that of the Hungarians. Rather than suffer the Austrian troops to march upon Hungary, they would draw their first and most terrific onslaught upon themselves. And while they thus nobly came forward for the support of their allies, the Hungarians, successful against Jellachich, drove him upon Vienna, and by their victory strengthened the force that was to attack that town. Under these circumstances, it was the clear duty of Hungary to support, without delay and with all disposable forces, not the Diet at Vienna, not the Committee of Safety or any other official body at Vienna, but the *Viennese Revolution*. And if Hungary should even have forgotten that Vienna had fought the first battle of Hungary, she owed it to her own safety not to forget that Vienna was the only outpost of Hungarian independence, and that after the fall of Vienna nothing could meet the advance of the Imperial troops against herself. Now, we know very well all the Hungarians can say and have said in defense of their inactivity during the blockade and storming of Vienna: the insufficient state of their own force, the refusal of the Diet or any other official body in Vienna to call them in, the necessity to keep on constitutional ground, and to avoid complications with the German Central Power. But the fact is, as to the insufficient state of the Hungarian army, that in the first days after the Viennese Revolution and the arrival of Jellachich, nothing was wanted in the shape of regular troops, as the Austrian regulars were very far from being concentrated; and that a courageous, unrelenting following up of the first advantage over Jellachich, even with nothing but the *Landsturm*[a] that had fought at Stuhlweissenburg, would have sufficed to effect a junction with the Viennese, and to adjourn to that day six months every concentration of an Austrian army. In war, and particularly in revolutionary warfare, rapidity of action until some decided advantage is gained is the first rule, and we have no hesitation in saying that upon *merely military grounds* Perczel ought not to have stopped until his junction with the Viennese was effected. There was certainly some risk, but who ever won a battle without risking something? And did the people of Vienna risk nothing when they drew upon themselves—they, a population of four hundred thousand—the forces that were to march to the conquest of twelve millions of Hungarians? The military fault committed by waiting until the Austrians had united, and by making the feeble demonstration at Schwechat which ended, as it deserved to do, in an inglorious defeat—this military fault certainly incurred more risks than a resolute march upon Vienna against the disbanded brigands of Jellachich would have done.[47]

---

[a] People's militia.— *Ed.*

But, it is said, such an advance of the Hungarians, unless authorized by some official body, would have been a violation of the German territory, would have brought on complications with the Central Power at Frankfort, and would have been, above all, an abandonment of the legal and constitutional policy which formed the strength of the Hungarian cause. Why, the official bodies in Vienna were nonentities! Was it the Diet, was it the popular Committees, who had risen for Hungary, or was it the people of Vienna, and they alone, who had taken to the musket to stand the brunt of the first battle for Hungary's independence? It was not this nor that official body in Vienna which it was important to uphold—all these bodies might, and would have been, upset very soon in the progress of the revolutionary development—but it was the ascendency of the revolutionary movement, the unbroken progress of popular action itself, which alone was in question, and which alone could save Hungary from invasion. What forms this revolutionary movement afterward might take, was the business of the Viennese, not of the Hungarians, so long as Vienna and German Austria at large continued their allies against the common enemy. But the question is, whether in this stickling of the Hungarian Government for some quasi-legal authorization, we are not to see the first clear symptom of that pretense to a rather doubtful legality of proceeding, which, if it did not save Hungary, at least told very well, at a later period, before the English middle-class audiences.

As to the pretext of possible conflicts with the Central Power of Germany at Frankfort, it is quite futile. The Frankfort authorities were *de facto* upset by the victory of the counter-revolution at Vienna; they would have been equally upset had the revolution, there, found the support necessary to defeat its enemies. And lastly, the great argument that Hungary could not leave legal and constitutional ground, may do very well for British free traders, but it will never be deemed sufficient in the eyes of history. Suppose the people of Vienna had stuck to "legal and constitutional" means on the 13th of March and on the 6th of October, what then of the "legal and constitutional" movement, and of all the glorious battles which, for the first time, brought Hungary to the notice of the civilized world? The very legal and constitutional ground, upon which it is asserted the Hungarians moved in 1848 and '49, was conquered for them by the exceedingly illegal and unconstitutional rising of the people of Vienna on the 13th of March. It is not to our purpose here to discuss the revolutionary history of Hungary, but it may be deemed proper if we observe that it is utterly useless to professedly use merely legal means of resistance against an enemy who scorns such scruples; and if we add, that had it not been for this eternal pretense of legality, which Görgey seized upon and turned against the Government, the devotion of Görgey's army to its General, and the disgraceful catastrophe of Világos, would have been impossible.[48] And when, at last, to save their honor, the Hungarians came across the Leitha, in the latter end of October 1848, was that not quite as illegal as any immediate and resolute attack would have been?

We are known to harbor no unfriendly feelings toward Hungary. We stood by her during the struggle; we may be allowed to say, that our paper, the *Neue Rheinische Zeitung*, has done more than any other to render the Hungarian cause popular in Germany, by explaining the nature of the struggle between the Magyar and Slavonian races, and by following up the Hungarian war in a series of articles which have had paid them the compliment of being plagiarized in almost every subsequent book upon the subject, the works of native Hungarians and "eye-witnesses" not excepted. We even now, in any future continental convulsion, consider Hungary as the necessary and natural ally of Germany. But we have been severe enough upon our own countrymen to have a right to speak out upon our neighbors; and then,we have here to record facts with historical impartiality, and we must say, that in this particular instance, the generous bravery of the people of Vienna was not only far more noble, but also more far-sighted than the cautious circumspection of the Hungarian Government. And, as Germans, we may further be allowed to say, that not for all the showy victories and glorious battles of the Hungarian campaign would we exchange that spontaneous, single-handed rising and heroic resistance of the people of Vienna, our countrymen, which gave Hungary the time to organize the army that could do such great things.

The second ally of Vienna was the German people. But they were everywhere engaged in the same struggle as the Viennese. Frankfort, Baden, Cologne, had just been defeated and disarmed. In Berlin and Breslau[a] the people were at daggers drawn with the army, and daily expected to come to blows. Thus it was in every local center of action. Everywhere questions were pending that could only be settled by the force of arms; and now it was that for the first time were severely felt the disastrous consequences of the continuation of the old dismemberment and decentralization of Germany. The different questions in every State, every province, every town were fundamentally the same; but they were brought forward everywhere under different shapes and pretexts, and had everywhere attained

---

[a] Polish name: Wrocław.— *Ed.*

different degrees of maturity. Thus it happened, that while in every locality the decisive gravity of the events at Vienna was felt, yet nowhere could an important blow be struck with any hope of bringing the Viennese succor or making a diversion in their favor; and there remained nothing to aid them but the Parliament and Central Power of Frankfort; they were appealed to on all hands, but what did they do?

The Frankfort Parliament and the bastard child it had brought to light by incestuous intercourse with the old German Diet, the so-called Central Power, profited by the Viennese movement to show forth their utter nullity. This contemptible Assembly, as we have seen, had long since sacrificed its virginity, and young as it was, it was already turning gray-headed and experienced in all the artifices of prating and pseudo-diplomatic prostitution. Of the dreams and illusions of power, of German regeneration and unity, that in the beginning had pervaded it, nothing remained but a set of Teutonic clap-trap phraseology that was repeated on every occasion, and a firm belief of each individual member in his own importance, as well as in the credulity of the public. The original naïveté was discarded; the representatives of the German people had turned practical men, that is to say, they had made it out that the less they did, and the more they prated, the safer would be their position as the umpires of the fate of Germany. Not that they considered their proceedings superfluous; quite the contrary, but they had found out that all really great questions, being to them forbidden ground, had better be let alone; and there, like a set of Byzantine doctors of the Lower Empire,[a] they discussed, with an importance and assiduity worthy of the fate that at last overtook them, theoretical dogmas long ago settled in every part of the civilized world, or microscopical practical questions which never led to any practical result. Thus, the Assembly being a sort of Lancastrian School[49] for the mutual instruction of members, and being, therefore, very important to themselves, they were persuaded it was doing even more than the German people had a right to expect, and looked upon every one as a traitor to the country who had the impudence to ask them to come to any result.

When the Viennese insurrection broke out, there was a host of interpellations, debates, motions, and amendments upon it, which of course led to nothing. The Central Power was to interfere. It sent two Commissioners, Messrs. Welcker, the ex-Liberal, and Mosle, to Vienna. The travels of Don Quixote and Sancho Panza form matter for an Odyssey in comparison to the heroic feats and wonderful

---

[a] Eastern Roman Empire.— *Ed.*

adventures of these two knights-errant of German Unity. Not daring to go to Vienna, they were bullied by Windischgrätz, wondered at by the idiot Emperor,[a] and impudently hoaxed by the Minister Stadion. Their despatches and reports are perhaps the only portion of the Frankfort transactions[b] that will retain a place in German literature; they are a perfect satirical romance, ready cut and dried, and an eternal monument of disgrace for the Frankfort Assembly and its government.

The left side of the Assembly had also sent two Commissioners to Vienna, in order to uphold its authority there—Messrs. Fröbel and Robert Blum. Blum, when danger drew near, judged rightly that here the great battle of the German Revolution was to be fought, and unhesitatingly resolved to stake his head on the issue. Fröbel, on the contrary, was of opinion that it was his duty to preserve himself for the important duties of his post at Frankfort. Blum was considered one of the most eloquent men of the Frankfort Assembly; he certainly was the most popular. His eloquence would not have stood the test of any experienced Parliamentary Assembly; he was too fond of the shallow declamations of a German dissenting preacher, and his arguments wanted both philosophical acumen and acquaintance with practical matter of fact. In politics, he belonged to "Moderate Democracy," a rather indefinite sort of thing, cherished on account of this very want of definiteness in its principles. But with all this, Robert Blum was by nature a thorough, though somewhat polished, plebeian, and in decisive moments his plebeian instinct and plebeian energy got the better of his indefinite and therefore indecisive political persuasion and knowledge. In such moments he raised himself far above the usual standard of his capacities.

Thus, in Vienna, he saw at a glance that here, and not in the midst of the would-be elegant debates of Frankfort, the fate of his country would have to be decided; he at once made up his mind, gave up all idea of retreat, took a command in the revolutionary force, and behaved with extraordinary coolness and decision. It was he who retarded for a considerable time the taking of the town and covered one of its sides from attack by burning the Tabor Bridge over the Danube. Everybody knows how after the storming he was arrested, tried by a court martial, and shot. He died like a hero. And the Frankfort Assembly, horror-struck as it was, yet took the bloody insult with a seeming good grace. A resolution was carried, which, by

---

[a] Ferdinand I.— *Ed.*

[b] A reference to the "Verhandlungen der deutschen verfassunggebenden Versammlung zu Frankfurt am Main" (see also present edition, Vol. 8, pp. 88-93).— *Ed.*

the softness and diplomatic decency of its language, was more an insult to the grave of the murdered martyr than a damning stain upon Austria. But it was not to be expected that this contemptible Assembly should resent the assassination of one of its members, particularly of the leader of the Left.

London, March, 1852

XIII

THE PRUSSIAN CONSTITUENT ASSEMBLY.
THE NATIONAL ASSEMBLY

[*New-York Daily Tribune,* No. 3432, April 17, 1852]

On the 1st of November Vienna fell, and on the 9th of the same month the dissolution of the Constituent Assembly in Berlin showed how much this event had at once raised the spirit and the strength of the counter-revolutionary party all over Germany.

The events of the summer of 1848 in Prussia are soon told. The Constituent Assembly, or rather "the Assembly elected for the purpose of agreeing upon a Constitution with the Crown," and its majority of representatives of the middle-class interest, had long since forfeited all public esteem by lending itself to all the intrigues of the Court, from fear of the more energetic elements of the population. They had confirmed, or rather restored, the obnoxious privileges of feudalism, and thus betrayed the liberty and the interest of the peasantry. They had neither been able to draw up a constitution, nor to amend in any way the general legislation. They had occupied themselves almost exclusively with nice theoretical distinctions, mere formalities, and questions of constitutional etiquette. The Assembly, in fact, was more a school of parliamentary *savoir vivre*[a] for its members, than a body in which the people could take any interest. The majorities were, besides, very nicely balanced, and almost always decided by the wavering *"Centers,"* whose oscillations from Right to Left, and *vice versa,* upset first the Ministry of Camphausen, then that of Auerswald and Hansemann. But while thus the Liberals, here as everywhere else, let the occasion slip out of their hands, the Court reorganized its elements of strength among the nobility, and the most uncultivated portion of the rural population, as well as in the army and bureaucracy. After

_____
[a] Good breeding.— *Ed.*

Hansemann's downfall, a ministry of bureaucrats and military officers, all staunch reactionists, was formed, which, however, seemingly gave way to the demands of the Parliament; and the Assembly, acting upon the commodious principle of "measures, not men," were actually duped into applauding this ministry, while they, of course, had no eyes for the concentration and organization of counter-revolutionary forces which that same ministry carried on pretty openly. At last, the signal being given by the fall of Vienna, the King[a] dismissed his ministers and replaced them by "men of action," under the leadership of the present Premier, M. Manteuffel. Then the dreaming Assembly at once awoke to the danger; it passed a vote of no confidence in the Cabinet, which was at once replied to by a decree removing the Assembly from Berlin, where it might, in case of a conflict, count upon the support of the masses, to Brandenburg, a petty provincial town dependent entirely upon the Government.[50] The Assembly, however, declared that it could not be adjourned, removed, or dissolved, except with its own consent. In the meantime, General Wrangel entered Berlin at the head of some forty thousand troops. In a meeting of the municipal magistrates and the officers of the National Guard, it was resolved not to offer any resistance. And now, after the Assembly and its constituents, the Liberal bourgeoisie, had allowed the combined reactionary party to occupy every important position and to wrest from their hands almost every means of defense, began that grand comedy of "passive and legal resistance" which they intended to be a glorious imitation of the example of Hampden and of the first efforts of the Americans in the War of Independence.[51] Berlin was declared in a state of siege, and Berlin remained tranquil; the National Guard was dissolved by the Government, and its arms were delivered up with the greatest punctuality. The Assembly was hunted down during a fortnight, from one place of meeting to another, and everywhere dispersed by the military, and the members of the Assembly begged of the citizens to remain tranquil. At last, the Government having declared the Assembly dissolved, it passed a resolution to declare the levying of taxes illegal,[52] and then its members dispersed themselves over the country to organize the refusal of taxes. But they found that they had been woefully mistaken in the choice of their means. After a few agitated weeks, followed by severe measures of the Government against the Opposition, every one gave up the idea of refusing the taxes in order to please a defunct Assembly that had not even had the courage to defend itself.

---

[a] Frederick William IV.— *Ed.*

Whether it was, in the beginning of November, 1848, already too late to try armed resistance, or whether a part of the army, on finding serious opposition, would have turned over to the side of the Assembly, and thus decided the matter in its favor, is a question which may never be solved. But in revolution, as in war, it is always necessary to show a strong front, and he who attacks is in the advantage; and in revolution, as in war, it is of the highest necessity to stake everything on the decisive moment, whatever the odds may be. There is not a single successful revolution in history that does not prove the truth of these axioms. Now, for the Prussian Revolution, the decisive moment had come in November, 1848; the Assembly, at the head, officially, of the whole revolutionary interest, did neither show a strong front, for it receded at every advance of the enemy; much less did it attack, for it chose even not to defend itself; and when the decisive moment came, when Wrangel, at the head of forty thousand men, knocked at the gates of Berlin, instead of finding, as he and all his officers fully expected, every street studded with barricades, every window turned into a loophole, he found the gates open and the streets obstructed only by peaceful Berliner burghers, enjoying the joke they had played upon him, by delivering themselves up, hands and feet tied, unto the astonished soldiers. It is true, the Assembly and the people, if they had resisted, might have been beaten; Berlin might have been bombarded, and many hundreds might have been killed, without preventing the ultimate victory of the royalist party. But that was no reason why they should surrender their arms at once. A well-contested defeat is a fact of as much revolutionary importance as an easily-won victory. The defeats of Paris, in June, 1848, and of Vienna, in October, certainly did far more in revolutionizing the minds of the people of these two cities than the victories of February and March. The Assembly and the people of Berlin would, probably, have shared the fate of the two towns above-named; but they would have fallen gloriously, and would have left behind themselves, in the minds of the survivors, a wish of revenge, which in revolutionary times is one of the highest incentives to energetic and passionate action. It is a matter of course that, in every struggle, he who takes up the gauntlet risks being beaten; but is that a reason why he should confess himself beaten, and submit to the yoke without drawing the sword?

In a revolution, he who commands a decisive position and surrenders it, instead of forcing the enemy to try his hands at an assault, invariably deserves to be treated as a traitor.

The same decree of the King of Prussia which dissolved the

Constituent Assembly also proclaimed a new Constitution,[a] founded upon the draft which had been made by a Committee of that Assembly, but enlarging, in some points, the powers of the Crown, and rendering doubtful, in others, those of the Parliament. This Constitution established two Chambers, which were to meet soon for the purpose of confirming and revising it.

We need hardly ask where the German National Assembly was during the "legal and peaceful" struggle of the Prussian Constitutionalists. It was, as usual, at Frankfort, occupied with passing very tame resolutions against the proceedings of the Prussian Government, and admiring the "imposing spectacle of the passive, legal, and unanimous resistance of a whole people against brutal force." The Central Government sent Commissioners to Berlin, to intercede between the Ministry and the Assembly; but they met the same fate as their predecessors at Olmütz, and were politely shown out. The Left of the National Assembly, i.e., the so-called Radical party, sent also their Commissioners; but after having duly convinced themselves of the utter helplessness of the Berlin Assembly, and confessed their own equal helplessness, they returned to Frankfort, to report progress, and to testify to the admirably peaceful conduct of the population of Berlin. Nay, more: when Mr. Bassermann, one of the Central Government's Commissioners, reported that the late stringent measures of the Prussian Ministers were not without foundation, inasmuch as there had of late been seen loitering about the streets of Berlin sundry savage-looking characters, such as always appear previous to anarchical movements (and which ever since have been named "Bassermannic characters"), these worthy deputies of the Left, and energetic representatives of the revolutionary interest, actually arose to make oath and testify that such was not the case! Thus, within two months, the total impotency of the Frankfort Assembly was signally proved. There could be no more glaring proofs that this body was totally inadequate to its task; nay, that it had not even the remotest idea of what its task really was. The fact, that both in Vienna and in Berlin the fate of the revolution was settled, that in both these capitals the most important and vital questions were disposed of, without the existence of the Frankfort Assembly ever being taken the slightest notice of—this fact alone is sufficient to establish that the body in question was a

---

[a] A reference to the following two documents published on one and the same day, December 5, 1848: "Verordnung, betreffend die Auflösung der zur Vereinbarung der Verfassung berufenen Versammlung" and "Verfassungsurkunde für den Preußischen Staat".— *Ed.*

mere debating-club, composed of a set of dupes, who allowed the governments to use them as a parliamentary puppet, shown to amuse the shopkeepers and petty tradesmen of petty States and petty towns, as long as it was considered convenient to divert the attention of these parties. How long this was considered convenient we shall soon see. But it is a fact worthly of attention, that among all the "eminent" men of this Assembly, there was not one who had the slightest apprehension of the part they were made to perform, and that even up to the present day, ex-members of the Frankfort Club have invariably organs of historical perception quite peculiar to themselves.

London, March, 1852

XIV

THE RESTORATION OF ORDER. DIET AND CHAMBERS

[*New-York Daily Tribune*, No. 3438, April 24, 1852]

The first months of the year 1849 were employed by the Austrian and Prussian Governments in following up the advantages obtained in October and November last. The Austrian Diet, ever since the taking of Vienna, had carried on a merely nominal existence in a small Moravian country-town, named Kremsier.[a] Here the Slavonian Deputies, who, with their constituents, had been mainly instrumental in raising the Austrian Government from its prostration, were singularly punished for their treachery against the European Revolution; as soon as the Government had recovered its strength, it treated the Diet and its Slavonian majority with the utmost contempt, and when the first successes of the imperial arms foreboded a speedy termination of the Hungarian war, the Diet, on the 4th of March, was dissolved and the deputies dispersed by military force.[53] Then at last the Slavonians saw that they were duped, and then they shouted: Let us go to Frankfort and carry on there the opposition which we cannot pursue here! But it was then too late, and the very fact that they had no other alternative than either to remain quiet or to join the impotent Frankfort Assembly—this fact alone was sufficient to show their utter helplessness.

Thus ended, for the present and most likely for ever, the attempts of the Slavonians of Germany to recover an independent national

---

[a] Czech name: Kroměříž.— *Ed.*

existence. Scattered remnants of numerous nations, whose nationality and political vitality had long been extinguished, and who in consequence had been obliged, for almost a thousand years, to follow in the wake of a mightier nation, their conqueror, the same as the Welsh in England, the Basques in Spain, the Bas-Bretons in France, and at a more recent period the Spanish and French Creoles in those portions of North America occupied of late by the Anglo-American race—these dying nationalities, the Bohemians, Carinthians, Dalmatians, &c., had tried to profit by the universal confusion of 1848, in order to restore their political *status quo* of A.D. 800. The history of a thousand years ought to have shown them that such a retrogression was impossible; that if all the territory east of the Elbe and Saale had at one time been occupied by kindred Slavonians, this fact merely proved the historical tendency, and at the same time the physical and intellectual power of the German nation to subdue, absorb, and assimilate its ancient eastern neighbors; that this tendency of absorption on the part of the Germans had always been and still was one of the mightiest means by which the civilization of western Europe had been spread in the east of that Continent; that it could only cease whenever the process of Germanization had reached the frontier of large, compact, unbroken nations, capable of an independent national life, such as the Hungarians and in some degree the Poles; and that, therefore, the natural and inevitable fate of these dying nations was to allow this progress of dissolution and absorption by their stronger neighbors to complete itself. Certainly this is no very flattering prospect for the national ambition of the Panslavistic dreamers who succeeded in agitating a portion of the Bohemian and South-Slavonian people; but can they expect that history would retrograde a thousand years in order to please a few phthisical bodies of men, who in every part of the territory they occupy are interspersed and surrounded by Germans, who from times almost immemorial have had for all purposes of civilization no other language but the German, and who lack the very first conditions of national existence, numbers and compactness of territory? Thus, the Panslavistic rising, which everywhere in the German and Hungarian Slavonic territories was the cloak for the restoration to independence of all these numberless petty nations, everywhere clashed with the European revolutionary movements, and the Slavonians, although pretending to fight for liberty, were invariably (the democratic portion of the Poles excepted) found on the side of despotism and reaction. Thus it was in Germany, thus in Hungary, thus even here and there in Turkey. Traitors to the popular cause, supporters and chief props to the Austrian Government's cabal, they placed themselves in the position of outlaws in the eyes of all revolutionary nations. And although nowhere the mass of the people had a part in the petty squabbles about nationality raised by the Panslavistic leaders, for the very reason that they were too ignorant, yet it will never be forgotten that in Prague, in a half-German town, crowds of Slavonian fanatics cheered and repeated the cry: "Rather the Russian knout than German Liberty!" After their first evaporated effort in 1848, and after the lesson the Austrian Government gave them, it is not likely that another attempt at a later opportunity will be made. But if they should try again under similar pretexts to ally themselves to the counter-revolutionary force, the duty of Germany is clear. No country in a state of revolution and involved in external war can tolerate a *Vendée*[54] in its very heart.

As to the Constitution proclaimed by the Emperor[a] at the same time with the dissolution of the Diet, there is no need to revert to it, as it never had a practical existence and is now done away with altogether. Absolutism has been restored in Austria to all intents and purposes ever since the 4th of March, 1849.

In Prussia, the Chambers met in February for the ratification and revision of the new Charter proclaimed by the King. They sat for about six weeks, humble and meek enough in their behavior toward the Government, yet not quite prepared to go the lengths the King and his ministers wished them to go. Therefore, as soon as a suitable occasion presented itself, they were dissolved.[55]

Thus both Austria and Prussia had for the moment got rid of the shackles of parliamentary control. The Governments now concentrated all power in themselves and could bring that power to bear wherever it was wanted: Austria upon Hungary and Italy, Prussia upon Germany. For Prussia, too, was preparing for a campaign by which "order" was to be restored in the smaller States.

Counter-revolution being now paramount in the two great centers of action of Germany, in Vienna and Berlin, there remained only the lesser States in which the struggle was still undecided, although the balance there, too, was leaning more and more against the revolutionary interest. These smaller States, we have said, found a common center in the National Assembly at Frankfort. Now, this so-called National Assembly, although its reactionist spirit had long been evident, so much so that the very people of Frankfort had risen in arms against it, yet its origin was of a more or less revolutionary nature; it occupied an abnormal, revolutionary position in January;

---

[a] Francis Joseph I.— *Ed.*

its competence had never been defined, and it had at last come to the decision—which, however, was never recognized by the larger States—that its resolutions had the force of law. Under these circumstances, and when the constitutionalist-monarchical party saw their positions turned by the recovering absolutists, it is not to be wondered that the liberal, monarchical bourgeoisie of almost the whole of Germany should place their last hopes upon the majority of this Assembly, just as the petty shopkeeping interest, the nucleus of the Democratic party, gathered in their growing distress around the minority of that same body which indeed formed the last compact parliamentary phalanx of Democracy. On the other hand, the larger Governments, and particularly the Prussian Ministry, saw more and more the incompatibility of such an irregular elective body with the restored monarchical system of Germany, and if they did not at once force its dissolution, it was only because the time had not yet come and because Prussia hoped first to use it for the furthering of its own ambitious purposes.

In the meantime, that poor Assembly itself fell into a greater and greater confusion. Its deputations and commissaries had been treated with the utmost contempt, both in Vienna and Berlin; one of its members,[a] in spite of his parliamentary inviolability, had been executed in Vienna as a common rebel. Its decrees were nowhere heeded; if they were noticed at all by the larger powers, it was merely by protesting notes which disputed the authority of the Assembly to pass laws and resolutions binding upon their governments. The Representative of the Assembly, the Central Executive Power, was involved in diplomatic squabbles with almost all the cabinets of Germany, and in spite of all their efforts neither Assembly nor Central Government could bring Austria or Prussia to state their ultimate views, plans, and demands. The Assembly, at last, commenced to see clearly, at least so far, that it had allowed all power to slip out of its hands, that it was at the mercy of Austria and Prussia, and that if it intended making a federal Constitution for Germany at all, it must set about the thing at once and in good earnest. And many of the vacillating members also saw clearly that they had been egregiously duped by the governments. But what were they, in their impotent position, able to do now? The only thing that could have saved them would have been promptly and decidedly to pass over into the popular camp; but the success, even of that step, was more than doubtful; and then, where in this helpless crowd of undecided, short-sighted, self-conceited beings who, when the eternal noise of

---

[a] Robert Blum.— *Ed.*

contradictory rumors and diplomatic notes completely stunned them, sought their only consolation and support in the everlastingly repeated assurance that they were the best, the greatest, the wisest men of the country, and that they alone could save Germany—where, we say, among these poor creatures, whom a single year of parliamentary life had turned into complete idiots, where were the men for a prompt and decisive resolution, much less for energetic and consistent action?

At last the Austrian Government threw off the mask. In its Constitution of the 4th of March it proclaimed Austria an indivisible monarchy, with common finances, system of customs-duties, of military establishments, thereby effacing every barrier and distinction between the German and non-German provinces. This declaration was made in the face of resolutions and articles of the intended federal Constitution, which had been already passed by the Frankfort Assembly. It was the gauntlet of war thrown down to it by Austria, and the poor Assembly had no other choice but to take it up. This it did with a deal of blustering, but which Austria, in the consciousness of her power, and of the utter nothingness of the Assembly, could well afford to allow to pass. And this precious representation, as it styled itself, of the German people, in order to revenge itself for this insult on the part of Austria, saw nothing better before it than to throw itself, hands and feet tied, at the feet of the Prussian Government. Incredible as it would seem, it bent its knees before the very ministers whom it had condemned as unconstitutional and anti-popular, and whose dismissal it had in vain insisted upon. The details of this disgraceful transaction, and the tragicomical events that followed, will form the subject of our next.

London, April, 1852

XV

THE TRIUMPH OF PRUSSIA

[New-York Daily Tribune, No. 3517, July 27, 1852]

We now come to the last chapter in the history of the German Revolution: the conflict of the National Assembly with the Governments of the different States, especially of Prussia; the insurrection of Southern and Western Germany, and its final overthrow by Prussia.

We have already seen the Frankfort National Assembly at work. We have seen it kicked at by Austria, insulted by Prussia, disobeyed by the lesser States, duped by its own impotent Central "Government," which again was the dupe of all and every prince in the country. But at last things began to look threatening for this weak, vacillating, insipid legislative body. It was forced to come to the conclusion that "the sublime idea of German Unity was threatened in its realization, "which meant neither more nor less than that the Frankfort Assembly, and all it had done and was about to do, were very likely to end in smoke. Thus it set to work in good earnest in order to bring forth as soon as possible its grand production, the "Imperial Constitution."

There was, however, one difficulty. What Executive Government was there to be? An Executive Council? No; that would have been, they thought in their wisdom, making Germany a Republic. A "President"? That would come to the same. Thus they must revive the old imperial dignity. But—as of course a prince was to be Emperor—who should it be? Certainly none of the *Dii minorum gentium*,[a] from Reuss-Schleiz-Greiz-Lobenstein-Ebersdorf[b] up to Bavaria[c]; neither Austria nor Prussia would have borne that. It could only be Austria or Prussia. But which of the two? There is no doubt that, under otherwise favorable circumstances, this august Assembly would be sitting up to the present day discussing this important dilemma without being able to come to a conclusion, if the Austrian Government had not cut the Gordian knot and saved them the trouble.

Austria knew very well that from the moment in which she could again appear before Europe with all her provinces subdued, as a strong and great European power, the very law of political gravitation would draw the remainder of Germany into her orbit, without the help of any authority which an imperial crown conferred by the Frankfort Assembly could give her. Austria had been far stronger, far freer in her movements, since she shook off the powerless crown of the German Empire—a crown which clogged her own independent policy, while it added not one iota to her strength, either within or without of Germany. And supposing the case that Austria could not maintain her footing in Italy and Hungary—why, then she was dissolved, annihilated in Germany too, and could never pretend to re-seize a crown which had slipped from her hands while she was in the full possession of her strength. Thus Austria at once declared against all imperialist resurrections, and

---

[a] Literally: junior gods; figuratively: second-rate personages.— *Ed.*
[b] Heinrich LXXII.— *Ed.*
[c] The reference is to the King of Bavaria, Maximilian II.— *Ed.*

plainly demanded the restoration of the German Diet, the only Central Government of Germany known and recognized by the treaties of 1815; and on the 4th of March, 1849, issued that Constitution which had no other meaning than to declare Austria an indivisible, centralized, and independent monarchy, distinct even from that Germany which the Frankfort Assembly was to reorganize.

This open declaration of war left, indeed, the Frankfort wiseacres no other choice but to exclude Austria from Germany, and to create out of the remainder of that country a sort of Lower Empire,[a] a "Little Germany," the rather shabby imperial mantle of which was to fall on the shoulders of his Majesty of Prussia. This, it will be recollected, was the renewal of an old project fostered already some six or eight years ago by a party of South and Middle German liberal *doctrinaires*,[b] who considered as a godsend the degrading circumstances by which their old crotchet was now again brought forward as the latest "new move" for the salvation of the country.

They accordingly finished, in February and March, 1849, the debate on the Imperial Constitution, together with the Declaration of Rights and the Imperial Electoral Law[56]; not, however, without being obliged to make, in a great many points, the most contradictory concessions—now to the Conservative or rather Reactionary party—now to the more advanced fractions of the Assembly. In fact, it was evident that the leadership of the Assembly, which had formerly belonged to the Right and Right Center (the Conservatives and Reactionists), was gradually, although slowly, passing toward the Left or Democratic side of that body. The rather dubious position of the Austrian Deputies in an Assembly which had excluded their country from Germany, and in which yet they were called upon to sit and vote, favored the derangement of its equipoise; and thus, as early as the end of February, the Left Center and the Left found themselves, by the help of the Austrian votes, very generally in a majority, while on other days the Conservative fraction of the Austrians, all of a sudden and for the fun of the thing, voting with the Right, threw the balance again on the other side. They intended by these sudden *soubresauts*[c] to bring the Assembly into contempt, which, however, was quite unnecessary, the mass of the people being long since convinced of the utter hollowness and futility of anything coming from Frankfort. What a specimen of a Constitution, in the

---

[a] Eastern Roman Empire.— *Ed.*
[b] See this volume, p. 22.— *Ed.*
[c] Jumps, leaps.— *Ed.*

Christian streets, they were fined if not more severely punished. It was under such foul oppressions, however, that the fortunes of his house took their rise and began to flourish. At the entrance of this street is still the bureau, the council-rooms of their imperial firm, where they receive tributes from the principalities and powers of the world. A poor devil of a Christian clerk sits there alone on Saturdays, to deal out small sums to travelers and others on letters of credit, etc.

Jews settled in Frankfort under some imperfect, dearly-paid protection of the German Emperors as early as the twelfth century. In 1339 their wretched habitations were set fire to by religious fanatics, called Flagellants. In 1462 they built in the present *Judengasse*, or New-Egypt, as it is sometimes named. Fire came upon them yet again in 1711. I roughly translate a brief account of the last conflagration, as illustrative of the spirit of that time: " Meanwhile, all the houses were burned up stock and branch, and indeed in such wise that not a single one of so many houses, nay, not so much as a stick of wood of an arm's length remained, which is surely marvelous. It was remarkable, also, that when one side of the street was burned down, the wind turned about as though it had finished there the business on which it was sent, and would now carry it on further; so that by this the other and greater part of the street was seized on by the fire and laid in ashes. The fire broke out almost in the middle of the street, in the house of the Rabbi Naphthali, their most famous Doctor. It is related for a certain truth, that when their Rabbi, who was besides a good Cabalist, was minded to teach his scholars the Cabala, and had kindled for experiment a great heap of wood in his house, he became confined in his incantation, and in place of conjuring the water-spirit to extinguish the fire kindled by him, called up the fire-spirits. Wherefore it was altogether in vain to try to save the smallest Jewish building. This is also to be considered in this conflagration, that of the many Christian houses near by, not a single one was consumed." Seeing on one side this account, written about one hundred years, and the persecutions and oppressions under which the Jews existed until the close of the last century; and seeing on the other side the friendly terms on which Jews and Catholics and Protestants now live and work together here, one would say the world had made progress. More, however, is to be made. Some additional measure of justice was dealt out to the Jews in the Revolution of 1848 : but they are not yet admitted to a full political equality with the Christian citizens of Frankfort. Just at this time the question of revising the constitution of the city is much discussed, and some propose, as one of the alterations, the admissibility of Jews to the Senate. With the present reactionary spirit of the German powers, it would seem, however, a dangerous time to at-

tiguing. Local events of the day, or some gone-to-seed item of foreign news, are the favorite topics of a low-toned conversation, freely punctuated with long whiffs of tobacco-smoke from the mouths of the interlocutors. As for helping out their rhetoric by any gesticulation or rising from their seats to command more attention, such French vivacity is never indulged in. The services of one hand are engaged to hold the pipe, while the other attends to the glass, and the rest of the body, once seated, never leaves its moorings till bedtime. These gentlemen must have had periods in their lives of greater mental activity than they indicate at these meetings, which are very possibly, to their habit, only an anodyne taken after the agitation of the day's business, as a preparation to full repose. They answer a questioning stranger intelligently and politely. May they sleep well! with quiet consciences and good digestions. They retire mostly before 10½ o'clock. The Frankforters generally are early to bed. Think of my coming home from Don Pasquale at the theater last night, at a little after 9 o'clock!

C. R. B.

GERMANY.

XV.

REVOLUTION AND COUNTER-REVOLUTION.

We now come to the last chapter in the history of the German Revolution : the conflict of the National Assembly with the Governments of the different States, especially of Prussia ; the insurrection of Southern and Western Germany, and its final overthrow by Prussia.

We have already seen the Frankfort National Assembly at work. We have seen it kicked at by Austria, insulted by Prussia, disobeyed by the lesser States, duped by its own impotent Central " Government," which again was the dupe of all and every prince in the country. But at last things began to look threatening for this weak, vacillating, insipid legislative body. It was forced to come to the conclusion that " the sublime idea of German Unity was threatened in its realization," —which meant neither more nor less than that the Frankfort Assembly, and all it had done and was about to do, were very likely to end in smoke. Thus t set to work in good earnest in order to bring forth as soon as possible its grand production, the "Imperial Constitution."

There was, however, one difficulty. What Executive Government was there to be ? An Executive Council ? No ; that would have been, they thought in their wisdom, making Germany a Republic. A " President" ? That would come to the same. Thus they must revive the old imperial dignity. But—as of course a prince was to be Emperor—who should it be? Certainly none of the *Dii minorum gentium*, from Reuss-Schleitz-Greitz-Lobenstein-Ebersdorf up to Bavaria; neither Austria nor Prussia would have borne that.

a disorder which penetrates its unfortunate victims with the solemn conviction that the whole world, its history and future, are governed and determined by a majority of votes in that particular representative body which has the honor to count them among its members, and that all and everything going on outside the walls of their house—wars, revolutions, railway-constructing, colonizing of whole new continents, California gold discoveries, Central American canals, Russian armies, and whatever else may have some little claim to influence upon the destinies of mankind—is nothing compared to the incommensurable events hinging upon the important question, whatever it may be, just at that moment occupying the attention of their honorable House. Thus it was the Democratic party of the Assembly, by effectually smuggling a few of their nostrums into the " Imperial Constitution," first became bound to support it, although in every essential point it flatly contradicted their own oft-proclaimed principles ; and at last, when this mongrel work was abandoned and bequeathed to them by its main authors, accepted the inheritance, and held out for this *monarchical* Constitution even in opposition to everybody who *then* proclaimed their own *republican* principles.

But it must be confessed that in this the contradiction was merely apparent. The indeterminate, self-contradictory, immature character of the Imperial Constitution was the very image of the immature, confused, conflicting political ideas of these democratic gentlemen. And if their own sayings and writings—as far as they could write—were not sufficient proof of this, their actions would furnish such proof; for among sensible people it is a matter of course to judge of a man not by his professions but by his actions; not by what he pretends to be, but by what he does and what he really is ; and the deeds of these heroes of German Democracy speak loud enough for themselves, as we shall learn by and by. However, the Imperial Constitution with all its appendages and paraphernalia was definitively passed, and on the 28th of March the King of Prussia was, by 290 votes, against 248 who abstained and some 200 who were absent, elected Emperor of Germany, *minus* Austria. The historical irony was complete ; the imperial farce executed in the streets of astonished Berlin, three days after the Revolution of March 18, 1848, by Frederick William IV. while in a state which elsewhere would come under the Maine Liquor Law—this disgusting farce, just one year afterward, had been sanctioned by the pretended Representative Assembly of all Germany. That, then, was the result of the German Revolution!

KARL MARX.

London, July, 1852.

Part of a page from the *New-York Daily Tribune* containing Engels' article from the series *Revolution and Counter-Revolution in Germany*

meantime, was framed under such jumping and counter-jumping, may easily be imagined.

.The Left of the Assembly—this *élite* and pride of revolutionary Germany, as it believed itself to be—was entirely intoxicated with the few paltry successes it obtained by the good-will, or rather the ill-will, of a set of Austrian politicians acting under the instigation and for the interest of Austrian despotism. Whenever the slightest approximation to their own not-very-well-defined principles had, in a homoeopathically diluted shape, obtained a sort of sanction by the Frankfort Assembly, these Democrats proclaimed that they had saved the country and the people. These poor, weak-minded men, during the course of their generally very obscure lives, had been so little accustomed to anything like success, that they actually believed their paltry amendments, passed with two or three votes' majority, would change the face of Europe. They had from the beginning of their legislative career been more imbued than any other fraction of the Assembly with that incurable malady, *parliamentary cretinism,* a disorder which penetrates its unfortunate victims with the solemn conviction that the whole world, its history and future, are governed and determined by a majority of votes in that particular representative body which has the honor to count them among its members, and that all and everything going on outside the walls of their house—wars, revolutions, railway-constructing, colonizing of whole new continents, California gold discoveries, Central American canals, Russian armies, and whatever else may have some little claim to influence upon the destinies of mankind—is nothing compared to the incommensurable events hinging upon the important question, whatever it may be, just at that moment occupying the attention of their honorable House. Thus it was the Democratic party of the Assembly, by effectually smuggling a few of their nostrums into the "Imperial Constitution," that first became bound to support it, although in every essential point it flatly contradicted their own oft-proclaimed principles; and at last, when this mongrel work was abandoned and bequeathed to them by its main authors, accepted the inheritance, and held out for this *monarchical* Constitution even in opposition to everybody who *then* proclaimed their own *republican* principles.

But it must be confessed that in this the contradiction was merely apparent. The indeterminate, self-contradictory, immature character of the Imperial Constitution was the very image of the immature, confused, conflicting political ideas of these democratic gentlemen. And if their own sayings and writings—as far as they could write—were not sufficient proof of this, their actions would furnish such proof; for among sensible people it is a matter of course to judge of a man not by his professions, but by his actions; not by what he pretends to be, but by what he does and what he really is; and the deeds of these heroes of German Democracy speak loud enough for themselves, as we shall learn by and by. However, the Imperial Constitution with all its appendages and paraphernalia was definitively passed, and on the 28th of March the King of Prussia was, by 290 votes against 248 who abstained and some 200 who were absent, elected Emperor of Germany, *minus* Austria. The historical irony was complete; the imperial farce executed in the streets of astonished Berlin, three days after the Revolution of March 18, 1848, by Frederick William IV,[57] while in a state which elsewhere would come under the Maine Liquor Law—this disgusting farce, just one year afterward, had been sanctioned by the pretended Representative Assembly of all Germany. That, then, was the result of the German Revolution!

London, July, 1852

XVI

THE NATIONAL ASSEMBLY AND THE GOVERNMENTS

[*New-York Daily Tribune*, No. 3537, August 19, 1852]

The National Assembly of Frankfort, after having elected the King of Prussia Emperor of Germany (*minus* Austria), sent a deputation to Berlin to offer him the crown, and then adjourned. On the 3d of April Frederick William received the Deputies. He told them that, although he accepted the right of precedence over all the other Princes of Germany, which this vote of the people's representatives had given him, yet he could not accept the Imperial crown as long as he was not sure that the remaining Princes acknowledged his supremacy and the Imperial Constitution conferring those rights upon him. It would be, he added, for the Governments of Germany to see whether this Constitution was such as could be ratified by them. At all events, Emperor or not, he always would be found ready, he concluded, to draw the sword against either the external or the internal foe. We shall soon see how he kept his promise in a manner rather startling for the National Assembly.

The Frankfort wiseacres, after profound diplomatic inquiry, at last came to the conclusion that this answer amounted to a refusal of the crown. They then (April 12) resolved: That the Imperial Constitution was the law of the land, and must be maintained; and not seeing their way at all before themselves, elected a Committee of Thirty, to make proposals as to the means how this Constitution could be carried out.

This resolution was the signal for the conflict between the Frankfort Assembly and the German Governments, which now broke out.

The middle classes, and especially the smaller trading class, had all at once declared for the new Frankfort Constitution. They could not await any longer the moment which was "to close the revolution." In Austria and Prussia the revolution had, for the moment, been closed by the interference of the armed power; the classes in question would have preferred a less forcible mode of performing that operation, but they had not had a chance; the thing was done, and they had to make the best of it, a resolution which they at once took and carried out most heroically. In the smaller States, where things had been going on comparatively smoothly, the middle classes had long since been thrown back into that showy, but resultless, because powerless, parliamentary agitation which was most congenial to themselves. The different States of Germany, as regarded each of them separately, appeared thus to have attained that new and definitive form which was supposed to enable them to enter, henceforth, the path of peaceful and constitutional development. There only remained one open question, that of the new political organization of the German Confederacy. And this question, the only one which still appeared fraught with danger, it was considered a necessity to resolve at once. Hence the pressure exerted upon the Frankfort Assembly by the middle classes, in order to induce it to get the Constitution ready as soon as possible; hence the resolution among the higher and lower bourgeoisie to accept and to support this Constitution, whatever it might be, in order to create a settled state of things without delay. Thus, from the very beginning, the agitation for the Imperial Constitution arose out of a reactionary feeling, and sprung up among those classes which were long since tired of the revolution.

But there was another feature in it. The first and fundamental principles of the future German Constitution had been voted during the first months of spring and summer, 1848—a time when popular agitation was still rife. The resolutions then passed—though completely reactionary *then*—now, after the arbitrary acts of the Austrian and Prussian Governments, appeared exceedingly liberal, and even democratic. The standard of comparison had changed. The Frankfort Assembly could not, without moral suicide, strike out these once-voted provisions, and model the Imperial Constitution upon those which the Austrian and Prussian Governments had dictated sword in hand. Besides, as we have seen, the majority in that Assembly had changed sides, and the Liberal and Democratic party were rising in influence. Thus the Imperial Constitution not only was distinguished by its apparently exclusive popular origin, but at the same time, full of contradiction as it was, it yet was the most liberal Constitution of all Germany. Its greatest fault was, that it was a mere sheet of paper, with no power to back its provisions.

Under these circumstances it was natural that the so-called Democratic party, that is, the mass of the petty trading class, should cling to the Imperial Constitution. This class had always been more forward in its demands than the Liberal Monarchico-Constitutional bourgeoisie; it had shown a bolder front, it had very often threatened armed resistance, it was lavish in its promises to sacrifice its blood and its existence in the struggle for freedom; but it had already given plenty of proofs that on the day of danger it was nowhere, and that it never felt more comfortable than the day after a decisive defeat, when everything being lost, it had at least the consolation to know that somehow or other the matter *was* settled. While, therefore, the adhesion of the large bankers, manufacturers and merchants was of a more reserved character, more like a simple demonstration in favor of the Frankfort Constitution, the class just beneath them, our valiant democratic shopkeepers, came forward in grand style and, as usual, proclaimed they would rather spill their last drop of blood than let the Imperial Constitution fall to the ground.

Supported by these two parties, the bourgeois adherents of Constitutional Royalty and the more or less democratic shopkeepers, the agitation for the immediate establishment of the Imperial Constitution gained ground rapidly, and found its most powerful expression in the Parliaments of the several States. The Chambers of Prussia, of Hanover, of Saxony, of Baden, of Württemberg, declared in its favor. The struggle between the Governments and the Frankfort Assembly assumed a threatening aspect.

The Governments, however, acted rapidly. The Prussian Chambers were dissolved, anti-constitutionally, as they had to revise and confirm the Constitution; riots broke out at Berlin, provoked intentionally by the Government; and the next day, the 28th of April, the Prussian Ministry issued a circular note, in which the Imperial Constitution was held up as a most anarchical and revolutionary document, which it was for the Governments of Germany to remodel and purify. Thus Prussia denied, point-blank, that sovereign constituent power which the wise men at Frankfort had always boasted of, but never established. Thus a Congress of Princes,[58] a renewal of the old Federal Diet, was called upon to sit in judgment on that Constitution which had already been promulgated as a law. And at the same time Prussia concentrated troops at Kreuznach, three days' march from Frankfort, and called upon the smaller States to follow its example by also dissolving their Chambers as soon as they should give their adhesion to the Frankfort Assembly. This example was speedily followed by Hanover and Saxony.

It was evident that a decision of the struggle by force of arms could not be avoided. The hostility of the Governments, the agitation among the people were daily showing themselves in stronger colors. The military were everywhere worked upon by the democratic citizens, and in the South of Germany with great success. Large mass meetings were everywhere held, passing resolutions to support the Imperial Constitution and the National Assembly, if need should be, with force of arms. At Cologne, a meeting of deputies of all the municipal councils of Rhenish Prussia took place for the same purpose. In the Palatinate, at Bergen, Fulda, Nuremberg, in the Odenwald, the peasantry met by myriads and worked themselves up into enthusiasm. At the same time, the Constituent Assembly of France dissolved, and the new elections were prepared amid violent agitation, while on the eastern frontier of Germany the Hungarians had within a month, by a succession of brilliant victories, rolled back the tide of Austrian invasion from the Theiss to the Leitha, and were every day expected to take Vienna by storm. Thus, popular imagination being on all hands worked up to the highest pitch, and the aggressive policy of the Governments defining itself more clearly every day, a violent collision could not be avoided, and cowardly imbecility only could persuade itself that the struggle was to come off peaceably. But this cowardly imbecility was most extensively represented in the Frankfort Assembly.

London, July, 1852

XVII

INSURRECTION

[*New-York Daily Tribune*, No. 3564, September 18, 1852]

The inevitable conflict between the National Assembly of Frankfort and the States' Government of Germany, at last broke out in open hostilities during the first days of May, 1849. The Austrian deputies, recalled by their Government, had already left the

Assembly and returned home, with the exception of a few members of the Left or Democratic party. The great body of the Conservative members, aware of the turn things were about to take, withdrew even before they were called upon to do so by their respective Governments. Thus, even independently of the causes which in the foregoing papers have been shown to strengthen the influence of the Left, the mere desertion of their posts by the members of the Right sufficed to turn the old minority into a majority of the Assembly. The new majority which, at no former time, had dreamt of ever obtaining that good fortune, had profited by their places on the opposition benches to spout against the weakness, the indecision, the indolence of the old majority and of its Imperial Lieutenancy. Now all at once, *they* were called on to replace that old majority. *They* were now to show what they could perform. Of course, *their* career was to be one of energy, determination, activity. *They*, the *élite* of Germany, would soon be able to drive onwards the senile Lieutenant of the Empire[a] and his vacillating ministers, and in case that was impossible, they would—there could be no doubt about it—by force of the sovereign right of the people, depose that impotent Government, and replace it by an energetic, indefatigable Executive, who would assure the salvation of Germany. Poor fellows! *their* rule—if rule it can be named where no one obeyed—was a still more ridiculous affair than even the rule of their predecessors.

The new majority declared that, in spite of all obstacles, the Imperial Constitution must be carried out, and *at once*; that on the 15th of July ensuing the people were to elect the deputies for the new House of Representatives, and that this House was to meet at Frankfort on the 22d of August following. Now, this was an open declaration of war against those Governments that had not recognized the Imperial Constitution, the foremost among which were Prussia, Austria, Bavaria, comprising more than three-fourths of the German population; a declaration of war which was speedily accepted by them. Prussia and Bavaria, too, recalled the deputies sent from their territories to Frankfort, and hastened their military preparations against the National Assembly; while, on the other hand, the demonstrations of the Democratic party (out of Parliament) in favor of the Imperial Constitution and of the National Assembly, acquired a more turbulent and violent character, and the mass of the working people, led by the men of the most extreme party, were ready to take up arms in a cause which, if it was not their own, at least gave them a chance of somewhat approaching their

---

[a] Archduke John of Austria.— *Ed.*

aims by clearing Germany of its old monarchical encumbrances. Thus everywhere the people and the Governments were at daggers drawn upon this subject; the outbreak was inevitable; the mine was charged, and it only wanted a spark to make it explode. The dissolution of the Chambers in Saxony, the calling in of the Landwehr (military reserve) in Prussia, the open resistance of the Governments to the Imperial Constitution, were such sparks; they fell, and all at once the country was in a blaze. In Dresden, on the 4th of May, the people victoriously took possession of the town and drove out the King[a] while all the surrounding districts sent reinforcements to the insurgents. In Rhenish Prussia and Westphalia the Landwehr refused to march, took possession of the arsenals and armed itself in defense of the Imperial Constitution. In the Palatinate the people seized the Bavarian Government officials and the public moneys, and instituted a Committee of Defense, which placed the province under the protection of the National Assembly. In Württemberg the people forced the King[b] to acknowledge the Imperial Constitution, and in Baden the army, united with the people, forced the Grand Duke[c] to flight and erected a Provisional Government. In other parts of Germany the people only awaited a decisive signal from the National Assembly to rise in arms and place themselves at its disposal.

The position of the National Assembly was far more favorable than could have been expected after its ignoble career. The Western half of Germany had taken up arms in its behalf; the military everywhere were vacillating; in the lesser States they were undoubtedly favorable to the movement. Austria was prostrated by the victorious advance of the Hungarians, and Russia, that reserve force of the German Governments, was straining all its powers in order to support Austria against the Magyar armies. There was only Prussia to subdue; and with the revolutionary sympathies existing in that country, a chance certainly existed of attaining that end. Everything, then, depended upon the conduct of the Assembly.

Now, insurrection is an art quite as much as war or any other, and subject to certain rules of proceeding, which, when neglected, will produce the ruin of the party neglecting them. Those rules, logical deductions from the nature of the parties and the circumstances one has to deal with in such a case, are so plain and simple that the short experience of 1848 had made the Germans pretty well acquainted with them. Firstly, never play with insurrection unless you are fully

---

[a] Frederick Augustus II.— *Ed.*
[b] William I.— *Ed.*
[c] Leopold.— *Ed.*

prepared to face the consequences of your play. Insurrection is a calculus with very indefinite magnitudes, the value of which may change every day; the forces opposed to you have all the advantage of organization, discipline and habitual authority; unless you bring strong odds against them, you are defeated and ruined. Secondly, the insurrectionary career once entered upon, act with the greatest determination, and on the offensive. The defensive is the death of every armed rising; it is lost before it measures itself with its enemies. Surprise your antagonists while their forces are scattering, prepare new successes, however small but daily; keep up the moral ascendant which the first successful rising has given to you; rally thus those vacillating elements to your side which always follow the strongest impulse, and which always look out for the safer side; force your enemies to a retreat before they can collect their strength against you; in the words of Danton, the greatest master of revolutionary policy yet known: *de l'audace, de l'audace, encore de l'audace!*[a]

What, then, was the National Assembly of Frankfort to do if it would escape the certain ruin which it was threatened with? First of all, to see clearly through the situation, and to convince itself that there was now no other choice than either to submit to the Governments unconditionally or take up the cause of the armed insurrection without reserve or hesitation. Secondly, to publicly recognize all the insurrections that had already broken out, and to call the people to take up arms everywhere in defense of the national representation, outlawing all princes, ministers, and others who should dare to oppose the sovereign people represented by its mandataries. Thirdly, to at once depose the German Imperial Lieutenant, to create a strong, active, *unscrupulous* Executive, to call insurgent troops to Frankfort for its immediate protection, thus offering at the same time a legal pretext for the spread of the insurrection, to organize into a compact body all the forces at its disposal, and, in short, to profit quickly and unhesitatingly by every available means for strengthening its position and impairing that of its opponents.

Of all this, the virtuous Democrats in the Frankfort Assembly did just the contrary. Not content with letting things take the course they liked, these worthies went so far as to suppress by their opposition all insurrectionary movements which were preparing. Thus, for instance, did Mr. Karl Vogt at Nuremberg. They allowed the insurrections of Saxony, of Rhenish Prussia, of Westphalia to be

---

[a] From Danton's speech made in the Legislative Assembly on September 2, 1792.— *Ed.*

suppressed without any other help than a posthumous, sentimental protest against the unfeeling violence of the Prussian Government. They kept up an underhand diplomatic intercourse with the South German insurrections, but never gave them the support of their open acknowledgment. They knew that the Lieutenant of the Empire sided with the Governments, and yet they called upon *him*, who never stirred, to oppose the intrigues of these Governments. The Ministers of the Empire, old Conservatives, ridiculed this impotent Assembly in every sitting, and they suffered it. And when William Wolff, a Silesian Deputy, and one of the editors of the *New Rhenish Gazette*,[a] called upon them to outlaw the Lieutenant of the Empire—who was, he justly said, nothing but the first and greatest traitor to the Empire[59]—he was hooted down by the unanimous and virtuous indignation of those democratic revolutionists! In short, they went on talking, protesting, proclaiming, pronouncing, but never had the courage nor the sense to act; while the hostile troops of the Governments drew nearer and nearer, and their own Executive, the Lieutenant of the Empire, was busily plotting with the German Princes their speedy destruction. Thus, even the last vestige of consideration was lost to this contemptible Assembly; the insurgents, who had risen to defend it, ceased to care any more for it, and when at last it came to a shameful end, as we shall see, it died without anybody taking any notice of its unhonored exit.

London, August, 1852

XVIII
PETTY TRADERS

[*New-York Daily Tribune*, No. 3576, October 2, 1852]

In our last we showed that the struggle between the German Governments on the one side, and the Frankfort Parliament on the other, had ultimately acquired such a degree of violence that in the first days of May a great portion of Germany broke out in open insurrection: first Dresden, then the Bavarian Palatinate, parts of Rhenish Prussia, and at last Baden.

In all cases, the *real fighting* body of the insurgents, that body which first took up arms and gave battle to the troops, consisted of the *working classes of the towns*. A portion of the poorer country population, laborers and petty farmers, generally joined them after

---

[a] *Neue Rheinische Zeitung.*— Ed.

the actual outbreak of the conflict. The greater number of the young men of all classes, below the capitalist class, was to be found, for a time at least, in the ranks of the insurgent armies, but this rather indiscriminate aggregate of young men very soon thinned as soon as the aspect of affairs took a somewhat serious turn. The students particularly, those "representatives of intellect," as they liked to call themselves, were the first to quit their standards, unless they were retained by the bestowal of officer's rank, for which they, of course, had very seldom any qualification.

The working class entered upon this insurrection as they would have done upon any other which promised either to remove some obstacles in their progress toward political dominion and social revolution, or at least to tie the more influential but less courageous classes of society to a more decided and revolutionary course than they had followed hitherto. The working class took up arms with a full knowledge that this was, in the direct bearings of the case, no quarrel of its own; but it followed up its only true policy: to allow no class that has risen on its shoulders (as the bourgeoisie had done in 1848) to fortify its class-government, without opening, at least, a fair field to the working class for the struggle for its own interests; and, in any case, to bring matters to a crisis, by which either the nation was fairly and irresistibly launched in the revolutionary career, or else the *status quo* before the revolution restored as near as possible, and thereby a new revolution rendered unavoidable. In both cases the working classes represented the real and well-understood interest of the nation at large, in hastening as much as possible that revolutionary course which, for the old societies of civilized Europe, has now become a historical necessity, before any of them can again aspire to a more quiet and regular development of its resources.

As to country people that joined the insurrection, they were principally thrown into the arms of the revolutionary party partly by the relatively enormous load of taxation, and partly of feudal burdens, pressing upon them. Without any initiative of their own, they formed the tail of the other classes engaged in the insurrection, wavering between the working men on one side, and the petty trading class on the other. Their own private social position, in almost every case, decided which way they turned; the agricultural laborer generally supported the city artisan, the small farmer was apt to go hand in hand with the small shopkeeper.

This class of petty tradesmen, the great importance and influence of which we have already several times adverted to, may be considered as the leading class of the insurrection of May, 1849. There being, this time, none of the large towns of Germany among the centers of the movement, the petty trading class, which in middling and lesser towns always predominates, found the means of getting the direction of the movement into its hands. We have, moreover, seen that, in this struggle for the Imperial Constitution and for the rights of the German Parliament, there were the interests of this peculiar class at stake. The Provisional Governments formed in all the insurgent districts represented in the majority of each of them this section of the people, and the length they went to may therefore be fairly taken as the measure of what the German petty bourgeoisie is capable of—capable, as we shall see, of nothing but ruining any movement that entrusts itself to its hands.

The petty bourgeoisie, great in boasting, is very impotent for action and very shy in risking anything. The *mesquin*[a] character of its commercial transactions and its credit operations is eminently apt to stamp its character with a want of energy and enterprise; it is, then, to be expected that similar qualities will mark its political career. Accordingly, the petty bourgeoisie encouraged insurrection by big words and great boasting as to what it was going to do; it was eager to seize upon power as soon as the insurrection, much against its will, had broken out; it used this power to no other purpose but to destroy the effects of the insurrection. Wherever an armed conflict had brought matters to a serious crisis, there the shopkeepers stood aghast at the dangerous situation created for them; aghast at the people who had taken their boasting appeals to arms in earnest; aghast at the power thus thrust into their own hands; aghast, above all, at the consequences for themselves, for their social positions, for their fortunes, of the policy in which they were forced to engage themselves. Were they not expected to risk "life and property," as they used to say, for the cause of the insurrection? Were they not forced to take official positions in the insurrection, whereby, in case of defeat, they risked the loss of their capital? And in case of victory, were they not sure to be immediately turned out of office and see their entire policy subverted by the victorious proletarians who formed the main body of their fighting army? Thus placed between opposing dangers which surrounded them on every side, the petty bourgeoisie knew not to turn its power to any other account than to let everything take its chance, whereby, of course, there was lost what little chance of success there might have been, and thus to ruin the insurrection altogether. Its policy or rather want of policy everywhere was the same, and, therefore, the insurrections of May, 1849, in all parts of Germany, are all cut out to the same pattern.

---

[a] Niggardly, cheeseparing.— *Ed.*

In Dresden, the struggle was kept on for four days in the streets of the town. The shopkeepers of Dresden, the "communal guard," not only did not fight, but in many instances favored the proceedings of the troops against the insurgents. These again consisted almost exclusively of working men from the surrounding manufacturing districts. They found *an able and cool-headed commander in the Russian refugee, Michael Bakunin,* who afterward was taken prisoner, and now is confined in the dungeons of Munkacs,[a] Hungary. The intervention of numerous Prussian troops crushed this insurrection.

In Rhenish Prussia, the actual fighting was of little importance. All the large towns being fortresses commanded by citadels, there could be only skirmishing on the part of the insurgents. As soon as a sufficient number of troops had been drawn together, there was an end to armed opposition.

In the Palatinate and Baden, on the contrary, a rich, fruitful province, and an entire State, fell into the hands of the insurrection. Money, arms, soldiers, warlike stores, everything was ready for use. The soldiers of the regular army themselves joined the insurgents; nay, in Baden, they were among the foremost of them. The insurrections in Saxony and Rhenish Prussia sacrificed themselves in order to gain time for the organization of this South-German movement. Never was there such a favorable position for a provincial and partial insurrection as this. A revolution was expected in Paris, the Hungarians were at the gates of Vienna, in all the central States of Germany not only the people, but even the troops, were strongly in favor of the insurrection, and only wanted an opportunity to join it openly. And yet the movement, having got once into the hands of the petty bourgeoisie, was ruined from its very beginning. The petty bourgeois rulers, particularly of Baden—M. Brentano at the head of them—never forgot that by usurping the place and prerogatives of the "lawful" sovereign, the Grand Duke,[b] they were committing high treason. They sat down in their ministerial armchairs with the consciousness of criminality in their hearts. What can you expect of such cowards? They not only abandoned the insurrection to its own uncentralized and therefore ineffective spontaneity, they actually did everything in their power to take the sting out of the movement, to unman, to destroy it. And they succeeded, thanks to the zealous support of that deep class of

---

[a] Ukrainian name: Mukachevo. (By that time Bakunin had been extradited by the Austrian authorities to tsarist Russia and imprisoned in the Peter and Paul Fortress in St. Petersburg.)— *Ed.*

[b] Leopold.— *Ed.*

politicians, the "Democratic" heroes of the petty bourgeoisie, who actually thought they were "saving the country," while they allowed themselves to be led by their noses by a few men of a sharper cast, such as Brentano.

As to the fighting part of the business, never were military operations carried on in a more slovenly, more stolid way than under the Badish General-in-Chief Sigel, an ex-Lieutenant of the regular army. Everything was got into confusion, every good opportunity was lost, every precious moment was loitered away with planning colossal but impracticable projects, until, when at last the talented Pole, Mieroslawski, took up the command, the army was disorganized, beaten, dispirited, badly provided for, opposed to an enemy four times more numerous, and withal he could do nothing more than fight, at Waghäusel, a glorious, though unsuccessful, battle, carry out a clever retreat, offer a last hopeless fight under the walls of Rastatt, and resign.[60] As in every insurrectionary war, where armies are mixed of well-drilled soldiers and raw levies, there was plenty of heroism and plenty of unsoldierlike, often inconceivable panic in the revolutionary army; but, imperfect as it could not but be, it had at least the satisfaction that four times its number were not considered sufficient to put it to the rout, and that a hundred thousand regular troops, in a campaign against twenty thousand insurgents, treated them, militarily, with as much respect as if they had had to fight the Old Guard of Napoleon.

In May the insurrection had broken out; by the middle of July, 1849, it was entirely subdued, and the first German Revolution was closed.

XIX
THE CLOSE OF THE INSURRECTION

[New-York Daily Tribune, No. 3594, October 23, 1852]

While the South and West of Germany was in open insurrection, and while it took the Governments from the first opening of hostilities at Dresden to the capitulation of Rastatt, rather more than ten weeks, to stifle this final blazing up of the first German Revolution, the National Assembly disappeared from the political theatre without any notice being taken of its exit.

We left this august body at Frankfort, perplexed by the insolent attacks of the Governments upon its dignity, by the impotency and treacherous listlessness of the Central Power it had itself created, by the risings of the petty trading class for its defense, and of the working class for a more revolutionary ultimate end. Desolation and despair reigned supreme among its members; events had at once assumed such a definite and decisive shape, that in a few days the illusions of these learned legislators, as to their real power and influence, were entirely broken down. The Conservatives, at the signal given by the Governments, had already retired from a body which henceforth could not exist any longer, except in defiance of the constituted authorities. The Liberals gave the matter up in utter discomfiture; they, too, threw up their commissions as representatives. Honorable gentlemen decamped by hundreds. From eight or nine hundred members the number had dwindled down so rapidly, that now 150, and a few days after 100, were declared a quorum. And even these were difficult to muster, although the whole of the Democratic party remained.

The course to be followed by the remnants of a Parliament was plain enough. They had only to take their stand openly and decidedly with the insurrection, to give it, thereby, whatever strength legality could confer upon it, while they themselves at once acquired an army for their own defense. They had to summon the Central Power to stop all hostilities at once; and if, as could be foreseen, this power neither could nor would do so, to depose it at once and put another more energetic Government in its place. If insurgent troops could not be brought to Frankfort (which, in the beginning, when the State Governments were little prepared and still hesitating, might have been easily done), then the Assembly could have adjourned at once to the very center of the insurgent district. All this, done at once, and resolutely, not later than the middle or end of May, might have opened chances both for the insurrection and for the National Assembly.

But such a determined course was not to be expected from the representatives of German shopocracy. These aspiring statesmen were not at all freed from their illusions. Those members who had lost their fatal belief in the strength and inviolability of the Parliament, had already taken to their heels; the Democrats, who remained, were not so easily induced to give up dreams of power and greatness which they had cherished for a twelvemonth. True to the course they had hitherto pursued, they shrunk back from decisive action until every chance of success, nay, every chance to succumb with, at least, the honors of war, had passed away. In order, then, to develop a factitious, busy-body sort of activity, the sheer impotence of which, coupled with its high pretensions, could not but excite pity and ridicule, they continued insinuating resolutions, addresses, and requests to an Imperial Lieutenant, who not even noticed them, to Ministers, who were in open league with the enemy. And when at last *William Wolff*, member for Striegau,[a] one of the editors of the *New Rhenish Gazette*,[b] the only really revolutionary man in the whole Assembly, told them that if they meant what they said, they had better give over talking and declare the Imperial Lieutenant, the chief traitor to the country, an outlaw at once; then the entire compressed virtuous indignation of these parliamentary gentlemen burst out with an energy which they never found when the Government heaped insult after insult upon them. Of course, for *Wolff's* proposition was the first sensible word spoken within the walls of St. Paul's Church[c]; of course, for it was the very thing that was to be done—and such plain language, going so direct to the purpose, could not but insult a set of sentimentalists, who were resolute in nothing but irresolution, and who, too cowardly to act, had once for all made up their minds that in doing nothing, they were doing exactly what was to be done. Every word which cleared up, like lightning, the infatuated but intentional nebulosity of their minds, every hint that was adapted to lead them out of the labyrinth where they obstinated themselves to take up as lasting an abode as possible, every clear conception of matters as they actually stood, was, of course, a crime against the majesty of this Sovereign Assembly.

Shortly after the position of the honorable gentlemen in Frankfort became untenable, in spite of resolutions, appeals, interpellations, and proclamations, they retreated, but not into the insurged districts; that would have been too resolute a step. They went to Stuttgart, where the Württemberg Government kept up a sort of expectative neutrality. There, at last, they declared the Lieutenant of the Empire to have forfeited his power, and elected from their own body a Regency of five.[61] This Regency at once proceeded to pass a Militia Law, which was actually in all due force sent to all the Governments of Germany. They, the very enemies of the Assembly, were ordered to levy forces in its defense! Then there was created—on paper, of course—an army for the defense of the National Assembly. Divisions, brigades, regiments, batteries, everything was regulated and ordained. Nothing was wanting but reality, for that army, of course, never was called into existence.

---

[a] Polish name: Strzegom.— *Ed.*

[b] *Neue Rheinische Zeitung.— Ed.*

[c] In St. Paul's Church, Frankfurt am Main, the National Assembly held its sessions from May 18, 1848 to May 30, 1849.— *Ed.*

One last scheme offered itself to the National Assembly. The Democratic population from all parts of the country sent deputations to place itself at the disposal of the Parliament, and to urge it on to a decisive action. The people, knowing what the intentions of the Württemberg Government were, implored the National Assembly to force that Government into an open and active participation with their insurgent neighbors. But No. The National Assembly, in going to Stuttgart, had delivered itself up to the tender mercies of the Württemberg Government. The members knew it, and repressed the agitation among the people. They thus lost the last remnant of influence which they might yet have retained. They earned the contempt they deserved, and the Württemberg Government, pressed by Prussia and the Imperial Lieutenant, put a stop to the Democratic farce by shutting up, on the 18th of June, 1849, the room where the Parliament met, and by ordering the members of the Regency to leave the country.

Next they went to Baden, into the camp of the insurrection, but there they were now useless. Nobody noticed them. The Regency, however, in the name of the Sovereign German People, continued to save the country by its exertions. It made an attempt to get recognized by foreign powers, by delivering *passports* to anybody who would accept of them. It issued proclamations and sent Commissioners to insurge those very districts of Württemberg whose active assistance it had refused when it was yet time; of course without effect. We have now under our eye an original report sent to the Regency by one of these Commissioners, Mr. Roesler (member for Oels[a]), the contents of which are rather characteristic. It is dated Stuttgart, 30th June, 1849. After describing the adventures of half-a-dozen of these Commissioners in a resultless search for cash, he gives a series of excuses for not having yet gone to his post, and then delivers himself of a most weighty argument respecting possible differences between Prussia, Austria, Bavaria and Württemberg, with their possible consequences. After having fully considered this, he comes, however, to the conclusion that there is no more chance. Next he proposes to establish relays of trustworthy men for the conveyance of intelligence, and a system of espionage as to the intentions of the Württemberg Ministry, and movements of the troops. This letter never reached its address, for when it was written the "Regency" had already passed entirely into the "foreign department," viz., Switzerland; and while poor Mr. Roesler troubled his head about the intentions of the formidable ministry of a

---

[a] Polish name: Oleśnica.— *Ed.*

sixth-rate kingdom, a hundred thousand Prussian, Bavarian, and Hessian soldiers had already settled the whole affair in the last battle under the walls of Rastatt.

Thus vanished the German Parliament, and with it the first and the last creation of the revolution. Its convocation had been the first evidence that there actually *had been* a revolution in Germany; and it existed as long as this, the first modern German Revolution, was not yet brought to a close. Chosen under the influence of the capitalist class by a dismembered, scattered, rural population, for the most part only awaking from the dumbness of feudalism, this Parliament served to bring in one body upon the political arena all the great popular names of 1820-1848, and then to utterly ruin them. All the celebrities of the middle-class Liberalism were here collected; the bourgeoisie expected wonders; it earned shame for itself and for its representatives. The industrial and commercial capitalist class were more severely defeated in Germany than in any other country; they were first worsted, broken, expelled from office in every individual State of Germany, and then put to rout, disgraced, and hooted in the Central German Parliament. Political Liberalism, the rule of the bourgeoisie, be it under a monarchical or republican form of government, is forever impossible in Germany.

In the latter period of its existence, the German Parliament served to disgrace forever that section which had ever since March, 1848, headed the official opposition, the Democrats representing the interests of the small trading, and partially of the farming class. That class was, in May and June, 1849, given a chance to show its means of forming a stable government in Germany. We have seen how it failed; not so much by adverse circumstances as by the actual and continual cowardice in all trying movements that had occurred since the outbreak of the revolution; by showing in politics the same short-sighted, pusillanimous, wavering spirit, which is characteristic of its commercial operations. In May, 1849, it had, by this course, lost the confidence of the real fighting mass of all European insurrections, the working class. But yet, it had a fair chance. The German Parliament belonged to it, exclusively, after the Reactionists and Liberals had withdrawn. The rural population was in its favor. Two-thirds of the armies of the smaller States, one-third of the Prussian army, the majority of the Prussian Landwehr (reserve or militia), were ready to join it, if it only acted resolutely, and with that courage which is the result of a clear insight in the state of things. But the politicians, who led on this class, were not more clear-sighted than the host of petty tradesmen which followed them. They proved even to be more infatuated, more ardently attached to delusions voluntarily kept up, more credulous, more incapable of resolutely dealing with facts than the Liberals. Their political importance, too, is reduced below the freezing point. But they not having actually carried their commonplace principles into execution, they were, under *very* favorable circumstances, capable of a momentary resurrection, when this last hope was taken from them, just as it was taken from their colleagues of the "pure Democracy" in France, by the *coup d'état* of *Louis Bonaparte*.

The defeat of the South-West German insurrection, and the dispersion of the German Parliament, bring the history of the first German Revolution to a close. We have now to throw a parting glance upon the victorious members of the counter-revolutionary alliance; we shall do this in our next letter.[62]

London, September 24, 1852

Karl Marx

[STATEMENT AND ACCOMPANYING LETTER TO THE EDITORIAL BOARD OF THE AUGSBURG *ALLGEMEINE ZEITUNG*] [63]

28 Dean Street,
Soho, London
October 4, 1851

TO THE EDITORIAL BOARD
OF THE AUGSBURG *ALLGEMEINE ZEITUNG*

Since the Editorial Board of the Augsburg *Allgemeine Zeitung* in a report from a Cologne correspondent dated September 26 has published a direct denunciation of me, I count upon your sense of justice to print the following reply in one of your forthcoming issues.

Yours truly,
Dr. *Karl Marx*

STATEMENT

A recondite report in the Augsburg *Allgemeine Zeitung*, dated Cologne, September 26,[a] makes out an absurd connection between me, Baroness von Beck and the Cologne arrests. I am alleged to have confided political secrets to Baroness von Beck which later in one way or another came into the hands of the authorities. I have seen Baroness von Beck only twice and that was in the presence of witnesses. On both occasions the matter concerned *exclusively* literary suggestions which I was compelled to reject since they proceeded from the completely false premise that I had some kind of connection with German newspapers. Having disposed of this matter, I never heard anything again of the Baroness until I learned of her sudden death. But I have never regarded the German refugees who were in daily contact with Frau von Beck as my friends any more than the Cologne correspondent of the Augsburg *Allgemeine Zeitung* or the "great" German men in London who turn emigration into a business and an official position. I have never considered it worth the trouble to reply to the mass of perfidiously

---

[a] See *Allgemeine Zeitung*, No. 273, September 30, 1851. Supplement.— *Ed.*

silly, crude and dishonest gossip in the German newspapers, which
either comes direct from London or is inspired from there. If I make
an exception this time it is only because the Cologne correspondent
of the Augsburg *Allgemeine Zeitung* tries to present the arrests in
Cologne, Dresden, etc., as *based* on my alleged indiscretions to
Baroness von Beck.

London, October 4, 1851

Karl Marx

The statement was first published
in the *Kölnische Zeitung*, No. 242,
October 9, 1851

The statement is printed according
to the newspaper; the accompanying letter is printed according to the
manuscript

Published in English for the first
time

Karl Marx

THE EIGHTEENTH BRUMAIRE
OF LOUIS BONAPARTE[64]

Written in December 1851-March 1852

First published as the first issue of the "non-periodic journal" *Die Revolution,* New York, 1852

Signed: *Karl Marx*

Printed according to the 1869 edition, checked with the 1852 and 1885 editions

Die Revolution,

Eine Zeitschrift in zwanglosen Heften.

Herausgegeben von

J. Weydemeyer.

~~~~~~~~~~~~

Erstes Heft.

~~~~~~~~~~~~

Der 18te Brumaire des Louis Napoleon

von

Karl Marx.

~~~~~~~~~~~~

New-York.

Expedition: Deutsche Vereins-Buchhandlung von Schmidt und Helmich.
William-Street Nr. 191.

1852.

Title-page of the journal *Die Revolution*, in which
The Eighteenth Brumaire of Louis Bonaparte
was published for the first time

I

Hegel remarks somewhere that all facts and personages of great importance in world history occur, as it were, twice. He forgot to add: the first time as tragedy, the second as farce.[65] Caussidière for Danton, Louis Blanc for Robespierre, the Montagne of 1848 to 1851[66] for the Montagne of 1793 to 1795, the Nephew for the Uncle. And the same caricature occurs in the circumstances attending the second edition of the eighteenth Brumaire![a]

Men make their own history, but they do not make it just as they please; they do not make it under circumstances chosen by themselves, but under circumstances directly encountered, given and transmitted from the past. The tradition of all the dead generations weighs like a nightmare on the brain of the living. And just when they seem engaged in revolutionising themselves and things, in creating something that has never yet existed, precisely in

---

[a] This passage reads as follows in the 1852 edition: "Hegel remarks somewhere that all facts and personages of great importance in world history occur, as it were, twice. He forgot to add: the first time as a great tragedy, the second as a miserable farce. Caussidière for Danton, Louis Blanc for Robespierre, the Montagne of 1848-51 for the Montagne of 1793-95, and the London constable with the first dozen indebted lieutenants that came along for the little corporal with his band of marshals![67] The eighteenth Brumaire of the idiot for the eighteenth Brumaire of the genius! And the same caricature in the circumstances attending the second edition of the *Eighteenth Brumaire*! The first time France on the verge of bankruptcy, this time Bonaparte himself on the threshold of the debtors' prison; then the coalition of the Great Powers on France's borders, this time the Ruge-Darasz coalition in England and the Kinkel-Brentano coalition in America; then a St. Bernard to cross, this time a company of gendarmes to be sent across the Jura; then more than a Marengo to be won, this time the Great Cross of the St. Andrew Order[68] to be earned and the respect of the Berlin *National-Zeitung* to be lost." — *Ed.*

such periods of revolutionary crisis they anxiously conjure up the spirits of the past to their service and borrow from them names, battle-cries and costumes in order to present the new scene of world history in this time-honoured disguise and this borrowed language. Thus Luther donned the mask of the Apostle Paul, the revolution of 1789 to 1814 draped itself alternately as the Roman Republic and the Roman Empire, and the revolution of 1848 knew nothing better to do than to parody, now 1789, now the revolutionary tradition of 1793 to 1795. In like manner a beginner who has learnt a new language always translates it back into his mother tongue, but he has assimilated the spirit of the new language and can freely express himself in it only when he finds his way in it without recalling the old and forgets his native tongue in the use of the new.

Consideration of this world-historical necromancy reveals at once a salient difference. Camille Desmoulins, Danton, Robespierre, Saint-Just, Napoleon, the heroes as well as the parties and the masses of the old French Revolution, performed the task of their time in Roman costume and with Roman phrases, the task of unchaining and setting up modern *bourgeois* society. The first ones knocked the feudal basis to pieces and mowed off the feudal heads which had grown on it. The other created inside France the conditions under which free competition could first be developed, parcelled landed property exploited and the unchained industrial productive forces of the nation employed; and beyond the French borders he everywhere swept the feudal institutions away, so far as was necessary to furnish bourgeois society in France with a suitable up-to-date environment on the European Continent. The new social formation once established, the antediluvian Colossi disappeared and with them resurrected Romanity—the Brutuses, Gracchi, Publicolas, the tribunes, the senators, and Caesar himself. Bourgeois society in its sober reality had begotten its true interpreters and mouthpieces in the Says, Cousins, Royer-Collards, Benjamin Constants and Guizots; its real commanders sat behind the counter, and the hogheaded Louis XVIII was its political chief. Wholly absorbed in the production of wealth and in peaceful competitive struggle, it no longer comprehended that ghosts from the days of Rome had watched over its cradle. But unheroic as bourgeois society is, it nevertheless took heroism, sacrifice, terror, civil war and battles of peoples to bring it into being. And in the classically austere traditions of the Roman Republic its gladiators found the ideals and the art forms, the self-deceptions that they needed in order to conceal from themselves the bourgeois limitations of the content of their struggles and to maintain their passion on the high plane of great historical tragedy. Similarly, at another stage of development, a century earlier, Cromwell and the English people had borrowed speech, passions and illusions from the Old Testament for their bourgeois revolution. When the real aim had been achieved, when the bourgeois transformation of English society had been accomplished, Locke supplanted Habakkuk.

Thus the resurrection of the dead in those revolutions served the purpose of glorifying the new struggles, not of parodying the old; of magnifying the given task in imagination, not of fleeing from its solution in reality; of finding once more the spirit of revolution, not of making its ghost walk about again.

From 1848 to 1851 only the ghost of the old revolution walked about, from Marrast, the *républicain en gants jaunes*,[a] who disguised himself as the old Bailly, down to the adventurer who hides his commonplace repulsive features under the iron death mask of Napoleon. An entire people, which had imagined that by means of a revolution it had imparted to itself an accelerated power of motion, suddenly finds itself set back into a defunct epoch and, in order that no doubt as to the relapse may be possible, the old dates arise again, the old chronology, the old names, the old edicts, which had long become a subject of antiquarian erudition, and the old myrmidons of the law, who had seemed long decayed. The nation feels like that mad Englishman in Bedlam who fancies that he lives in the times of the ancient Pharaohs and daily bemoans the hard labour that he must perform in the Ethiopian mines as a gold digger, immured in this subterranean prison, a dimly burning lamp fastened to his head, the overseer of the slaves behind him with a long whip, and at the exits a confused welter of barbarian mercenaries, who understand neither the forced labourers in the mines nor one another, since they speak no common language. "And all this is expected of me," sighs the mad Englishman, "of me, a freeborn Briton, in order to make gold for the old Pharaohs." "In order to pay the debts of the Bonaparte family," sighs the French nation. The Englishman, so long as he was in his right mind, could not get rid of the fixed idea of making gold. The French, so long as they were engaged in revolution, could not get rid of the memory of Napoleon, as the election of December 10[69] proved. They hankered to return from the perils of revolution to the fleshpots of Egypt,[70] and December 2, 1851 was the answer. They have not only a caricature of the old Napoleon, they have the old Napoleon himself, caricatured as he must appear in the middle of the nineteenth century.

---

[a] Republican in yellow gloves.— *Ed.*

The social revolution of the nineteenth century cannot draw its poetry from the past, but only from the future. It cannot begin with itself before it has stripped off all superstition about the past. Earlier revolutions required recollections of past world history in order to dull themselves to their own content. In order to arrive at its own content, the revolution of the nineteenth century must let the dead bury their dead.[a] There the words went beyond the content; here the content goes beyond the words.

The February revolution was a surprise attack, a *taking* of the old society *unawares*, and the people proclaimed this unexpected *coup de main* as a deed of historic importance, ushering in the new epoch. On December 2 the February revolution is conjured away by a cardsharper's trick, and what seems overthrown is no longer the monarchy but the liberal concessions that were wrung from it by centuries of struggle. Instead of *society* having conquered a new content for itself, it seems that the *state* only returned to its oldest form, to the shamelessly simple domination of the sabre and the cowl. This is the answer to the *coup de main* of February 1848, given by the *coup de tête*[b] of December 1851. Easy come, easy go. Meanwhile the intervening time has not passed by unused. During the years 1848 to 1851 French society made up, and that by an abbreviated because revolutionary method, for the studies and experiences which, in a regular, so to speak, textbook course of development, would have had to precede the February revolution, if it was to be more than a ruffling of the surface. Society now seems to have fallen back behind its point of departure; it has in truth first to create for itself the revolutionary point of departure, the situation, the relations, the conditions under which alone modern revolution becomes serious.

Bourgeois revolutions, like those of the eighteenth century, storm swiftly from success to success, their dramatic effects outdo each other, men and things seem set in sparkling brilliants, ecstasy is the everyday spirit, but they are short-lived, soon they have attained their zenith, and a long crapulent depression seizes society before it learns soberly to assimilate the results of its storm-and-stress period. On the other hand, proletarian revolutions, like those of the nineteenth century, criticise themselves constantly, interrupt themselves continually in their own course, come back to the apparently accomplished in order to begin it afresh, deride with unmerciful thoroughness the inadequacies, weaknesses and paltrinesses of their

---

[a] Cf. Matthew 8 : 22.— *Ed.*
[b] Rash act.— *Ed.*

first attempts, seem to throw down their adversary only in order that he may draw new strength from the earth and rise again, more gigantic, before them, and recoil again and again from the indefinite prodigiousness of their own aims, until a situation has been created which makes all turning back impossible, and the conditions themselves cry out:

> Hic Rhodus, hic salta!
> Here is the rose, here dance![71]

For the rest, every fairly competent observer, even if he had not followed the course of French development step by step, must have had a presentiment that an unheard-of fiasco was in store for the revolution. It was enough to hear the self-complacent howl of victory with which Messieurs the Democrats congratulated each other on the beneficial consequences of the second Sunday in May 1852.[72] In their minds the second Sunday in May 1852 had become a fixed idea, a dogma, like the day on which Christ should reappear and the millennium begin, in the minds of the Chiliasts.[73] As ever, weakness had taken refuge in a belief in miracles, fancied the enemy overcome when it had only conjured him away in imagination, and lost all understanding of the present in a passive glorification of the future in store for it and of the deeds it had *in petto*[a] but which it merely did not want as yet to make public. Those heroes who seek to disprove their proven incapacity by offering each other their sympathy and getting together in a crowd had tied up their bundles, collected their laurel wreaths in advance and were just then engaged in discounting on the exchange market the republics *in partibus*[b] for which they had already providently organised the government personnel with all the calm of their unassuming disposition. December 2 struck them like a thunderbolt from a clear sky, and the peoples that in periods of pusillanimous depression gladly let their inward apprehension be drowned out by the loudest bawlers will have perhaps convinced themselves that the times are past when the cackle of geese could save the Capitol.

The Constitution, the National Assembly, the dynastic parties, the blue and the red republicans, the heroes of Africa,[74] the

---

[a] In reserve.— *Ed.*

[b] *In partibus infidelium*—literally: in parts inhabited by infidels. The words are added to the title of Roman Catholic bishops holding purely nominal dioceses in non-Christian countries. In the figurative sense they mean: "not really existing".— *Ed.*

thunder from the platform, the sheet lightning of the daily press, the entire literature, the political names and the intellectual reputations, the civil law and the penal code, the *liberté, égalité, fraternité* and the second Sunday in May 1852—all has vanished like a phantasmagoria before the spell of a man whom even his enemies do not make out to be a magician. Universal suffrage seems to have survived only for a moment, in order that with its own hand it may make its last will and testament before the eyes of all the world and declare in the name of the people itself: "All that comes to birth is fit for overthrow, as nothing worth." [a]

It is not enough to say, as the French do, that their nation was taken unawares. A nation and a woman are not forgiven the unguarded hour in which the first adventurer that came along could violate them. [b] The riddle is not solved by such turns of speech, but merely formulated differently. It remains to be explained how a nation of thirty-six million can be surprised and delivered unresisting into captivity by three swindlers.

Let us recapitulate in general outline the phases that the French Revolution went through from February 24, 1848 to December 1851.

Three main periods are unmistakable: *the February period;* May 4, 1848 to May 28, 1849: *the period of the constitution of the republic* or *of the Constituent National Assembly;* May 28, 1849 to December 2, 1851: *the period of the constitutional republic* or *of the Legislative National Assembly.* [c]

The *first period,* from February 24, or the overthrow of Louis Philippe, to May 4, 1848, the meeting of the Constituent Assembly, the *February period* proper, may be described as the *prologue* to the revolution. Its character was officially expressed in the fact that the government improvised by it declared itself that it was *provisional* and, like the government, everything that was mooted, attempted or enunciated during this period proclaimed itself to be only *provisional.* Nothing and nobody ventured to lay claim to the right of existence and of real action. All the elements that had prepared or determined the revolution, the dynastic opposition, [75] the republican bourgeoisie, the democratic-republican petty bourgeoisie and the Social-Democratic workers, provisionally found their place in the February *government.*

---

[a] Goethe, *Faust,* Erster Teil, "Studierzimmer".— *Ed.*

[b] The 1852 edition has here: "could violate and appropriate them".— *Ed.*

[c] Here and below in the German editions of 1852, 1869 and 1885 the date of the opening of the Legislative Assembly is given inaccurately as May 29, 1849.— *Ed.*

It could not be otherwise. The February days originally aimed at an electoral reform, by which the circle of the politically privileged among the possessing class itself was to be widened and the exclusive domination of the finance aristocracy overthrown. When it came to the actual conflict, however, when the people mounted the barricades, the National Guard maintained a passive attitude, the army offered no serious resistance and the monarchy ran away, the republic appeared to be a matter of course. Every party construed it in its own way. Having secured it arms in hand, the proletariat impressed its stamp upon it and proclaimed it to be a *social republic*. There was thus indicated the general content of the modern revolution, a content which[a] was in most singular contradiction to everything that, with the material available, with the degree of education attained by the masses, under the given circumstances and relations, could be immediately realised in practice. On the other hand, the claims of all the remaining elements that had collaborated in the February revolution were recognised by the lion's share that they obtained in the government. In no period do we, therefore, find a more confused mixture of high-flown phrases and actual uncertainty and clumsiness, of more enthusiastic striving for innovation and more thorough domination of the old routine, of more apparent harmony of the whole of society and more profound estrangement of its elements. While the Paris proletariat still revelled in the vision of the wide prospects that had opened before it and indulged in earnest discussions on social problems, the old forces of society had grouped themselves, rallied, reflected and found unexpected support in the mass of the nation, the peasants and petty bourgeois, who all at once stormed on to the political stage, after the barriers of the July monarchy had fallen.

The *second period*, from May 4, 1848 to the end of May 1849, is the period of the *constitution*, the *foundation*, *of the bourgeois republic*. Directly after the February days not only had the dynastic opposition been surprised by the republicans and the republicans by the Socialists, but all France by Paris. The National Assembly, which met on May 4, 1848, had emerged from the national elections and represented the nation. It was a living protest against the aspirations of the February days and was to reduce the results of the revolution to the bourgeois scale. In vain the Paris proletariat, which immediately grasped the character of this

---

[a] The 1852 edition has here: "as cannot be otherwise in the prologue to a drama".— *Ed.*

National Assembly, attempted on May 15, a few days after it met, forcibly to negate its existence, to dissolve it, to disintegrate again into its constituent parts the organic form in which the proletariat was threatened by the reacting spirit of the nation.[76] As is known, May 15 had no other result save that of removing Blanqui and his comrades, that is, the real leaders of the proletarian party,[a] from the public stage for the entire duration of the cycle we are considering.

The *bourgeois monarchy* of Louis Philippe can be followed only by a *bourgeois republic*, that is to say, whereas a limited section of the bourgeoisie ruled in the name of the king, the whole of the bourgeoisie will now rule on behalf of the people. The demands of the Paris proletariat are utopian nonsense, to which an end must be put. To this declaration of the Constituent National Assembly the Paris proletariat replied with the *June insurrection*, the most colossal event in the history of European civil wars. The bourgeois republic triumphed. On its side stood the finance aristocracy, the industrial bourgeoisie, the middle class, the petty bourgeois, the army, the lumpenproletariat organised as the Mobile Guard,[77] the intellectuals, the clergy and the rural population. On the side of the Paris proletariat stood none but itself. More than 3,000 insurgents were butchered after the victory, and 15,000 were deported without trial. With this defeat the proletariat recedes into the *background* of the revolutionary stage. It attempts to press forward again on every occasion, as soon as the movement appears to make a fresh start, but with ever decreased expenditure of strength and always slighter results. As soon as one of the social strata situated above it gets into revolutionary ferment, the proletariat enters into an alliance with it and so shares all the defeats that the different parties suffer, one after another. But these subsequent blows become the weaker, the greater the surface of society over which they are distributed. The more important leaders of the proletariat in the Assembly and in the press successively fall victim to the courts, and ever more equivocal figures come to head it. In part it throws itself into *doctrinaire experiments, exchange banks and workers' associations, hence into a movement in which it renounces the revolutionising of the old world by means of the latter's own great, combined resources, and seeks, rather, to achieve its salvation behind society's back, in private fashion, within its limited conditions of existence, and hence necessarily suffers*

---

[a] The 1852 edition has: "the real leaders of the proletarian party, the revolutionary Communists".— *Ed.*

shipwreck. It seems to be unable either to rediscover revolutionary greatness in itself or to win new energy from the connections newly entered into, until *all classes* with which it contended in June themselves lie prostrate beside it. But at least it succumbs with the honours of the great, world-historic struggle; not only France, but all Europe trembles at the June earthquake, while the ensuing defeats of the upper classes are so cheaply bought that they require barefaced exaggeration by the victorious party to be able to pass for events at all, and become the more ignominious the further the defeated party is from the proletarian party.

The defeat of the June insurgents, to be sure, had indeed prepared and levelled the ground on which the bourgeois republic could be founded and built up, but it had shown at the same time that in Europe the questions at issue are other than that of "republic or monarchy". It had revealed that here *bourgeois republic* signifies the unlimited despotism of one class over other classes. It had proved that in countries with an old civilisation, with a developed formation of classes, with modern conditions of production and with an intellectual consciousness in which all traditional ideas have been dissolved by the work of centuries, *the republic* signifies *in general only the political form of the revolutionising of bourgeois society* and not its *conservative form of life*, as, for example, in the United States of North America, where, though classes already exist, they have not yet become fixed, but continually change and interchange their component elements in constant flux, where the modern means of production, instead of coinciding with a stagnant surplus population, rather compensate for the relative deficiency of heads and hands, and where, finally, the feverish, youthful movement of material production, which has to make a new world its own, has left neither time nor opportunity for abolishing the old spirit world.

During the June days all classes and parties had united in the *Party of Order* against the proletarian class as the *Party of Anarchy*, of socialism, of communism. They had "saved" society from "*the enemies of society*". They had given out the watch-words of the old society, "*property, family, religion, order*", to their army as passwords and had proclaimed to the counter-revolutionary crusaders: "By this sign thou shalt conquer!" [78] From this moment, as soon as one of the numerous parties which had gathered under this sign against the June insurgents seeks to hold the revolutionary battlefield in its own class interest, it goes down before the cry: "Property, family, religion, order." Society is saved just as often as the circle of its rulers contracts, as a more exclusive interest is maintained against a wider one. Every demand of the simplest bourgeois financial reform, of the most ordinary liberalism, of the most formal republicanism, of the most shallow democracy, is simultaneously castigated as an "attempt on society" and stigmatised as "socialism". And, finally, the high priests of "religion and order"[a] themselves are driven with kicks from their Pythian tripods, hauled out of their beds in the darkness of night, put in prison-vans, thrown into dungeons or sent into exile; their temple is razed to the ground, their mouths are sealed, their pens broken, their law torn to pieces in the name of religion, of property, of the family, of order. Bourgeois fanatics for order are shot down on their balconies by mobs of drunken soldiers, their domestic sanctuaries profaned, their houses bombarded for amusement—in the name of property, of the family, of religion and of order. Finally, the scum of bourgeois society forms the *holy phalanx of order* and the hero Krapülinski[b] installs himself in the Tuileries as the "*saviour of society*".

II

Let us pick up the threads of the development once more.

The history of the *Constituent National Assembly* since the June days is the *history of the domination and the disintegration of the republican faction of the bourgeoisie,* of that faction which is known by the names of tricolour republicans, pure republicans, political republicans, formalist republicans, etc.

Under the bourgeois monarchy of Louis Philippe it had formed the *official* republican *opposition* and consequently a recognised component part of the political world of the day. It had its representatives in the Chambers and a considerable sphere of influence in the press. Its Paris organ, the *National,* was considered just as respectable in its way as the *Journal des Débats.* Its character corresponded to this position under the constitutional monarchy. It was not a faction of the bourgeoisie held together by great common interests and marked off by specific conditions of production. It was a clique of republican-minded bourgeois,

---

[a] In the German original: "Religion und Ordnung". According to the list of misprints in the 1852 edition, this should read: "Religion der Ordnung" ("religion of order") but the correction was not introduced into the 1869 and 1885 editions.— *Ed.*

[b] *Krapülinski*—one of the main characters in Heine's poem "Zwei Ritter" (*Romanzero*). Here Marx alludes to Louis Bonaparte.— *Ed.*

writers, lawyers, officers and officials that owed its influence to the personal antipathies of the country against Louis Philippe, to memories of the old republic, to the republican faith of a number of enthusiasts, above all, however, to *French nationalism*, whose hatred of the Vienna treaties[79] and of the alliance with England it always kept awake. A large part of the following that the *National* had under Louis Philippe was due to this concealed imperialism, which could consequently confront it later, under the republic, as a deadly rival in the person of Louis Bonaparte. It fought the finance aristocracy, as did all the rest of the bourgeois opposition. Polemics against the budget, which were closely connected in France with fighting the finance aristocracy, procured popularity too cheaply and material for puritanical leading articles[a] too plentifully, not to be exploited. The industrial bourgeoisie was grateful to it for its slavish defence of the French protectionist system, which it accepted, however, more on national grounds than on grounds of national economy; the bourgeoisie as a whole, for its vicious denunciation of communism and socialism. For the rest, the party of the *National* was *purely republican*, that is, it demanded a republican instead of a monarchist form of bourgeois rule and, above all, the lion's share of this rule. On the conditions of this transformation it was by no means clear. On the other hand, what was clear as daylight to it and was publicly acknowledged at the reform banquets in the last days of Louis Philippe, was its unpopularity with the democratic petty bourgeois and, in particular, with the revolutionary proletariat. These pure republicans, as is, indeed, the way with pure republicans, were already on the point of contenting themselves in the first instance with a regency of the Duchess of Orleans,[80] when the February revolution broke out and assigned their best-known representatives a place in the Provisional Government. From the start, they naturally had the confidence of the bourgeoisie and a majority in the Constituent National Assembly. The *socialist* elements of the Provisional Government were excluded forthwith from the Executive Commission which the National Assembly formed when it met, and the party of the *National* took advantage of the outbreak of the June insurrection to discharge the *Executive Commission*[81] also, and therewith to get rid of its closest rivals, the *petty-bourgeois*, or *democratic*, *republicans* (Ledru-Rollin, etc.). Cavaignac, the general of the bourgeois republican party who commanded the June massacre, took the place of the Executive Commission with

---

[a] Marx uses the English words "leading articles".— *Ed.*

a sort of dictatorial authority. Marrast, former editor-in-chief of the *National,* became the perpetual president of the Constituent National Assembly, and the ministries, as well as all other important posts, fell to the portion of the pure republicans.

The republican bourgeois faction, which had long regarded itself as the legitimate heir of the July monarchy, thus found its fondest hopes exceeded; it attained power, however, not as it had dreamed under Louis Philippe, through a liberal revolt of the bourgeoisie against the throne, but through a rising of the proletariat against capital, a rising laid low with grape-shot. What it had pictured to itself as the *most revolutionary* event occurred in reality as the *most counter-revolutionary.* The fruit fell into its lap, but it fell from the tree of knowledge, not from the tree of life.

The exclusive *rule of the bourgeois republicans* lasted only from June 24 to December 10, 1848. It is summed up in the *drafting of a republican constitution* and in the *state of siege of Paris.*

The new *Constitution* was at bottom only the republicanised edition of the constitutional Charter of 1830.[82] The narrow electoral qualification of the July monarchy, which excluded even a large part of the bourgeoisie from political rule, was incompatible with the existence of the bourgeois republic. In lieu of this qualification, the February revolution had at once proclaimed direct universal suffrage. The bourgeois republicans could not undo this event. They had to content themselves with adding the limiting proviso of a six months' residence in the constituency. The old organisation of the administration, of the municipal system, of the judicial system, of the army, etc., continued to exist inviolate, or, where the Constitution changed it, the change concerned the table of contents, not the contents; the name, not the subject matter.

The inevitable general staff of the freedoms of 1848, personal freedom, freedom of the press, of speech, of association, of assembly, of education and of religion, etc., received a constitutional uniform, which made them invulnerable. For each of these freedoms is proclaimed as the *absolute* right of the French *citoyen,* but always with the marginal note that it is unlimited so far as it is not limited by the "*equal rights of others* and the *public safety*" or by "laws" which are intended to mediate just this harmony of individual freedoms with one another and with the public safety. For example: "Citizens have a right to associate, to meet peacefully and unarmed, to petition, and express their opinions through the press and elsewhere. *The enjoyment of these rights has*

no other limit, than the equal rights of others, and the public safety."
(Chapter II of the French Constitution, § 8.)—"The right of
tuition is free. The freedom of tuition shall be *enjoyed* on the
conditions fixed by law, and under the supervision of the state."
(*Ibidem,* § 9.)—"The home of every citizen is inviolable *except* in
the forms prescribed by law." (Chapter II, § 3.) Etc., etc.—The
Constitution, therefore, constantly refers to future *organic* laws
which are to implement those marginal notes and regulate the
enjoyment of these unrestricted freedoms in such manner that
they will conflict neither with one another nor with the public
safety. And later, these organic laws were brought into being by
the friends of order and all those freedoms regulated in such
manner that the bourgeoisie in its enjoyment of them finds itself
unhindered by the equal rights of the other classes. Where it
forbids these freedoms entirely to "the others" or permits
enjoyment of them under conditions that are just so many police
traps, this always happens solely in the interest of "*public safety*",
that is, the safety of the bourgeoisie, as the Constitution prescribes.
In the following period, both sides accordingly appeal with
complete justice to the Constitution: the friends of order, who
abrogated all these freedoms, as well as the democrats, who
demanded all of them. For each paragraph of the Constitution
contains its own antithesis, its own Upper and Lower House,
namely, freedom in the general phrase, abrogation of freedom in
the marginal note. Thus, so long as the *name* of freedom was
respected and only its actual realisation prevented, of course in a
legal way, the constitutional existence of freedom remained intact,
inviolate, however mortal the blows dealt to its existence *in actual
life.*

This Constitution, made inviolable in so ingenious a manner, was
nevertheless, like Achilles, vulnerable in one point, not in the heel,
but in the head, or rather in the two heads in which it wound
up—the *Legislative Assembly,* on the one hand, the *President,* on the
other. Glance through the Constitution and you will find that only
the paragraphs in which the relationship of the President to the
Legislative Assembly is defined are absolute, positive, non-
contradictory, incapable of distortion. For here it was a question of
the bourgeois republicans safeguarding themselves. §§ 45-70 of the
Constitution are so worded that the National Assembly can remove
the President constitutionally, whereas the President can remove
the National Assembly only unconstitutionally, only by setting
aside the Constitution itself. Here, therefore, it challenges its
forcible destruction. It not only sanctifies the division of powers,

like the Charter of 1830, it widens it into an intolerable
contradiction. The *play of the constitutional powers*, as Guizot termed
the parliamentary squabble between the legislative and executive
power, is in the Constitution of 1848 continually played *va-banque*.[a]
On one side are 750 representatives of the people, elected by
universal suffrage and eligible for re-election; they form an
uncontrollable, indissoluble, indivisible National Assembly, a National Assembly that enjoys legislative omnipotence, decides in the
last instance on war, peace and commercial treaties, alone
possesses the right of amnesty and, by its permanence, perpetually
holds the front of the stage. On the other side is the President,
with all the attributes of royal power, with authority to appoint
and dismiss his ministers independently of the National Assembly,
with all the resources of the executive power in his hands,
bestowing all posts and disposing thereby in France of the
livelihoods of at least a million and a half people, for so many
depend on the five hundred thousand officials and officers of
every rank. He has the whole of the armed forces behind him. He
enjoys the privilege of pardoning individual criminals, of suspend-
ing National Guards, of discharging, with the concurrence of the
Council of State, general, cantonal and municipal councils elected
by the citizens themselves. Initiative and direction are reserved to
him in all treaties with foreign countries. While the Assembly
constantly performs on the boards and is exposed to daily public
criticism, he leads a secluded life in the Elysian Fields,[b] and that
with Article 45 of the Constitution before his eyes and in his heart,
crying to him daily: "*Frère, il faut mourir!*"[83] Your power ceases on
the second Sunday of the lovely month of May in the fourth year
after your election! Then your glory is at an end, the piece is not
played twice and if you have debts, see to it betimes that you pay
them off with the 600,000 francs squandered on you by the
Constitution, unless, perchance, you should prefer to go to
Clichy[84] on the second Monday of the lovely month of
May!—Thus, whereas the Constitution assigns actual power to the
President, it seeks to secure moral power for the National
Assembly. Apart from the fact that it is impossible to create a
moral power by paragraphs of law, the Constitution here
abrogates itself once more by having the President elected by all

---

[a] Staking one's all.— *Ed.*

[b] A pun: Elysian Fields was a synonym of paradise in antiquity; in Paris the *Champs
Elysées* (Elysian Fields) is the name of the avenue where Louis Bonaparte's official
residence was.— *Ed.*

Frenchmen through direct suffrage. While the votes of France are split up among the 750 members of the National Assembly, they are here, on the contrary, concentrated on a *single* individual. While each separate representative of the people represents only this or that party, this or that town, this or that bridgehead, or even only the mere necessity of electing some one of the 750, where neither the cause nor the man is closely examined, *he* is the elect of the nation and the act of his election is the trump that the sovereign people plays once every four years. The elected National Assembly stands in a metaphysical relation, but the elected President in a personal relation, to the nation. The National Assembly, indeed, exhibits in its individual representatives the manifold aspects of the national spirit, but in the President this national spirit finds its incarnation. As against the Assembly, he possesses a sort of divine right; he is President by the grace of the people.

Thetis, the sea goddess, had prophesied to Achilles that he would die in the bloom of youth. The Constitution, which, like Achilles, had its weak spot, had also, like Achilles, its presentiment that it must go to an early death. It was sufficient for the constitution-making pure republicans to cast a glance from the lofty heaven of their ideal republic at the profane world to perceive how the arrogance of the royalists, the Bonapartists, the Democrats, the Communists as well as their own discredit grew daily in the same measure as they approached the completion of their great legislative work of art, without Thetis on this account having to leave the sea and communicate the secret to them. They sought to cheat destiny by a catch in the Constitution, through § 111 of it, according to which every motion for a *revision of the Constitution* must be supported by at least three-quarters of the votes, cast in three successive debates between which an entire month must always lie, with the added proviso that no fewer than 500 members of the National Assembly vote. Thereby they merely made the impotent attempt still to exercise, when only a parliamentary minority, as which they already saw themselves prophetically in their mind's eye, a power which at the present moment, when they commanded a parliamentary majority and all the resources of governmental authority, was slipping daily more and more from their feeble hands.

Finally the Constitution, in a melodramatic paragraph, entrusts itself "to the vigilance and the patriotism of the whole French people and every single Frenchman", after it had previously entrusted in another paragraph the "vigilant" and "patriotic"

Frenchmen to the tender penal attentions of the High Court of Justice, the "*haute cour*", invented by it for the purpose.

Such was the Constitution of 1848 which, on December 2, 1851, was not overthrown by a head, but fell down at the touch of a mere hat; this hat, to be sure, was a three-cornered Napoleonic one.

While the bourgeois republicans in the Assembly were busy devising, discussing and voting this Constitution, Cavaignac outside the Assembly maintained the *state of siege of Paris.* The state of siege of Paris was the midwife of the Constituent Assembly in its travail of republican creation. If the Constitution is subsequently put out of existence by bayonets, it must not be forgotten that it was likewise by bayonets, and these turned against the people, that it had to be protected in its mother's womb, and by bayonets that it had to be brought into existence. The forefathers of the "respectable republicans" had sent their symbol, the tricolour, on a tour round Europe. They themselves in turn produced an invention that of itself made its way over the whole Continent, but returned to France with ever renewed love until it has now become naturalised in half her departments—the *state of siege.* A splendid invention, periodically employed in every ensuing crisis in the course of the French Revolution. But barrack and bivouac, which were thus periodically laid on French society's head to compress its brain and render it quiet; sabre and musket, which were periodically allowed to act as judges and administrators, as guardians and censors, to play policemen and do night watchman's duty; moustache and uniform, which were periodically trumpeted forth as the highest wisdom of society and as its rector—were not barrack and bivouac, sabre and musket, moustache and uniform finally bound to hit upon the idea of rather saving society once and for all by proclaiming their own regime as the highest and freeing civil society completely from the trouble of governing itself? Barrack and bivouac, sabre and musket, moustache and uniform were bound to hit upon this idea all the more as they might then also expect better cash payment for their higher services, whereas from the merely periodical state of siege, and the transient rescues of society at the bidding of this or that bourgeois faction, little of substance was gleaned save some killed and wounded and some friendly bourgeois grimaces. Should not the military at last one day play state of siege in their own interest and for their own benefit, and at the same time besiege the bourgeois purses? Moreover, be it noted in passing, one must not forget that *Colonel Bernard*, the same military commission president who under Cavaignac had 15,000 insurgents deported without trial, is at this moment again at the head of the military commissions active in Paris.

Whereas, with the state of siege in Paris, the respectable, the pure republicans planted the nursery in which the praetorians of December 2, 1851 were to grow up, they on the other hand deserve praise for the reason that, instead of exaggerating the national sentiment as under Louis Philippe, they now, when they had command of the national power, crawled before foreign countries, and, instead of setting Italy free, let her be reconquered by Austrians and Neapolitans.[85] Louis Bonaparte's election as President on December 10, 1848 put an end to the dictatorship of Cavaignac and to the Constituent Assembly.

In § 44 of the Constitution it is stated: "The President of the French Republic must never have lost his status of a French citizen." The first President of the French republic, L. N. Bonaparte, had not merely lost his status of a French citizen, had not only been an English special constable, he was even a naturalised Swiss.[86]

I have discussed elsewhere the significance of the election of December 10.[a] I will not revert to it here. It is sufficient to remark here that it was a *reaction of the peasants*, who had had to pay the costs of the February revolution, against the remaining classes of the nation, a *reaction of the country against the town*. It met with great approval in the army, for which the republicans of the *National* had provided neither glory nor additional pay, among the big bourgeoisie, who hailed Bonaparte as a bridge to the monarchy, and among the proletarians and petty bourgeois, who hailed him as a scourge for Cavaignac. I shall have an opportunity later of going more closely into the relationship of the peasants to the French Revolution.

The period from December 20, 1848[b] until the dissolution of the Constituent Assembly, in May 1849, comprises the history of the downfall of the bourgeois republicans. After having founded a republic for the bourgeoisie, driven the revolutionary proletariat out of the field and reduced the democratic petty bourgeoisie to silence for the time being, they are themselves thrust aside by the mass of the bourgeoisie, which justly impounds this republic as *its property*. This bourgeois mass was, however, *royalist*. One section of it, the big

---

[a] See present edition, Vol. 10, pp. 80-82.— *Ed.*

[b] The day of the expiry of Cavaignac's powers and of Louis Bonaparte's accession to the presidency.— *Ed.*

landowners, had ruled during the *Restoration* and was accordingly *Legitimist*. The other, the finance aristocracy and big industrialists, had ruled during the July monarchy and was consequently *Orleanist*. The high dignitaries of the army, the university, the church, the bar, the Academy and of the press were to be found on either side, though in various proportions. Here, in the bourgeois republic, which bore neither the name *Bourbon* nor the name *Orleans*, but the name *Capital*, they had found the form of state in which they could rule *conjointly*. The June insurrection had already united them in the "Party of Order". Now it was necessary, in the first place, to remove the coterie of bourgeois republicans who still occupied the seats of the National Assembly. Just as brutal as these pure republicans had been in their misuse of physical force against the people, just as cowardly, mealy-mouthed, spiritless, broken and incapable of fighting were they now in their retreat, when it was a question of maintaining their republicanism and their legislative rights against the executive power and the royalists. I need not relate here the ignominious story of their dissolution. It was a fading-away, not a going-under. Their history has come to an end forever, and, both inside and outside the Assembly, they figure in the following period only as memories, memories that seem to regain life whenever the mere name of Republic is once more the issue and as often as the revolutionary conflict threatens to sink down to the lowest level. I may remark in passing that the journal which gave its name to this party, the *National*, was converted to socialism in the following period.[a]

Before we finish with this period we must still cast a retrospective glance at the two powers, one of which annihilated the other on December 2, 1851, whereas from December 20, 1848 until the exit of the Constituent Assembly, they had lived in conjugal relations. We mean Louis Bonaparte, on the one hand, and the party of the coalitioned royalists, the Party of Order, of the big bourgeoisie, on the other. On acceding to the presidency, Bonaparte at once formed a ministry of the Party of Order, at the head of which he placed

---

[a] Here, to avoid repetition (see below, pp. 180-81), Marx leaves out the following paragraph printed in the 1852 edition: "Hence the history of the constitution or foundation of the French Republic falls into three periods: May 4 to June 24, 1848—struggle of all classes and class adjuncts united in February under the leadership of the bourgeois republicans against the proletariat, frightful defeat of the proletariat; June 25, 1848 to December 10, 1848—rule of the bourgeois republicans, drafting of the Constitution, state of siege in Paris, Cavaignac's dictatorship; December 20, 1848 to the end of May 1849—struggle of Bonaparte and the Party of Order against the republican Constituent Assembly, defeat of the latter, end of the bourgeois republicans."— *Ed.*

Odilon Barrot, the old leader, *nota bene,* of the most liberal faction of
the parliamentary bourgeoisie. M. Barrot had at last secured the
ministerial portfolio, the spectre of which had haunted him since
1830, and what is more, the premiership in the ministry; but not, as
he had imagined under Louis Philippe, as the most advanced leader
of the parliamentary opposition, but with the task of putting a
parliament to death, and as the confederate of all his arch-enemies,
Jesuits and Legitimists. He brought the bride home at last, but only
after she had been prostituted. Bonaparte seemed to efface himself
completely. This party acted for him.

The very first meeting of the council of ministers resolved on the
expedition to Rome, which, it was agreed, should be undertaken
behind the back of the National Assembly and the means for which
were to be wrested from it by false pretences. Thus they began by
swindling the National Assembly and secretly conspiring with the
absolutist powers abroad against the revolutionary Roman Republic.
In the same manner and with the same manoeuvres Bonaparte
prepared his coup of December 2 against the royalist Legislative
Assembly and its constitutional republic. Let us not forget that the
same party which formed Bonaparte's ministry on December 20,
1848, formed the majority of the Legislative National Assembly on
December 2, 1851.

In August the Constituent Assembly had decided to dissolve only
after it had worked out and promulgated a whole series of organic
laws that were to supplement the Constitution. On January 6, 1849,
the Party of Order had a deputy named Rateau move that the
Assembly should let the organic laws go and rather decide on its *own
dissolution.* Not only the ministry, with Odilon Barrot at its head, but
all the royalist members of the National Assembly bullied it,
suggesting that its dissolution was necessary for the restoration of
credit, for the consolidation of order, for putting an end to the
indefinite provisional arrangements and for establishing a definitive
state of affairs; that it hampered the efficiency of the new
government and sought to prolong its existence merely out of
malice; that the country was tired of it. Bonaparte took note of all
this invective against the legislative power, learnt it by heart and
proved to the parliamentary royalists, on December 2, 1851, that he
had learnt from them. He reiterated their own catchwords against
them.

The Barrot ministry and the Party of Order went further. They
caused *petitions to the National Assembly* to be made throughout
France, in which this body was kindly requested to disappear. They
thus led the unorganised popular masses into the attack against the

National Assembly, the constitutionally organised expression of the
people. They taught Bonaparte to appeal from parliamentary
assemblies to the people. At length, on January 29, 1849, the day had
come on which the Constituent Assembly was to decide concerning
its own dissolution. The National Assembly found the building
where its sessions were held occupied by the military; Changarnier,
the general of the Party of Order, in whose hands the supreme
command of the National Guard and troops of the line had been
united, held a great military review in Paris, as if a battle were
impending, and the coalitioned royalists threateningly declared to
the Constituent Assembly that force would be employed if it should
prove unwilling.[a] It was willing, and bargained itself only a very short
deadline. What was January 29 but the coup d'état of December 2,
1851, only carried out by the royalists with Bonaparte against the
republican National Assembly? The gentlemen did not notice, or did
not wish to notice, that Bonaparte availed himself of January 29,
1849 to have a portion of the troops march past him in front of the
Tuileries, and seized with avidity on just this first public summoning
of the military power against the parliamentary power to suggest
Caligula. They, to be sure, saw only their Changarnier.

A factor that particularly motivated the Party of Order in forcibly
cutting short the duration of the Constituent Assembly's life were the
organic laws supplementing the Constitution, such as the education
law, the law on religious worship, etc. To the coalitioned royalists it
was most important that they themselves should make these laws and
not let them be made by the republicans, who had grown mistrustful.
Among these organic laws, however, was also a law on the
responsibility of the President of the republic. In 1851 the Legislative
Assembly was occupied with the drafting of just such a law, when
Bonaparte anticipated this coup with the coup of December 2. What
would the coalitioned royalists not have given in their parliamentary
winter campaign of 1851 to have found the Responsibility Law ready
to hand, and drawn up, at that, by a mistrustful, hostile, republican
Assembly!

After the Constituent Assembly had itself shattered its last weapon
on January 29, 1849, the Barrot ministry and the friends of order
hounded it to death, left nothing undone that could humiliate it and
wrested from the impotent, self-despairing Assembly laws that cost it
the last remnant of respect in the eyes of the public. Bonaparte,

---

[a] The original says: "dass man Gewalt anwenden werde, wenn sie nicht willig
sei"—an ironic paraphrase of a passage from Goethe's poem "Der Erlkönig": "Und
bist du nicht willig, so brauch ich Gewalt" ("And if you're unwilling, I'll get you by
force").— *Ed.*

occupied with his fixed Napoleonic idea,[87] was brazen enough publicly to exploit this degradation of the parliamentary power. For when, on May 8, 1849, the National Assembly passed a vote of censure of the ministry[a] because of the occupation of Civitavecchia by Oudinot, and ordered it to bring back the Roman expedition to its ostensible purpose,[88] Bonaparte published the same evening in the *Moniteur* a letter to Oudinot, in which he congratulated him on his heroic exploits and, in contrast to the pen-pushing parliamentarians, already posed as the generous protector of the army. The royalists smiled at this. They regarded him simply as their dupe. Finally, when Marrast, the President of the Constituent Assembly, believed for a moment that the safety of the National Assembly was endangered and, relying on the Constitution, requisitioned a colonel and his regiment, the colonel declined, cited discipline in his support and referred Marrast to Changarnier, who scornfully refused him with the remark that he did not like *baïonnettes intelligentes*.[b] In November 1851, when the coalitioned royalists wanted to begin the decisive struggle with Bonaparte, they sought to put through in their notorious *Questors' Bill* the principle of the direct requisition of troops by the President of the National Assembly.[89] One of their generals, Le Flô, had signed the Bill. In vain did Changarnier vote for it and Thiers pay homage to the far-sighted wisdom of the former Constituent Assembly. The *War Minister, Saint-Arnaud,* answered him as Changarnier has answered Marrast—and to the acclamation of the Montagne!

Thus the *Party of Order,* when it was not yet the National Assembly, when it was still only the ministry had itself stigmatised the *parliamentary regime*. And it makes an outcry when December 2, 1851 banished this regime from France!

We wish it a happy journey.

III

On May 28, 1849 the Legislative National Assembly met. On December 2, 1851 it was dispersed. This period covers the span of life of the *constitutional or parliamentary republic*.[c]

---

[a] The resolution of the Constituent Assembly on the Roman expedition, passed on May 7, 1849, was published in *Le Moniteur universel* the following day.— *Ed.*

[b] Bayonets which thought.— *Ed.*

[c] Here, to avoid repetition (see below, p. 181), Marx leaves out the following paragraph printed in the 1852 edition: "It falls into three main periods: *May 28, 1849 to June 13, 1849*, struggle between democracy and the bourgeoisie, *defeat of the*

In the first French Revolution the rule of the *Constitutionalists* is followed by the rule of the *Girondins* and the rule of the *Girondins* by the rule of the *Jacobins.* Each of these parties relies on the more progressive party for support. As soon as it has brought the revolution far enough to be ûnable to follow it further, still less to go ahead of it, it is thrust aside by the bolder ally that stands behind it and sent to the guillotine. The revolution thus moves along an ascending line.

It is the reverse with the revolution of 1848. The proletarian party appears as an appendage of the petty-bourgeois-democratic party. It is betrayed and dropped by the latter on April 16, May 15,[90] and in the June days. The democratic party, in its turn, leans on the shoulders of the bourgeois-republican party. The bourgeois republicans no sooner believe themselves well established than they shake off the troublesome comrade and support themselves on the shoulders of the Party of Order. The Party of Order hunches its shoulders, lets the bourgeois republicans tumble and throws itself on the shoulders of armed force. It fancies it is still sitting on its shoulders when, one fine morning, it perceives that the shoulders have turned into bayonets. Each party kicks back at the one behind, which presses upon it, and leans against the one in front, which pushes backwards. No wonder that in this ridiculous posture it loses its balance and, having made the inevitable grimaces, collapses with curious capers. The revolution thus moves in a descending line. It finds itself in this state of retrogressive motion before the last February barricade has been cleared away and the first revolutionary authority constituted.

The period that we have before us comprises the most motley mixture of crying contradictions: constitutionalists who conspire openly against the Constitution; revolutionists who are confessedly constitutional; a National Assembly that wants to be omnipotent and always remains parliamentary; a Montagne that finds its vocation in patience and counters its present defeats by prophesying future victories; royalists who form the *patres conscripti*[a] of the republic and are forced by the situation to keep the hostile royal houses, to which they adhere, abroad, and the republic, which they hate, in France; an

---

petty-bourgeois or democratic party; June 13, 1849 to May 31, 1850, parliamentary dictatorship of the bourgeoisie, i.e., of the coalitioned Orleanists and Legitimists or of the Party of Order, a dictatorship which makes itself complete by *abolishing universal suffrage; May 31, 1850 to December 2, 1851,* struggle between the bourgeoisie and Bonaparte, *overthrow of bourgeois rule, end of the constitutional or parliamentary republic.*" — *Ed.*

[a] Conscript fathers—collective designation of senators in Ancient Rome.— *Ed.*

executive power that finds its strength in its very weakness and its respectability in the contempt that it calls forth; a republic that is nothing but the combined infamy of two monarchies, the Restoration and the July monarchy, with an imperial label—alliances whose first proviso is separation; struggles whose first law is indecision; wild, inane agitation in the name of tranquillity; most solemn preaching of tranquillity in the name of revolution; passions without truth, truths without passion; heroes without heroic deeds, history without events; development, whose sole driving force seems to be the calendar, made wearisome through constant repetition of the same tensions and relaxations; antagonisms that periodically seem to work themselves up to a climax only to lose their sharpness and fall away without being able to resolve themselves; pretentiously paraded exertions and philistine terror at the danger of the world coming to an end, and at the same time the pettiest intrigues and court comedies played by the world redeemers, who in their *laissez-aller*[a] remind us less of the Day of Judgment than of the times of the Fronde[91]—the official collective genius of France brought to naught by the artful stupidity of a single individual; the collective will of the nation, as often as it speaks through universal suffrage, seeking its appropriate expression through the inveterate enemies of the interests of the masses, until at length it finds it in the self-will of a freebooter. If any section of history has been painted grey on grey,[b] it is this. Men and events appear as inverted Schlemihls, as shadows that have lost their bodies. The revolution itself paralyses its own bearers and endows only its adversaries with passionate forcefulness. When the "red spectre", continually conjured up and exorcised by the counter-revolutionaries,[92] finally appears, it appears not with the Phrygian cap of anarchy on its head, but in the uniform of order, in *red breeches*.

We have seen that the ministry which Bonaparte installed on December 20, 1848, on his Ascension Day,[c] was a ministry of the Party of Order, of the Legitimist and Orleanist coalition. This Barrot-Falloux ministry had outlived the republican Constituent Assembly, whose term of life it had more or less violently cut short, and found itself still at the helm. Changarnier, the general of the allied royalists, continued to unite in his person the general command of the First Army Division and of the National Guard of

---

[a] Letting things take their course.— *Ed.*

[b] G. W. F. Hegel, *Grundlinien der Philosophie des Rechts. Vorrede.*— *Ed.*

[c] On that day Louis Bonaparte took up his residence at the Presidential palace in the Champs Elysées (see also footnote "b" on p. 116 of this volume).— *Ed.*

Paris. Finally, the general elections had secured the Party of Order a large majority in the National Assembly. Here the deputies and peers of Louis Philippe encountered a hallowed host of Legitimists, for whom many of the nation's ballots had become transformed into admission cards to the political stage. The Bonapartist representatives of the people were too sparse to be able to form an independent parliamentary party.[a] They appeared merely as the *mauvaise queue*[b] of the Party of Order. Thus the Party of Order was in possession of governmental power, the army and the legislative body, in short, of the whole of state power; it had been morally strengthened by the general elections, which made its rule appear as the will of the people, and by the simultaneous triumph of the counter-revolution on the whole continent of Europe.

Never did a party open its campaign with greater resources or under more favourable auspices.

The shipwrecked *pure republicans* found that they had melted down to a clique of about fifty men in the Legislative National Assembly, the African generals Cavaignac, Lamoricière and Bedeau at their head. The great opposition party, however, was formed by the *Montagne*. The *Social-Democratic* party had given itself this parliamentary baptismal name. It commanded more than 200 of the 750 votes of the National Assembly and was consequently at least as powerful as any one of the three factions of the Party of Order taken by itself. Its numerical inferiority compared with the entire royalist coalition seemed compensated by special circumstances. Not only did the elections in the departments show that it had gained a considerable following among the rural population. It counted in its ranks almost all the deputies from Paris; the army had made a confession of democratic faith by the election of three non-commissioned officers,[c] and the leader of the Montagne, Ledru-Rollin, in contradistinction to all the representatives of the Party of Order, had been raised to the parliamentary peerage by five departments, which had pooled their votes for him. In view of the inevitable clashes of the royalists among themselves and of the whole Party of Order with Bonaparte, the Montagne thus seemed to have all the elements of success before it on May 28, 1849. A fortnight later it had lost everything, honour included.[d]

---

[a] The 1852 edition further has: "They were sufficiently represented to count as figures in a general call-up against the republican armed forces."— *Ed.*

[b] Pitiful appendage.— *Ed.*

[c] Boichot and Rattier, elected in Paris, and Commissaire, elected in Alsace.— *Ed.*

[d] Paraphrase of the famous dictum, "All is lost save honour", which is ascribed to King Francis I of France.— *Ed.*

Before we pursue parliamentary history further, some remarks are necessary to avoid common misconceptions regarding the whole character of the epoch that lies before us. Looked at with the eyes of democrats, the period of the Legislative National Assembly is concerned with what the period of the Constituent Assembly was concerned with: the simple struggle between republicans and royalists. The movement itself, however, they sum up in the *one* shibboleth: "*reaction*"—night, in which all cats are grey and which permits them to reel off their night watchman's commonplaces. And, to be sure, at first sight the Party of Order reveals a tangled knot of different royalist factions, which not only intrigue against each other—each seeking to elevate its own pretender to the throne and exclude the pretender of the opposing faction—but also all unite in common hatred of, and common attacks on, the "republic". In opposition to this royalist conspiracy the Montagne, for its part, appears as the representative of the "republic". The Party of Order appears to be perpetually engaged in a "reaction", directed against press, association and the like, neither more nor less than in Prussia, and which, as in Prussia, is carried out in the form of brutal police intervention by the bureaucracy, the gendarmerie and the law courts. The "Montagne", for its part, is just as continually occupied in warding off these attacks and thus defending the "eternal rights of man" as every so-called people's party has done, more or less, for a century and a half. If one looks at the situation and the parties more closely, however, this superficial appearance, which veils the *class struggle* and the peculiar physiognomy of this period,[a] disappears.

Legitimists and Orleanists, as we have said, formed the two great factions of the Party of Order. Was what held these factions fast to their pretenders and kept them apart from one another nothing but lily and tricolour, House of Bourbon and House of Orleans, different shades of royalism, was it their royalist faith at all? Under the Bourbons, *big landed property* had governed, with its priests and lackeys; under the Orleans, high finance, large-scale industry, large-scale trade, that is, *capital*, with its retinue of lawyers, professors and smooth-tongued orators. The Legitimate monarchy was merely the political expression of the hereditary rule of the lords of the soil, as the July monarchy was only the political expression of the usurped rule of the bourgeois parvenus. What kept the two factions apart, therefore, was not any so-called principles, it was their

---

[a] The 1852 edition has here: "and thus turns it into a gold-mine for pub politicians and republican stalwarts".— *Ed.*

material conditions of existence, two different kinds of property, it was the old contrast between town and country, the rivalry between capital and landed property. That at the same time old memories, personal enmities, fears and hopes, prejudices and illusions, sympathies and antipathies, convictions, articles of faith and principles bound them to one or the other royal house, who is there that denies this? Upon the different forms of property, upon the social conditions of existence, rises an entire superstructure of different and distinctly formed sentiments, illusions, modes of thought and views of life. The entire class creates and forms them out of its material foundations and out of the corresponding social relations. The single individual, to whom they are transmitted through tradition and upbringing, may imagine that they form the real motives and the starting-point of his activity. While Orleanists and Legitimists, while each faction sought to make itself and the other believe that it was loyalty to their two royal houses which separated them, facts later proved that it was rather their divided interests which forbade the unification of the two royal houses. And as in private life one differentiates between what a man thinks and says of himself and what he really is and does, so in historical struggles one must still more distinguish the language and the imaginary aspirations of parties from their real organism and their real interests, their conception of themselves from their reality. Orleanists and Legitimists found themselves side by side in the republic, with the same claims. If each side wished to effect the *restoration* of its *own* royal house against the other, that merely signified that each of the *two great interests* into which the *bourgeoisie* is split—landed property and capital—sought to restore its own supremacy and the subordination of the other. We speak of two interests of the bourgeoisie, for large landed property, despite its feudal coquetry and pride of race, has been rendered thoroughly bourgeois by the development of modern society. Thus the Tories in England long imagined that they were enthusiastic about monarchy, the church and the beauties of the old English Constitution, until the day of danger wrung from them the confession that they are enthusiastic only about *rent*.[a]

The coalitioned royalists carried on their intrigues against one another in the press, in Ems, in Claremont,[93] outside parliament. Behind the scenes they donned their old Orleanist and Legitimist liveries again and once more engaged in their old tourneys. But on the public stage, in their grand performances of state,[94] as a great

---

[a] Cf. this volume, p. 328.—*Ed.*

parliamentary party, they put off their respective royal houses with mere obeisances and adjourned the restoration of the monarchy *ad infinitum.* They did their real business as the *Party of Order,* that is, under a *social,* not under a *political* title; its representatives of the bourgeois world-order, not as knights of errant princesses; as the bourgeois class against other classes, not as royalists against the republicans. And as the Party of Order they exercised more unrestricted and sterner domination over the other classes of society than ever previously under the Restoration or under the July monarchy, a domination which, in general, was only possible under the form of the parliamentary republic, for only under this form could the two great divisions of the French bourgeoisie unite, and thus put the rule of their class instead of the regime of a privileged faction of it on the order of the day. If, nevertheless, they, as the Party of Order, also insulted the republic and expressed their repugnance of it, this happened not merely as a result of royalist memories. Instinct taught them that the republic, true enough, makes their political rule complete, but at the same time undermines its social foundation, since they must now confront the subjugated classes and contend against them without mediation, without the concealment afforded by the crown, without being able to divert the national interest by their subordinate struggles among themselves and with the monarchy. It was a feeling of weakness that caused them to recoil from the pure conditions of their own class rule and to yearn for the former more incomplete, more undeveloped and precisely on that account less dangerous forms of this rule. On the other hand, every time the coalitioned royalists come into conflict with the pretender that confronts them, with Bonaparte, every time they believe their parliamentary omnipotence endangered by the executive power, every time, therefore, that they must produce their political title to their rule, they come forward as *republicans* and not as *royalists,* from the Orleanist Thiers, who warns the National Assembly that the republic divides them least,[a] to the Legitimist Berryer, who, on December 2, 1851, as a tribune swathed in a tricoloured sash, harangues the people assembled before the town hall of the tenth *arrondissement* in the name of the republic. To be sure, a mocking echo calls back to him: Henry V! Henry V!

As against the coalitioned bourgeoisie, a coalition between petty bourgeois and workers had been formed, the so-called *Social-Democratic* party. The petty bourgeois saw themselves badly re-

---

[a] Marx has in mind the speech delivered by Thiers in the Legislative Assembly on January 17, 1851.— *Ed.*

warded after the June days of 1848, their material interests imperilled and the democratic guarantees which were to ensure the implementation of these interests called in question by the counter-revolution. Accordingly, they came closer to the workers. On the other hand, their parliamentary representation, the *Montagne*, thrust aside during the dictatorship of the bourgeois republicans, had in the last half of the life of the Constituent Assembly reconquered its lost popularity through the struggle with Bonaparte and the royalist ministers. It had concluded an alliance with the socialist leaders. In February 1849, banquets celebrated the reconciliation. A joint programme was drafted, joint election committees were set up and joint candidates put forward. The revolutionary point was broken off from the social demands of the proletariat and a democratic turn given to them; the purely political form was stripped from the democratic claims of the petty bourgeoisie and their socialist point turned outward. Thus arose *Social-Democracy*. The new *Montagne*, the result of this combination, contained, apart from some working-class supernumeraries and some members of the socialist sects, the same elements as the old Montagne, only numerically stronger. However, in the course of development, it had changed with the class that it represented. The peculiar character of Social-Democracy is epitomised in the fact that democratic-republican institutions are demanded as a means, not of superseding two extremes, capital and wage labour, but of weakening their antagonism and transforming it into harmony. However different the means proposed for the attainment of this end may be, however much it may be embellished with more or less revolutionary notions, the content remains the same. This content is the reformation of society in a democratic way, but a reformation within the bounds of the petty bourgeoisie. Only one must not form the narrow-minded notion that the petty bourgeoisie, on principle, wishes to enforce an egoistic class interest. Rather, it believes that the *special* conditions of its emancipation are the *general* conditions within which alone modern society can be saved and the class struggle avoided. Just as little must one imagine that the democratic representatives are indeed all shopkeepers[a] or enthusiastic supporters of shopkeepers. In their education and individual position they may be as far apart from them as heaven from earth. What makes them representatives of the petty bourgeoisie is the fact that in their minds they do not get beyond the limits which the latter do not get beyond in life, that they are consequently driven, theoretically, to the same problems and

---

[a] Marx uses the English word.— *Ed.*

solutions to which material interest and social position drive the latter in practice. This is, in general, the relationship between the *political* and *literary representatives* of a class and the class they represent.

After the analysis we have given, it is obvious that if the Montagne continually contends with the Party of Order for the republic and the so-called rights of man, neither the republic nor the rights of man are its final end, any more than an army which one wants to deprive of its weapons and which resists has taken the field in order to remain in possession of its own weapons.

Immediately, as soon as the National Assembly met, the Party of Order provoked the Montagne. The bourgeoisie now felt the necessity of making an end of the democratic petty bourgeoisie, just as a year before it had realised the necessity of getting rid of the revolutionary proletariat. Only the situation of the adversary was different. The strength of the proletarian party lay in the streets, that of the petty bourgeoisie in the National Assembly itself. It was therefore a question of decoying them out of the National Assembly into the streets and causing them to smash their parliamentary power themselves, before time and circumstances could consolidate it. The Montagne galloped headlong into the trap.

The bombardment of Rome by the French troops was the bait that was thrown to it. It violated Article V of the Constitution which forbids the French Republic to employ its military forces against the freedom of another people.[95] In addition to this, Article 54 prohibited any declaration of war on the part of the executive power without the assent of the National Assembly, and by its resolution of May 8, the Constituent Assembly had disapproved of the Roman expedition. On these grounds Ledru-Rollin brought in a bill of impeachment against Bonaparte and his ministers on June 11, 1849. Exasperated by the wasp stings of Thiers, he actually let himself be carried away to the point of threatening that he would defend the Constitution by every means, even with arms in hand. The Montagne rose to a man and repeated this call to arms. On June 12, the National Assembly rejected the bill of impeachment, and the Montagne left the parliament. The events of June 13 are known: the proclamation issued by a section of the Montagne, declaring Bonaparte and his ministers "outside the Constitution"[a]; the street procession of the democratic National Guards, who, unarmed as they were, dispersed on encountering the troops of Changarnier, etc., etc. A part of the Montagne fled abroad; another part was

---

[a] "Déclaration de la Montagne au peuple français. Paris, 12 juin [1849]" — *Ed.*

arraigned before the High Court at Bourges,[96] and a parliamentary regulation subjected the remainder to the schoolmasterly surveillance of the President of the National Assembly.[a] Paris was again declared in a state of siege and the democratic part of its National Guard dissolved. Thus the influence of the Montagne in parliament and the power of the petty bourgeois in Paris were broken.

Lyons, where June 13 had given the signal for a bloody insurrection of the workers,[97] was, along with the five surrounding departments, likewise declared in a state of siege, a condition that has continued up to the present moment.

The bulk of the Montagne had left its vanguard in the lurch, having refused to sign its proclamation. The press had deserted, only two journals[b] having dared to publish the *pronunciamento*. The petty bourgeois betrayed their representatives, in that the National Guards either stayed away or, where they appeared, hindered the erection of barricades. The representatives had duped the petty bourgeois, in that the alleged allies from the army were nowhere to be seen. Finally, instead of gaining an accession of strength from it, the democratic party had infected the proletariat with its own weakness and, as is usual with the great deeds of democrats, the leaders had the satisfaction of being able to charge their "people" with desertion, and the people the satisfaction of being able to charge its leaders with fraud.

Seldom had an action been announced with more noise than the impending campaign of the Montagne, seldom had an event been trumpeted with greater certainty or longer in advance than the inevitable victory of democracy. Most assuredly, the democrats believe in the trumpets before whose blasts the walls of Jericho fell down.[c] And as often as they stand before the ramparts of despotism, they seek to imitate the miracle. If the Montagne wished to triumph in parliament, it should not have called to arms. If it called to arms in parliament, it should not have acted in parliamentary fashion in the streets. If the peaceful demonstration was meant seriously, then it was folly not to foresee that it would be given a war-like reception. If a real struggle was intended, then it was odd to lay down the weapons with which it would have to be waged. But the revolutionary threats of the petty bourgeois and their democratic representatives are mere attempts to intimidate the antagonist. And when they have run into a blind alley, when they have sufficiently compromised themselves to

---

[a] André Dupin.— *Ed.*
[b] *La Réforme* and *La Démocratie pacifique.— Ed.*
[c] Cf. Joshua 6 : 5 and 6 : 20.— *Ed.*

make it necessary to give effect to their threats, then this is done in an ambiguous fashion that avoids nothing so much as the means to the end and tries to find excuses for succumbing. The blaring overture that announced the contest dies away in a faint grumble as soon as the struggle has to begin, the actors cease to take themselves *au sérieux*, and the action collapses completely, like a pricked balloon.

No party exaggerates its means more than the democratic, none deludes itself more light-mindedly over the situation. Since a section of the army had voted for it, the Montagne was now convinced that the army would revolt for it. And on what occasion? On an occasion which, from the standpoint of the troops, had no other meaning than that the revolutionists took the side of the Roman soldiers against the French soldiers. On the other hand, the recollections of June 1848 were still too fresh to allow of anything but a profound aversion on the part of the proletariat towards the National Guard and a thoroughgoing mistrust of the democratic chiefs on the part of the chiefs of the secret societies. To iron out these differences, it was necessary for great common interests to be at stake. The violation of an abstract paragraph of the Constitution could not provide these interests. Had not the Constitution been repeatedly violated, according to the assurance of the democrats themselves? Had not the most popular journals branded it as counter-revolutionary botch-work? But the democrat, because he represents the petty bourgeoisie, that is, a *transition class,* in which the interests of two classes are simultaneously mutually blunted, imagines himself elevated above class antagonism generally. The democrats concede that a privileged class confronts them, but they, along with all the rest of the nation, form the *people.* What they represent is the *people's rights*; what interests them is the *people's interests.* Accordingly, when a struggle is impending, they do not need to examine the interests and positions of the different classes. They do not need to weigh their own resources too critically. They have merely to give the signal and the *people,* with all its inexhaustible resources, will fall upon the *oppressors.* Now, if in practice their interests prove to be uninteresting and their potency impotence, then either the fault lies with pernicious sophists, who split the *indivisible people* into different hostile camps, or the army was too brutalised and blinded to comprehend that the pure aims of democracy are also the best thing for it, or the whole thing has been wrecked by a detail in its execution, or else an unforeseen accident has this time spoilt the game. In any case, the democrat comes out of the most disgraceful defeat just as immaculate as he was innocent when he went into it, with the newly-won conviction that he is bound to win, not that he himself and his party have to give up the old standpoint, but, on the contrary, that conditions have to ripen to suit him.

Accordingly, one must not imagine the Montagne, decimated and broken though it was, and humiliated by the new parliamentary regulation, as being particularly miserable. If June 13 had removed its chiefs, it made room, on the other hand, for men of lesser calibre, whom this new position flattered. If their impotence in parliament could no longer be doubted, they were entitled now to confine their actions to outbursts of moral indignation and blustering declamation. If the Party of Order affected to see embodied in them, as the last official representatives of the revolution, all the terrors of anarchy, they could in reality be all the more insipid and modest. They consoled themselves, however, for June 13 with the profound utterance: But if they dare to attack universal suffrage, well then—then we'll show them what we are made of! *Nous verrons!*[a]

So far as the Montagnards who fled abroad are concerned, it is sufficient to remark here that Ledru-Rollin, because in barely a fortnight he had succeeded in ruining irretrievably the powerful party at whose head he stood, now found himself called upon to form a French government *in partibus*[b]; that to the extent that the level of the revolution sank and the official bigwigs of official France became more dwarf-like, his figure in the distance, removed from the scene of action, seemed to grow in stature; that he could figure as the republican pretender for 1852, and that he issued periodical circulars to the Wallachians and other peoples, in which the despots of the Continent are threatened with the deeds of himself and his confederates. Was Proudhon altogether wrong when he cried to these gentlemen: "*Vous n'êtes que des blagueurs*"?[c]

On June 13 the Party of Order had not only broken the Montagne, it had effected the *subordination of the Constitution to the majority decisions of the National Assembly*. And it understood the republic thus: that the bourgeoisie rules here in parliamentary forms, without, as in a monarchy, encountering any barrier such as the veto power of the executive or the right to dissolve parliament. This was a *parliamentary republic*, as Thiers termed it.[d] But when on June 13 the bourgeoisie secured its omnipotence within the house of parliament, did it not afflict parliament itself, vis-à-vis the executive

---

[a] We shall see.— *Ed.*

[b] Here in the sense of "abroad". See also footnote on pp. 5, 107, 282.— *Ed.*

[c] "You are nothing but braggarts." From Proudhon's letter "Aux citoyens Ledru-Rollin, Charles Delescluze, Martin Bernard, et consorts, Rédacteurs du *Proscrit*, à Londres" published in the newspaper *Le Peuple* in July 1850.— *Ed.*

[d] In his speech in the Legislative Assembly on January 17, 1851.— *Ed.*

authority and the people, with incurable weakness by expelling its most popular part? By surrendering numerous deputies without further ado on the demand of the courts, it abolished its own parliamentary immunity. The humiliating regulations to which it subjected the Montagne exalted the President of the republic in the same measure as they degraded the individual representatives of the people. By branding an insurrection for the protection of the constitutional charter an anarchic act aiming at the subversion of society, it precluded the possibility of its appealing to insurrection should the executive authority violate the Constitution in relation to it. And by the irony of history, the general who on Bonaparte's instructions bombarded Rome and thus provided the immediate occasion for the constitutional revolt of June 13, that very *Oudinot* had to be the man offered by the Party of Order imploringly and unavailingly to the people as general on behalf of the Constitution against Bonaparte on December 2, 1851. Another hero of June 13, *Vieyra*, who was lauded from the tribune of the National Assembly for the brutalities that he had committed in the democratic newspaper offices at the head of a gang of National Guards belonging to high finance circles—this same Vieyra had been initiated into Bonaparte's conspiracy and played an essential part in depriving the National Assembly in the hour of its death of any protection by the National Guard.

June 13 had still another meaning. The Montagne had wanted to force the impeachment of Bonaparte. Its defeat was therefore a direct victory for Bonaparte, his personal triumph over his democratic enemies. The Party of Order gained the victory; Bonaparte had only to cash in on it. He did so. On June 14 a proclamation could be read on the walls of Paris in which the President, reluctantly, against his will, as it were, compelled by the sheer force of events, comes forth from his cloistered seclusion and, posing as misunderstood virtue, complains of the calumnies of his opponents and, while he seems to identify his person with the cause of order, rather identifies the cause of order with his person. Moreover, the National Assembly had, it is true, subsequently approved the expedition against Rome, but Bonaparte had taken the initiative in the matter. After having re-installed the High Priest Samuel in the Vatican, he could hope to enter the Tuileries as King David.[98] He had won the priests over to his side.

The revolt of June 13 was confined, as we have seen, to a peaceful street procession. No martial laurels were, therefore, to be won against it. Nevertheless, at a time as poor as this in heroes and events, the Party of Order transformed this bloodless battle into a second

Austerlitz.[99] Platform and press praised the army as the power of
order, in contrast to the popular masses, representing the impotence
of anarchy, and extolled Changarnier as the "bulwark of society", a
deception in which he himself finally came to believe. Surreptitious-
ly, however, the corps that seemed doubtful were transferred from
Paris, the regiments which had shown at the elections the most
democratical sentiments were banished from France to Algiers, the
turbulent spirits among the troops were relegated to penal
detachments, and finally the isolation of the press from the barracks
and of the barracks from civil society was systematically carried
out.

Here we have reached the decisive turning-point in the history of
the French National Guard. In 1830 it was decisive in the overthrow
of the Restoration. Under Louis Philippe every rebellion in which
the National Guard stood on the side of the troops miscarried. When
in the February days of 1848 it evinced a passive attitude towards the
insurrection and an equivocal one towards Louis Philippe, he gave
himself up for lost and actually was lost. Thus the conviction took
root that the revolution could not be victorious *without* the National
Guard, nor the army *against* it. This was the superstition of the
army in regard to civilian omnipotence. The June days of 1848,
when the entire National Guard, with the troops of the line, put
down the insurrection, had strengthened the superstition. After
Bonaparte's assumption of office, the position of the National Guard
was to some extent weakened by the unconstitutional union, in the
person of Changarnier, of the command of its forces with the
command of the First Army Division.

Just as the command of the National Guard appeared here as an
attribute of the military commander-in-chief, so the National Guard
itself now appeared as only an appendage of the troops of the line.
Finally, on June 13 its power was broken, and not only by its partial
disbandment, which from this time on was periodically repeated all
over France, until mere fragments of it were left behind. The
demonstration of June 13 was, above all, a demonstration of the
democratic National Guards. They had not, to be sure, borne their
arms, but worn their uniforms against the army; precisely in this
uniform, however, lay the talisman. The army convinced itself that
this uniform was a piece of woollen cloth like any other. The spell
was broken. In the June days of 1848 bourgeoisie and petty
bourgeoisie stood united as the National Guard with the army
against the proletariat; on June 13, 1849 the bourgeoisie let the
petty-bourgeois National Guard be dispersed by the army; on
December 2, 1851 the National Guard of the bourgeoisie itself had

vanished, and Bonaparte merely registered this fact when he subsequently signed the decree for its disbandment. Thus the bourgeoisie had itself smashed its last weapon against the army, but it had to smash it the moment the petty bourgeoisie no longer stood behind it as a vassal, but before it as a rebel, as in general it was bound to destroy all its means of defence against absolutism with its own hand as soon as it had itself become absolute.

Meanwhile, the Party of Order celebrated the reconquest of a power that seemed lost in 1848 only to be found again, freed from its restraints, in 1849, celebrated by means of invectives against the republic and the Constitution, of curses on all future, present and past revolutions, including that which its own leaders had made, and in laws by which the press was muzzled, association destroyed and the state of siege regulated as an organic institution. The National Assembly then adjourned from the middle of August to the middle of October, after having appointed a permanent commission for the period of its absence. During this recess the Legitimists intrigued with Ems, the Orleanists—with Claremont, Bonaparte—by means of princely tours, and the Departmental Councils—in deliberations on a revision of the Constitution: incidents which regularly recur in the periodic recesses of the National Assembly and which I propose to discuss only when they become events. Here it may merely be remarked, in addition, that it was impolitic for the National Assembly to disappear for considerable intervals from the stage and leave only a *single*, albeit sorry, figure to be seen at the head of the republic, that of Louis Bonaparte, while to the scandal of the public the Party of Order fell asunder into its royalist component parts and followed its conflicting desires for Restoration. As often as the confused noise of *parliament* grew silent during these recesses and its body dissolved in the nation, it became unmistakably clear that only *one* thing was still wanting to complete the true form of this republic: to make the *former's* recess permanent and replace the *latter's* inscription: *Liberté, Égalité, Fraternité* by the unambiguous words: Infantry, Cavalry, Artillery!

IV

In the middle of October 1849 the National Assembly met once more. On November 1 Bonaparte surprised it with a message in which he announced the dismissal of the Barrot-Falloux ministry and the formation of a new ministry. No one has ever sacked lackeys with less ceremony than Bonaparte his ministers. The kicks that were

intended for the National Assembly were given in the meantime to
Barrot and Co.

The Barrot ministry, as we have seen, had been composed of
Legitimists and Orleanists, a ministry of the Party of Order.
Bonaparte had needed it to dissolve the republican Constituent
Assembly, to bring about the expedition against Rome and to break
the democratic party. Behind this ministry he had seemingly effaced
himself, surrendered governmental power into the hands of the
Party of Order and donned the modest character mask that the
responsible editor of a newspaper wore under Louis Philippe, the
mask of the *homme de paille*.[a] He now threw off a mask which was no
longer the light veil behind which he could hide his physiognomy,
but an iron mask which prevented him from displaying a physiognomy of his own. He had appointed the Barrot ministry in order to
blast the republican National Assembly in the name of the Party of
Order; he dismissed it in order to declare his own name independent
of the National Assembly of the Party of Order.

Plausible pretexts for this dismissal were not lacking. The Barrot
ministry neglected even the decencies that would have let the
President of the republic appear as a power side by side with the
National Assembly. During the recess of the National Assembly
Bonaparte published a letter to Edgar Ney in which he seemed to
disapprove of the liberal attitude of the Pope,[b] just as in opposition to
the Constituent Assembly he had published a letter in which he
commended Oudinot for the attack on the Roman Republic. When
the National Assembly now voted the budget for the Roman
expedition, Victor Hugo, out of alleged liberalism, brought up this
letter for discussion.[c] The Party of Order with scornfully incredulous
outcries stifled the idea that Bonaparte's ideas could have any
political importance. Not one of the ministers took up the gauntlet
for him. On another occasion Barrot, with his well-known hollow
rhetoric, let fall from the platform words of indignation concerning
the "abominable intrigues" that, according to his assertion, went on
in the immediate entourage of the President. Finally, while the
ministry obtained from the National Assembly a widow's pension for
the Duchess of Orleans it rejected any proposal to increase the Civil
List of the President. And in Bonaparte the imperial pretender was
so intimately bound up with the adventurer down on his luck that the

---

    [a] Man of straw.— *Ed.*

    [b] Pius IX. The 1852 and 1869 editions have "illiberal attitude of the Pope"; the
correction was made in the 1885 edition.— *Ed.*

    [c] In his speech in the Legislative Assembly on October 19, 1849.— *Ed.*

one great idea, that he was called to restore the empire, was always supplemented by the other, that it was the mission of the French people to pay his debts.

The Barrot-Falloux ministry was the first and last *parliamentary ministry* that Bonaparte brought into being. Its dismissal forms, accordingly, a decisive turning-point. With it the Party of Order lost, never to reconquer it, an indispensable post for the maintenance of the parliamentary regime, the lever of executive power. It is immediately obvious that in a country like France, where the executive power commands an army of officials numbering more than half a million individuals and therefore constantly maintains an immense mass of interests and livelihoods in the most absolute dependence; where the state enmeshes, controls, regulates, superintends and tutors civil society from its most comprehensive manifestations of life down to its most insignificant stirrings, from its most general modes of being to the private existence of individuals; where through the most extraordinary centralisation this parasitic body acquires an ubiquity, an omniscience, a capacity for accelerated mobility and an elasticity which finds a counterpart only in the helpless dependence, in the loose shapelessness of the actual body politic—it is obvious that in such a country the National Assembly forfeits all real influence when it loses command of the ministerial posts, if it does not at the same time simplify the administration of the state, reduce the army of officials as far as possible and, finally, let civil society and public opinion create organs of their own, independent of the governmental power. But it is precisely with the maintenance of that extensive state machine in its numerous ramifications that the *material interests* of the French bourgeoisie are interwoven in the closest fashion. Here it finds posts for its surplus population and makes up in the form of state salaries for what it cannot pocket in the form of profit, interest, rents and honorariums. On the other hand, its *political interests* compelled it to increase daily the repressive measures and therefore the resources and the personnel of the state power, while at the same time it had to wage an uninterrupted war against public opinion and mistrustfully mutilate, cripple, the independent organs of the social movement, where it did not succeed in amputating them entirely. Thus the French bourgeoisie was compelled by its class position to annihilate, on the one hand, the vital conditions of all parliamentary power, and therefore, likewise, of its own, and to render irresistible, on the other hand, the executive power hostile to it.

The new ministry was called the d'Hautpoul ministry. Not that General d'Hautpoul had received the rank of Prime Minister.

Rather, simultaneously with Barrot's dismissal, Bonaparte abolished this dignity, which, true enough, condemned the President of the republic to the status of the legal nonentity of a constitutional monarch, but of a constitutional monarch without throne or crown, without sceptre or sword, without irresponsibility, without imprescriptible possession of the highest state dignity, and, worst of all, without a Civil List. The d'Hautpoul ministry contained only one man of parliamentary standing, the money-lender *Fould,* one of the most notorious of the high financiers. To his lot fell the ministry of finance. Look up the quotations on the Paris *bourse* and you will find that from November 1, 1849 onwards the French *fonds*[a] rise and fall with the rise and fall of Bonapartist stocks. While Bonaparte had thus found his ally in the *bourse,* he at the same time took possession of the police by appointing Carlier Police Prefect of Paris.

Only in the course of development, however, could the consequences of the change of ministers come to light. To begin with, Bonaparte had taken a step forward only to be driven backward all the more conspicuously. His brusque message was followed by the most servile declaration of allegiance to the National Assembly. As often as the ministers dared to make a diffident attempt to introduce his personal fads as legislative proposals, they themselves seemed to carry out, against their will only and compelled by their position, comical commissions of whose fruitlessness they were convinced in advance. As often as Bonaparte blurted out his intentions behind the ministers' backs and played with his "*idées napoléoniennes*",[100] his own ministers disavowed him from the tribune of the National Assembly. His usurpatory longings seemed to make themselves heard only in order that the malicious laughter of his opponents might not be muted. He behaved like an unrecognised genius, whom all the world takes for a simpleton. Never did he enjoy the contempt of all classes in fuller measure than during this period. Never did the bourgeoisie rule more absolutely, never did it display more ostentatiously the insignia of domination.

I have not here to write the history of its legislative activity, which is summarised during this period in two laws: in the law reestablishing the *wine tax* and the *education law* abolishing unbelief.[101] If wine drinking was made harder for the French, they were presented all the more plentifully with the water of true life. If in the law on the wine tax the bourgeoisie declared the old, hateful French tax system to be inviolable, it sought through the education law to

---

[a] Government securities.— *Ed.*

ensure among the masses the old state of mind that put up with the tax system. One is astonished to see the Orleanists, the liberal bourgeois, these old apostles of Voltairianism and eclectic philosophy, entrust to their hereditary enemies, the Jesuits, the superintendence of the French mind. But although in regard to the pretenders to the throne, Orleanists and Legitimists could part company, they understood that to secure their united rule necessitated the uniting of the means of repression of two epochs, that the means of subjugation of the July monarchy had to be supplemented and strengthened by the means of subjugation of the Restoration.

The peasants, disappointed in all their hopes, crushed more than ever by the low level of grain prices on the one hand, and by the growing burden of taxes and mortgage debts on the other, began to bestir themselves in the departments. They were answered by a drive against the schoolmasters, who were made subject to the clergy, by a drive against the *maires*,[a] who were made subject to the prefects, and by a system of espionage, to which all were made subject. In Paris and the large towns reaction itself has the physiognomy of its epoch and challenges more than it strikes down. In the countryside it becomes dull, mean, petty, tiresome and vexatious, in a word, the gendarme. One understands how three years of the regime of the gendarme, consecrated by the regime of the priest, were bound to demoralise the immature masses.

Whatever amount of passion and declamation might be employed by the Party of Order against the minority from the tribune of the National Assembly, its speech remained as monosyllabic as that of the Christians, whose words were to be: Yea, yea; nay, nay![b] As monosyllabic on the platform as in the press. Flat as a riddle whose answer is known in advance. Whether it was a question of the right of petition or the tax on wine, freedom of the press or free trade, the clubs or the municipal charter, protection of personal freedom or regulation of the state budget, the watchword constantly recurs, the theme remains always the same, the verdict is ever ready and invariably reads: "*Socialism!*" Even bourgeois liberalism is declared *socialistic*, bourgeois enlightenment socialistic, bourgeois financial reform socialistic. It was socialistic to build a railway, where a canal already existed, and it was socialistic to defend oneself with a cane when one was attacked with a rapier.

This was not merely a figure of speech, fashion or party tactics. The bourgeoisie had a true insight into the fact that all the weapons

---

[a] Mayors.— *Ed.*
[b] Matthew 5 : 37.— *Ed.*

which it had forged against feudalism turned their points against itself, that all the means of education which it had produced rebelled against its own civilisation, that all the gods which it had created had fallen away from it. It understood that all the so-called civil freedoms and organs of progress attacked and menaced its *class rule* at its social foundation and its political summit simultaneously, and had therefore become "*socialistic*". In this menace and this attack it rightly discerned the secret of socialism, whose import and tendency it judges more correctly than so-called socialism is able to judge itself; the latter can, accordingly, not comprehend why the bourgeoisie callously hardens its heart against it, whether it sentimentally bewails the sufferings of mankind, or in Christian spirit prophesies the millennium and universal brotherly love, or in humanistic style drivels on about mind, education and freedom, or in doctrinaire fashion excogitates a system for the conciliation and welfare of all classes. What the bourgeoisie did not grasp, however, was the logical conclusion that its *own parliamentary regime*, that its *political rule* in general, was now also bound to meet with the general verdict of condemnation as being *socialistic*. As long as the rule of the bourgeois class had not been organised completely, as long as it had not acquired its pure political expression, the antagonism of the other classes, likewise, could not appear in its pure form, and where it did appear could not take the dangerous turn that transforms every struggle against the state power into a struggle against capital. If in every stirring of life in society it saw "tranquillity" imperilled, how could it want to maintain at the head of society a *regime of unrest*, its own regime, the *parliamentary regime*, this regime that, according to the expression of one of its spokesmen, lives in struggle and by struggle? The parliamentary regime lives by discussion; how shall it forbid discussion? Every interest, every social institution, is here transformed into general ideas, debated as ideas; how shall any interest, any institution, sustain itself above thought and impose itself as an article of faith? The struggle of the orators on the platform evokes the struggle of the scribblers of the press; the debating club in parliament is necessarily supplemented by debating clubs in the salons and ale houses; the representatives, who constantly appeal to public opinion, give public opinion the right to speak its real mind in petitions. The parliamentary regime leaves everything to the decision of majorities; how shall the great majorities outside parliament not want to decide? When you play the fiddle at the top of the state, what else is to be expected but that those down below dance?

Thus, by now stigmatising as "*socialistic*" what it had previously extolled as "*liberal*", the bourgeoisie confesses that its own interests dictate that it should be delivered from the danger of its *own rule*; that, in order to restore tranquillity in the country, its bourgeois parliament must, first of all, be laid to rest; that, in order to preserve its social power intact, its political power must be broken; that the individual bourgeois can continue to exploit the other classes and to enjoy undisturbed property, family, religion and order only on condition that their class be condemned along with the other classes to similar political nullity; that, in order to save its purse, it must forfeit the crown, and the sword that is to safeguard it must at the same time be hung over its own head as a sword of Damocles.

In the domain of the interests of the general citizenry, the National Assembly showed itself so unproductive that, for example, the discussions on the Paris-Avignon railway, which began in the winter of 1850, were still not ripe for conclusion on December 2, 1851. Wherever it did not repress, or react, it was stricken with incurable barrenness.

While Bonaparte's ministry partly took the initiative in framing laws in the spirit of the Party of Order, and partly even outdid that party's harshness in its execution and administration, he, on the other hand, by childishly silly proposals sought to win popularity, to bring out his opposition to the National Assembly, and to hint at a secret reserve that was only temporarily prevented by conditions from making its hidden treasures available to the French people. Such was the proposal to decree an increase in pay of four sous a day to the non-commissioned officers. Such was the proposal of an honour system lending-bank for the workers. Money as a gift and money on tick, it was with prospects such as these that he hoped to allure the masses. Donations and loans—the financial science of the lumpenproletariat, whether of high degree or low, is restricted to this. Such were the only springs which Bonaparte knew how to set in motion. Never has a pretender speculated more stupidly on the stupidity of the masses.

The National Assembly flared up repeatedly over these unmistakable attempts to gain popularity at its expense, over the growing danger that this adventurer, whom his debts spurred on and no established reputation held back, would venture a desperate coup. The discord between the Party of Order and the President had taken on a threatening character when an unexpected event threw him back repentant into its arms. We mean the *by-elections of March 10, 1850*. These elections were held for the purpose of filling the representatives' seats that after June 13 had been rendered vacant by imprisonment or exile. Paris elected only Social-Democratic candidates.[a] It even concentrated most of the votes on an insurgent of June 1848, on Deflotte. Thus did the Parisian petty bourgeoisie, in alliance with the proletariat, revenge itself for its defeat on June 13, 1849. It seemed to have disappeared from the battlefield at the moment of danger only to reappear there on a more propitious occasion with more numerous fighting forces and with a bolder battle cry. One circumstance seemed to heighten the peril of this election victory. The army voted in Paris for the June insurgent against La Hitte, a minister of Bonaparte's, and in the departments largely for the Montagnards, who here, too, though indeed not so decisively as in Paris, maintained the ascendancy over their adversaries.

Bonaparte saw himself suddenly confronted with the revolution once more. As on January 29, 1849, as on June 13, 1849, so on March 10, 1850, he disappeared behind the Party of Order. He made obeisance, he pusillanimously begged pardon, he offered to appoint any ministry it pleased at the behest of the parliamentary majority, he even implored the Orleanist and Legitimist party leaders, the Thiers, the Berryers, the Broglies, the Molés, in brief, the so-called burgraves,[102] to take the helm of state themselves. The Party of Order proved unable to take advantage of this opportunity that would never return. Instead of boldly possessing itself of the power offered, it did not even compel Bonaparte to reinstate the ministry dismissed on November 1; it contented itself with humiliating him by its forgiveness and adjoining M. *Baroche* to the d'Hautpoul ministry. As public prosecutor this Baroche had stormed and raged before the High Court at Bourges, the first time against the revolutionists of May 15,[103] the second time against the democrats of June 13, both times because of an attack on the National Assembly. None of Bonaparte's ministers subsequently contributed more to the degradation of the National Assembly, and after December 2, 1851, we meet him once more as the comfortably-installed and highly-paid Vice-President of the Senate. He had spat in the revolutionists' soup in order that Bonaparte might finish them off.

The Social-Democratic party, for its part, seemed only to try to find pretexts for putting its own victory once again in doubt and for blunting its point. Vidal, one of the newly elected representatives of Paris, had been elected simultaneously in Strasbourg. He was induced to decline the election for Paris and accept it for Strasbourg. And so, instead of making its victory at the polls definitive and

---

[a] François Vidal, Hippolyte Carnot and Paul Deflotte.— *Ed.*

thereby compelling the Party of Order at once to contest it in parliament, instead of thus forcing the adversary to fight at the moment of popular enthusiasm and a favourable mood in the army, the democratic party wearied Paris during the months of March and April with a new election campaign, let the aroused popular passions wear themselves out in this repeated provisional election game, let the revolutionary energy satiate itself with constitutional successes, dissipate itself in petty intrigues, hollow declamations and sham movements, let the bourgeoisie rally and make its preparations, and, lastly, weakened the significance of the March elections by a sentimental commentary in the April by-election, that of the election of Eugène Sue. In a word, it made an April Fool of March 10.

The parliamentary majority understood the weakness of its antagonists. Its seventeen burgraves—for Bonaparte had left to it the direction of and responsibility for the attack—drew up a new electoral law, the introduction of which was entrusted to M. Faucher, who solicited this honour for himself. On May 8 he introduced the law by which universal suffrage was to be abolished, a residence of three years in the locality of the election to be imposed as a condition on the voters and, finally, the proof of this residence made dependent in the case of workers on a certificate from their employers.

Just as the democrats had, in revolutionary fashion, agitated and raged during the constitutional election contest, so now, when it was necessary to prove the serious nature of those electoral victories arms in hand, did they in constitutional fashion preach order, majestic calm (*calme majestueux*), lawful action, that is to say, blind subjection to the will of the counter-revolution, which imposed itself as the law. During the debate the Mountain put the Party of Order to shame by asserting, against the latter's revolutionary passion, the dispassionate attitude of the philistine who keeps within the law, and by striking it down with the fearful reproach that it proceeded in a revolutionary manner. Even the newly elected deputies were at pains to prove by their decorous and discreet action what a misconception it was to decry them as anarchists and construe their election as a victory for revolution. On May 31 the new electoral law went through. The Montagne contented itself with smuggling a protest into the pocket of the President. The electoral law was followed by a new press law, by which the revolutionary newspapers were entirely suppressed.[104] They had deserved their fate. The *National* and *La Presse*, two bourgeois organs, were left behind after this deluge as the most advanced outposts of the revolution.

We have seen how during March and April the democratic leaders had done everything to embroil the people of Paris in a sham fight, how after May 8 they did everything to restrain them from a real fight. In addition to this, we must not forget that the year 1850 was one of the most splendid years of industrial and commercial prosperity, and the Paris proletariat was therefore fully employed. But the election law of May 31, 1850 excluded it from any participation in political power. It cut it off from the very arena of the struggle. It threw the workers back into the position of pariahs which they had occupied before the February revolution. By letting themselves be led by the democrats in face of such an event and forgetting the revolutionary interests of their class for momentary ease and comfort, they renounced the honour of being a conquering power, surrendered to their fate, proved that the defeat of June 1848 had put them out of the fight for years and that the historical process would for the present again have to go on *over* their heads. As far as petty-bourgeois democracy is concerned, which on June 13 had cried: "But if once universal suffrage is attacked, then we'll show them", it now consoled itself with the contention that the counter-revolutionary blow which had struck it was no blow and the law of May 31 no law. On the second Sunday in May 1852, every Frenchman would appear at the polling place with ballot in one hand and sword in the other. With this prophecy it rested content. Lastly, the army was disciplined by its superior officers for the elections of March and April 1850, just as it had been disciplined for those of May 28, 1849. This time, however, it said decidedly: "The revolution shall not dupe us a third time."

The law of May 31, 1850 was the coup d'état of the bourgeoisie. All its conquests over the revolution hitherto had only a provisional character. They were endangered as soon as the existing National Assembly retired from the stage. They depended on the hazards of a new general election, and the history of elections since 1848 irrefutably proved that the bourgeoisie's moral sway over the mass of the people was lost in the same measure as its actual domination developed. On March 10 universal suffrage declared itself directly against the domination of the bourgeoisie; the bourgeoisie answered by outlawing universal suffrage. The law of May 31 was, therefore, one of the necessities of the class struggle. On the other hand, the Constitution required a minimum of two million votes to make an election of the President of the republic valid. If none of the candidates for the presidency obtained this minimum, the National Assembly was to choose the President from among the five[a]

---

[a] The original mistakenly says here: "among the three".— *Ed.*

candidates to whom the largest number of votes would fall. At the time when the Constituent Assembly made this law, ten million voters were registered on the rolls. In its view, therefore, a fifth of the people entitled to vote was sufficient to make the presidential election valid. The law of May 31 struck at least three million votes off the electoral rolls, reduced the number of people entitled to vote to seven million and, nevertheless, retained the legal minimum of two million for the presidential election. It therefore raised the legal minimum from a fifth to nearly a third of the effective votes, that is, it did everything to smuggle the election of the President out of the hands of the people and into the hands of the National Assembly. Thus through the electoral law of May 31 the Party of Order seemed to have made its rule doubly secure, by surrendering the election of the National Assembly and that of the President of the republic to this stationary section of society.

V

As soon as the revolutionary crisis had been weathered and universal suffrage abolished, the struggle between the National Assembly and Bonaparte broke out again.

The Constitution had fixed Bonaparte's salary at 600,000 francs. Barely six months after his installation he succeeded in increasing this sum to twice as much, for Odilon Barrot wrung from the Constituent National Assembly an extra allowance of 600,000 francs a year for so-called representation moneys. After June 13 Bonaparte had caused similar requests to be voiced, this time without eliciting response from Barrot. Now, after May 31, he at once availed himself of the favourable moment and caused his ministers to propose a Civil List of three million in the National Assembly. A long life of adventurous vagabondage had endowed him with the most developed antennae for feeling out the weak moments when he might squeeze money from his bourgeois. He practised regular *chantage*.[a] The National Assembly had violated the sovereignty of the people with his assistance and his cognizance. He threatened to denounce its crime to the tribunal of the people unless it loosened its purse-strings and purchased his silence with three million a year. It had robbed three million Frenchmen of their franchise. He demanded, for every Frenchman out of circulation, a franc in circulation, precisely three million francs. He, the elect of six million, claimed damages

---

[a] Blackmail.— *Ed.*

for the votes out of which he said he had retrospectively been cheated. The Commission of the National Assembly refused this importunate person. The Bonapartist press threatened. Could the
National Assembly break with the President of the republic at a
moment when it had fundamentally and definitely broken with the
mass of the nation? It rejected the annual Civil List, it is true, but
it granted a single extra allowance of 2,160,000 francs. It thus
rendered itself guilty of the double weakness of granting the
money and of showing at the same time by its vexation that it
granted it unwillingly. We shall see later for what purpose
Bonaparte needed the money. After this vexatious aftermath,
which followed on the heels of the abolition of universal suffrage
and in which Bonaparte exchanged his humble attitude during the
crisis of March and April for challenging impudence to the
usurpatory parliament, the National Assembly adjourned for three
months, from August 11 to November 11. In its place it left
behind a Permanent Commission of twenty-eight members, which
contained no Bonapartists, but did contain some moderate
republicans. The Permanent Commission of 1849 had included
only Order men and Bonapartists. But at that time the Party of
Order declared itself in permanence against the revolution. This
time the parliamentary republic declared itself in permanence
against the President. After the law of May 31, this was the only
rival that still confronted the Party of Order.

When the National Assembly met once more in November 1850,
it seemed that, instead of the petty skirmishes it had hitherto had
with the President, a great and ruthless struggle, a life-and-death
struggle between the two powers, had become inevitable.

As in 1849 so during this year's parliamentary recess, the Party
of Order had broken up into its individual factions, each occupied
with its own restoration intrigues, reinforced by the death of Louis
Philippe. The Legitimist king, Henry V, had even nominated a
formal ministry which resided in Paris and in which members of
the Permanent Commission held seats. Bonaparte, in his turn, was
therefore entitled to make tours of the French departments and,
according to the disposition of the town that he favoured with his
presence, to divulge, now covertly, now more overtly, his own
restoration plans and canvass votes for himself. On these
processions, which the great official *Moniteur* and the little private
Moniteurs of Bonaparte naturally had to celebrate as triumphal
processions, he was constantly accompanied by persons affiliated with
the *Society of December 10.* This society dates from the year 1849. On
the pretext of founding a benevolent society, the lumpenproletariat

of Paris had been organised into secret sections, each section being led by Bonapartist agents, with a Bonapartist general[a] at the head of the whole. Alongside decayed *roués* with dubious means of subsistence and of dubious origin, alongside ruined and adventurous offshoots of the bourgeoisie, were vagabonds, discharged soldiers, discharged jailbirds, escaped galley slaves, rogues, mountebanks, *lazzaroni*,[105] pickpockets, tricksters, gamblers, *maquereaus*,[b] brothel keepers, porters, *literati*, organ-grinders, rag-pickers, knife grinders, tinkers, beggars—in short, the whole indefinite, disintegrated mass, thrown hither and thither, which the French term *la bohème*; from this kindred element Bonaparte formed the core of the Society of December 10. A "benevolent society"—in so far as, like Bonaparte, all its members felt the need of benefiting themselves at the expense of the labouring nation. This Bonaparte, who constitutes himself *chief of the lumpenproletariat*, who here alone rediscovers in mass form the interests which he personally pursues, who recognises in this scum, offal, refuse of all classes the only class upon which he can base himself unconditionally, is the real Bonaparte, the Bonaparte *sans phrase*.[c] An old crafty *roué*, he conceives the historical life of the nations and their performances of state as comedy in the most vulgar sense, as a masquerade where the grand costumes, words and postures merely serve to mask the pettiest knavery. Thus on his expedition to Strasbourg, where a trained Swiss vulture had played the part of the Napoleonic eagle. For his irruption into Boulogne he puts some London lackeys into French uniforms. They represent the army.[107] In his Society of December 10, he assembles 10,000 rogues who are to play the part of the people, as Nick Bottom that of the lion.[d] At a moment when the bourgeoisie itself played the most complete comedy, but in the most serious manner in the world, without infringing any of the pedantic conditions of French dramatic etiquette, and was itself half deceived, half convinced of the solemnity of its own performance of state, the adventurer, who took the comedy as plain comedy, was bound to win. Only when he has eliminated his solemn opponent, when he himself now takes his imperial role seriously and under the Napoleonic mask imagines he is the real Napoleon, does he become the victim of his own

---

[a] Jean Pierre Piat.—*Ed.*

[b] Procurers.—*Ed.*

[c] The 1852 edition adds: "unmistakable even when he later, in the fullness of power, paid off the debt to some of his erstwhile fellow conspirators, alongside the revolutionaries, by having them transported to Cayenne".[106]—*Ed.*

[d] The reference is to Shakespeare's *A Midsummer Night's Dream*, Act I, Scene 2.—*Ed.*

conception of the world, the serious buffoon who no longer takes world history for a comedy but his comedy for world history. What the national *ateliers*[108] were for the socialist workers, what the *Gardes mobiles* were for the bourgeois republicans, the Society of December 10, the party fighting force characteristic of Bonaparte, was for him. On his journeys the detachments of this society packing the railways had to improvise a public for him, stage public enthusiasm, roar *vive l'Empereur*, insult and beat up republicans, of course under the protection of the police. On his return journeys to Paris they had to form the advance guard, forestall counter-demonstrations or disperse them. The Society of December 10 belonged to him, it was *his* work, his very own idea. Whatever else he appropriates is put into his hands by the force of circumstances; whatever else he does, the circumstances do for him or he is content to copy from the deeds of others. But Bonaparte with official phrases about order, religion, family and property in public, before the citizens, and with the secret society of the Schufterles and Spiegelbergs, the society of disorder, prostitution and theft, behind him—that is Bonaparte himself as original author, and the history of the Society of December 10 is his own history. Now it had happened by way of exception that people's representatives belonging to the Party of Order came under the cudgels of the Decembrists. Still more. Yon, the Police Commissioner assigned to the National Assembly and charged with watching over its safety, acting on the deposition of a certain Allais, advised the Permanent Commission that a section of the Decembrists had decided to assassinate General Changarnier and Dupin, the President of the National Assembly, and had already designated the individuals who were to perpetrate the deed. One can understand the terror of M. Dupin. A parliamentary enquiry into the Society of December 10, that is, the profanation of the Bonapartist secret world, seemed inevitable. Just before the meeting of the National Assembly Bonaparte providently disbanded his society, naturally only on paper, for in a detailed memoir at the end of 1851 Police Prefect Carlier still sought in vain to move him to really break up the Decembrists.

The Society of December 10 was to remain the private army of Bonaparte until he succeeded in transforming the public army into a Society of December 10. Bonaparte made the first attempt at this shortly after the adjournment of the National Assembly, and precisely with the money just wrested from it. As a fatalist, he lives in the conviction that there are certain higher powers which man, and the soldier in particular, cannot withstand. Among these powers he counts, first and foremost, cigars and champagne, cold poultry and garlic sausage. Accordingly, to begin with, he treats officers and non-commissioned officers in his Elysée apartments to cigars and champagne, to cold poultry and garlic sausage. On October 3 he repeats this manoeuvre with the mass of the troops at the St. Maur review, and on October 10 the same manoeuvre on a still larger scale at the Satory army parade. The Uncle remembered the campaigns of Alexander in Asia, the Nephew the triumphal marches of Bacchus in the same land. Alexander was a demigod, to be sure, but Bacchus was a god and moreover the tutelary deity of the Society of December 10.

After the review of October 3, the Permanent Commission summoned the War Minister d'Hautpoul. He promised that these breaches of discipline should not recur. We know how on October 10 Bonaparte kept d'Hautpoul's word. As Commander-in-Chief of the Paris army, Changarnier had commanded at both reviews. He, simultaneously a member of the Permanent Commission, chief of the National Guard, the "saviour" of January 29 and June 13, the "bulwark of society", the candidate of the Party of Order for presidential honours, the suspected Monk of two monarchies, had hitherto never acknowledged himself as the subordinate of the War Minister, had always openly derided the republican Constitution and had pursued Bonaparte with an ambiguous lordly protection. Now he was consumed with zeal for discipline against the War Minister and for the Constitution against Bonaparte. While on October 10 a section of the cavalry raised the shout: "*Vive Napoléon! Vivent les saucissons!*", Changarnier arranged that at least the infantry marching past under the command of his friend Neumayer should preserve an icy silence. As a punishment, the War Minister relieved General Neumayer of his post in Paris at Bonaparte's instigation, on the pretext of appointing him commanding general of the fourteenth and fifteenth army divisions. Neumayer refused this exchange of posts and so had to resign. Changarnier, for his part, published an order of the day on November 2, in which he forbade the troops to indulge in political outcries or demonstrations of any kind while under arms. The Elysée newspapers attacked Changarnier; the papers of the Party of Order attacked Bonaparte; the Permanent Commission held repeated secret sessions in which it was repeatedly proposed to declare the country in danger; the army seemed divided into two hostile camps, with two hostile general staffs, one in the Elysée where Bonaparte, the other in the Tuileries where Changarnier, lived. It seemed that only the meeting of the National Assembly was needed to give the signal for battle. The French public judged this friction between Bonaparte and Changarnier like that English journalist who characterised it in the following words:

> "The political housemaids of France are sweeping away the glowing lava of the revolution with old brooms and wrangle with one another while they do their work."

Meanwhile, Bonaparte hastened to remove the War Minister, d'Hautpoul, to pack him off in all haste to Algiers and to appoint General Schramm War Minister in his place. On November 12 he sent to the National Assembly a message of American prolixity, overloaded with detail, redolent of order, desirous of reconciliation, constitutionally acquiescent, treating of all and sundry, but not of the *questions brûlantes*[a] of the moment. As if in passing, he made the remarks that according to the express provisions of the Constitution the President alone could dispose of the army. The message closed with the following words of great solemnity:

> "*Above all things, France demands tranquillity.... But bound by an oath, I shall keep within the narrow limits that it has set for me....* As far as I am concerned, elected by the people and owing my power to it alone, I shall always bow to its lawfully expressed will. Should you resolve at this session on a revision of the Constitution, a Constituent Assembly will regulate the position of the executive power. If not, then the people will solemnly pronounce its decision in 1852. But whatever the solutions of the future may be, let us come to an understanding, so that passion, surprise or violence may never decide the destiny of a great nation.... What occupies my attention, above all, is not who will rule France in 1852, but how to employ the time I have at my disposal so that the intervening period may pass by without agitation or disturbance. I have opened my heart to you with sincerity; you will answer my frankness with your trust, my good endeavours with your co-operation, and God will do the rest."[b]

The respectable, hypocritically moderate, virtuously commonplace language of the bourgeoisie reveals its deepest meaning in the mouth of the autocrat of the Society of December 10 and the picnic hero of St. Maur and Satory.

The burgraves of the Party of Order did not delude themselves for a moment concerning the trust that this opening of the heart deserved. About oaths they had long been *blasé*; they numbered in their midst veterans and virtuosos of political perjury. Nor had they failed to hear the passage about the army. They observed with annoyance that in its discursive enumeration of recently enacted laws the message passed over the most important law, the electoral law, in studied silence, and moreover, in the event of there being no revision of the Constitution, left the election of the President in 1852 to the people. The electoral law was the leaden ball chained to the feet of

---

[a] Burning questions.— *Ed.*
[b] *Le Moniteur universel*, No. 317, November 13, 1850.— *Ed.*

the Party of Order, which prevented it from walking and so much the more from storming forward! Moreover, by the official disbandment of the Society of December 10 and the dismissal of the War Minister d'Hautpoul, Bonaparte had with his own hand sacrificed the scapegoats on the altar of the country. He had blunted the edge of the expected collision. Finally, the Party of Order itself anxiously sought to avoid, to mitigate, to gloss over any decisive conflict with the executive power. For fear of losing its conquests over the revolution, it allowed its rival to carry off the fruits thereof. "Above all things, France demands tranquillity." This was what the Party of Order had cried to the revolution since February,[a] this was what Bonaparte's message cried to the Party of Order. "Above all, France demands tranquillity." Bonaparte committed acts that aimed at usurpation, but the Party of Order committed "unrest" if it raised a row about these acts and construed them hypochondriacally. The sausages of Satory were quiet as mice when no one spoke of them. "Above all, France demands tranquillity." Bonaparte demanded, therefore, that he be left in peace to do as he liked and the parliamentary party was paralysed by a double fear, by the fear of again evoking revolutionary unrest and by the fear of itself appearing as the instigator of unrest in the eyes of its own class, in the eyes of the bourgeoisie. Consequently, since France demanded tranquillity above all things, the Party of Order dared not answer "war" after Bonaparte had talked "peace" in his message. The public, which had anticipated scenes of great scandal at the opening of the National Assembly, was cheated of its expectations. The opposition deputies, who demanded the submission of the Permanent Commission's minutes on the October events, were outvoted by the majority. On principle, all debates that might cause excitement were eschewed. The proceedings of the National Assembly during November and December 1850 were without interest.

At last, towards the end of December, guerrilla warfare began over a number of prerogatives of parliament. The movement got bogged down in petty squabbles regarding the prerogatives of the two powers, since the bourgeoisie had done away with the class struggle for the moment by abolishing universal suffrage.

A judgment for debt had been obtained from the court against Mauguin, one of the people's representatives. In answer to the enquiry of the President of the Court, the Minister of Justice, Rouher, declared that a warrant for the debtor's arrest should be

---

[a] 1848.— *Ed.*

issued without further ado. Mauguin was thus thrown into the debtors' jail. The National Assembly flared up when it learned of the assault. Not only did it order his immediate release, but it even had him fetched forcibly from Clichy the same evening, by its *greffier*.[a] In order, however, to confirm its faith in the sanctity of private property and with the idea at the back of its mind of opening, in case of need, an asylum for Montagnards who had become troublesome, it declared imprisonment of people's representatives for debt permissible after previously obtaining its consent. It forgot to decree that the President might also be locked up for debt. It destroyed the last semblance of the immunity that enveloped the members of its own body.

It will be remembered that, acting on the information given by a certain Allais, Police Commissioner Yon had denounced a section of the Decembrists for planning the murder of Dupin and Changarnier. In reference to this, at the very first sitting the questors made the proposal that parliament should form a police force of its own, paid out of the private budget of the National Assembly and absolutely independent of the Prefect of Police. The Minister of the Interior, Baroche, protested against this invasion of his domain. A miserable compromise on this matter was concluded, according to which, although the police commissioner of the Assembly was to be paid out of its private budget and to be appointed and dismissed by its questors, this would only happen after previous agreement with the Minister of the Interior. Meanwhile criminal proceedings had been taken by the government against Allais, and here it was easy to represent his information as a hoax and through the mouth of the public prosecutor to cast ridicule upon Dupin, Changarnier, Yon and the whole National Assembly. Thereupon, on December 29, the Minister Baroche writes a letter to Dupin in which he demands Yon's dismissal. The Bureau of the National Assembly decides to retain Yon in his position, but the National Assembly, alarmed by its violence in the Mauguin affair and accustomed when it has ventured a blow at the executive power to receive two blows from it in return, does not sanction this decision. It dismisses Yon as a reward for his professional zeal and robs itself of a parliamentary prerogative indispensable against a man who does not decide by night in order to execute by day, but who decides by day and executes by night.[b]

---

[a] Clerk.— *Ed.*

[b] An allusion to the fact that Bonaparte staged his coup d'état on the night of December 1, 1851.— *Ed.*

We have seen how on great and striking occasions during the months of November and December the National Assembly avoided or quashed the struggle with the executive power. Now we see it compelled to take it up on the pettiest occasions. In the Mauguin affair it confirms the principle of imprisoning people's representatives for debt, but reserves the right to have it applied only to representatives it dislikes, and wrangles over this infamous privilege with the Minister of Justice. Instead of availing itself of the alleged murder plot to decree an enquiry into the Society of December 10 and irredeemably unmask Bonaparte before France and Europe in his true character of chief of the Paris lumpenproletariat, it lets the conflict be degraded to a point where the only issue between it and the Minister of the Interior is which of them has the authority to appoint and dismiss a police commissioner. Thus, during the whole of this period, we see the Party of Order compelled by its equivocal position to dissipate and fragment its struggle with the executive power in petty jurisdictional squabbles, chicanery, legalistic hairsplitting, and delimitational disputes, and to make the most ridiculous matters of form the substance of its activity. It does not dare to take up the conflict at the moment when this has significance from the standpoint of principle, when the executive power has really exposed itself and the cause of the National Assembly would be the cause of the nation. By so doing it would give the nation its marching orders, and it fears nothing more than that the nation should move. On such occasions it accordingly rejects the motions of the Montagne and proceeds to the order of the day. The question at issue in its larger aspects having thus been dropped, the executive power calmly bides the time when it can again take up the same question on petty and insignificant occasions, when this is, so to speak, of only local parliamentary interests. Then the repressed rage of the Party of Order breaks out, then it tears away the curtain from the stage-set, then it denounces the President, then it declares the republic in danger, but then, also, its fervour appears absurd and the occasion for the struggle seems a hypocritical pretext or altogether not worth fighting about. The parliamentary storm becomes a storm in a teacup, the fight becomes an intrigue, the conflict a scandal. While the revolutionary classes gloat with malicious joy over the humiliation of the National Assembly, for they are just as enthusiastic about the parliamentary prerogatives of this Assembly as the latter is about the public liberties, the bourgeoisie outside parliament does not understand how the bourgeoisie inside parliament can waste time over such petty squabbles and imperil tranquillity by such pitiful rivalries with the President. It becomes confused by a strategy that makes peace at the moment when all the world is expecting battles, and attacks at the moment when all the world believes peace has been made.

On December 20, Pascal Duprat interpellated the Minister of the Interior concerning the Gold Bars Lottery. This lottery was a "daughter of Elysium".[a] Bonaparte with his faithful followers had brought her into the world and Police Prefect Carlier had placed her under his official protection, although French law forbids all lotteries with the exception of raffles for charitable purposes. Seven million lottery tickets at a franc apiece, the profits ostensibly to be devoted to shipping Parisian vagabonds to California. On the one hand, golden dreams were to supplant the socialist dreams of the Paris proletariat, and the seductive prospect of the first prize to replace the doctrinaire right to work. Naturally, the Paris workers did not recognise in the glitter of the California gold bars the inconspicuous francs that were enticed out of their pockets. In the main, however, the matter was nothing short of a downright swindle. The vagabonds who wanted to open California gold mines without troubling to leave Paris were Bonaparte himself and his debt-ridden cronies. The three million voted by the National Assembly had been squandered in riotous living; in one way or another the coffers had to be replenished. In vain had Bonaparte opened a national subscription for the building of so-called *cités ouvrières*, and figured at the head of the list himself with a considerable sum. The hard-hearted bourgeois waited mistrustfully for him to pay up his share and since this, naturally, did not ensue, the speculation in socialist castles in the air fell straightway to the ground. The gold bars proved a better draw. Bonaparte & Co. were not content to pocket part of the excess of the seven million over the bars to be allotted in prizes; they manufactured false lottery tickets; they issued ten, fifteen and even twenty tickets with the same number—a financial operation in the spirit of the Society of December 10! Here the National Assembly was confronted not with the fictitious President of the republic, but with Bonaparte in the flesh. Here it could catch him in the act, in conflict not with the Constitution but with the *Code pénal*. If on Duprat's interpellation it proceeded to the day's agenda, this did not happen merely because Girardin's motion that it should declare itself "*satisfait*" reminded the Party of Order of its own systematic corruption. The bourgeois and, above all, the bourgeois inflated into

---

[a] The phrase "Tochter aus Elysium" occurs in Schiller's poem "An die Freude" as an epithet of joy. Marx uses it as a pun to allude to Louis Bonaparte's official residence in the Champs Elysées.— *Ed.*

a statesman, supplements his practical meanness by theoretical extravagance. As a statesman he becomes, like the state power that confronts him, a higher being that can only be fought in a higher, consecrated fashion.

Bonaparte, who precisely because he was a Bohemian, a princely lumpenproletarian, had the advantage over a rascally bourgeois in that he could conduct a dirty struggle, now saw, after the Assembly had itself guided him with its own hand across the slippery ground of the military banquets, the reviews, the Society of December 10, and, finally, the *Code pénal,* that the moment had come when he could pass from an apparent defensive to the offensive. The minor defeats meanwhile sustained by the Minister of Justice, the Minister of War, the Minister of the Navy and the Minister of Finance,[a] through which the National Assembly signified its snarling displeasure, troubled him little. He not only prevented the ministers from resigning and thus recognising the sovereignty of parliament over the executive power, but could now consummate what he had begun during the recess of the National Assembly: the severance of the military power from parliament, the *removal of Changarnier.*

An Elysée paper[b] published an order of the day alleged to have been addressed during the month of May to the First Army Division, and therefore proceeding from Changarnier, in which the officers were recommended, in the event of an insurrection, to give no quarter to the traitors in their own ranks, but to shoot them immediately and refuse the National Assembly the troops, should it requisition them. On January 3, 1851 the Cabinet was interpellated concerning this order of the day. For the investigation of this matter it requests a breathing space, first of three months, then of a week, finally of only twenty-four hours. The Assembly insists on an immediate explanation. Changarnier rises and declares that there never was such an order of the day. He adds that he will always hasten to comply with the demands of the National Assembly and that in case of a clash it can count on him. It receives his declaration with indescribable applause and passes a vote of confidence in him. It abdicates, it decrees its own impotence and the omnipotence of the army by placing itself under the private protection of a general; but the general deceives himself when he puts at its command against Bonaparte a power that he only holds as a fief from the same Bonaparte and when, in his turn, he expects to be protected by this parliament, by his own protégé in need of protection. Changarnier,

---

[a] Rouher, Schramm, Romain-Desfossés and Fould.— *Ed.*
[b] *La Patrie,* January 2, 1851.— *Ed.*

however, believes in the mysterious power with which the bourgeoisie has endowed him since January 29, 1849. He considers himself the third power, existing side by side with both the other state powers. He shares the fate of the rest of this epoch's heroes, or rather saints, whose greatness consists precisely in the biassed great opinion of them that their party creates in its own interests and who shrink to everyday figures as soon as circumstances call on them to perform miracles. Unbelief is, in general, the mortal enemy of these reputed heroes and real saints. Hence their dignified moral indignation at the dearth of enthusiasm displayed by wits and scoffers.

The same evening, the ministers were summoned to the Elysée; Bonaparte insists on the dismissal of Changarnier; five ministers refuse to sign it; the *Moniteur* announces a ministerial crisis, and the press of the Party of Order threatens to form a parliamentary army under Changarnier's command. The Party of Order had constitutional authority to take this step. It merely had to appoint Changarnier President of the National Assembly and requisition any number of troops it pleased for its protection. It could do so all the more safely as Changarnier still actually stood at the head of the army and the Paris National Guard and was only waiting to be requisitioned together with the army. The Bonapartist press did not as yet even dare to question the right of the National Assembly directly to requisition troops, a legal scruple that in the given circumstances did not promise any success. That the army would have obeyed the orders of the National Assembly is probable when one bears in mind that Bonaparte had to search all Paris for eight days in order, finally, to find two generals—Baraguay d'Hilliers and Saint-Jean d'Angély—who declared themselves ready to countersign Changarnier's dismissal. That the Party of Order, however, would have found in its own ranks and in parliament the necessary number of votes for such a resolution is more than doubtful, when one considers that eight days later 286 votes detached themselves from the party and that in December 1851, at the last hour for decision, the Montagne still rejected a similar proposal. Nevertheless, the burgraves might, perhaps, still have succeeded in spurring the mass of their party to a heroism that consisted in feeling themselves secure behind a forest of bayonets and accepting the services of an army that had deserted to their camp. Instead of this, on the evening of January 6, Messrs. the Burgraves betook themselves to the Elysée in order to make Bonaparte desist from dismissing Changarnier by using statesmanlike phrases and urging considerations of state. Whomever one seeks to persuade, one acknowledges as master of the situation. On January 12 Bonaparte, assured by this step, appoints a new ministry in which the leaders of the old ministry, Fould and Baroche, remain. Saint-Jean d'Angély becomes War Minister, the *Moniteur* publishes the decree dismissing Changarnier, and his command is divided between Baraguay d'Hilliers, who receives the First Army Division, and Perrot, who receives the National Guard. The bulwark of society has been dismissed, and while this does not cause any tiles to fall from the roofs, quotations on the *bourse* are, on the other hand, going up.

By repulsing the army, which places itself in the person of Changarnier at its disposal, and so surrendering the army irrevocably to the President, the Party of Order declares that the bourgeoisie has forfeited its vocation to rule. A parliamentary ministry no longer existed. Having now indeed lost its grip on the army and National Guard, what effective means remained to it with which simultaneously to maintain the usurped power of parliament over the people and its constitutional power against the President? None. Only the appeal to powerless principles, to principles that it had itself always interpreted merely as general rules, which one prescribes for others in order to be able to move all the more freely oneself. The dismissal of Changarnier and the falling of the military power into Bonaparte's hands closes the first part of the period we are considering, the period of struggle between the Party of Order and the executive power. War between the two powers has now been openly declared, is openly waged, but only after the Party of Order has lost both arms and soldiers. Without the ministry, without the army, without the people, without public opinion, after its Electoral Law of May 31 no longer the representative of the sovereign nation, *sans* eyes, *sans* ears, *sans* teeth, *sans* everything,[a] the National Assembly had undergone a gradual transformation into an *ancient French Parliament*[109] that has to leave action to the government and content itself with growling remonstrances *post festum*.[b]

The Party of Order receives the new ministry with a storm of indignation. General Bedeau recalls to mind the mildness of the Permanent Commission during the recess, and the excessive consideration it had shown by waiving the publication of its minutes. The Minister of the Interior[c] now himself insists on the publication of these minutes, which by this time have naturally become as dull as

[a] Shakespeare, *As You Like It*, Act II, Scene 7.— *Ed.*
[b] After the feast, that is, belatedly.— *Ed.*
[c] Baroche.— *Ed.*

ditch-water, disclose no fresh facts and have not the slightest effect on the *blasé* public. Upon Rémusat's proposal the National Assembly retires into its offices and appoints a "Committee for Extraordinary Measures". Paris departs the less from the rut of its everyday routine, since at this moment trade is prosperous, manufactories are busy, corn prices low, foodstuffs overflowing and the savings banks receive fresh deposits daily. The "extraordinary measures" that parliament has announced with so much noise fizzle out on January 18 in a no-confidence vote against the ministers without General Changarnier even being mentioned. The Party of Order had been forced to frame its motion in this way in order to secure the votes of the republicans, as of all the measures of the ministry, Changarnier's dismissal is precisely the only one which the republicans approve of, while the Party of Order is in fact not in a position to censure the other ministerial acts, which it had itself dictated.

The no-confidence vote of January 18 was passed by 415 votes to 286. Thus, it was carried only by a *coalition* of the extreme Legitimists and Orleanists with the pure republicans and the Montagne. Thus it proved that the Party of Order had lost in conflicts with Bonaparte not only the ministry, not only the army, but also its independent parliamentary majority, that a squad of representatives had deserted from its camp, out of fanaticism for conciliation, out of fear of the struggle, out of lassitude, out of family regard for the state salaries of their kinsmen, out of speculation on ministerial posts becoming vacant (Odilon Barrot), out of sheer egoism, which makes the ordinary bourgeois always inclined to sacrifice the general interest of his class for this or that private motive. From the first, the Bonapartist representatives adhered to the Party of Order only in the struggle against the revolution. The leader of the Catholic party, Montalembert, had already at that time thrown his influence into the Bonapartist scale, since he despaired of the parliamentary party's prospects of life. Lastly, the leaders of this party, Thiers and Berryer, the Orleanist and the Legitimist, were compelled openly to proclaim themselves republicans, to confess that their hearts were royalist but their heads republican, that the parliamentary republic was the sole possible form for the rule of the bourgeoisie as a whole. Thus they were compelled, before the eyes of the bourgeois class itself, to stigmatise the restoration plans, which they continued indefatigably to pursue behind parliament's back, as an intrigue as dangerous as it was foolish.

The no-confidence vote of January 18 hit the ministers and not the President. But it was not the ministry, it was the President who had dismissed Changarnier. Should the Party of Order impeach Bonaparte himself? On account of his restoration desires? The latter merely supplemented their own. On account of his conspiracy in connection with the military reviews and the Society of December 10? They had buried these themes long since under simple orders of the day. On account of the dismissal of the hero of January 29 and June 13, the man who in May 1850 threatened to set fire to all four corners of Paris in the event of a rising? Their allies of the Montagne and Cavaignac did not even allow them to raise the fallen bulwark of society by means of an official declaration of sympathy. They themselves could not deny the President the constitutional authority to dismiss a general. They only raged because he made an unparliamentary use of his constitutional right. Had they not continually made an unconstitutional use of their parliamentary prerogative, particularly in regard to the abolition of universal suffrage? They were therefore reduced to moving within strictly parliamentary limits. And it took that peculiar malady which since 1848 has raged all over the Continent, *parliamentary cretinism*, which holds those infected by it fast in an imaginary world and robs them of all sense, all memory, all understanding of the rude external world—it took this parliamentary cretinism for those who had destroyed all the conditions of parliamentary power with their own hands, and were bound to destroy them in their struggle with the other classes, still to regard their parliamentary victories as victories and to believe they hit the President by striking at his ministers. They merely gave him the opportunity to humiliate the National Assembly afresh in the eyes of the nation. On January 20 the *Moniteur* announced that the resignation of the entire ministry had been accepted. On the pretext that no parliamentary party any longer had a majority, as the vote of January 18, this fruit of the coalition between Montagne and royalists, proved, and pending the formation of a new majority, Bonaparte appointed a so-called transition ministry, not one member of which was a member of parliament, all being absolutely unknown and insignificant individuals, a ministry of mere clerks and copyists. The Party of Order could now work to exhaustion playing with these marionettes; the executive power no longer thought it worth while to be seriously represented in the National Assembly. The more his ministers were pure dummies, the more manifestly Bonaparte concentrated the whole executive power in his own person and the more scope he had to exploit it for his own ends.

In coalition with the Montagne, the Party of Order revenged itself by rejecting the grant to the President of 1,800,000 francs, which the chief of the Society of December 10 had compelled his ministerial clerks to propose. This time a majority of only 102 votes decided the matter; thus 27 fresh votes had fallen away since January 18; the dissolution of the Party of Order was making progress. At the same time, in order that there might not for a moment be any mistake about the meaning of its coalition with the Montagne, it scorned even to consider a proposal signed by 189 members of the Montagne calling for a general amnesty of political offenders. It sufficed for the Minister of the Interior, a certain Vaïsse, to declare that the tranquillity was only apparent, that in secret great agitation prevailed, that in secret ubiquitous societies were being organised, the democratic papers were preparing to come out again, the reports from the departments were unfavourable, the Geneva refugees were directing a conspiracy spreading by way of Lyons over all Southern France, France was on the verge of an industrial and commercial crisis, the manufacturers of Roubaix had reduced working hours, that the prisoners of Belle Isle[110] were in revolt—it sufficed for even a mere Vaïsse to conjure up the red spectre, and the Party of Order rejected without discussion a motion that would certainly have won the National Assembly immense popularity and thrown Bonaparte back into its arms. Instead of letting itself be intimidated by the executive power with the prospect of fresh disturbances, it ought rather to have allowed the class struggle a little elbow-room, so as to keep the executive power dependent on itself. But it did not feel equal to the task of playing with fire.

Meanwhile, the so-called transition ministry continued to vegetate until the middle of April. Bonaparte wearied and befuddled the National Assembly with continual new ministerial combinations. Now he seemed to want to form a republican ministry with Lamartine and Billault, now a parliamentary one with the inevitable Odilon Barrot, whose name may never be missing when a dupe is necessary, then a Legitimist ministry with Vatimesnil and Benoist d'Azy, and then again an Orleanist one with Maleville. While he thus kept the different factions of the Party of Order in tension against one another and alarmed them as a whole by the prospect of a republican ministry and the consequent inevitable restoration of universal suffrage, he at the same time engendered in the bourgeoisie the conviction that his honest efforts to form a parliamentary ministry were being frustrated by the irreconcilability of the royalist factions. The bourgeoisie, however, cried out all the louder for a "strong government"; it found it all the more unpardonable to leave France "without administration" the more a general commercial crisis seemed now to be approaching and won recruits for socialism in the towns, just as the ruinously low price of corn did in the countryside. Trade became daily slacker, the unemployed hands increased perceptibly, ten thousand workers, at least, were breadless in Paris, innumerable factories stood idle in Rouen, Mulhouse, Lyons, Roubaix, Tourcoing, St. Etienne, Elbeuf, etc. Under these circumstances Bonaparte could venture, on April 11, to restore the ministry of January 18: Messrs. Rouher, Fould, Baroche, etc., reinforced by M. Léon Faucher, whom the Constituent Assembly during its last days had, with the exception of five votes cast by ministers, unanimously stigmatised by a vote of no-confidence for sending out false telegrams. The National Assembly had therefore gained a victory over the ministry on January 18, had struggled with Bonaparte for three months, only to have Fould and Baroche on April 11 admit the puritan Faucher as a third member into their ministerial alliance.[a]

In November 1849 Bonaparte had contented himself with an *unparliamentary* ministry, in January 1851 with an *extra-parliamentary* one, and on April 11 he felt strong enough to form an *anti-parliamentary* ministry, which harmoniously combined in itself the no-confidence votes of both Assemblies, the Constituent and the Legislative, the republican and the royalist. This gradation of ministries was the thermometer with which parliament could measure the decrease of its own vital heat. By the end of April the latter had fallen so low that Persigny, in a personal interview, could urge Changarnier to go over to the camp of the President. Bonaparte, he assured him, regarded the influence of the National Assembly as completely destroyed, and the proclamation was already prepared that was to be published after the coup d'état, which was kept steadily in view but was by chance again postponed. Changarnier informed the leaders of the Party of Order of the obituary notice, but who believes that bedbug bites are fatal? And parliament, stricken, disintegrated and putrescent as it was, could not prevail upon itself to see in its duel with the grotesque chief of the Society of December 10 anything but a duel with a bedbug. But Bonaparte answered the Party of Order as Agesilaus did King Agis: "*I seem to you an ant, but one day I shall be a lion.*" [111]

---

[a] An ironic paraphrase of the expression "in eurem Bunde der dritte" ("the third member in your alliance") from Schiller's poem "Die Bürgschaft".— *Ed.*

VI

The coalition with the Montagne and the pure republicans, to which the Party of Order saw itself condemned in its unavailing efforts to maintain possession of the military power and to reconquer supreme control of the executive power, proved incontrovertibly that it had forfeited its independent *parliamentary majority*. On May 28 the mere power of the calendar, of the hour hand of the clock, gave the signal for its complete disintegration. With May 28 the last year of the life of the National Assembly began. It had now to decide for continuing the Constitution unaltered or for revising it. But revision of the Constitution, that implied not only rule of the bourgeoisie or of petty-bourgeois democracy,[a] democracy or proletarian anarchy, parliamentary republic or Bonaparte, it implied at the same time Orleans or Bourbon! Thus fell in the midst of parliament the apple of discord that was bound to inflame openly the conflict of interests which split the Party of Order into hostile factions. The Party of Order was a combination of heterogeneous social substances. The question of revision generated a political temperature at which the product again decomposed into its original constituents.

The interest of the Bonapartists in a revision was simple. For them it was above all a question of abolishing Article 45, which forbade Bonaparte's re-election and the prorogation of his authority. No less simple appeared the position of the republicans. They unconditionally rejected any revision; they saw in it a universal conspiracy against the republic. Since they commanded *more than a quarter of the votes* in the National Assembly and, according to the Constitution, three-quarters of the votes were required for a resolution for revision to be legally valid and for the convocation of a revising Assembly, they only needed to count their votes to be sure of victory. And they were sure of victory.

As against these clear positions, the Party of Order found itself caught in inextricable contradictions. If it should reject revision, it would imperil the *status quo*, since it would leave Bonaparte only one way out, that of force, and since on the second Sunday in May 1852, at the decisive moment, it would be surrendering France to revolutionary anarchy, with a President who had lost his authority, with a parliament which for a long time had not possessed it and with a people that meant to reconquer it. If it voted for constitutional

---

[a] According to the list of misprints in the 1852 edition, this passage should read: "rule of the bourgeoisie or petty-bourgeois democracy"; however, Marx did not reproduce this alteration in the 1869 edition.— *Ed.*

revision, it knew that it voted in vain and would be bound to fail constitutionally because of the veto of the republicans. If it unconstitutionally declared a simple majority vote to be binding, then it could hope to dominate the revolution only if it subordinated itself unconditionally to the sovereignty of the executive power, then it would make Bonaparte master of the Constitution, of its revision and of itself. A merely partial revision which would prolong the authority of the President would pave the way for imperial usurpation. A general revision which would shorten the existence of the republic would bring the dynastic claims into unavoidable conflict, for the conditions of a Bourbon and the conditions of an Orleanist restoration were not only different, they were mutually exclusive.

The parliamentary republic was more than the neutral territory on which the two factions of the French bourgeoisie, Legitimists and Orleanists, large landed property and industry, could dwell side by side with equality of rights. It was the unavoidable condition of their *common* rule, the sole form of state in which their general class interest subjected to itself at the same time both the claims of their particular factions and all the remaining classes of society. As royalists they fell back into their old antagonism, into the struggle for the supremacy of landed property or of money, and the highest expression of this antagonism, its personification, was their kings themselves, their dynasties. Hence the resistance of the Party of Order to the *recall of the Bourbons*.

The Orleanist and people's representative Creton had in 1849, 1850 and 1851 periodically introduced a motion for the revocation of the decree exiling the royal families. Parliament, also periodically, presented the spectacle of an Assembly of royalists that obdurately barred the gates through which their exiled kings might return home. Richard III had murdered Henry VI, remarking that he was too good for this world and belonged in heaven.[a] The royalists declared France too bad to possess her kings again. Constrained by force of circumstances, they had become republicans and repeatedly sanctioned the popular decision that banished their kings from France.

A revision of the Constitution—and circumstances compelled taking it into consideration—called in question, along with the republic, the common rule of the two bourgeois factions, and revived, with the possibility of a monarchy, the rivalry of the interests which it had predominantly represented by turns, the struggle for

---

[a] Shakespeare, *Richard III*, Act I, Scene 2.—*Ed.*

the supremacy of one faction over the other. The diplomats of the Party of Order believed they could settle the struggle by an amalgamation of the two dynasties, by a so-called *fusion* of the royalist parties and their royal houses. The real fusion of the Restoration and the July monarchy was the parliamentary republic, in which Orleanist and Legitimist colours were obliterated and the various species of bourgeois disappeared in the bourgeois as such, in the bourgeois genus. Now, however, Orleanist was to become Legitimist and Legitimist Orleanist. Royalty, in which their antagonism was personified, was to embody their unity; the expression of their exclusive factional interests was to become the expression of their common class interest; the monarchy was to do what only the abolition of two monarchies, the republic, could do and had done. This was the philosopher's stone, to produce which the doctors of the Party of Order racked their brains. As if the Legitimist monarchy could ever become the monarchy of the industrial bourgeois or the bourgeois monarchy ever become the monarchy of the hereditary landed aristocracy. As if landed property and industry could fraternise under *one* crown, when the crown could only descend to one head, the head of the elder brother or of the younger. As if industry could come to terms with landed property at all, so long as landed property does not decide itself to become industrial. If Henry V should die tomorrow, the Count of Paris would not on that account become the king of the Legitimists unless he ceased to be the king of the Orleanists. The philosophers of fusion, however, who became more vociferous in proportion as the question of revision came to the fore, who had provided themselves with an official daily organ in the *Assemblée nationale* and who are again at work even at this very moment (February 1852), considered the whole difficulty to be due to the opposition and rivalry of the two dynasties. The attempts to reconcile the Orleans family with Henry V, begun since the death of Louis Philippe, but, like the dynastic intrigues generally, played at only while the National Assembly was in recess, during the *entr'actes*, behind the scenes, more sentimental coquetry with the old superstition than seriously meant business, now became grand performances of state, enacted by the Party of Order on the public stage, instead of in amateur theatricals, as hitherto. The couriers sped from Paris to Venice, from Venice to Claremont,[112] from Claremont to Paris. The Count of Chambord issues a manifesto in which "with the help of all the members of his family" he announces not his, but the "national" restoration. The Orleanist Salvandy throws himself at the feet of Henry V. The Legitimist chiefs, Berryer, Benoist d'Azy, Saint-Priest, travel to Claremont in order to persuade the Orleans set, but in vain. The fusionists perceive too late that the interests of the two bourgeois factions neither lose exclusiveness nor gain pliancy when they culminate in the form of family interests, the interests of two royal houses. If Henry V were to recognise the Count of Paris as his successor—the sole success that the fusion could achieve at best—the House of Orleans would not win any claim that the childlessness of Henry V had not already secured to it, but it would lose all claims that it had gained through the July revolution. It would waive its original claims, all the titles that it had wrested from the older branch of the Bourbons in almost a hundred years of struggle; it would barter away its historical prerogative, the prerogative of the modern kingdom, for the prerogative of its genealogical tree. The fusion, therefore, would be nothing but a voluntary abdication of the House of Orleans, its resignation to Legitimacy, a repentant withdrawal from the Protestant state church into the Catholic. A withdrawal, moreover, that would not even bring it to the throne which it had lost, but to the throne's steps, on which it had been born. The old Orleanist ministers, Guizot, Duchâtel, etc., who likewise hastened to Claremont to announce the fusion, in fact represented merely the hangover from the July revolution, the despair felt in regard to the bourgeois monarchy and the monarchism of the bourgeois, the superstitious belief in Legitimacy as the last charm against anarchy. Imagining themselves mediators between Orleans and Bourbon, they were in reality merely Orleanist renegades, and the Prince of Joinville received them as such. On the other hand, the viable, bellicose section of the Orleanists, Thiers, Baze, etc., convinced Louis Philippe's family all the more easily that if any directly monarchist restoration presupposed the fusion of the two dynasties and if any such fusion presupposed abdication of the House of Orleans, it was, on the contrary, wholly in accord with the tradition of their forefathers to recognise the republic for the moment and wait until events permitted the conversion of the presidential chair into a throne. Rumours of Joinville's candidature were circulated, public curiosity was kept in suspense and, a few months later, in September, after the rejection of revision, his candidature was publicly proclaimed.

The attempt at a royalist fusion of Orleanists with Legitimists had thus not only failed; it had destroyed their *parliamentary fusion*, their common republican form, and had broken up the Party of Order into its original component parts; but the more the estrangement between Claremont and Venice grew, the more their settlement broke down and the Joinville agitation gained ground, so much the more eager and earnest became the negotiations between Bonaparte's minister Faucher and the Legitimists.

The disintegration of the Party of Order did not stop at its original elements. Each of the two great factions, in its turn, underwent decomposition anew. It was as if all the old nuances that had formerly fought and jostled one another within each of the two circles, whether Legitimist or Orleanist, had thawed out again like dry infusoria on contact with water, as if they had acquired anew sufficient vital energy to form groups of their own and independent antagonisms. The Legitimists dreamed that they were back among the controversies between the Tuileries and the Pavillon Marsan, between Villèle and Polignac.[113] The Orleanists relived the golden days of the tourneys between Guizot, Molé, Broglie, Thiers and Odilon Barrot.

That part of the Party of Order which was eager for revision, but was divided again on the limits to revision, a section composed of the Legitimists led by Berryer and Falloux, on the one hand, and by La Rochejaquelein, on the other, and of the conflict-weary Orleanists led by Molé, Broglie, Montalembert and Odilon Barrot, agreed with the Bonapartist representatives on the following indefinite and broadly framed motion:

"With the object of restoring to the nation the full exercise of its sovereignty, the undersigned representatives move that the Constitution be revised."[a]

At the same time, however, they unanimously declared through their reporter Tocqueville that the National Assembly had not the right to move the *abolition of the republic*, that this right was vested solely in the Revising Chamber. For the rest, the Constitution might be revised only in a "*legal*" *manner*, hence only if the constitutionally prescribed three-quarters of the number of votes were cast in favour of revision. On July 19, after six days of stormy debate, revision was rejected, as was to be anticipated. Four hundred and forty-six votes were cast for it, but two hundred and seventy-eight against. The extreme Orleanists, Thiers, Changarnier, etc., voted with the republicans and the Montagne.

Thus the majority of parliament declared against the Constitution, but this Constitution itself declared for the minority and that its vote was binding. But had not the Party of Order subordinated the Constitution to the parliamentary majority on May 31, 1850, and on June 13, 1849? Up to now, was not its whole policy based on the

---

[a] The motion was tabled at the sitting of the Legislative Assembly on June 2, 1851. See *Le Moniteur universel*, No. 154, June 3, 1851.— *Ed.*

subordination of the paragraphs of the Constitution to the decisions of the parliamentary majority? Had it not left to the democrats the Old Testament-style superstitious belief in the letter of the law, and castigated the democrats for it? At the present moment, however, revision of the Constitution meant nothing but continuation of the presidential authority, just as continuation of the Constitution meant nothing but Bonaparte's deposition. Parliament had declared for him, but the Constitution declared against parliament. He therefore acted in the sense of parliament when he tore up the Constitution, and he acted in the sense of the Constitution when he dispersed parliament.

Parliament had declared the Constitution and, with the latter, its own rule to be "beyond the majority"; by its vote it had abolished the Constitution and prorogued the presidential power, while declaring at the same time that neither can the one die nor the other live so long as it itself continues to exist. Those who were to bury it were standing at the door. While it debated on revision, Bonaparte removed General Baraguay d'Hilliers, who had proved irresolute, from the command of the First Army Division and appointed in his place General Magnan, the victor of Lyons,[114] the hero of the December days, one of his creatures, who under Louis Philippe had already compromised himself more or less in Bonaparte's favour on the occasion of the Boulogne expedition.

The Party of Order proved by its decision on revision that it knew neither how to rule nor how to serve; neither how to live nor how to die; neither how to endure the republic nor how to overthrow it; neither how to uphold the Constitution nor how to throw it overboard; neither how to co-operate with the President nor how to break with him. To whom, then, did it look for the solution of all the contradictions? To the calendar, to the course of events. It ceased to presume to sway the events. It therefore challenged the events to assume sway over it, and thereby challenged the power to which in the struggle against the people it had surrendered one attribute after another until it itself stood impotent before this power. In order that the head of the executive power might be able the more undisturbedly to draw up his plan of campaign against it, strengthen his means of attack, select his tools and fortify his positions, it resolved precisely at this critical moment to retire from the stage and adjourn for three months, from August 10 to November 4.

The parliamentary party was not only dissolved into its two great factions, each of these factions was not only split within itself, but the Party of Order in parliament had fallen out with the Party of Order *outside* parliament. The spokesmen and scribes of the bourgeoisie, its platform and its press, in short, the ideologists of the bourgeoisie and the bourgeoisie itself, the representatives and the represented, were alienated from one another and no longer understood each other.

The Legitimists in the provinces, with their limited horizon and their unlimited enthusiasm, accused their parliamentary leaders, Berryer and Falloux, of deserting to the Bonapartist camp and of defection from Henry V. Their minds, pure as the fleur-de-lis,[a] believed in the fall of man, but not in diplomacy.

Far more fateful and decisive was the breach of the commercial bourgeoisie with its politicians. It reproached them, not as the Legitimists reproached theirs, with having abandoned their principles, but, on the contrary, with clinging to principles that had become useless.

I have already indicated above that since Fould's entry into the ministry the section of the commercial bourgeoisie which had held the lion's share of power under Louis Philippe, namely, the *finance aristocracy*, had become Bonapartist. Fould represented not only Bonaparte's interests in the *bourse*, he represented at the same time the interests of the *bourse* before Bonaparte. The position of the finance aristocracy is most strikingly depicted in a passage from its European organ, the London *Economist*. In its issue of February 1, 1851, its Paris correspondent writes:

"Now we have it stated from numerous quarters that above all things France demands tranquillity. The President declares it in his message to the Legislative Assembly[b]; it is echoed from the tribune; it is asserted in the journals; it is announced from the pulpit; *it is demonstrated by the sensitiveness of the public funds at the least prospect of disturbance, and their firmness the instant it is made manifest that the executive is victorious.*"

In its issue of November 29, 1851, *The Economist* declares in its own name:

"*The President is the guardian of order, and is now recognised as such on every Stock Exchange of Europe.*"

The finance aristocracy, therefore, condemned the parliamentary struggle of the Party of Order with the executive power as a *disturbance of order*, and celebrated every victory of the President over its ostensible representatives as a *victory of order*. By finance aristocracy must here be understood not merely the great loan

---

[a] The emblem of the Bourbon dynasty.— *Ed.*

[b] The message of November 12, 1850 (see this volume, p. 152).— *Ed.*

promoters and speculators in public funds, in regard to whom it is immediately obvious that their interests coincide with the interests of the state power. All modern finance, the whole of the banking business, is interwoven in the closest fashion with public credit. A part of their business capital is necessarily invested and put out at interest in quickly convertible public funds. Their deposits, the capital placed at their disposal and distributed by them among merchants and industrialists, are partly derived from the dividends of holders of government securities. If in every epoch the stability of the state power was like Moses and the prophets to the entire money market and to the priests of this money market, why not all the more so today, when every deluge threatens to sweep away the old states, and the old state debts with them?

The *industrial bourgeoisie*, too, in its fanaticism for order, was angered by the squabbles of the parliamentary Party of Order with the executive power. After their vote of January 18 on the occasion of Changarnier's dismissal, Thiers, Anglas, Sainte-Beuve, etc., received from their constituents, precisely in the industrial districts, public reproofs in which their coalition with the Montagne was specifically scourged as high treason to order. If, as we have seen, the boastful taunts, the petty intrigues which marked the struggle of the Party of Order with the President merited no better reception, then, on the other hand, this bourgeois party, which required its representatives to allow the military power to pass from its own parliament to an adventurous pretender without offering resistance, was not even worth the intrigues that were squandered in its interests. It proved that the struggle to maintain its *public* interests, its own *class interests*, its *political power*, only troubled and upset it, as it was a disturbance of private business.

With barely an exception, the bourgeois dignitaries of the departmental towns, the municipal authorities, the judges of the Commercial Courts, etc., everywhere received Bonaparte on his tours in the most servile manner, even when, as in Dijon, he made an unrestrained attack on the National Assembly, and especially on the Party of Order.[a]

When trade was good, as it still was at the beginning of 1851, the commercial bourgeoisie raged against any parliamentary struggle, lest trade be put out of humour. When trade was bad, as it continually was from the end of February 1851, the commercial

---

[a] L.-N. Bonaparte, "Réponse [au discours du maire de Dijon au banquet offert par la ville à M. le Président de la République, le 1 juin 1851]", *Le Moniteur universel*, No. 154, June 3, 1851.— *Ed.*

bourgeoisie accused the parliamentary struggles of being the cause
of stagnation and cried out for them to stop in order that trade might
start again. The revision debates came precisely in this bad period.
Since the question here was whether the existing form of state was to
be or not to be, the bourgeoisie felt itself all the more justified in
demanding from its representatives the ending of this torturous
provisional arrangement and at the same time the maintenance of
the *status quo*. There was no contradiction in this. By the end of the
provisional arrangement it understood precisely its continuation, the
postponement to a distant future of the moment when a decision had
to be reached. The *status quo* could be maintained in only two ways:
prolongation of Bonaparte's authority or his constitutional retirement and the election of Cavaignac. A section of the bourgeoisie
desired the latter solution and knew no better advice to give its
representatives than to keep silent and leave the burning question
untouched. They were of the opinion that if their representatives did
not speak, Bonaparte would not act. They wanted an ostrich
parliament that would hide its head in order to remain unseen.
Another section of the bourgeoisie desired, because Bonaparte was
already in the presidential chair, to leave him sitting in it, so that
everything might remain in the same old rut. They were indignant
because their parliament did not openly infringe the Constitution
and abdicate without ceremony.

The General Councils of the departments, those provincial
representative bodies of the big bourgeoisie, which met from August
25 on during the recess of the National Assembly, declared almost
unanimously for revision, and thus against parliament and in favour
of Bonaparte.

Still more unequivocally than in falling out with its *parliamentary
representatives* did the bourgeoisie display its wrath against its literary
representatives, its own press. The sentences of ruinous fines and
shameless terms of imprisonment, on the verdicts of bourgeois
juries, for every attack by bourgeois journalists on Bonaparte's
usurpationist desires, for every attempt by the press to defend the
political rights of the bourgeoisie against the executive power,
astonished not merely France, but all Europe.

While the *parliamentary Party of Order*, by its clamour for
tranquillity, as I have shown, committed itself to quiescence, while it
declared the political rule of the bourgeoisie to be incompatible with
the safety and existence of the bourgeoisie, by destroying with its
own hands in the struggle against the other classes of society all the
conditions for its own regime, the parliamentary regime, the
extra-parliamentary mass of the bourgeoisie, on the other hand, by its

servility towards the President, by its vilification of parliament, by its brutal maltreatment of its own press, invited Bonaparte to suppress and annihilate its speaking and writing section, its politicians and its *literati*, its platform and its press, in order that it might then be able to pursue its private affairs with full confidence in the protection of a strong and unrestricted government. It declared unequivocally that it longed to get rid of its own political rule in order to get rid of the troubles and dangers of ruling.

And this extra-parliamentary bourgeoisie,[a] which had already rebelled against the purely parliamentary and literary struggle for the rule of its own class and betrayed the leaders of this struggle, now dares after the event to indict the proletariat for not having risen in a bloody struggle, a life-and-death struggle on its behalf! This bourgeoisie, which every moment sacrificed its general class interests, that is, its political interests, to the narrowest and most sordid private interests, and demanded a similar sacrifice from its representatives, now moans that the proletariat has sacrificed its [the bourgeoisie's] ideal political interests to its [the proletariat's] material interests. It poses as a lovely being that has been misunderstood and deserted in the decisive hour by the proletariat misled by socialists. And it finds a general echo in the bourgeois world. Naturally, I do not speak here of hole-and-corner German politicians and opinionated boobies. I refer, for example, to the already quoted *Economist*, which as late as November 29, 1851, that is, four days prior to the coup d'état, had declared Bonaparte to be the "guardian of order", but the Thiers and Berryers to be "anarchists", and on December 27, 1851, after Bonaparte had quieted these anarchists, is already vociferous concerning the treason to "the skill, knowledge, discipline, mental influence, intellectual resources and moral weight of the middle and upper ranks" committed by the masses of "ignorant, untrained, and stupid *proletaires*". The stupid, ignorant and vulgar mass was none other than the bourgeois mass itself.

In the year 1851, France had admittedly passed through a kind of minor trade crisis. The end of February showed a decline in exports compared with 1850; in March trade suffered and factories closed down; in April the position of the industrial departments appeared as desperate as after the February days; in May business had still not revived; as late as June 28 the holdings of the Bank of France showed, by the enormous growth of deposits and the equally great

---

[a] The 1852 edition has: "And this miserable, cowardly extra-parliamentary bourgeoisie,..." — *Ed.*

decrease in advances on bills of exchange, that production was at a standstill, and it was not until the middle of October that a progressive improvement of business again set in. The French bourgeoisie attributed this trade stagnation to purely political causes, to the struggle between parliament and the executive power, to the precariousness of a merely provisional form of state, to the terrifying prospect of the second Sunday in May 1852. I will not deny that all these circumstances had a depressing effect on some branches of industry in Paris and the departments. But in every case this influence of the political conditions was only local and inconsiderable. Does this require further proof than the fact that the improvement of trade set in towards the middle of October, at the very moment when the political situation grew worse, the political horizon darkened and a thunderbolt from Elysium[a] was expected at any moment? For the rest, the French bourgeois, whose "skill, knowledge, spiritual insight and intellectual resources" reach no further than his nose, could throughout the period of the Great Exhibition in London[115] have found the cause of his commercial misery right under his nose. While in France factories were closed down, in England commercial bankruptcies broke out. While in April and May the industrial panic reached a climax in France, in April and May the commercial panic reached a climax in England. The French woollen industry suffered alongside the English, and the French silk manufacture with the English too. True, the English cotton mills continued working, but no longer at the same profits as in 1849 and 1850. The only difference was that the crisis in France was industrial, in England commercial; that while in France the factories stood idle, in England they extended operations, but under less favourable conditions than in preceding years; that in France it was exports, in England imports which were hardest hit. The common cause, which is naturally not to be sought within the bounds of the French political horizon, was obvious. The years 1849 and 1850 were years of the greatest material prosperity and of an over-production that appeared as such only in 1851. At the beginning of this year it was given a further special impetus by the prospect of the Great Exhibition. In addition there were the following special circumstances: first, the partial failure of the cotton crop in 1850 and 1851, then the certainty of a bigger cotton crop than had been expected; first the rise, then the sudden fall, in short, the fluctuations in the price of cotton. The crop of raw silk, in France

---

[a] A pun: Elysium here means both the skies and the Presidential palace in the Champs Elysées.— *Ed.*

at least, had turned out to be even below the average yield. Woollen manufacture, finally, had expanded so much since 1848 that the production of wool could not keep pace with it and the price of raw wool rose out of all proportion to the price of woollen manufactures. Here, then, in the raw material of three industries producing for the world market, we have already threefold material for a stagnation in trade. Apart from these special circumstances, the apparent crisis of 1851 was nothing else but the halt which over-production and over-speculation invariably make in describing the industrial cycle, before they summon all their strength in order to rush feverishly through the final phase of this cycle and arrive once more at their starting-point, the *general trade crisis*. During such intervals in the history of trade commercial bankruptcies break out in England, while in France industry itself is reduced to idleness, being partly forced into retreat by the competition, just then becoming intolerable, of the English in all markets, and being partly singled out for attack as a luxury industry by every business stagnation. Thus, besides the general crises, France goes through national trade crises of her own, which are nevertheless determined and conditioned far more by the general state of the world market than by French local influences. It will not be without interest to contrast the judgment of the English bourgeois with the prejudice of the French bourgeois. In its annual trade report for 1851, one of the largest Liverpool houses writes:

"Few years have more thoroughly belied the anticipations formed at their commencement than the one just closed; instead of the great prosperity which was almost unanimously looked for it has proved one of the most discouraging that has been seen for the last quarter of a century—this, of course, refers to the mercantile, not to the manufacturing classes. And yet there certainly were grounds for anticipating the reverse at the beginning of the year—stocks of produce were moderate, money was abundant, and food was cheap, a plentiful harvest well secured, unbroken peace on the Continent, and no political or fiscal disturbances at home; indeed, the wings of commerce were never more unfettered.... To what source, then, is this disastrous result to be attributed? We believe to *over-trading* both in imports and exports. Unless our merchants will put more stringent limits to their freedom of action, nothing but a *triennial* panic can keep us in check."[a]

Now picture to yourself the French bourgeois, how in the throes of this business panic his trade-crazy brain is tortured, set in a whirl and stunned by rumours of coups d'état and the restoration of universal suffrage, by the struggle between parliament and the executive power, by the Fronde between Orleanists and Legitimists,

---

[a] "The Spirit of the Annual Trade Circulars. The Year That Is Past", *The Economist*, No. 437, January 10, 1852.— *Ed.*

by the communist conspiracies in the south of France,. by alleged *Jacqueries* in the departments of Nièvre and Cher, by the advertisements of the different candidates for the presidency, by the cheapjack slogans of the journals, by the threats of the republicans to uphold the Constitution and universal suffrage by force of arms, by the gospels of the émigré heroes *in partibus*,[a] who announced that the world would come to an end on the second Sunday in May 1852—think of all this and you will understand why in this unspeakable, deafening chaos of fusion, revision, prorogation, constitution, conspiration, coalition, emigration, usurpation and revolution, the bourgeois madly snorts at his parliamentary republic: "*Rather an end with terror than terror without end!*"

Bonaparte understood this cry. His power of comprehension was sharpened by the growing turbulence of creditors who, with each sunset which brought settling day, the second Sunday in May 1852, nearer, saw a movement of the stars protesting their earthly bills of exchange. They had become veritable astrologers. The National Assembly had blighted Bonaparte's hopes of a constitutional prorogation of his authority; the candidature of the Prince of Joinville forbade further vacillation.

If ever an event has, well in advance of its coming, cast its shadow before it, it was Bonaparte's coup d'état. As early as January 29, 1849, barely a month after his election, he had made a proposal about it to Changarnier. In the summer of 1849 his own Prime Minister, Odilon Barrot, had covertly denounced the policy of coups d'état; in the winter of 1850 Thiers had openly done so. In May 1851 Persigny had sought once more to win Changarnier for the coup; the *Messager de l'Assemblée* had published an account of these negotiations. During every parliamentary storm, the Bonapartist journals threatened a coup d'état, and the nearer the crisis drew, the louder grew their tone. In the orgies that Bonaparte kept up every night with men and women of the swell mob,[b] as soon as the hour of midnight approached and rich libations had loosened tongues and fired imaginations, the coup d'état was fixed for the following morning. Swords were drawn, glasses clinked, representatives were thrown out of the window, and the imperial mantle fell upon Bonaparte's shoulders, until the following morning banished the spook once more and astonished Paris learned, from vestals of little reticence and from indiscreet paladins, of the danger it had once again escaped. During the months of September and October

---

[a] Abroad.— *Ed.*
[b] Marx uses the English expression "swell mob".— *Ed.*

rumours of a coup d'état followed thick and fast. Simultaneously, the shadow took on colour, like a variegated daguerreotype. Look up the September and October copies of the organs of the European daily press and you will find, word for word, intimations like the following: "Paris is full of rumours of a coup d'état. The capital is to be filled with troops during the night, and the next morning is to bring decrees which will dissolve the National Assembly, declare the department of the Seine in a state of siege, restore universal suffrage and appeal to the people. Bonaparte is said to be seeking ministers for the execution of these illegal decrees." The reports that bring these tidings always end with the fateful word *"postponed"*. The coup d'état was ever the fixed idea of Bonaparte. With this idea he had again set foot on French soil. He was so obsessed by it that he continually betrayed it and blurted it out. He was so weak that, just as continually, he gave it up again. The shadow of the coup d'état had become so familiar to the Parisians as a spectre that they were not willing to believe in it when it finally appeared in the flesh. What allowed the coup d'état to succeed was, therefore, neither the reticent reserve of the chief of the Society of December 10 nor the fact that the National Assembly was caught unawares. If it succeeded, it succeeded despite *his* indiscretion and with *its* foreknowledge, a necessary, inevitable result of antecedent development.

On October 10 Bonaparte announced to his ministers his decision to restore universal suffrage; on the 16th they handed in their resignations; on the 26th Paris learned of the formation of the Thorigny ministry. Police Prefect Carlier was simultaneously replaced by Maupas; the head of the First Army Division, Magnan, concentrated the most reliable regiments in the capital. On November 4 the National Assembly resumed its sittings. It had nothing better to do than to recapitulate in a short, succinct form the course it had gone through and to prove that it was buried only after it had died.

The first post that it forfeited in the struggle with the executive power was the ministry. It had solemnly to admit this loss by accepting at full value the Thorigny ministry, a mere sham. The Permanent Commission had received M. Giraud with laughter when he presented himself in the name of the new ministers. Such a weak ministry for such strong measures as the restoration of universal suffrage! Yet the precise object was to get nothing through *in* parliament, but everything *against* parliament.

On the very first day of its re-opening, the National Assembly received the message from Bonaparte in which he demanded the restoration of universal suffrage and the abolition of the law of May 31, 1850. The same day his ministers introduced a decree to this effect. The National Assembly at once rejected the ministry's motion of urgency and rejected the law itself on November 13 by 355 votes to 348. Thus, it tore up its mandate once more; it once more confirmed the fact that it had transformed itself from the freely elected representatives of the people into the usurpatory parliament of a class; it acknowledged once more that it had itself cut in two the muscles which connected the parliamentary head with the body of the nation.

If by its motion to restore universal suffrage the executive power appealed from the National Assembly to the people, the legislative power appealed by its Questors' Bill from the people to the army. This Questors' Bill was to establish its right of directly requisitioning troops, of forming a parliamentary army. While it thus designated the army as the arbitrator between itself and the people, between itself and Bonaparte, while it recognised the army as the decisive state power, it had to confirm, on the other hand, the fact that it had long given up its claim to dominate this power. By debating its right to requisition troops, instead of requisitioning them at once, it betrayed its doubts about its own powers. By rejecting the Questors' Bill, it made public confession of its impotence. This bill was defeated, its proponents lacking 108 votes of a majority. The Montagne thus decided the issue. It found itself in the position of Buridan's ass, not, indeed, between two bundles of hay with the problem of deciding which was the more attractive, but between two showers of blows with the problem of deciding which was the harder. On the one hand, there was the fear of Changarnier; on the other, the fear of Bonaparte. It must be confessed that the position was no heroic one.

On November 18 an amendment was moved to the law on municipal elections introduced by the Party of Order, to the effect that instead of three years', one year's domicile should suffice for municipal electors. The amendment was lost by a single vote, but this one vote immediately proved to be a mistake. By splitting up into its hostile factions, the Party of Order had long ago forfeited its independent parliamentary majority. It showed now that there was no longer any majority at all in parliament. The National Assembly had become *incapable of transacting business.* Its atomised constituents were no longer held together by any force of cohesion; it had drawn its last breath; it was dead.

Finally, a few days before the catastrophe, the extra-parliamentary mass of the bourgeoisie was solemnly to confirm once more its breach with the bourgeoisie in parliament. Thiers, as a parliamentary hero infected more than the rest with the incurable disease of parliamentary cretinism, had, after the death of parliament, hatched out, together with the Council of State, a new parliamentary intrigue, a Responsibility Law by which the President was to be firmly held within the limits of the Constitution. Just as, on laying the foundation stone of the new market halls in Paris on September 15, Bonaparte, like a second Masaniello, had enchanted the *dames des halles*, the fishwives—to be sure, one fishwife outweighed seventeen burgraves in real power; just as after the introduction of the Questors' Bill he enraptured the lieutenants he regaled in the Elysée, so now, on November 25, he swept off their feet the industrial bourgeoisie, which had gathered at the circus to receive at his hands prize medals for the London Industrial Exhibition. I shall give the significant portion of his speech as reported in the *Journal des Débats*[a]:

> "With such unhoped-for successes, I am justified in reiterating how great the French Republic would be if it were permitted to pursue its real interests and reform its institutions, instead of being constantly disturbed by demagogues, on the one hand, and by monarchist hallucinations, on the other. (Loud, stormy and repeated applause from every part of the amphitheatre.) The monarchist hallucinations hinder all progress and all important branches of industry. In place of progress nothing but struggle. One sees men who were formerly the most zealous supporters of the royal authority and prerogative become partisans of a Convention merely in order to weaken the authority that has sprung from universal suffrage. (Loud and repeated applause.) We see men who have suffered most from the Revolution, and have deplored it most, provoke a new one, and merely in order to fetter the nation's will.... I promise you tranquillity for the future, etc., etc. (Bravo, bravo, a storm of bravos.)"

Thus the industrial bourgeoisie applauds with servile bravos the coup d'état of December 2, the annihilation of parliament, the downfall of its own rule, the dictatorship of Bonaparte. The thunder of applause on November 25 had its answer in the thunder of cannon on December 4,[116] and it was on the house of Monsieur Sallandrouze, who had clapped most, that they clapped most of the bombs.

Cromwell, when he dissolved the Long Parliament, went alone into its midst, drew out his watch in order that it should not continue to exist a minute after the time limit fixed by him, and drove out each one of the members of parliament with jovial humorous taunts. Napoleon, smaller than his prototype, at least betook himself on the eighteenth Brumaire to the legislative body and read out to it,

---

[a] For November 26, 1851.—*Ed.*

though in a faltering voice, its sentence of death. The second Bonaparte, who, moreover, found himself in possession of an executive power very different from that of Cromwell or Napoleon, sought his model not in the annals of world history, but in the annals of the Society of December 10, in the annals of the criminal courts. He robs the Bank of France of twenty-five million francs, buys General Magnan with a million, the soldiers with fifteen francs apiece and liquor, comes together with his accomplices secretly like a thief in the night, has the houses of the most dangerous parliamentary leaders broken into and Cavaignac, Lamoricière, Le Flô, Changarnier, Charras, Thiers, Baze, etc., dragged from their beds, the key points of Paris and the parliamentary building occupied by troops, and cheapjack placards posted early in the morning on all the walls, proclaiming the dissolution of the National Assembly and the Council of State, the restoration of universal suffrage and the placing of the Seine department in a state of siege. In like manner, he inserted a little later in the *Moniteur*[a] a false document which asserted that influential parliamentarians had grouped themselves round him and formed a state *consulta*.

The rump parliament, assembled in the *mairie* building of the tenth *arrondissement* and consisting mainly of Legitimists and Orleanists, votes the deposition of Bonaparte amid repeated cries of "Long live the Republic", unavailingly harangues the gaping crowds before the building and is finally led off in the custody of African sharpshooters, first to the d'Orsay barracks, and later packed into prison vans and transported to the prisons of Mazas, Ham and Vincennes. Thus ended the Party of Order, the Legislative Assembly and the February revolution.

Before hastening to close, let us briefly summarise the latter's history:

I. *First period*. From February 24 to May 4, 1848. February period. Prologue. Universal brotherhood swindle.

II. *Second period*. Period of constituting the republic and of the Constituent National Assembly.

    1. May 4 to June 25, 1848. Struggle of all classes against the proletariat. Defeat of the proletariat in the June days.

    2. June 25 to December 10, 1848. Dictatorship of the pure bourgeois republicans. Drafting of the Constitution. Proclamation of a state of siege in Paris. The bourgeois dictatorship set aside on December 10 by the election of Bonaparte as President.

---

[a] For December 3, 1851.— *Ed.*

3. December 20, 1848 to May 28, 1849. Struggle of the Constituent Assembly with Bonaparte and with the Party of Order in alliance with him. End of the Constituent Assembly. Fall of the republican bourgeoisie.

III. *Third period.* Period of the *constitutional republic* and of the *Legislative National Assembly.*

1. May 28, 1849 to June 13, 1849. Struggle of the petty bourgeoisie with the bourgeoisie and with Bonaparte. Defeat of the petty-bourgeois democracy.

2. June 13, 1849 to May 31, 1850. Parliamentary dictatorship of the Party of Order. It completes its rule by abolishing universal suffrage, but loses the parliamentary ministry.

3. May 31, 1850 to December 2, 1851. Struggle between the parliamentary bourgeoisie and Bonaparte.

a) May 31, 1850 to January 12, 1851. Parliament loses the supreme command of the army.

b) January 12 to April 11, 1851. It is worsted in its attempts to regain the administrative power. The Party of Order loses its independent parliamentary majority. Its coalition with the republicans and the Montagne.

c) April 11, 1851 to October 9, 1851. Attempts at revision, fusion, prorogation. The Party of Order dissolves into its separate constituents. The breach of the bourgeois parliament and bourgeois press with the mass of the bourgeoisie hardens.

d) October 9 to December 2, 1851. Open breach between parliament and the executive power. Parliament performs its dying act and succumbs, left in the lurch by its own class, by the army and by all the remaining classes. End of the parliamentary regime and of bourgeois rule. Victory of Bonaparte. Empire restored as parody.

VII

On the threshold of the February revolution, the *social republic* appeared as a phrase, as a prophecy. In the June days of 1848, it was drowned in the blood of the *Paris proletariat,* but it haunts the subsequent acts of the drama like a ghost. The *democratic republic* announces its arrival. On June 13, 1849 it is dissipated together with its *petty bourgeois,* who have taken to their heels, but in its flight it blows its own trumpet with redoubled boastfulness. The *parliamentary republic*, together with the bourgeoisie, takes possession of the entire stage; it enjoys its existence to the full, but December 2, 1851 buries it to the accompaniment of the anguished cry of the coalitioned royalists: "Long live the Republic!"[a]

The French bourgeoisie balked at the power of the working proletariat; it has brought the lumpenproletariat to power, with the chief of the Society of December 10 at the head. The bourgeoisie kept France in breathless fear of the future terrors of red anarchy; Bonaparte discounted this future for it when, on December 4, he had the eminent bourgeois of the Boulevard Montmartre and the Boulevard des Italiens shot down at their windows by the liquor-inspired army of order. The bourgeoisie apotheosised the sword; the sword rules it. It destroyed the revolutionary press; its own press has been destroyed. It placed popular meetings under police supervision; its salons are under the supervision of the police. It disbanded the democratic National Guards; its own National Guard is disbanded. It imposed a state of siege; a state of siege is imposed upon it. It supplanted the juries by military commissions; its juries are supplanted by military commissions. It subjected public education to the sway of the priests; the priests subject it to their own education.[b] It transported people without trial; it is being transported without trial. It repressed every stirring in society by means of the state power; every stirring in its society is suppressed by the state power. Out of enthusiasm for its purse, it rebelled against its own politicians and men of letters; its politicians and men of letters are swept aside, but its purse is being plundered now that its mouth has been gagged and its pen broken. The bourgeoisie never wearied of crying out to the revolution what Saint Arsenius cried out to the Christians: "*Fuge, tace, quiesce!* Flee, be silent, keep still!" Bonaparte cries to the bourgeoisie: "*Fuge, tace, quiesce!* Flee, be silent, keep still!"

The French bourgeoisie had long ago found the solution to Napoleon's dilemma: "*Dans cinquante ans, l'Europe sera républicaine ou cosaque*."[c] It had found the solution to it in the "*république cosaque*".

---

[a] The 1852 edition has the following paragraph here: "The social and the democratic republic suffered defeats, but the parliamentary republic, the republic of the royalist bourgeoisie foundered, as did the pure republic, the republic of the bourgeois republicans."— *Ed.*

[b] According to the list of misprints in the 1852 edition, the second part of this sentence should read as follows: "the priests subjected themselves to their own education". However, this alteration was not reproduced in the 1869 edition.— *Ed.*

[c] "In fifty years Europe will be republican or Cossack." (The words are taken from the book by Las Cases, *Mémorial de Sainte-Hélène*.)— *Ed.*

No Circe, by means of black magic, has distorted that work of art, the bourgeois republic, into a monstrous shape. That republic has lost nothing but the semblance of respectability.[a] Present-day France[b] was contained in a finished state within the parliamentary republic. It only required a bayonet thrust for the abcess to burst and the monster to spring forth before our eyes.[c]

---

[a] In the 1852 edition this sentence reads as follows: "That republic has lost nothing but its rhetoric arabesques, its manners, in a word, the semblance of respectability."— *Ed.*

[b] France after the coup d'état of 1851.— *Ed.*

[c] In the 1852 edition two paragraphs follow here:

"The immediate aim of the February revolution was to overthrow the Orleans dynasty and that part of the bourgeoisie which ruled under it. It was not until December 2, 1851 that this aim was achieved. Then the immense possessions of the house of Orleans, the real basis of its influence, were confiscated, and what had been expected after the February revolution came to pass after December: the imprisonment, flight, deposition, banishment, disarming and humiliation of the men who from 1830 on had wearied France with their appeals. But only part of the commercial bourgeoisie ruled under Louis Philippe. Its other factions formed a dynastic and a republican opposition or stood entirely outside the so-called legal country [Marx has *legalen Landes*, which is a translation of the French expression *pays légal*]. Only the parliamentary republic included all factions of the commercial bourgeoisie in its political sphere. Moreover, under Louis Philippe the commercial bourgeoisie excluded the landowning bourgeoisie. Only the parliamentary republic placed them side by side as possessing equal rights, wedded the July monarchy to the Legitimist monarchy and amalgamated two epochs of the rule of property into one. Under Louis Philippe the privileged part of the bourgeoisie concealed its rule beneath the crown; in the parliamentary republic the rule of the bourgeoisie—after it had united all its elements and made its empire the empire of its class—revealed itself. So the revolution had first created the form in which the rule of the bourgeois class received its broadest, most general and ultimate expression and could therefore also be overthrown, without being able to rise again.

"Only now was the sentence executed which was passed in February upon the Orleanist bourgeoisie, i.e. the most viable faction of the French bourgeoisie. Now a crushing blow was struck at its parliament, its legal courts, its commercial courts, its provincial representations, its notary's office, its university, its tribune and its tribunals, its press and its literature, its administrative income and its court fees, its army salaries and its state pensions, in its spirit and in its body. *Blanqui* had made the disbanding of the bourgeois guards the first demand on the revolution, and the bourgeois guards, who in February extended their hand to the revolution in order to hinder its progress, disappeared from the scene in December. The Pantheon itself is again turned into an ordinary church. With the last form of the bourgeois regime, the spell too has been broken which transfigured its eighteenth-century founders into saints. Therefore when on December 2 Guizot learned about the success of the coup d'état, he exclaimed: *C'est le triomphe complet et définitif du socialisme! This is the complete and final triumph of socialism!* That means: this is the final and complete collapse of the rule of the bourgeoisie."— *Ed.*

Why did the Paris proletariat not rise in revolt after December 2?[a]

The overthrow of the bourgeoisie had as yet been only decreed: the decree had not been carried out. Any serious insurrection of the proletariat would at once have put fresh life into the bourgeoisie, would have reconciled it with the army and ensured a second June defeat for the workers.

On December 4 the proletariat was incited by bourgeois and *épicier*[b] to fight. On the evening of that day several legions of the National Guard promised to appear, armed and uniformed, on the scene of battle. For the bourgeois and the *épicier* had got wind of the fact that in one of his decrees of December 2 Bonaparte abolished the secret ballot and enjoined them to record their "yes" or "no" in the official registers after their names. The resistance[c] of December 4 intimidated Bonaparte. During the night he caused placards to be posted on all the street corners of Paris, announcing the restoration of the secret ballot. The bourgeois and the *épicier* believed that they had gained their end. Those who failed to appear next morning were the bourgeois and the *épicier*.

By a *coup de main* during the night of December 1 to 2, Bonaparte had robbed the Paris proletariat of its leaders, the barricade commanders. An army without officers, averse to fighting under the banner of the Montagnards because of the memories of June 1848 and 1849 and May 1850,[d] it left to its vanguard, the secret societies, the task of saving the insurrectionary honour of Paris, which the bourgeoisie had so unresistingly surrendered to the soldiery that, later on, Bonaparte could sneeringly give as his motive for disarming the National Guard—his fear that its arms would be turned against itself by the anarchists![e]

"*C'est le triomphe complet et définitif du socialisme!*" Thus Guizot characterised December 2. But if the overthrow of the parliamentary republic contains within itself the germ of the triumph of the proletarian revolution, its immediate and palpable result was *the victory of Bonaparte over parliament, of the executive power over the*

---

[a] In the 1852 edition this paragraph reads as follows: "Why did the proletariat not rescue the bourgeoisie? Implied in this is the question: Why did the Paris proletariat not rise in revolt after December 2?"—*Ed.*

[b] Pejorative term for shopkeeper.—*Ed.*

[c] In the 1852 edition: "The bloody resistance".—*Ed.*

[d] In the 1852 edition the beginning of this sentence reads as follows: "An army without officers, too enlightened by its memories of June 1848 and 1849 and May 1850 to fight under the banner of the Montagnards, it was therefore correctly assessing its own strength and the general situation when...."—*Ed.*

In the 1852 edition: "his fear, not that it would turn its arms against him, but that the anarchists would turn them against itself".—*Ed.*

legislative power, of force without words over the force of words.[a] In parliament the nation made its general will the law, that is, it made the law of the ruling class its general will. Before the executive power it renounces all will of its own and submits to the superior command of an alien will, to authority. The executive power, in contrast to the legislative power, expresses the heteronomy of a nation, in contrast to its autonomy. France, therefore, seems to have escaped the despotism of a class only to fall back beneath the despotism of an individual, and, what is more, beneath the authority of an individual without authority. The struggle seems to be settled in such a way that all classes, equally impotent and equally mute, fall on their knees before the rifle butt.

But the revolution is thorough. It is still journeying through purgatory. It does its work methodically. By December 2, 1851 it had completed one half of its preparatory work; it is now completing the other half. First it perfected the parliamentary power, in order to be able to overthrow it. Now that it has attained this, it perfects the *executive power*, reduces it to its purest expression, isolates it, sets it up against itself as the sole target, in order to concentrate all its forces of destruction against it. And when it has done this second half of its preliminary work, Europe will leap from its seat and exultantly exclaim: Well burrowed, old mole![b]

This executive power with its enormous bureaucratic and military organisation, with its extensive and artificial state machinery, with a host of officials numbering half a million, besides an army of another half million, this appalling parasitic body, which enmeshes the body of French society like a net and chokes all its pores, sprang up in the days of the absolute monarchy, with the decay of the feudal system, which it helped to hasten. The seignorial privileges of the landowners and towns became transformed into so many attributes of the state power, the feudal dignitaries into paid officials and the motley pattern of conflicting medieval plenary powers into the regulated plan of a state authority whose work is divided and centralised as in a factory. The first French Revolution, with its task of breaking all separate local, territorial, urban and provincial powers in order to create the civil unity of the nation, was bound to develop what the absolute monarchy had begun: the centralisation, but at the same time the extent, the attributes and the agents of governmental power. Napoleon perfected this state machinery. The

---

[a] The 1852 edition adds: "Thus the one power of the old state is at first only freed from its limitation, becoming an unlimited, absolute power."—*Ed.*

[d] A reference to Shakespeare, *Hamlet*, Act I, Scene 5.—*Ed.*

Legitimist monarchy and the July monarchy added nothing but a greater division of labour, growing in the same measure as the division of labour within bourgeois society created new groups of interests, and, therefore, new material for state administration. Every *common* interest was straightway severed from society, counterposed to it as a higher, *general* interest, snatched from the activity of society's members themselves and made an object of government activity, whether it was a bridge, a schoolhouse and the communal property of a village community, or the railways, the national wealth and the national university of France. Finally, in its struggle against the revolution, the parliamentary republic found itself compelled to strengthen, along with the repressive measures, the resources and centralisation of governmental power. All revolutions perfected this machine instead of breaking it. The parties that contended in turn for domination regarded the possession of this huge state edifice as the principal spoils of the victor.

But under the absolute monarchy, during the first revolution, under Napoleon, bureaucracy was only the means of preparing the class rule of the bourgeoisie. Under the Restoration, under Louis Philippe, under the parliamentary republic, it was the instrument of the ruling class, however much it strove for power of its own.

Only under the second Bonaparte does the state seem to have made itself completely independent.[a] As against civil society, the state machine has consolidated its position so thoroughly that the chief of the Society of December 10 suffices for its head, a casual adventurer from abroad, raised up as leader by a drunken soldiery, which he has bought with liquor and sausages, and which he must continually ply with more sausage. Hence the downcast despair, the feeling of most dreadful humiliation and degradation that oppresses the breast of France and makes her catch her breath. She feels dishonoured.[b]

And yet the state power is not suspended in mid air. Bonaparte

---

[a] In the 1852 edition this sentence reads thus: "Only under the second Bonaparte does the state seem to have made itself independent of society and subjected it." The text went on as follows: "The independence of the executive power emerges into the open when its chief no longer requires genius, its army no longer requires glory, and its bureaucracy no longer requires moral authority in order to justify itself." — *Ed.*

[b] The 1852 edition further has: "Just as Napoleon hardly left her any excuse for freedom, so the second Bonaparte no longer left her any excuse for servitude." — *Ed.*

represents a class, and the most numerous class of French society at that, the *small-holding peasantry.*

Just as the Bourbons were the dynasty of big landed property and just as the Orleans were the dynasty of money, so the Bonapartes are the dynasty of the peasants, that is, the mass of the French people. Not the Bonaparte who submitted to the bourgeois parliament, but the Bonaparte who dispersed the bourgeois parliament is the chosen man of the peasantry. For three years the towns had succeeded in falsifying the meaning of the election of December 10 and in cheating the peasants out of the restoration of the empire. The election of December 10, 1848 has been consummated only by the coup d'état of December 2, 1851.

The small-holding peasants form a vast mass, the members of which live in similar conditions but without entering into manifold relations with one another. Their mode of production isolates them from one another instead of bringing them into mutual intercourse. The isolation is increased by France's bad means of communication and by the poverty of the peasants. Their field of production, the smallholding, admits of no division of labour in its cultivation, no application of science and, therefore, no diversity of development, no variety of talent, no wealth of social relationships. Each individual peasant family is almost self-sufficient; it itself directly produces the major part of its consumption and thus acquires its means of life more through exchange with nature than in intercourse with society. A smallholding, a peasant and his family; alongside them another smallholding, another peasant and another family. A few score of these make up a village, and a few score of villages make up a department. In this way, the great mass of the French nation is formed by simple addition of homologous magnitudes, much as potatoes in a sack form a sack of potatoes. Insofar as millions of families live under economic conditions of existence that separate their mode of life, their interests and their culture from those of the other classes, and put them in hostile opposition to the latter, they form a class. Insofar as there is merely a local interconnection among these small-holding peasants, and the identity of their interests begets no community, no national bond and no political organisation among them, they do not form a class. They are consequently incapable of enforcing their class interests in their own name, whether through a parliament or through a convention. They cannot represent themselves, they must be represented. Their representative must at the same time appear as their master, as an authority over them, as an unlimited governmental power that protects them against the other classes and sends them rain and sunshine from above. The political influence of the small-holding peasants, therefore, finds its final expression in the executive power subordinating society to itself.[a]

Historical tradition gave rise to the belief of the French peasants in the miracle that a man named Napoleon would bring all the glory back to them. And an individual turned up who gives himself out as the man because he bears the name of Napoleon, as a result of the *Code Napoléon,* which lays down that *la recherche de la paternité est interdite.*[b] After a vagabondage of twenty years and after a series of grotesque adventures, the legend finds fulfilment and the man becomes Emperor of the French. The fixed idea of the Nephew was realised, because it coincided with the fixed idea of the most numerous class of the French people.

But, it may be objected, what about the peasant risings in half of France,[117] the raids on the peasants by the army, the mass incarceration and transportation of peasants?

Since Louis XIV, France has experienced no similar persecution of the peasants "for demagogic practices".[118]

But let there be no misunderstanding. The Bonaparte dynasty represents not the revolutionary, but the conservative peasant; not the peasant that strikes out beyond the condition of his social existence, the smallholding, but rather the peasant who wants to consolidate this holding; not the country folk who, linked up with the towns, want to overthrow the old order through their own energies, but on the contrary those who, in stupefied seclusion within this old order, want to see themselves and their smallholdings saved and favoured by the ghost of the empire. It represents not the enlightenment, but the superstition of the peasant; not his judgment, but his prejudice; not his future, but his past; not his modern Cévennes, but his modern Vendée.[119]

The three years' rigorous rule of the parliamentary republic had freed a part of the French peasants from the Napoleonic illusion and had revolutionised them, even if only superficially; but the bourgeoisie violently repressed them whenever they set themselves in motion. Under the parliamentary republic the modern and the traditional consciousness of the French peasant contended for mastery. This progress took the form of an incessant struggle between the schoolmasters and the priests. The bourgeoisie struck down the schoolmasters. For the first time the peasants made efforts

---

[a] In the 1852 edition the end of the sentence reads as follows: "...the executive power subordinating parliament and the state subordinating society to itself".— *Ed.*

[b] Inquiry into paternity is forbidden.— *Ed.*

to behave independently in the face of the activity of the government. This was shown in the continual conflict between the *maires* and the prefects. The bourgeoisie deposed the *maires*. Finally, during the period of the parliamentary republic, the peasants of different localities rose against their own offspring, the army. The bourgeoisie punished them with states of siege and punitive expeditions. And this same bourgeoisie now cries out about the stupidity of the masses, the *vile multitude*,[a] that has betrayed it to Bonaparte. It has itself forcibly strengthened the imperial sentiments of the peasant class, it conserved the conditions that form the birthplace of this peasant religion. The bourgeoisie, to be sure, is bound to fear the stupidity of the masses as long as they remain conservative, and the insight of the masses as soon as they become revolutionary.

In the risings after the coup d'état, a part of the French peasants protested, arms in hand, against their own vote of December 10, 1848. The school they had gone through since 1848 had sharpened their wits. But they had made themselves over to the underworld of history; history held them to their word, and the majority was still so prejudiced that in precisely the reddest departments the peasant population voted openly for Bonaparte. In its view, the National Assembly had hindered his progress. He had now merely broken the fetters that the towns had imposed on the will of the countryside. In some parts the peasants even entertained the grotesque notion of a convention side by side with Napoleon.

After the first revolution had transformed the peasants from semi-villeins into freeholders, Napoleon confirmed and regulated the conditions on which they could exploit undisturbed the soil of France which had only just fallen to their lot and slake their youthful passion for property. But what is now causing the ruin of the French peasant is his smallholding itself, the division of the land, the form of property which Napoleon consolidated in France. It is precisely the material conditions which made the French feudal peasant a small-holding peasant and Napoleon an emperor. Two generations have sufficed to produce the inevitable result: progressive deterioration of agriculture, progressive indebtedness of the agriculturist. The "Napoleonic" form of property, which at the beginning of the nineteenth century was the condition for the liberation and enrichment of the French country folk, has developed in the course of this century into the law of their enslavement and pauperisation.

---

[a] An expression used by Thiers in his speech in the Legislative Assembly on May 24, 1850.— *Ed.*

And precisely this law is the first of the "*idées napoléoniennes*" which the second Bonaparte has to uphold. If he still shares with the peasants the illusion that the cause of their ruin is to be sought, not in this small-holding property itself, but outside it, in the influence of secondary circumstances, his experiments will burst like soap bubbles when they come in contact with the relations of production.[a]

The economic development of small-holding property has radically changed the relation of the peasants to the other classes of society. Under Napoleon, the fragmentation of the land in the countryside supplemented free competition and the beginning of big industry in the towns.[b] The peasant class was the ubiquitous protest against the landed aristocracy which had just been overthrown.[c] The roots that small-holding property struck in French soil deprived feudalism of all nutriment. Its landmarks formed the natural fortifications of the bourgeoisie against any *coup de main* on the part of its old overlords. But in the course of the nineteenth century the feudal lords were replaced by urban usurers; the feudal obligation that went with the land was replaced by the mortgage; aristocratic landed property was replaced by bourgeois capital. The smallholding of the peasant is now only the pretext that allows the capitalist to draw profits, interest and rent from the soil, while leaving it to the tiller of the soil himself to see how he can extract his wages. The mortgage debt burdening the soil of France imposes on the French peasantry payment of an amount of interest equal to the annual interest on the entire British national debt. Small-holding property, in this enslavement by capital to which its development inevitably pushes forward, has transformed the mass of the French nation into troglodytes.[d] Sixteen million peasants (including women and children) dwell in hovels, a large number of which have but one opening, others only two and the most favoured only three. And windows are to a house what the five senses are to the head. The bourgeois order, which at the beginning of the century set the state to stand guard over the newly arisen smallholding and manured it with laurels, has become a vampire that sucks out its blood and brains and throws them into the

---

[a] The 1852 edition adds: "depriving that illusion of its last hiding place and at best making the disease more acute".— *Ed.*

[b] The 1852 edition further has: "Even the advantages given to the peasant class were in the interest of the new bourgeois order. This newly created class was the all-round extension of the bourgeois regime beyond the gates of the towns, its realisation on a national scale."— *Ed.*

[c] The 1852 edition further has: "If it was favoured most of all, it was also suited most of all as a point of attack for the restoration of feudalism."— *Ed.*

[d] In the 1852 edition: "into a nation of troglodytes".— *Ed.*

alchemist's cauldron of capital. The *Code Napoléon* is now nothing but a *codex* of distraints, forced sales and compulsory auctions. To the four million (including children, etc.) officially recognised paupers, vagabonds, criminals and prostitutes in France must be added five million who hover on the margin of existence and either have their haunts in the countryside itself or, with their rags and their children, continually desert the countryside for the towns and the towns for the countryside. The interests of the peasants, therefore, are no longer, as under Napoleon, in accord with, but in opposition[a] to the interests of the bourgeoisie, to capital. Hence the peasants find their natural ally and leader in the *urban proletariat,* whose task is the overthrow of the bourgeois order. But *strong and unlimited govern-ment*—and this is the second *"idée napoléonienne",* which the second Napoleon has to carry out—is called upon to defend this "material" order by force. This *"ordre matériel"* also serves as the catchword in all of Bonaparte's proclamations against the rebellious peasants.

Besides the mortgage which capital imposes on it, the small-holding is burdened by *taxes.* Taxes are the source of life for the bureaucracy, the army, the priests and the court, in short, for the whole apparatus of the executive power. Strong government and heavy taxes are identical. By its very nature, small-holding property forms a suitable basis for an all-powerful and innumerable bureaucracy. It creates a uniform level of relationships and persons over the whole surface of the land. Hence it also permits of uniform action from a supreme centre on all points of this uniform mass. It annihilates the aristocratic intermediate grades between the mass of the people and the state power. On all sides, therefore, it calls forth the direct interference of this state power and the interposition of its immediate organs. Finally, it produces an unemployed surplus population for which there is no place either on the land or in the towns, and which accordingly reaches out for state offices as a sort of respectable alms, and provokes the creation of state posts.[b] By the new markets which he opened at the point of the bayonet, by the plundering of the Continent, Napoleon repaid the compulsory taxes

---

[a] In the 1852 edition: "in the deadliest opposition".— *Ed.*

[b] The 1852 edition further has: "Under Napoleon this numerous government personnel was not only directly productive in that it provided for the new peasantry, by state coercion, in the form of public works, etc., what the bourgeoisie was still unable to provide with the resources of private industry. The state taxes were an essential means of coercion for maintaining exchange between town and country. Otherwise the smallholder would, in peasant self-complacency, have broken off the connection with the towns as was the case in Norway and in part of Switzerland."— *Ed.*

with interest. These taxes were a spur to the industry of the peasant, whereas now they rob his industry of its last resources and complete his inability to resist pauperism. And an enormous bureaucracy, well-braided and well-fed, is the "*idée napoléonienne*" which is most congenial of all to the second Bonaparte. How could it be otherwise, seeing that alongside the actual classes of society he is forced to create an artificial caste, for which the maintenance of his regime becomes a bread-and-butter question? Accordingly, one of his first financial operations was the raising of officials' salaries to their old level and the creation of new sinecures.

Another "*idée napoléonienne*" is the domination of the *priests* as an instrument of government. But while in its accord with society, in its dependence on natural forces and its submission to the authority which protected it from above, the smallholding that had newly come into being was naturally religious, the smallholding that is ruined by debts, at odds with society and authority, and driven beyond its own limitations naturally becomes irreligious. Heaven was quite a pleasing accession to the narrow strip of land just won, especially as it makes the weather; it becomes an insult as soon as it is thrust forward as substitute for the smallholding. The priest then appears as only the anointed bloodhound of the earthly police—another "*idée napoléonienne*".[a] On the next occasion, the expedition against Rome will take place in France itself, but in a sense opposite to that of M. de Montalembert.[120]

Lastly, the culminating point of the "*idées napoléoniennes*" is the preponderance of the *army*. The army was the *point d'honneur* of the small-holding peasants, it was they themselves transformed into heroes, defending their new possessions against the outer world, glorifying their recently won nationhood, plundering and revolutionising the world. The uniform[b] was their own state dress; war was their poetry; the smallholding, extended and rounded off in imagination, was their fatherland, and patriotism the ideal form of their sense of property. But the enemies against whom the French peasant has now to defend his property are not the Cossacks; they are the *huissiers*[c] and the tax collectors. The smallholding lies no longer in the so-called fatherland, but in the register of mortgages.

---

[a] In the 1852 edition this sentence reads as follows: "The priest then appears as only the anointed bloodhound of the earthly police—another '*idée napoléonienne*'— whose duty under the second Bonaparte is not, as under Napoleon, to watch the enemies of the peasant regime in the towns, but Bonaparte's enemies in the country."—*Ed.*

[b] In the 1852 edition: "The dazzling uniform".—*Ed.*

[c] Bailiffs.—*Ed.*

The army itself is no longer the flower of the peasant youth; it is the swamp-flower of the peasant lumpenproletariat. It consists in large measure of *remplaçants*, of substitutes, just as the second Bonaparte is himself only a *remplaçant*, the substitute for Napoleon. It now performs its deeds of valour by hunting down the peasants like chamois, and in organised drives, by doing *gendarme* duty, and if the internal contradictions of his system chase the chief of the Society of December 10 over the French border, his army, after some acts of brigandage, will reap, not laurels, but thrashings.

One sees: all "*idées napoléoniennes*" *are ideas of the undeveloped small-holding in the freshness of its youth*; for the smallholding that has outlived its day they are an absurdity. They are only the hallucinations of its death struggle, words that are transformed into phrases, spirits transformed into ghosts.[a] But the parody of the empire was necessary to free the mass of the French nation from the weight of tradition and to work out in pure form the opposition between the state power and society. With the progressive undermining of small-holding property, the state structure erected upon it collapses. The centralisation of the state that modern society requires arises only on the ruins of the military-bureaucratic government machinery which was forged in opposition to feudalism.[b]

The condition of the French peasants provides us with the answer to the riddle of the *general elections of December 20 and 21*, which bore the second Bonaparte up Mount Sinai, not to receive laws, but to give them.[c]

Manifestly, the bourgeoisie had now no choice but to elect

---

[a] The 1852 edition adds: "appropriate costumes transformed into absurd fancy dress".— *Ed.*

[b] Instead of the last two sentences, the 1852 edition has: "The demolition of the state machine will not endanger centralisation. Bureaucracy is only the low and brutal form of a centralisation that is still afflicted with its opposite, with feudalism. When he is disappointed in the Napoleonic Restoration, the French peasant will part with his belief in his smallholding, the entire state edifice erected on this smallholding will fall to the ground and *the proletarian revolution will obtain that chorus without which its solo becomes a swan song in all peasant countries.*"— *Ed.*

[c] In the 1852 edition: "but to give and execute them". Then follows this passage: "Of course in those fateful days the French nation committed a mortal sin against democracy, which daily prays on its knees: Holy Universal Suffrage, plead for us! The believers in Universal Suffrage are naturally unwilling to dispense with the miraculous power which has worked such great things with them, which has transformed Bonaparte II into a Napoleon, a Saul into a Paul and a Simon into a Peter. The popular spirit speaks to them through the ballot box as the God of the Prophet Ezekiel spoke to the dry bones: '*Haec dicit dominus deus ossibus suis: Ecce, ego intromittam in vos spiritum et vivetis.*' Thus saith the Lord God unto these bones: Behold, I will cause breath to enter into you, and ye shall live'" [Ezekiel 37 : 5].— *Ed.*

Bonaparte.[a] When the puritans at the Council of Constance[121] complained of the dissolute lives of the popes and wailed about the necessity of moral reform, Cardinal Pierre d'Ailly thundered at them: "Only the devil in person can still save the Catholic Church, and you ask for angels." In like manner, after the coup d'état, the French bourgeoisie cried: Only the chief of the Society of December 10 can still save bourgeois society! Only theft can still save property; only perjury, religion; bastardy, the family; disorder, order!

As the executive authority which has made itself an independent power, Bonaparte feels it to be his mission to safeguard "bourgeois order". But the strength of this bourgeois order lies in the middle class. He looks on himself, therefore, as the representative of the middle class and issues decrees in this sense. Nevertheless, he is somebody solely due to the fact that he has broken the political power of this middle class and daily breaks it anew. Consequently, he looks on himself as the adversary of the political and literary power of the middle class. But by protecting its material power, he generates its political power[b] anew. The cause must accordingly be kept alive; but the effect, where it manifests itself, must be done away with. But this cannot pass off without slight confusions of cause and effect, since in their interaction both lose their distinguishing features. New decrees that obliterate the border line. As against the bourgeoisie, Bonaparte looks on himself, at the same time, as the representative of the peasants and of the people in general, who wants to make the lower classes of the people happy within the framework of bourgeois society. New decrees that cheat the "true Socialists"[122] of their statecraft in advance. But, above all, Bonaparte looks on himself as the chief of the Society of December 10, as the representative of the lumpenproletariat, to which he himself, his entourage, his government and his army belong, and whose prime consideration is to benefit itself and draw California lottery prizes from the state treasury. And he vindicates his position as chief of the Society of December 10 with decrees, without decrees and despite decrees.

This contradictory task of the man explains the contradictions of his government, the confused, blind to-ing and fro-ing which seeks now to win, now to humiliate first one class and then another and arrays all of them uniformly against him, whose practical uncertainty forms a highly comical contrast to the imperious, categorical style of

---

[a] The 1852 edition further has: "Despotism or anarchy? Naturally it voted for despotism."— *Ed.*

[b] In the 1852 edition: "its public, its political power".— *Ed.*

the government decrees, a style which is faithfully copied from the uncle.[a]

Industry and trade, hence the business affairs of the middle class, are to prosper in hothouse fashion under the strong government. The grant of innumerable railway concessions. But the Bonapartist lumpenproletariat is to enrich itself. The initiated play *tripotage*[b] on the *bourse* with the railway concessions. But no capital is forthcoming for the railways. Obligation of the Bank to make advances on railway shares. But, at the same time, the Bank is to be exploited for personal ends and therefore must be cajoled. Release of the Bank from the obligation to publish its report weekly. Leonine agreement of the Bank with the government. The people are to be given employment. Initiation of public works. But the public works increase the obligations of the people in respect of taxes. Hence reduction of the taxes by an onslaught on the *rentiers*, by conversion of the five per cent bonds to four-and-a-half per cent. But, once more, the middle class must receive a *douceur*.[c] Therefore doubling of the wine tax for the people, who buy it *en détail*,[d] and halving of the wine tax for the middle class, who drink it *en gros*.[e] Dissolution of the actual workers' associations, but promises of miracles of association in the future. The peasants are to be helped. Mortgage banks that expedite their getting into debt and accelerate the concentration of property. But these banks are to be used to make money[f] out of the confiscated estates of the House of Orleans. No capitalist wants to agree to this condition, which is not in the decree, and the mortgage bank remains a mere decree, etc., etc.

Bonaparte would like to appear as the patriarchal benefactor of all classes. But he cannot give to one class without taking from another. Just as at the time of the Fronde it was said of the Duke of Guise that he was the most *obligeant* man in France because he had turned all his estates into his partisans' obligations to him, so Bonaparte would fain be the most *obligeant* man in France and turn all the property, all the labour of France into a personal obligation to himself. He would like to steal the whole of France in order to be able to make a present of her to France or, rather, in order to be able to buy France anew with

---

[a] The 1852 edition further has: "So the haste and precipitateness of these contradictions is to ape the many-sided activities and promptness of the Emperor."— *Ed*

[b] Hanky-panky.— *Ed*

[c] Sop.— *Ed*

[d] Retail.— *Ed*

[e] Wholesale.— *Ed*

[f] In the 1852 edition: "to make money for oneself".— *Ed*

French money, for as the chief of the Society of December 10 he must needs buy what ought to belong to him. And all the state institutions, the Senate, the Council of State, the legislative body, the Legion of Honour, the soldiers' medals, the wash-houses, the public works, the railways, the *état-major*[a] of the National Guard excluding privates, and the confiscated estates of the House of Orleans—all become parts of the institution of purchase. Every place in the army and in the government machine becomes a means of purchase. But the most important feature of this process, whereby France is taken in order to be given back, is the percentages that find their way into the pockets of the head and the members of the Society of December 10 during the transaction. The witticism with which Countess L.,[b] the mistress of M. de Morny, characterised the confiscation of the Orleans estates: "*C'est le premier vol* de l'aigle*"[c] is applicable to every flight of this *eagle*, which is more like a *raven*.[123] He himself and his adherents call out to one another daily like that Italian Carthusian admonishing the miser who, with boastful display, counted up the goods on which he could yet live for years to come: "*Tu fai conto sopra i beni, bisogna prima far il conto sopra gli anni.*"** Lest they make a mistake in the years, they count the minutes. A gang of shady characters push their way forward to the court, into the ministries, to the head of the administration and the army, a crowd of the best of whom it must be said that no one knows whence he comes, a noisy, disreputable, rapacious *bohème* that crawls into braided coats with the same grotesque dignity as the high dignitaries of Soulouque. One can visualise clearly this upper stratum of the Society of December 10, if one reflects that *Véron-Crevel**** is its preacher of morals and *Granier de Cassagnac* its thinker. When Guizot, at the time of his ministry, utilised this Granier on a hole-and-corner newspaper against the dynastic opposition, he used to boast of him with the quip: "*C'est le roi des drôles*," "he is the king of buffoons."[d] One would do wrong to recall the Regency[124] or Louis XV in connection with Louis Bonaparte's court and clique. For "often already, France has

---

* *Vol* means flight and theft.

** "Thou countest thy goods, thou shouldst first count thy years."

*** In his novel *Cousine Bette*, Balzac delineates the thoroughly dissolute Parisian philistine in Crevel, a character based on Dr. Véron, owner of the *Constitutionnel.*

---

[a] General Staff.— *Ed.*

[b] Lehon.— *Ed.*

[c] "It is the first flight (theft) of the eagle."— *Ed.*

[d] Quoted in the article by Dupont "Chronique de l'Interieur", *Voix du Proscrit*, No. 8, December 15, 1850.— *Ed.*

experienced a government of mistresses; but never before a government of *hommes entretenus.*" *ª

Driven by the contradictory demands of his situation and being at the same time, like a conjurer, under the necessity of keeping the public gaze fixed on himself, as Napoleon's substitute, by springing constant surprises, that is to say, under the necessity of executing a coup d'état *en miniature* every day, Bonaparte throws the entire bourgeois economy into confusion, violates everything that seemed inviolable to the revolution of 1848, makes some tolerant of revolution, others desirous of revolution, and produces actual anarchy in the name of order, while at the same time stripping its halo from the entire state machine, profanes it and makes it at once loathsome and ridiculous. The cult of the Holy Coat of Trier[125] he duplicates in Paris with the cult of the Napoleonic imperial mantle. But when the imperial mantle finally falls on the shoulders of Louis Bonaparte, the bronze statue of Napoleon will crash from the top of the Vendôme Column.[126]

---

* The words quoted are those of Madame Girardin.

ª *Hommes entretenus*: kept men. The 1852 edition further has: "And Cato, who took his life to be able to associate with heroes in the Elysian Fields! Poor Cato!"— *Ed.*

Frederick Engels

ENGLAND [127]

I

The English Whigs are decidedly unlucky. Hardly has Palmerston fallen from office for having "left England without an ally, indeed without a friend on the Continent of Europe", hardly has the first commotion surrounding his fall [128] subsided, when the whole press is resounding with cries of war and in this connection is bringing to light a morass of maladministration in the departments of war and the navy sufficient to break the neck of more than one ministry.

Ever since 1846 various military figures had been drawing the country's attention to the possibility of an invasion of England if there was a war with France. At that time the danger of such a war was too remote however, and the Quixotic manner adopted by these first alarmists merely excited laughter. General Head in particular acquired a not exactly enviable celebrity from that time on by his continual appeals to the nation to strengthen the national defences. In this context it should not be forgotten moreover that the aged Wellington was likewise declaring the existing coastal fortifications to be extremely inadequate.

Louis Napoleon's coup d'état however suddenly imparted a completely new significance to this debate. John Bull at once realised that the French military dictatorship, that parody of the Consulate, would in all probability embroil France in war, and that in these circumstances an attempt might very well be made to avenge Waterloo. [129] The most recent exploits of the English military forces were not exactly brilliant; at the Cape the Kaffirs were consistently victorious, and even on the Slave Coast an attempted English landing had been decisively beaten off by naked Negroes, despite European tactics and cannon. [130] What would be

the fate of the English soldiers once they came up against the far
more dangerous "Africans" from the proving-ground of
Algeria?[131] And who could guarantee that such an unscrupulous
adventurer as Louis Bonaparte would not one morning, without
the tedious formality of a declaration of war, appear on the
English coast with ten or twelve steamships packed full of troops
and a dozen ships of the line to back them up, and attempt a
march on London?

It was undeniably a serious matter; the Government at once
gave orders for new batteries to be installed at the entrances to the
major harbours on the south and south-east coasts. But the public
also took the matter seriously, and in a way which threatened to
become very disagreeable for the Government. In particular there
were some enquiries into the availability of forces, and it was
found that at that moment, even if Ireland were reduced to the
bare minimum, not more than 25,000 men and 36 cannon with
draught-animals could be turned out for the defence of Great
Britain, and that, as to the fleet, at present *not one ship* of
significance in the ports was ready to sail to prevent a landing. It
was found, as the Kaffir war had already shown, that the
equipment of the British soldier impedes his mobility and is
thoroughly unpractical; it was found that his weapons are by no
means on a par with those of other European armies, and that
there is not a soldier in England with a gun remotely comparable
to the Prussian needle-gun or the rifle used by the French
sharpshooters and riflemen. In the Commissariat of the Navy cases
of quite outrageous corruption and negligence were discovered, all
of which was exaggerated to mammoth proportions by alarmists and
place-hunters.

The affair would seem at first sight only to concern the English
aristocrats, rentiers and bourgeois who would be the first to suffer
from a French invasion and possible conquest. But it must not be
forgotten that the independent development of England, the slow
but sure fighting-out of the conflict between bourgeoisie and
proletariat, a conflict which is furthest advanced here, is of the
utmost importance for the development of Europe as a whole.
Although this peculiarly methodical development in England may,
as in 1848 and previously in the years following 1793, sometimes
be a temporary obstacle in the path of the momentarily victorious
revolutionaries of the Continent, fundamentally it is nevertheless
of a far more revolutionary nature than all these transient
continental struggles put together. Whilst the great French
Revolution foundered on the conquest of Europe, England

8*

revolutionised society with the steam engine, conquered the world market, increasingly wrested power from all those classes left behind by history and prepared the ground for the great, decisive struggle between the industrial capitalist and the industrial worker. It was of the greatest significance for the development of the whole of Europe that Napoleon never managed to fling 150,000 men across from Boulogne to Folkestone and to conquer England with the veterans of the Republican armies. During the Restoration, when the Continent was left to the tender mercies of those myrmidons of legitimacy [132] so aptly portrayed by Béranger, in England the party of the die-hards, the Tories, was suffering its first major rupture caused by Canning's Ministry, which already had very bourgeois features, and Canning and later Peel were beginning that gradual undermining of the English Constitution which has since continued without pause and which must very shortly reach the point where the whole rotten edifice comes crashing to the ground. This undermining of the old institutions of England and the basis of this undermining process, the incessant revolutionising of English society by large-scale industry are quietly going on, heedless of whether revolution or counter-revolution is for the moment carrying the day on the Continent; and if this movement is slow, it is however sure and never takes a backward step. The defeat of the Chartists on April 10, 1848, [133] was exclusively a defeat and decisive rejection of foreign political influence; it is not continental political upheavals but world-wide trade crises, direct material blows calling into question the livelihood of each individual, which are the mainsprings of development in England. And now, when there are unmistakable signs that the final removal from political power of all the traditional classes by the industrial bourgeoisie and thus the dawn of the decisive day of battle between it and the industrial proletariat are imminent, a disturbance of this development now, even a temporary conquest of England by the rapacious praetorians of December 2, would have the gravest consequences for the European movement as a whole. Only in England has industry attained such dimensions that it is the focal point of the whole national interest, of all the conditions of existence for every class. But industry consists on the one hand of the industrial bourgeoisie and on the other of the industrial proletariat, and all the other elements comprising the nation are increasingly grouped around these opposed classes. Here therefore, where the only point that matters is who shall rule, the industrial *capitalists* or the industrial *workers*, here, if anywhere, is the ground where the class struggle in its modern form can be decided and where the industrial proletariat on the one hand has the strength to win political power and on the other finds the material means, the productive forces which enable it to make a total social revolution and ultimately to eliminate class contradictions. And it is certainly the supreme interest of the whole proletarian party in Europe to ensure that this development in England, which is leading to the greatest intensification of the contradiction between the two industrial classes and ultimately to the defeat of the ruling class by the oppressed, is not as a result of foreign conquest deflected, its momentum diminished and the decisive struggle postponed for an indefinite period.

What, then, are the prospects?

First and foremost, a country such as Great Britain, which without Ireland numbers 22 million and with Ireland 29 million inhabitants, cannot be simply taken by surprise attack. The alarmists cite the example of Carthage, which, dispersing its fleets and armies to its remotest possessions, twice succumbed to a surprise attack by the Romans.[134] But, apart from the totally altered conditions of warfare, the Roman landing in Africa in the Second Punic War only became possible after the flower of the Carthaginian armies had been destroyed in Spain and Italy and the Punic fleets driven from the Mediterranean; the surprise attack was no such thing but a very substantial military operation and the quite natural culmination of a long war which in its final stages ran consistently in Rome's favour. And the Third Punic War was scarcely a war at all but simply the crushing of the weaker party by a party ten times stronger; it was somewhat like Napoleon's confiscation of the Venetian Republic.[135] At present, however, France does not stand where she did in 1797, nor does England resemble Venice at the end of its days.

Napoleon considered at least 150,000 men necessary to conquer England. At that time England admittedly had many more soldiers at her disposal but also a much smaller population and industrial resources. And nowadays, however insignificant the available power of the English at this moment may be, at least as many would be required to conquer England. A glance at the map shows that any invasion army which landed in England would have to advance at least as far as the Tees, the Tyne or even the Tweed; if it halted at any point short of that, all the resources of the industrial districts would remain in the hands of the defenders, and in the face of the ever growing power of the latter it would have to man lines extremely deficient in marked military features

and far too extended for its forces. The area south of the
above-mentioned rivers, i.e. England proper, numbers 16 million
inhabitants and would demand the detaching of such forces to
secure communications, lay siege to or occupy the coastal
fortifications and suppress the inevitable national uprising, that
only very few would remain available for effective operations on
the Scottish border. And however well they were commanded, it is
unlikely that fewer than 150,000 men could conquer England and
prevail in the face of rebellion within the country and regular
warfare from the direction of Scotland and Ireland.

Now, by fresh levies and skilled concentration 150,000 men can
of course be assembled at some point on the north coast of France,
but this would take at least a month or two. And in this time
England could concentrate quite a respectable naval force in the
Channel, partly by calling on the Tagus fleet[136] and steamships
from other nearby stations, and partly by mobilising the ships laid
up in the ports, whilst within a further month all the steamships
and some of the sailing ships from the Atlantic stations and from
Malta and Gibraltar could be to hand. The landing army would
therefore have to be ferried across, if not all at once, then at least
in a few large detachments, since sooner or later communications
with France would in any case be interrupted. At least 50,000 men
would have to be landed at a time and the whole army therefore
in three crossings. And furthermore, men-of-war could not be
used at all or only to a limited extent for the transporting of
troops in this operation, since they would have to ward off the
English fleet. And France could not assemble transport for 50,000
men along with the necessary artillery and munitions in her
Channel ports within six weeks, even if she were to requisition
neutral shipping. However each day by which the expedition is
postponed represents a further advantage for England, for time is
all she needs in order to concentrate her fleet and train her
recruits.

If however consideration of the English fleet precludes ferrying
the landing army of 150,000 men across in more than three
detachments, consideration of England's land-power must also
forbid any soldier worth his salt to risk the crossing to England
with fewer than 50,000 men at a time. We have seen that in the
circumstances most favourable to an invasion, the English would
still have a period of one or two months to prepare for such a
contingency; only someone who did not know them could assume
them to be incapable of organising a land-army in this time which
would have no difficulty in driving an advance guard of 50,000

men into the sea before support arrived. It should be remembered
that embarkation can only take place between Cherbourg and
Boulogne and the landing only between the Isle of Wight and
Dover, i.e. within a stretch of coast that is at no point more than
four days' good marching distance from London. It should be
remembered that embarkation and landing depend on wind and
tide, that the English fleet in the Channel would offer resistance,
and that between the first and second landings perhaps eight to
ten days and at the very least four would therefore elapse, since
the main body of the troops would have to be transported in
sailing ships and picked up along the entire length of the coast
from Cherbourg to Boulogne; a "camp at Boulogne"[137] cannot be
set up on the spur of the moment. In these circumstances it is
unlikely that anything will be attempted until at least 70,000-
80,000 men can be flung across at one time, and for this purpose
transport would first have to be found, which in turn requires
time. However, since with each week by which the expedition is
delayed, England's defensive strength will grow more rapidly than
the enemy's transport and naval power, the attackers' position will
become increasingly unfavourable; they will soon reach the point
where they cannot risk anything unless they are able to ferry
150,000 men across at one time, and even they would encounter
such resistance that they would be certain of eventual annihilation
unless a reserve of some 100,000 men were subsequently
despatched.

In a word, the conquest of England cannot be accomplished by
means of a surprise attack. If the whole Continent were to unite to
that end, it would need a year merely to find and assemble
transport alone—more than England needs to put her coasts into
a state of defence, concentrate a navy which would be a match for
all the continental fleets combined and could prevent them joining
forces, and assemble an army which would make it impossible for
any enemy to remain on English soil.

National feeling amongst the English is at this particular
moment more intense than at any time since 1815, and the grave
danger of an invasion would lend it an altogether new impetus.
Furthermore, the population of Great Britain is by no means as
unmilitary as it is made out to be; the bourgeoisie, the petty
bourgeoisie and the proletariat of the big cities are admittedly
much less familiar with fire-arms and therefore less fitted for the
conduct of civil war than the corresponding classes on the
Continent. But the population as a whole has a great deal of
warlike spirit and contains very useful military elements. Nowhere

are there more hunters and poachers, i.e. semi-trained light infantry and sharpshooters; and the 40,000-50,000 mechanics and engineers are better prepared for the arms workshops, the artillery and service in the engineering corps than any comparable number of chosen men in whatever continental country one cares to name. The ground itself, almost entirely devoid of major military features virtually up to the Scottish border, is hilly broken country, tailor-made for small-scale warfare. And if hitherto guerrilla warfare has only been successful in comparatively sparsely populated countries, in the case of a serious attack England in particular might well be able to demonstrate that in very densely populated countries, e.g. in the almost continuous labyrinth of buildings in Lancashire and West Yorkshire, guerrilla warfare can be rather effective.

With regard to raids aimed at plundering the wealthy ports, destroying depots and so on, England is at present admittedly in an exposed position. The fortifications are scarcely worth mentioning. Provided there are no ships lying at Spithead it is possible to sail calmly right up to the entrance of Southampton Water and land sufficient troops to exact a levy of whatever size desired from Southampton. Woolwich could perhaps be occupied and destroyed at present although this would be a somewhat greater undertaking. Liverpool's only defence is a pitiful battery of 18 iron ship's cannon lacking any form of aiming device and manned by eight to ten artillerymen and half a company of infantry. But with the exception of Brighton, all the important English coastal towns are situated within deep bays or far up rivers and have natural defences in the form of sand-banks and rocks with which only the native pilots are familiar. Any attacker attempting to find his way without a pilot through these narrow channels, which are mostly only navigable by large ships at high tide, runs the risk of losing more than he could hope to make away with, and if such an expedition met with any resistance or the slightest unexpected obstacle it would have as disastrous an outcome as the Danish expedition against Eckernförde in 1849.[138] On the other hand a rapid landing of 10,000-20,000 men from steamships in some rural area and a short plundering raid against small country towns, the positive results of which would necessarily be meagre, would admittedly be very easy to accomplish and could not be prevented at all at present.

All these fears would however melt away of their own accord as soon as the Tagus fleet, the North American squadron and some of the steamboats pursuing the slave-ships between Brazil and

Africa were recalled to England and at the same time the ships laid up in the naval ports were mobilised. That would suffice to prevent any surprise attack and delay any serious attempt at invasion long enough to allow England to take the necessary further action.

Meanwhile the alarm will have the positive effect of terminating the absurd policy of maintaining 800 floating cannon in the Mediterranean, 1,000 in the Atlantic and 300 each in the Pacific and the Indian Ocean, whilst there is not a single ship to protect the coasts at home; and of engaging in interminable and inglorious wars with Negroes and Kaffirs, while troops are urgently needed in the home country. The cumbersome, heavy and in every respect antiquated equipment of the army, the boundless carelessness and nonchalance of the military and naval administration, and the gross nepotism, the bribery and the fraud in these departments will by and large be eliminated. The industrial bourgeoisie will finally rid itself of the Peace Congress and Peace Society humbug, which exposed it to so much well-deserved mockery and did such harm to its political progress and thus to the whole development of England. And if war were to break out, it may very easily happen, owing to the well-known irony of world history which is enjoying an unprecedented vogue at present, that Messrs. Cobden and Bright, in their dual capacity as members of the Peace Society [139] and as men who may become ministers in the near future, would have to wage a stubborn war, perhaps against the whole continent.

Manchester, January 23, 1852

II

Parliament is due to meet next Tuesday, on February 3. Of the three principal issues which will take up the early debates, we have briefly discussed two already: Palmerston's dismissal [140] and the state of the defences in the event of a war with France. There remains the third, which for the development of England is by far the most important: *electoral reform.*

The new Reform Bill which Russell is due to present at the very outset will provide sufficient opportunity to examine the general significance of electoral reform in England more closely. For today, since we are only concerned with communicating and elucidating a number of rumours about this bill, the observation will suffice that in this whole matter the immediate issue is solely how much of their political power will be retained by the reactionary or conservative classes, i.e. the landed aristocracy, the rentiers, the stock-exchange speculators, the colonial landowners, the shipping magnates and a section of the merchants and bankers, and how much they will surrender to the industrial bourgeoisie, which heads all the progressive and revolutionary classes. For the present we are not concerned here with the proletariat at all.

The Daily News, the voice of the industrial bourgeoisie in London and a good source in such matters, gives some information about the Whig Ministry's new Reform Bill. According to this information, the intended reforms would touch upon three aspects of the British electoral system.

Hitherto every Member of Parliament had to show that he owned landed property worth at least £300 before he could be admitted. However this condition, in many cases embarrassing, was almost always evaded by bogus purchases and bogus contracts. It had long ago become ineffective as far as the industrial bourgeoisie was concerned; it is now to be dropped completely. Its abolition is one of the "six points" of the proletarian People's Charter,[141] and it is interesting to observe how one of these six points (they are all six very middle-class and have already been implemented in the United States) is already being officially acknowledged.

Hitherto the electoral system was organised in the following way: according to ancient English custom some Members were sent by the counties[a] and some by the towns. Any person wanting to vote in a county had either to own land with an annual value of £2 entirely in his own right (freehold property)[b] or hold rented land with an annual value of £50. In the towns on the other hand any man could vote who occupied a house whose rent was £10 and who paid the poor-rate corresponding to that amount. Whilst in those towns which sent Members, the mass of small tradesmen and craftsmen, i.e. all the petty bourgeoisie, were admitted to the suffrage by this arrangement, in the county elections the aristocracy's tenants-at-will,[c] i.e. tenants who could be given notice to quit from one year to the next and who were therefore

---

[a] Engels uses the English term.— *Ed.*

[b] In the original version the German expression is followed by the English term "freehold property" in brackets.— *Ed.*

[c] Engels uses the English term.— *Ed.*

completely dependent on their landlords, represented the over-whelming majority. Last year Mr. Locke King proposed extending the norm of £10 rents, which applied in the towns, to the counties as well, and obtained a large majority for this proposal against the ministers in a sparsely attended House. It is said that Russell now intends to reduce the amount for the counties to £10 and for the towns to £5. The effect of such a measure would be very significant. In the towns it would immediately give the franchise to the better paid among the proletariat, which would make the election of Chartist representatives in some large towns very probable, whilst in the medium-sized and smaller towns the industrial bourgeoisie would receive an enormous increase in votes and in parliamentary seats. And in the counties all citizens of small and moderate means in small towns without their own parliamentary representatives would at once be admitted to the suffrage; they would constitute the overwhelming majority in most cases and by their numbers and relative independence of the few great noble families who control the counties at present they would put an end to the electoral terrorism hitherto practised by these magnates. Furthermore this rural petty bourgeoisie is even now increasingly succumbing to the influence of the industrial bourgeoisie and would thus open up a significant number of the counties to them.

The electoral constituencies have hitherto varied enormously in size and importance; the number of representatives bore no relationship whatsoever to the size of the population or number of electors. One or two hundred electors in one place sent as many representatives as six to eleven thousand electors in another place. This inequality was particularly marked in the towns; and particularly the small towns with few electors were the scene of the most scandalous bribery (e.g. St. Albans) or absolute electoral dictatorship by this or that great landowner. According to the report in *The Daily News* eight of the smallest towns with the right to elect a Member of Parliament are now to be deprived of their representatives and the remaining small towns which elect Members of Parliament are to be lumped together with other neighbouring country towns, up to now represented only in the counties, in such a way that the size of the electorate is significantly increased. This would resemble the system of urban grouping which has existed in Scotland ever since the Union with England (1707).[142] That the industrial bourgeoisie may likewise expect an increase of political power from such a measure, timid though it is, is proved by the outstanding importance which they have for a long time attached to the equalisation of the electoral constituencies, over and above any other issue of parliamentary reform. In addition it is reported that London and Lancashire, in other words two of the principal centres of the industrial bourgeoisie, are to receive increased representation in Parliament.

If Russell really intends to present this Bill, then according to past experience, this is indeed a great deal for the little man. It appears that Peel's laurels will not let him rest and that he too has resolved to be "bold" for once. This boldness is admittedly accompanied by all the timorousness and cautious circumspection of the English Whig, and in the present state of public opinion in England will appear bold to no one but himself and his Whig colleagues. But after the hesitation, vacillation and second thoughts, after the repeated and always unsuccessful putting-out of feelers with which this diminutive peer has occupied his time since the end of the previous session, one might never-theless have expected less than the above proposals—always providing of course that he does not change his mind before Tuesday.[143]

The industrial bourgeoisie, it does not need to be spelled out, are demanding a great deal more than that. They are demanding household suffrage,[a] i.e. the vote for every man occupying a house or part of a house on which he is required to pay rates, voting by ballot and a total revision of constituency boundaries to ensure equal representation for equal numbers of electors and equal wealth. They will haggle hard and long with the ministry and extract every possible concession from it before agreeing a price for their support. The English industrialist is a good businessman and will certainly dispose of his vote for the highest price obtainable.

Incidentally it is already now becoming evident that even the above ministerial minimum of electoral reform cannot but have the effect of strengthening the power of that class which already controls England in practice and is making giant strides towards the political recognition of its hegemony: the industrial bourgeoisie. The proletariat, whose independent struggle for its own interests against the industrial bourgeoisie will not begin until such time as the political supremacy of that class is established, the proletariat will in any circumstances also derive some advantage from this electoral reform. How great this advantage will be however depends simply on whether the debate and eventual

---

    a Engels uses the English term.— Ed.

establishment of electoral reform occurs *before* the trade crisis breaks or rather coincides with it; for the proletariat, for the time being, only plays an active part, at the front of the stage, at great moments of decision, like Fate in classical tragedy.

Manchester, January 30, 1852

Written on January 23 and 30, 1852

First published in Russian in the journal *Letopisi marksizma*, Vol. IV, 1927

Signed: *F. Engels*

Printed according to the manuscript

Published in English for the first time

Karl Marx and Frederick Engels

TO THE EDITOR OF *THE TIMES*[144]

Sir,

The destruction of the last remnants of an independent press on the Continent has made it the honourable duty of the English press to record every act of illegality and oppression in that quarter of Europe. Allow me, therefore, through your columns, to lay before the public a fact, which shows that the judges in Prussia are quite on a level with the political menials of Louis Napoleon.

You know what a valuable *moyen de gouvernement*[a] a well got-up conspiracy may turn out, if brought forward at the proper moment. The Prussian government, in order to render their parliament pliable, wanted such a plot in the beginning of last year. Accordingly, numbers of persons were arrested, and the police was set to work all over Germany. But nothing was made out, and after all, but a few individuals were ultimately retained in prison at Cologne, under the pretext of being the chiefs of a widespread revolutionary organisation. The principal of them are Dr. Becker and Dr. Bürgers, two gentlemen connected with the press, Dr. Daniels, Dr. Jacobi and Dr. Klein, medical practitioners two of whom had honourably filled the arduous duties of a physician to the administration of the poor, and M. Otto, director of extensive chemical works, and well known in his country by his attainments in chemical science. There being, however, no evidence against them, their release was expected every day. But while they were in prison, the "Disciplinary Law" was promulgated, enabling the government, by a very short and easy proceeding, to rid themselves of any obnoxious judicial functionary. The effect of this enactment upon the hitherto slow and languishing proceedings against the above-named gentlemen was

---

[a] Means of government.— *Ed.*

almost instantaneous. Not only were they placed *au secret*, denied every communication with each other or their friends, even by letter, and deprived of books and writing materials (allowed, in Prussia, to the meanest felon before conviction); but the judicial proceedings took a quite different turn. The *Chambre du Conseil* (you know we are judged, in Cologne, by the *Code Napoléon*) was at once found ready to make out a case against them, and the matter went before the Senate of Accusation, a body of judges fulfilling the functions of an English Grand Jury.[145] It is to the unparalleled judgment of this body that I beg particularly to draw your attention. In this judgment there occurs, literally translated, the following extraordinary passage:

> "Considering, that no reliable evidence has been brought forward, that, therefore, no case having been made out, *there exists no reason for maintaining the indictment*"—(the prisoners are ordered to be set at liberty, you suppose, is the necessary conclusion? Not it indeed)—"the whole of the minutes and documents is to be returned to the *juge d'instruction*[a] for a fresh investigation."

This means, then, that after a detention of ten months, during which time neither the activity of the police nor the acumen of the counsel for the Crown have been able to make out the shadow of a case—the whole proceeding is to begin again from the beginning, in order, perhaps, after another year's investigation, to be handed over a third time to the *juge d'instruction*!

The explanation of such a glaring breach of the law is this: the government are just now preparing the organisation of a High Court of Justice to be made up of the most subservient materials. As a defeat before a jury would be certain, the government must delay the final trial of this affair until it may go before this new Court, which of course, will give every guarantee to the Crown and none to the prisoners.

Would it not be far more honourable for the Prussian government to pass sentence at once, by Royal Decree, upon the prisoners, in the way M. Louis Bonaparte has done?

I am, Sir, your most obedient servant.

London, 29 January 1852

A Prussian[b]

First published in German in the book: *Der Briefwechsel zwischen Friedrich Engels und Karl Marx*, Erster Band, Stuttgart, 1913

Printed according to Engels' rough copy in English

---

[a] Examining magistrate.— *Ed.*
[b] The signature is in Marx's hand.— *Ed.*

Frederick Engels

REAL CAUSES WHY THE FRENCH PROLETARIANS REMAINED COMPARATIVELY INACTIVE IN DECEMBER LAST[146]

I

[*Notes to the People*, No. 43, February 21, 1852]

Ever since the 2nd of December last, the whole interest that foreign, or at least continental politics may excite, is taken up by that lucky and reckless gambler, Louis Napoleon Bonaparte. "What is he doing? Will he go to war, and with whom? Will he invade England?" These questions are sure to be put wherever continental affairs are spoken of.

And certainly there is something startling in the fact of a comparatively unknown adventurer, placed by chance at the head of the executive power of a great republic, seizing, between sunset and sunrise, upon all the important posts of the capital, driving the parliament like chaff to the winds, suppressing metropolitan insurrection in two days, provincial tumults in two weeks, forcing himself, in a sham election, down the throat of the whole people, and establishing, in the same breath, a constitution which confers upon him all the powers of the state.[147] Such a thing has not occurred, such a shame has not been borne by any nation since the praetorian legions of declining Rome put up the empire to auction and sold it to the highest bidder. And the middle-class press of this country, from *The Times* down to *The Weekly Dispatch*, has never, since the days of December, allowed any occasion to pass without venting its virtuous indignation upon the military despot, the treacherous destroyer of his country's liberties, the extinguisher of the press, and so forth.

Now, with every due contempt for Louis Napoleon, we do not think it would become an organ of the working-class[a] to join in this chorus of high-sounding vituperation in which the respective

---

[a] *Notes to the People*.— *Ed.*

papers of the stockjobbers, the cotton-lords, and the landed aristocracy strive to out-blackguard each other. These gentlemen might as well be remembered of the real state of the question. *They* have every reason to cry out, for whatever Louis Napoleon took from others, he took it not from the working-classes, but from those very classes whose interests in England the aforesaid portion of the press represents. Not that Louis Napoleon would not, quite as gladly, have robbed the working-classes of anything that might appear desirable to him, but it is a fact that in December last the French working-classes could not be robbed of anything, because everything worth taking had already been taken from them during the three years and a half of middle-class parliamentary government that had followed the great defeats of June 1848. In fact, what, on the eve of the 2nd of December, remained to be taken from them? The suffrage? They had been stripped of that by the Electoral Law of May 1850. The right of meeting? That had long been confined to the "safe" and "well-disposed" classes of society. The freedom of the press? Why, the real proletarian press had been drowned in the blood of the insurgents of the great battle of June, and that shadow of it which survived for a time, had long since disappeared under the pressure of gagging laws, revised and improved upon every succeeding session of the National Assembly.[148] Their arms? Every pretext had been taken profit of, in order to ensure the exclusion from the National Guard of all working-men, and to confine the possession of arms to the wealthier classes of society.

Thus the working-classes had, at the moment of the late *coup d'état*, very little, if anything, to lose in the chapter of political privileges. But, on the other hand, the middle and capitalist classes were at that time in possession of political omnipotence. Theirs was the press, the right of meeting, the right to bear arms, the suffrage, the parliament. Legitimists and Orleanists, landholders and fundholders, after thirty years' struggle, had at last found a neutral ground in the republican form of government. And for them it was indeed a hard case to be robbed of all this, in the short space of a few hours, and to be reduced at once to the state of political nullity to which they themselves had reduced the working people. That is the reason why the English "respectable" press is so furious at Louis Napoleon's lawless indignities. As long as these indignities, either of the executive government or the parliament, were directed against the working-classes, why that, of course, was right enough, but as soon as a similar policy was extended to "the better sort of people," the "wealthy intellects of the nation," ah, that was quite different, and it behoved every lover of liberty to raise his voice in defence of "principle."

The struggle, then, on the 2nd of December lay principally between the middle-classes and Louis Napoleon, the representative of the army. That Louis Napoleon knew this, he showed by the orders given to the army during the struggle of the 4th, to fire principally upon "the gentlemen in broad-cloth." The glorious battle of the boulevards is known well enough; and a series of volleys upon closed windows and unarmed *bourgeois* was quite sufficient to stifle, in the middle-class of Paris, every movement of resistance.

On the other hand, the working-classes, although they could no longer be deprived of any direct political privilege, were not at all disinterested in the question. They had to lose, above all, the great chance of May 1852, when all powers of the state were to expire simultaneously, and when, for the first time since June 1848, they expected to have a fair field for a struggle; and aspiring as they were to political supremacy, they could not allow any violent change of government to occur, without being called upon to interpose between the contending parties as supreme umpires, and to impose to them their will as the law of the land. Thus, they could not let the occasion pass without showing the two opposing forces that there was a third power in the field, which, if momentarily removed from the theatre of official and parliamentary contentions, was yet ever ready to step in as soon as the scene was changed to its own sphere of action,—to the *street.* But then, it must not be forgotten that even in this case the proletarian party laboured under great disadvantages. If they rose against the usurper, did they not virtually defend and prepare the restoration and dictatorship of that very parliament which had proved their most relentless enemy? And if they at once declared for a revolutionary government, would they not, as was actually the case in the provinces, frighten the middle-class so much as to drive them to a union with Louis Napoleon and the army? Besides, it must be remembered that the very strength and flower of the revolutionary working-class have been either killed during the insurrection of June, or transported and imprisoned under innumerable *different* pretences ever since that event. And finally, there was this one fact which was alone sufficient to ensure to Napoleon the neutrality of the great majority of the working-classes: *Trade was excellent,* and Englishmen know it well enough, that with a fully employed and well-paid working-class, no agitation, much less a revolution, can be got up.

It is now very commonly said in this country that the French must be a set of old women or else they would not submit to such treatment. I very willingly grant that, as a nation, the French deserve, at the present moment, such adorning epithets. But we all know that the French are, in their opinions and actions, more dependent upon success than any other civilised nation. As soon as a certain turn is given to events in this country, they almost without resistance follow up that turn, until the last extreme in that direction has been reached. The defeat of June 1848 gave such a counter-revolutionary turn to France and, through her, to the whole continent. The present ascension of the Napoleonic empire is but the crowning fact of a long series of counter-revolutionary victories, that filled up the three last years; and once engaged upon the declivity, it was to be expected that France would go on falling until she reached the bottom. How near she may be to that bottom it is not easy to say; but that she is getting nearer to it very rapidly every one must see. And if the past history of France is not to be belied by future deeds of the French people, we may safely expect that the deeper the degradation, the more sudden and the more dazzling will be the result. Events, in these times of ours, are succeeding each other at a tremendously rapid rate, and what it took formerly a nation a whole century to go through, is now-a-days very easily overcome in a couple of years. The old empire lasted fourteen years; it will be exceedingly lucky for the imperial eagle if the revival, upon the most shabby scale, of this piece of performance will last out so many months. And then?

II

[*Notes to the People*, No. 48, March 27, 1852]

Although at a first glance it might appear that in the present moment Louis Napoleon, in France, sways with undisturbed omnipotence, and that, perhaps, the only power, besides his own, is that of courtly intrigues that beset him on all sides, and plot against each other for the purpose of obtaining sole favour with, and influence over, the French autocrat; yet, in reality, things are quite different. The whole secret of Louis Napoleon's success is this, that by the traditions of his name he has been placed in a position to hold, for a moment, *the balance of the contending classes of French society.* For it is a fact that under the cloak of the state of siege by military despotism which now veils France, the struggle of

216 Frederick Engels

the different classes of society is going on as fiercely as ever. That struggle, having been carried on for the last four years with powder and shot has only now taken a different form. In the same way as any protracted war will exhaust and fatigue the most powerful nation, so has the open, bloody war of the last year fatigued and momentarily exhausted the *military* strength of the different classes. But class-war is independent of actual warfare, and not always needs barricades and bayonets to be carried on with; class-war is inextinguishable as long as the various classes with their opposed and conflicting interests and social positions are in existence; and we have not yet heard that since the blessed advent of the mock-Napoleon, France had ceased to count among her inhabitants large landed proprietors, and agricultural labourers, or *métayers,* large money-lenders, and small mortgaged freeholders, capitalists, and working-men.

The position of the different classes in France is just this: the revolution of February had for ever upset the power of the large bankers and stockjobbers; after their downfall every other class of the populations of the towns had had their day. First, the working-men, during the days of the first revolutionary excitement,—then the petty republican shopkeepers under Ledru-Rollin,—then the republican fraction of the bourgeoisie under Cavaignac,—lastly, the united royalist middle-classes, under the late National Assembly. None of these classes had been able to hold fast the power they for a moment possessed; and latterly, among the ever reappearing divisions of the legitimist royalists, or the landed interest, and the Orleans royalists, or the moneyed interest, it appeared inevitable that power would again slip from their hands, and return to those of the working-class, who themselves might be expected to have become fitter to turn it to account. But then there was another mighty class in France, mighty, not by the large individual properties of its members, but by its numbers and its very wants. That class—the small, mortgaged freeholders, making up at least three-fifths of the French nation—was slow to act, and slow to be acted upon, as all rural populations; it stuck to its old traditions, distrusted the wisdom of the apostles of all parties from the towns, and remembering that it had been happy, free from debt, and comparatively rich in the time of the Emperor,[a] laid, by the means of universal suffrage, the executive power in the hands of his nephew. The active agitation of the democratic socialist party, and

---

[a] Napoleon I.—*Ed.*

more still the disappointment which Louis Napoleon's measures soon prepared for them, led part of this peasant-class into the ranks of the Red party; but the mass of them stuck to their traditions, and said that if Louis Napoleon had not yet proved the Messiah he was expected to be, it was the fault of the National Assembly that gagged him. Besides the mass of the peasantry, Louis Napoleon, himself a species of lofty swell-mob's man, and surrounded by the élite of the fashionable swell mob, found support in the most degraded and dissolute portion of the population of the towns. This element of strength he united into a paid body called the "Society of the 10th of December." Thus, relying upon the peasantry for the vote; upon the mob for noisy demonstrations, upon the army, ever ready to upset a government of parliamentary talkers, pretending to speak the voice of the working-classes, he could quietly wait for the moment when the squabbles of the middle-class parliament would allow him to step in and assume a more or less absolute sway over those classes, none of which, after a four years' bloody struggle, had proved strong enough to seize upon a lasting supremacy. And this he did on the 2nd of December last.

Thus the reign of Louis Napoleon is not superseding the class-war. It merely suspends for a while the bloody outbreaks which mark from time to time the efforts of this or that class to gain or maintain political power. None of these classes were strong enough to venture at a new battle, with any chance of success. The very division of classes favoured, for the time being, Napoleon's projects. He upset the middle-class parliament, and destroyed the political power of the middle-class; might not the proletarians rejoice at this? And certainly, the proletarians could not be expected to fight for an assembly that had been their most deadly enemy! But at the same time Louis Napoleon's usurpation menaced the common fighting-ground of all classes, and the last vantage-grounds of the working-class—the Republic; why, as soon as the working-men stood up for the defence of the Republic, the middle-class joined the very man that had just ousted them in order to defeat, in the working-class, the common enemy of society. Thus it was in Paris—thus in the provinces,—and the army won an easy victory over the contending and opposing classes; and after the victory, the millions of the imperialist peasantry stepped in with their vote, and with the help of official falsifications, established the government of Louis Napoleon as that of the representative of almost unanimous France.

But even now, class struggles and class interests are at the bottom of every important act of Louis Napoleon's, as we shall see in our next.

III

[*Notes to the People*, No. 50, April 10, 1852]

We repeat: Louis Napoleon came to power because the open war carried on during the last four years between the different classes of French society had worn them out, had shattered their respective fighting armies, and because under such circumstances, for a time at least, the struggle of these classes can only be carried on in a peaceful and legal way, by competition, by trades' organisations, and by all the different means of pacific struggle by which the opposition of class against class has now been carried on in England for above a century. Under these circumstances it is in a manner of speaking in the interest of all contending classes that ·a so-called *strong government* should exist which might repress and keep down all those minor, local and scattered outbreaks of open hostility, which, without leading to any result, trouble the development of the struggle in its new shape by retarding the recovery of strength for a new pitched battle. This circumstance may in some way explain the undeniable general acquiescence of the French in the present government. How long it may be ere both the working and capitalist classes may have regained strength and self-reliance enough to come out and openly claim, each for themselves, the dictatorship of France, of course nobody can tell; but at the rate events are going now-a-days, either of these classes will most likely be brought into the field unexpectedly, and thus the fight of class against class in the streets may be renewed long before, from the relative or absolute strength of the parties, such an occurrence might seem probable. For, if the French revolutionary, that is the working-class party, has to wait till it is again in the same conditions of strength as in February 1848, it might resign itself to submissive passiveness of some ten years, which it certainly will not do; and at the same time, a government like that of Louis Napoleon is placed in the necessity, as we shall see by and by, to entangle itself and France into such difficulties as ultimately must be solved by a great revolutionary blow. We will not speak of the chances of war, nor of other occurrences which may, or may not come to pass; we will only mention one event which is as sure to come as the sun is sure to rise tomorrow morning, and that is a

Vol. II.]   Saturday, March 27, 1852.   [*No. 48.*]

Read in this Number "Current Notes, No. 1"

Read in this Number "Chartist Reports, 1."

NOTES

TO

THE PEOPLE.

BY

ERNEST JONES,

OF THE MIDDLE TEMPLE, BARRISTER AT LAW,

Author of the Wood Spirit, Lord Lindsay, My Life, History of the Working Classes, Confessions of a King, Recollections of a Student, The New World, Beldagon Church, Painter of Florence, Canterbury versus Rome. &c., &c.

PRICE TWOPENCE.

CONTENTS:

London:

J. PAVEY, 47, HOLYWELL STREET.

1852.

Green & Co., Printers, 32, Castle Street, Holborn.

Read in this Number "Continental Notes."

Title-page of the journal *Notes to the People*, in which Engels' article "Real Causes Why the French Proletarians Remained Comparatively Inactive in December Last" was published

[Vol. II.] Saturday, March 27, 1852. [No. 48.

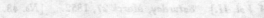

Read in this Number—Cromwell's Epitaph ?
Read in this Number—Continental Notes.

NOTES TO THE PEOPLE.

BY

ERNEST JONES,

OF THE MIDDLE TEMPLE, BARRISTER AT LAW.

Author of the Wood Spirit, Lord Lindsay, My Life, History of the
Working Classes, Confessions of a King, Recollections of a Wandering
Pen, New Religion, Beldagon Church, Painter of Florence,
Factories, &c., &c., &c.

PRICE TWOPENCE.

CONTENTS.

London:

J. PAVEY, 47, HOLYWELL STREET.

1852.

general commercial and industrial revulsion. The bad trade and bad harvests of 1846 and 1847, made the revolution of 1848; and there are ten chances to one, that in 1853 trade, all over the world, will be far deeper uprooted and far more lastingly upset than ever it was before.[149] And who is there who thinks the ship, Louis Napoleon sails in, [is] sea-worthy enough to stand the gales that then must of necessity spring up?

But let us look at the position in which the bastard-eagle found himself on the evening of his victory. He had for supporters the army, the clergy, and the peasantry. He had been opposed in his attempt by the middle-class (comprising the large landed proprietors), and the Socialists or revolutionary working-men. Once at the head of the government, he had not only to retain those parties that brought him there, but also to gain over, or at least to conciliate to the new state of things, as many as possible of those that had opposed him hitherto. As to the army, the clergy, the government officials and the members of that conspiracy of place-hunters by which he had long since surrounded himself, direct bribes, ready money, open plunder of the public resources, was the only thing required; and we have seen how quick Louis Napoleon has been at coming down with the cash, or at finding out berths for his friends which gave them glorious opportunities for enriching themselves at once. Look at DeMorny, who went into office a beggar, crushed by a load of debts, and who, four weeks afterwards, walked out again with debts paid and what even in the neighbourhood of Belgrave Square[150] would be called a handsome independence besides! But to deal with the peasantry, with the large landed proprietors, with the funds, monied, manufacturing, shipping, trading and shop-keeping interests, and lastly with that most formidable question of the century, the labour-question—that was quite another thing. For all the silencing measures of the government notwithstanding, the interests of these different classes remained as opposed as ever, although there was no longer a press, a parliament, a meeting-platform to proclaim this unpleasant fact; and thus, whatever the government might try to do for one class, was sure to hurt the interest of another. Whatever Louis Napoleon might attempt, he was to be met everywhere by the question, "who pays the piper?"—a question which has upset more governments than all other questions, Militia questions, Reform questions, &c., together. And although Louis Napoleon has already made his predecessor Louis Philippe contribute a good share to pay the piper,[151] yet the piper requires a good deal more.

We shall begin, in our next, to trace the position of the different classes of society in France, and to inquire how far there were any means at the disposal of the present government to improve that position. We shall at the same time review what that government has attempted and will most likely attempt later on for this purpose, and thus we shall collect materials from which to draw a correct conclusion as to the position and future chances of the man who is now doing his best to bring into disrepute the name of Napoleon.

Written in February-early April 1852

First published in the weekly *Notes to the People*, Nos. 43, 48 and 50; February 21, March 27 and April 10, 1852

Reproduced from *Notes to the People*

Karl Marx

STATEMENT
[SENT TO THE EDITORIAL BOARD
OF THE *KÖLNISCHE ZEITUNG*]

A report dated Paris, February 25 in No. 51 of the *Kölnische Zeitung* includes the following item à propos of the so-called Franco-German conspiracy[152]:

"Several of the accused, who have fled, among them a certain A. Majer, who is described as an *agent of Marx and his confederates*...."

The falsehood of this assertion, which generously accords me not only "confederates" but an "agent" as well, is proved by the following facts: A. Majer, one of the most intimate friends of Herr K. Schapper and the former Prussian lieutenant Willich, acted as book-keeper to the Refugee Committee headed by them.[153] I learned of the departure from London of this personage, who is a complete stranger to me, from a letter written by a friend[a] in Geneva in which he reported that a certain A. Majer was purveying the most absurd gossip about me. Finally I read in French newspapers that this A. Majer is a "politician".

London, March 3, 1852

Karl Marx

First published in the *Kölnische Zeitung*, No. 57, March 6, 1852

Printed according to the newspaper

---

[a] Probably Ernst Dronke.— *Ed.*

224

Karl Marx

GENERAL KLAPKA[154]

The following programme of General Klapka, which we have received from a reliable source, is to be handed to Kossuth on his arrival in London. It shows how greatly Kossuth's authority has been shaken among his more important supporters. It reads as follows:

POLITICAL PROGRAMME

As I am retiring from the arena of all political activity for a while, and perhaps for a long time, and do not wish that my principles and views should be incorrectly interpreted, I herewith declare to my friends:

1) No dictatorship, neither in the Fatherland nor outside it, so long as the decision of the nation has not been given on this matter.

2) In deference to the majority of my compatriots and in accordance with my own conviction, I recognise our honoured fellow-citizen Ludwig Kossuth as the head of the Hungarian Refugee Association, but at the same time I declare that I regard the clinging to the position and title of Governor as wholly incompatible with the basic principle of our revolutionary activity and very harmful to our cause.

3) With regard to our activity abroad.

   a) For the conduct of affairs, besides the appointed head, several members elected by all the émigrés should together with him constitute the Central Committee.

   b) The distribution of financial support obtained by exploiting Hungarian popularity must be guided not by personal conditions, but solely by the circumstances of the case, whether one is a loyal son of the Fatherland, what service one has rendered to the Fatherland, and whether in general one has any claim to support. Accordingly, the money intended by the Central Committee for private support must be administered in a non-partisan and public manner by committees which are elected by the respective refugee organisations themselves.

With regard to our activity at home.

As soon as Hungary is in a position to embark on a life and death struggle against its tyrants, those who will then stand at the head of the public cause should have the duty to convene in the shortest possible term a Constituent National

Assembly on the basis of universal suffrage as the sole revolutionary power, and the Government must be merely a creation of this Assembly.

4) Since it cannot be our task to interfere in the activity of the future representatives of the nation and already now draft a Constitution for our Fatherland, we can merely indicate those principles through which we expect the future prosperity of the Fatherland, its revival, power and welfare, and the guarantee of an indissoluble union of all the nationalities; these principles, however, if we wish to take into account the spirit and past of our nation, are liberty, equality and fraternity applied equally to both individuals and nationalities.

Those are my personal principles. But since providence, without taking into account our petty reasoning, often exerts its decisive influence on the fate of nations precisely where it is least expected, and since in my view the question of the future constitution of Hungary is at present only of secondary importance, whereas the throwing off of the Austrian yoke, which threatens our national existence with complete destruction, is a primary and vital question, I therefore declare that both my sword and my influence shall serve any foreign power whose aim is the overthrow of the Austrian dynasty as well as the restoration of the independence and political existence of Hungary.

April 1852

Georg Klapka
General

From the above programme one can very accurately judge Klapka's character. He firmly adheres to a position between two stools; he would like to appear independent and energetic, but is not strong enough for that. Natural instinct is stronger than his will. He wants Kossuth and also does not want him. With one hand he caresses him, with the other hand he slaps him in the face, but in order to soften the blows he puts on silk gloves. Klapka forgets that a box on the ears whether delivered with or without gloves always remains a box on the ears and that a vain, irritable, ambitious man like Kossuth is as little likely to forget a small insult as a big one. Vacillating, irresolute people like Klapka always have the misfortune of doing everything by halves. By this programme Klapka demonstrates his political immaturity, and the concluding sentence bears the stamp of clumsiness and of imprudence. Klapka forgets that an untimely word often suffices to betray entire plans. We hope that General Klapka will never be in a situation in which he has to regret the clumsiness of Klapka the diplomat.

Written in the first half of May 1852

First published in: Marx and Engels, *Works*, Second Russian Edition, Vol. 44, Moscow 1977

Printed according to the manuscript, which is in Jenny Marx's handwriting

Published in English for the first time

Karl Marx and Frederick Engels

THE GREAT MEN OF THE EXILE[155]

Written in May-June 1852

First published in Russian in
Marx-Engels Archives, Book 5,
Moscow-Leningrad, 1930

Printed according to the manuscript

I

"Sing, immortal soul,
the redemption of fallen mankind"[a]—
through Gottfried Kinkel.

Gottfried Kinkel was born some 40 years ago. The story of his life has been made available to us in an autobiography, *Gottfried Kinkel. Wahrheit ohne Dichtung. Biographisches Skizzenbuch.*[b] Edited by Adolph Strodtmann (Hamburg, Hoffmann & Campe, 1850, octavo).[c]

Gottfried is the hero of that democratic Siegwart epoch[156] that flooded Germany with endless torrents of patriotic melancholy and tearful lament. He made his debut as a commonplace lyrical Siegwart.

We are indebted to Strodtmann the Apostle, whose "narrative compilation" we follow here, both for the diary-like fragments in which Gottfried's pilgrimage on this earth is presented to the reader, and for the glaring lack of discretion of the revelations they contain.

Bonn, February-September 1834

"Like his friend, Paul Zeller, young Gottfried studied Protestant theology and his industry and piety earned him the respect of his celebrated teachers (Sack, Nitzsch and Bleek)" (p. 5).

From the very beginning he is "obviously immersed in weighty speculations" (p. 4), he is "cross and gloomy" (p. 5) as befits a *grand homme en herbe.*[d] "Gottfried's gloomily flashing brown eyes"

---

[a] F. G. Klopstock, *Der Messias,* Erster Gesang.—*Ed.*

[b] *Truth without Poetry. A Biographical Sketch-Book.* Apparently an allusion to Goethe's *Dichtung und Wahrheit (Poetry and Truth).—Ed.*

[c] The second volume of Strodtmann's book on Kinkel was published in 1851.—*Ed.*

[d] A budding genius.—*Ed.*

"observed" some youths "in brown jackets and pale-blue overcoats"; he at once sensed that these youths "wished to make up
for their inner emptiness by outer show" (p. 6). His moral
indignation is explained by the fact that Gottfried had "defended
Hegel and Marheineke" when these lads had called Marheineke a
"blockhead"; later, when he goes to study in Berlin and is himself
in the position of having to learn from Marheineke, he characterises him in his diary with the following belletristic dictum (p. 61):

> I tell you what: your groping theorist
> Is like a beast led round and round and round
> By evil spirits on a barren ground
> Near to the verdant pastures he has missed.[a]

Gottfried has clearly forgotten that other verse in which
Mephistopheles makes fun of the student thirsting for knowledge:

> So, knowledge and fair reason you'll despise.[b]

However, the whole moralising student scene serves merely as
an introduction enabling the future liberator of the world to make
the following revelation (p. 6).
Gottfried:

> "This race will not perish, unless a war comes.... Only strong remedies can raise
> this age up from the mire!"
> "A new Flood with you as a second and improved edition of Noah!" his friend
> replied.

The pale-blue overcoats have helped Gottfried to the point
where he can proclaim himself the "*Noah* in a new Flood". His
friend adds the following comment that might well have served as
the motto to the whole biography.

> "My father and I have often had occasion to smile at your *passion for unclear
> ideas*!"

Throughout these confessions of a beautiful soul[c] we find
repeated only one "clear idea", namely that Kinkel was a great
man from the moment of his conception. The most trivial things
that occur to all trivial people become momentous events; the
petty joys and sorrows that every student of theology experiences
in a more interesting form, the conflicts with bourgeois conditions
to be found by the dozen in every seminary and consistory in

---

[a] Goethe, *Faust*, Erster Teil, "Studierzimmer" (translation by Philip Mayne,
Penguin Books, 1949).—*Ed.*

[b] Ibid.—*Ed.*

[c] "Bekenntnisse einer schönen Seele" (Confessions of a Beautiful Soul) is the
title of Book 6 of Goethe's novel *Wilhelm Meisters Lehrjahre.*—*Ed.*

Germany become world-shaking events from which Gottfried, overwhelmed by *Weltschmerz*, fashions a perpetual comedy.[a]

The family of his "friend Paul" leaves Bonn and returns to Württemberg. Gottfried stages this event in the following manner.

Gottfried loves Paul's sister and uses the occasion to say that he has "already been in love twice before"! His present love, however, is no ordinary love but a "fervent and authentic act of divine worship" (p. 13). Gottfried climbs the Drachenfels together with friend Paul and against this romantic backcloth he breaks into dithyrambs:

"Farewell to friendship!—I shall find a brother in our Saviour;—Farewell to love—Faith shall be my bride;—Farewell to sisterly loyalty—I am come to the commune of many thousands of just souls! Away then, O my youthful heart, learn to be alone with your God; struggle with him until you conquer him and force him to give you a new name, that of holy Israel, which no one knows but he who receives it!—I give you greetings, you glorious rising sun, image of my awakening soul!" (p. 17).

Thus the departure of his friend gives Gottfried the opportunity to sing an ecstatic hymn to his own soul. As if that were not enough, his friend must also sing a hymn. For while Gottfried exults ecstatically he speaks "with solemn voice and glowing countenance", he "forgets the presence of his friend", "his gaze is transfigured", "his voice inspired", etc. (p. 17)—in short, we have the vision of the Prophet Elijah as it appears in the Bible complete in every detail.

"Smiling sorrowfully Paul looked at him with his loyal gaze and said: 'You have a mightier heart in your bosom than I and *will surely outdistance me*—but let me be your friend—even when I am far away.' Joyfully Gottfried clasped the proferred hand and renewed the ancient covenant" (p. 18).

Gottfried has got what he wants from this Transfiguration on the Mount. Friend Paul, who has just been laughing at "Gottfried's passion for unclear ideas", humbles himself before the name of "holy Israel" and acknowledges Gottfried's superiority and future greatness. Gottfried is as pleased as Punch and graciously condescends to renew the ancient covenant.

---

[a] The following passage is crossed out in the manuscript: "Thus we find that these confessions consistently present a double aspect—there is firstly the *comedy*, the amusing way in which Gottfried interprets the smallest trivia as signs of his future greatness and in anticipation of this casts himself in relief, and then there is the *rodomontade*, his mendacious manner of complacently embellishing in retrospect every little occurrence in his theologico-lyrical past. Having established these two basic features we can follow the further developments of Gottfried's story."—*Ed.*

* * *

The scene changes. It is the birthday of Kinkel's mother, the
wife of Pastor Kinkel of Upper Cassel. The family festival is used
to proclaim that "the lady, like the mother of our Lord, was called
Mary" (p. 20)—certain proof that Gottfried, too, was destined to
be a saviour and redeemer. Thus in the first twenty pages the
most insignificant events have been used to present our student of
theology in the role of *Noah,* the *holy Israel, Elijah,* and, lastly,
Christ.

* * *

Inevitably, Gottfried, who on the whole has experienced
nothing, constantly dwells on his inner feelings. The pietism that
has stuck to this parson's son and budding scholar of divinity is
well adapted both to his innate emotional instability and his
coquettish preoccupation with his own person. We learn that his
mother and sister were both strict pietists and that Gottfried was
very conscious of his own sinfulness. The conflict of this pious
sense of sin with the "carefree and sociable *joie de vivre*" of the
ordinary student appears in Gottfried, as befits his world-historical
mission, in terms of a struggle between religion and poetry. The
pint of beer that the parson's son from Upper Cassel downs with
the other students becomes the fateful chalice in which Faust's
twin spirits are locked in battle. In the description of his pietistic
family life we see his "Mother Mary" combat as sinful "Gottfried's
penchant for the theatre" (p. 28), a momentous conflict designed
to prefigure the poet of the future but which in fact merely
highlights Gottfried's love of the theatrical. The harpy-like pietism
of his sister Johanna is said to be shown by an incident in which
she is supposed to have boxed the ears of a five-year-old girl for
inattention in church—sordid family gossip whose inclusion would
be incomprehensible were it not for the revelation at the end of
the book that this same sister Johanna put up the strongest
opposition to Gottfried's marriage to Frau Mockel.

The fact that in Seelscheid Gottfried preached "a wonderful
sermon about the wilting wheat" is recounted as an event.

* * *

The Zeller family and "beloved Elise" at last take their
departure. We learn that Gottfried "squeezed the girl's hand

passionately" and murmured the greeting, "Elise, farewell! I must say no more". This interesting story is followed by the first of Siegwart's laments.

"Destroyed!" "Silent." "Most agonising torment!" "Burning brow." "Deepest sighs." "His mind was lacerated by the wildest pains," etc. (p. 37).

It turns the whole Elijah scene into the purest comedy, performed for the benefit of his "friend Paul" and himself. Paul again makes his appearance in order to whisper into the ear of Siegwart, who is sitting there alone and wretched: "This kiss is for my Gottfried" (p. 38).

And Gottfried cheers up.

"My plan to see my sweet love again, honourably and *not without a name,* is firmer than ever" (p. 38).

Neither considerations about the name he expects to make nor bragging of the laurels he claims in advance are wanting even amid the pangs of love. Gottfried uses the intermezzo to commit his love to paper in extravagant and vainglorious terms, to make sure that the world is not deprived of even his diary-feelings. But the scene has not yet reached its climax. The faithful Paul has to point out to the world-storming maestro that if Elise were to remain stationary while he continued to develop, she might not satisfy him later on.

"O no!" said Gottfried. "This heavenly budding flower whose first leaves have scarcely opened already smells so sweetly. How much greater will be her beauty when ... the burning summer *ray* of manly *vigour* unfolds her *innermost calix!*" (p. 40).

Paul finds himself reduced to answering this sordid image by remarking that rational arguments mean nothing to poets.

"'And all your wisdom will not protect you from the whims of life better than our *lovable* folly,' Gottfried replied *with a smile*" (p. 40).

What a moving picture: Narcissus smiling to himself! The gauche student suddenly enters as the lovable fool, Paul becomes Wagner and admires the great man, and the great man "smiles", "indeed, he smiles a kind, gentle smile". The climax is saved.

*   *   *

Gottfried finally manages to leave Bonn. He gives this summary of his educational attainments there:

"Unfortunately I am gradually moving further away from Hegelianism; although my greatest wish is to be a rationalist,[157] I am at the same time a supernaturalist and a mystic, *if necessary* I am even a pietist" (p. 45).

This self-analysis requires no commentary.

* * *

Berlin, October 1834-August 1835

Leaving his narrow family and student environment Gottfried arrives in Berlin. In comparison with Bonn, Berlin is relatively metropolitan but of this we find no trace in Gottfried any more than we find evidence of his involvement in the scientific activity of the day. Gottfried's diary entries confine themselves to the emotions he experiences together with his new *compagnon d'aventure,* Hugo Dünweg from Barmen, and also to the minor hardships of an indigent theologian: his money difficulties, shabby coats, employment as a reviewer, etc. His life stands in no relation to the public life of the city, but only to the Schlössing family, in which Dünweg passes for *Master Wolfram*[a] and Gottfried for *Master Gottfried von Strasbourg* (p. 67). Elise fades gradually from his heart and he conceives a new itch for Fräulein Maria Schlössing. Unfortunately he learns of Elise's engagement to someone else and he sums up his Berlin feelings and aspirations as a "*dark* longing for a woman he could [call] *wholly* his own".

However, Berlin must not be abandoned without making the inevitable point:

"Before he left Berlin old Weiss" (the producer) "took him *once again* into the theatre. A strange feeling came over the youth as the friendly old man led him into the great auditorium where the busts of German dramatists have been placed and with a gesture towards a few empty niches said meaningfully:

"'*There are still some vacant places.*'"

Yes, indeed, there is still a place vacant awaiting our Platenite Gottfried who solemnly allows an old *farceur*[b] to present him with the exquisite pleasure of "future immortality".

Bonn, Autumn 1835-Autumn 1837

"Constantly vacillating between art, life and science, unable to reach a decision, active in all three without firm commitment, he intended to learn, to gain and to be creative in all three as much as his indecision would permit" (p. 89).

---

[a] Wolfram von Eschenbach.— *Ed.*
[b] Comedian.— *Ed.*

Having thus discovered himself to be an irresolute dilettante, Gottfried returns to Bonn. Of course, the feeling that he is a dilettante does not deter him from taking his licentiate examination and from becoming a *Privatdozent* at the University of Bonn.

"Neither Chamisso nor Knapp had published the poems he had sent them in their pocket almanacs[a] and this hurt him greatly" (p. 99).

This is the public debut of the great man who in private circles lives on intellectual tick on the promise of his future eminence. From this time on he definitely becomes a dubious local celebrity in belletristic student circles until the moment when a grazing shot in Baden suddenly turns him into the hero of German philistinism.

"But more and more there arose in Kinkel's breast the yearning for a firm, true love, a yearning that no devotion to work could dispel" (p. 103).

The first victim of this yearning is a certain Minna. Gottfried dallies with Minna and sometimes for the sake of variety he acts the compassionate Mahadeva who allows the maiden to worship him[b] while he meditates on the state of her health.

"Kinkel could have loved her had he been able to deceive himself about her condition; but his *love* would have *killed* the wilting rose even more quickly. Minna was the first girl that could understand him; but she was a second Hecuba and would have borne him torches and not children, and through them the passion of the parents would have burned down their own house as Priam's passion burned Troy. Yet he could not abandon her, his heart bled for her, *he was indeed wretched not through love, but through pity*."

The godlike hero whose love is supposed to kill, like the sight of Jupiter, is nothing but an ordinary self-regarding young coxcomb who in the course of his marriage-studies tries out the role of the cad for the first time. Moreover, his revolting meditations on her health and its possible effects on any future children are turned into base speculations by the fact that he prolongs the relationship for his own pleasure and breaks it off only when it provides him with the excuse for yet another melodramatic scene.

Gottfried goes on a journey to visit an uncle whose son has just died; at the midnight hour in the room where the corpse is laid out he stages a scene from a Bellini opera with his cousin, Mlle Elise II. He becomes engaged to her, "in the presence of the

---

[a] An allusion to the *Deutscher Musenalmanach* (ed. Adelbert von Chamisso and Gustav Schwab) and to *Christoterpe. Ein Taschenbuch für christliche Leser* (ed. Albert Knapp).— *Ed.*

[b] Cf. Goethe's poem "Der Gott und die Bajadere".— *Ed.*

dead", and on the following morning he is fortunately accepted by his uncle as his future son-in-law.

"Now that he was lost to her forever, he often thought of Minna and of the moment when he would see her again. But he did not fear this moment as she could have no claims on a heart that was already pledged" (p. 117).

The new engagement means nothing but the opportunity to bring about a dramatic collision in his relationship with Minna, in which "duty and passion" confront each other. This collision is produced in the most philistine and rascally way because in his own mind our bonhomme denies Minna's legal claims upon his heart which is already "pledged". The virtuous man is of course not at all disturbed by the need to compound this cowardly lie to himself by reversing the order of events in the matter of his "pledged heart".

Gottfried has plunged into the interesting necessity of being forced to break "a poor, great heart".

"After a pause Gottfried went on: 'At the same time, dear Minna, I feel I owe you an apology—I have perhaps sinned against you—the hand which I let you have yesterday with such feelings of friendship, that hand is no longer free—I am engaged!'" (p. 123).

Our melodramatic student takes good care not to mention that this engagement took place a few hours after he had given her his hand "with such feelings of friendship".

"Oh God!—Minna—can you forgive me?" (*loc. cit.*)

"I am a man and must be faithful to my *duty*—I *must* not love you! But I have not deceived you" (p. 124).

After this moral duty which has been contrived after the event, it only remains to produce the unbelievable, a theatrical reversal of the whole relationship so that instead of Minna forgiving him, our moral priest forgives the deceived woman. With this in mind he conceives the possibility that Minna "might hate him from afar" and he follows this supposition up with this final moral:

"'I would gladly forgive you for that and if that should happen you can be assured of my forgiveness in advance. And now farewell, my duty calls me, I must leave you!' He slowly left the arbour.... From that hour on Gottfried was unhappy" (p. 124).

The actor and conceited lover is transformed into the hypocritical priest who extricates himself from the affair with an unctuous blessing; Siegwart's sham conflicts of love have led to the happy result that he is able in his imagination to think himself unhappy.

It finally becomes apparent that all of these arranged love stories were nothing but Gottfried's coquettish flirtation with himself. The whole affair amounts to no more than that our priest, who dreams of his future immortality, has enacted Old Testament stories and modern lending-library phantasies after the manner of Spiess, Clauren and Cramer so that he may indulge his vanity by posing as a romantic hero.

"Rummaging among his books he came across Novalis' *Ofterdingen*, the book that had so often inspired him to write poetry a year before. While still at school he and some friends had founded a society by the name of *Teutonia* with the aim of increasing their understanding of German history and literature. In this society he had assumed the name of *Heinrich von Ofterdingen*.... Now the meaning of this name became clear to him. He *saw himself as that same Heinrich* in the charming little town at the foot of the Wartburg and a longing for the '*blue flower*' took hold of him with overwhelming force. Minna could not be the glorious fairy-tale blossom, nor could his bride, however anxiously he probed his heart. Dreaming, he read on and on, the phantastic world of magic enveloped him and he ended by hurling himself weeping into a chair, thinking of the '*blue flower*'."

Gottfried here unveils the whole romantic lie which he had woven around himself; the carnival pursuit of disguising oneself as other people is his authentic "inner being". Earlier on he had called himself Gottfried von Strasbourg; now he appears as *Heinrich von Ofterdingen* and he is searching not for the "blue flower" but for a woman who will acknowledge his claims to be Heinrich von Ofterdingen. And in the end he really did find the "blue flower", a little faded and yellow, in a woman who played the much longed-for comedy in his interest and in her own.

The sham Romanticism, the travesty and the caricature of ancient stories and romances which Gottfried *re-lives* to make up for the lack of any inner substance of his own, the whole emotional swindle of his vacuous encounters with Mary, Minna and Elise I and II have brought him to the point where he thinks that his experiences are on a par with those of Goethe. Just as Goethe after experiencing the storms of love suddenly set out for Italy and there wrote his [Roman] *Elegies*, so too Gottfried thinks that his day-dreams of love qualify him for an expedition to Rome. Goethe must have had a premonition of Gottfried:

> And as the whale has his lice
> I can have them too.[a]

---

[a] Goethe, *Zahme Xenien.*—Ed.

Italy, October 1837-March 1838

The expedition to Rome opens in Gottfried's diary with a lengthy account of the journey from Bonn to Coblenz.

This new epoch begins as the previous one had concluded, namely with a narrative richly embellished by allusions to the experiences of others. While on the steamer Gottfried recalls the "splendid passage in Hoffmann" where he "made Master Johannes Wacht produce a highly artistic work immediately after enduring the most overwhelming grief".[158] As a confirmation of the "splendid passage" Gottfried follows up his "overwhelming grief" about Minna by "*meditating*" about a "tragedy he had *long since intended to write*" (p. 140).

During Kinkel's journey from Coblenz to Rome the following events take place:

"The friendly letters he frequently received from his fiancée and which he answered for the most part on the spot, dispelled his gloomy thoughts" (p. 144).

"His love for the beautiful Elise II struck root deeply in the youth's yearning bosom" (p. 146).

* * *

In Rome we find:

"On his arrival in Rome Kinkel had found a letter from his fiancée awaiting him which further intensified his love for her and caused the image of Minna to fade even more into the background. His heart assured him that Elise could make him happy and he gave himself up to this feeling with the purest passion.... Only now did he realise what love is" (p. 151).

We see that Minna, whom formerly he only loved "out of pity", has re-entered the emotional scene. In his relationship with Elise his dream is that she can make him happy, not he her. And yet in his "blue flower" fantasy he had already said that the fairy-tale blossom which had given him such a poetic itch could be neither Elise nor Minna. But his newly aroused feelings for these two girls now serve as part of the mise en scène for a new conflict.

"Kinkel's poetry seemed to be slumbering in Italy" (p. 151).

Why?

"Because he still lacked *form*" (p. 152).

We learn later that a six-month stay in Italy enabled him to bring the "*form*" back to Germany well wrapped up. As Goethe had written his *Elegies* in Rome so Kinkel too thinks up an elegy called *The Awakening of Rome* (p. 153).

* * *

Kinkel's maid brings him a letter from his fiancée. He opens it joyfully—

"and sank back on his bed with a cry. Elise announced that a wealthy man, a Dr. D. with an extensive practice and even a riding horse (!), had asked for her hand in marriage. As it would probably be a long time before he, Kinkel, an indigent theologian, would have a permanent position she asked him to release her from the bonds that tied her to him".

A complete reminiscence of *Menschenhass und Reue*.[a]

Gottfried "annihilated", "terrible petrification", "dry eyed", "thirst for revenge", "dagger", "the bosom of his rival", "heart-blood of his enemy", "cold as ice", "maddening pain", etc. (pp. 156 and 157).

In these "sorrows and joys of a poor theologian" it is the thought that she had "spurned" him for the sake of the "uncertain possession of earthly goods" (p. 157) that gives most pain to our unhappy student. Having been moved by the obligatory theatrical feelings he finally rises to the following consolation:

"She was unworthy of you—and you still possess the pinions of genius that will bear you aloft high above this dark misery! *And when one day your fame encircles the globe* the false woman will find a judge in her own heart!—Who knows, perhaps one day in the years to come *her children* will seek me out to implore my aid and *I would not wish to evade that rashly*" (p. 157).

Having, inevitably, enjoyed in advance the exquisite pleasure of "his future fame encircling the globe", he thus reveals himself to be a common clerical philistine. He speculates that later on Elise's children might perhaps come to beg alms from the great poet—and he would "not wish to evade that rashly". And why? Because Elise "prefers a riding horse" to the "future fame" of which he constantly dreams, because she prefers "earthly goods" to the farce he intends to perform with himself in the role of Heinrich von Ofterdingen. Old Hegel was quite right when he pointed out that a noble consciousness always turns into a base one.[b]

Bonn, Summer 1838-Summer 1843
(*Intrigue and Love*)[c]

Having furnished a caricature of Goethe in Italy, Gottfried now resolves on his return to enact Schiller's *Kabale und Liebe*.

---

[a] A drama by August Kotzebue.—*Ed.*
[b] G. W. F. Hegel, *Phänomenologie des Geistes*, VI. Der Geist.—*Ed.*
[c] *Intrigue and Love*—a tragedy by Schiller.—*Ed.*

Though his heart is rent with *Weltschmerz* Gottfried feels "better than ever" physically (p. 167). His intention is "to establish literary fame for himself through his works" (p. 169), which does not however prevent him from acquiring a cheaper fame without work later on when his "works" failed to do what was expected of them.

The "dark longing" which Gottfried always experiences when he pursues a "female of the species" finds expression in a remarkably rapid succession of promises of marriage and engagements. The promise of marriage is the classical method by which the strong man and the superior mind "of the future" seeks to conquer his beloved ones and bind them to him in reality. As soon as he thinks he has found a little blue flower that might help him to play the part of Heinrich von Ofterdingen, the poet's gentle and hazy sentimentality assumes the firm shape of the student's dream of adding to the ideal affinity the bond of "duty". No sooner are the first greetings over than offers of marriage fly in all directions *à tort et à travers*[a] towards every daisy and water lily in sight. This bourgeois hunt puts in an even more revolting light the feeble wheedling coquetry with which Gottfried constantly opens his heart to reveal "the great torments of the poet".

Thus after his return from Italy Gottfried naturally has to "promise" marriage yet again. The object of his passion on this occasion was directly chosen by his sister, the lady Johanna, whose fanatical pietism has already been immortalised by the exclamations in Gottfried's diary.

"Bögehold had just recently announced his engagement to Fräulein Kinkel, and Johanna, who interfered more obtrusively than ever in her brother's affairs of the heart, now conceived the wish, for a number of reasons and family considerations which are better passed over in silence, that Gottfried should *reciprocate* and marry Fräulein Sophie Bögehold, her fiancé's sister" (p. 172). It goes without saying that "Kinkel *could not but* feel drawn to a gentle girl.... And she was indeed a dear, innocent maiden" (p. 173). "In the most tender fashion"—it goes without saying—"Kinkel asked for her hand which was joyfully promised him by her happy parents as soon as"—it goes without saying—"he had obtained a secure post and was in a position to lead his bride home as"—it goes without saying—"a professor or owner of a quiet parsonage."

On this occasion our passionate student set down in elegant verses an account of that tendency towards marriage that forms such a constant ingredient of his adventures.

> Nothing else can stir my passion
> So much as a small white hand.

---

[a] Indiscriminately.—*Ed.*

Everything else, eyes, lips, locks, is dismissed as a mere "trifle".

> All these fail to stir his passion
> But her shapely, small white hand (p. 174).

He describes the flirtation that he begins with Fräulein Sophie Bögehold at the command of "his more than ever obtrusive sister Johanna" and because of the constant stimulus of his longing for a "hand", as "deep, firm and tranquil" (p. 175). Above all "it is the *religious* element that predominates in this new love" (p. 176).

In Gottfried's romances the religious element takes the place either of the novelistic or of the theatrical element. Where he cannot devise dramatic effects to achieve new Siegwart situations he applies religious feelings to adorn these banal episodes with the patina of higher meaning. Siegwart becomes a pious Jung-Stilling, who had likewise received such miraculous strength from God that even though three women perished beneath his manly chest he was still able repeatedly to "lead home" a new love.

* * *

We come finally to the fateful catastrophe of this eventful story of his life, to Stilling's meeting with *Johanna Mockel,* who had formerly borne the married name of Mathieux. Here Gottfried discovered a female Kinkel, his romantic *alter ego.* Only she was harder, smarter, less confused and thanks to her mature age she had left her youthful illusions behind her.

What Mockel had in common with Kinkel was the fact that her talents too had gone unrecognised by the world. She was repulsive and vulgar; her first marriage had been "unhappy". She possessed musical talents but not enough to make a great stir with her compositions or technical mastery. In Berlin her attempt to imitate the stale childhood antics of Bettina[a] had led to a fiasco. Her character had been soured by her experiences. Even though she shared with Kinkel the foppish affectation of inflating the ordinary events of her life so as to invest them with "greater solemnity", owing to her more advanced age she nevertheless felt a *need* for love (according to Strodtmann) that was more pressing than her need for the poetic drivel that accompanies it. Whereas Kinkel was feminine in this respect, Mockel was masculine. Hence nothing could be more natural than for such a person to enter with joy into Kinkel's comedy of the misunderstood beautiful souls

---

[a] Bettina von Arnim.— *Ed.*

and to play it to a mutually satisfying conclusion, i.e. to acknowledge Siegwart's fitness for the role of Heinrich von Ofterdingen and to allow him to discover that she was the "blue flower".

Kinkel, having been led to his third or fourth fiancée by his sister, is now introduced into a new labyrinth of love by Mockel.

Gottfried now finds himself in the "social swim" (p. 190), i.e. in one of those little "circles" consisting of the professors or other "worthies" of German university towns. Only in the lives of Teutonic Christian students can such societies mark a new epoch. Mockel sings and is applauded. At table it is arranged that Gottfried should sit next to her and here the following scene takes place:

"'It must be a glorious feeling,' Gottfried opined, 'to fly through the joyous world on the pinions of genius, admired by all.'—'That's what you *imagine*,' Mockel exclaimed. 'I hear that you have a great gift for poetry. Perhaps people will scatter incense for you *also* ... and I shall ask you then whether you are happy, if you are not...'—'If I am not?' Gottfried asked, as she paused" (p. 188).

The bait had been put out for our clumsy lyrical student. Mockel then informs him that she had recently heard

"him preaching about the yearning of Christians to return to their faith and she had thought about how resolutely the handsome youth must have renounced the world who had aroused a timid longing even in her for the harmless childhood slumber with which the echo of faith now lost had once surrounded her" (p. 189).

Gottfried was "enchanted" (p. 189) by such politeness. He was tremendously pleased to discover that "Mockel was unhappy" (loc. cit.). He immediately resolved "to devote his passionate enthusiasm for the faith of salvation at the hands of Jesus Christ to bringing back this sorrowing soul *too* into the fold" (loc. cit.). As Mockel was a Catholic the friendship was formed on the imaginary basis of the task of recovering a soul "in the service of the Almighty", a comedy in which Mockel too was willing to participate.

*   *   *

"In 1840 Kinkel was appointed as an assistant in the Protestant community in Cologne, where he went every Sunday morning to preach" (p. 193).

This comment of the biographer may serve as an excuse for a brief discussion of Kinkel's position as a theologian. "In 1840" the critical movement had already mercilessly dissected the content of the Christian faith; with Bruno Bauer scientific [criticism] had reached the point of open conflict with the state. It is at this juncture that Kinkel makes his debut as a preacher. But as he lacks both the energy of the orthodox and the understanding that would enable him to see theology objectively, he comes to terms with Christianity on the level of lyrical and declamatory sentimentality à la Krummacher. He presents Christ as a "friend and leader", he seeks to do away with "ugliness" in the formal aspects of Christianity, and for the content he substitutes a hollow phraseology. The device by means of which content is replaced by form and ideas by phrases has produced a host of declamatory priests in Germany whose last offshoots had of course to lead to *democracy*. But whereas in theology at least a superficial knowledge is still essential here and there, in the democratic movement, where an orotund but vacuous rhetoric, *nullité sonore,*[a] makes intellect and an insight into realities completely superfluous, an empty phraseology came into its own. Kinkel, whose theological studies had led to nothing beyond the making of sentimental extracts of Christianity in the manner of Clauren, was in speech and in his writings the epitome of this fraudulent pulpit oratory that is also described as "poetic prose" and which he oddly enough now made the basis of his "poetic mission". His poetastering, moreover, is [not][b] aimed at planting true laurels but only red rowan berries with which he beautifies the highway of trivia. This same feebleness of character which attempts to overcome conflicts not by resolving their content but by clothing them in a facile form is visible too in the way he lectures at the university. The struggle to abolish the old scholastic pedantry is sidestepped by means of a "free and easy" attitude which turns the lecturer into a student and exalts the student placing him on an equal footing with the lecturer. This school then produced a whole generation of Strodtmanns, Schurzes and suchlike who eventually were able to make use of their phraseology, their knowledge and their unexacting "lofty mission" only in the democratic movement.

* * *

The new love-affair develops into the story of *Gockel, Hinkel und Gackeleia.*[c]

---

[a] A noisy nothingness.—*Ed.*

[b] The manuscript is damaged here.—*Ed.*

[c] An allusion to Clemens Brentano's fairy-tale about Gockel, Hinkel and Gackeleia (Cock, Hen and Chick). A comic effect is achieved here because of the similarity between *Gockel* (Cock) and Mockel, and *Hinkel* (Hen) and Kinkel.—*Ed.*

The year 1840 was a turning point in the history of Germany. On the one hand, the critical application of Hegel's philosophy to theology and politics had brought about a scientific revolution. On the other hand, from Frederick William IV's accession to the throne dates the emergence of a bourgeois movement whose constitutional aspirations still had a wholly radical appearance—from the vague "political poetry" of the period to the new phenomenon of a daily press which constituted a revolutionary power.

What was Gottfried doing during this period? Together with Mockel he founded the *Maikäfer, eine Zeitschrift für Nicht-Philister*[a] (p. 209) and the May-Bug Club. The aim of this paper was nothing more than

"to provide a cheerful and enjoyable evening for a group of friends once a week and to give the participants the opportunity to present their works for criticism by a benevolent, artistically-minded audience" (pp. 209-10).

The real purpose of the May-Bug Club was to solve the riddle of the blue flower. The meetings took place in Mockel's house, and their object was the acclamation of Mockel as "Queen" (p. 210) and of Kinkel as "Minister" (p. 255) by a group of insignificant literary students. Here the two misunderstood beautiful souls found it possible to make up for the "injustice the harsh world had done them" (p. 296); they could recognise each other in the roles of Heinrich von Ofterdingen and the blue flower. Gottfried, to whom the copying of other people's roles had become second nature, must have felt happy to have at last created a real "*amateur theatre*" (p. 254). The farce was itself the prelude to practical developments:

"These evenings provided the opportunity to see Mockel also in the house of her parents" (p. 212).

Moreover, the May-Bug Club copied also the Hainbund[159] in Göttingen, only with the difference that the latter represented a stage in the development of German literature while the former remained on the level of an insignificant local caricature. The "merry May-Bugs" (p. 254), for instance, Sebastian Longard, Leo Hasse, C. A. Schlönbach, were, as the apologetic biographer admits, pale, insipid, indolent, unimportant youths (pp. 211 and 298).

---

[a] *May-Bug, a Journal for Non-Philistines.—Ed.*

* * *

Naturally, Gottfried soon began to make "comparisons" (p. 221) between Mockel and his fiancée, but he had "had no time hitherto"—much against his habit—"for the customary reflections on weddings and matrimony" (p. 219). In a word, he stood like Buridan's ass between the two bundles of hay, unable to decide between them. But with her greater maturity and very practical bent Mockel "clearly discerned the invisible bond" (p. 225); she resolved to give "chance or the will of God" (p. 229) a helping hand.

"At a time of day when Gottfried was usually prevented by his scholarly work as a teacher from seeing Mockel, he one day went to visit her and as he quietly approached her room he heard the sound of a mournful song. Pausing to listen he heard this song:

> You draw nigh! And like the dawn
> There trembles on my cheeks, etc., etc.,
> Many a nameless pain.
> Alas, you feel them not!

"A long drawn-out, melancholy chord concluded her song and faded gradually in the breeze" (pp. 230 and 231).

Gottfried crept away unobserved, as he imagined, and having arrived home again he found the situation very interesting. He wrote a number of despairing sonnets in which he compared Mockel to the Lorelei (p. 233). In order to escape from the Lorelei and to remain true to Fräulein Sophie Bögehold he tried to obtain a post as a teacher in Wiesbaden, but was rejected. This accident was compounded by a further intervention by fate which proved to be decisive. Not only was "the sun striving to leave the sign of Virgo" (p. 236), but also Gottfried and Mockel took a trip down the Rhine in a skiff; their skiff was overturned by an approaching steam-boat and Gottfried swam ashore bearing Mockel.

"As he drew towards the shore he felt her heart close to his and was suddenly overwhelmed by the feeling that only *this* woman would be able to make him happy" (p. 238).

This time Gottfried at last experienced not an imaginary but a real scene from a novel, from the *Wahlverwandtschaften*.[a] This decided the matter; he broke off his engagement to Sophie Bögehold.

---

[a] *Elective Affinities,* a novel by J. W. Goethe.—*Ed.*

* * *

First love, then the intrigue. In the name of the Presbytery Pastor Engels protested to Gottfried that the marriage of a divorced woman and a Catholic to a Protestant preacher was offensive. Gottfried replied by appealing to the eternal rights of man and made the following points with a good deal of unction.

1. "It was no crime for him to have drunk coffee with the lady in Hirzekümpchen" (p. 249).
2. "The matter was ambiguous as he had not announced in public either that he intended to marry the lady, or that he did not intend to do so" (p. 251).
3. "As far as faith was concerned, no one can know what the future holds in store" (p. 250).
"And now, may I ask you to step inside and have a cup of coffee" (p. 251).

With this cliché Gottfried and Pastor Engels, who could not resist such an invitation, left the stage. In this way, quietly and yet forcefully, Gottfried was able to resolve the conflict with the existing conditions.

* * *

The following extract serves to illustrate the effect of the May-Bug Club on Gottfried:

"It was June 29, 1841. On this day the first anniversary of the May-Bug Club was to be celebrated on a grand scale" (p. 253). "A shout as of one voice arose to decide who should carry off the prize. Modestly Gottfried bent his knee before the Queen, who placed the inevitable laurel wreath on his glowing brow, while the setting sun cast its brightest rays over the transfigured countenance of the poet" (p. 285).

The solemn dedication of the imagined poetic fame of Heinrich von Ofterdingen is followed by the feelings and the wishes of the blue flower. That evening Mockel sang a May-Bug anthem she had composed which ends with the following stanza summarising the whole trend:

> And what's the moral of the tale?
> Fly, May-Bug, fly!
> A man who's old will ne'er find a wife,
> So make haste, do not waste your life,
> Fly, May-Bug, fly!

The ingenuous biographer remarks that "the invitation to marriage contained in the stanza was wholly free of any ulterior motives" (p. 255). Gottfried perceived the ulterior motives but "did not wish to evade rashly" the opportunity of being crowned for two further years before the whole May-Bug Club and of being an object of passion. So he married Mockel on May 22, 1843, after she had become a member of the Protestant Church despite her lack of faith. This was done on the absurd pretext that "definite articles of faith are less important in the Protestant Church than the *ethical* idea" (p. 315).

> So that's the moral of the tale:
> Trust not blue flowers, bright or pale.

* * *

Gottfried had entered into the relationship with Mockel on the pretext of leading her out of her unbelief into the Protestant Church. Mockel now demanded *Das Leben Jesu*[a] by Strauss and lapsed again into her unbelief,

"and with a heavy heart he followed her on the path of doubt into the abysses of negation. Together with her he toiled through the labyrinthine jungle of modern philosophy" (p. 308).

He is driven into negation not by the development of philosophy which was already having an effect on the masses but by the intervention of a chance emotional relationship.

What he brings with him out of the labyrinth of philosophy is revealed in his diaries:

"I should like to see whether the mighty current flowing from Kant to Feuerbach will drive me out into—*pantheism!!*" (p. 308).

As though this current did not go beyond pantheism, and as though Feuerbach were the last word in German philosophy!

"The key-stone of my life," the diary goes on to say, "is not historical knowledge, but a coherent system, and the core of theology is not ecclesiastical history, but dogma" (*ibid.*).

As if German philosophy had not dissolved the coherent systems into historical knowledge and the core of dogma into ecclesiastical history! These confessions clearly reveal the counter-revolutionary democrat for whom the movement is nothing more than a means by which to arrive at a few incontrovertible eternal truths as worthless points of rest.

However, Gottfried's apologetic book-keeping of his whole development will enable the reader to judge which revolutionary factor lay concealed in this melodramatic, play-acting theologian.

---

[a] D. F. Strauss, *The Life of Jesus.*— *Ed.*

II

This brings to a close the first act of the drama of Kinkel's life and nothing worthy of mention then occurs before the outbreak of the February revolution. The publishing house of Cotta accepted his poems but without offering him a royalty and most of the copies remained unsold until that stray bullet in Baden gave a poetic nimbus to the author and created a market for his products.

Incidentally, our biographer omits mention of one significant fact. The self-confessed goal of Kinkel's desires was that he should die as an old theatre director: his ideal was a certain Eisenhut who together with his troupe used to roam up and down the Rhine as a travelling pickle-herring and who afterwards went mad.

Alongside his Bonn lectures with their rhetoric of the pulpit, Gottfried also gave a number of theological and aesthetic performances in Cologne from time to time. When the February revolution broke out, he concluded them with this prophetic utterance:

"The thunder of battle reverberates over to us from Paris and opens a new and glorious era for Germany and the whole continent of Europe. The raging storm will be followed by Zephyr's blissful breeze of freedom. On this day is born the great, fruitful epoch of — *constitutional monarchy!*"

The constitutional monarchy expressed its thanks to Kinkel for this compliment by appointing him associate professor. Such recognition could however not suffice for our *grand homme en herbe*. The constitutional monarchy showed no eagerness to cause his "fame to encircle the globe". Moreover, the laurels Freiligrath had collected for his recent political poems prevented the crowned May-Bug poet from sleeping. Heinrich von Ofterdingen, therefore, wheeled to the left and became first a constitutional democrat and then a republican democrat (*honnête et modéré*). He set out to become a deputy but the May elections took him neither to Berlin nor to Frankfurt. Despite this initial setback he pursued his objective undismayed and it can truthfully be said that he did not spare himself. He wisely limited himself at first to his immediate environment. He founded the *Bonner Zeitung*, a modest local product distinguished only by the peculiar feebleness of its democratic rhetoric and its naive patriotic ignorance. He elevated the May-Bug Club to the rank of a democratic students' club and from this there duly flowed a host of disciples that bore the Master's renown into every village of the district of Bonn and

forced Professor Kinkel upon every assembly. He himself poli-
ticked with the grocers in their club, he extended a brotherly
hand to the worthy manufacturers and even hawked the warm
breath of freedom among the peasantry of Kindenich and
Seelscheid. Above all he reserved his sympathy for the honourable
trade of master craftsmen. He wept together with them over the
decay of handicrafts, the terrible effects of free competition, the
modern dominance of capital and of machines. Together with
them he devised plans to restore the guild system and to prevent
the competition of non-guild masters. So as to do everything of
which he was capable he set down the results of his club
deliberations with the petty master craftsmen in the pamphlet
entitled *Handwerk, errette Dich!*[a]

Lest there be any doubt as to Herr Kinkel's position and to the
significance of his little tract for Frankfurt and the nation, he
dedicated it to the "thirty members of the economic committee of
the Frankfurt National Assembly".

Heinrich von Ofterdingen's researches into the "beauty" of the
handicrafts led him immediately to the discovery that "the
handicrafts are at present divided by a yawning chasm" (p. 5).
This chasm consists in the fact that some artisans "frequent the
clubs of the grocers and officials" (what progress!) and that others
do not do this, and also in the fact that some artisans are educated
and others are not. Despite this chasm the author regards the
artisans' associations and assemblies springing up everywhere in
the beloved fatherland and the agitation for enhancing the
position of the handicrafts (we recall the programmes à la
Winkelblech[160] of 1848) as a gratifying symptom. In order to
contribute his mite of good advice to this beneficent movement he
devises his own programme of salvation.

He begins by examining how the evil effects of *free competition*
can be remedied by restricting it but without eliminating it
altogether. The solutions he proposes are these:

"A youth who lacks the requisite ability and maturity should be debarred by law
from becoming a master" (p. 20).

"No master shall be permitted to have more than one apprentice at any given
time" (p. 29).

"An examination must also be introduced for teaching a craft" (p. 30).

"The master of an apprentice must unfailingly attend the examination" (p. 31).

"On the question of maturity it should become mandatory that henceforth no
one may become a master before completion of his twenty-fifth year" (p. 42).

---

[a] "Handicraft, save yourself!"—*Ed.*

"As evidence of ability every candidate for the title of master should henceforth be required to pass an examination and moreover in public" (p. 43).

"In this context it is of vital importance that the examination should be free" (p. 44).

"All provincial masters of the same guild must likewise submit themselves" to these examinations (p. 55).

Friend Gottfried, who is himself engaged in political peddling, desires to abolish "itinerant trading or peddling" in other, profane wares on the grounds of its dishonesty (p. 60).

"A manufacturer of craft goods desires to withdraw his assets from the business to his own advantage and, dishonestly, to the disadvantage of his creditors. Like all ambivalent things, this phenomenon too is described by a foreign word: it is called bankruptcy. He therefore quickly takes his finished products to some neighbouring towns and sells them there to the highest bidder" (p. 64). These auctions—"in actual fact a sort of garbage that our dear neighbour, commerce, disposes of in the garden of handicraft"—must be abolished.

(Would it not be much simpler, Friend Gottfried, to go to the root of the matter and abolish bankruptcy itself?)

"It is true that fairs are in a special position" (p. 65). "In these circumstances the law will have to let the various towns and villages call an assembly of all the citizens to decide by majority vote (!) whether existing fairs should be retained or abolished" (p. 68).

Gottfried now comes to the "vexed question" of the relationship between handicraft and machine industry and brings to light the following:

"Let everyone *sell only those goods that he himself can produce with his own hands*" (p. 80). "Because machines and handicraft have gone their own ways they have strayed from their true paths and now both are in a sorry plight" (p. 84).

He wishes to unite them by getting the artisans, such as the bookbinders of a town, to combine and maintain a machine.

"As they use the machine only for themselves and only when they have an order they will be able to produce more cheaply than the merchant who owns a factory" (p. 85). "Capital will be broken by combination" (p. 84). (And combination will be broken by capital.)

He then generalises his ideas about "the purchase of a machine to rule lines, and to cut paper and cardboard" (p. 85) by the united certificated bookbinders of Bonn and conceives the notion of a "machine chamber".

"Confederations of the various guild masters must set up businesses everywhere, similar to the factories of individual businessmen though on a smaller scale. These will work to order, exclusively for the benefit of local masters. They will not accept commissions from other employers" (p. 86). A specific feature of these machine chambers is the fact that "a commercial management" will only "be needed initially" (ibid). "Every idea as novel as this one," Gottfried exclaims "ecstatically", "can only be put into practice when all the details have been thought out in a very calm matter of fact way." He urges "each handicraft to perform this analysis for itself"! (pp. 87, 88).

There follows a polemic against competition from the state in the shape of the labour performed by the inmates of prisons, reminiscences about a colony of criminals ("the creation of a human Siberia", p. 102), and finally an attack on the "so-called handicraft companies and handicraft commissions" in the armed forces. The aim here is to relieve the army burden for the artisan by inducing the state to commission goods from the guild masters that it could itself produce more cheaply.

"The problems of competition are thus disposed of" (p. 109).

Gottfried's second important point touches on the material aid which the craftsmen are to receive from the state. Gottfried regards the state solely from the point of view of an official and hence arrives at the opinion that the easiest and surest way to help the artisan is by the Treasury advancing money to erect trade halls, set up loan offices, etc. How the Treasury is to get the funds is the "ugly" side of the problem and, naturally enough, cannot be investigated here.

Lastly, our theologian inevitably lapses into the role of moral preacher. He reads the artisans a moral lecture on self-help. He firstly mentions the "complaints about long-term borrowing and about discounts" (p. 136), and invites the artisan to consider the following moral question: "Do you always fix the same, unchanging price, my friend, for every job of work that you undertake?" (p. 132). On this occasion he also warns the artisan against making extortionate demands on "wealthy Englishmen". "The root of the whole evil," Gottfried imagines, "is the system of annual accounts" (p. 139). This is followed by Jeremiads about the way in which the artisans carry on in the taverns and their wives indulge their love of finery (pp. 140 ff.).

The means by which the handicrafts can improve their position are "the corporation, the sickness fund and the artisans' court of arbitration" (p. 146); and lastly, the workers' educational associations (p. 153). The following is his final statement about these educational associations:

"And finally song combined with oratory will create a bridge to *dramatic performances* and *the artisan theatre* which must constantly be kept in view as the ultimate objective of these aesthetic strivings. Only when the labouring classes learn once more how to move on the *stage* will their artistic education be complete" (pp. 174-75).

Gottfried has thus succeeded in changing the artisan into a comedian and has arrived back at his own situation.

But this whole flirtation with the guild aspirations of the master craftsmen in Bonn achieved also a practical result. In return for the solemn promise to table a motion to set up guilds, Gottfried's election as Member for Bonn in the imposed Lower Chamber[161] was contrived. "From this moment on Gottfried felt" happy.

He set off at once for Berlin and as he believed that it was the intention of the government to establish a permanent "corporation" of licensed master legislators in the Lower Chamber, he acted as if he were to stay there for ever and decided to send for his wife and child. But then the Chamber was dissolved and friend Gottfried, bitterly disappointed, had to leave his parliamentary bliss and go back to Mockel.

Soon afterwards the conflict between the Frankfurt Assembly and the [German] governments broke out and this led to the movements in South Germany and on the Rhine. The Fatherland called and Gottfried obeyed. Siegburg was the site of an arsenal for the army reserve, and next to Bonn Siegburg was the place where Gottfried had sown the seed of freedom most frequently. He joined forces with his friend Anneke, a former lieutenant, and summoned all his loyal followers to a march on Siegburg. They were to assemble at the rope ferry. More than a hundred were supposed to come, but when after waiting a long time Gottfried counted the heads of the faithful[a] there were barely thirty—and of these only three were students, to the undying shame of the May-Bug Club! Undaunted, Gottfried and his band crossed the Rhine and marched towards Siegburg. The night was dark and it was drizzling. Suddenly the sound of horses' hooves could be heard behind our valiant heroes. They took cover at the side of the road, a patrol of lancers galloped by: miserable knaves had talked too freely and the authorities had got wind of it. The march was now futile and had to be abandoned. The pain that Gottfried felt in his breast that night can only be compared with the torments he experienced when both Knapp and Chamisso declined to print his first poetic efforts in their magazines.

After this he could remain no longer in Bonn, but did not the Palatinate provide great scope for his activities? He went to Kaiserslautern and as he had to have a job he obtained a sinecure in the War Office (it is said that he was put in charge of naval

---

[a] A line from Schiller's "Lied von der Glocke".—*Ed.*

affairs[a]). But he continued to earn his living by hawking around his ideas about freedom and the people's paradise among the peasants of the region and it is said that his reception in a number of reactionary districts was anything but cordial. Despite these minor misfortunes Kinkel could be seen on every highroad, striding along purposefully, his travelling bag slung over his shoulder, and from this point on he appears in all the newspapers invariably accompanied by his travelling bag.

But the uprising in the Palatinate was quickly terminated and we discover Kinkel again in Karlsruhe, where instead of the travelling bag he carries a musket, which now becomes his permanent emblem. This musket is said to have had a very *beautiful* aspect, i.e. a butt and stock made of mahogany and it was certainly an artistic, aesthetic musket; there was also an *ugly* aspect to it and this was the fact that friend Gottfried could neither load, nor see, nor shoot, nor march. So much so that a friend asked him why *he* was going into battle at all. Whereupon Gottfried replied: Well, the fact is that I can't return to Bonn, I have to live!

Thus Gottfried joined the ranks of the warriors in the corps of the chivalrous Willich. As a number of his comrades-in-arms have reliably reported, Gottfried served as a common partisan, sharing all the vicissitudes of this company with humility. He was as merry and friendly in bad times as in good, but he was mostly on the cart for the exhausted and the sick. At Rastatt,[162] however, this unsullied witness to truth and justice was to undergo the test from which he would emerge unblemished and as a martyr to the plaudits of the whole German nation. The exact details of this exploit have not yet been established with any accuracy. All that is known is that a troop of partisans got lost in a skirmish and a few shots were fired on their flank; that a bullet grazed our Gottfried's head and he fell to the ground with the cry "I am dead"; that although he was not dead he could not accompany the others on the retreat and was taken to a farm house where he turned to the worthy Black Forest peasants with the words "Save me—I am Kinkel!"; finally, that he was discovered there by the Prussians, who dragged him off into Babylonian captivity.

III

With his capture a new stage began in Kinkel's life, a stage that at the same time opened a new era in the history of German

---

[a] The Palatinate had no coast-line.—*Ed.*

philistinism. No sooner had the May-Bug Club heard the news of his capture than they wrote to all the German papers that Kinkel, the great poet, was in danger of being summarily shot and that it was the duty of the German people, especially the educated among them, and above all the women and girls, to do everything to save the life of the imprisoned poet. Kinkel himself composed a poem[a] at about this time, as we are told, in which he compared himself to "Christ, his friend and teacher", adding: "My blood is shed for you." From this point on his emblem is the *lyre*. In this way Germany suddenly learned that Kinkel was a poet, and a great poet, and from this moment on the mass of German philistines and aestheticising drivellers joined in the farce of the blue flower put on by our Heinrich von Ofterdingen.

In the meantime the Prussians brought him before a military tribunal. For the first time after a long interval he had an opportunity to try out one of those moving appeals to the tear ducts of his audience which—according to Mockel—had brought him such applause earlier on as an assistant preacher in Cologne. Cologne was destined soon to witness his most glorious performance in this sphere. He made a speech in his own defence before the tribunal which unfortunately, owing to the indiscretion of a friend, was later made available to the public through the medium of the Berlin *Abend-Post*.[b] In this speech Kinkel "guards" himself

"against any identification of his actions with the dirt and filth which recently, I know, unfortunately tagged on to this revolution".[163]

After this rabid revolutionary speech Kinkel was sentenced to twenty years detention in a fortress, but as an act of grace this was reduced to prison with hard labour. He was then removed to Naugard,[c] where he was reported to have been employed in spinning wool, and so just as formerly he had appeared with the emblem first of the travelling bag, then the musket and then the lyre, he now appears in association with the *spinning wheel*. We shall see him later wandering over the ocean accompanied by the emblem of the purse.

In the meantime a curious event took place in Germany. It is well known that the German philistine is endowed by nature with a beautiful soul. Now he found his most cherished illusions cruelly shattered by the hard blows of the year 1849. Not a single hope

[a] G. Kinkel, "Mein Vermächtnis".—*Ed.*

[b] G. Kinkel, "Vertheidigungsrede vor dem preussischen Kriegsgericht zu Rastatt am 4. August 1849" (*Abend-Post*, Nos. 78 and 79, April 5 and 6, 1850).—*Ed.*

[c] The Polish name is Novogard.—*Ed.*

had become reality and even the fast-beating hearts of young men began to despair about the fate of the fatherland. Every heart yielded to a melancholy languor and the need began to be universally felt for a democratic Christ, for a real or imagined sufferer who in his torments would bear the sins of the philistine world with the fortitude of a lamb and whose suffering would epitomise in extreme form the inert, chronic nostalgia of the whole of philistinism. The May-Bug Club, with Mockel at its head, set out to satisfy this universal need. And indeed, who better fitted for the task of enacting this great passion farce than our captive passion flower, Kinkel at the spinning wheel, able to emit endless floods of pathetic sentimental tears, who was in addition preacher, professor of fine arts, deputy, political colporteur, musketeer, newly discovered poet and old impresario all rolled into one? Kinkel was the man of the moment and as such he was immediately accepted by the German philistines. Every paper abounded in anecdotes, vignettes, poems, reminiscences of the captive poet, his sufferings in prison were magnified a thousand-fold and took on mythical stature; at least once a month his hair was reported to have gone grey; in every bourgeois meeting-place and at every tea-party he was remembered with solicitude; the daughters of the educated classes sighed over his poems, and old maids, who knew what yearning is, wept freely in various cities of the fatherland at the thought of his shattered manhood. All other profane victims of the movement, all who had been shot, who had fallen in battle or who had been imprisoned, disappeared into naught beside this one sacrificial lamb, beside this man after the hearts of the philistines male and female. For him alone did the rivers of tears flow, and indeed, he alone was able to respond to them in kind. In short, we have the perfect image of the *democratic Siegwart epoch*, which yielded in nothing to the literary Siegwart epoch of the preceding century, and Siegwart-Kinkel never felt more at home in any role than in this one where he appeared to be great not because of what he did but because of what he did not do. He seemed great not by dint of his strength and his powers of resistance but through his weakness and by feebly breaking down in a situation where his only task was to survive with decorum and sentiment. Mockel, however, was able and experienced enough to take practical advantage of the public's soft heart and she immediately organised a highly efficient industry. She caused all of Gottfried's published and unpublished works, which now suddenly became valuable and *en vogue*, to be printed and propagated among the public; she also took the occasion to

dispose of her own life experiences from the insect world, e.g. her
Story of a Firefly[a]; she employed the May-Bug Strodtmann to
assemble Gottfried's most secret diary-feelings and prostitute them
to the public for a considerable sum of money; she organised
collections of every kind and in general she displayed undeniable
commercial talent and great perseverance in converting the
feelings of the educated public into hard cash. In addition she had
the great satisfaction

"of seeing the greatest men of Germany, such as Adolf Stahr, meeting daily in
her little room".

The climax of this whole Siegwart mania was to be reached at
the Assizes in Cologne where Gottfried gave a guest performance
in the spring of 1850. This was the trial resulting from the
attempted uprising in Siegburg and Kinkel was brought to
Cologne for the occasion. As Gottfried's diaries play such a
prominent part in this sketch it will be appropriate if we too insert
an excerpt from the diary of an eyewitness.

"Kinkel's wife visited him in gaol. She welcomed him from behind the grill with
verses; he replied, I understand, in hexameters; whereupon they both sank to their
knees before each other, and the prison inspector, an old sergeant-major, who was
standing by wondered whether he was dealing with madmen or clowns. When
asked later by the chief public prosecutor about the content of their conversation
he declared that the couple had indeed spoken German but that he could not make
head or tail of it. Whereupon Frau Kinkel is supposed to have retorted that a man
who was so wholly innocent of art and literature should not be made an inspector."

When he faced the jury Kinkel wriggled his way out by acting
the pure tear-jerker, the poetaster of the Siegwart period of the
vintage of *Werther's Sufferings*.[b]

"'Members of the Court, Gentlemen of the Jury—the blue eyes of my
children—the green waters of the Rhine—it is no dishonour to shake the hand of
the proletarian—the pallid lips of the prisoner—the gentle air of one's
home'"[c]—and similar muck: that was what the whole famous speech amounted to
and the public, the jury, the prosecution and even the police shed their bitterest
tears and the trial closed with a unanimous acquittal and a no less unanimous
weeping and sobbing. Kinkel is doubtless a dear, good man but he is also a
repulsive mixture of religious, political and literary reminiscences."

It was very upsetting indeed.

---

[a] An allusion to G. Kinkel's *Lebenslauf eines Johannisfünkchens*.—*Ed.*

[b] Goethe, *Die Leiden des jungen Werthers*.—*Ed.*

[c] G. Kinkel, "Vertheidigungsrede vor dem Geschworenengerichte zu Köln am
2. Mai 1850".—*Ed.*

Fortunately this period of misery was soon terminated by the romantic liberation of Kinkel from Spandau gaol. His escape was a re-enactment of the story of Richard Lionheart and Blondel,[164] with the difference that this time it was Blondel who was in prison while Lionheart played on the barrel-organ outside and that Blondel was an ordinary itinerant minstrel and Lionheart was basically hardly more than a chicken heart. Lionheart was in fact the student Schurz from the May-Bug Club, a little intriguer with great ambitions and limited achievements who was however intelligent enough to have seen through the "German Lamartine"! Not long after the escape student Schurz declared in Paris that he, who was using Kinkel, knew very well that Kinkel was no *lumen mundi*,[a] whereas he, Schurz, and none other was destined to be the future president of the German Republic. This manikin, one of those students "in brown jackets and pale-blue overcoats" whom Gottfried had once followed with his "gloomily flashing eyes", succeeded in freeing Kinkel at the cost of sacrificing some poor devil of a warder who is now doing time elevated by the feeling of being a martyr for freedom—the freedom of Gottfried Kinkel.

IV

We next meet Kinkel again in *London*, and this time, thanks to his prison fame and the sentimentality of the German philistines, he has become the greatest man in Germany. Mindful of his sublime mission friend Gottfried was able to exploit all the advantages of the moment. His romantic escape gave new impetus to the Kinkel cult in Germany and he adroitly directed this onto a path that was not without beneficial material consequences. At the same time this metropolis provided the much venerated man with a new, complex arena in which to receive even greater acclaim. He did not hesitate: he had to become the lion of the season.[b] With this in mind he refrained for the time being from all political activity and withdrew into the seclusion of his home in order to grow a beard, without which no prophet can succeed. After that he visited Dickens, the English liberal newspapers, the German businessmen in the City and especially the aesthetic Jews in that place. He was all things to all men: to one a poet, to another a patriot in general, professor of fine arts to a third, Christ to the

---

[a] Luminary.—*Ed.*
[b] Marx and Engels use the English word.—*Ed.*

fourth, the great long-suffering Odysseus to the fifth. To everyone, however, he appeared as the gentle, artistic, benevolent and humanitarian Gottfried. He did not rest until Dickens had eulogised him in the *Household Words*,[a] until the *Illustrated News*[b] had published his portrait. He mobilised the few Germans in London who had been involved in the Kinkel mania even at a distance to invite him ostensibly to lecture on modern drama; tickets to these lectures flooded into the homes of the local German businessmen. No running around, no advertisement, no charlatanism, no importunity, no humiliation in front of this audience was beneath him; in return, however, he did not go unrewarded. Gottfried sunned himself complacently in the mirror of his own fame and in the gigantic mirror of the Crystal Palace[165] of the world. And we may say that he now felt tremendously content.

There was no lack of praise for his lectures (see *Kosmos*).

Kosmos: "Kinkel's Lectures"

"While looking once at Döbler's misty images I was surprised by the whimsical question of whether it was possible to produce such chaotic creations in 'words', whether it was possible to utter misty images. It is no doubt unpleasant for the critic to have to confess, at the very outset, that in this case his critical autonomy will vibrate against the galvanised nerves of a stimulating reminiscence, as the fading sound of a dying note echoes in the strings. Nevertheless I would prefer to renounce any attempt at a bewigged and boring analysis of pedantic insensitivity than to deny that tone which the charming muse of the German refugee caused to resonate in my receptive *imagination*. This keynote of Kinkel's paintings, this sounding board of his chords is the sonorous, creative, formative and gradually shaping 'word'—'*modern thought*'. The human '*judgment*' of this thought leads truth out of the chaos of mendacious traditions, and places it, as the inviolable property of mankind, under the protection of spiritually active, logical minorities who will lead mankind from a credulous ignorance to a state of more sceptical science. It is the task of the science of doubt to profane the mysticism of pious deceit, to undermine the absolutism of a stupefied tradition; through scepticism, that ceaselessly labouring guillotine of philosophy, to decapitate accepted authority and to lead the nations out of the misty regions of theocracy by means of revolution into the luscious meadows of democracy" (of nonsense). "The sustained, unflagging search in the annals of mankind, and the understanding of man himself, is the great task of all revolutionaries and this had been understood by that proscribed poet-rebel who on three recent Monday evenings uttered his 'dissolving views'[c] before a bourgeois audience in the course of his lectures on the history of the modern theatre."

"A Worker"[166]

---

[a] Charles Dickens, "Gottfried Kinkel; A Life in Three Pictures", *Household Words*, No. 32, November 2, 1850.— *Ed.*

[b] *Illustrated London News.— Ed.*

[c] The English expression is used in the original.— *Ed.*

It is generally claimed that *this worker* is a very close relation of Kinkel's—namely Mockel—as indeed seems likely from the use of such expressions as "sounding board", "fading sound", "chords" and "galvanised nerves".

However, even this period of hard-earned self-satisfaction was not to last forever. The Last Judgment on the existing world order, the democratic day of judgment, namely the much celebrated May 1852,[167] was drawing ever closer. In order to confront this day all booted and spurred Gottfried Kinkel had to don his political lion's skin once more: he had to make contact with the "emigration".

So we come to the London "emigration", this hotchpotch of former members of the Frankfurt Parliament, the Berlin National Assembly, and Chamber of Deputies, of gentlemen from the Baden campaign, giants from the comedy of the Imperial Constitution,[168] writers without a public, loudmouths from the democratic clubs and congresses, twelfth-rate journalists and so forth.

The great men of the Germany of 1848 had been on the point of coming to a sticky end when the victory of the "tyrants" rescued them, swept them out of the country and made saints and martyrs of them. They were saved by the counter-revolution. The course of continental politics brought most of them to London, which thus became their European centre. It is evident that in this situation something had to happen, something had to be arranged to remind the public daily of the existence of these world liberators. It was necessary at all costs to preclude the impression that universal history might be able to proceed without the intervention of these mighty men. The more this refuse of mankind found itself hindered by its own impotence as much as by the prevailing situation from undertaking any real action, the more zealously did it indulge in spurious activity whose imagined deeds, imagined parties, imagined struggles and imagined interests had been so noisily trumpeted abroad by those involved. The less able these people were to bring about a new revolution in fact, the more they had to anticipate this eventuality in their minds, to share out the plum jobs in advance and enjoy the prospect of future power. The form taken by this self-important activity was that of a mutual insurance club of would-be great men and the reciprocal guarantee of government posts.

V

The first attempt to create such an "organisation" took place as early as the spring of 1850. A magniloquent "Draft Circular to German Democrats, printed in manuscript form" was hawked around London together with a "Covering Letter to the Leaders".[a] The Circular and Covering Letter invited the readers to found a united democratic church. The immediate aim was to form a Central Bureau to deal with the affairs of German *émigrés*,[169] to set up a joint administration for refugee problems, to start a printing press in London, and to unite all patriots against the common enemy, etc. The emigration should then become the centre of the internal movement, the organisation of the emigration was to be the beginning of a comprehensive democratic organisation, those outstanding personalities who were without means should as members of the Central Bureau be paid salaries raised by taxes levied on the German people. This tax proposal seemed all the more appropriate as "the German emigration had gone abroad not merely without a respectable hero but, what is even worse, without common *assets*". The document does not conceal that the Hungarian, Polish and French committees already in existence provided the model for this "organisation" and the whole of it is redolent of a certain envy of the privileged position of these prominent allies.

The Circular was the joint production of Herr Rudolph *Schramm* and Herr Gustav *Struve*, behind whom lay concealed the merry figure of Herr Arnold *Ruge*, a corresponding member living in Ostend at the time.

Herr *Rudolph Schramm*—a rowdy, loudmouthed and extremely muddleheaded little man whose life-motto came from *Rameau's Nephew*:

"I would rather be an impudent windbag than not exist at all."[b]

When at the height of his power, Herr Camphausen would gladly have given the forward young Crefelder an important post, had it been seemly thus to elevate a mere junior official. Thanks to bureaucratic etiquette Herr Schramm found only the career of a democrat still open to him. And in this profession he really did

---

[a] R. Schramm, G. Struve, "Entwurf eines Rundschreibens an deutsche Demokraten; als Manuscript gedruckt. Begleitschreiben an die Führer".—*Ed.*

[b] Denis Diderot, *Rameau's Neffe*. Aus dem Manuscript übersetzt von J. W. Goethe.—*Ed.*

advance at one point to the post of President of the Democratic Club in Berlin and with the support of some Left-wing Members of Parliament he later became the Deputy for Striegau[a] in the Berlin National Assembly. Here the normally so loquacious Schramm distinguished himself by his obstinate silence, which was accompanied, however, by an uninterrupted series of grunts. After the Constituent Assembly had been dissolved our democratic man of the people wrote a pamphlet in support of a constitutional monarchy[b] but he was not re-elected. Later, at the time of the Brentano government, he appeared momentarily in Baden and there in the "Club of Resolute Progress"[170] he became acquainted with Struve. On his arrival in London he declared his intention of withdrawing from all political activity, for which reason he forthwith published the circular referred to above. Essentially an unsuccessful bureaucrat, Herr Schramm imagined that his family relations qualified him to represent the radical bourgeoisie in exile and he did indeed present a fair caricature of the radical bourgeois.

Gustav Struve is one of the more important figures of the emigration. At the very first glimpse of his leathery appearance, his protuberant eyes with their sly, stupid expression, the mat gleam on his bald pate and his half Slav, half Kalmuck features, one cannot doubt that one is in the presence of an unusual man. And this impression is confirmed by his low, guttural voice, his sentimental and unctuous manner of speaking and the solemn gravity of his deportment. To be just it must be said that faced with the greatly increased difficulties of distinguishing oneself these days, our Gustav tried at least to be different from his fellow citizens; part prophet, part speculator, part bunion healer—he centred his activities on all kinds of odd peripheral matters and made propaganda for the strangest assortment of causes. For example, being a Russian he suddenly took it into his head to enthuse about the cause of German freedom after he had been employed in a supernumerary capacity in the Russian embassy to the Federal Diet[171] and had written a little pamphlet in defence of the Diet.[c] Regarding his own skull as the normal human cranium, he vigorously applied himself to phrenology and from then on he refused to trust anyone whose skull he had not yet felt and

---

[a] The Polish name is Strzegom.—*Ed.*

[b] R. Schramm, *Der Standpunkt der Demokratie in und zur octroyirten zweiten Kammer.*—*Ed.*

[c] G. Struve, *Erster Versuch auf dem Felde des deutschen Bundesrechts.*—*Ed.*

examined. He also gave up eating meat and preached the gospel of strict vegetarianism; he was, moreover, a weather-prophet, he inveighed against tobacco and was prominent in the interest of the ethics of German Catholicism [172] and water-cures. Given his thoroughgoing hatred of concrete knowledge it was natural that he should be in favour of free universities in which the four faculties [173] would be replaced by the study of phrenology, physiognomy, chiromancy and necromancy. It was also quite in character for him persistently to maintain that he was a great writer precisely because his mode of writing was the antithesis of everything that could be held to be stylistically acceptable.

In the early forties Gustav had already invented the *Deutscher Zuschauer*, a little paper that he published in Mannheim, that he patented and that pursued him everywhere as a fixed idea. He also made the discovery at around this time that Rotteck's *Weltgeschichte* and the Rotteck-Welcker *Staats-Lexikon*, the two works that had been his Old and New Testaments, were out of date and in need of a new *democratic* edition. This revision Gustav undertook without delay and published an extract from it in advance under the title *Grundzüge der Staatswissenschaft*. Since 1848, moreover, the revision had become "an undeniable necessity, for the late Rotteck had not experienced the events of recent years".

In the meantime there broke out in Baden in quick succession the three "popular uprisings" [174] that have been depicted by Gustav as the very centre of the whole modern course of world history.[a] Driven into exile by the very first of these revolts (Hecker's) and engaged in publishing his *Deutscher Zuschauer* once again, this time in Basle, he was dealt a hard blow by fate when the publisher in Mannheim continued to print the *Deutscher Zuschauer* there under a different editor. The battle between the true and the false *Deutscher Zuschauer* was so bitterly fought that neither paper survived. To compensate for this Gustav devised a constitution for the German Federal Republic[b] in which Germany was to be divided into 24 republics, each with a president and two chambers; he appended a neat map on which the whole plan could be clearly seen.

In September 1848 the second insurrection began, in which our Gustav acted as both Caesar and Socrates. He used the time granted him on German soil to issue serious warnings to the Black Forest peasantry about the deleterious effects of smoking tobacco.

---

[a] G. Struve, *Geschichte der drei Volkserhebungen in Baden.—Ed.*
[b] G. Struve, *Die Grundrechte des deutschen Volkes.—Ed.*

In Lörrach he published his *Moniteur* with the title of *Government Organ—German Free State—Freedom, Prosperity, Education.*[a] This publication contained *inter alia* the following decree:

"Article[1]. The extra tax of 10 per cent imposed by the aforesaid on goods imported from Switzerland is hereby abolished; Article 2. *Christian Müller, the Customs Officer, is given the task of implementing the measure.*"

He was accompanied in all his trials by his faithful Amalia, who subsequently published a romantic account of them.[b] She was also active in administering the oath to captured gendarmes; it was her custom to fasten a red band around the arm of every one who swore allegiance to the German free state and to give him a kiss. Unfortunately Gustav and Amalia were taken prisoner and languished in gaol where the imperturbable Gustav at once resumed his republican translation of Rotteck's *Weltgeschichte* until he was at last liberated by the outbreak of the third insurrection. Gustav now became a member of a real provisional government and the mania for provisional governments was now added to his other fixed ideas. As President of the War Council he hastened to introduce as much muddle as possible into his department and to recommend the "traitor" Mayerhofer for the post of Minister for War (vide Goegg, *Rückblick*,[c] Paris, 1851). Later he vainly aspired to the post of Foreign Minister and to have 60,000 florins placed at his disposal. Herr Brentano soon relieved our Gustav of the burdens of government and Gustav now headed the opposition in the "Club of Resolute Progress". He delighted above all in opposing the very measures of Brentano which he himself had supported. Even though the Club was disbanded and Gustav had to flee to the Palatinate, this disaster had its positive side for it enabled him to issue one further number of the inevitable *Deutscher Zuschauer* in Neustadt an der Haardt—this compensated Gustav for much undeserved suffering. A further satisfaction was that he was successful in a by-election in some remote corner of the uplands and was nominated member of the Baden Constituent Assembly, which meant that he could now return in an official capacity. In this Assembly Gustav only distinguished himself by the following three proposals that he put forward in Freiburg: 1) On June 28: everyone who wants to negotiate with the enemy to be

---

[a] *Republikanisches Regierungs-Blatt.* It appeared with the subtitle: *Deutsche Republik! Wohlstand, Bildung, Freiheit für Alle!—Ed.*

[b] Amalie Struve, *Erinnerungen aus den badischen Freiheitskämpfen.—Ed.*

[c] A. Goegg, *Rückblick auf die Badische Revolution unter Hinweisung auf die gegenwärtige Lage Teutschlands* (published anonymously).—*Ed.*

declared a traitor. 2) On June 30: a new provisional government to be formed in which Struve would have a seat and a vote. 3) On the same day that the previous motion was defeated he proposed that as the defeat at Rastatt had rendered all resistance futile the uplands should be spared the terrors of war and that therefore all officials and soldiers should receive ten days' wages and members of the Assembly should receive ten days' expenses together with travelling costs and then they should all repair to Switzerland to the accompaniment of trumpets and drums. When this proposal too was rejected Gustav at once set out for Switzerland on his own and having been driven from thence by James Fazy's stick he retreated to London, where he came to the fore with yet another discovery, namely the *six scourges of mankind.* These six scourges were: the princes, the nobles, the priests, the bureaucracy, the standing army, mammon and bedbugs. The spirit in which Gustav interpreted the late Rotteck can be gauged from the further discovery that mammon was the invention of Louis Philippe. Gustav preached the gospel of the six scourges in the *Deutsche Londoner Zeitung,*[a] which belonged to the ex-Duke of Brunswick. He was tolerably rewarded for this activity and in return he gratefully bowed to the ducal censorship. So much for Gustav's relations with the first scourge, the princes. As for his relationship with the nobles, the second scourge, our moral and religious republican had visiting cards printed on which he figured as "Baron von Struve". If his relations with the remaining scourges were less amicable this cannot be his fault. Gustav then made use of his leisure time in London to devise a republican calendar in which the saints were replaced by right-minded men and the names "Gustav" and "Amalia" were particularly prominent. The months were given German designations in imitation of those in the calendar of the French Republic and there were a number of similar beneficial and commonplace innovations. Moreover his favourite fixed ideas made their appearance again in London: to revive the *Deutscher Zuschauer* and the Club of Resolute Progress and to form a provisional government. On all these matters he found himself of one mind with Schramm and in this way the Circular came into being.

The third member of the alliance,[b] the great *Arnold Ruge* with his air of a sergeant-major still waiting for civilian employment,

---

[a] G. Struve, "Abschiedsbrief Struve's Havre, 7. Oktober 1849", *Deutsche Londoner Zeitung,* No. 238, October 26, 1849.— *Ed.*

[b] Paraphrase of the last line of Schiller's "Die Bürgschaft".— *Ed.*

outshines the whole of the emigration. It cannot be said that this noble man commends himself by his notably handsome exterior; Paris acquaintances were wont to sum up his Pomeranian-Slav features with the word "ferret-face" (*figure de fouine*). Arnold Ruge, the son of peasants of the isle of Rügen, had endured seven years in Prussian prisons for demagogic agitation.[175] He threw himself wildly into Hegelian philosophy as soon as he had realised that once he had leafed through Hegel's *Encyclopädie* he could dispense with the study of all other science. He also developed the principle (which he advanced in a short story and which he attempted to practise on his friends—poor Herwegh can vouch for the truth of this) of *profiting* from marriage and accordingly he early acquired a "material basis" in this manner.

With the help of his Hegelian phrases and his material basis he merely contrived to become door-keeper to German philosophy. In the *Hallische Jahrbücher* and the *Deutsche Jahrbücher* it was his task to announce and to trumpet the names of rising luminaries and he showed that he was not without talent in exploiting them for his own literary purposes. Unfortunately, the period of philosophical anarchy very soon supervened, that period when science no longer had a universally acknowledged king, when Strauss, B. Bauer and Feuerbach fought among themselves and when the most diverse alien elements began to disrupt the simplicity of the classical doctrine. Our Ruge looked on helplessly; he no longer knew which path to take; his Hegelian categories had always operated in a vacuum, now they ran completely amok and he suddenly felt a strong desire for a mighty movement where people were not very particular about thought and writing.

Ruge played the same role in the *Hallische Jahrbücher* as the late bookseller Nicolai had done in the old *Berlinische Monatsschrift.* Like the latter his ambition was to print the works of others and, in so doing, to derive material advantage and also to quarry literary sustenance for the effusions of his own brain. The only difference was that in *rewriting* his collaborators' articles, in this literary digestive process with its inevitable end product, our Ruge went much further than did his model. Moreover, Ruge was not the door-keeper of German Enlightenment, he was the Nicolai of modern German philosophy and was able to conceal the natural banality of his genius behind a thick hedge of speculative jargon. Like Nicolai he fought valiantly against *Romanticism* because it had long since been demolished philosophically by Hegel in his *Aesthetik* and by Heine from the point of view of literature in *Die romantische Schule.* But unlike Hegel, Ruge agreed with Nicolai in arrogating to himself the right as an anti-Romantic to set up a vulgar philistinism and above all his own philistinic self as an ideal of perfection. With this in mind and so as to defeat the enemy on his own ground, Ruge went in for making verses. No Dutchman could have achieved the dull flatness of these poems which Ruge hurled so challengingly into the face of Romanticism.

And in general our Pomeranian thinker did not really feel at ease in Hegelian philosophy. Able as he was in detecting contradictions he was all the more feeble in resolving them and he had a very understandable horror of dialectics. The upshot was that the crudest possible contradictions dwelt peaceably together in his dogmatic brain and that his powers of understanding, never very agile, were nowhere more at home than in such mixed company. It sometimes happened that in his own way he imbibed simultaneously two articles by two different writers and conflated them into a single new product, without noticing that they had been written from two opposing viewpoints. Always getting stuck in his contradictions he sought to extricate himself by asserting in his arguments with theorists that his deficient reasoning was due to his practical sense, and on the other hand telling the practical people that his practical clumsiness and inconsistency was the height of theoretical achievement. He would end by maintaining that it was precisely his own entanglement in insoluble contradictions, his chaotically uncritical faith in the purport of all popular slogans that showed him to be a man of *"principle"*.

Before we go on to concern ourselves with the further career of our Maurice of Saxony, as he liked to style himself in his intimate circle of friends, we would point to two qualities which made their appearance already in the *Jahrbücher*. The first is his *mania for manifestos*. No sooner had anyone hatched any kind of novel opinion that Ruge believed to have a future than he would issue a manifesto. As no one reproaches him with ever having given birth to an original thought, such manifestos were always a suitable opportunity to claim this novel idea as his property in a more or less declamatory fashion. This would be followed by the attempt to form a party, a group, a *"mass"* which would stand behind him and to whom he could act as sergeant-major. We shall see later to what unbelievable heights of perfection Ruge had developed the art of fabricating manifestos, proclamations and pronunciamentos.

The second quality is the particular *diligence* in which Arnold excels. As he does not care to study overmuch, or as he puts it "to transfer ideas from one library into another",[a] he prefers "to gain his knowledge fresh from life", in other words, to note down conscientiously every evening all the novel or bright ideas or "anecdotes" that he has heard, read, or just picked up during the day. As opportunity arises these materials are then made to contribute to Ruge's daily stint which he performs just as conscientiously as his other bodily needs. It is this that his admirers refer to when they say that he cannot hold his ink. The subject of his daily literary production is a matter of complete indifference; what is vital is that Ruge should be able to immerse every possible topic in that wonderful stylistic sauce that goes with everything, just like the English who enjoy their Soyer's relish[b] or Worcester sauce[c] equally with fish, fowl, cutlets or anything else. This daily stylistic *diarrhoea* he likes to designate the "*strikingly beautiful form*" and he regards it as adequate grounds for passing himself off as an "artist".

Contented as Ruge was to be the Swiss guard of German philosophy he still had a secret sorrow gnawing at his innermost vitals. He had not written a single large book and had daily to envy the happy Bruno Bauer who had published eighteen fat volumes while still a young man. To remedy this incongruity Ruge had one and the same essay printed three times in one and the same volume under different titles and then brought out the same volume in a number of different formats. In this way Arnold Ruge's *Collected Works*[d] came into being and even today he derives much pleasure from counting them every morning volume by volume as they stand there neatly bound in his library, whereupon he exclaims joyfully: "And anyway, Bruno Bauer is a man without principles!"

Even though Arnold did not manage to comprehend the Hegelian philosophy, he did succeed in representing one Hegelian category in his own person. He was the very incarnation of "*the honest consciousness*" and was strengthened in this when he made the pleasant discovery in the *Phänomenologie*—which otherwise remained a sealed book to him—that the honest consciousness "always has pleasure in itself".[e] Though it wears its integrity on its sleeve the honest consciousness uses it to conceal the petty malice

[a] A. Ruge, *Unsre letzten zehn Jahre.*—*Ed.*
[b] Marx and Engels use the English words "Soyer's relish".—*Ed.*
[c] Marx and Engels say "Warwickshire sauce".—*Ed.*
[d] A. Ruge, *Gesammelte Schriften.*—*Ed.*
[e] G. W. F. Hegel, *Phänomenologie des Geistes.* VI. Der Geist.—*Ed.*

and crotchetiness of the philistine; it has the right to allow itself every kind of base action because it knows that its baseness springs from honest motives. Its very stupidity becomes a virtue because it is an irrefutable proof that it stands up for its principles. Despite every *arrière pensée* it is firmly convinced of its own integrity and the more it intends to perpetrate a deception or a *mesquine*[a] base act, the more open and trustworthy does it appear. Beneath the halo of good intentions all the petty meannesses of the philistine become transformed into as many virtues; sordid self-interest appears purified when presented as a piece of self-sacrifice; cowardice appears disguised as a higher form of courage; baseness becomes magnanimity; and the coarse manners and obtrusiveness of the peasant become ennobled, and indeed transfigured into the signs of uprightness and good humour. This is the gutter in which the contradictions of philosophy, democracy and phrase-mongering in general all strangely merge; such a man is moreover richly endowed with all the vices, the mean and petty qualities, with the slyness and the stupidity, the avarice and the clumsiness, the servility and the arrogance, the untrustworthiness and the bonhomie of the emancipated serf, the peasant: philistine and ideologist, atheist and slogan worshipper, absolute ignoramus and absolute philosopher all in one—that is Arnold Ruge as Hegel foretold him in 1806.

After the *Deutsche Jahrbücher* were suppressed Ruge transported his family to Paris in a carriage specially built for the purpose. Here, his unlucky star brought him into contact with *Heine*, who honoured him as the man who "had translated Hegel into Pomeranian". Heine asked him whether Prutz was not a pseudonym of his, which Ruge could deny in good conscience. However, it was not possible to make Heine believe that our Arnold was not the author of Prutz's poems. Incidentally, Heine discovered very soon that even though Ruge had no talent he knew very well how to give the appearance of being a man of character. Thus it came about that friend Arnold gave Heine the idea for his *Atta Troll.* If Ruge did not immortalise his sojourn in Paris by writing a great work he nevertheless deserves our thanks for the one Heine produced for him. In gratitude the poet wrote for him this well-known epitaph:

> Atta Troll, reforming bear,
> Pure and pious; a passionate husband,

---

[a] Petty.—*Ed.*

> By the Zeitgeist led astray
> A backwoods sansculotte,
> Dances badly but ideals
> Dwell within his shaggy breast
> Often stinking very strongly—
> Talent none, but Character![a]

In Paris our Arnold experienced the misfortune of becoming involved with the Communists. He published articles by *Marx* and *Engels* in the *Deutsch-Französische Jahrbücher*[b] that contained views running directly counter to those he had himself announced in the Preface, an accident to which the Augsburg *Allgemeine Zeitung*[c] drew his attention but which he bore with philosophical resignation.

To overcome an innate social awkwardness our Ruge has collected a small number of curious anecdotes that could be used on any occasion. He calls these anecdotes *yarns*. His preoccupation with these yarns, sustained over many years, finally led to the transformation of all events, situations and circumstances into a series of pleasant or unpleasant, good or bad, important or trivial, interesting or boring yarns. The Paris bustle, the many new impressions, socialism, politics, the Palais-Royal,[176] the cheapness of the oysters—all these things wrought so powerfully on the mind of this unfortunate man that his head began to spin permanently and irremediably and Paris for him became an unlimited storehouse of yarns. He himself hit upon the idea of using wood shavings to make coats for the proletariat and in general he had a foible for industrial yarns for which he could never find any shareholders.

When the politically better known Germans were expelled from France,[177] Ruge contrived to avoid this fate by presenting himself to Minister Duchâtel as a *savant sérieux*.[d] He evidently had in mind the "scholar" in Paul de Kock's *Amant de la lune*, who established himself as a *savant* by means of an original way of making corks pop into the air.[e]

---

[a] Heinrich Heine, *Atta Troll*, Caput XXIV.—*Ed.*

[b] The reference is to Marx's articles "On the Jewish Question" and "Contribution to the Critique of Hegel's Philosophy of Law. Introduction", and to Engels' articles "Outlines of a Critique of Political Economy" and "The Condition of England. *Past and Present* by Thomas Carlyle"(see present edition, Vol. 3).—*Ed.*

[c] "Frankreich. Die ersten Proben der deutsch-französischen Jahrbücher" (anon.), *Allgemeine Zeitung* (Augsburg), No. 70, March 10, 1844.—*Ed.*

[d] A true scholar.—*Ed.*

[e] This refers to Saucissard, a character in Paul de Kock's novel.—*Ed.*

Shortly afterwards Arnold went to Switzerland where he met
K. *Heinzen*, a former Dutch non-commissioned officer, Cologne
writer and Prussian tax sub-inspector. These two were soon bound
together by bonds of the most intimate friendship. Heinzen
learnt philosophy from Ruge, Ruge learnt politics from Heinzen.
From this time on we detect in Ruge a growing necessity to appear
as a philosopher *par excellence* only among the coarser elements of
the German movement, a fate that led him down and down until
at last he was accepted as a philosopher only by "Friends of Light"
ministers (Dulon), German-Catholic parsons (Ronge) and Fanny
Lewald. At the same time, however, anarchy was growing apace in
German philosophy. Stirner's *Unique,* [Stein's] *Socialism and Communism,*[a] etc., all these recent intruders, caused Ruge's head to spin
quite intolerably; a great leap had to be ventured. So Ruge escaped
into *humanism,* the catch-phrase with which all confusionists in
Germany, from Reuchlin to Herder, have covered up their
embarrassment. This catch-phrase seemed all the more appropriate
as Feuerbach had only recently "rediscovered man" and Arnold
fastened on to it with such desperation that he has not let go of it to
this day. But while still in Switzerland Arnold made yet another,
incomparably greater discovery. This was that "the ego by *appearing
frequently* before the public asserts itself as a *character*".[b] From this
point on a new field of activity opened for Arnold. He now elevated
the most shameless meddling and importunity into a principle. Ruge
had to take part in everything and to poke his nose into everything.
No hen could lay an egg without Ruge "editing the *rationale*" of this
"event".[178] Contact had to be maintained at all costs with some
obscure local paper where there was a chance of making frequent
appearances. He no longer wrote a single newspaper article without
signing his name and, where possible, mentioning himself. The
principle of the frequent appearance had to be extended to every
article; an article had first to appear in letter form in the European
papers and (after Heinzen's emigration to New York) in the
American papers also; then it was printed as a pamphlet and finally
reprinted in the collected works.

Thus equipped, our Ruge could return to Leipzig to obtain
definitive recognition of his *character.* But once arrived all was not a
bed of roses. His old friend Wigand, the bookseller, had very

---

[a] M. Stirner, *Der Einzige und sein Eigenthum.* L. Stein, *Der Socialismus und
Communismus des heutigen Frankreichs.—Ed.*

[b] A. Ruge, *Unsre letzten zehn Jahre.—Ed.*

successfully replaced him in the role of Nicolai and as no other post was vacant Ruge fell into gloomy reflections on the transitoriness of all yarns. This was his situation when the German revolution broke out.

It brought sudden relief to our Arnold too. The mighty movement in which even the clumsiest could easily swim with the current had finally got underway and Ruge went at once to Berlin where he intended to fish in troubled waters. As a *revolution* had just broken out he felt that it would be appropriate for him to come forward with proposals for *reform*. So he founded a paper with that name. The pre-revolutionary *Réforme* of Paris had been the most untalented, ignorant and boring paper in France. The Berlin *Reform* demonstrated that it was possible to surpass its French model and that one could unhesitatingly offer the German public such an incredible journal even in the "metropolis of intelligence". On the assumption that Ruge's clumsy language was the best guarantee for the profound content lying behind it Arnold was elected to the Frankfurt Parliament as Member for Breslau.[a] Here he saw his chance as editor of the democratic Left wing to come forward with an absurd *manifesto*.[b] Apart from that he distinguished himself only by his passion for issuing *manifestos* for European *peoples' congresses,* and hastened to add his voice to the general wish that Prussia should be integrated into Germany. Later, on his return to Berlin, he demanded that Germany should be integrated into Prussia and Frankfurt into Berlin, and when he finally decided to become a peer of Saxony he demanded that Germany and Prussia should both be integrated into Dresden.

His parliamentary activity brought him no laurels other than the fact that his own party despaired at his clumsy ineptitude. At the same time his *Reform* was going downhill, a situation that could only be remedied, as he thought, by his personal presence in Berlin. As an "honest consciousness" he naturally discovered a strictly political pretext for his resignation and in fact he demanded that the whole of the Left should leave with him. Naturally, they refused and Ruge went to Berlin alone. Once there, he discovered that modern conflicts can best be resolved by the "*Dessau method*", as he termed the small state, a model of constitutional democracy. Then during the siege of Vienna he again drew up a *manifesto* in which General

---

[a] The Polish name is Wrocław.— *Ed.*
[b] A. Ruge, "Motivirtes Manifest der radical-demokratischen Partei in der constituirenden Nationalversammlung zu Frankfurt am Main", *Die Reform,* No. 66, June 7, 1848.— *Ed.*

Wrangel was exhorted to march against Windischgrätz and to free Vienna.[a] He even obtained the approval of the Democratic Congress for this curious document under the pretext that it had already been set up with the signature and printed.[179] Finally, when Berlin itself was in a state of siege, Herr Ruge went to Manteuffel and made proposals concerning the *Reform,* which were however rejected. Manteuffel told him that he wished all opposition papers were like the *Reform*; the *Neue Preussische Zeitung* was much more dangerous—an utterance which the naïve Ruge, with triumphant pride, hastened to report through the length and breadth of Germany. Arnold became an enthusiastic advocate of *passive resistance,*[180] which he himself put into practice by leaving his paper, editors and everything in the lurch and running away. Active flight is evidently the most resolute form of passive resistance. The counter-revolution had supervened and Ruge fled before it all the way from Berlin to London without stopping.

At the time of the May uprising in Dresden Arnold placed himself at the head of the movement in Leipzig together with his friend Otto Wigand and the city council. He and his companions issued a vigorous *manifesto* to the citizens of Dresden urging them to fight bravely—in Leipzig, it went on, Ruge, Wigand and the city fathers were watching, and whoever did not desert himself would not be deserted by Heaven. Scarcely had the manifesto been published when our brave Arnold took to his heels and fled to Karlsruhe.

In Karlsruhe he felt unsafe even though the Baden troops were standing on the Neckar and hostilities were a long way from breaking out. He asked Brentano to send him to Paris as ambassador. Brentano permitted himself the joke of giving him the post for 12 hours revoking it next morning, just when Ruge was about to depart. Undaunted, Ruge went to Paris together with Schütz and Blind, the official representatives of the Brentano government, and once there made such a spectacle of himself that Oppenheim, his former editor, announced in the official *Karlsruher Zeitung*[b] that Herr Ruge was not in Paris in any official capacity but merely "*on his own initiative*". Having once been taken along by Schütz and Blind to see Ledru-Rollin, Ruge suddenly interrupted the diplomatic negotiations with a terrible diatribe against the Germans in the presence of the Frenchman so that his colleagues finally had to withdraw discomfited and compromised. June 13[c]

---

[a] A. Ruge, "An das deutsche Volk!"—*Ed.*

[b] On May 31, 1849.—*Ed.*

[c] On that day a peaceful demonstration was dispersed in Paris, and this signified the defeat of the Montagne Party.—*Ed.*

came and dealt our Arnold such a severe blow that for no reason at all he took to his heels and did not pause to take breath again until he found himself in London, on free British soil. Referring to this flight later he compared himself to Demosthenes.[a]

In London Ruge first attempted to be introduced as the Baden provisional ambassador. He then tried to gain acceptance in the English press as a great German thinker and writer but was always turned away on the grounds that the English were too materialistic to understand German philosophy. He was also asked about his works—a request which Ruge could answer only with a sigh while the image of Bruno Bauer once again rose up before his eyes. For even his *Collected Works*, what were they but pamphlets reprinted again and again? And they were not even pamphlets but merely newspaper articles in pamphlet form, and basically they were not even newspaper articles but only the muddled fruits of his reading. Something had to be done and so Ruge wrote two articles for the *Leader*[b] in which under the pretext of an analysis of German democracy he declared that in Germany "*humanism*" was now the order of the day as represented by Ludwig Feuerbach and Arnold Ruge, the author of the following works: 1) *Die Religion unsrer Zeit,* 2) *Die Demokratie und der Sozialismus,* 3) *Die Philosophie und die Revolution.* These three epoch-making works which have not appeared in the bookshops to this day are, it goes without saying, nothing more than new titles arbitrarily applied to old essays of Ruge's. Simultaneously he resumed his daily stints when for his own edification, for the benefit of the German public and to the horror of Herr Brüggemann he began to retranslate articles into German that had somehow got out of the *Kölnische Zeitung* and into the *Morning Advertiser.* Not exactly burdened with laurels he withdrew to Ostend

---

[a] The following paragraph is crossed out in the manuscript: "The question arises here: why in particular is Herr A. Ruge in England? In the year 1849 Herr Ruge began to realise at least one thing: that his position in Germany was very untenable, very compromised, and that he needed to be transferred to distant soil to maintain a sort of pretext for his frequent appearances. There are no external reasons whatever to keep him away from the Continent. When he turned his back on the Berlin state of siege, his editors stayed behind; when he withdrew from Leipzig, Wigand and his other associates stayed there without a hair falling from their heads; he did not take part in any compromising activities in Baden any more than he did in Paris. But precisely because Ruge is *no refugee* in the usual sense of the word, he considers it so important to hold an official position in the emigration."— *Ed.*

[b] A. Ruge, "The German Democratic Party. 1. The Origin and Elements of the Party. 2. The Revolution and the Present Condition of Parties and of the Nation". *The Leader,* Nos. 39 and 40, December 21 and 28, 1850.— *Ed.*

where he found the leisure necessary to his preparations for the role of the worldly-wise *Confusius*[a] *of the German emigration.*

Just as Gustav represents the vegetable nature and Gottfried the sensibility of German *petty-bourgeois* philistinism, Arnold represents its *reason* or rather its *unreason.* Unlike Arnold Winkelried [181] he does not open up a *path* to freedom; he is in his own person the *gutter* of freedom[b]; Ruge stands in the German revolution like the notices seen at the corners of certain streets: it is permitted to pass water here.

We return at last to our circular with its covering latter. It fell flat and the first attempt to create a united democratic church came to nought. Schramm and Gustav later declared that failure was due solely to the circumstance that Ruge could neither speak French nor write German. But then the great men again set to work.

> Chè ciascun oltra moda era possente,
> Come udirete nel canto seguente.[c]

VI

Rodomonte[d] K. *Heinzen* had arrived in London from Switzerland at the same time as Gustav. Karl Heinzen had for many years made a living from his threat to destroy "tyranny" in Germany. After the outbreak of the February revolution he went so far as to attempt, with unheard-of courage, to inspect German soil from the vantage point of Schuster Island.[e] He then betook himself to Switzerland where from the safety of Geneva he again thundered against the "tyrants and oppressors of the people" and took the opportunity to declare that "Kossuth is a great man, but Kossuth has forgotten about fulminating silver".[f] Heinzen's horror of bloodshed had turned him into the alchemist of the revolution. He dreamt of an explosive substance that would blast the whole of European reaction into the air in a trice, without its user even getting his fingers burnt. He had a particular aversion to walking amid a shower of bullets and

---

[a] A pun on Confucius.— *Ed.*

[b] In German a play on words: *der Freiheit eine Gasse*—a path to freedom, and *der Freiheit eine Gosse*—a gutter of freedom.—*Ed.*

[c] For puissant were they all beyond compare,
    As in our next canto you shall hear (Boiardo, *L'Orlando innamorato*, Canto 17).—*Ed.*

[d] A character from Ariosto's *Orlando furioso.*— *Ed.*

[e] Near Basle.— *Ed.*

[f] K. Heinzen, "Der Mord", *Die Evolution*, No. 4, January 26, 1849.—*Ed.*

to ordinary warfare in which high principle is no defence against them. Under the government of Herr Brentano he even risked a revolutionary visit to Karlsruhe. As he did not receive the reward he thought due to him for his heroic deeds he at first resolved to edit the *Moniteur*[a] of that "traitor" Brentano. But when the Prussians advanced he declared that Heinzen would not "let himself be shot" for that traitor Brentano.[b] Under the pretext of forming an *élite* corps where political principles and military organisation would complement each other, i.e. where military cowardice would pass for political courage, his constant search for the ideal volunteer corps made him retrace his steps until he had regained the familiar territory of Switzerland. *Sophiens Reise von Memel nach Sachsen*[182] was more bloody than Rodomonte's revolutionary journey. On his arrival in Switzerland he declared that there were no longer any real men in Germany, that the authentic fulminating silver had not yet been discovered, that the war was not being conducted on revolutionary principles but in the ordinary way, with powder and lead, and that he intended to revolutionise Switzerland as Germany was a lost cause. In the secluded idyll of Switzerland and with the bizarre dialect they speak there it was easy for Rodomonte to pass for a German writer and even for a dangerous man. He achieved his aim. He was expelled and despatched to London at federal expense. Rodomonte Heinzen had not directly participated in the European revolution; but, undeniably, he had moved about extensively on its behalf. When the February revolution broke out he collected "revolutionary contributions" in New York, so as to hasten to the aid of his country, and advanced as far as the Swiss border. When the March Association's[183] revolution collapsed he retired from Switzerland to beyond the Channel at the expense of the Swiss Federal Council. He had the satisfaction of making the revolution pay for his advance and the counter-revolution for his retreat.

In the Italian epics of chivalry we constantly encounter mighty, broad-shouldered giants armed with enormous cudgels who, despite the fact that they lash about them wildly and make a frightening din in battle, never manage to hit their foes but only the trees in the vicinity. Herr Heinzen is such an Ariostian giant in political literature. Endowed by nature with a churlish figure and huge masses of flesh, he interpreted these gifts to mean that he was destined to be a great man. His weighty physical appearance determines his whole literary posture which is physical through and

---

[a] *Karlsruher Zeitung.—Ed.*
[b] K. Heinzen, *Einige Blicke auf die badisch-pfälzische Revolution.—Ed.*

through. His opponents are always small, mere dwarfs, who can barely reach his ankles and whom he can survey with his knee-cap. When, however, he should indeed make a physical appearance, our *uomo membruto*[a] takes refuge in literature or in the courts. Thus scarcely had he reached the safety of English soil when he wrote a tract on moral courage.[b] Or again, our giant allowed a certain Herr Richter to thrash him so frequently and so thoroughly in New York that the magistrate, who at first only imposed insignificant fines, finally, in recognition of his doggedness, sentenced the dwarf Richter to pay 200 dollars damages.

The natural complement to this great physique, so healthy in every fibre, is the *healthy commonsense*,which Herr Heinzen ascribes to himself in the highest possible degree. It is inevitable that a man with such commonsense will turn out to be a "natural" genius who has learnt nothing, a barbarian innocent of literature and science. By virtue of his commonsense (which he also calls "his perspicacity" and which allows him to tell Kossuth that he has "advanced to the extreme frontiers of thought"), he learns only from hearsay or the newspapers. He is therefore always behind the times and always wears the coat that literature cast off some years previously, while rejecting as immoral and reprehensible the new modern dress he has as yet been unable to become familiar with. But when he has once assimilated a thing his faith in it is quite unshakable; it transforms itself into something that has grown naturally, that is self-evident, that everyone must appreciate and that only the malicious, the stupid or the sophist will pretend not to grasp. Such a robust body and healthy commonsense must of course have also some honest, solid *principles*, and he even shows to advantage when he takes the craze for principles to extremes. In this field Heinzen is second to none. He draws attention to his principles at every opportunity, every argument is met by an appeal to principle, everyone who fails to understand him or whom he does not understand is demolished by the argument that he has no principles and that his insincerity and pure ill-will are such that he would deny that day was day and night night. To deal with these base disciples of Ahriman he summons up his muse, indignation; he curses, rages, boasts, preaches, and foaming at the mouth he roars out the most tragicomical tirades. He demonstrates what can be achieved in the

---

[a] Strong-arm man.— *Ed.*

[b] K. Heinzen, "Lehren der Revolution", *Deutsche Londoner Zeitung*, Nos. 241 and 242, November 9 and 16, 1849.— *Ed.*

field of literary invective by a man to whom Börne's wit and literary accomplishment are equally alien. As the muse is, so is the style. An eternal cudgel,[a] but a commonplace cudgel with knots that are not even original or sharp. Only when he encounters scientific terms does he feel momentarily at a loss. He is then like that Billingsgate fishwife with whom O'Connell became involved in a shouting match and whom he silenced by replying to a long string of insults: You are all that and worse: you are a *triangulus isosceles,* you are a *parallelepipedon*!

From the earlier history of Herr Heinzen mention should be made of the fact that he was in the Dutch colonies, where he advanced not indeed to the rank of general but to that of non-commissioned officer, a slight for which he later on always treated the Dutch as a nation without principles. Later we find him back in Cologne as a sub-inspector of taxes and in this capacity he wrote a comedy in which his healthy commonsense vainly strove to satirise the philosophy of Hegel.[b] He was more at home in the gossip columns of the *Kölnische Zeitung,* in the feuilleton, where he let fall some weighty words about the quarrels in the Cologne Carnival Club, the institute from which all the great men of Cologne have graduated. His own sufferings and those of his father, a forester, in their struggle with superiors assumed the proportions of events of universal significance, as easily happens when the men of healthy commonsense contemplate their small personal problems. He gives an account of them in his *Preussische Büreaukratie,* a book much inferior to Venedey's[c] and containing nothing more than the complaints of a petty official against the higher authorities. The book involved him in a trial and although the worst he had to fear was six months in gaol he thought his head was in danger and fled to Brussels. From here he demanded that the Prussian government should not only grant him a safe conduct but also that they should suspend the whole French legal procedure and give him a jury trial for an ordinary offence.[184] The Prussian government issued a warrant for his arrest; he replied with a *Steckbrief*[d] against the Prussian government in which he preached *inter alia* moral resistance and

---

[a] Cf. Grimm's fairy-tale "Tischlein deck dich, Esel streck dich, Knüppel aus dem Sack" ("The Wishing-Table, the Gold Ass, and the Cudgel in the Sack").—*Ed.*

[b] K. Heinzen, *Doktor Nebel, oder: Gelehrsamkeit und Leben.*—*Ed.*

[c] J. Venedey, *Preussen und Preussenthum.*—*Ed.*

[d] *Steckbrief,* the title of Heinzen's book, means both a description of a person wanted by the police and a warrant of arrest.—*Ed.*

constitutional monarchy and condemned revolution as immoral
and jesuitical. From Brussels he went to Switzerland. Here, as we
saw above, he met friend Arnold and from him he learned not
only his philosophy but also a very useful method of self-
enrichment. Just as Arnold sought to assimilate the ideas of his
opponents in the course of polemising against them, so Heinzen
learned to acquire ideas new to him by attacking and *reviling*
them. Hardly had be become an atheist when with all the zeal of
the proselyte he immediately plunged into a furious polemic
against poor old Follen because the latter saw no reason to become
an atheist in his old age. Having had his nose rubbed in the Swiss
Federal Republic his healthy commonsense developed to the point
where he desired to introduce the Federal Republic into Germany
too. The same commonsense came to the conclusion that this
could not be done without a revolution and so Heinzen became a
revolutionary. He then began a trade in pamphlets[a] which in the
coarsest tones of the Swiss peasant preached immediate "assault"
and death to the princes, from whom all the evils of the world
stem. He looked for committees in Germany who would drum up
the cost of printing and would distribute these pamphlets, and this
led naturally to the growth of a large-scale begging industry which
first exploited the party members and then reviled them. Old
Itzstein could give further particulars about that. These pamphlets
gave Heinzen a great reputation among itinerant German wine
salesmen who praised him everywhere as a brave "reckless
fighter".

From Switzerland he went to America. Here, although his Swiss
rustic style enabled him to pass as a genuine poet, he nevertheless
very quickly managed to ride the New York *Schnellpost*[b] to death.

Having returned to Europe in the wake of the February
revolution, he sent despatches to the *Mannheimer Abendzeitung*
announcing the arrival of the great Heinzen[c] and he also
published a pamphlet to revenge himself on Lamartine,[d] who
with his whole government had ignored him despite his mandate
as official representative of the American Germans. He did not
wish to go back to Prussia as he still feared for his head despite
the March revolution and the amnesty. He would wait until the
nation summoned him. As this did not happen he resolved to

---

[a] K. Heinzen, *Teutsche Revolution. Gesammelte Flugschriften.*—*Ed.*

[b] *Deutsche Schnellpost für Europäische Zustände.*—*Ed.*

[c] K. Heinzen, "Vom Rhein, 12. April" and "Meine Erklärung", *Mannheimer Abendzeitung*, Nos. 105 and 107, April 15 and 17, 1848.—*Ed.*

[d] K. Heinzen, *Frankreichs "Brüderlicher Bund mit Deutschland".*—*Ed.*

stand *in absentia* for the Hamburg constituency to the Frankfurt Parliament: his hope was that he would compensate for being a bad speaker by the loudness of his voice—but he was defeated.

Having arrived in London after the termination of the Baden uprising, he became indignant with the young people who had forgotten this great man of *before* the revolution and of *after* the revolution, and who caused him to sink into oblivion. He had always been nothing more than *l'homme de la veille* or *l'homme du lendemain*, he was never *l'homme du jour* or even *de la journée*.[a] As the authentic fulminating silver had still not been discovered, new weapons had to be found to combat the reaction. He called for two million heads so that he could be a dictator and wade up to the ankles in blood—shed by others. His real aim was, of course, merely to create a scandal; the reaction had transported him to London at its own expense; by means of an expulsion order from England it would now, so Heinzen hoped, send him gratis to New York. The coup failed and its only consequence was that the radical French papers called him a fool who shouted for two million heads only because he had never risked his own. But to cap it all, he had published his bloodthirsty sanguinary article in the *Deutsche Londoner Zeitung*[b] owned by the ex-Duke of Brunswick—in return for a cash payment, of course.

Gustav and Heinzen had a high opinion of each other for a considerable time. Heinzen praised Gustav as a sage and Gustav praised Heinzen as a fighter. Heinzen had scarcely been able to wait for the end of the European revolution so that he could put an end to the "ruinous disunity in the democratic German *emigration*" and to re-open his pre-March business. He put forward "a programme of the Germanic revolutionary party in the shape of a draft proposal for discussion".[c] This programme was distinguished by the invention of a special ministry to cater for "the all-important need for public playgrounds, battlegrounds" (minus hail of bullets) "and gardens" and was notable also for the decree "abolishing the privileges of the male sex especially in marriage" (especially also in thrusting manoeuvres[d] in war, see Clausewitz). This programme was actually no more than a

---

[a] He had always been nothing more than yesterday's man or tomorrow's man, he was never the man of today or even the man of the day.— *Ed.*

[b] K. Heinzen, "Lehren der Revolution" (see this volume, p. 276) —*Ed.*

[c] [K. Heinzen,] "Programm der deutschen Revolutionspartei. Als Entwurf und Vorschlag der Diskussion preisgegeben". *Westdeutsche Zeitung*, No. 64, March 16, 1850.—*Ed.*

[d] *Stosstaktik.—Ed.*

diplomatic note from Heinzen to Gustav as no one else cared a straw about it. And instead of the hoped-for unification it brought about the immediate separation of the two capons; Heinzen demanded that during the "revolutionary transition period" there should be a single dictator who should moreover be a Prussian and, to preclude all misunderstandings, he added: "No soldier can be appointed dictator." Gustav, on the other hand, demanded a triumvirate comprising two Badeners and himself. Moreover, Gustav thought that Heinzen had included in his prematurely published programme an "idea" stolen from him. This put an end to the second attempt at unification and Heinzen, denied recognition by the whole world, receded into obscurity until, in the autumn of 1850, he found English soil too hot for him and sailed off to New York.

VII

GUSTAV AND THE COLONY OF RENUNCIATION

After the indefatigable Gustav had made an unsuccessful attempt to establish a *Central Refugee Committee* together with Friedrich Bobzin, Habbegg, Oswald, Rosenblum, Cohnheim, Grunich and other "outstanding" men, he made his way towards Yorkshire. For here, so he believed, a magic garden would flower and in it, unlike the garden of Alcine, virtue would rule instead of vice. An old Englishman with a sense of humour, whom our Gustav had bored with his theories, took him at his word and gave him a few acres of moor in Yorkshire on the express condition that he would there found a "Colony of Renunciation", a colony in which the consumption of meat, tobacco and spirits would be strictly prohibited, only a vegetarian diet would be permitted and where every colonist would be obliged to read a chapter from Struve's book on constitutional law[a] at his morning prayers. Moreover, the colony was to be self-supporting. Accompanied by his Amalia, by his Swabian wall-flower Schnauffer and by a few other of his faithfuls, Gustav placed his trust in God and went to found the "Colony of Renunciation". Of the colony it must be reported that it contained little "prosperity", much culture and unlimited "freedom" to be bored and to grow thin. One fine morning our Gustav uncovered a dreadful plot. His companions who did not share Gustav's ruminant constitution, and with whom

---

[a] G. Struve, *Grundzüge der Staatswissenschaft.—Ed.*

the vegetarian fare did not agree, had resolved behind his back to slaughter the old cow, the only one and whose milk provided the chief source of income of the "Colony of Renunciation". Gustav wrung his hands and shed bitter tears at this malevolence against a fellow creature. He indignantly dissolved the colony and decided to become a wet Quaker[185] unless he succeeded in reviving the *Deutscher Zuschauer* or establishing a "provisional government" in London.

VIII

Arnold, who was anything but content with the seclusion of his life in Ostend and who longed for a "frequent appearance" before the public, heard of Gustav's misfortune. He resolved to return to England at once and, by climbing on Gustav's shoulders, to hoist himself into the pentarchy of European democracy. For in the meantime the European Central Committee[186] had been formed consisting of Mazzini, Ledru-Rollin and Darasz. Mazzini was its soul. Ruge thought he could smell a vacant position. In his *Proscrit* Mazzini had indeed introduced General Ernst *Haug*, his own invention, as the German Associate but for decency's sake it was not possible to nominate such a completely unknown person onto the Central Committee. Our Ruge was not unaware of the fact that Gustav had had dealings with Mazzini in Switzerland. He himself was acquainted with Ledru-Rollin but unfortunately Ledru-Rollin was not acquainted with him. So Arnold took up residence in Brighton and flattered and cajoled the unsuspecting Gustav, promised to help him found a *Deutscher Zuschauer* in London and even to undertake as a joint venture the democratic publication of the Rotteck-Welcker *Staats-Lexikon* with Ruge paying the costs. At the same time he introduced our Gustav as a great man and collaborator into the local German paper which in accordance with his principles he always had on tap (this time it happened to be the *Bremer Tages-Chronik* of the "Friend of Light" minister Dulon). One good deed deserves another: Gustav presented Arnold to Mazzini. As Arnold's French was wholly incomprehensible there was nothing to prevent him from introducing himself to Mazzini as the greatest man in Germany and in particular as her greatest "thinker". The canny Italian idealist at once realised that Arnold was the man he was looking for, the *homme sans conséquence*[a] who would provide the German counter-signature of his anti-papal Bulls. Thus Arnold Ruge became the fifth wheel on

---

[a] Nonentity.— *Ed.*

the state coach of the European centre of democracy. When an
Alsatian asked Ledru what on earth possessed him to make an ally of
such a "*bête*", Ledru replied brusquely: "*C'est l'homme de Mazzini.*" [a]
When Mazzini was asked why he became involved with Ruge,[b] a man
bereft of all ideas, he answered slyly: "*C'est précisément pourquoi je l'ai
pris.*" [c] Mazzini himself had every reason to avoid people with ideas.
Arnold Ruge, however, saw his wildest dreams come true and for the
moment he even forgot Bruno Bauer.

When the time came for him to sign Mazzini's first manifesto he
sadly recalled the days when he had presented himself to
Professor Leo in Halle and old Follen in Switzerland as a
Trinitarian on one occasion and as a humanist atheist on another.
This time he was obliged with Mazzini to declare himself for *God*
and against princes. However, Arnold's philosophic conscience had
already been largely enfeebled by his association with Dulon and
other clerics among whom he passed for a philosopher. Even in
his best days our Arnold could not entirely suppress a certain
foible for religion in general and moreover his "honest consciousness" kept on whispering to him: Sign, Arnold! *Paris vaut bien une
messe.*[d] One does not become fifth wheel on the coach of the
provisional government of Europe *in partibus*[e] for nothing.
Reflect, Arnold! All you have to do is sign a manifesto every two
weeks, and even as a "*membre du parlement allemand*",[f] in the
company of the greatest men in all Europe. And bathed in
perspiration, Arnold signs. A curious joke, he murmurs. *Ce n'est
que le premier pas qui coûte.*[g] He had copied this last sentence into
his notebook the previous night. However, Arnold had not yet
come to the end of his trials. The European Central Committee
had issued a series of manifestos to Europe, to the French, the
Italians, the Wasserpolacken [187] and the Wallachians and now,
following the great battle at Bronzell,[188] it was *Germany's* turn. In
his draft Mazzini attacked the Germans for their lack of
cosmopolitan spirit, and in particular, for their arrogant treatment

---

[a] "He is Mazzini's man."— *Ed.*

[b] The original has Ledru, probably a slip of the pen.— *Ed.*

[c] "I took him for that very reason."— *Ed.*

[d] Paris is well worth a mass—the words attributed to Henry IV, King of
France.— *Ed.*

[e] *In partibus infidelium*—literally in parts inhabited by infidels. The words are
added to the title of Roman Catholic bishops appointed to purely nominal dioceses in
non-Christian countries.— *Ed.*

[f] "Member of the German Parliament".— *Ed.*

[g] It is only the first step that is difficult.— *Ed.*

of Italian salami vendors, organ-grinders, confectioners, dormouse tamers and mouse-trap sellers. Taken aback, Arnold confessed that it was true. He went further. He declared his readiness to cede the Italian Tyrol and Istria to Mazzini. But this was not enough. He had not only to appeal to the conscience of the German people, but also to attack them where they were most vulnerable. Arnold received instructions that this time he was to have an opinion, as he represented the German element. He felt like the student Jobs.[a] He scratched himself thoughtfully behind his ear and after long reflection he stuttered: "Since the age of Tacitus the German bards sing baritone.[b] In winter they kindle fires on all the mountains so as to warm their feet."

The bards, the baritone and fires on all the mountains! That will certainly give German freedom a lift! thought Mazzini with a grin. The bards, the baritone, fires on all the mountains and German freedom went into the manifesto[c] as *douceur*[d] for the German nation. To his astonishment Arnold Ruge had passed the examination and understood for the first time with what little wisdom the world is governed. From that moment on he despised Bruno Bauer more than ever for all his eighteen hefty tomes written while he was still young.

While Arnold in the wake of the European Central Committee was signing *warlike* manifestos with God, for Mazzini and against the princes, the *peace movement* was spreading not only in England, under the aegis of Cobden, but even beyond the North Sea. So that in Frankfurt am Main the Yankee swindler, Elihu Burritt, together with Cobden, Jaup, Girardin and the Red Indian Ka-gi-ga-gi-wa-wa-be-ta could hold a Peace Congress.[189] Our Arnold was just itching to avail himself of the opportunity to make one of his "frequent appearances" and to produce a manifesto. So he proclaimed himself a corresponding member of the Frankfurt Assembly and sent it an extremely confused Peace Manifesto[e] translated out of Cobden's speeches into his own speculative Pomeranian. Various Germans drew Arnold's attention to the contradiction between his warlike attitude in the Central Commit-

---

[a] The hero of K. A. Kortum's satirical poem *Die Jobsiade.—Ed.*

[b] Probably ironical for *Baritus*, the battle song of the Teutons.—*Ed.*

[c] Manifesto of the Central Committee of European Democracy of November 13, 1850, published in *La voix du proscrit*, No. 4, November 17, 1850.—*Ed.*

[d] Sop.—*Ed.*

[e] "A letter from Dr. Arnold Ruge, member for Breslau in the German Parliament, at Frankfort. Presented by the Delegates from Brighton to the Peace Congress assembled at Frankfort, August, 1850.—*Ed.*

tee and his peace manifesto Quakerism. He would reply: "Well, there you have the contradictions. That's the dialectic for you. In my youth I studied Hegel." His "honest consciousness" was eased by the thought that Mazzini knew no German and it was therefore not hard to pull the wool over his eyes.

Moreover, Arnold's relationship with Mazzini promised to become even more secure thanks to the protection of *Harro Harring* who had just landed in Hull. For with Harring a new and highly symptomatic character steps onto the stage.

IX

The great drama of the democratic emigration of 1849 to 1852 had been preceded by a prelude eighteen years previously: the emigration of demagogues in 1830 and 1831.[190] Even though with the passage of time most of the emigrants of this first wave had been ousted from the stage, there still remained a few worthy remnants who, stoically indifferent to the course of history and the effect of their action, continued to work as agitators, devised global plans, formed provisional governments and hurled proclamations into the world in every direction. It is obvious that the business experience of these seasoned swindlers greatly surpassed that of the younger generation. It was this very acumen acquired through eighteen years practice in conspiring, scheming, intriguing, proclaiming, duping, showing off and pushing oneself to the fore that gave Mr. Mazzini—supported by three straw men of much smaller experience in such matters—the audacity and the assurance to install himself as the Central Committee of European Democracy.

No one was more favoured by circumstances to become the very type of the *émigré* agitator than our friend *Harro Harring*. And indeed he did become the prototype whom all our great men of the exile, all the Arnolds, Gustavs and Gottfrieds, have striven more or less consciously and with varying success to emulate. They may even equal him if circumstances are not unfavourable, but they will hardly surpass him.

Harro, who like Caesar has himself described his great deeds (London, 1852),[a] was born on the "Cimbrian Peninsula"[b] and

---

[a] H. Harring, *Historisches Fragment über die Entstehung der Arbeiter-Vereine und ihren Verfall in Communistische Speculationen* (the passages quoted in this chapter are mostly taken from this book).— *Ed.*

[b] Old name for Jutland.— *Ed.*

belongs to that visionary North-Frisian race which has already been shown by Dr. Clement to have produced all the great nations of the world.

"Already in early youth" he attempted to "set the seal of action upon his enthusiasm for the cause of the peoples" by going to *Greece* in 1821.[191] We see how friend Harro had an early premonition of his mission to be everywhere where confusion reigned. Later on

"a strange fate led him to the source of absolutism, to the vicinity of the Tsar and he had seen through the Jesuitism of constitutional monarchy in *Poland*[192]".

Thus in Poland as well Harro fought for freedom. But "the crisis in the history of Europe following the fall of Warsaw led him to deep reflection", and his reflection led him to the idea of "national democracy", which he at once "documented in the work: *Die Völker*, Strasbourg, March 1832". It is worth remarking that this work was almost quoted at the Hambach Festival.[193] At the same time he published his "republican poems: 'Blutstropfen'; 'Die Monarchie, oder die Geschichte vom König *Saul*'; 'Männer-Stimmen, zu Deutschlands Einheit'" and edited the journal *Deutschland* in Strasbourg. All these and even his future writings had the unexpected good fortune to be banned by the Federal Diet on November 4, 1831. This was the only thing the worthy fighter still lacked; only now did he achieve the reputation he deserved and also the martyr's crown. So that he could exclaim:

"My writings were widely known and evoked a warm response in the hearts of the people. They were mostly distributed *gratis*. In the case of some of them I did not even recover the costs of printing."

But new honours still awaited him. Already in November 1831 Herr Welcker had vainly attempted in a long letter "to convert him to the *vertical horizon* of constitutionalism". And now, in January 1832, there came a visit from Herr Malten, a well-known Prussian agent abroad, who proposed that he should enter Prussian service. What double recognition this was—and from the enemy too! Enough, Malten's offer triggered off

"the idea that in the face of this dynastic treachery he should advance the concept of Scandinavian nationality", and "from that time on at least the *word* Scandinavia was reborn after having been forgotten for centuries".

In this manner our North Frisian from Söderjylland[a] who did not know himself whether he was a German or a Dane acquired at

---

[a] The Frisian name for South Jutland.— *Ed.*

least an imaginary nationality whose first consequence was that the men of Hambach would have nothing to do with him.

With all these events behind him Harro's fortune was made. Veteran of freedom in Greece and Poland, the inventor of the "democracy of nationality", re-discoverer of the word "Scandinavia", acknowledged by the ban of the Federal Diet to be a poet, thinker and journalist, a martyr, a great man esteemed even by his enemies, a man whose allegiance constitutionalists, absolutists and republicans vied with each other to possess and, with all that, empty-headed and confused enough to believe in his own greatness—what then was needed to make his happiness complete? But Harro was a conscientious man and as his fame grew so did the demands which he made upon himself. What was missing was a great work that would present in an artistic, entertaining and popular form the great doctrines of freedom, the idea of the democracy of nationality and all the sublime struggles for freedom on the part of the youthful Europe arising before his very eyes. None but a poet and thinker of the first rank could produce such a work and none but Harro could be this man. Thus arose the first three plays of the "dramatic cycle *Das Volk*, comprising twelve plays in all, one of them in Danish", a labour to which the author devoted ten years of his life. Unfortunately eleven of these twelve plays have "hitherto remained in manuscript".

However, this dallying with the muse was not to last forever.

"In the winter of 1832-1833 a movement was prepared in Germany—which was brought to a tragic end in the riot in Frankfurt.[194] I was entrusted with the task of taking the fortress (?) of Kehl on the night of April 6. Men and weapons were at the ready."

Unfortunately it all came to nothing and Harro had to retire to the depths of France, where he wrote his "*Worte eines Menschen*". From there he was summoned to Switzerland by the Poles arming themselves for their march on Savoy. Here he became "associated with their General Staff", wrote a further two plays of his dramatic cycle *Das Volk*, and made the acquaintance of Mazzini in Geneva. The whole brimstone gang consisting of Polish, French, German, Italian and Swiss adventurers under the command of the noble Ramorino then made their famous raid into Savoy.[195] In this campaign our Harro felt "the value of his life and strength". But as the other freedom fighters felt "the value of their lives" no less than Harro and no doubt had just as few illusions about their "strength", the exploit ended badly and they returned to Switzerland beaten, dishevelled and in disarray.

This campaign was all that was needed to make the band of emigrant knights fully conscious of the terror they inspired in the tyrants. As long as the after-effects of the July revolution still caused isolated insurrections in France, Germany or Italy, as long as someone or other was still standing behind them, our émigré heroes felt themselves to be but atoms in the seething masses —more or less privileged, prominent atoms, to be sure, but in the last analysis they were still atoms. But as these insurrections gradually grew feebler, as the great mass of "cowards", of the "half-hearted" and the "men of little faith" retired from the putschist swindles and as our knights felt increasingly lonely, so their self-esteem grew in proportion. If the whole of Europe became craven, stupid and selfish, how could the loyal men fail to grow in their own estimation, for they were the priests who kept the sacred fires of hatred for all tyrants burning in their breasts and who maintained the traditions of the great era of virtue and love of freedom for a more vigorous generation! If they too deserted the flag the tyrants would be safe for ever. So like the democrats of 1848 they saw in every defeat a guarantee of future victory and they gradually transformed themselves more and more into itinerant Don Quixotes with dubious sources of income. Once arrived at this point, they could venture upon their greatest act of heroism, the foundation of *"Young Europe"* [196] whose Charter of Brotherhood was edited by Mazzini and signed in Berne on April 15, 1834. Harro joined it as an

"initiator of the Central Committee, adoptive member of Young Germany and Young Italy and also as representative of the Scandinavian branch" which he "still represents today".

The date of the Charter of Brotherhood marks for our Harro the great epoch from which calculations are made forwards and backwards, as up to now from the birth of Christ. It is the high point of his life. He was co-dictator of Europe *in partibus* and although the world knew nothing of him he was one of the most dangerous men alive. No one stood behind him but his many unpublished works, a few German artisans in Switzerland and a dozen political speculators who had seen better days—but for that very reason he could claim that all nations were on his side. For it is the fate of all great men not to be recognised by their own age whereas the future belongs to them for that very reason. And this future—our Harro had it in black and white in his bag in the form of the Charter of Brotherhood.

But now began Harro's decline. His first sorrow was that "Young Germany [197] split off from Young Europe in 1836". But Germany was duly punished for that. For owing to this split *"nothing had been prepared* for a national movement in Germany in the spring of 1848" and this is why everything ended so miserably.

But a much greater sorrow for our Harro was the emergence of communism. We learn from him that the founder of communism was none other than

"the cynic Johannes Müller from Berlin, the author of a very interesting pamphlet on Prussian policy, Altenburg 1831", who went to England where "he had no option but to tend swine in Smithfield Market at the crack of dawn".

Communism soon began to spread among the German artisans in France and Switzerland and it became a very dangerous enemy for our Harro as it cut off the only market for his writings. This was due to the "indirect communist censorship" from which poor Harro has suffered to this very day and indeed is now suffering more than ever, as he sadly confesses and "as the fate of his drama *Die Dynastie* proves".

This indirect communist censorship even succeeded in driving our Harro from Europe and so he went to Rio de Janeiro (in 1840) where he lived for a time as a painter. "Using his time conscientiously here as everywhere", he published a new work:

"*Poesie eines Scandinaven* (2,000 copies) which has been distributed so widely among sea-faring people that it has, as it were, become the favourite oceanic reading matter".

However, his "scrupulous sense of obligation towards Young Europe" unfortunately caused him soon to return to Europe. He

"hastened to Mazzini in London and soon perceived the danger that threatened the cause of the European peoples from communism".

New deeds awaited him. The Bandiera brothers were preparing for their expedition to Italy.[198] To support them and to embroil the forces of despotism in a diversion, Harro

"returned to South America to do everything possible with Garibaldi to further the idea of the future of the nations by establishing a United States of South America".

But the despots had got wind of his mission and Harro took to his heels. He sailed to New York.

"Out on the ocean I was very active intellectually and wrote among other things a drama, *Die Macht der Idee*, which belonged to the dramatic cycle *Das Volk*—this too has remained in manuscript up to now!"

From South America he brought with him to New York a mandate alleging a connection with *Humanidad.*

The news of the February revolution inspired him to produce a pamphlet in French, *La France réveillée,* and while embarking for Europe,

"I documented my love for my country once again in some poems, *Scandinavia*".

He arrived in Schleswig-Holstein. Here,

"after an absence of twenty-seven years", he discovered "an unheard-of confusion in the concepts of international law, democracy, republic, socialism and communism, which lay like rotting hay and straw in the Augean stables of party strife and national hatred".

No wonder, for his

"political writings and" his "whole striving and activities since 1831 had remained alien and unknown in those frontier provinces of my home country".

The Augustenburg party[199] had suppressed him for eighteen years by means of a conspiracy of silence. To deal with this he girt on a sabre, a rifle, four pistols and six daggers and called for the formation of a volunteer corps, but in vain. After various adventures he finally landed in Hull. Here he hastened to issue two circulars—to the people of Schleswig-Holstein, and to the Scandinavians and Germans[a] and even sent a note, as has been reported, to two Communists in London with this message:

"Fifteen thousand workers in Norway asked me to tell you that they extend the hand of brotherhood to you."

Despite this curious appeal he soon became a sleeping partner of the European Central Committee again, thanks to the Charter of Brotherhood, and he also became

"night watchman and employee of a young firm of brokers in Gravesend on the Thames where my task was to drum up trade among ships' captains in nine different languages until I was required to practise deceit, a thing which the philosopher Johannes Müller was at least spared in his capacity as swineherd".

Harro summarised his action-packed life as follows:

"It can easily be calculated that apart from my poems I have given away more than 18,000 copies of my writings in German (their price in Hamburg varies from 10 shillings to 3 marks, and accordingly their value amounts to around 25,000 marks in toto) to the democratic movement. I have never been reimbursed for the printing costs, let alone received any profit for myself."

---

[a] "Sendschreiben an die 'Schleswig-Holsteiner'", November 29, 1850, and "Sendschreiben an die Skandinaven und an die Deutschen", February 3, 1851.— *Ed.*

With this we bring the adventures of our demagogic Hidalgo from the South Jutland Mancha to a close. In Greece and in Brazil, on the Weichsel [a] and on La Plata, in Schleswig-Holstein and in New York, in London and in Switzerland: at different times the representative of Young Europe and of the South-American *Humanidad*, painter, night watchman and employee, peddler of his own writings; among Wasserpolacken one day and gauchos the next, and ships' captains the day after that; unacknowledged, abandoned, ignored but everywhere an itinerant knight of freedom thoroughly despising ordinary bourgeois work—our hero at all times in all countries and in all circumstances remains himself: with the same confusion, the same pretentious obtrusiveness, the same faith in himself, and in spite of all the world he will never cease to say, write and print that since 1831 he has been the mainspring of world history.

X

Despite his unexpected successes hitherto Arnold had not yet arrived at the goal of his labours. As Germany's representative by the grace of Mazzini, he was under the obligation on the one hand to obtain confirmation of his appointment at least by the German emigration and, on the other hand, to present the Central Committee with people who accepted his leadership. He did indeed claim that in Germany "there was a clearly defined part of the people behind him" but this hind portion could scarcely inspire much confidence in Mazzini and Ledru as long as they could see nothing but the Ruge front portion. In short, Arnold had to look around among the émigrés for a "clearly defined" tail.

At about this time Gottfried Kinkel came to London and together with him or soon afterwards a number of other exiles partly from France, partly from Switzerland and Belgium: Schurz, Strodtmann, Oppenheim, Schimmelpfennig, Techow, etc. These new arrivals, some of whom had already tried their hand at forming provisional governments in Switzerland, infused new life into the London emigration and for our Arnold the moment seemed more favourable than ever. At the same time Heinzen again took over the *Schnellpost* in New York and so Arnold could now make his "frequent appearances" on the other side of the ocean as well as in the little paper in Bremen.[b] Should Arnold ever find his Strodtmann the

---

[a] Vistula.— *Ed.*
[b] *Bremer Tages-Chronik.—Ed.*

A page of the manuscript of *The Great Men of the Exile* (the main text is in Engels' hand, the addition in Marx's)

latter would surely declare the monthly files of the *Schnellpost* from the beginning of 1851 on to be a priceless source of information. This infinitely feeble mixture of gossip, silliness and nastiness, this ant-like self-importance with which Arnold deposits his droppings, has to be seen to be believed. While Heinzen portrays Arnold as a European Great Power, Arnold treats Heinzen as an American newspaper oracle. He tells him the secrets of European diplomacy and in particular the latest daily events in the world history of this emigration. Arnold sometimes figures as the anonymous correspondent in London and Paris in order to keep the American public informed of some of the great Arnold's fashionable movements.[a]

"Once again Arnold Ruge has the Communists by the throat"—"Arnold Ruge *yesterday*" (dated from Paris so that the dating gives the old joker away) "made an excursion from Brighton to London." And again: "Arnold Ruge to Karl Heinzen: Dear Friend and Editor.... Mazzini sends you his greetings.... Ledru-Rollin *gives you his permission* to translate his pamphlet on the June 13th" and so on.

A letter from America has this comment to make:

"As I see from Ruge's letters" (in the *Schnellpost*) "Heinzen must be writing Ruge" (privately) "all sorts of funny stories about the importance of his paper in America, while Ruge seems to act as if he were a major European government. Whenever Ruge imparts a momentous piece of information to Heinzen, he never omits to add: You can ask other newspapers in the States to reprint this. As if they would wait for Ruge's authorisation if they found the news worth reprinting. Incidentally, I have never seen these momentous reports actually appear anywhere else despite Herr Ruge's advice and permission."

Father Ruge employed both this little paper and the *Bremer Tages-Chronik* to win over newly arrived emigrants by flattery: Kinkel is here now, the poet of genius and patriot; Strodtmann, a great writer; Schurz, a young man as amiable as he is bold, and a whole array of distinguished revolutionary warriors.

Meanwhile in contrast to the Mazzini Committee a *plebeian* European Committee was formed with the support of the "inferior refugees" and the émigré riff-raff of the various European nations. At the time of the battle of Bronzell this committee had issued a manifesto[b] that included the following outstanding German signatories: Gebert, Majer, Dietz, Schärttner, Schapper, Willich.[200] This document was couched in peculiar French and contained as the latest piece of information the news that at that moment (November 10, 1850) the Holy Alliance of Tyrants had assembled 1,330,000 soldiers backed by another 700,000 armed henchmen in reserve, that "the

---

[a] Marx and Engels use the English words "fashionable movements".— *Ed.*

[b] This manifesto of November 10, 1850 was published in *Le Constitutionnel* on November 18, 1850.— *Ed.*

German papers and the committee's own contacts" had revealed to it the secret intentions of the Warsaw conferences,[201] and that these were to massacre all the republicans of Europe. This was followed by the inevitable call to arms. This *manifeste-Fanon-Caperon-Gouté*, as it was described by the *Patrie* (to which they sent it), was overwhelmed with ridicule by the counter-revolutionary press. The *Patrie* called it

"the manifesto of the *dii minorum gentium*, written without chic, without style and equipped with only the most banal clichés, *serpents, sicaires* and *égorgements*[a]".

The *Indépendance belge* states that it was written by the *soldats les plus obscurs de la démagogie,*[b] poor devils who had sent it to its correspondent in London even though this paper was conservative. So great was their longing to get into print; as penalty, the paper would not publish the names of the signatories. Despite their attempts to beg from the reaction these noble people did not manage to obtain recognition as conspirators and as dangerous men.

The establishment of this rival firm spurred Arnold on to even greater efforts. Together with Struve, Kinkel, R. Schramm, Bucher, etc., he tried to found a *Volksfreund,* or, if Gustav were to insist, a *Deutscher Zuschauer*. But the plan fell through. Partly because the others resisted Arnold's protectorate, partly because our "good-humoured" Gottfried demanded payment in cash whereas Arnold shared Hansemann's view that in money matters there is no room for good humour.[c] Arnold's particular aim was to impose a levy on the Reading Circle, a club of German watchmakers, well-paid workers and petty bourgeois, but in this too he was frustrated.

But soon there arose another opportunity for Arnold to make one of his "frequent appearances". Ledru and his supporters among the French émigrés could not let February 24 (1851) pass without a "fraternal celebration" of the nations of Europe. In fact only the French and the Germans attended. Mazzini did not come and excused himself by letter; Gottfried, who was present, went home fuming because his mute presence failed to produce the magical effect he expected; Arnold lived to see the day when his friend Ledru pretended not to know him, and became so confused when he rose to speak that he did not produce the French speech he had

---

[a] G. de Molinari, "Un nouveau manifeste rouge", *La Patrie*, No. 332, November 28, 1850; *dies minorum gentium* means "minor gods"; *serpents, sicaires* and *égorgements* means "snakes", "assassins" and "massacres".— *Ed.*

[b] Most obscure soldiers of demagogy (*L'Indépendance belge*, No. 323, November 19, 1850).— *Ed.*

[c] From Hansemann's speech at a sitting of the United Diet in Berlin on June 8, 1847.— *Ed.*

prepared and which had been approved in high places; he just stammered a few words in German and,exclaiming: *À la restauration de la révolution!*[a], retreated precipitately causing a general shaking of heads.

On the same day a rival banquet took place under the auspices of the competing committee referred to above. Annoyed that the Mazzini-Ledru committee had not invited him to join them from the beginning, Louis Blanc took himself off to the refugee mob, declaring that "the aristocracy of talent must also be abolished". The whole lower emigration was assembled. The chivalrous Willich presided. The hall was festooned with flags and the walls were emblazoned with the names of the greatest men of the people: Waldeck between Garibaldi and Kossuth, Jacoby between Blanqui and Cabet, Robert Blum between Barbès and Robespierre. That coquettish fop Louis Blanc read out in a whining voice an address from his old yes-men, the future peers of the social republic, the delegates of the Luxemburg of 1848.[202] Willich read out an address from Switzerland, the signatures to which had partly been collected under false pretences, and their ostentatious and indiscreet publication led afterwards to the mass expulsion of the signatories. From Germany no message had arrived. Then speeches. Despite the boundless fraternal love boredom could be seen on every face.

The banquet gave rise to a highly edifying scandal which, like all the heroic deeds of the European central mob-committee, unfolded within the pages of the counter-revolutionary press. It had struck observers as very strange that during the banquet a certain Barthélemy should have given an extremely grandiose eulogy of *Blanqui* in the presence of Louis Blanc. The puzzle was now elucidated. The *Patrie* printed a toast that Blanqui, in response to a request, had sent from Belle-Île to the orator at the banquet.[203] In the toast he made a blunt and powerful attack on the whole provisional government of 1848 and on M. Louis Blanc in particular. The *Patrie* expressed astonishment that this toast had been suppressed during the banquet. Louis Blanc at once wrote to *The Times*[b] declaring that Blanqui was an abominable intriguer and had never sent such a toast to the banquet committee. The committee, consisting of Messrs. Blanc, Willich, Landolphe, Schapper, Barthélemy and Vidil, announced simultaneously in the *Patrie* that they had never received the toast. The *Patrie*, however, did not publish the declaration until it had made inquiries of M. Antoine, Blanqui's

---

[a] To the restoration of the revolution!—*Ed.*
[b] L. Blanc, "To the Editor of *The Times*", March 3 [,1851].—*Ed.*

brother-in-law, who had given it the text of the toast. Beneath the declaration of the banquet committee it printed M. Antoine's reply [a]: he had sent the toast to Barthélemy, one of the signatories of the declaration, and had received an acknowledgement from him. Whereupon M. Barthélemy was forced to admit that it was true that he had lied. He had indeed received the toast but had thought it unsuitable and had therefore not informed the committee of it. But before this, behind Barthélemy's back his co-signatory, the French ex-captain Vidil, had also written to the *Patrie*,[b] saying that his honour as a soldier and his sense of truth compelled him to confess that he himself, Louis Blanc, Willich and all the other signatories of the first declaration of the committee had lied. The committee had consisted of 13 members and not 6. They had all seen Blanqui's toast, they had discussed it and after a long debate agreed to suppress it by a majority of 7 votes to 6. He had been one of the six who had voted *in favour* of reading it in public.

It is easy to imagine the joy of the *Patrie* when it received Barthélemy's declaration after Vidil's letter. It printed the letter with this preface [c]:

"We have often asked ourselves, and it is a difficult question to answer, whether the demagogues are notable more for their boastfulness or their stupidity. A fourth letter from London has increased our perplexity. There they are, we do not know how many poor wretches, who are so tormented by the longing to write and to see their names published in the *reactionary* press that they are undeterred even by the prospect of infinite humiliation and mortification. What do they care for the laughter and the indignation of the public—the *Journal des Débats*, the *Assemblée nationale* and the *Patrie* will publish their stylistic exercises; to achieve this no cost to the cause of cosmopolitan democracy can be too high.... In the name of literary commiseration we therefore include the following letter from 'citizen' Barthélemy—it is a novel, and, we hope, the last proof of the authenticity of Blanqui's famous toast whose existence they first all denied and now fight among themselves for the right to acknowledge."

XI

"The force of actual events", to use one of Arnold's pungently beautiful forms, now took the following course. On February 24, Ruge had compromised himself and the German émigrés in the

---

[a] ["La déclaration de la commission du Banquet des Egaux du 1 mars 1851"]; G. Antoine, "À M. le rédacteur du journal *La Patrie*" [le 6 mars 1851,] *La Patrie*, No. 66, March 7, 1851.—*Ed.*

[b] [J. Vidil, "Au rédacteur du journal *La Patrie*, le 8 mars 1851,] *La Patrie*, No. 69, March 10, 1851.—*Ed.*

[c] *La Patrie*, No. 71, March 12, 1851.—*Ed.*

presence of foreigners. Hence the few émigrés who still felt inclined to go along with him felt insecure and without backing. Arnold put the blame on the division in the emigration and pressed harder than ever for unity. Compromised as he was, he still reached eagerly for the chance to compromise himself further.

Hence the *anniversary of the March revolution in Vienna* was used to give a German banquet. The chivalrous Willich declined the invitation; as he belonged to "citizen" Louis Blanc he could not collaborate with "citizen" Ruge who belonged to "citizen" Ledru. Likewise the ex-deputies Reichenbach, Schramm, Bucher, etc., shunned Ruge. Not counting the silent guests there appeared Mazzini, Ruge, Struve, Tausenau, Haug, Ronge and Kinkel—all of whom spoke.

Ruge filled the role of the "complete fool", as even his friends say. The Germans present were however to experience even greater things. Tausenau's clowning, Struve's croaking, Haug's chattering, Ronge's litanies turned the whole audience to stone and the majority drifted away even before that flower of rhetoric, Jeremiah-Kinkel, who had been saved for the dessert, could begin his speech. "In the name of the martyrs" for the martyrs, Gottfried spoke as a martyr and uttered lachrymose words of reconciliation to all, "from the simple defender of the constitution down to the red republican".[a] At the same time as all these republicans, and even red republicans, like Kinkel, groaned away in this fashion, they also grovelled before the English constitution in humble adoration, a contradiction to which the *Morning Chronicle* deigned to draw their attention the following morning.

However, the same evening Ruge saw the fulfilment of his desires, as can be seen from a proclamation whose most brilliant sections we offer here:

"TO THE GERMANS!

"Brothers and friends in the fatherland! We, the undersigned, constitute at present, and until such time as you decide differently, the committee for German affairs" (irrespective which affairs).

"The Central Committee of European Democracy has sent us Arnold *Ruge*, the Baden revolution has sent us Gustav *Struve*, the Viennese revolution has sent us Ernst *Haug*, the religious movement has sent us Johannes *Ronge*, and prison has sent us Gottfried *Kinkel*; we have invited the Social-Democratic workers to send a representative to our midst.

"German brothers! Events have deprived you of your freedom ... we know that you are incapable of abandoning your freedom for ever, and we have" (according

---

[a] "Eine Rede Kinkel's" (March 13). *Bremer Tages-Chronik*, No. 531, March 25, 1851.—*Ed.*

to Arnold) "omitted nothing" (in the way of committees and manifestos) "that might accelerate your recovery of it.

"When we ... when we gave our support and our guarantee to the Mazzini loan, when we ... when we ... initiated the holy alliance of peoples against the unholy alliance of their oppressors, we only did, we are sure of it, what you wished with all your hearts to see done.... The tyrants have been arraigned before the universal court of mankind in the .great trial of freedom" (and while Arnold is the public prosecutor, the "tyrants" can sleep in peace). "... Arson, murder, devastation, hunger and bankruptcy will soon be widespread throughout Germany.

"You have the example of France before your eyes—smouldering with fury it is more united than ever in its determination to liberate itself" (who the devil could have predicted December 2![a])—"Look at Hungary, even the Croats have been converted" (thanks to the *Deutscher Zuschauer* and Ruge's coats made from sawdust)—"and believe us, for we know, when we say that Poland is immortal" (Mr. Darasz confided this piece of information to them under solemn oath of secrecy).

"Force against force—that is the justice that is being prepared. And we shall leave nothing undone to bring into being a *more effective provisional government*" (aha!) "than the Pre-parliament and a more potent arm of the people than the National Assembly"[204] (see below what these gentlemen brought into being when they attempted to lead each other by the nose).

"Our draft proposals concerning the finances and the press" (Order No. 1 and 2 of the strong provisional government—the Customs Officer, Christian Müller, is given the task of implementing this measure) "shall be presented to you separately. They deal mainly with business affairs. We wish only to say that every purchase of the Italian loan will be of immediate benefit to our committee and to our cause and that for the moment you can help in a practical way above all by ensuring a *liberal supply of money*. We shall then *know how to translate this money into public opinion and public power*" (with Arnold as translator) "... We say to you: *Subscribe 10 million francs and we shall liberate the Continent!*

"Germans, remember..." (that you sing baritone and kindle fires on the mountains[b]) "... lend us your thoughts" (at present they are almost as much in demand as money), "your purse" (yes, don't forget that) "and your arm! We expect your zeal to increase with the intensity of your oppression and that the committee shall be adequately strengthened for the hour of decision by your present assistance." (If not, they would have to resort to liquor, which would be against Gustav's principles.)

"All democrats are *instructed* to publicise our proclamation" (the Customs Officer, Christian Müller, will take care of the rest).

"London, March 13, 1851

The Committee for German Affairs
*Arnold Ruge, Gustav Struve, Ernst Haug,
Johannes Ronge, Gottfried Kinkel*[c]"

---

[a] The reference is to Louis Bonaparte's coup d'état in France on December 2, 1851.—*Ed.*

[b] See this volume, p. 283.—*Ed.*

[c] The proclamation was published (without the salutation and signatures) in the *Bremer Tages-Chronik*, No. 534, March 28, 1851.—*Ed.*

Our readers are acquainted with Gottfried, they are also acquainted with Gustav; Arnold's "frequent appearances" have likewise been repeated often enough. So there remain but two members of the "effective provisional government" whom we have still to introduce.

Johannes *Ronge* or Johannes Kurzweg,[a] as he likes to be known in his intimate circle, has certainly not written the *Apocalypse*. There is nothing mysterious about him; he is banal, hackneyed, as insipid as water, especially lukewarm dish-water. As is well known Johannes became famous when he refused to permit the Holy Coat of Trier[205] to intercede for him—though it is wholly unimportant who intercedes for Johannes. When Johannes first made his appearance the elderly Paulus expressed his regrets that Hegel was dead as *now* he would no longer be able to regard him as shallow, and the late Krug was lucky to be dead as he thereby escaped the danger of acquiring a reputation for profundity. Johannes is one of those phenomena often met with in history who several centuries after the rise and fall of a movement expound the content of this movement in a most feeble and colourless manner to philistines of a certain kind and to eight-year-old children as if it were the latest discovery. Such a profession does not last very long, and soon our Johannes found himself in a situation in Germany which became daily more difficult. His watered-down version of the German Enlightenment went out of fashion and Johannes made a pilgrimage to England where we see him re-appear, without any notable success, as the rival of Padre Gavazzi. The ungainly, sallow, tedious village parson naturally paled by the side of the fiery, histrionic Italian monk, and the English bet heavily that this boring Johannes could not be the man who had set the deep-thinking German nation in motion. But he was consoled by Arnold Ruge, who found that the German Catholicism of our Johannes was remarkably similar to his own brand of atheism.

Ludwig von Hauck had been a captain of engineers in the Imperial Austrian army, then in 1848 co-editor of the constitution in Vienna, later still as leader of a battalion in the Viennese National Guard he defended the gate of the Imperial Palace against the Imperial army on October 30 with great courage, abandoning his post only after all was lost. He escaped to Hungary, joined up with Bem's army in Transylvania where in

---

[a] *Kurzweg* here means blunt, frank, outspoken.—*Ed.*

consequence of his valour he advanced to the rank of colonel in the general staff. After Görgey surrendered at Világos [206] Ludwig Hauck was taken prisoner and died like a hero on one of the gallows that the Austrians erected in Hungary to avenge their repeated defeats and to express their fury at the Russian protection, which had become intolerable to them. In London Haug was long thought to be the Hauck who had been taken prisoner, an officer who had greatly distinguished himself in the Hungarian campaign. However, it now seems to be established that he is not the late Hauck. Just as he was unable to prevent Mazzini from improvising him into a general after the fall of Rome, [207] so too he could do nothing to stop Arnold Ruge from transforming him into the representative of the Viennese revolution and a member of the strong provisional government. Later he gave aesthetic lectures about the economic foundations of the cosmogony of universal history from a geological standpoint and with musical accompaniment. Among the *émigrés* this melancholic man is known as the poor wretch, or as the French say, *la bonne bête.*

Arnold could not believe his good fortune. He had a manifesto, a strong provisional government, a loan of ten million francs and even a tiny weekly magazine with the modest title *Kosmos,* edited by General Haug.

The manifesto disappeared unread and without leaving a trace. The *Kosmos* died of exhaustion in the third number, the money failed to roll in, the provisional government dissolved into its components once more.

At first, the *Kosmos* contained advertisements for Kinkel's lectures,[a] for the worthy Willich's appeals for money for the Schleswig-Holstein refugees and for Göhringer's saloon. It contained further among other things a lampoon by Arnold. The old joker invented a certain hospitable friend called Müller in Germany whose friend, Schulze,[b] he pretended to be. Müller expresses astonishment at what he reads in the papers about English hospitality; he fears that all this "sybaritism" may distract Schulze from his "affairs of state"—but he does not grudge him this as when Schulze returns to Germany he will be so overwhelmed by state affairs that he will have to deny himself the pleasures of Müller's hospitality. Finally, Müller exclaims:

---

[a] See this volume, p. 258.—*Ed.*

[b] Müller and Schulze are the characters of many German popular jokes.—*Ed.*

"Surely it was not the traitor Radowitz, but Mazzini, Ledru-Rollin, Citizen Willich, Kinkel and *yourself*" (Arnold Ruge) "who were invited to Windsor Castle?"

If after all this the *Kosmos* collapsed after the third issue the failure could certainly not be put down to lack of publicity, for at every possible English meeting the speakers would find it pressed into their hands with the request to recommend it as they would find their own principles specially represented in it.

Scarcely had the subscriptions for the ten-million-franc loan been opened when suddenly the rumour arose that a list of contributors to a fund to dispatch Struve (and Amalia) to America was circulating in the City.

"When the committee resolved to publish a German weekly with Haug as editor, Struve protested as he wanted the post of editor for himself and wished to call the journal *Deutscher Zuschauer*. Thereupon he resolved to go to America."

Thus far the report in the *Deutsche Schnellpost* of New York. It remains silent about the fact (and Heinzen had his reasons for this) that as Gustav was a collaborator on the Duke of Brunswick's *Deutsche Londoner Zeitung* Mazzini had struck his name off the list of the German committee. Gustav soon acclimatised his *Deutscher Zuschauer* in New York. But soon after came the news from over the ocean: "Gustav's *Zuschauer* is dead." As he says, this was not for the lack of people who put their name down as subscribers, nor because he had no leisure for writing but simply because of a dearth of *paying* subscribers. However, the democratic revision of Rotteck's *Weltgeschichte* could not be postponed any longer, so great was the need for it, and as he had already begun it 15 years previously he would send the subscribers a corresponding number of pages of the *Weltgeschichte* instead of the *Deutscher Zuschauer*. But he would have to request payment in advance for this, to which in the circumstances no one could object. As long as Gustav had remained on this side of the Atlantic Heinzen depicted him along with Ruge as the greatest man in Europe. No sooner had he reached the other side than a terrific row began between them. Gustav writes:

"When on June 6 in Karlsruhe Heinzen saw that guns were being brought up [208] he left for Strasbourg in female company."

Whereupon Heinzen called Gustav a "soothsayer".

When the *Kosmos* was about to founder, Arnold was busy broadcasting its virtues in the journal of the stalwart Heinzen, and at about the time when the strong provisional government was disintegrating, Rodomonte-Heinzen was proclaiming "*military obedience*" towards it in his journal. Heinzen's love of the military in peacetime is well known.

"Shortly after Struve's departure *Kinkel* too resigned from the committee, which was thereby reduced to impotence" (New York *Deutsche Schnellpost,* No. 23).

Thus the "strong provisional government" dwindled still further and only Messrs. Ruge, Ronge and Haug remained in it. Even Arnold realised that with this Trinity nothing at all could be brought into existence, let alone a cosmos. Nevertheless through all the permutations, variations and combinations it remained the nucleus of all the committees he subsequently formed. An indefatigable man, he saw no reason to throw in his hand; after all his aim was merely to do something that would have the appearance of action, the semblance of profound political schemes, something that, above all, would provide matter for self-important talk, frequent appearances and complacent gossip.

As for Gottfried, his dramatic lectures for respectable city-merchants[a] did not allow him to compromise himself. But on the other hand it was altogether too evident that the purpose of the manifesto of March 13 was none other than to provide support for the place Herr Arnold had usurped in the European Central Committee. Even Gottfried had afterwards to realise this, but it was not in his interest to grant Ruge such recognition. So it came to pass that shortly after the manifesto had been published, the *Kölnische Zeitung* printed a declaration by that *dama acerba,*[b] Mockel. Her husband, she wrote, had not signed the appeal, he was not interested in public loans and had resigned from the newly-formed committee. Whereupon Arnold gossiped in the New York *Schnellpost* to the effect that admittedly Kinkel had been prevented by illness from signing the manifesto, but he gave his approval, the plan to issue it had been conceived in his room, he himself had undertaken to dispatch a number of copies to Germany and he only left the committee because it elected General Haug president in preference to himself. Arnold accompanied this declaration with annoying attacks on Kinkel's vanity, calling him "absolute martyr" and the "democratic Beckerath", and with insinuations against Frau Johanna Kinkel, who had access to such taboo journals as the *Kölnische Zeitung.*

---

[a] Marx and Engels use the English words "city-merchants".—*Ed.*

[b] *Kölnische Zeitung,* No. 114, May 13, 1851; *dama acerba*—strict woman.—*Ed.*

However, Arnold's seed had not fallen on stony soil. Kinkel's "beautiful soul" resolved to turn the tables on his rivals and to raise the treasure of revolution alone. Johanna's statement repudiating this ridiculous scheme had scarcely appeared in the *Kölnische Zeitung* when on his own initiative our Gottfried launched an appeal for a loan in the transatlantic papers with the comment that the money should be sent to the man "who inspires the most confidence". And who could this man be but Gottfried Kinkel? For the time being he demanded an advance payment of £500 sterling with which to manufacture revolutionary paper money. Ruge, not to be outdone, had the *Schnellpost* declare that he was the treasurer of the Democratic Central Committee and that Mazzini notes were already available and could be purchased from him. Whoever wished to lose £500 sterling would certainly do better to take the available notes than to speculate in something that did not yet exist. And Rodomonte-Heinzen roared that unless Herr Kinkel abandoned his manoeuvres he would be branded publicly as an "enemy of the revolution". Gottfried had counter-articles published in the *New-Yorker Staatszeitung*, the direct rival of the *Schnellpost*. In this way full-scale hostilities were in progress on the other side of the Atlantic while kisses of Judas were still being exchanged on this side.

But by issuing an appeal for a national loan in his own name Gottfried had somewhat shocked the democratic rank and file, as he soon realised. To make good his blunder he now declared that

"this appeal for money, for a German national loan did not proceed from him. In all likelihood what had happened was that some all too zealous friends in America had made free with his name".

This declaration provoked the following answer from Dr. Wiss in the New York *Schnellpost*:

"It is generally known that the appeal to agitate for a German loan *was sent to me by Gottfried Kinkel with the urgent request* to publicise it in all the German newspapers, and I am ready and willing to show this letter to anyone who is in doubt on this point. If Kinkel has really made that statement the only honourable course for him to pursue is to retract it publicly and to publish my correspondence with him to show the party that I was quite independent and that as far as he is concerned I did certainly not exhibit 'an excess of zeal'. If he has not issued the statement it is Kinkel's duty to declare publicly that the journalist responsible for printing it is an evil slanderer, or if there had been a misunderstanding, an irresponsible and unscrupulous gossip. For my part I am unable to believe Kinkel capable of such unmitigated perfidy. Dr. C. Wiss" (*Wochenblatt der Deutschen Schnellpost*, New York).

What was Kinkel to do? Once again he thrust his *aspra donzella*[a] into the breach, he stated that Mockel was the "irresponsible and unscrupulous gossip", he claimed that his wife had promoted the loan behind his back. It cannot be denied that this tactic was highly "aesthetic".

Thus did our Gottfried sway like a reed, now advancing, now retreating, now launching a project, now dissociating himself from it, always tacking to adjust to the wind of popularity. While he officially allowed the aesthetic bourgeoisie to fête and feast him in London as the martyr of the revolution, behind the backs of the same people he indulged in forbidden commerce with the mob[b] of the emigration as represented by Willich. While living in circumstances that could be described as luxurious in comparison with his modest situation in Bonn, he wrote to St. Louis that he was living as befitted the "representative of poverty".[c] In this way he behaved towards the bourgeoisie as etiquette required, and at the same time he showed due respect to the proletariat. But as a man whose imagination far outweighed his understanding he could not help falling into the bad manners and the arrogant postures of the parvenu and this alienated many a pompous philistine émigré from him. Wholly characteristic of him was the article on the Great Exhibition that he wrote for the *Kosmos*. He admired nothing so much as the giant mirror that was exhibited in the Crystal Palace. For him, the objective world reduces itself to a mirror, the subjective world to a cliché. Under the pretext of seeing the beautiful side of everything he dallies with everything and this dallying he calls poetry, self-sacrifice or religion, as the occasion demands. Fundamentally, everything is used to gratify himself. It is inevitable that in practice he should bring into prominence the ugly side, since imagination turns into lies and enthusiasm into baseness. It was moreover to be expected that Gottfried would soon cast off his lion's skin when he fell into the hands of old, experienced clowns like Gustav and Arnold.

XII

The Great Exhibition inaugurated a new epoch in the emigration. The great throng of German philistines that flooded into

---

[a] Raw virgin.—*Ed.*

[b] Marx and Engels use the English word.—*Ed.*

[c] G. Kinkel, "Der Brief an die Bürger von St. Louis", *Bremer Tages-Chronik*, No. 507, February 25, 1851.—*Ed.*

London during the summer, felt ill at ease in the bustle of the great Crystal Palace and in the even larger town of London with its noise, its din and its clamour. And when the burden and labour of the day,[a] the dutiful inspection of the Exhibition and the other sights had been completed in the sweat of his brow, the German philistine could recover at his ease at the Hanau landlord of Schärttner or the Star landlord of Göhringer, with their beery cosiness, their smoke-filled fug and their public-house politics. Here "one could meet the whole of the fatherland" and in addition all the greatest men of Germany could be seen gratis. There they all sat, the members of parliament, the deputies of Chambers, the generals, the club orators of the wonderful period of 1848 and 1849, they smoked their pipes just like ordinary people and debated the loftiest interests of the fatherland day after day *coram publico*[b] and with unshakable dignity. This was the place where for the price of a few bottles of extremely cheap wine the German citizen could discover exactly what went on at the most secret meetings of the European cabinets. This was the place where he could learn to within a minute when "it would all start". In the meantime one bottle after another was started and all the parties went home unsteadily but strengthened in the knowledge that they had made their contribution to the salvation of the fatherland. Never has the emigration drunk more and cheaper than during the period when the solvent masses of German philistines were in London.

The true organisation of the emigration was in fact this *tavern organisation* presided over by Silenus-Schärttner in Long Acre which experienced its heyday thanks to the Exhibition. Here the true Central Committee sat in perpetual session. All other committees, organisations, party formations were just trimmings, the patriotic arabesques of this primeval German tavern society of idlers.

In addition the emigration was strengthened at the time by the arrival of Messrs. Meyen, Faucher, Sigel, Goegg, Fickler, etc.

Meyen, a little hedgehog who through an oversight had come into the world without spines, was, under the name *Poinsinet*, once described by Goethe in this way:

"In literature, as in society, one encounters such curious, stout little manikins. Endowed with some small talent they endeavour always to claim the attention of the public and as they can easily be overlooked, they are the source of much

---

[a] Cf. Matthew 20 : 12.—*Ed.*
[b] In public.—*Ed.*

amusement. However, they always manage to profit sufficiently. They live, act, are mentioned and are accorded a favourable reception. Their failures do not disconcert them; they regard them as exceptional and hope that the future will bring them great successes. Poinsinet is a figure of this sort in the French literary world. It goes almost beyond belief to see what has been done with him, how he has been misled and mystified and even his sad death by drowning in Spain does not diminish the ridiculous impression made by his life, just as a frog made of fireworks does not attain to dignity by concluding a lengthy series of sputters with a loud bang."[a]

On the other hand, writers contemporary with him pass on the following information: *Eduard Meyen* belonged to the "Resolute" group which represented the Berlin intelligentsia as against the mass stupidity of the rest of Germany. He too had a Meyen-Bug Club in Berlin with his friends Mügge, Klein, Zabel, Buhl, etc. Each of these Meyen bugs sat on his own small leaf.[b] Eduard Meyen's paper was called the *Mannheimer Abendblättchen*[c] and here, every week, after enormous efforts, he deposited a small green turd of correspondence. Our Meyen-bug really did progress to the point in 1845 when he was *about* to publish a monthly periodical; contributions from various people landed on his desk, the publisher waited but the whole project collapsed because Eduard after eight months in cold sweat declared that he could not finish the prospectus. As Eduard took all his childish activities seriously he was regarded in Berlin after the March revolution as a man who took the movement seriously. In London he worked together with Faucher on a German edition of the *Illustrated London News* under the editorship and censorship of an old woman who had known some German twenty years before, but he was discarded as useless after he had attempted with great tenacity to insert his profound articles about sculpture that he had published ten years previously in Berlin. But when, later on, the Kinkel emigration made him their secretary he realised that he was a practical *homme d'état*[d] and he announced in a lithographed leaflet that he had arrived at the "tranquillity of a point of view". After his death a whole heap of titles for future projects will be found among his papers.

Conjointly with Meyen we must necessarily consider *Oppenheim*, his co-editor and co-secretary. It has been claimed that Oppenheim is not so much a man as an allegorical figure: the

---

[a] Goethe, "Anmerkungen über Personen und Gegenstände, deren in dem Dialog Rameau's Neffe erwähnt wird".— *Ed.*

[b] *Blättchen*—"small leaf" and "small newspaper".—*Ed.*

[c] *Mannheimer Abendzeitung.—Ed.*

[d] Statesman.— *Ed.*

goddess of boredom, it is reported, came down to Frankfurt am Main and assumed the shape of this son of a Jewish jeweller. When Voltaire wrote: *"Tous les genres sont bons, excepté le genre ennuyeux"*,[a] he must have had a premonition of our Heinrich Bernhard Oppenheim. We prefer Oppenheim the writer to Oppenheim the orator. His writings may be avoided, but his spoken delivery—*c'est impossible.* The pythagorean metempsychosis may have some foundation in reality but the name borne by Heinrich Bernhard Oppenheim in former ages can no longer be discovered as no man ever made a name for himself through being an unbearable chatterbox. His life may be epitomised by its three climactic moments: Arnold Ruge's editor—Brentano's editor—Kinkel's editor.

The third member of the alliance[b] is Herr Julius *Faucher.* He is one of those Berlin Huguenots who know how to exploit their minor talent with great commercial adroitness. He made his public debut as the Ensign Pistol of the Free Trade Party in which capacity he was employed by Hamburg commercial interests to make propaganda. During the revolutionary disturbances they allowed him to preach free trade in the apparently chaotic form of anarchism. When this ceased to be relevant to the times he was dismissed and, with Meyen, became joint editor of the Berlin *Abend-Post.* Under the pretence of wishing to abolish the state and introduce anarchy he refrained from dangerous opposition towards the existing government and when, later on, the paper failed because it could not afford the deposit, the *Neue Preussische Zeitung* commiserated with Faucher, the only respectable writer among the democrats.[c] This cosy relationship with the *Neue Preussische Zeitung* soon became so intimate that our Faucher began to act as its correspondent in London. Faucher's activity in émigré politics did not last long; his free trade inclined him towards commerce where he found his true calling, to which he returned with great energy and in which he achieved results never seen before: namely a *price list* that assesses his goods according to a completely sliding scale. As is well known, the *Breslauer Zeitung* was indiscreet enough to inform the general public of this document.

---

[a] All styles are good except the tiresome kind (Voltaire, *L'enfant prodigue,* Preface).—*Ed.*

[b] Cf. Schiller, "Die Bürgschaft" (see this volume, pp. 163 and 264).—*Ed.*

[c] This refers to two items published in the *Neue Preussische Zeitung* on July 20 and 21, 1850, in the section "Berliner Zuschauer".—*Ed.*

This three-star constellation of the Berlin intelligentsia is confronted with the three-star constellation of strong South-German principles: Sigel, Fickler, Goegg.

Franz *Sigel,* whom his friend Goegg describes as

"a short, beardless man, bearing a strong resemblance to Napoleon", is, again according to Goegg, "a hero", "a man of the future", "above all a genius, intellectually creative and constantly hatching new plans".

Between ourselves, General Sigel is a young Baden lieutenant of principle and ambition. He read in an account of the campaigns of the French Revolution that the step from second lieutenant to supreme commander is mere child's play, and from that moment on this little beardless man firmly believed that Franz Sigel must become supreme commander in a revolutionary army. His wish was granted thanks to the Baden insurrection of 1849 and a popularity with the army arising from a confusion of names.[a] The battles he fought on the Neckar and did not fight in the Black Forest are well known; his retreat to Switzerland has been praised even by his enemies as a timely and correct manoeuvre. His military plans here bear witness to his study of the revolutionary wars. In order to remain faithful to the revolutionary tradition hero Sigel, ignoring the enemy and operational and withdrawal lines and similar bagatelles, went conscientiously from one Moreau position to the next. And if he did not manage to parody Moreau's campaigns in every detail, if he crossed the Rhine at Eglisau and not at Paradies, this was the fault of the enemy, who was too ignorant to appreciate such a learned manoeuvre. In his orders of the day and in his instructions Sigel emerges as a preacher and if he has an inferior style to Napoleon, he has more principle. Later, he concerned himself with devising a handbook for revolutionary officers in all branches of the service, from which we are in a position to offer the following important extract:

"An officer of the revolution must carry the following articles according to regulations: 1 head-covering and cap, 1 sabre with belt, 1 black, red and yellow[b] camel-hair sash, 2 pairs of black leather gloves, 2 battle coats, 1 cloak, 1 pair of cloth trousers, 1 tie, 2 pairs of boots or shoes, 1 black leather travelling case—12" wide, 10" high, 4" deep, 6 shirts, 3 pairs of underpants, 8 pairs of socks, 6 handkerchiefs, 2 towels, 1 washing and shaving kit, 1 writing case, 1 writing tablet with letters patent, 1 clothes brush, 1 copy of service regulations."

Joseph Fickler—

---

[a] See this volume, p. 324.—*Ed.*
[b] The colours representing German unity.—*Ed.*

"the model of a decent, resolute, imperturbably tenacious man of the people whom the people of the whole Upper Baden and lake district supported as one man and whose struggles and sufferings over many years had earned him a popularity approaching that of Brentano" (according to the testimony of his friend Goegg).

As befits a decent, resolute, imperturbably tenacious man of the people, Joseph Fickler has a fleshy full-moon face, a fat neck and a paunch to match. The only fact known about his early life is that he earned a livelihood[a] with the aid of a carving from the fifteenth century and with relics relating to the Council of Constance.[209] He allowed travellers and foreign art-lovers to inspect these curiosities in exchange for money and incidentally sold them "antique" souvenirs of which Fickler, as he loved to relate with great self-satisfaction, would constantly order a new "antique" supply.

His only deeds during the revolution were firstly his arrest by Mathy after the Pre-parliament and, second, his arrest by Römer in Stuttgart in June 1849. Thanks to these arrests he managed to avoid compromising himself. The Württemberg democrats later deposited 1,000 guilders as bail for him, whereupon Fickler went to Thurgau incognito, and to the great distress of his guarantors no more was heard of him. It is undeniable that he successfully translated the feelings and opinions of the lakeside peasants into printers' ink in the *Seeblätter*; incidentally in view of his friend Ruge he is of the opinion that much study makes people stupid and for this reason he warned his friend Goegg not to visit the library of the British Museum.

Amandus Goegg, amiable, as his name indicates,

"is no great orator, but an unassuming citizen whose noble and modest bearing earns him the friendship of people everywhere" (*Westamerikanische Blätter*).

From sheer nobility Goegg became a member of the provisional government in Baden, where, as he admits, he could do nothing against Brentano and in all modesty he assumed the title of Dictator. No one denies that his achievements as Finance Minister were modest. In all modesty he proclaimed the "Social-Democratic Republic" in Donaueschingen the day before the final retreat to Switzerland, a retreat for which the orders had already been given. In all modesty he later declared (see Heinzen's *Janus*, 1852) that the Paris proletariat had lost on December 2 because it did not possess his own French-Badenese democratic experience nor

---

[a] Marx and Engels use the English word.—*Ed.*

the insights available elsewhere in the French parts of South Germany. Anyone who desires further proofs of Goegg's modesty and of the existence of a "Goegg party", will find them in the book *Rückblick auf die badische Revolution,* etc., Paris 1851, written by himself. A fitting climax to his modesty came in a public meeting in Cincinnati when he declared that

"reputable men had visited him in Zurich after the bankruptcy of the Baden revolution and had announced that in the Baden revolution men of all the German tribes had taken part. It was therefore to be regarded as a German matter just as the Roman revolution was an Italian matter. As he was the man who had held out, they said that he must *become the German Mazzini.* His modesty compelled him to refuse."

Why? A man who was once "Dictator" and who is moreover the bosom friend of "Napoleon" Sigel, could surely also "*become the German Mazzini*".

Once the emigration was augmented *au grand complet*[a] by these and similar less noteworthy arrivals, it could proceed to those mighty battles that the reader shall learn of in the next canto.

XIII

Chi mi darà la voce e le parole,
E un proferir magnanimo e profondo!
Che mai cosa piu fiera sotto il sole
Non fu veduta in tutto quanto il mondo;
L'altre battaglie fur rose e viole,
Al raccontar di questa mi confondo;
Perchè il valor, e'l pregio della terra
A fronte son condotti in questa guerra.
(Boiardo, *Orlando innamorato,* Canto 27)

Now who will give me words and who the tongue,
To sing of such brave deeds in sonorous sounds!
For ne'er was strife upon this earth begun
More proudly fought on bloodier battle grounds;
Compared to this all other wars are roses
To tell of it my lyric art confounds
For on this earth there ne'er was seen such glory
Or noble valour bright as in this story.

The latest fashionable arrivals[b] had replenished the emigration and the time had now come when the *émigrés* had to attempt to "*organise*" themselves on a larger scale so as to make up a full

---

[a] To its full extent.—*Ed.*
[b] Marx and Engels use the English words "fashionable arrivals".—*Ed.*

dozen. As might have been expected, these attempts degenerated into bitter feuds. The paper war conducted in the transatlantic journals now reached its climax. The privations of individuals, intrigues, plots, self-praise—the great men spent their energies in such paltry activities. But the emigration had gained something, a history of its own, lying outside world history, its own political pettifoggery alongside public affairs. And the very fact that they fought each other led each to believe in the importance of the other. Beneath the façade of all these strivings and conflicts lay the speculation in democratic party funds, the Holy Grail,[210] and this transformed these transcendental rivalries, these disputes about Emperor Barbarossa's beard, into ordinary competition between fools. Anyone who wishes to study the source material relating to this great war between the frogs and the mice[a] will find all pertinent documents in the New York *Schnellpost*, the *New-Yorker Deutsche Zeitung*, the *Allgemeine Deutsche Zeitung* and the *Staatszeitung*, in the Baltimore *Correspondent*, in the *Wecker* and in other German-American papers. However, this display of alleged connections and imagined conspiracies, this whole hue and cry raised by the émigrés was not without serious consequences. It provided the governments with the pretext they needed to arrest many people in Germany, to obstruct the movement throughout the country and to use these wretched strawmen in London as scarecrows with which to frighten the German middle classes. Far from constituting any danger to existing circumstances these heroes of the exile wish only that Germany should be as silent as the grave so that their voice might be heard the better and that the general level of thought should decline so far that even men of their stature might appear outstanding.

The newly-arrived South German worthies, since they were not committed to any side, found themselves in an excellent position in London to mediate between the various cliques and, at the same time, to gather the mass of émigrés around the leaders as a kind of chorus. Their sturdy sense of duty impelled them not to forgo this opportunity.

At the same time, however, they could already see Ledru-Rollin where he saw himself, namely in the chair of the president of the French Republic. As the closest neighbours of France it was vital for them to obtain recognition from the provisional government of France as the provisional chiefs of Germany. Sigel especially

---

[a] A reference to *Batrachomyomachia* — *The Battle of the Frogs and the Mice* — a mock-heroic Greek poem, which parodies Homer's *Iliad.— Ed.*

wished to see his supreme command guaranteed by Ledru. But the only way to Ledru led over Arnold's corpse. Besides, they were still impressed by Arnold's *persona* and he still passed as the philosophical northern light who would illumine their South-German twilight. So they turned first of all to *Ruge*.

On the opposing side stood in the first instance *Kinkel* with his immediate entourage—Schurz, Strodtmann, Schimmelpfennig, Techow, etc.; then came the former members of parliament[a] and deputies of Chambers, led by *Reichenbach* with Meyen and Oppenheim as the representatives of literature; and, lastly, Willich with his flock which, however, remained in the background. The roles were distributed as follows: Kinkel as a passion-flower represents the German philistines in general; Reichenbach as a count represents the bourgeoisie; Willich as Willich represents the proletariat.

The first thing to say about August *Willich* is that Gustav always felt secretly mistrustful of him because of his pointed skull signifying that the enormous overgrowth of self-esteem had stunted all other qualities. A German philistine who once caught sight of ex-Lieutenant Willich in a London pub snatched up his hat and fled exclaiming: My God, he looks just like Jesus Christ, our Lord! In order to increase the similarity Willich became a carpenter for a while before the revolution. Later on he emerged as a partisan leader in the campaign in Baden and the Palatinate.

The partisan leader, a descendant of the old Italian condottiere, is a peculiar phenomenon of more recent wars, especially in Germany. The partisan leader, accustomed to act on his own initiative, is reluctant to subordinate himself to a general supreme command. His men owe their allegiance only to him, but he is likewise wholly dependent on them. For this reason the discipline in a volunteer corps is something rather special; according to circumstances it may be savagely strict, but mostly it is extremely lax. The partisan leader cannot always act the martinet, he must often flatter his men and win them over individually with the aid of physical caresses; the normal military qualities are of little use here and boldness must be supplemented by other characteristics if the leader is to retain the respect of his subordinates. If he is not noble he must at least have a magnanimous consciousness, to be complemented as always by cunning, crafty intrigue and covert practical baseness. In this way he not only wins over his soldiers but also captivates the inhabitants, surprises the enemy, and the

---

[a] The Frankfurt National Assembly.— *Ed.*

originality of his character is acknowledged especially by his opponents. But all this does not suffice to hold together a volunteer corps, most of whose members either come from the lumpenproletariat or are rapidly assimilated into it. What is needed in addition is a lofty idea. The partisan leader must therefore have a nucleus of fixed ideas, he must be a man of principle who always keeps in mind his mission to redeem the world. By means of sermons delivered to his men and sustained didactic propaganda he must impart a consciousness of this lofty idea to every man individually and in this way transform the whole troop into sons within the faith. If this lofty idea is tinged with philosophy or mysticism or anything that surpasses normal understanding, if it is something Hegelian by nature (as was the case with the idea that General Willisen tried to infuse into the Prussian army[211]), then so much the better. For this ensures that the noble consciousness will enter into each and every partisan and the deeds of the whole corps thereby attain to a speculative consecration which exalts them far above the level of ordinary unreflecting courage, and the fame of such a troop depends less on its achievements than on its messianic calling. The strength of a troop can only be enhanced if all the warriors are made to swear an oath that they will not survive the destruction of the cause for which they are fighting and would prefer to be massacred to the last man beneath the last apple tree on the frontier while singing a hymn. Of course, such a troop and such a leader inevitably feel degraded by contact with ordinary profane soldiers and they will make every effort either to keep at a distance from the army or else to shake off the society of the uncircumcised as quickly as possible. They hate nothing more than a large army and a large war where their cunning buttressed by a lofty incentive can achieve little if it disregards the normal rules of war. Thus the partisan leader must be a crusader in the full sense of the word, he must be Peter the Hermit and Walther the Pauper rolled into one. Faced with the heterogeneous elements and the informal mode of life of his corps he must always uphold virtue. He must not allow his men to drink him under the table and so he should rather drink in solitude, for instance at night in bed. If it should happen to him, as it might to any fallible human being, that he find himself returning to barracks late at night after inordinate indulgence in the pleasures of this life, he will take care [not] to enter through the main gate, but will return by a roundabout route and climb unnoticed over the wall to avoid giving offence. Feminine charms should leave him cold, but it will make a good impression if he, as Cromwell did with his non-commissioned officers, takes a tailor's apprentice into his bed from time to time. In general he cannot lead too strict and ascetic a life. Behind the *cavaliere della ventura*[a] stand the *cavalieri del dente*[b] of his corps who live mainly from requisitions and free quarters, to which Walther the Pauper has to turn a blind eye and even for that reason Peter the Hermit has always to be at hand with the consolation that such unpleasant measures are only taken to save the country and are therefore in the interest of the victims themselves.

All the qualities that the partisan leader displays in wartime re-appear in peacetime in a modified form, but one that can scarcely be regarded as an improvement. Above all else he must preserve the core of the regiment for a new corps and must keep his recruiting officers in a state of constant activity. The core, consisting of the remnants of the volunteer corps and the general mob of émigrés, is put into barracks either at government expense (as in Besançon[212]) or by some other means. Life in the barracks must not lack spiritual consecration and it is provided by a barracks communism that invests the disdain of ordinary civilian occupations with a higher significance. As this communist barracks is no longer subject to the articles of war, but only to the moral authority and the dictates of self-sacrifice, it is inevitable that brawls should break out over the communal funds. From these disputes moral authority does not always emerge unscathed. If there is an artisans' club anywhere in the vicinity it can be employed as a recruiting base and the artisans are given the prospect of a jolly life full of adventures in exchange for the oppressive work of the present. By pointing to the higher ethical significance of the barracks for the future of the proletariat, it is even possible to induce the club to make financial contributions. In both the barracks and the club the sermonising and the patriarchal and gossipy style of personal relations will not fail to impress. Even in peacetime the partisan does not lose his indispensable assurance and just as formerly every setback spurred him on to proclaim victory on the morrow, so now he is for ever expounding on the moral certainty and the physical inevitability that *it* will "start" within the next fortnight. As he must needs have an enemy and as the noble man is necessarily opposed by the ignoble ones he discovers in them a raging hostility towards

---

[a] Knight of fortune.— *Ed.*
[b] Knights of the knapsack.— *Ed.*

himself, he imagines that they hate him merely because of his well-deserved popularity and would gladly poison him or stab him. With this in mind he always conceals a long dagger beneath his pillow.

Just as the partisan leader in war will never succeed unless he assumes that the population reveres him, likewise in peace he will not indeed manage to form any lasting political associations but he will constantly suppose them to exist and from this all sorts of strange mystifications can arise. The talent for requisitioning and obtaining free quarters appears again in the form of a cosy parasitism. By contrast, the strict asceticism of our Orlando, like everything that is noble and great, is subject to terrible temptations in times of peace. Boiardo says in Canto 24:

> Turpin claims that the Count of Brava
> Was virginal and chaste his whole life long.
> Of that you may believe, Sirs, what you will—

But it is also well known that later the beautiful Angelica's eyes caused Count of Brava to lose his reason and Astolf had to go to the moon to recover it for him, as Master Lodovico Ariosto so charmingly narrates.[a] Our modern Orlando, however, mistook himself for the poet who tells how he, too, loved so greatly that he lost his reason and tried to find it with his lips and hands on the bosom of his Angelica and was thrown out of the house for his pains.

In politics the partisan leader will display his superiority in all the methods of small-scale warfare. In conformity with the notion of a partisan he will go from one party to the next.[b] *Mesquines*[c] intrigues, sordid prevarication, the occasional lie, morally outraged perfidy will be the natural symptoms of the noble consciousness. His faith in his mission and in the higher meaning of his words and deeds will induce him to declare emphatically: "I never lie!" The fixed ideas become a splendid cloak for his secret treachery and cause the simpletons of the emigration, who have *no* ideas *at all*, to conclude that he, the man of fixed ideas, is simply a fool. And our worthy slyboots could desire nothing better.

Don Quixote and Sancho Panza rolled into one, as much in love with his knapsack as with his fixed ideas, with the free provisions of the itinerant knight as much as with renown, Willich is the man

---

[a] In *L'Orlando furioso*, Canto 34.— *Ed*.
[b] A pun on the word *Parteigänger* (partisan) the second component of which is derived from an old German word meaning "to go", "to walk".— *Ed*
[c] Petty.— *Ed*.

of the duodecimo[a] war and the microscopic intrigue. He conceals his cunning beneath the mask of character. His real future lies in the prairies of the Rio Grande del Norte.

Concerning the relations between the two wings of the emigration we have described, a letter from Herr Goegg in the *Deutsche Schnellpost* in New York is very revealing:

"They" (the South Germans) "resolved to bolster up the reputation of the *moribund* Central Committee by attempting to unite with the other factions. But there is little prospect of success for this well-intentioned idea. Kinkel continues to intrigue, has formed a committee consisting of his rescuer,[b] his biographer[c] and several Prussian lieutenants.[d] The committee is to work in secret, to expand, if possible to gain possession of the democratic funds, and then suddenly appear publicly as the powerful Kinkel party. This is neither honest nor just nor sensible!"

How "honest" the intentions to unite of the South Germans were can be seen from the following letter from Herr Sigel to the same newspaper:

"If we, the few men with *honourable* intentions, have in part also resorted to conspiracies, this is due to the need to protect ourselves against the vile perfidy and the presumptuousness of Kinkel and his colleagues and to show them that they are not born to rule. *Our chief aim* was to force Kinkel to come to a large meeting in order to prove to him and to what he calls his close political friends that not all that glitters is gold. The devil take the instrument" (Schurz), "the devil take the singer too"[e] (Kinkel) (*Wochenblatt der New-Yorker Deutschen Zeitung*, September 24, 1851).

The strange constitution of the two factions that rebuke each other for being "North German" and "South German" can be seen from the fact that at the head of the South-German elements stood the "mind" of Ruge, while at the head of the North-German side were the "feelings" of Kinkel.

In order to understand the great struggle that was now waged we must waste a few words on the diplomacy of these two world-shaking parties.

Arnold (and his henchmen likewise) was concerned above all to form a "private society" with the official *appearance* of "revolutionary activity". This society would then give rise to his beloved "Committee *for* German Affairs" and this committee would then propel Ruge into the European Central Committee. Arnold had

---

a Diminutive.—*Ed.*
b Carl Schurz.—*Ed.*
c Adolf Strodtmann.—*Ed.*
d Gustav Techow and Alexander Schimmelpfennig.—*Ed.*
e Goethe, *Faust*, Erster Teil, "Nacht", "Strasse vor Gretchens Türe".—*Ed.*

been indefatigable in his efforts to realise this aim since the summer of 1850. He had hoped that the South Germans would provide "that happy medium where he could dominate in comfort". The official establishment of the emigration and the formation of committees was therefore the necessary policy of Arnold and his allies.

Kinkel and his associates, on the other hand, had to try and undermine everything that could legitimise the position Ruge had arrogated to himself in the European Central Committee. In reply to his appeal for a preliminary subscription of £500 sterling Kinkel had received the promise of some money from New Orleans, whereupon he had formed a *secret finance committee* together with Willich, Schimmelpfennig, Reichenbach, Techow, Schurz, etc. They reasoned: once we have the money we shall have the emigration; once we have the emigration we shall also have the government in Germany. Their aim, therefore, was to occupy the whole emigration mainly with formal meetings but to foil any attempt at setting up an official organisation that went beyond a "loosely organised society" and above all to frustrate all proposals to form committees. This would delay the enemy faction, block its activities and enable them to manoeuvre behind its backs.

Both factions, i.e. "the distinguished men", had one thing in common: they both led the mass of émigrés by the nose, did not inform them of their real objectives, wanted to use them merely as a foil and to drop them as soon as they had served their purpose.

Let us take a look at these democratic Machiavellis, Talleyrands and Metternichs and see how they treat each other.

Scene 1. July 14, 1851.—After "a private understanding with Kinkel to make common cause had fallen through", Ruge, Goegg, Sigel, Fickler and Ronge invited the distinguished men of all factions to a meeting in Fickler's home on July 14. Twenty-six people appeared. Fickler proposed that a "private circle" of German refugees should be formed and this should create a "business committee for the advancement of revolutionary objectives". This was opposed mainly by Kinkel and six of his supporters. After a violent debate lasting several hours Fickler's motion was passed (16 votes to 10). Kinkel and the minority declared themselves unable to participate any further and took their departure.

Scene 2. July 20.—The above majority constituted itself as an association. Joined, among others, by *Tausenau*, who had been introduced by Fickler.

If Ronge is the Luther and Kinkel the Melanchthon then Herr Tausenau is the *Abraham a Sancta Clara* of the German democrats.

If the two haruspices in Cicero could not look each other in the face without laughing[a] then Herr Tausenau cannot catch sight of his own earnest features in the mirror without bursting into laughter. If Ruge had discovered in the Badeners people whom *he* impressed, Fate now had its revenge when it introduced to him the Austrian Tausenau, a man who impressed *him.*

At the suggestion of Goegg and Tausenau the negotiations were postponed in order to try once again to bring about a union with Kinkel's faction.

Scene 3. July 27.—Meeting in the Cranbourne Hotel. The "distinguished" emigration *au grand complet.*[b] Kinkel's group appeared but not with the intention of joining the association already in existence; on the contrary, they pressed for the formation of an "open discussion club *without* a business committee and without *definite objectives*". Schurz, who acted as young Kinkel's mentor throughout all these parliamentary negotiations, proposed:

"The present society should form itself into a private political association with the name *German Émigré Club* and should accept as new members other citizens from among the German refugees on the nomination of a member and after a majority vote in favour."

Passed unanimously. The club resolved to meet every Friday.

"The passing of this motion was welcomed with general applause and with the cry: 'Long Live the German Republic!!!' Everyone felt that they had done their duty by being prepared to make concessions and that they had achieved something positive serving the cause of revolution" (Goegg, *Wochenblatt der* [*Deutschen*] *Schnellpost,* August 20, 1851).

Eduard Meyen was so delighted with this success that he exclaimed in his lithographed report:

"The whole emigration now form a coherent phalanx up to and including Bucher and with the sole exception of the incorrigible Marx clique."

This same notice of Meyen's can be found also in the Berlin lithographed ministerial reports.[c]

In this way, thanks to a general willingness to make concessions and to the accompaniment of three cheers for the German Republic, the great *Émigré Club,* which was to hold such inspiring meetings and which was to dissolve in satisfaction a few weeks

---

[a] Cicero, in his book *De divinatione,* quotes this remark by Cato the Elder. The haruspices were diviners in ancient Rome basing their predictions on the inspection of the entrails of sacrificial animals.—*Ed.*

[b] There to a man.—*Ed.*

[c] *Preussische Lithographische Correspondenz.—Ed.*

after Kinkel's departure for America, came into being. Its dissolution did not of course prevent it from playing an important part as a living entity in America.

Scene 4. August 1.—Second meeting in the Cranbourne Hotel.

"Unfortunately we must already report today that the expectations raised by the formation of this club have been disappointed" (Goegg, *loc. cit.*, August 27).

Without first obtaining a majority decision, Kinkel introduced six Prussian refugees and six Prussian visitors to the Great Exhibition into the club. *Damm** (President, former President of the Baden Constituent Assembly) expressed his astonishment at this treacherous infringement of the statutes.

Kinkel explained:

"The club is only a *loosely* organised society with no other purpose than for people to get to know each other and to have discussions that are open to everyone. It is therefore desirable for visitors to attend the meetings of the society in large numbers."

Student *Schurz* attempted to cover up quickly for his Professor's lack of tact by moving an amendment to permit the admission of visitors. Motion passed. Abraham a Sancta Clara *Tausenau* rose and put the following two important motions with a perfectly straight face:

"1. A commision" ("*the*" committee) "should be set up to give a detailed report every week on current affairs, particularly in Germany. These reports are to be preserved in the archive of the society and published at an appropriate time. 2. There should be a commission" ("*the*" committee) "to deposit in the archive all possible details concerning violations of the law and acts of cruelty towards the supporters of democracy committed by the servants of the reaction during the last three years and at the present time."

Reichenbach opposed this vigorously: "He saw suspicious motives lurking behind these innocuous proposals and also the wish to use the election of these commissions as a device to give the meeting an *offical* character not desired by himself or his friends."

Schimmelpfennig and *Schurz*: "These commissions could arrogate powers unto themselves that might be of a conspiratorial nature and gradually lead to an *official committee*."

Meyen: "*I want words, not deeds*."

* "Damm is here!"
"Who is here?"
"Damm is here!"
"Who?"
"Damm, Damm, surely you know Damm?" [a]

---

[a] Paraphrase of a German song.—*Ed.*

According to Goegg's account, the majority seemed inclined to accept the motions; Machiavelli *Schurz* proposed an adjournment. Abraham a Sancta Clara *Tausenau* being good-natured agreed to the proposal. *Kinkel* expressed the opinion that

"the vote should be postponed until the next meeting chiefly because his group appeared to be in the minority that evening and he and his friends would be unable in the circumstances to regard the vote as binding *on their conscience*".

Adjournment agreed.

Scene 5. August 8.—Third meeting in the Cranbourne Hotel. Discussion of the Tausenau motions.—Ignoring the agreement, Kinkel-Willich had brought along the "rank and file refugees", *le menu peuple*,[a] so as to "bind their conscience" this time.—*Schurz* moved an amendment proposing voluntary lectures on current affairs, and in accordance with a pre-arranged plan Meyen immediately volunteered to speak on Prussia, Schurz on France, Oppenheim on England and Kinkel on America and the future (since his immediate future lay in America).— *Tausenau's* proposals were rejected. He declared emotionally that his only wish was to sacrifice his just anger on the altar of the fatherland and to remain within the bosom of his allies. But the Ruge-Fickler faction at once assumed the outraged indignation of beautiful souls who have been swindled.

Intermezzo.—Kinkel had at last received £160 sterling from New Orleans and together with other renowned celebrities he was supposed to invest it for the revolution. The Ruge-Fickler faction, already embittered by the recent vote, now learned of this. They had no time to lose, action was essential. A new emigration swamp came into being and its idle stagnant existence was decked out with the name of the "*Agitation Union*". Its members were Tausenau, Frank, Goegg, Sigel, Hertle, Ronge, Haug, Fickler and Ruge. The Union immediately announced in the English press:

"Its aims are not to discuss but to work, it would produce not words but works[b] and above all it appeals to like-minded comrades to send money contributions. The Agitation Union appoints *Tausenau* to be its executive leader and its agent in its external business. It also recognises *Ruge's* position in the European Central Committee" (as Imperial Administrator) "as well as his previous activity on behalf of and in the name of the German people."[c]

---

[a] The common folk.— *Ed.*

[b] "Words" and "works" are in English in the manuscript.—*Ed.*

[c] K. Tausenau, "The German Agitation Union of London", *The Leader*, No. 73, August 16, 1851.—*Ed.*

It is easy to recognise the prototype, comprising Ruge, Ronge and Haug, in the new combination. Thus after the struggles and the efforts of so many years Ruge had finally reached his goal: he was acknowledged to be the fifth wheel on the central coach of democracy and had a clearly—all too clearly—defined part of the people behind him, consisting of eight men in all. But even this pleasure was poisoned for him as his recognition was purchased at the cost of an indirect slight and was agreed to only on the condition imposed by the peasant Fickler that Ruge should henceforth cease to "broadcast his rubbish to the whole world". The coarse Fickler regarded as "distinguished" only those writings by Ruge which he had not read and did not need to read.

Scene 6. August 22.—The Cranbourne Hotel. Firstly, there was a "diplomatic master-stroke" (vide Goegg) on the part of *Schurz*: he proposed the formation of a general refugee committee to comprise six members taken from the different factions together with five co-opted members of the already existing Refugee Committee of the Willich Artisan Association. (This would have given the Kinkel-Willich faction a permanent majority.) Agreed. The elections were carried out but rejected by the members of the Rugean part of the state, which meant the complete collapse of the diplomatic master-stroke. How seriously this refugee committee was meant to be taken can be seen from the fact that four days later Willich resigned from the Committee of Artisans and Refugees, which had only had a nominal existence for a long time, following upon repeated, wholly disrespectful revolts on the part of the "rank and file refugees" which had made the dissolution of the committee an inevitability for a considerable time.

Question concerning the emergence in public of the Agitation Union. Motion: that the Émigré Club should have nothing to do with the Agitation Union and should publicly dissociate itself from all its actions. Furious attacks on the "agitators" Goegg and Sigel junior (i.e. senior, see below[a]) in their presence. Rudolf *Schramm* declared that his old friend Ruge was a minion of Mazzini and a "gossipy old woman". *Et tu, Brute!* Goegg retorted, not as a great orator but as an ordinary citizen, and he launched a bitter attack on the ambiguous, slack, perfidious, unctuous Kinkel.

"It is irresponsible to prevent those who wish to work from doing so, but these people want a fictitious, inactive association so that this clique can use it as a cover for certain purposes."

---

[a] See this volume, p. 324.—*Ed.*

When Goegg referred to the public announcement of the Agitation Union in the English papers, *Kinkel* rose majestically and said that

"he already controlled the whole American press and had taken steps to ensure his control of the French press too".

The motion of the German faction was passed and provoked a declaration from the "agitators" that the members of their Union could no longer remain within the Émigré Club.

Thus arose the terrible gulf between the Émigré Club and the Agitation Union which gapes through the whole history of the modern world. The most curious fact about it is that both creatures only survived until their separation and now they vegetate in the Kaulbachian battle of the ghosts[213] that is still waged in German-American meetings and papers and will apparently continue to the end of time.

The whole meeting was all the more stormy as the undisciplined Schramm went so far as to attack Willich as well, claiming that the Emigré Club brought itself into disrepute by its connections with that knight. The chairman, who happened to be the timorous Meyen, had already lost control several times in despair. But the debate about the Agitation Union and the resignation of its members brought the tumult to a climax. To the accompaniment of shouts, drumming, blustering, threats and raging the edifying meeting went on until 2 a.m. when the landlord turned off the gas and so plunged the heated antagonists into darkness. This brought all plans to save the nation to a sad end.

At the end of August the chivalrous Willich and the cosy Kinkel made an attempt to smash the Agitation Union by putting the following proposal to the worthy Fickler:

"He should join with them and their closer political friends in forming a *finance committee* to manage the money that had come in from New Orleans. This committee should continue to function until it was possible to set up a public finance committee of the Revolution. However, the acceptance of this offer would imply the dissolution of all German revolutionary and agitation societies that had existed hitherto."

The worthy Fickler rejected the idea of this "imposed, secret and irresponsible committee" with indignation.

"How," he exclaimed, "can a mere finance committee hope to unite all the revolutionary parties around it? The money that has arrived and that is still to come can never suffice to persuade the widely divergent strands of the democrats to sacrifice their autonomy."

Thus instead of achieving the hoped-for destruction of the Agitation Union this attempted seduction enabled Tausenau to declare that the breach between the two mighty parties of Emigration and Agitation had now become irreparable.

XIV

To show how pleasantly the war was waged between Agitation and Emigration we append here a few excerpts from the German-American papers.

AGITATION

Ruge declares that Kinkel is an "agent of the Prince of Prussia". Another agitator discovers that the outstanding men of the Émigré Club consist of

"Pastor Kinkel together with three Prussian lieutenants, two insipid Berlin *literati* and one student".

Sigel writes:

"It cannot be denied that Willich has gained some support. But when a man has been a preacher for three years and only tells people what they wish to hear, he would have to be very stupid not to be able to win some of them over. The Kinkelites are attempting to take these supporters over. The Willich supporters are whoring with the Kinkel supporters."

A fourth agitator declares that Kinkel's supporters are "idolators".

Tausenau gives this description of the Émigré Club:

"Divergent interests beneath the mask of conciliatoriness, the systematic deception to obtain majorities, the emergence of unknown quantities as organising party leaders, attempts to impose a secret finance committee and all the other manoeuvres and subterfuges with which *immature politicians* have always tried to control the fates of their country in exile, while the first glow of the revolution disperses all such vanities like a morning mist."

Lastly, Rodomonte-Heinzen announces that the only reputable refugees in England personally known to him were Ruge, Goegg, Fickler and Sigel. The members of the Émigré Club were "egoists, royalists and communists". Kinkel was "an incurably vain fool and a theorising aristocrat", Meyen, Oppenheim, Willich, etc., were people "who do not even come up to his, Heinzen's, knee and as for Ruge, they do not even reach to his ankle" (New York *Schnellpost*, *New-Yorker Deutsche Zeitung*, *Wecker*, etc., 1851).

EMIGRATION

"What is the purpose of an imposed committee that stands in mid-air, that confers authority on itself although it has not done any work, has not been elected and has not asked the people whom it claims to represent whether they wish to be represented by such men?"

"Everyone who knows Ruge, knows that the mania for proclamations is his incurable disease."—"In parliament[a] Ruge did not even acquire the influence of a Raveaux or a Simon of Trier".—"Where revolutionary energy in action, organisational work, discretion or reticence are necessary, Ruge is dangerous because he cannot hold his tongue, he cannot hold his ink and always claims that he represents everybody. When Ruge meets Mazzini and Ledru-Rollin this is translated into Rugean and published in all the papers as: Germany, France and Italy have banded together fraternally to serve the revolution."—"This pretentious imposition of a committee, this boastful inactivity determined Ruge's most intimate and intelligent friends, such as Oppenheim, Meyen and Schramm, to join forces with other men."—"Behind Ruge there is no clearly defined section of the people, but only a clearly outlined pigtail of peace."

"How many hundreds of people ask themselves daily who is this Tausenau and there is no one, no one who can give an answer. Here and there you can find a Viennese who will assure you that he is one of those democrats from Vienna with whom the reaction used to reproach the Viennese democrats so as to put them in a bad light. But that is the concern of the Viennese. At any rate Tausenau is an unknown factor, and it is even less known whether he is a factor at all."

"Let us take another look at these worthy men who regard everyone else as an immature politician. Sigel, the supreme commander. If anyone ever asks the muse of history how such an insipid nonentity was given the supreme command she will be completely at a loss for a reply. Sigel is only his brother's[b] brother. His brother became a popular officer as a result of his critical remarks about the government, remarks which had been provoked by his frequent arrests for disorderly behaviour. The young Sigel thought this reason enough in the early confusion prevailing at the outbreak of revolution to proclaim himself supreme commander and minister of war. The Baden artillery, which had often proved its worth, had plenty of older and more experienced officers who should have taken precedence over this young Lieutenant Sigel, and they were more than a little indignant when they had to obey an unknown young man whose inexperience was only matched by his incompetence. But there was Brentano, who was so mindless and treacherous as to permit anything that might ruin the revolution.... The total incompetence that Sigel displayed during the whole Baden campaign.... It is certainly noteworthy that Sigel left the bravest soldiers of the republican army in the lurch at Rastatt and in the Black Forest without the reinforcements he had *promised* while he himself drove around Zurich with the epaulettes and the carriage of Prince von Fürstenberg and paraded as an interesting unfortunate supreme commander. This is the well-known magnitude of this mature politician who, understandably proud of his earlier heroic deeds, imposed himself as supreme commander for a second time, on this occasion in the Agitation Union. This is the great well-known man, the brother of his brother."

---

[a] The Frankfurt National Assembly.—*Ed.*
[b] Albert Sigel's.—*Ed.*

"It is really laughable when such people" (as the agitators) "reproach others with half-heartedness, for they are *political nonentities* who neither half nor whole are anything at all."—"Personal ambition is the whole secret of their fundamental position."—"As a society the Agitation Union has meaning only for a very limited group, like a literary circle or a billiard club, and therefore it has no claim to be taken into consideration or given a voice."—"You yourselves have cast the dice! Let the uninitiated be initiated so that they may judge for themselves what kind of people you are!"—(Baltimore *Correspondent.*)

One must say that in their understanding of each other these gentlemen have almost achieved an understanding of themselves.

XV

In the meantime the secret finance committee of the "émigrés" had elected a managing committee consisting of Kinkel, Willich and Reichenbach and it now resolved to take serious measures in connection with the German loan. As reported in the New York *Schnellpost,* the *New-Yorker Deutsche Zeitung* and the Baltimore *Correspondent* at the end of 1851, student Schurz was sent on a mission to France, Belgium and Switzerland where he sought out all old, forgotten, and vanished parliamentarians, imperial regents,[214] deputies of Chambers and other noteworthy men, right down to the late Raveaux, to get them to guarantee the loan. The forgotten unfortunates hastened to give their guarantee. For what else was the guarantee of the loan if not a mutual guarantee of government posts *in partibus*[a]; and Messrs. Kinkel, Willich and Reichenbach likewise obtained by this means guarantees of *their* future prospects. And these worried worthies in Switzerland were so obsessed with "organisation" and the guarantee of future posts that they had long before worked out a plan by which government posts would be awarded according to seniority—which produced a terrible scandal about who were to have Nos. 1, 2 and 3. In short, student Schurz brought back the guarantee in his pocket and so they all went to work. Some days earlier Kinkel had, it is true, promised in another meeting with the "agitators" that he would not go ahead with an "Emigration" loan without them. For that very reason he departed taking the signatures of the guarantors and *carte blanche* from Reichenbach and Willich—ostensibly to find customers for his aesthetic lectures in the north of England, but in reality to go to Liverpool and embark for New York where he

---

[a] See this volume, p. 282.—*Ed.*

hoped like *Perceval* to find the *Holy Grail,* the gold of the democratic parties.

And now begins that sweet-sounding, strange, magniloquent, fabulous, true and adventurous story of the great battles fought on both sides of the Atlantic Ocean between the Émigrés and the Agitators. It was a war waged with renewed bitterness and with indefatigable persistence. In it we witness Gottfried's crusade in the course of which he contends with Kossuth and after great labours and indescribable temptations he finally returns home with the Grail in the bag.

> Or, bei signori, io vi lascio al presente,
> E se voi tornerete in questo loco,
> Diró questa battaglia dov'io lasso
> Ch'un altra non fu mai di tal fracasso.
>   (Boiardo, Canto 26)

> And there, kind Sirs, I leave you for the present,
> If one day you return unto this place
> I'll give you further news of this great war
> So full of mighty deeds ne'er done before.

NEW-YORK DAILY TRIBUNE.

VOL. XII......NO. 3,540.   NEW-YORK, SATURDAY, AUGUST 21, 1852.   PRICE TWO CENTS

Karl Marx

THE ELECTIONS IN ENGLAND.—
TORIES AND WHIGS[215]

London, Friday, August 6, 1852

The results of the General Election for the British Parliament are now known. This result I shall analyze more fully in my next letter.[a]

What were the parties which during this electioneering agitation opposed or supported each other?

Tories, Whigs, Liberal Conservatives (Peelites), Free Traders, *par excellence* (the men of the Manchester School,[216] Parliamentary and Financial Reformers), and lastly, the Chartists.

Whigs, Free Traders and Peelites coalesced to oppose the Tories. It was between this coalition on one side, and the Tories on the other, that the real electoral battle was fought. Opposed to Whigs, Peelites, Free Traders and Tories, and thus opposed to entire official England, were the Chartists.

The political parties of Great Britain are sufficiently known in the United States. It will be sufficient to bring to mind, in a few strokes of the pen, the distinctive characteristics of each of them.

Up to 1846 the Tories passed as the guardians of the traditions of Old England. They were suspected of admiring in the British Constitution the eighth wonder of the world; to be *laudatores temporis acti,*[b] enthusiasts for the throne, the High Church,[217] the privileges and liberties of the British subject. The fatal year, 1846, with its repeal of the Corn Laws,[218] and the shout of distress which

---

[a] See this volume, pp. 348-53.— *Ed.*
[b] People who laud the past (Horace, *De Arte Poetica,* 173).— *Ed.*

this repeal forced from the Tories, proved that they were enthusiasts for nothing but the rent of land, and at the same time disclosed the secret of their attachment to the political and religious institutions of Old England. These institutions are the very best institutions, with the help of which the *large landed property*—the landed interest—has hitherto ruled England, and even now seeks to maintain its rule. The year 1846 brought to light in its nakedness the *substantial class interest* which forms the *real base* of the Tory party. The year 1846 tore down the traditionally venerable lion's hide, under which Tory class interest had hitherto hidden itself. The year 1846 transformed the Tories into *Protectionists*. Tory was the sacred name, Protectionist is the profane one; Tory was the political battle-cry, Protectionist is the economical shout of distress; Tory seemed an idea, a principle; Protectionist is an interest. Protectionists of what? Of their own revenues, of the rent of their own land. Then the Tories, in the end, are Bourgeois as much as the remainder, for where is the Bourgeois who is not a protectionist of his own purse? They are distinguished from the other Bourgeois, in the same way as the rent of land is distinguished from commercial and industrial profit. Rent of land is conservative, profit is progressive; rent of land is national, profit is cosmopolitical; rent of land believes in the State Church, profit is a dissenter by birth.[219] The repeal of the Corn Laws in 1846 merely recognized an already accomplished fact, a change long since enacted in the elements of British civil society, viz., the subordination of the landed interest under the moneyed interest, of property under commerce, of agriculture under manufacturing industry, of the country under the city. Could this fact be doubted since the country population stands, in England, to the towns' population in the proportion of one to three? The substantial foundation of the power of the Tories was the rent of land. The rent of land is regulated by the price of food. The price of food, then, was artificially maintained at a high rate by the Corn Laws. The repeal of the Corn Laws brought down the price of food, which in its turn brought down the rent of land, and with sinking rent broke down the real strength upon which the political power of the Tories reposed.

What, then, are they trying to do now? To maintain a political power, the social foundation of which has ceased to exist. And how can this be attained? By nothing short of a *Counter-Revolution*, that is to say, by a reaction of the State against Society. They strive to retain forcibly institutions and a political power which are condemned from the very moment at which the rural population found itself outnumbered three times by the population of the towns. And such an attempt must necessarily end with their destruction; it must accelerate and make more acute the social development of England; it must bring on a crisis.

The Tories recruit their army from the farmers, who either have not yet lost the habit of following their landlords as their natural superiors, or who are economically dependent upon them, or who do not yet see that the interest of the farmer and the interest of the landlord are no more identical than the respective interests of the borrower and of the usurer. They are followed and supported by the Colonial Interest, the Shipping Interest, the State Church Party, in short, by all those elements which consider it necessary to safeguard their interests against the necessary results of modern manufacturing industry, and against the social revolution prepared by it.

Opposed to the Tories, as their hereditary enemies, stand the *Whigs*, a party with whom the American Whigs[220] have nothing in common but the name.

The British Whig, in the natural history of politics, forms a species which, like all those of the amphibious class, exists very easily, but is difficult to describe. Shall we call them, with their opponents, Tories out of office? or, as continental writers love it, take them for the representatives of certain *popular* principles? In the latter case we should get embarrassed in the same difficulty as the historian of the Whigs, Mr. Cooke, who, with great *naïveté*, confesses in his "History of Parties" that it is indeed a certain number of "liberal, moral and enlightened principles" which constitutes the Whig party, but that it was greatly to be regretted that during the more than a century and a half that the Whigs have existed, they have been, when in office, always prevented from carrying out these principles. So that in reality, according to the confession of their own historian, the Whigs represent something quite different from their professed "liberal and enlightened principles." Thus they are in the same position as the drunkard brought up before the Lord Mayor, who declared that he represented the Temperance principle but from some accident or other always got drunk on Sundays.

But never mind their principles; we can better make out what they are in historical fact; what they carry out, not what they once believed, and what they now want other people to believe with respect to their character.

The Whigs, as well as the Tories, form a fraction of the large landed property of Great Britain. Nay, the oldest, richest and

most arrogant portion of English landed property is the very
nucleus of the Whig party.

What, then, distinguishes them from the Tories? The Whigs are
the *aristocratic representatives* of the Bourgeoisie, of the industrial
and commercial middle class. Under the condition that the
Bourgeoisie should abandon to them, to an oligarchy of aristocratic families, the monopoly of government and the exclusive
possession of office, they make to the middle class, and assist it in
conquering, all those concessions, which in the course of social and
political development have shown themselves to have become
unavoidable and *undelayable*. Neither more nor less. And as often as
such an unavoidable measure has been passed, they declare loudly
that herewith the end of historical progress has been obtained;
that the whole social movement has carried its ultimate purpose,
and then they "cling to finality." [221] They can support, more easily
than the Tories, a decrease of their rental revenues, because they
consider themselves as the heaven-born farmers of the revenues of
the British Empire. They can renounce the monopoly of the Corn
Laws, as long as they maintain the monopoly of government as
their family property. Ever since the "glorious revolution" of
1688 [222] the Whigs, with short intervals, caused principally by the
first French Revolution and the consequent reaction, have found
themselves in the enjoyment of the public offices. Whoever recalls
to his mind this period of British history, will find no other
distinctive mark of Whigdom but the maintenance of their family
oligarchy. The interests and principles which they represent
besides, from time to time, do not belong to the Whigs; they are
forced upon them by the development of the industrial and
commercial class, the Bourgeoisie. After 1688 we find them united
with the Bankocracy, just then rising into importance, as we find
them in 1846, united with the Millocracy. The Whigs as little
carried the Reform Bill of 1831,[223] as they carried the Free Trade
Bill of 1846. Both Reform movements, the political as well as the
commercial, were movements of the Bourgeoisie. As soon as either
of these movements had ripened into irresistibility; as soon as, at
the same time, it had become the safest means of turning the
Tories out of office, the Whigs stepped forward, took up the
direction of the Government, and secured to themselves the
governmental part of the victory. In 1831 they extended the
political portion of reform as far as was necessary in order not to
leave the middle class entirely dissatisfied; after 1846 they
confined their Free Trade measures so far as was necessary, in
order to save to the landed aristocracy the greatest possible

amount of privileges. Each time they had taken the movement in hand in order to prevent its forward march, and to recover their own posts at the same time.

It is clear that from the moment when the landed aristocracy is no longer able to maintain its position as an independent power, to fight, as an independent party, for the government position, in short, that from the moment when the Tories are definitively overthrown, British history has no longer any room for the Whigs. The aristocracy once destroyed, what is the use of an aristocratic representation of the Bourgeoisie against this aristocracy?

It is well known that in the Middle Ages the German Emperors put the just then arising towns under Imperial Governors, "*advocati*," to protect these towns against the surrounding nobility. As soon as growing population and wealth gave them sufficient strength and independence to resist, and even to attack the nobility, the towns also drove out the noble Governors, the *advocati*.

The Whigs have been these *advocati* of the British middle class, and their governmental monopoly must break down as soon as the landed monopoly of the Tories is broken down. In the same measure as the middle class has developed its in- dependent strength, they have shrunk down from a party to a coterie.

It is evident what a distastefully heterogeneous mixture the character of the British Whigs must turn out to be: Feudalists, who are at the same time Malthusians, money-mongers with feudal prejudices, aristocrats without point of honour, Bourgeois without industrial activity, finality-men with progressive phrases, progres- sists with fanatical Conservatism, traffickers in homeopathical fractions of reforms, fosterers of family-nepotism, Grand Masters of corruption, hypocrites of religion, Tartuffes of politics. The mass of the English people has a sound aesthetical common sense. It has an instinctive hatred against everything motley and ambiguous, against bats and Russellites. And then, with the Tories, the mass of the English people, the urban and rural proletariat, has in common the hatred against the "money- monger." With the Bourgeoisie it has in common the hatred against aristocrats. In the Whigs it hates the one and the other, aristocrats and Bourgeois, the landlord who oppresses, and the money lord who exploits it. In the Whigs it hates the oligarchy which has ruled over England for more than a century, and by which the people is excluded from the direction of its own affairs.

The Peelites (Liberals and Conservatives[a]) are no party; they are merely the *souvenir* of a party man, of the late Sir Robert Peel. But Englishmen are too prosaical, for a *souvenir* to form, with them, the foundation for anything but elegies. And now, that the people have erected brass and marble monuments to the late Sir Robert Peel in all parts of the country, they believe they are able so much the more to do without those perambulant Peel monuments, the Grahams, the Gladstones, the Cardwells, etc. The so-called Peelites are nothing but this staff of bureaucrats which Robert Peel had schooled for himself. And because they form a pretty complete staff, they forget for a moment that there is no army behind them. The Peelites, then, are old supporters of Sir Robert Peel, who have not yet come to a conclusion as to what party to attach themselves to. It is evident that a similar scruple is not a sufficient means for them to constitute an independent power.

Remain the Free Traders and the Chartists, the brief delineation of whose character will form the subject of my next.

Written on August 2, 1852

First published in the *New-York Daily Tribune*, No. 3540, August 21, 1852; reprinted in *The People's Paper*, No. 22, October 2, 1852

Signed: *Karl Marx*

Reproduced from the *New-York Daily Tribune* and checked with *The People's Paper*

---

[a] *The People's Paper* has here "Liberal Conservatives"; "Liberals and Conservatives" in the *New-York Daily Tribune* is apparently a mistake.— *Ed.*

The People's Paper,

THE CHAMPION OF
POLITICAL JUSTICE AND UNIVERSAL RIGHT.

No. 23.]   LONDON, SATURDAY, OCTOBER 9, 1852.   [Price Fourpence

Karl Marx

THE CHARTISTS[224]

London, Tuesday, August 10, 1852

While the Tories, the Whigs, the Peelites—in fact, all the parties we have hitherto commented upon—belong more or less to the past, the Free Traders (the men of the Manchester School, the Parliamentary and Financial Reformers) are the *official representatives of modern English society*, the representatives of that England which rules the market of the world. They represent the party of the self-conscious Bourgeoisie, of industrial capital striving to make available its social power as a political power as well, and to eradicate the last arrogant remnants of feudal society. This party is led on by the most active and most energetic portion of the English Bourgeoisie—the *manufacturers*. What they demand is the complete and undisguised ascendancy of the Bourgeoisie, the open, official subjection of society at large under the laws of modern, Bourgeois production, and under the rule of those men who are the directors of that production.[a] By Free Trade they mean the unfettered movement of capital, freed from all political, national and religious shackles. The soil is to be a marketable commodity, and the exploitation of the soil is to be carried on according to the common commercial laws. There are to be manufacturers of food as well as manufacturers of twist and cottons, but no longer any lords of the land. There are, in short, not to be tolerated any political or social restrictions, regulations or monopolies, unless they proceed from "the eternal laws of political economy," that is, from the conditions under which Capital produces and distributes. The struggle of this party against the old

---

[a] In *The People's Paper* the words "and under the rule of those men who are the directors of that production" are omitted.— *Ed.*

English institutions, products of a superannuated, an evanescent stage of social development, is resumed in the watchword: *Produce as cheap as you can, and do away with all the faux frais of production* (with all superfluous, unnecessary expenses in production). And this watchword is addressed not only to the private individual, but to the *nation at large* principally.

Royalty, with its "barbarous splendors," its court, its civil list and its flunkeys—what else does it belong to but to the *faux frais* of production? The nation can produce and exchange without royalty; away with the crown. The sinecures of the nobility, the House of Lords? *faux frais* of production. The large standing army? *faux frais* of production. The Colonies? *faux frais* of production. The State Church, with its riches, the spoils of plunder or of mendicity? *faux frais* of production. Let parsons compete freely with each other, and everyone pay them according to his own wants. The whole circumstantial routine of English Law, with its Court of Chancery?[225] *faux frais* of production. National wars? *faux frais* of production. England can exploit foreign nations more cheaply while at peace with them.

You see, to these champions of the British Bourgeoisie, to the men of the Manchester School, every institution of Old England appears in the light of a piece of machinery as costly as it is useless, and which fulfils no other purpose than to prevent the nation from producing the greatest possible quantity at the least possible expense, and to exchange its products in freedom. Necessarily, their last word is the *Bourgeois Republic*, in which free competition rules supreme in all spheres of life; in which there remains altogether that *minimum* only of government which is indispensable for the administration, internally and externally, of the common class interest and business of the Bourgeoisie; and where this minimum of government is as soberly, as economically organized as possible. Such a party, in other countries, would be called *democratic*. But it is necessarily revolutionary, and the complete annihilation of Old England as an aristocratic country is the end which it follows up with more or less consciousness. Its nearest object, however, is the attainment of a Parliamentary reform which should transfer to its hands the legislative power necessary for such a revolution.

But the British Bourgeois are not excitable Frenchmen. When they intend to carry a Parliamentary reform they will not make a Revolution of February. On the contrary. Having obtained, in 1846, a grand victory over the landed aristocracy by the repeal of the Corn Laws, they were satisfied with following up the material advantages of this victory, while they neglected to draw the necessary political and economical conclusions from it, and thus enabled the Whigs to reinstate themselves into their hereditary monopoly of government. During all the time, from 1846 to 1852, they exposed themselves to ridicule by their battle-cry: Broad principles and practical (read *small*) measures. And why all this? Because in every violent movement they are obliged to appeal to the *working class*. And if the aristocracy is their vanishing opponent the working class is their arising enemy. They prefer to compromise with the vanishing opponent rather than to strengthen the arising enemy, to whom the future belongs, by concessions of a more than apparent importance. Therefore, they strive to avoid every forcible collision˙ with the aristocracy; but historical necessity and the Tories press them onwards. They cannot avoid fulfilling their mission, battering to pieces Old England, the England of the Past; and the very moment when they will have conquered exclusive political dominion, when political dominion and economical supremacy will be united in the same hands, when, therefore, the struggle against capital will no longer be distinct from the struggle against the existing Government—from that very moment will date the *social revolution of England*.

We now come to the *Chartists*, the politically active portion of the British *working class*. The six points of the Charter which they contend for contain nothing but the demand of *Universal Suffrage*, and of the conditions without which Universal Suffrage would be illusory for the working class; such as the ballot, payment of members, annual general elections. But Universal Suffrage[a] is the equivalent for political power for the working class of England, where the proletariat forms the large majority of the population, where, in a long, though underground[b] civil war, it has gained a clear consciousness of its position as a class, and where even the rural districts know no longer any peasants, but only landlords, industrial capitalists (farmers) and hired laborers. The carrying of Universal Suffrage in England would, therefore, be a far more socialistic

---

[a] The editors of *The People's Paper* after the words "annual general elections" added the word "etc." (they referred to the two remaining points of the Charter: equal constituencies and abolition of property qualification for candidate members). After the words "But Universal Suffrage" they added "with its adjuncts".— *Ed.*

[b] *The People's Paper* has here "disguised".— *Ed.*

measure than anything which has been honored with that name on the Continent.

Its inevitable result, here, is *the political supremacy of the working class.*

I shall report, on another occasion, on the revival and the reorganization of the Chartist Party. For the present I have only to treat of the recent election.[a]

To be a voter for the British Parliament, a man must occupy, in the Boroughs, a house rated at £10 to the poor's-rate, and, in the counties, he must be a freeholder[226] to the annual amount of 40 shillings, or a leaseholder to the amount of £50. From this statement alone it follows, that the Chartists could take, officially, but little part in the electoral battle just concluded. In order to explain the actual part they took in it, I must recall to mind a peculiarity of the British electoral system:

Nomination day and Declaration day! Show of hands and Poll!

When the candidates have made their appearance on the day of election, and have publicly harangued the people, they are elected, in the first instance, by the show of hands, and every hand has the right to be raised, the hand of the non-elector as well as that of the elector. For whomsoever the majority of the hands are raised, that person is declared, by the returning officer, to be (provisionally) elected by show of hands. But now the medal shows its reverse. The election by show of hands was a mere ceremony, an act of formal politeness toward the "sovereign people," and the politeness ceases as soon as privilege is menaced. For if the show of hands does not return the candidates of the privileged electors, these candidates demand a poll; only the privileged electors can take part in the poll, and whosoever has there the majority of votes is declared duly elected. The first election, by show of hands, is a show satisfaction allowed, for a moment, to public opinion, in order to convince it, the next moment, the more strikingly of its impotency.

It might appear that this election by show of hands, this dangerous formality, had been invented in order to ridicule universal suffrage, and to enjoy some little aristocratic fun at the

---

[a] In *The People's Paper* the text of the four paragraphs that follow (ending with the words: "...that the working masses stood up, on the nomination days, in their own name.") is omitted. Instead of it, the following text is added by the editors, in square brackets: "The author here analyses the British electoral system, and then proceeds." — *Ed.*

expense of the "rabble" (expression of Major Beresford, Secretary of War). But this would be a delusion, and the old usage, common originally to all Teutonic nations, could drag itself traditionally down to the nineteenth century, because it gave to the British class-Parliament, cheaply and without danger, an appearance of popularity. The ruling classes drew from this usage the satisfaction that the mass of the people took part, with more or less passion, in their sectional interests as its national interests. And it was only since the Bourgeoisie took an independent station at the side of the two official parties, the Whigs and Tories, that the working masses stood up, on the nomination days, in their own name. But in no former year has the contrast of show of hands and poll, of Nomination day and Declaration day, been so serious, so well defined by opposed principles, so threatening, so general, upon the whole surface of the country, as in this last election of 1852.

And what a contrast! It was sufficient to be named by show of hands in order to be beaten at the poll.[a] It was sufficient to have had the majority at a poll, in order to be saluted, by the people, with rotten apples and brickbats. The duly elected members of Parliament, before all, had a great deal to do, in order to keep their own parliamentary bodily selves in safety. On one side the majority of the people, on the other the twelfth part of the whole population, and the fifth part of the sum total of the male adult inhabitants of the country. On one side enthusiasm, on the other bribery. On one side parties disowning their own distinctive signs, Liberals pleading the conservatism, Conservatives proclaiming the liberalism of the views; on the other, the people, proclaiming their presence and pleading their own cause. On one side a worn-out engine which, turning incessantly in its vicious circle, is never able to move a single step forward, and the impotent process of friction by which all the official parties gradually grind each other into dust; on the other, the advancing mass of the nation, threatening to blow up the vicious circle and to destroy the official engine.

I shall not follow up, over all the surface of the country, this contrast between nomination and poll, of the threatening electoral demonstration of the working class, and the timid electioneering manoeuvres of the ruling classes. I take one borough from the mass, where the contrast is concentrated in a focus: the Halifax election. Here the opposing candidates were: Edwards (Tory); Sir

---

[a] In *The People's Paper* this sentence is omitted.—*Ed.*

Charles Wood (late Whig Chancellor of the Exchequer, brother-in-law to Earl Grey); Frank Crossley (Manchester man); and finally Ernest Jones, the most talented, consistent and energic representative of Chartism. Halifax being a manufacturing town, the Tory had little chance. The Manchester man Crossley was leagued with the Whigs. The serious struggle, then, lay only between Wood and Jones, between the Whig and the Chartist.[a]

"Sir Charles Wood made a speech of about half an hour, perfectly inaudible at the commencement, and, during its latter half, for the disapprobation of the immense multitude. His speech, as reported by the reporter, who sat close to him, was merely a recapitulation of the Free Trade measures passed, and an attack on Lord Derby's Government, and a laudation of '*the unexampled prosperity of the country and the people!'*—[Hear, hear.] He did not propound one single new measure of reform; and but faintly, in very few words, hinted at Lord John Russell's bill for the franchise." [227]

I give a more extensive abstract of E. Jones's speech, as you will not find it in any of the great London ruling-class papers.[b]

"Ernest Jones, who was received with immense enthusiasm, then spoke as follows: Electors and Non-electors, you have met upon a great and solemn festival. To-day, the Constitution recognizes Universal Suffrage in theory that it may, perhaps, deny it in practice on the morrow. To-day the representatives of two systems stand before you, and you have to decide beneath which you shall be ruled for seven years. Seven years—a little life! I summon you to pause upon the threshold of those seven years: to-day they shall pass slowly and calmly in review before you: to-day decide, you 20,000 men, that perhaps five hundred may undo your will to-morrow. [Hear, hear.] I say the representatives of two systems stand before you. Whig, Tory, and money-mongers are on my left, it is true, but they are all as one. The money-monger says, buy cheap and sell dear. The Tory says, buy dear, sell dearer. Both are the same for labor. But the former system is in the ascendant, and pauperism rankles at its root. That system is based on foreign competition. Now, I assert, that under the buy cheap and sell dear principle, brought to bear on foreign competition, the ruin of the working and small trading classes must go on. Why? Labor is the creator of all wealth. A man must work before a grain is grown, or a yarn is woven. But there is no self-employment for the working-man in this country. Labor is a hired commodity—labor is a thing in the market that is bought and sold; consequently, as labor creates all wealth, labor is the first thing bought—'Buy cheap! buy cheap!' Labor is bought in the cheapest market. But now comes the next: 'Sell dear! sell dear!' Sell what? *Labor's produce.*

---

[a] The quotation that follows is omitted in *The People's Paper.* Instead of it, the following text is added by the editors, in square brackets: "Here follows an extract from the speech of Sir Charles Wood, which, as familiar to our readers, we do not give." The report of Wood's speech at the election meeting on July 6, 1852, and Ernest Jones's speech given below are quoted from the article "The Halifax Election" published in *The People's Paper,* No. 12, July 24, 1852.— *Ed.*

[b] In *The People's Paper* all of the text that follows, except for the concluding paragraph, is omitted and the following note is added by the editors in square brackets: "Here the speech of Ernest Jones is quoted, which we likewise omit."— *Ed.*

To whom? To the foreigner—aye! and to *the laborer himself*—for labor, not being self-employed, the laborer is *not* the partaker of the first fruits of his toil. 'Buy cheap, sell dear.' How do you like it? 'Buy cheap, sell dear.' Buy the working-man's labor cheaply, and sell back to that very working-man the produce of his own labor dear! The principle of inherent loss is in the bargain. The employer buys the labor cheap—he sells, and on the sale he must make a profit; he sells to the working-man himself—and thus every bargain between employer and employed is a deliberate cheat on the part of the employer. Thus labor has to sink through eternal loss, that capital may rise through lasting fraud. But the system stops not here. *This is brought to bear on foreign competition—which means, we must ruin the trade of other countries, as we have ruined the labor of our own.* How does it work? The high-taxed country has to undersell the low-taxed. Competition abroad is constantly increasing—consequently cheapness must increase constantly also. Therefore, wages in England must keep constantly falling. And how do they effect the fall? By *surplus labor.* How do they obtain the surplus labor? By monopoly of the land, which drives more hands than are wanted into the factory. By monopoly of machinery, which drives those hands into the street—by woman labor which drives the man from the shuttle—by child labor which drives the woman from the loom. Then planting their foot upon that living base of surplus, they press its aching heart beneath their heel, and cry 'Starvation! Who'll work? A half loaf is better than no bread at all'—and the writhing mass grasps greedily at their terms. [Loud cries of "Hear, hear."] Such is the system for the working-man. But Electors! How does it operate on you? How does it affect home trade, the shopkeeper, poor's-rate and taxation? For every increase of competition abroad, there must be an increase of cheapness at home. Every increase of cheapness in labor is based on increase of labor surplus, and this surplus is obtained by an increase of machinery. I repeat, how does this operate on you! The Manchester Liberal on my left establishes a new patent, and throws three hundred men as a surplus in the streets. Shopkeepers! Three hundred customers less. Rate payers! Three hundred paupers more. [Loud cheers.] But, mark me! The evil stops not there. These three hundred men operate first to bring down the wages of those who remain at work in their own trade. The employer says, 'Now I reduce your wages.' The men demur. Then he adds: 'Do you see those three hundred men who have *just* walked out—*you may change places if you like*, they're sighing to come in on any terms, for they're starving.' The men feel it, and are crushed. Ah! you Manchester Liberal! Pharisee of politics! those men are listening—have I got you now? But the evil stops not yet. Those men, driven from their own trade, seek employment in others, when they swell the surplus, and bring wages down. The low paid trades of to-day were the high paid once—the high paid of to-day will be the low paid soon. Thus the purchasing power of the working classes is diminished every day, and with it dies home trade. Mark it, shopkeepers! your customers grow poorer, and your profits less, while your paupers grow more numerous and your poor's-rates and your taxes rise. Your receipts are smaller, your expenditure is more large. You get less and pay more. How do you like the system? On you the rich manufacturer and landlord throw the weight of poor's-rate and taxation. Men of the middle class! You are the tax-paying machine of the rich. They create the poverty that creates their riches, and they make you pay for the poverty they have created. The landlord escapes it by privilege, the manufacturer by repaying himself out of the wages of his men, and that reacts on you. How do you like the system? Well, that is the system upheld by the gentlemen on my left. What then do I propose? I have shown the wrong. That is something. But I do more; I stand here to show the right, and prove it so." (Loud cheers.)

Ernest Jones then went on to expose his own views on political and economical reform, and continued as follows:

"'Electors and Non-electors, I have now brought before you some of the social and political measures, the immediate adoption of which I advocate now, as I did in 1847. But, because I tried to extend *your* liberties, *mine* were curtailed. [Hear, hear.] Because I tried to rear the temple of freedom for you all, I was thrown into the cell of a felon's jail; and there, on my left, sits one of my chief jailers. [Loud and continued groans, directed towards the left.] Because I tried to give voice to truth, I was condemned to silence. For two years and one week he cast me into a prison in solitary confinement on the silent system, without pen, ink, or paper, but oakum picking as a substitute.— Ah! [turning to Sir Charles Wood] it was your turn for two years and one week; it is mine this day. I summon the angel of retribution from the heart of every Englishman here present. [An immense burst of applause.] Hark! you feel the fanning of his wings in the breath of this vast multitude! [Renewed cheering, long continued.] You may say this is not a public question. But it is! [Hear, hear.] It is a public question, for the man who cannot feel for the wife of the prisoner, will not feel for the wife of the working-man. He who will not feel for the children of the captive will not feel for the children of the labor-slave. ["Hear, hear", and cheers.] His past life proves it, his promise of to-day does not contradict it. Who voted for Irish coercion, the gagging bill, and tampering with the Irish press? The Whig! There he sits! Turn him out! Who voted fifteen times against Hume's motion for the franchise; Locke King's on the counties; Ewart's for short Parliaments; and Berkeley's for the ballot? The Whig—there he sits; turn him out! Who voted against the release of Frost, Williams, and Jones? The Whig—there he sits; turn him out! Who voted against inquiry into colonial abuses and in favor of Ward and Torrington, the tyrants of Ionia and Ceylon?—The Whig—there he sits; turn him out! Who voted against reducing the Duke of Cambridge's salary of £12,000, against all reductions in the army and navy; against the repeal of the window-tax, and 48 times against every other reduction of taxation, his own salary included? The Whig—there he sits; turn him out! Who voted against a repeal of the paper duty, the advertisement duty, and the taxes on knowledge? The Whig—there he sits; turn him out! Who voted for the batches of new bishops, vicar rates, the Maynooth grant, against its reduction, and against absolving dissenters [228] from paying Church rates? The Whig—there he sits; turn him out! Who voted against all inquiry into the adulteration of food? The Whig—there he sits; turn him out! Who voted against lowering the duty on sugar, and repealing the tax on malt? The Whig—there he sits; turn him out! Who voted against shortening the nightwork of bakers, against inquiry into the condition of frame-work knitters, against medical inspectors of workhouses, against preventing little children from working before six in the morning, against parish relief for pregnant women of the poor, and against the Ten Hours Bill? The Whig—there he sits; turn him out! Turn him out, in the name of humanity and of God! Men of Halifax! Men of England! the two systems are before you. Now judge and choose!' [It is impossible to describe the enthusiasm kindled by this speech, and especially at the close; the voice of the vast multitude, held in breathless suspense during each paragraph, came at each pause like the thunder of a returning wave, in execration of the representative of Whiggery and class rule. Altogether, it was a scene that will long be unforgotten. On the show of hands being taken, very few, and those chiefly of the hired or intimidated, were held up for Sir C. Wood; but almost everyone present raised both hands for Ernest Jones, amidst cheering and enthusiasm it would be impossible to describe.]

"The Mayor declared Mr. Ernest Jones and Mr. Henry Edwards to be elected by show of hands. Sir C. Wood and Mr. Crossley then demanded a poll."

What Jones had predicted took place; he was nominated by 20,000 votes, but the Whig Sir Charles Wood and the Manchester man Crossley were elected by 500 votes.

Written on August 2, 1852

First published in the *New-York Daily Tribune*, No. 3543, August 25, 1852; reprinted in the *Semi-Weekly Tribune*, August 27, the *New-York Weekly Tribune*, No. 573, September 4, and in an abridged form in *The People's Paper*, No. 23, October 9, 1852
Signed: *Karl Marx*

Reproduced from the *New-York Daily Tribune* and checked with *The People's Paper*

Karl Marx

CORRUPTION AT ELECTIONS[229]

London, Friday, August 20, 1852

Just before the late House of Commons separated, it resolved to heap up as many difficulties as possible for its successors in their way to Parliament. It voted a Draconian law against bribery, corruption, intimidation, and electioneering sharp practices in general.

A long list of questions is drawn up, which, by this enactment, may be put to petitioners or sitting members, the most searching and stringent that can be conceived.[a] They may be required on oath to state who were their agents, and what communications they held with them. They may be asked and compelled to state, not only what they know, but what they "believe, conjecture, and suspect," as to money expended either by themselves or any one else acting—authorized or not authorized—on their behalf. In a word, no member can go through the strange ordeal without risk of perjury, if he have the slightest idea that it is possible or likely that any one has been led to overstep on his behalf the limits of the law.

Now, even supposing this law to take it for granted that the new legislators will use the same liberty as the clergy, who only believe *some* of the Thirty-Nine Articles,[230] yet contrive to sign them *all*, yet there remain, nevertheless, clauses sufficient to make the new Parliament the most virginal assembly that ever made speeches and passed laws for the three kingdoms. And in juxtaposition with the general election immediately following, this law secures to the Tories the glory, that under their administration the greatest purity of election has been theoretically proclaimed and the greatest

---

[a] "Election Bribery and Corruption", *The Times*, No. 21160, July 6, 1852.—*Ed.*

amount of electoral corruption has been practically carried out.

"A fresh election is proceeded with, and here a scene of *bribery, corruption, violence, drunkenness and murder* ensues, *unparalleled* since the times the old Tory monopoly reigned supreme before. We actually hear of soldiers with loaded guns, and bayonets fixed, taking Liberal electors by force, dragging them under the landlord's eyes to vote against their own consciences, and these soldiers, shooting with deliberate aim the people who dared to sympathize with the captive electors, and committing wholesale murder on the unresisting people! [Allusion to the event at Six Mile Bridge, Limerick, County Clare.] It may be said: That was in Ireland! Ay, and in England they have employed their police to break the stalls of those opposed to them; they have sent their organized gangs of midnight ruffians prowling through the streets to intercept and intimidate the Liberal electors; they have opened the cesspools of drunkenness; they have showered the gold of corruption, as at Derby, and in almost every contested place they have exercised systematic intimidation."[a]

Thus far Ernest Jones's *People's Paper*. Now, after this Chartist weekly paper, hear the weekly paper of the opposite party, the most sober, the most rational, the most moderate organ of the industrial Bourgeoisie, *The London Economist*:

"We believe we may affirm, at this general election, there has been more *truckling*, more *corruption*, more *intimidation*, more *fanaticism* and more *debauchery* than on any previous occasion.... It is reported that bribery has been more extensively resorted to at this election than for many previous years.... Of the amount of intimidation and undue influence of every sort which has been practised at the late election, it is probably impossible to form an exaggerated estimate.... And when we sum up all these things—the brutal drunkenness, the low intrigues, the wholesale corruption, the barbarous intimidation, the integrity of candidates warped and stained, the honest electors who are ruined, the feeble ones who are suborned and dishonored; the lies, the stratagems, the slanders, which stalk abroad in the daylight, naked and not ashamed—the desecration of holy words, the soiling of noble names—we stand aghast at the holocaust of victims, of destroyed bodies and lost souls, on whose funeral pile a new Parliament is reared."[b]

The means of corruption and intimidation were the usual ones: direct Government influence. Thus on an electioneering agent at Derby, arrested in the flagrant act of bribing, a letter was found from Major Beresford, the Secretary at War, wherein that same Beresford opens a credit upon a commercial firm for electioneering monies. *The Poole Herald* publishes a circular from the Admiralty-House to the half-pay officers, signed by the commander-in-chief of a naval station, requesting their votes for the ministerial candidates.—Direct force of arms has also been employed, as at Cork, Belfast, Limerick (at which latter place eight

---

[a] Ernest Jones, "The Reign of the Tories", *The People's Paper*, No. 15, August 14, 1852.— *Ed.*

[b] "The Cost of a New Parliament", *The Economist*, No. 467, August 7, 1852.— *Ed.*

persons were killed).—Threats of ejectment by landlords against their farmers, unless they voted with them. The Land Agents of Lord Derby herein gave the example to their colleagues.—Threats of exclusive dealing against shopkeepers, of dismissal against workmen, intoxication, etc., etc.—To these *profane* means of corruption *spiritual* ones were added by the Tories; the royal proclamation against Roman Catholic Processions[a] was issued in order to inflame bigotry and religious hatred; the No-Popery cry was raised everywhere. One of the results of this proclamation were the Stockport Riots.[231] The Irish priests, of course, retorted with similar weapons.

The election is hardly over, and already a single Queen's Counsel has received from twenty-five places instructions to invalidate the returns to Parliament on account of bribery and intimidation. Such petitions against elected members have been signed, and the expenses of the proceedings raised at Derby, Cockermouth, Barnstaple, Harwich, Canterbury, Yarmouth, Wakefield, Boston, Huddersfield, Windsor, and a great number of other places. Of eight to ten Derbyite members it is proved that, even under the most favorable circumstances, they will be rejected on petition.

The principal scenes of this bribery, corruption and intimidation were, of course, the agricultural counties and the Peers' Boroughs, for the conservation of the greatest possible number of which latter, the Whigs had expended all their acumen in the Reform Bill of 1831. The constituencies of large towns and of densely populated manufacturing counties were, by their peculiar circumstances, very unfavorable ground for such manoeuvres.

Days of general election are in Britain traditionally the bacchanalia of drunken debauchery, conventional stock-jobbing terms for the discounting of political consciences, the richest harvest times of the publicans. As an English paper says, "these recurring *saturnalia* never fail to leave enduring traces of their pestilential presence."[b] Quite naturally so. They are saturnalia in the ancient Roman sense of the word. The master then turned servant, the servant turned master. If the servant be master for one day, on that day brutality will reign supreme. The masters were the grand dignitaries of the ruling classes, or sections of classes, the servants formed the mass of these same classes, the

---

[a] Victoria R., "A Proclamation", June 15, 1852. *The Times,* No. 21143, June 16, 1852.— *Ed.*

[b] "The Cost of a New Parliament", *The Economist,* No. 467, August 7, 1852.— *Ed.*

privileged electors encircled by the mass of the non-electors, of those thousands that had no other calling than to be mere hangers-on, and whose support, vocal or manual, always appeared desirable, were it only on account of the theatrical effect.

If you follow up the history of British elections for a century past or longer, you are tempted to ask, not why British Parliaments were so bad, but on the contrary, how they managed to be even as good as they were, and to represent as much as they did, though in a dim refraction, the actual movement of British society. Just as opponents of the representative system must feel surprised on finding that legislative bodies in which the abstract majority, the accident of the mere number is decisive, yet decide and resolve according to the necessities of the situation—at least during the period of their full vitality. It will always be impossible, even by the utmost straining of logical deductions, to derive from the relations of mere numbers the necessity of a vote in accordance with the actual state of things; but from a given state of things the necessity of certain relations of members will always follow as of itself. The traditional bribery of British elections, what else was it, but another form, as brutal as it was popular, in which the relative strength of the contending parties showed itself? Their respective means of influence and of dominion, which on other occasions they used in a *normal* way, were here enacted for a few days in an abnormal and more or less burlesque manner. But the premise remained, that the candidates of the rivaling parties represented the interests of the mass of the electors, and that the privileged electors again represented the interests of the non-voting mass, or rather, that this voteless mass had, as yet, no specific interest of its own. The Delphic priestesses had to become intoxicated by vapors to enable them to find oracles; the British people must intoxicate itself with gin and porter to enable it to find its oracle-finders, the legislators. And where these oracle-finders were to be looked for, that was a matter of course.

This relative position of classes and parties underwent a radical change from the moment the industrial and commercial middle classes, the Bourgeoisie, took up its stand as an official party at the side of the Whigs and Tories, and especially from the passing of the Reform Bill in 1831. These Bourgeois were in no wise fond of costly electioneering manoeuvres, of *faux frais* of general elections. They considered it cheaper to compete with the landed aristocracy by general moral, than by personal pecuniary means. On the other hand they were conscious of representing a universally predominant interest of modern society. They were, therefore, in a position to demand that electors should be ruled by their common national interests, not by personal and local motives, and the more they recurred to this postulate, the more the latter species of electoral influence was, by the very composition of constituencies, centered in the landed aristocracy, but withheld from the middle classes. Thus the Bourgeoisie contended for the principle of moral elections and forced the enactment of laws in that sense, intended, each of them, as safeguards against the local influence of the landed aristocracy; and indeed, from 1831 down, bribery adopted a more civilized, more hidden form, and general elections went off in a more sober way than before. When at last the mass of the people ceased to be a mere chorus, taking a more or less impassioned part in the struggle of the official heroes, drawing the lots among them, rioting, in bacchantic carouse, at the creation of parliamentary divinities, like the Cretan Curetes[a] at the birth of Jupiter,[232] and taking pay and treat for such participation in their glory—when the Chartists surrounded in threatening masses the whole circle within which the official election struggle must come off, and watched with scrutinizing mistrust every movement taking place within it—then an election like that of 1852 could not but call for universal indignation, and elicit even from the conservative *Times*, for the first time, some words in favor of general suffrage, and make the whole mass of the British Proletariat shout as with one voice. The foes of Reform, they have given Reformers the best arguments; such is an election under the class system; such is a House of Commons with such a system of election!

In order to comprehend the character of bribery, corruption and intimidation, such as they have been practised in the late election, it is necessary to call attention to a fact which operated in a parallel direction.

If you refer to the general elections since 1831, you will find that, in the same measure as the pressure of the voteless majority of the country upon the privileged body of electors was increasing, as the demand was heard louder, from the middle classes, for an extension of the circle of constituencies, from the working class, to extinguish every trace of a similar privileged circle—that in the same measure the number of electors who actually voted grew less and less, and the constituencies thus more and more contracted themselves. Never was this fact more striking than in the late election.

---

[a] Instead of "Curetes" the *New-York Daily Tribune* has here "Centaurs" by mistake.— *Ed.*

Let us take, for instance, London. In the City the constituency numbers 26,728; only 10,000 voted. The Tower Hamlets number 23,534 registered electors; only 12,000 voted. In Finsbury, of 20,025 electors, not one-half voted. In Liverpool, the scene of one of the most animated contests, of 17,433 registered electors, only 13,000 came to the polls.

These examples will suffice. What do they prove? The apathy of the privileged constituencies. And this apathy, what proves it? That they have outlived themselves—that they have lost every interest in their own political existence. This is in no wise apathy against politics in general, but against a species of politics, the result of which, for the most part, can only consist in helping the Tories to oust the Whigs, or the Whigs to conquer the Tories. The constituencies feel instinctively that the decision lies no longer either with Parliament, or with the making of Parliament. Who repealed the Corn Laws? Assuredly not the voters who had elected a Protectionist Parliament, still less the Protectionist Parliament itself, but only and exclusively the pressure from without. In this pressure from without, in other means of influencing Parliament than by voting, a great portion even of electors now believe. They consider the hitherto lawful mode of voting as an antiquated formality, but from the moment Parliament should make front against the pressure from without, and dictate laws to the nation in the sense of its narrow constituencies, they would join the general assault against the whole antiquated system of machinery.

The bribery and intimidation practised by the Tories were, then, merely violent experiments for bringing back to life dying electoral bodies which have become incapable of production, and which can no longer create decisive electoral results and really national Parliaments. And the result? The old Parliament was dissolved, because at the end of its career it had dissolved into sections which brought each other to a complete standstill. The new Parliament begins where the old one ended; it is paralytic from the hour of its birth.

Written about August 16, 1852

First published in the *New-York Daily Tribune*, No. 3552, September 4, 1852; reprinted in the *Semi-Weekly Tribune*, September 7, the *New-York Weekly Tribune*, No. 574, September 11, and in *The People's Paper*, No. 24, October 16, 1852

Signed: *Karl Marx*

Reproduced from the *New-York Daily Tribune* and checked with *The People's Paper*

Karl Marx

RESULT OF THE ELECTIONS[233]

London, Friday, August 27, 1852

I propose now to consider the results of the late general election.

If we resume Whigs, Free Traders and Peelites, under the generic name of the Opposition, thus in common oppose them to the Tories, we find the statistics of the new Parliament to express evidently the great antagonism alluded to in a preceding letter[a]—the antagonism of *city* and *country.*

There were elected in *England,* in the Boroughs 104 Ministerialists, 215 Oppositionists; but in the Counties 109 Ministerialists and only 32 Oppositionists. From the Counties, the strongholds of the Tories, must be deducted the richest and most influential ones: the West Riding of Yorkshire, South Lancashire, Middlesex, East Surrey and others, possessing a population of four millions, out of the ten millions who compose the population of the Counties, independent of the towns sending members to Parliament.

In *Wales,* the results of the elections in town and country are exactly opposed to each other: the Boroughs here elected 10 Oppositionists and 3 Ministerialists, the Counties 11 Ministerialists, and 3 Oppositionists.

Scotland shows us the contrast in its clearest form. The Boroughs, to 25 Oppositionists, elected not a single Ministerialist. The Counties sent 14 Ministerialists and 13 Oppositionists.

In *Ireland* the proportion is different from what it shows itself in Great Britain. In Ireland the national party is the strongest in the country where the population is more directly under the influence of the Catholic clergy, while in the towns of the North English and

---

[a] See this volume, p. 344.— *Ed.*

Protestant elements predominate. Here, then, the proper seat of
Opposition is the country, though with the present mode of election
this cannot show itself so very strikingly. In Ireland the Boroughs
sent 14 Ministerial and 25 Opposition, the Counties 24 Ministerial
and 35 Opposition.

If you ask me now which party has conquered at the elections, the
reply is, they have each and all defeated the Tories, for they
evidently are in a minority, in spite of bribery, intimidation, and
Government influence. The most correct statements give: Ministerial, 290; Liberals or collective Opposition, 337; doubtful, 27. Now,
even if you add these 27 doubtfuls to the Ministerial strength, there
remains a majority of twenty for the Liberals. The Tories, however,
had calculated upon a majority of 336 at least. But leaving out of the
question this numerical minority, the Tories succumbed in the
elective struggle, for their leading men were forced to deny their
own protectionist principles. Of 290 Derbyites 20 pronounced
against all and every sort of protection, and of the remainder many,
even Disraeli[a] himself, against the Corn Laws.

Lord Derby had assured in his parliamentary declarations[b] that he
would change the commercial policy of the country only if supported
by a large majority—so little did he anticipate that he would find
himself in a minority. Though, therefore, the result of the election is
far from corresponding to the sanguine expectations of the Tories,
it is yet far more favorable to them than the Opposition ever
expected.

No party has been defeated more severely than the Whigs—and in
that very point where the inherent strength of this party lies: in its
old ministers. The mass of the Whigs confounds itself on one hand
with the Free Traders, on the other with the Peelites. The real vital
principle of British Whiggery concentrates itself in its official head.
The chief of the late Whig Ministry, Lord John Russell, has been
re-elected, it is true, by the City of London; but in the city election of
1847 Mr. Masterman (Tory) stood 415 votes below Lord J. Russell.
In the election of 1852 he stood 819 votes above him, and headed the
poll. Eleven members of the late Whig Government have been right
down turned out of their Parliamentary seats, viz.: Sir W. G. Craig,
Lord of the Treasury; R. M. Bellew, Lord of the Treasury; Sir

___

[a] See Disraeli's address to the electors of the County of Buckingham on June 2,
1852, and his speech at a dinner of the electors of this county on July 14, 1852, *The
Times*, Nos. 21135 and 21168, June 7 and July 15, 1852.—*Ed.*

[b] The reference is to his speech in the House of Lords made on May 24, 1852, *The
Times*, No. 21124, May 25, 1852.—*Ed.*

D. Dundas, Judge-Advocate-General [a]; Sir G. Grey, Home Secretary; J. Hatchell, Attorney-General for Ireland; G. Cornewall Lewis, Secretary to the Treasury; Lord C. E. Paget, Secretary to the Master-General of the Ordnances; J. Parker, Secretary to Admiralty; Sir W. Somerville, Secretary for Ireland; Admiral Stewart, Lord of the Admiralty; and to these you may add Mr. Bernal, the Chairman of Committees.[234] In short, since the Reform Bill, the Whigs have not experienced a similar rout.

The Peelites, whose numbers were already feeble in the late Parliament, have shrunk to an even less considerable group, and many of their most important men have lost their seats, for instance Cardwell, Ewart (both for Liverpool); Greene (Lancaster [b]); Lord Mahon (Hertford); Roundell Palmer (Plymouth), & c. The greatest sensation was created by the defeat of Cardwell, not only on account of the importance of the town represented by him, but also on account of his personal relations to the late Sir R. Peel. He is, with Lord Mahon, his literary executor. Cardwell was defeated because he supported the repeal of the Navigation Laws,[235] and because he would not join the No Popery cry; and the Church and State party influenced the elections considerably in Liverpool.

"That very busy and very money-making community," observes an English Free Trade paper on this occasion,[c] "has little time to cultivate religious feelings, it must rely, therefore, on the priesthood, and become an instrument in their hands."

Besides this, the electors of Liverpool are not, like those of Manchester, "men," but "gentlemen," and striving for the old orthodoxy faith is a main requisite of a gentleman.

The Free Traders, lastly, have lost some of their best known names at the electoral contest; thus, at Bradford Col. Thompson (alias Old Mother Goose), one of the oldest preachers and literary representatives of Free Trade; at Oldham, W. J. Fox, one of their most renowned agitators and most witty speakers; Bright and Gibson themselves beat at Manchester, the stronghold of the party, their Whig opponents by a comparatively weak majority only. It is, however, a matter of course that, under the existing electoral system, the Manchester School counts not, and cannot count, upon a Parliamentary majority. But it had, nevertheless, boasted for many

---

[a] The New-York Daily Tribune has here "Judge-Advocate of Scotland".— Ed.

[b] The New-York Daily Tribune has here "Lanark".— Ed.

[c] The Economist. (The quotation is from the article "The Elections" published in its issue No. 463, July 10, 1852.)—Ed.

years, that if only the Whigs were turned out and the Tories returned to office, it would excite a tremendous agitation and perform heroic deeds. And now, instead, we see it again, in the late electoral battle, modestly go hand in hand with the Whigs, and this alone is equal to a moral defeat.

If thus none of the official parties has obtained a victory, if, on the contrary, all of them have been beaten in their turn, the British nation retains the consolation that, though no party, yet a profession, is more imposingly represented in Parliament than ever—the profession of *lawyers.* The House of Commons will count above a hundred lawyers in its ranks, and this number of jurisconsults is perhaps no favorable augury, neither for a party that it will gain its action before Parliament, nor for Parliament that it will carry a verdict with the nation.

According to the numerical proportions stated, there is no doubt of it—the total opposition disposes of a negative majority against the Tories. By united operations, it can upset the Ministry in the very first days after the meeting of Parliament. It is, itself, incapable of forming a durable Administration from its own body. A fresh dissolution and a fresh General Election would be necessary; a fresh General Election, in its turn, would only necessitate a fresh dissolution. In order to break through this vicious circle, a Parliamentary reform is needed. And antiquated parties and a new Parliament will even prefer Tory rule to such a heroic operation.

The Tories, though in a minority compared to the combined opposition, are yet the strongest faction of Parliament, if every party is considered separately. They are, besides, entrenched in the strongholds of office, they have a well disciplined, compact, pretty homogenous army to back them, and they are, finally, certain that their game is played out for ever if they lose this time. Opposed to them is a coalition of four armies, each under a different chief, composed of badly amalgamated fractions, divided by interest, principle, *souvenirs* and passions, mutinous against paramount parliamentary discipline, watching jealously their respective pretensions.

The *parliamentary* proportions of the different Oppositionist sections, as a matter of course, in no ways correspond to their *national* proportions. Thus it is that the Whigs in Parliament still form the most numerous mass of the Opposition, the nucleus around which the other sections group themselves; and this is the more dangerous as this party, in its imagination always at the head of the Administration, is far more eager to back out of the pretensions of its allies than to beat the common enemy. The Peelite, the second Oppositional section, counts 38 members, directed by Sir J. Graham, S. Herbert and Gladstone. Sir J. Graham speculates upon an alliance with the men of the Manchester School. He aspires too much to the premiership, to feel any inclination of helping the Whigs to recover their old Government monopoly. On the other hand, many of the Peelites share the conservative views of the Tories, and the Liberals can count upon their regular support in questions of commercial policy only.

"In many other topics," says a liberal paper, "it will be easy for Ministers so to frame their measures as to secure a great majority of them."[a]

The Free Traders, *par excellence,* stronger than in the last Parliament, are said to number 113 members. The struggle with the Tories will force them more onwards than will be considered advisable by the cautious policy of the Whigs.

The Irish Brigade,[236] finally, about 63 strong, since the death of King Dan,[b] not exactly smothered by laurels, but in a position to hold, numerically, the balance of power, shares nothing with the British Opposition party but the hatred against Derby. In the British Parliament it represents Ireland against England. For a somewhat lengthy campaign no Parliamentary party can with certainty count upon its support.

If, in a few words, we resume the results of the preceding disquisition, viz.: that the Tories are opposed by a negative majority, but not by a party which in their stead could seize the helm of Government—that their downfall necessarily would bring on a Parliamentary reform—that their army is compact, homogenous, disciplined and in possession of the Government fortresses—that the Opposition is a conglomerate of four different sections—that coalition armies always fight badly and maneuver clumsily—that even the negative majority only amounts to 20 or 30 votes—that one-fourth of Parliament, 173 members, are new men, who will anxiously avoid anything that could endanger their dearly-bought seats—we come necessarily to the result that the Tories will possess the strength, not to vanquish, but to force on things to a crisis. And to this they appear resolved. The fear of such a crisis, which would revolutionize the whole of the official superficies of England, speaks through every organ of the London daily and weekly press. *The*

---

[a] "The Results of the Elections", *The Economist,* No. 465, July 24, 1852.—*Ed.*
[b] Daniel O'Connell.—*Ed.*

Times, The Morning Chronicle, The Daily News, The Spectator, The Examiner—they all shout out, because they all of them have their fears. They would prefer reasoning the Tories out of office by hard words, and thus prevent the crisis. The collision will come over them in spite of all hard words and of all virtuous indignation.

Written about August 16, 1852

First published in the *New-York Daily Tribune*, No. 3558, September 11, 1852; reprinted in the *Semi-Weekly Tribune* [No. 762], September 14, and in *The People's Paper*, No. 25, October 23, 1852

Signed: *Karl Marx*

Reproduced from the *New-York Daily Tribune* and checked with *The People's Paper*

Karl Marx

MOVEMENTS OF MAZZINI AND KOSSUTH.— LEAGUE WITH LOUIS NAPOLEON.—PALMERSTON [237]

London, Tuesday, September 28, 1852

The following are authentic facts with regard to the movements among the Italian and Hungarian emigration:

Some time since the Hungarian Gen. Vetter traveled through all Italy on a commission from Kossuth and Mazzini with the passport of a painter who is a citizen of the United States. He was accompanied by the Hungarian cantatrice, Madame Ferenczi, who gave concerts. By this means he penetrated into the higher official circles, while the communications from Mazzini of which he was the bearer opened to him the doors of the secret societies. He traversed the entire country, from Turin and Genoa, by way of Milan, to Rome and Naples. He has lately returned to England and made his report, to the great astonishment of Mr. Mazzini, the archangel of the Democracy. The gist of Vetter's statements is briefly that Italy has become perfectly *materialistic*; that the traffic in silk, oil, and other products of the country forms to such an extent the all-absorbing theme of the day, and that the middle class (Mazzini's great reliance) reckon with such fearful exactness the expenses and losses which the revolution has occasioned, and accordingly seek so earnestly to repair the same by the most zealous devotion to industry, that it is absolutely *impossible to think of a revolutionary movement being commenced by Italy*. In that country, says Vetter in this document, no rising can take place until the French crater shall again vomit fire, especially as the revolutionary part of the population *par excellence* are discouraged by long persecution and by the continual failure of their plans, and, above all, have not the masses to support them.

Upon this report of Vetter's, Mazzini, after having raved so loudly and so foolishly against France, found himself compelled, *volens nolens*, once more to resign the *initiative* to the old Babylon.

But, having determined on again making a league with France, with what party do you suppose these gentlemen have begun to treat? *With Mr. Louis Bonaparte.*

Kossuth, in accord with Mazzini, sent one Kiss to Paris, to enter into relations with the Bonapartists. Kiss had formerly been acquainted with the sons of Jérôme Bonaparte. He amuses himself in Paris, in coffee houses and other houses, hangs around Pierre Bonaparte, scatters incense before him, and writes splendid reports to Kossuth. Now, the liberation of Hungary by the firm of L. Napoleon and Kossuth, is no longer a matter of doubt. The chief of revolutionists has made an alliance of life and death with the "tyrant."

Previous to all this, the old Lelewel, the Pole, and Tadeusz Gorzowski, a Russian priest, had come to London in the name of the so-called Polish Centralization,[238] and had laid before Kossuth and Mazzini the plan for an insurrection, whose turning point should be the co-operation of Bonaparte. Their special friend in London was a Count Lanckoroński, who is also an imperial Russian agent, and their plan had the signal honor of being revised and corrected in St. Petersburg beforehand. This Count Lanckoroński is now at Paris, to look after Kiss, whence he goes to Ostend to receive new instructions from St. Petersburg.

Kiss has sent to Kossuth from Paris all sorts of assurances, which would be at home in a book of fables, but which in the fabulous condition of French affairs are perhaps true. It is said that Kossuth has received an autograph letter from Louis Napoleon, inviting him *to come to Paris.* Kossuth is having copies of this letter circulated in all the counties of Hungary. In that country he has prepared everything for a general outbreak. Even royal-imperial officials are in the complot. Kossuth hopes to commence the affair in October.

So far I have given you nothing more than an almost verbal repetition of what has been communicated to me. If now you ask what is my opinion of the matter, it is that Louis Bonaparte desires to kill two flies with a single blow. He intends to ingratiate himself with Kossuth and Mazzini, and then to betray them to the Austrians, in return for which the latter will give their consent to his assumption of the imperial crown of France. Besides, he thinks that Kossuth and Mazzini will lose all their influence in the revolutionary party as soon as it is known that they have been negotiating, or have formed a connection with him. Moreover, he finds among the Absolute Powers a strong opposition to his mounting the throne, and, adventurer as he is, it is very possible, though not very probable, that he is disposed to try his hand with the conspirators.

As for what concerns Italy in particular, Louis Bonaparte looks forward to adding Lombardy and Venice to his own dominions, while Naples will fall to his cousin Murat. A fine prospect for Signor Mazzini!

Having again touched upon Italy, let me communicate another piece of intelligence. The Countess Visconti, one of the heroines of the last Italian struggle for freedom, was here not long since and had a long conversation with Lord Palmerston. His Lordship told her that he hoped before the end of the present year to stand at the head of the British Government, and that Europe should then march toward a speedy transformation. Italy, especially, could no longer be left in the claws of Austria, because no country could, in the long run, be governed by powder and lead. In all this Palmerston gave out that he expected to find an ally in France. His desire was, however, that Lombardy, in case of a general movement, should at once be annexed to Piedmont, and the question of making it a republic be left entirely to the future.

For my part, I am convinced that the veteran Palmerston is under the greatest illusions, and in particular does not understand that, even if he still possesses some influence in parliamentary coteries, he has none in the country itself.

Written on September 28, 1852

First published in the *New-York Daily Tribune*, No. 3590, and the *Semi-Weekly Tribune*, No. 773, October 19, 1852; reprinted in the *New-York Weekly Tribune*, No. 580, October 23, 1852

Reproduced from the *New-York Daily Tribune*

Karl Marx

PAUPERISM AND FREE TRADE.—
THE APPROACHING COMMERCIAL CRISIS [239]

London, Friday, October 15, 1852

In a malt-house in Banbury, Mr. Henley, President of the Board of Trade, lately explained to his assembled farming friends that Pauperism had decreased but by circumstances which had nothing to do with free trade; and above all, by the *famine of Ireland*, the discovery of gold abroad, the exodus of Ireland, the great demand consequent thereon for British shipping, &c., &c.[a] We must confess that "the famine" is quite as radical a remedy against Pauperism as arsenic is against rats.

"At least," observes *The London Economist*, "the Tories must admit the existing prosperity and its natural result, the emptied workhouses."[b]

The Economist then attempts to prove to this incredulous President of the Board of Trade, that workhouses have emptied themselves in consequence of free trade, and that if free trade is allowed to take its full development, they are likely to disappear altogether from the British soil. It is a pity that *The Economist's* statistics do not prove what they are intended to prove.

Modern industry and commerce, it is well known, pass through periodical cycles of from 5 to 7 years, in which they, in regular succession, go through the different states of quiescence—next improvement—growing confidence—activity—prosperity—excitement—over-trading—convulsion—pressure—stagnation—distress—ending again in quiescence.

Recollecting this fact, we will revert to the statistics of *The Economist*.

---

[a] See Henley's speech at a Tory banquet in Banbury on September 28, 1852, *The Times*, No. 21234, September 30, 1852.—*Ed.*

[b] "Mr. Henley and Pauperism", *The Economist*, No. 475, October 2, 1852.—*Ed.*

From 1834, when the sum expended for the relief of the poor amounted to £6,317,255, it fell to a minimum of £4,044,741 in 1837. From that date it rose again every year until 1843, when it reached £5,208,027. In 1844, '45 and '46, it again fell to £4,954,204, and rose again in 1847 and '48, in which latter year it amounted to £6,180,764,—almost as high as in 1834, before the introduction of the new Poor Law.[240] In 1849, '50, '51 and '52 it fell again to £4,724,619. But the period of 1834-37 was a period of prosperity; that of 1838-42, a period of crisis and stagnation; 1843-46, a period of prosperity; 1847 and '48, a period of crisis and stagnation, and 1849-1852 again a period of prosperity.

What, then, prove these statistics? In the best of cases, the common-place tautology that British pauperism rises and falls with the alternate periods of stagnation and prosperity, independently of either free trade or protection. Nay, in the free trade year of 1852 we find the Poor Law expenditures higher by £679,878 than in the year of protection, 1837, in spite of the Irish Famine,[241] the "nuggets" of Australia, and the steady stream of emigration.

Another British Free Trade paper attempts to prove that exports rise with free trade, and prosperity with exports, and that with prosperity pauperism must decrease and finally disappear; and the following figures are to prove this. The number of able-bodied human beings doomed to subsist by parish support was:

> Jan. 1, 1849, in 590 Unions, 201,644
> Jan. 1, 1850, in 606 Unions, 181,159
> Jan. 1, 1851, in 606 Unions, 154,525

Comparing herewith the export lists, we find, for exports of British and Irish manufacture:

> 1848 .... £48,946,395
> 1849 58,910,833
> 1850 65,756,035

And what proves this table? An increase of exports of £9,964,438 redeemed above 20,000 persons from pauperism in 1849; a further increase of £6,845,202 redeemed 26,634 more in 1850. Now, even supposing free trade to do entirely away with the industrial cycles and their vicissitudes, then the redemption of the total number of able-bodied paupers would, under the present system, require an additional increase of the foreign trade of £50,000,000 annually, that is to say, an increase of very near 100 per cent. And these sober-minded Bourgeois statisticians have the courage to speak of "Utopists."—Verily, there are no greater Utopists in existence than these Bourgeois optimists.

I have just got hold of the documents published by the Poor Law Board. They prove indeed that we are experiencing a numerical decrease of paupers against 1848 and 51. But from these papers there follows at the same time: From 1841-'44 the average of paupers was 1,431,571—1845-'48 it was 1,600,257. In 1850 there were 1,809,308 paupers receiving in-door and out-door relief, and in 1851 they numbered 1,600,329, or rather more than the average of 1845-'48. Now, if we compare these numbers with the population as verified by the census, we find that there were in 1841-'48, 89 paupers to every 1,000 of the population, and 90 in 1851. Thus in reality pauperism has increased above the average of 1841-'48, and that in spite of free trade, famine, prosperity, in spite of the nuggets of Australia and the stream of emigration.

I may notice on this occasion, that the number of criminals has increased also, and a glance at *The Lancet*, a medical journal, shows that the adulteration and poisoning of articles of food has hitherto kept up apace with free trade. Every week *The Lancet* causes a new panic in London by unraveling fresh mysteries. This paper has established a complete commission of inquiry of physicians, chemists, &c., for the examination of the articles of food sold in London. Poisoned coffee, poisoned tea, poisoned vinegar, poisoned cayenne, poisoned pickles—everything mixed up with poison—that is the regular winding up of the reports of this commission.

Either side of the Bourgeois commercial policy, Free Trade or Protection, is, of course, equally incapable of doing away with facts that are the mere necessary and natural results of the economical base of Bourgeois society. And a matter of a million of paupers in the British workhouses is as inseparable from British prosperity, as the existence of eighteen to twenty millions in gold in the Bank of England.

This once settled in reply to the Bourgeois phantasts, who on one hand hold up as a result of Free Trade what is a mere necessary concomitant of every period of prosperity in the commercial cycles, or who, on the other hand, expect things from Bourgeois prosperity which it cannot possibly bring about. This once settled, there can be no doubt that the year 1852 is one of the most signal years of prosperity England ever enjoyed. The public revenue, in spite of the repeal of the window tax, the shipping returns, the export lists, the quotations of the money

market, above all, the unprecedented activity in the manufacturing
districts, bears an irrefutable testimony to this fact.

But the most superficial knowledge of commercial history from
the beginning of the nineteenth century, suffices to convince
anybody that the moment is approaching when the commercial
cycle will enter the phase of *excitement*, in order thence to pass
over to those of over-speculation and convulsion. "Not at all!"
shout the Bourgeois optimists. "In no previous period of
prosperity was there less speculation than in the present one. Our
present prosperity is founded upon the production of articles of
immediate usefulness, which enter into consumption almost as
rapidly as they can be brought to market, which leave to the
producer an adequate profit, and stimulate renewed and enlarged
production."

In other words, what distinguishes this present prosperity is the
fact that the existing surplus capital has thrown, and is throwing
itself, directly into industrial production. According to the late
report of Mr. Leonard Horner, Inspector General of Factories,
there took place in 1851 an increase in cotton factories alone equal
to 3,717 horse power.[a] His enumeration of factories in course of
construction is almost endless. Here a spinning mill with 150 horse
power, there a weaving shed for 600 looms for colored goods,
another spinning factory for 60,000 spindles and 620 horse power,
another for spinning and weaving with 200, another with 300
horse power, etc. The largest, however, is building near Bradford
(Yorkshire) for the manufacture of Alpaca and mixed goods.

"The magnitude of this concern, which is being erected for Mr. Titus Salt, may be
inferred from the fact that it is calculated to cover six statute acres of ground. The
principal building will be a massive stone edifice of considerable architectural
pretensions, having a single room in it 540 feet long, and the machinery will include
the latest inventions of acknowledged merit. The engines to move this immense mass
of machinery are being made by Messrs. Fairbairn, of Manchester, and they are
calculated to work 1,200 horse power. The gas works alone will be equal to those of a
small town, and will be erected upon White's hydrocarbon system, at a cost of £4,000.
It is calculated that 5,000 lights will be required, consuming 100,000 cubic feet of gas
per diem. In addition to this extensive factory, Mr. Salt is building 700 cottages for the
workpeople in its immediate neighborhood."

What, then, follows this enormous investment of capital for
immediate industrial production? That the crisis will not come?

_____

[a] Cited from the article "Cotton Manufactures" published in *The Times*, No.
21227, September 22, 1852. The quotation that follows is also taken from this
article.— *Ed.*

By no means; but on the contrary, that it will take a far more dangerous character than in 1847, when it was more commercial and monetary than industrial. This time it will fall with its heaviest weight upon the *manufacturing* districts. Let the unequaled stagnation of 1838-'42 be recalled to mind, which, too, was a direct result of industrial over-production. The more surplus capital concentrates itself in industrial production, instead of dividing its stream amongst the manifold channels of speculation, the more extensive, the more lasting, the more direct will the crisis fall upon the working masses and upon the very *élite* of the middle class. And if, in the moment of revulsion, the whole overwhelming mass of goods on the market already takes at once the form of lumbering ballast, how much more must this be the case with these numerous enlarged or newly-erected factories, just far enough advanced to begin to work, and for which it is of vital importance to set to work at once? If every time when capital deserts its habitual commercial channels of circulation, this desertion creates a panic which reaches even into the parlor of the Bank of England, how much more so a similar *sauve qui peut* in a moment when an immense amount has thus been turned into fixed capital in the shape of mills, machinery, etc., which begin to work only at the outbreak of the crisis, or which partially require further sums of circulating capital before they can be got into workable condition.

I take from *The Friend of India* another fact significative of the character of the approaching crisis. From a statement of the commerce of Calcutta in 1852 therein contained, it results that the value of cotton goods, twist and yarn imported into Calcutta in 1851, amounted to £4,074,000, or nearly two-thirds of the whole trade. In this year the whole amount of these imports will be larger still. The imports into Bombay, Madras, Singapore, are not even comprised herein. But the crisis of 1847 has given such revelations of Indian trade, that nobody can retain the slightest doubt of the final results of an industrial prosperity, in which the imports of "our Indian Empire" count for two-thirds of the whole.

So much as to the character of the state of convulsion which is to follow in the wake of the present state of prosperity. That this convulsion will come down in 1853, is prognosticated by many symptoms, especially the plethora of gold at the Bank of England, and the particular circumstances under which this large influx of bullion takes place.

At this moment there are £21,353,000 in bullion in the vaults of the Bank of England. It has been attempted to explain this influx by the surplus production of gold in Australia and California. A simple glance at facts proves the incorrectness of this view.

The increased quantity of bullion in the Bank of England represents, in reality, nothing but the diminished import of other commodities; in other words a large surplus of exports over imports. The last trade lists show, in fact, a considerable decrease of imports in hemp, sugar, tea, tobacco, wines, wool, grains, oils, cocoa, flour, indigo, hides, potatoes, bacon, pork, butter, cheese, hams, lard, rice, and almost all the manufactures of the European continent and of British India.[a] There was an evident over-importation in 1850 and 1851, and this, as well as the increased price of bread-stuffs on the Continent in consequence of a bad harvest, tends to keep down imports. The imports of cotton and flax alone show an increase.

This surplus of exports over imports explains why the rate of exchange is favorable for England. On the other hand, the balancing by gold of this excess of exports, causes a large portion of British capital to lie idle and to go to increase the reserves of the banks. The banks as well as private individuals hunt up every means to invest this idle capital. Hence the present abundance of loanable capital and the low rate of interest. First-class paper is at $1^3/_4$ and 2 per cent. Now, if you compare any history of trade, say Tooke's *History of Prices*, you find that the coincidence of these symptoms: unusual accumulation of bullion in the cellars of the Bank of England, excess of exports over imports, favorable rate of exchange, abundance of loanable capital, and low rate of interest, regularly opens, in the commercial cycle, that phase where prosperity passes into excitement, where on one hand over-trading in imports, on the other, wild speculations in all sorts of attractive bubbles, is sure to begin. But this state of excitement itself, is only the precursor of the state of convulsion. Excitement is the highest apex of prosperity; it does not produce the crisis, but it provokes its outbreak.

I know very well that the official economical *fortune-tellers* of England will consider this view exceedingly heterodox. But when since "Prosperity Robinson,"[b] the famous Chancellor of the Exchequer, who in 1825, just before the appearance of the crisis, opened Parliament with the prophecy of immense and unshakeable prosperity—when have these Bourgeois optimists ever

---

[a] See "Accounts Relating to Trade and Navigation. For the Eight Months Ended September 5, 1852", *The Economist*, No. 476, October 9, 1852.— *Ed.*

[b] Frederick John Robinson, Viscount Goderich.— *Ed.*

foreseen or predicted a crisis? There never was a single period of prosperity, but they profited by the occasion to prove that *this time* the medal was without a reverse, that the inexorable *fate* was *this time* subdued. And on the day, when the crisis broke out, they held themselves harmless by chastising trade and industry with moral, common-place preaching against want of foresight and caution.

The peculiar state of politics created by this momentary commercial and industrial prosperity, will form the subject of my next letter.

Written on October 12, 1852

First published in the *New-York Daily Tribune*, No. 3601, November 1, 1852; reprinted in the *Semi-Weekly Tribune*, No. 776, November 2, and in the *New-York Weekly Tribune*, No. 582, November 6, 1852

Signed: *Karl Marx*

Reproduced from the *New-York Daily Tribune*

Karl Marx

POLITICAL CONSEQUENCES
OF THE COMMERCIAL EXCITEMENT [242]

London, Tuesday, October 19, 1852

My last letter described the present industrial and commercial situation of this country; let us now draw the political consequences therefrom.

If the outbreak of the anticipated industrial and commercial revulsion will give a more dangerous and revolutionary character to the impending struggle with the Tories, the present prosperity is, for the moment, the most valuable ally to the Tory party; an ally, which, indeed, will not enable them to re-enact the Corn Laws, abandoned already by themselves, but which effectually consolidates their political power and assists them in carrying on a social reaction that, if let alone, would necessarily end in the conquest of substantial class-advantages, as it has been from its beginning started in the name of a substantial class-interest. No Corn Laws, says Disraeli,[a] but a fresh settlement of taxes in the interest of the oppressed farmers. But why are farmers oppressed? Because they, for the most part, continue to pay the old protectionist rates of rent, while the old protectionist price of corn is gone the way of all flesh. The aristocracy will not abate the rent of their land, but they will introduce a new mode of taxation which shall make up, to the farmers, for the surplus farmers have to pay into the pockets of the aristocracy.

I repeat that the present commercial prosperity is favorable to Tory reaction. Why?

---

[a] In his address to the electors of the County of Buckingham on June 2, 1852 and in his speech at a dinner of the electors of this county on July 14, 1852, *The Times*, Nos. 21135 and 21168, June 7 and July 15, 1852.— *Ed.*

"Patriotism," complains *Lloyd's Weekly Newspaper*, "patriotism is apt to go to sleep in the cupboard if meat and drink be there. Hence, free trade is the present security of the Earl of Derby; he lies on a bed of roses plucked by Cobden and Peel."[a]

The mass of the people is fully employed and more or less well off—always deducting the paupers inseparable from British prosperity; it is therefore not at present a very malleable material for political agitation. But what, above all things, enables Derby to carry out his machinations, is the fanaticism with which the *middle class* has thrown itself into the mighty process of industrial production, erecting of mills, constructing of machinery, building of ships, spinning and weaving of cotton and wool, storing of warehouses, manufacturing, exchanging, exporting, importing, and other more or less useful proceedings, the purpose of which, to them, is always the making of money. The Bourgeoisie, in this moment of brisk trade—and it very well knows that these happy moments are getting more and more few and far between—will and must make money, much money; nothing but money. It leaves to its politicians *ex professo* the task of watching the Tories. But the politicians *ex professo* (compare, for instance, Joseph Hume's letter to *The Hull Advertiser*[b]) complain justly that, deprived of pressure from without, they can agitate as little as the human frame could react without the pressure of the atmosphere.

The Bourgeoisie have, indeed, a sort of uneasy divination that in the high regions of government something suspicious is brewing, and that the Ministry *exploits* not overscrupulously the political apathy in which prosperity has thrown them. They, therefore, sometimes give the Ministry a warning through their organs in the press. For instance:

"To what extent the democracy [read the Bourgeoisie] may carry their present *wise* forbearance, their respect for their own power and for the rights of others, making no attempt to strengthen themselves by doing as the aristocracy have done, we cannot foresee; but the aristocracy must not infer, from the general conduct of the democracy, that they will never depart from moderation." [London *Economist*.[c]]

But Derby replies: Do you think I am fool enough to be frightened by you now, when the sun shines, and to be idle until

---

[a] "Mr. Hume's 'Rope of Sand'", *Lloyd's Weekly Newspaper*, No. 516, October 10, 1852.— *Ed.*

[b] Dated September 15, 1852, *The Hull Advertiser*, September 24, 1852.— *Ed.*

[c] "Lord John Russell and the Democracy", *The Economist*, No. 475, October 2, 1852.— *Ed.*

commercial storms and stagnation of trade give you the time to mind politics more clearly?

The plan of the Tory campaign shows itself every day.

The Tories began by chicaning open-air meetings; they prosecute, in Ireland, newspapers which contain articles unpleasant to them; they indict, in this moment, for seditious libel, the agents of the Peace Society,[243] who have distributed pamphlets against the use of the lash in the militia. In this quiet manner, they push back, wherever they can, the isolated opposition of the street and of the press.

In the meantime, they avoid every great and public rupture with their opponents, by delaying the meeting of Parliament, and by preparing everything in order to occupy it, when met, with the funeral "of a dead Duke,[a] instead of the interests of a living people". [Radical Paper.[b]] In the first week of November, Parliament will meet. But before January there can be no question of a serious beginning of the session.

And how do the Tories fill up the meantime? With the Registration campaign and the formation of the militia.

In the Registration campaign the object is to throw out or to prevent their opponents from entering the new lists of parliamentary electors for the ensuing year, by making out this or that objection which legally prevents a man from being registered a voter. Each political party is represented by its lawyers, and carries on the action at its own expense, and the revising barristers, named by the Chief Justice of the Queen's Bench,[244] decide on the admissibility of claims or objections. This campaign has hitherto had its principal theater in Lancashire and Middlesex. In order to get up the money for the campaign in North Lancashire, the Tories circulated lists of subscription on which Lord Derby himself had put down his name for the liberal sum of £500. The extraordinary number of 6,749 objections to voters have been taken in Lancashire, viz, 4,650 for South, and 2,099 for North Lancashire. For the former, the Tories objected to 3,557 qualifications; the Liberals to 1,093; for the latter, the Tories, to 1,334 qualifications; the Liberals to 765. (This, of course, merely amongst County voters, independently of the voters for the Boroughs, situated in that County.) The Tories were victorious in Lancashire. In the County of Middlesex there were expunged

---

[a] Duke of Wellington.— Ed.

[b] The People's Paper (in the article "Lord Derby and the People"), No. 23, October 9, 1852.— Ed.

from the registers 353 Radicals and 140 Conservatives—the Conservatives thus gaining 200 votes.

In this battle, the Tories stand on one side—the Whigs, with the men of the Manchester School, on the other. The latter, it is pretty well known, have formed freehold land societies—machines for manufacturing new voters. The Tories leave the machines alone, but destroy their products. Mr. Shadwell, revising barrister for Middlesex, gave decisions by which great numbers of the freehold land society voters have been disfranchised, declaring that a plot of land did not confer the franchise unless it had cost £50. As this was a question of fact and not of law, there is no appeal from this decision to the Court of Common Pleas.[245] Everybody conceives that this distinction of fact and law gives to the revising barristers, always open to the influence of the existing Ministry, the greatest power in composing the new voters' lists.

And what do these great efforts of the Tories, and the direct interference of their leader in the Registration campaign, prognosticate?

That the Earl of Derby has no very sanguine hopes for the continuance of his new Parliament, that he is inclined to dissolve it in case of resistance on its part, and that in the meantime he seeks to prepare, by the revising barristers, a conservative majority for another general election.

And while thus the Tories, on one hand, hold in reserve the Parliament-making machine placed at their disposal by the Registration campaign, they carry out, on the other hand, the Militia Bill, which places at their disposal the necessary bayonets for carrying out even the most reactionary acts of Parliament, and for supporting in tranquillity the frowns of the Peace Society.

"With Parliament to give it a legal semblance, with an armed militia to give it an active power, what may not the reaction do in England?"—exclaims the organ of the Chartists.[a]

And the death of the "Iron Duke," of the common-sense-hero of Waterloo, has in this particular critical moment freed the aristocracy of an importune guardian angel, who had experience enough in warfare to sacrifice, often enough, apparent victories to a well-covered retreat, and the brilliant offensive to a timely compromise. Wellington was the moderator of the House of Lords; he held in decisive moments often 60 and more proxies; he

---

[a] *The People's Paper* (in the article "Lord Derby and the People"), No. 23, October 9, 1852.— *Ed.*

prevented the Tories from declaring open war against the Bourgeoisie and against public opinion. But now, with a conflict-seeking Tory Ministry under the direction of a sporting character,[a] the House of Lords,

"instead of being, as under the guidance of the Duke, the steady ballast of the State, may become the top-hamper that may endanger its safety."

This latter notion, that the lordly ballast is necessary to the safety of the State, does of course not belong to us, but to the liberal *London Daily News*. The present Duke of Wellington, hitherto Marquis of Douro, has at once passed from the Peelite into the Tory camp. And thus there is every sign that the aristocracy are about to make the most reckless efforts to reconquer the lost ground, and to bring back the golden times of 1815 to 1830. And the Bourgeoisie, in this moment, has no time to agitate, to revolt, not even to get up a proper show of indignation.

Written on October 12, 1852

First published in the *New-York Daily Tribune*, No. 3602, November 2, 1852; reprinted in the *Semi-Weekly Tribune*, No. 777, November 5, and the *New-York Weekly Tribune*, No. 582, November 6, 1852

Signed: *Karl Marx*

Reproduced from the *New-York Daily Tribune*

---

[a] Earl of Derby.— *Ed.*

Karl Marx

POLITICAL PARTIES AND PROSPECTS[246]

London, Tuesday, November 2, 1852

We continue the deduction of political consequences which follow unavoidably in the wake of the present commercial and industrious prosperity.

In the midst of this atmosphere of universal industrial activity, of accelerated commercial interchange, of political indifference, deprived of any pressure from without, parliamentary parties complete in perfect tranquillity the process of their own dissolution.

"The Peelites and the Russellites gravitate at this moment toward each other in the strongest manner. The Peelites, those indispensable 'statesmen', not being able to do anything by themselves, now want to be received into the kinship of the governing family. Only look how much their organ, *The Morning Chronicle*, praises the very indifferent speech of Lord John Russell, at Perth."

Thus speaks *The Morning Herald*, the semi-official organ of the Government.

Quite the contrary, says *The Guardian*. Only listen to Mr. Henley, the President of the Board of Trade, speaking in the malt-house of Banbury to the circle of his farmer-friends:

"This party," declares Mr. Henley, "had principles of its own, and had stuck to them. Free Trade or Protection was an open question, and had only been made a party question by the late Sir Robert Peel." He speaks respectfully of the Peelites: "There was now no substantial obstacle to the reunion of the *great Conservative Party*."[a]

---

[a] J. W. Henley's speech at a Tory banquet in Banbury on September 28 and the comments on it that follow are quoted from the article "The Week" in *The Guardian*, No. 357, October 6, 1852.—*Ed.*

That's just it, exclaims *The Guardian*; sink Protection, and revive Conservatism. In other words, *The Guardian* supposes that the Peelites are ready—the Corn Laws left out of the question—to enter into a reactionary alliance with the Tories. And *The Daily News* reports as a fact, that a portion of Peelites has already passed into the Derbyite camp.[a] But a portion of the Whigs, too, is suspected of the same offense—and it would be nothing miraculous, considering that their aristocratic nucleus is formed by a clique of place-hunters. There is, for instance, Lord Dalhousie. My Lord was a Minister under Peel, in the liberal period of government. After the downfall of Peel, Russell offered him a seat in his new Cabinet. In common with the Duke of Newcastle, Lord St. Germans, and other members of the former Government, he supported in the Upper House the maneuvers of the Whigs, and was rewarded, on a vacancy, with the Governor-Generalship of India, that most splendid prize of all in the oligarchic lottery. He turned it to the greatest economical account. The Whigs boasted of the "unprecedented" sacrifice they had made in alienating so highly coveted an office from their own immediate connection. And now, at this present moment, the lure held out to Lord Dalhousie is the Wardenship of the Cinque Ports, a sinecure of thousands a year.[247] Our man is said not to be overburdened with patrimonial wealth and to consider it his patriotic duty to secure the Cinque Ports against a surprise, even under a Derby Ministry.

Similar bits of *chronique scandaleuse*, anecdotes of negotiations of this or that Whig as to the lowest price at which he is to make himself over to the Tories, are found by dozens in the Liberal weekly press. They prove the profound corruption of the Whig party; but their importance disappears before the schism between its two principal leaders, Russell and Palmerston. We had already known, some time ago, incidents connected with recent election contests in which the part taken by Lord Palmerston in support of the ministerial candidates seemed unaccountable, as the Liberal papers expressed themselves. Now, one fine morning, Palmerston's own organ, *The Morning Post*, brings out a leader,[b] referring to the rumors that Palmerston either was to enter the Cabinet as Secretary of State and leader of the Commons, or in case of a speedy dissolution of the Derby Ministry, to form a new cabinet with those fragments of it which might not have become quite

---

[a] The reference is to the leading article in *The Daily News* of October 12, 1852.— *Ed.*
[b] *The Morning Post*, October 7, 1852.— *Ed.*

"impossible." *The Morning Post,* finding upon the whole these rumors very attractive, declares that it does not speak in Lord Palmerston's name, but in its own private name. But Palmerston, in despite of all the pressing and even importunate calls of the Whig and Liberal press, does not think it proper to refute the calumniating report. The Peelite *Morning Chronicle* mentions these rumors[a] in a tone which plainly shows that Gladstone & Co. would not feel any *horror vacui*[b] at the idea of similar amalgamations. *The Daily News,* a paper of the Manchester School, discovers this circumstance, and indignantly calls upon the traitors among Whigs and Peelites to join themselves openly to Derby.[c] Thus you see how every one of the Parliamentary *coteries* which have hitherto one after the other taken hold of the political helm, is distrusting all others and its own members, how they accuse each other of desertion, corruption, compromise and yet each and all admit, that, leaving the Corn Laws out of the question, there is nothing in the way of their joining the Derbyites but personal rancor and personal ambition. They occupy toward Derby about the same position as, before the 2d December last, the different fractions of the Party of Order toward Bonaparte.

That the opposition is awaiting the coming Parliamentary campaign in a rather pusillanimous mood, is easily explained.

Little John Russell received the freedom of the burgh of Perth in a little bag, and replied, after a giant dinner, in a little speech, the most important part of which was the following declaration:

"We are bound in justice, as well as, I think, directed by *policy, to wait until those measures are produced which are to give to the agricultural interest,* to the colonial interest, to the shipping interest, all the compensation of which they have hitherto been unjustly deprived [laughter]—those admirable measures which are to put an end to a long contest."[d]

The only daily paper of which Russell yet disposes, *The Globe* (evening paper), gives on the above the following commentary: "Any such opposition, as was urged against Sir R. Peel in 1835, would involve a certainty of failure," on account of the rivalries of the various Liberal leaders.[e] Thus the experiment to upset the Derby Cabinet at the very outset of the session, by a compact vote

---

[a] In its leading article of October 5, 1852.— *Ed.*

[b] *Horror vacui*—fear of death (literally: fear of vacuum).— *Ed.*

[c] The reference is to the leading article in *The Daily News* of October 12, 1852.— *Ed.*

[d] John Russell, Speech at a dinner in Perth on September 24, 1852, *The Times,* No. 21291, September 27, 1852.— *Ed.*

[e] Quoted from the leading article in *The Globe,* September 28, 1852.— *Ed.*

of the coalesced opposition, has been entirely abandoned, and Lord John Russell remains faithful to his part, being the first to sound the retreat. And as to the prospects of Parliamentary opposition at large, its chief, Mr. J. Hume, makes the following confession in his letter to *The Hull Advertiser*:

"If my experience, as regards the Irish members hitherto in the House of Commons, is to be taken, the material is not likely to be of that substance to be moulded and kept in proper position, or under the influence of any leader. The Irish members are too extravagant, too ardent, too strongly imbued with Ireland's wrongs and her sufferings. At present nothing, as far as I know, has been done toward a union of Liberals who may be doubtful of the acts of the Derby Administration; and when I look to the hollow professions of those who preceded Lord Derby (the Whigs), and on their throwing up the cards rather than play out the game for the popular cause, by calling on the Reformers to join them, I cannot have much confidence in anything they may do to promote the union of parties. Indeed, they must be left, I fear, to chew the cud, whilst the Derbyites are committing all kinds of misgovernment to forward their own cause, and to benefit their supporters; and it will only be *after considerable time* of such conduct that there can be any chance of a People's party being formed."[a]

John Bright, the actual chief of the Manchester School, has indeed attempted, in his after-dinner speech to the manufacturers of Belfast, to make good by cajoleries to the Irish members the attacks of Joseph Hume,[b] but in all matters of Parliamentary discipline "Old Joe's" opinion is an authority.

Thus the Parliamentary opposition is completely despairing of itself.

Nay, the old Parliamentary opposition has so far outlived itself that its Nestor, Hume, at the end of his long career now publicly declares that there is in the House of Commons no "People's party." Whatever was there called so, was a mere "rope of sand."

Thus, general dissolution, universal weakness and impotency in the camp of the Opposition.

Written on October 16, 1852   Reproduced from the newspaper

First published in the *New-York Daily Tribune*, No. 3625, November 29, 1852

Signed: *Karl Marx*

---

[a] Joseph Hume, Letter to *The Hull Advertiser* written on September 15, 1852, *The Hull Advertiser*, September 24, 1852.— *Ed.*

[b] John Bright, Speech at a dinner in Belfast on October 4, 1852, *The Times*, No. 21240, October 7, 1852.— *Ed.*

Karl Marx

[ATTEMPTS TO FORM A NEW OPPOSITION PARTY][248]

London, Tuesday, November 9, 1852

In the same measure as the hitherto predominating parties dissolve themselves, and as their distinctive marks are effaced, the want of a new opposition party is felt, as a matter of course. This want finds an expression in different ways.

Lord John Russell, in his already quoted speech,[a] takes the lead. Part of the alarm raised by Lord Derby, he says, had sprung from the rumors that he, Lord J. Russell, had adopted "highly democratical opinions." "Well, I need not say on that subject that this rumor was totally unfounded; that it has no circumstances on which it rested." Nevertheless, he pronounces himself a Democrat, and then explains the harmless meaning of the word:

"The people of this country are, in other words, the Democracy of the country. Democracy has as fair a right to the enjoyment of its rights as monarchy or nobility. Democracy does not mean to diminish any of the prerogatives of the Crown. Democracy does not attempt to take away any of the lawful privileges of the House of Lords. What, then, is this Democracy? The growth of wealth, the growth of intellect, the forming of opinions more enlightened and more calculated to carry on in an enlightened manner the Government of the world. But I will say more. I will say that the manner of dealing with that increase of the position of the Democracy could not be *according to the old system of restraint with which I was but too familiar*. On the contrary, Democracy ought to be maintained and encouraged, there ought to be given a legitimate and legal organ to that power and influence."

"Lord John Russell," exclaims *The Morning Herald* in reply, "has one set of principles for office and another set of principles for opposition. When in office, his principle is to do nothing, and when out of office, to pledge himself to everything."

---

[a] See this volume, p. 371.— *Ed.*

What in all the world may *The Morning Herald* mean by "nothing," if it calls the above trash, pronounced by Lord John Russell, "everything!" and if it menaces little John Russell, for his king-loving, lords-respecting, bishop-conserving "Democracy," with the fate of Frost, Williams & Co.! But the humor of the thing is that Lord Derby, in the House of Lords, announces himself as the prominent opponent of "Democracy," and speaks of Democracy as of the only party against which it is worthwhile to struggle.[a] And in steps the inevitable John Russell with an examination of what this Democracy is, viz., the growth of wealth, of the intellect of this wealth, and of its claims to influence Government through public opinion and through legal organs. Thus, then, Democracy is nothing but the claims of the Bourgeoisie, the industrious and commercial middle class. Lord Derby stands up as the opponent, Lord John Russell volunteers as the standard-bearer of this Democracy. Both of them agree in the implicit confession, that the ancient feuds within their own class, the aristocracy, are no longer of any interest to the country. And Russell is quite prepared to drop the name of Whig for that of Democrat, if this be the *conditio sine qua non* for turning his opponents out. The Whigs, in this case, would in fact continue to play the same part, and appear officially as the servants of the middle class. Thus, Russell's plan of a party reorganisation is confined to the adoption of a new party name.

Joseph Hume, too, considers the formation of a new "people's party" a necessity. But he says that on tenant-right and similar propositions it cannot be formed. "On these matters you could not muster a hundred out of the 654 members to unite." What, then, is his nostrum?

"The people's league or party, or union, must agree on one point—say the ballot; and after carrying that one point, proceed from step to step to other points. And while the movement must begin with a few individual[b] members of the House of Commons, it cannot succeed until the people out of doors and the electors shall see the necessity of doing their part, and of giving support to the small party of the people in Parliament."[c]

This same Hume was one of the drawers-up of the People's Charter.[249] From the People's Charter and its six points, he

---

[a] See Derby's speech in the House of Lords on March 15, 1852, *The Times*, No. 21064, March 16, 1852.— *Ed.*

[b] *The Hull Advertiser* has here "Radical".— *Ed.*

[c] Joseph Hume, Letter to *The Hull Advertiser*, September 15, 1852, *The Hull Advertiser*, September 24, 1852. Below the same letter is quoted.— *Ed.*

retreated to the "little Charter" of the financial and parliamentary reformers with only three points,[250] and now we see him reduced to one point, the ballot. What success he promises to himself from his new nostrum, he will tell us himself in the concluding words of his letter to *The Hull Advertiser*:

"Tell me how many editors will risk to give their support to a party that, as Parliament is now composed, *can never succeed to power?*"

Now, as this new party does not mean to change for the present anything in the composition of Parliament, but confines itself to the ballot, it will, by its own confession, never succeed to power. What is the good of forming a party of *impotence*, and of openly confessed impotence?

Next to Joseph Hume, there is another attempt made for the creation of a new party. This is the so-called *National Party*. Instead of the People's Charter, this party would make universal suffrage its *exclusive* shibboleth, and thus leave out those very conditions which can alone make the movement for universal suffrage a national movement and secure to it popular support. I shall hereafter have occasion to recur to this National Party. It consists of ex-Chartists who wish to conquer *respectability* for themselves, and of Radicals, middle-class ideologists, who wish to get hold of the Chartist movement. Behind them—whether "Nationals" are aware of it or not—you find the parliamentary and financial reformers, the men of the Manchester School, urging them on and using them as their vanguard.

Now, what cannot but be evident to everyone in all these miserable compromises and backslidings, these huntings after weakly expediency, these vacillations and quack *nostra*, is this:—Catiline is at the gates of the city,[a] a decisive struggle is drawing near, the opposition knows its unpopularity, its incapacity for resistance, and all the attempts at the formation of new centers of defense agree in one point only, in a "going backwards policy." The "National Party" retreats from the Charter to General Suffrage, Joe Hume from General Suffrage to the ballot, a third from the ballot to the equalization of electoral districts, and so forth, until at last we arrive at Johnny Russell, who has nothing to give out for a battle-cry but the mere name of democracy. Lord J. Russell's Democracy would be, practically speaking, the ul-

---

[a] The expression "Catiline is at the gates of the city" ("Catilina est aux portes") belongs to Goupil de Préfelne, a deputy of the French Constituent Assembly of 1789, and is a paraphrased ancient Roman expression of the period of the Second Punic War: "Hannibal ad partes."—*Ed.*

timatum of the National Party, of Hume's "people's party," and of all the other party shams, if any one of them had anything like vitality about it.

But on the one hand, the political flaccidity and indifference consequent upon a period of material prosperity, on the other hand the conviction that nevertheless the Tories are menacing mischief—on the one hand, the certainty on the part of the *Bourgeois* leaders that they will very soon require the people to back them, on the other hand the knowledge acquired by some popular leaders that the people are too indolent to create, for the moment, a movement of their own—all these circumstances produce the phenomenon that parties attempt to make themselves acceptable to each other, and that the different factions of the opposition out of Parliament attempt a union by making to each other concessions, from the most advanced faction downwards until at last they again arrive at what Lord J. Russell is pleased to call democracy.

Of the attempts at creating a self-styled "National Party," Ernest Jones justly remarks:

"The People's Charter is the most comprehensive measure of political reform in existence, and the Chartists are the only truly national party of political and social reformers in Great Britain."[a]

And R. G. Gammage, one of the members of the Chartist Executive,[251] thus addresses the people:

"Would you then refuse the co-operation of the middle classes? Certainly not, if that co-operation is offered on fair and honorable terms. And what are these terms? They are easy and simple; adopt the Charter, and having adopted that Charter, unite with its friends who are already organized for its achievement. If you refuse to do this, you must either be opposed to the Charter itself, or, piqueing yourselves upon your class superiority, you must imagine that superiority to entitle you to leadership. In the first case, no honest Chartist can unite with you, in the second, no working man ought so far to lose his self-respect as to succumb to your class prejudices. Let the working men trust their own power alone, receiving honest aid from whatever sources, but acting as though their salvation depended upon their own exertions."[b]

The mass of the Chartists, too, are at the present moment absorbed by material production; but on all points the nucleus of

---

[a] Ernest Jones, "The Race of Shams", *The People's Paper*, No. 23, October 9, 1852.— *Ed.*

[b] Robert George Gammage, "Respectable Democracy", *The People's Paper*, No. 23, October 9, 1852.— *Ed.*

the party is reorganized, and the communications re-established, in England as well as in Scotland, and in the event of a commercial and political crisis, the importance of the present noiseless activity at the headquarters of Chartism will be felt all over Great Britain.

Written on October 16, 1852

First published in the *New-York Daily Tribune*, No. 3622, November 25, and the *Semi-Weekly Tribune*, No. 783, November 26, 1852

Signed: *Karl Marx*

Reproduced from the *New-York Daily Tribune*

Karl Marx and Frederick Engels

[PUBLIC STATEMENT
TO THE EDITORS OF THE ENGLISH PRESS]²⁵²

Sir,—The undersigned call your attention to the attitude of the Prussian Press, including even the most reactionary papers, such as the *Neue Preussische Zeitung,* during the pending trial of the Communists at Cologne, and to the honourable discretion they observe, at a moment where scarcely a third part of the witnesses have been examined, when none of the produced documents have been verified, and not a word has fallen yet from the defence. While those papers, at the worst, represent the Cologne prisoners and the undersigned, their London friends, in accordance with the public accuser, as "dangerous conspirators who alone are responsible for the whole history of Europe of the latter four years, and for all the revolutionary commotions of 1848 and 1849"—there are in London two public organs, *The Times* and *The Daily News* which really have not hesitated to represent the Cologne prisoners and the undersigned as a "gang of sturdy beggars," swindlers, etc.ᵃ The undersigned address to the English public the same demand which the defensors of the accused have addressed to the public in Germany—to suspend their judgment, and to wait for the end of the trials. Were they to give further explanations at the present time, the Prussian government might obtain the means of baffling a revelation of police-tricks, perjury, forgery of documents, falsification of dates, thefts, etc., unprecedented even in the records of Prussian political justice. When that revelation shall have been made in the course of the present proceedings, public opinion in England will know how to qualify the anonymous

---

ᵃ The reference is to an item by the Berlin correspondent of *The Times* written on October 9, 1852 and published in *The Times,* No. 21245, October 13, 1852. —*Ed.*

scribes of *The Times* and *Daily News*, who constitute themselves the advocates and mouthpieces of the most infamous and subaltern government spies.

We are, Sir, yours fraternally,

F. *Engels*
F. *Freiligrath*
K. *Marx*
W. *Wolff*

London, October 28th

Published in *The People's Paper*, No. 26, *The Spectator*, No. 1270, *The Examiner*, No. 2335, *The Morning Advertiser*, *The Leader*, No. 136, October 30, 1852

Reproduced from *The People's Paper* and checked with the other newspapers

Karl Marx

THE TRIALS AT COLOGNE

TO THE EDITOR OF *THE MORNING ADVERTISER*

Sir,—I beg to offer you my best thanks for the generous protection you have afforded to the cause of my friends, the prisoners at Cologne.[a] While the defence will bring to light the series of unscrupulous acts committed by the agents of the Prussian police, even during the progress of this trial, I wish to inform you of the last trick that has been had recourse to, in order to prove a criminal correspondence between myself and the Cologne prisoners. According to the report of the *Kölnische Zeitung,* of October 29, Mr. Stieber, the councillor of police, has produced another of his documents—a ridiculous letter, purporting to be in my handwriting, in which I am made to recommend one of my pretended agents "to push under the doors of acknowledged democrats, at Crefeld, 50 copies of the *Red Catechism,*[b] and to choose for the execution of commission the midnight-hour of June 5, 1852." [c]

For the sake of my accused friends, I hereby declare,—

1. That the letter in question is not written by myself.

2. That I learned its existence only from the *Kölnische Zeitung* of 29th inst.

3. That I never saw the so-called *Red Catechism.*

4. That I never caused any copies of the "Red" to be circulated, in whatever manner.

---

[a] The reference is to the statement in defence of the Cologne prisoners published by *The Morning Advertiser* (see this volume, pp. 378-79).— *Ed.*

[b] Moses Hess, *Rother Kathechismus für das deutsche Volk.*— *Ed.*

[c] Quoted from the minutes of the Cologne trial published in the *Kölnische Zeitung* from October 5 to November 13, 1852, under the title *Assisen-Procedur gegen D. Herm. Becker und Genossen. Anklage wegen hochverrätherischen Complottes.*— *Ed.*

This declaration, made also before the magistrate in Marlborough Street, and consequently as valid as an oath, I have sent by post to Cologne. By your inserting it in the columns of your paper, you will the more oblige me, as that would be the most effective means of preventing the Prussian police from intercepting the document.

I am, Sir, your obedient servant,

Dr. *Charles Marx*

London, October 30, 1852—
28, Dean Street, Soho

Published in *The Morning Advertiser*, November 2, and *The People's Paper*, No. 27, November 6, 1852

Reproduced from *The Morning Advertiser* and checked with *The People's Paper*

Karl Marx

KOSSUTH, MAZZINI, AND LOUIS NAPOLEON [253]

TO THE EDITOR OF *THE N. Y. TRIBUNE*

Sir: My letter of 28th of September last, containing revelations as to the movements of Kossuth and Mazzini,[a] has, I perceive, elicited considerable animadversion, and given the Democratic press occasion for a vast amount of superfluous declamation, abuse and bluster.

I have ascertained that Kossuth has no part in this clamor. If he had himself ventured a denial of my assertions, I should have returned to the subject, and given incontestable evidence for the facts adduced.

However, my letter was not intended as an attack on Kossuth, but rather as a *warning*. In politics a man may ally himself, for a given object, with the devil himself—only he must be sure that he is cheating the devil, instead of the devil cheating him.

As to the gentleman who has taken upon himself *authoritatively* to refute me, I beg to remind him of an old proverb: *Amicus incommodus ab inimico non differt.*[b]

To the gentlemen of the Democratic press, and especially of the German Democratic press, who, as usual, have yelled the loudest, I say they are all bigoted Crypto-Royalists. These gentlemen cannot do without kings, gods and popes. Scarcely got out of the leading strings of their old rulers, they manufacture new ones for themselves, and grow indignant at those "infidels and rebels" who

---

[a] See this volume, pp. 354-56.— *Ed.*
[b] An awkward friend does not differ from an enemy.— *Ed.*

render themselves obnoxious by publishing unpleasant truths, revealing compromising facts and thus committing *lese*-majesty and sacrilege against the newly-elevated Democratic gods and kings.

London, November 16, 1852

Your private correspondent

Published in the *New-York Daily Tribune,*
No. 3627, December 1, 1852

Reproduced from the newspaper

Karl Marx and Frederick Engels

A FINAL DECLARATION
ON THE LATE COLOGNE TRIALS[254]

TO THE EDITOR OF *THE MORNING ADVERTISER*

Sir,—The undersigned discharge a duty to themselves and towards their now condemned friends at Cologne, by laying before the English public a statement of facts connected with the recent monster trial in that city, which have not been made sufficiently known by the London press.

Eighteen months have been wasted on the mere getting up of the evidence for this trial. During the whole of that time our friends have been kept in solitary confinement, deprived of all means of occupation and even of books; those who became ill were refused proper medical treatment, or if they obtained it, the condition in which they were placed prevented them from benefiting thereby. Even after the "act of accusation" had been communicated to them, they were prohibited, in direct violation of the law, from conferring with their lawyers. And what were the pretexts for this protracted cruel imprisonment? After the lapse of the first nine months the "Chamber of Accusation" declared that there were no grounds on which a charge could be maintained, and that, therefore, the instruction had to be recommended. It was recommended. Three months later, at the opening of the assizes, the public accuser[a] pleaded that the mass of the evidence

---

[a] Otto Saedt.— *Ed.*

had grown into a larger bulk than he had as yet been able to digest. And after three further months the trial was again adjourned, on the ground of the illness of one of the chief Government witnesses.

The real cause of all this delay was the fear of the Prussian Government to confront the meagre substance of the facts with the pompously announced "unheard-of revelations." At last, the Government succeeded in selecting a jury, such as the Rhenish provinces had never yet beheld, composed of six reactionary nobles, four members of the *haute finance*, and two members of the bureaucracy.

Now, what was the evidence laid before this jury? Merely the absurd proclamations and correspondence of a set of ignorant phantasts, importance-seeking conspirators, the tools and associates at once of one Cherval, an avowed agent of the police. The greater part of those papers were formerly in the possession of a certain Oswald Dietz in London. During the Great Exhibition[255] the Prussian police, while Dietz was absent from his home, had his drawers broken open, and thus obtained the desired documents by a common theft. These papers, in the first instance, furnished the means of discovering the so-called Franco-German plot at Paris.[256] Now, the proceedings at Cologne proved, that those conspirators, and Cherval, their Paris agent, were the very political opponents of the defendants and their undersigned London friends. But the public accuser pleaded, that a mere personal quarrel had prevented the latter from taking part in the plot of Cherval and his associates. By such an argumentation it was intended to prove the moral complicity of the Cologne defendants in the Paris plot; and while the accused of Cologne were thus made responsible for the acts of their very enemies, the professed friends of Cherval and his associates were produced by the Government in court, not at the bar like the defendants—nay, in the witness-box, to depose against them. This, however, appeared too bad. Public opinion forced the Government to look out for less equivocal evidence. The whole of the police machinery was set to work under the direction of one Stieber, the principal Government witness at Cologne, royal councillor of police, and chief of the Berlin criminal police. In the sitting of October 23rd, Stieber announced, that an extraordinary courier from London had delivered to him most important documents, proving, undeniably, the complicity of the accused in an alleged conspiracy with the undersigned.

"Amongst other documents, the courier had brought him the original minute-book of the sittings of the secret society, presided over by Dr. Marx, and with whom the defendants had been in correspondence." [a]

Stieber, however, entangled himself in discordant statements as to the date on which his courier was to have reached him. Dr. Schneider, the leading counsel for the defence, charged him directly with perjury, upon which Stieber ventured no other reply than to fall back upon his dignity of the representative of the Crown, entrusted with a most important mission from the very highest authority of the State. As to the minute-book, Stieber declared twice on oath, that it was the "genuine minute-book of the London Communist Society," but later on, closely pressed by the defence, he admitted that it might be a mere book of notes, taken by one of his spies. At length, from his own evidence, the book was proved to be a deliberate forgery, and its origin traced back to three of Stieber's London agents, Greif, Fleury, and Hirsch. The latter has since admitted that he composed the book under the guidance of Fleury and Greif. So decisive was the evidence at Cologne on this point, that even the public accuser declared Stieber's important documents a "most unfortunate book," a mere forgery. The same personage refused to take notice of a letter forming part of the Government evidence, in which the handwriting of Dr. Marx had been imitated; that document, too, having turned out a gross and palpable forgery. In the same manner every other document brought forward in order to prove, not the revolutionary tendencies, but the actual participation of the accused in some distant plot, turned out a forgery of the police. So great were the Government's fears of an exposure, that it not only caused the post to retain all documents addressed to the counsel for the defence, but the latter to be intimidated by Stieber, with a threatened prosecution for his "criminal correspondence" with the undersigned.

If now, in spite of the absence of all convincing proof, a verdict has, nevertheless, been obtained,[257] that result has only become possible, at the hands even of such a jury, by the retroactive application of the new criminal code, under which *The Times* and the Peace Society[258] themselves might at any time be tried on the formidable charge of high treason. Moreover, the trial at Cologne had assumed, by its duration, and by the extraordinary means

---

[a] Here and elsewhere the quotations are taken from the minutes of the Cologne trial published in the *Kölnische Zeitung* from October 5 to November 13, 1852, under the title *Assisen-Procedur gegen D. Herm. Becker und Genossen. Anklage wegen hochverrätherischen Complottes.—Ed.*

employed on the part of the prosecution, such vast dimensions, that an acquittal would have equalled a condemnation of the Government; and a conviction prevailed generally in the Rhenish provinces, that the immediate consequence of an acquittal would be the suppression of the entire institution of the jury.

We are, Sir, your most obedient servants,

F. *Engels*
F. *Freiligrath*
K. *Marx*
W. *Wolff*

London, November 20, 1852

Published in *The Morning Advertiser*,
No. 19168, November 29, 1852

Reproduced from the newspaper

Frederick Engels

THE LATE TRIAL AT COLOGNE[259]

London, Wednesday, December 1, 1852

You will have ere this received by the European papers numerous reports of the Communist Monster Trial at Cologne, Prussia, and of its result. But as none of the reports is anything like a faithful statement of the facts, and as these facts throw a glaring light upon the political means by which the Continent of Europe is kept in bondage, I consider it necessary to revert to this trial.

The Communist or Proletarian party, as well as other parties, had lost, by suppression of the rights of association and meeting, the means of giving to itself a *legal* organization on the Continent. Its leaders, besides, had been exiled from their countries. But no political party can exist without an organization; and that organization which both the Liberal bourgeois and the Democratic shopkeeping class were enabled more or less to supply by the social station, advantages, and long-established, everyday intercourse of their members, the proletarian class, without such social station and pecuniary means, was necessarily compelled to seek in secret association. Hence, both in France and Germany, sprang up those numerous secret societies which have, ever since 1849, one after another been discovered by the police and prosecuted as conspiracies; but if many of them were really conspiracies, formed with the actual intention of upsetting the Government for the time being—and he is a coward that under certain circumstances would not conspire, just as he is a fool who, under other circumstances, would do so—there were some other societies which were formed with a wider and more elevated purpose, which knew, that the upsetting of an existing Government was but a passing stage in the great impending struggle, and which intended to keep together and to prepare the party, whose nucleus they formed, for the last, decisive combat which must one day or another crush forever in Europe the domination, not of mere "tyrants," "despots" and "usurpers," but of a power far superior, and far more formidable than theirs; that of capital over labor.

The organization of the advanced Communist party in Germany [260] was of this kind. In accordance with the principles of its "Manifesto" (published in 1848) and with those explained in the series of articles on *Revolution and Counter-Revolution in Germany*,[a] published in *The New-York Daily Tribune*, this party never imagined itself capable of producing, at any time and at its pleasure, that revolution which was to carry its ideas into practice. It studied the causes that had produced the revolutionary movements of 1848, and the causes that made them fail. Recognizing the social antagonism of classes at the bottom of all political struggles, it applied itself to the study of the conditions under which one class of society can and must be called on to represent the whole of the interests of a nation, and thus politically to rule over it. History showed to the Communist party, how, after the landed aristocracy of the Middle Ages, the monied power of the first capitalists arose and seized the reins of Government; how the social influence and political rule of this *financial* section of capitalists was superseded by the rising strength, since the introduction of steam, of the *manufacturing* capitalists, and how at the present moment two more classes claim their turn of domination, the petty trading class, and the industrial working class. The practical revolutionary experience of 1848-49 confirmed the reasonings of theory, which led to the conclusion that the democracy of the petty traders must first have its turn, before the Communist working class could hope to permanently establish itself in power and destroy that system of wages-slavery which keeps it under the yoke of the bourgeoisie. Thus the secret organization of the Communists could not have the direct purpose of upsetting the *present* governments of Germany. Being formed to upset not these, but the insurrectionary government, which is sooner or later to follow them, its members might, and certainly would, individually lend an active hand to a revolutionary movement against the present *status quo* in its time; but the *preparation* of such a movement, otherwise than by secret spreading of Communist opinions by the masses, could not be an object of the Association.[b] So well was this foundation of the society understood by the majority of its members, that when the place-hunting ambition of some tried to turn it into a

---

[a] See this volume, pp. 3–96.— *Ed.*
[b] The Communist League.— *Ed.*

conspiracy for making an *ex tempore* revolution, they were speedily turned out.

Now, according to no law upon the face of the earth, could such an association be called a plot, a conspiracy for purposes of high treason. If it was a conspiracy, it was one against, not the existing Government, but its probable successors. And the Prussian Government was aware of it. That was the cause why the eleven defendants were kept in solitary confinement during eighteen months, spent, on the part of the authorities, in the strangest judicial feats. Imagine, that after eight months' detention, the prisoners were remanded for some months more, "there being no evidence of any crime against them!" And when at last they were brought before a jury, there was not a single overt act of a treasonable nature proved against them. And yet they were convicted, and you will speedily see how.

One of the emissaries of the society[a] was arrested in May, 1851, and from documents found upon him, other arrests followed. A Prussian police officer, a certain *Stieber*, was immediately ordered to trace the ramifications, in London, of the pretended plot. He succeeded in obtaining some papers connected with the above-mentioned seceders from the society, who had, after being turned out, formed an actual conspiracy in Paris and London. These papers were obtained by a double crime. A man named Reuter was bribed to break open the writing desk of the secretary of the society,[b] and steal the papers therefrom. But that was nothing yet. This theft led to the discovery and conviction of the so-called Franco-German plot, in Paris,[261] but it gave no clue as to the great Communist Association. The Paris plot, we may as well here observe, was under the direction of a few ambitious imbeciles and political *chevaliers d'industrie*[c] in London, and of a formerly convicted forger, then acting as a police spy in Paris[d]; their dupes made up, by rapid declamations and blood-thirsty rantings, for the utter insignificance of their political existence.

The Prussian police, then, had to look out for fresh discoveries. They established a regular office of secret police at the Prussian Embassy in London. A police agent, Greif by name, held his odious vocation under the title of an *attaché* to the Embassy—a step which would suffice to put all Prussian Embassies out of the pale of international law, and which even the Austrians have not yet dared

---

[a] Peter Nothjung.— *Ed.*
[b] Oswald Dietz.— *Ed.*
[c] Adventurers, swindlers.— *Ed.*
[d] Julien Cherval.— *Ed.*

to take. Under him worked a certain Fleury, a merchant in the City of London, a man of some fortune and rather respectably connected, one of those low creatures who do the basest actions from an innate inclination to infamy. Another agent was a commercial clerk named Hirsch, who, however, had already been denounced as a spy on his arrival. He introduced himself into the society of some German Communist refugees in London, and they, in order to obtain proofs of his real character, admitted him for a short time. The proofs of his connection with the police were very soon obtained, and Mr. Hirsch, from that time, absented himself. Although, however, he thus resigned all opportunities of gaining the information he was paid to procure, he was not inactive. From his retreat in Kensington, where he never met one of the Communists in question, he manufactured every week pretended reports of pretended sittings of a pretended Central Committee of that very conspiracy which the Prussian police could not get hold of. The contents of these reports were of the most absurd nature; not a Christian name was correct, not a name correctly spelt, not a single individual made to speak as he would be likely to speak. His master, Fleury, assisted him in this forgery, and it is not yet proved that "*Attaché*" Greif can wash his hands of these infamous proceedings. The Prussian Government, incredible to say, took these silly fabrications for gospel truth, and you may imagine what a confusion such depositions created in the evidence to be brought before the jury. When the trial came on, Mr. Stieber, the already mentioned police officer, got into the witness-box, swore to all these absurdities, and, with no little self-complacency, maintained that he had a secret agent in the very closest intimacy with those parties in London who were considered the prime movers in this awful conspiracy. This secret agent was very secret indeed, for he had hid his face for eight months in Kensington, for fear he might actually see one of the parties whose most secret thoughts, words and doings he pretended to report week after week.

Messrs. Hirsch and Fleury, however, had another invention in store. They worked up the whole of the reports they had made into an "original Minute Book" of the sittings of the secret supreme committee, whose existence was maintained by the Prussian police; and Mr. Stieber, finding that this book wondrously agreed with the reports already received from the same parties, at once laid it before the jury, declaring upon his oath that after serious examination and according to his fullest conviction that book was genuine. It was then that most of the absurdities reported by Hirsch were made public. You may imagine the surprise of the pretended members of that secret committee when they found things stated of them which they never knew before. Some who were baptized William, were here christened Louis or Charles; others, at the time they were at the other end of England, were made to have pronounced speeches in London; others were reported to have read letters they never had received; they were made to have met regularly on a Thursday, when they used to have a convivial reunion, once a week, on Wednesdays; a working man, who could hardly write, figured as one of the takers of minutes and signed as such; and they all of them were made to speak in a language which, if it may be that of Prussian police stations, was certainly not that of a reunion in which literary men, favorably known in their country, formed the majority. And, to crown the whole, a receipt was forged for a sum of money, pretended to have been paid by the fabricators to the pretended secretary of the fictitious Central Committee for this book; but the existence of this pretended secretary rested merely upon a hoax that some malicious Communist had played upon the unfortunate Hirsch.

This clumsy fabrication was too scandalous an affair not to produce the contrary of its intended effect. Although the London friends of the defendants were deprived of all means to bring the facts of the case before the jury—although the letters they sent to the counsel for the defense were suppressed by the post—although the documents and affidavits they succeeded in getting into the hands of these legal gentlemen were not admitted in evidence, yet the general indignation was such that even the public accusers,[a] nay, even Mr. Stieber—whose oath had been given as a guarantee for the authenticity of that book—were compelled to recognize it as a forgery.

This forgery, however, was not the only thing of the kind of which the police was guilty. Two or three more cases of the sort came out during the trial. The documents stolen by Reuter were interpolated by the police so as to disfigure their meaning. A paper, containing some rabid nonsense, was written in a handwriting imitating that of Dr. Marx, and for a time it was pretended that it had been written by him, until at last the prosecution was obliged to acknowledge the forgery. But for every police infamy that was proved as such, there were five or six fresh ones brought forward, which could not, at the moment, be unveiled, the defense being taken by surprise, the proofs having to be got from London, and every correspondence of the counsel for the defense with the London Communist refugees being in open court treated as complicity in the alleged plot!

---

[a] Otto Saedt and August Seckendorf.— *Ed.*

That Greif and Fleury are what they are here represented to be has been stated by Mr. Stieber himself, in his evidence; as to Hirsch, he has before a London magistrate confessed that he forged the "Minute Book" by order and with the assistance of Fleury, and then made his escape from this country in order to evade a criminal prosecution.

The Government could stand few such branding disclosures as came to light during the trial. It had a jury such as the Rhenish Province had not yet seen. Six nobles, of the purest reactionist water, four Lords of Finance, two Government officials. These were not the men to look closely into the confused mass of evidence heaped before them during six weeks, when they heard it continually dinned into their ears that the defendants were the chiefs of a dreadful Communist conspiracy, got up in order to subvert everything sacred—property, family, religion, order, government and law! And yet, had not the Government, at the same time, brought it to the knowledge of the privileged classes, that an acquittal in this trial would be the signal for the suppression of the jury; and that it would be taken as a direct political demonstration—as a proof of the middle-class liberal opposition being ready to unite even with the most extreme revolutionists—the verdict would have been an acquittal. As it was, the retroactive application of the new Prussian code enabled the Government to have seven prisoners convicted, while four merely were acquitted, and those convicted were sentenced to imprisonment varying from three to six years,[262] as you have, doubtless, already stated at the time the news reached you.

Written about November 29, 1852

First published in the *New-York Daily Tribune*, No. 3645, December 22 and the *Semi-Weekly Tribune*, No. 791, December 24, 1852

Signed: *Karl Marx*

Reproduced from the *New-York Daily Tribune*

Karl Marx

**REVELATIONS
CONCERNING THE COMMUNIST TRIAL
IN COLOGNE** [263]

Written from the end of October to the beginning of December 1852

First published anonymously as a separate pamphlet: *Enthüllungen über den Kommunisten-Prozess zu Köln*, Basel, 1853

Printed according to the text of the 1875 edition checked with the 1853 and 1885 editions

Enthüllungen

über den

Kommunisten-Prozeß

zu Köln.

Basel,

Buchdruckerei von Chr. Krüsi.

1853.

Title-page of the first edition of Marx's work
Revelations Concerning the Communist Trial in Cologne

I

PRELIMINARIES

On May 10, 1851 Nothjung was arrested in Leipzig and Bürgers, Röser, Daniels, Becker and the others were arrested shortly after. The arrested men appeared before the Court of Assizes in Cologne on October 4, 1852 on a charge of "treasonable conspiracy" against the Prussian state. Thus the preliminary detention (in solitary confinement) had lasted a year and a half.

When Nothjung and Bürgers were arrested the police discovered copies of the *Manifesto of the Communist Party*,[a] the "Rules of the Communist League" (a communist propaganda society), two Addresses of the Central Authority of this League [b] as well as a number of addresses and other publications. A week after Nothjung's arrest had become public knowledge there were house-searches and arrests in Cologne. So if there had still been something to discover it would certainly have disappeared by then. And in fact the haul yielded only a few irrelevant letters. A year and a half later when the accused finally appeared before the jury, the *bona fide* material in the possession of the prosecution had not been augmented by a single document. Nevertheless as we are assured by the Public Prosecutor's office (represented by von Seckendorf and Saedt) all government departments of the Prussian state had undertaken the most strenuous and many-sided activity. What then had they been doing? *Nous verrons!*

The unusually long period of pre-trial detention was explained in the most ingenious way. At first it was claimed that the Saxon government refused to extradite Bürgers and Nothjung to Prussia.

---

[a] See present edition, Vol. 6, pp. 477-519.— *Ed.*
[b] See present edition, Vol. 10, pp. 277-87, 371-77.— *Ed.*

The court in Cologne appealed in vain to the ministry in Berlin, which appealed in vain to the authorities in Saxony. The Saxon authorities however relented. Bürgers and Nothjung were handed over. By October 1851 enough progress had been made at last for the files to be presented to the indictment board of the Cologne Court of Appeal. The board ruled that "there was no factual evidence of an indictable offence and ... the investigation must therefore start again from the beginning". Meanwhile the zeal of the courts had been kindled by a recently approved disciplinary law which enabled the Prussian government to dismiss any official of the judiciary who incurred its displeasure. Accordingly the case was dismissed on this occasion because there was no evidence of an indictable offence. At the following quarterly session of the assizes it had to be postponed because there was too much evidence. The mass of documents was said to be so huge that the prosecutor was unable to digest it. Gradually he did digest it, the bill of indictment was presented to the prisoners and the action was due to be heard on July 28. But in the meantime the great driving wheel of the government's case, Chief of Police Schulz, fell ill. The accused had to sit in gaol for another three months awaiting an improvement in Schulz's health. Fortunately Schulz died, the public became impatient and the government had to ring up the curtain.

Throughout this whole period the police authorities in Cologne, the police headquarters in Berlin and the Ministries of Justice and of the Interior had continually intervened in the investigations, just as Stieber, their worthy representative, was to intervene later on as witness in the public court proceedings in Cologne. The government succeeded in assembling a jury that is quite unprecedented in the annals of the Rhine Province. In addition to members of the upper bourgeoisie (Herstadt, Leiden, Joest), there were city patricians (von Bianca, vom Rath), country squires (Häbling von Lanzenauer, Freiherr von Fürstenberg, etc.), two Prussian government officials, one of them a royal chamberlain (von Münch-Bellinghausen) and finally a Prussian professor (Kräusler). Thus in this jury every one of the ruling classes in Germany was represented and only these classes were represented.

With this jury the Prussian government, it seems, could stop beating about the bush and make the case into a political trial pure and simple. The documents seized from Nothjung, Bürgers and the others and admitted by them to be genuine did not indeed prove the existence of a plot; in fact they did not prove the existence of any action provided for in the *Code pénal*.[264] But they showed conclusively the hostility of the accused to the existing government and the existing social order. However what the intelligence of the legislators had failed to achieve might well be made good by the conscience of the jury. Was it not a stratagem of the accused that they should have conducted their hostile activities directed against the existing social order in such a way that they did not violate any article of the Code? Does a disease cease to be infectious because it is not listed in the Police Medical Register? If the Prussian government had restricted itself to using the material actually available to prove the harmfulness of the accused and if the jury had confined itself to rendering them harmless by its verdict of guilty, who could censure either government or jury? Who indeed but the foolish dreamer who imagines that a Prussian government and the ruling classes in Prussia are strong enough to give even their opponents a free rein as long as they confine themselves to discussion and propaganda.

However the Prussian government had deprived itself of the opportunity of using this broad highway of political trials. Owing to the unusual delay in bringing the case before the court, the Ministry's direct intervention in the proceedings, the mysterious hints about unheard-of horrors, the rodomontade about a conspiracy ensnaring the whole of Europe and, finally, the signally brutal treatment of the prisoners, the trial was swollen into a *procès monstre*, the eyes of the European press were upon it and the curiosity and suspicions of the public were fully aroused. The Prussian government had put itself in a position in which for decency's sake the prosecution was simply obliged to produce evidence and the jury to demand it. The jury itself had to face another jury, the jury of public opinion.

To rectify its first blunder, the government was forced into a second one. The police, who had acted as examining magistrates during the preliminary investigation, had to appear as witnesses during the trial. By the side of the ordinary Public Prosecutor the government had to put an extraordinary one, beside the Public Prosecutor's office the police, beside a Saedt and Seckendorf a Stieber together with his Wermuth, his griffin Greif and his little Goldheim.[a] It was inevitable that yet another government department should intervene in court and, by virtue of the miraculous powers of the police, should continuously supply the facts whose shadows the legal prosecution had pursued in vain. The court was so thoroughly aware of the position that with the most laudable

---

[a] A play on the names of the three police agents: the word *Wermuth* means vermouth, wormwood and also bitterness; *Greif*—griffin, and *Goldheimchen* (diminutive of Goldheim)—golden cricket.— *Ed.*

resignation the President, the judge and the prosecutor abandoned their functions to Stieber the Police Superintendent and the witness and continually disappeared behind him. Before we proceed to elucidate these revelations made by the police, revelations which form the basis of the "indictable offence" that the indictment board was unable to discover, one more preliminary observation remains to be made.

It became evident from the papers seized from the accused, as well as from their own statements, that a German communist society had existed with a central authority originally based in London. On September 15, 1850, the Central Authority split. The majority—referred to in the indictment[a] as the "*Marx party*"—moved the seat of the Central Authority to Cologne. The minority, which was later expelled from the League by the group in Cologne, established itself as an independent central authority in London and founded a separate league[265] in London and on the continent. The indictment refers to this minority and its supporters as the "*Willich-Schapper party*".

Saedt-Seckendorf claim that the split in the London Central Authority had its origin solely in personal disagreements. Long before Saedt-Seckendorf the "chivalrous Willich" had spread the most vicious rumours among the London émigrés about the causes of the split and had found in Herr Arnold Ruge, that fifth wheel on the state coach of European Central Democracy,[266] and in others of the same sort, people who were willing to act as channels leading to the German and American press. The democrats realised that they could gain an easy victory over the Communists by making the "chivalrous Willich" the impromptu representative of the Communists. The "chivalrous Willich" for his part realised that the "Marx party" could not reveal the causes of the split without betraying the existence of a secret society in Germany and in particular exposing the Central Authority in Cologne to the paternal attention of the Prussian police. This situation no longer obtains and so we may cite a few passages from the minutes of the last session of the London Central Authority, dated September 15, 1850.[b]

In support of his motion calling for separation, Marx said inter alia the following which is given here verbatim:

"The point of view of the minority is dogmatic instead of critical, idealistic instead of materialistic. They regard not the real conditions

[a] "Königlicher Rheinischer Appellationsgerichtshof zu Köln. Anklageschrift gegen 1) Peter Gerhard Roeser, 2) Johann Heinrich Georg Bürgers, 3) Peter Nothjung u.a."—*Ed.*
[b] See present edition, Vol. 10, pp. 625-29.—*Ed.*

but a *mere effort of will* as the driving force of the revolution. Whereas we say to the workers: 'You will have to go through 15, 20, 50 years of civil wars and national struggles not only to bring about a change in society but also to change yourselves, and prepare yourselves for the exercise of political power', you say on the contrary: 'Either we seize power at once, or else we might as well just take to our beds.' Whereas we are at pains to show the German workers in particular how rudimentary the development of the German proletariat is, you appeal to the patriotic feelings and the class prejudice of the German artisans, flattering them in the grossest way possible, and this is a more popular method, of course. Just as the word '*people*' has been given an aura of sanctity by the democrats, so you have done the same for the word '*proletariat*'. Like the democrats you substitute the catchword of revolution for revolutionary development," etc., etc.

Herr Schapper's verbatim reply was as follows:

"I have voiced the opinion attacked here because I am in general an enthusiast in this matter. The question at issue is whether we ourselves chop off a few heads right at the start or whether it is our own heads that will fall." (Schapper even promised to lose his own head in a year, i.e. on September 15, 1851.) "In France the workers will come to power and thereby we in Germany too. Were this not the case I would indeed take to my bed; in that event I would be able to enjoy a different material position. If we come to power we can take such measures as are necessary to ensure the rule of the proletariat. I am a fanatical supporter of this view but the Central Authority favours the very opposite," etc., etc.

It is obvious that it was not for personal reasons that the Central Authority was divided. But it would be just as wrong to speak of a difference of principle. The Schapper-Willich party have never laid claim to the dignity of having their own ideas. Their own contribution is the peculiar misunderstanding of other people's ideas which they set up as dogmas and, reducing these to a phrase, they imagine to have made them their own. It would be no less incorrect to agree with the prosecution in describing the Willich-Schapper party as the "party of action", unless by action one understands indolence concealed behind beerhouse bluster, simulated conspiracies and meaningless pseudo-alliances.

II

THE DIETZ ARCHIVE

The document found in the possession of the accused, the *Manifesto of the Communist Party*, which had been printed before the February revolution and had been available from booksellers for some years, could neither in its form nor in its aims be the programme of a "plot". The confiscated *Addresses* of the Central Authority were concerned exclusively with the relations of the Communists to the future democratic government and therefore not to the government of Frederick William IV. Lastly, the "Rules" were indeed the rules of a secret propaganda society, but the *Code pénal* prescribes no penalties for secret societies. The ultimate aim of this propaganda is said to be the destruction of existing society; but the Prussian state has already perished once and could perish ten times more and indeed for good and all without the existing social order being even the slightest bit harmed. The Communists can help accelerate the dissolution of bourgeois society and yet leave the dissolution of the Prussian state in the hands of bourgeois society. If a man whose immediate aim was the overthrow of the Prussian state were to preach the destruction of the social order as a means to this end he would be like that deranged engineer who wished to blow up the whole planet in order to remove a rubbish-heap.

But if the final goal of the League is the *overthrowing of the social order*, the method by which this is to be achieved is necessarily that of *political revolution* and this entails the overthrow of the Prussian state, just as an earthquake entails the overthrow of a chicken-house. The accused, however, proceed in fact from the outrageous assumption that the present Prussian government would collapse without their having to lift a finger. They accordingly did not found a league to overturn the present government of Prussia, and were not guilty of any "treasonable conspiracy".

Has anyone ever accused the early Christians of aiming at the overthrow of some obscure Roman prefect? The Prussian political philosophers from Leibniz to Hegel have laboured to dethrone God, and if I dethrone God I also dethrone the king who reigns by the grace of God. But has anyone ever prosecuted them for *lèse-majesté* against the house of Hohenzollern?

From whatever angle one looked at it, when the *corpus delicti* was subjected to public scrutiny it vanished like a ghost. The complaint of the indictment board [a] that there was "*no indictable offence*" remained valid and the "*Marx* party" was spiteful enough to refrain from providing *one single iota for the indictment* during the whole year and a half of the preliminary investigation.

Such an embarrassing situation had to be remedied. The Willich-Schapper party, in conjunction with the police, remedied it.

---

[a] A pun in the original: *Klage des Anklagesenats* (*Klage* means complaint, accusation, indictment; *Anklagesenat*, indictment board).— *Ed.*

Let us see how Herr Stieber, the midwife of this party, introduces it into the trial in Cologne. (See Stieber's testimony in the sitting of October 18, 1852.[a])

While Stieber was in London in the spring of 1851, allegedly to protect the visitors to the Great Exhibition[267] from pilferers and thieves,[b] the Berlin police headquarters sent him a copy of the papers found in *Nothjung's* home.

> "*In particular,*" Stieber swore, "my attention was directed to the conspirators' archive which according to *papers found in Nothjung's home were in the possession of a certain Oswald Dietz in London and which would undoubtedly contain the whole correspondence of the League's members.*"

The conspirators' archive? The whole correspondence of the League's members? But Dietz was the secretary of the Willich-Schapper Central Authority. If the archive of a conspiracy was in his possession it was the archive of the Willich-Schapper conspiracy. If Dietz had correspondence belonging to the League it could only be the correspondence of the separate league that was hostile to the accused in Cologne. But even more became clear from the scrutiny of the documents found in Nothjung's home, namely that nothing in them points to the fact of Oswald Dietz being the keeper of an archive. Moreover, how should Nothjung, who was in Leipzig, know what was not even known to the "*Marx* party" in London?

Stieber could not say outright: Now note this, Gentlemen of the Jury! I have made amazing discoveries in London. Unfortunately they refer to a conspiracy with which the accused in Cologne have nothing to do and which it is not the task of the Cologne jury to judge, but which provided a pretext for keeping the accused in solitary confinement for one and a half years. Stieber could not say this. The intervention of Nothjung was indispensable to create even the semblance of a connection between the revelations and documents from London and the trial in Cologne.

Stieber then swore on oath that a man offered to buy the archive for cash from Oswald Dietz. The plain fact is that a certain Reuter, a Prussian police spy who has never belonged to a communist society, lived in the same house as Dietz and, during the latter's absence,

---

[a] The testimony of witnesses such as Stieber and other evidence produced during the Cologne trial is quoted by Marx from the minutes of the trial published in the *Kölnische Zeitung* between October 5 and November 13, 1852, under the heading "Assisen-Procedur gegen D. Herm. Becker und Genossen. Anklage wegen hochverrätherischen Complottes".— *Ed.*

[b] Poking fun at Stieber, Marx forms the words "Stiebern" and "Diebern" evidently derived from *Stieber*—which literally means retriever—and *Dieb*—thief.— *Ed.*

broke into his desk and stole his papers. That Herr Stieber paid him
for the theft is quite credible, but this would hardly have protected
Stieber from a journey to Van Diemen's Land [268] if the manoeuvre
had become public knowledge while he was in London.

On August 5, 1851, Stieber, who was in Berlin, received from
London the Dietz archive, "in a bulky parcel wrapped in stout
oil-cloth", which turned out to be a heap of documents consisting of
"60 separate items". To this Stieber could swear, and at the same
time he swore that the parcel he received on August 5, 1851
contained also letters from the leading district in Berlin dated
August 20, 1851. If someone were to assert that Stieber was
perjuring himself when he claimed that he received on August 5,
1851 letters dated August 20, 1851, Stieber would justly retort that a
royal Prussian counsellor, like the Evangelist Matthew, has the right
to perform chronological miracles.

En passant. From the list of documents stolen from the Willich-
Schapper party and from the dates of these documents it follows that
although the party had been warned by Reuter's burglary, it still
constantly found ways and means of having its documents stolen and
allowing them to fall into the hands of the Prussian police.

When Stieber found himself in possession of the treasure
wrapped in stout oil-cloth he was beside himself with joy. "The
whole network," he swore, "lay revealed before my eyes." And
what did the treasure-trove contain about the "Marx party" and
the accused in Cologne? According to Stieber's own testimony,
nothing at all except for

"the original of a declaration by several members of the Central Authority, who
obviously formed the nucleus of the 'Marx party'; it was dated London, September 17,
1850, and concerned their resignation from the communist society consequent on the
well-known breach of September 15, 1850".

Stieber says so himself but even in this simple statement he is
unable simply to confine himself to the facts. He is compelled to
raise them to a higher plane in order to make them truly worthy
of the police. For the original declaration[a] contained nothing more
than a statement of three lines to the effect that the majority-
members of the former Central Authority and their friends were
resigning from the *public Workers' Society* of Great Windmill
Street [269]; but they did not resign from a "*communist society*".

Stieber could have spared his correspondents the oil-cloth and
his authorities the postal dues. He had only to rummage[b] through

---

    [a] See present edition, Vol. 10, p. 483.— *Ed.*
    [b] Here Marx plays on the name *Stieber* and the verb *durchstiebern*, which means
rummage, scan, search.— *Ed.*

the various German papers of September 1850 and he would have found in black and white the declaration of the "nucleus of the Marx party" announcing their resignation from the Refugee Committee[270] and also from the Workers' Society of Great Windmill Street.

The immediate product of Stieber's researches was then the amazing discovery that the "nucleus of the Marx party" had resigned from the public Society of Great Windmill Street on September 17, 1850. "The whole network of the Cologne plot lay revealed before his eyes." But the public couldn't believe their eyes.[a]

III
THE CHERVAL PLOT

Stieber, however, was able to make the most of his stolen treasure-trove. The papers that had come into his possession on August 5, 1851, led to the discovery of the so-called "Franco-German plot in Paris".[271] They contained six reports sent from Paris by *Adolph Majer*, an emissary of Willich-Schapper, as well as five reports from the leading district in Paris to the Willich-Schapper Central Authority. (Stieber's testimony in the sitting of October 18.) Stieber then went on a diplomatic pleasure trip to Paris and there he made the personal acquaintance of the great Carlier who in the recent notorious affair of the Gold Bullion Lottery[b] had just delivered proof that though a great enemy of the Communists, he was an even greater friend of other people's private property.

"Accordingly I went to Paris in September 1851. Carlier, the Prefect of Police there at the time, was most eager and ready to lend me his support.... With the aid of French police agents the threads laid bare in the London letters were speedily and surely traced; we were able to track down the addresses of the various leaders of the conspiracy and to keep all their movements, and especially all their meetings and correspondence, under observation. Some very sinister things came to light.... I was compelled to yield to Prefect Carlier's demands and measures were taken during the night of September 4, 1851." (Stieber's testimony of October 18.)

Stieber left Berlin in September. Let us assume it was September 1. At best he could have arrived in Paris on the evening of the

---

[a] In the German the last sentence has a dual meaning, either "The public, however, couldn't believe his [i.e. Stieber's] eyes" or "The public, however, couldn't believe their eyes".— *Ed.*

[b] See this volume, pp. 156-57.— *Ed.*

2nd. On the night of the 4th measures were taken. Thirty-six hours remain then for the conference with Carlier and for the necessary steps to be taken. In these thirty-six hours not only were the addresses of the various leaders "tracked down"; but *all* their movements, *all* their meetings and *all* their correspondence were "kept under observation", that is of course after their "addresses had been tracked down". Stieber's arrival not only inspires the "French police agents" with a miraculous "speed and sureness", it also makes the conspiratorial leaders "eager and ready" to perpetrate so many movements, meetings and so much correspondence within twenty-four hours that already the following evening measures can be taken against them.

But it is not enough that on September 3 the addresses of the individual leaders should have been traced and all their movements, meetings and correspondence put under observation:

"French police agents," Stieber swears, "found an opportunity to be present at the meetings of the conspirators and to hear their decisions about the plan of campaign for the next revolution."

No sooner have the police agents observed the meetings than the observation gives them an opportunity to be present, and no sooner have they been present at one meeting than it becomes several meetings, and no sooner has it become several meetings than decisions are adopted about the plan of campaign during the next revolution—and all this on the same day. On that very same day when Stieber first meets Carlier, Carlier's police discover the addresses of the various leaders, the various leaders meet Carlier's police, invite them to their meetings that very day, hold a whole series of meetings on the same day for their benefit and cannot part from them without hastily adopting decisions on the plan of campaign for the next revolution.

However eager and ready Carlier might be—and no one will doubt his readiness to uncover a communist plot three months before the coup d'état—Stieber ascribes more to him than he could achieve. Stieber asks miracles of the police; he does not merely ask for them, he believes them; he does not merely believe them, he swears to them on oath.[a]

"At the beginning of this venture, i.e. the taking of measures, first of all a French police inspector and I personally arrested the dangerous Cherval, the ringleader of the French Communists. He resisted vigorously and a stubborn struggle ensued."

---

[a] A pun: Marx has *er beschwört sie*, which can mean "he swears to them on oath" or "he invokes, or entreats, them".— *Ed.*

Thus Stieber's testimony of October 18.

"Cherval made an attempt on my life in Paris, in my own home where he had broken in during the night. In the course of the ensuing struggle my wife, who came to my aid, was wounded."

Thus Stieber's further testimony of October 27.

On the night of the 4th, Stieber intervenes at Cherval's dwelling and it comes to fisticuffs in which Cherval resists. On the night of the 3rd, Cherval intervenes at Stieber's dwelling and it comes to fisticuffs in which Stieber resists. But it was precisely on the 3rd that a veritable *entente cordiale* obtained between conspirators and police agents as a result of which so many great deeds were performed in one day. It is now alleged that not only the conspirators were found out by Stieber on the 3rd, but Stieber too was found out on the 3rd by the conspirators. While Carlier's agents discovered the addresses of the conspirators, the conspirators discovered Stieber's address. While he played the role of an "observer" towards them, they pursued an active role towards him. While he was dreaming about their plot against the government, they were engaged in an assault on his person.

Stieber's testimony of October 18 continues:

"In the course of the struggle" (this is Stieber on the attack) "I observed that Cherval was endeavouring to put a piece of paper into his mouth and swallow it. Only with great difficulty was it possible to retrieve one half of the paper, the other half being already devoured."

So the paper was situated in Cherval's mouth, between his teeth in fact, for only one half was retrieved, the other half having already been devoured. Stieber and his henchman, a police inspector or whoever, could only retrieve the other half by placing their hands in the jaws of the "dangerous Cherval". Against such an onslaught *biting* was the most obvious method of defence that Cherval could adopt, and the Paris papers actually reported that Cherval had bitten Frau Stieber; in that scene however Stieber was assisted not by his wife but by the police inspector. On the other hand, Stieber declares that when Cherval assaulted him in his own home, it was Frau Stieber who had been wounded while coming to his aid. If one compares Stieber's statements with the reports of the Paris papers it would appear that on the night of the 3rd Cherval bit Frau Stieber in an attempt to save the papers that Herr Stieber tore from between his teeth on the night of the 4th. Stieber will retort that Paris is a city of miracles and that long before him La Rochefoucauld had said that in France everything is possible.[272]

Putting the belief in miracles to one side for a moment it seems that the first miracles arose because Stieber compressed into *one* day, September 3, a whole series of events that were in reality spread over a long period of time, while the latter miracles arose when he claimed of different events that happened in one place and on one evening that they occurred in two places on two eyenings. Let us confront his tale from *A Thousand and One Nights* with the actual facts. But first one very strange fact, though by no means a miracle.[a] Stieber tore from Cherval one half of the paper that had been swallowed. What was in the retrieved half? The whole that Stieber wanted.

"This paper," he swears, "contained a vital instruction for Gipperich, the emissary in Strasbourg, together with his *complete address.*"

Now for the facts of the matter.

We know from Stieber that he received the Dietz archive in a stout oil-cloth wrapping on August 5, 1851. On August 8 or 9, 1851, a certain Schmidt arrived in Paris. Schmidt, it seems, is the name inevitably assumed by Prussian police agents travelling incognito. In 1845-46 Stieber travelled through the Silesian Mountains under the name of Schmidt. *Fleury*, his London agent, went as Schmidt to Paris in 1851. Here he searched for the various leaders of the Willich-Schapper conspiracy and lit upon Cherval. He pretended that he had fled from Cologne rescuing the League's cash-box with 500 talers. He produced credentials from Dresden and various other places and spoke about reorganising the League, uniting the different parties, as the schisms were caused solely by personal disagreements (the police preached unity and union even then), and promised to use the 500 talers to inject fresh life into the League. Schmidt gradually made the acquaintance of various leaders of the Willich-Schapper communities in Paris. He not only learned their addresses, but visited them, watched their post, observed their movements, found his way into their meetings and, as an *agent provocateur*, egged them on. Cherval in particular became more boastful than ever as Schmidt lavished more and more admiration on him, hailing him as the League's great unknown, as the "Great Chief" who was only unaware of his own importance, a fate that had befallen many a great man. One evening when Schmidt went with Cherval to a meeting of the League, the latter read out his famous letter to

---

[a] Here Marx plays on the words *verwunderlich*—strange, surprising, amazing, and *Wunder*—wonder, miracle.— *Ed.*

Gipperich before sending it off. In this way Schmidt learned of Gipperich's existence. "As soon as Gipperich returns to Strasbourg," Schmidt observed, "we can give him an order for the 500 talers lying in Strasbourg. Here is the address of the man who is holding the money. Give me in exchange Gipperich's address to send it as a credential to the man to whom Gipperich will present himself." In this way Schmidt obtained Gipperich's address. On the same evening a quarter of an hour after Cherval posted the letter to Gipperich, a message was sent by electric telegraph and Gipperich was arrested, his house was searched and the famous letter was intercepted. Gipperich was *arrested before Cherval.*

Some little while after this Schmidt informed Cherval that a man called Stieber who was a member of the Prussian police had arrived in Paris. He had not only learned his address but had also heard from a waiter in a café opposite that Stieber had conferred about having him (Schmidt) arrested. Cherval was the man who could give this wretched Prussian policeman a lesson he would not easily forget. "We'll throw him in the Seine" was Cherval's answer. They agreed to gain entry into Stieber's house the next day under some pretext or other in order to confirm that he was there and to make a mental note of his personal appearance. The next evening our heroes really set out on their expedition. As they approached their goal Schmidt expressed the opinion that it would be better if Cherval were to enter the house while he patrolled in front of it. "Just ask the porter for Stieber," he went on, "and when Stieber lets you in tell him that you want to speak to Herr Sperling and ask him whether he has brought the expected bill of exchange from Cologne. Oh, and one thing more. Your white hat is too conspicuous, it is too democratic. There, take my black one." They exchanged hats, Schmidt prepared to stand guard, Cherval pulled the bell-rope and found himself in Stieber's house. The porter doubted whether Stieber was at home and Cherval was about to withdraw when a woman's voice called from upstairs: "Yes, Stieber is at home." Cherval followed the voice and the trail led to an individual wearing green spectacles who identified himself as Stieber. Cherval then produced the formula agreed on about Sperling and the bill of exchange. "That won't do," Stieber interrupted him quickly. "You come into my house, ask for me, are shown up, then you try to withdraw, etc. I find that is extremely suspicious." Cherval answered brusquely. Stieber pulled the bell, several men appeared immediately, they surrounded Cherval, Stieber reached for his coat pocket from where a letter was visible. It did not in fact contain Cherval's instructions to

Gipperich, but it was a letter from Gipperich to Cherval. Cherval tried to eat the letter, Stieber attempted to take it from his mouth, Cherval hit out and bit and lashed out. Husband Stieber tried to save one half, wife Stieber the other half and an injury was all the reward she had for her zeal. The noise of the scene brought all the other tenants from their apartments. Meanwhile one of Stieber's types had thrown a gold watch downstairs and while Cherval was shouting: "Spy!" Stieber and Co. screamed: "Stop thief!" The porter recovered the gold watch and the cry of "Stop thief!" became general. Cherval was arrested and on his way out he was met at the door not by his friend Schmidt but by four or five soldiers.

When confronted with the facts, all the miracles invoked[a] by Stieber disappear. His agent Fleury had been at work for over three weeks, he not only laid bare the threads of the plot, he also helped to weave them. Stieber had only to arrive from Berlin and he could exclaim: Veni, vidi, vici![b] He could present Carlier with a ready-made plot and Carlier needed only to be "willing" to intervene. There was no need for Frau Stieber to be bitten by Cherval on the 3rd because Herr Stieber put his hand into Cherval's mouth on the 4th. There was no need for Gipperich's address and the appropriate instructions to be salvaged whole from the jaws of the "dangerous Cherval", like Jonah from the whale's belly,[c] after they have been half eaten. The only miracle that remains is the miraculous faith of the jurymen to whom Stieber dares to serve up seriously such fairy tales. Genuine representatives of the obtuse thinking of loyal subjects![273]

"In prison, after I had shown Cherval to his great astonishment," Stieber swears (in the sitting of October 18), "all his original reports which he had sent to London, he realised that I knew all and made a frank confession to me."

The papers that Stieber showed Cherval at first were by no means his original reports to London. Only afterwards were these together with other documents from the Dietz archive sent to Stieber from Berlin. He first showed Cherval a circular signed by Oswald Dietz that Cherval had just received and a few of the most recent letters from Willich. How did Stieber get possession of these? While Cherval was occupied biting and fighting Herr and Frau Stieber the valiant Schmidt-Fleury hurried to Mme Cherval,

---

[a] A pun: *beschworenen* can mean both "invoked" and "sworn to".— *Ed.*

[b] "I came, I saw, I conquered" thus, according to Plutarch, Caesar announced his victory at Zela, on August 2, 47 B.C. over Pharnaces II, King of Bosporus.— *Ed.*

[c] Jonah 2:10.— *Ed.*

an Englishwoman (Fleury being a German businessman in London naturally speaks English) and told her that her husband had been arrested, that the danger was great, that she should hand over his papers so that he might be compromised no further, and that Cherval had instructed him to give them to a third person. As proof that he came as a genuine emissary he showed her the white hat he had taken from Cherval because it looked too democratic. Thus Fleury obtained the letters from Mme Cherval and Stieber obtained them from Fleury.

At any rate he now had a more favourable base from which to operate than previously in London. He could simply steal the Dietz archive, but he could concoct Cherval's evidence. Accordingly (in the sitting on October 18) he makes his Cherval expatiate about "contacts in Germany" as follows:

"He had lived in the Rhineland for a considerable time and more particularly he had been in Cologne in 1848. There he made the acquaintance of Marx and the latter admitted him to the League, which he then zealously propagated in Paris on the basis of elements already existing there."

In 1846 Cherval was nominated and admitted to the League in London by Schapper at a time when Marx was in Brussels and was himself not yet a member of the League.[274] So Cherval could not be admitted to the same League by Marx in Cologne in 1848.

On the outbreak of the March revolution Cherval went to Rhenish Prussia for a few weeks but from there returned to London where he remained without interruption from the end of spring 1848 until the summer of 1850. He cannot therefore at the same time "have zealously propagated the League in Paris" unless Stieber, who performs chronological miracles, also finds *spatial* miracles within his powers and can even confer the quality of ubiquity on third persons.

Only after his expulsion from Paris did Marx come to know Cherval superficially along with a hundred other workers when he joined the Workers' Society in Great Windmill Street in London in September 1849. So he cannot have met him in Cologne in 1848.

At first Cherval told Stieber the truth on all these points. Stieber tried to compel him to make false statements. Did he succeed? We have only Stieber's testimony that he did, and that is a shortcoming. Stieber's prime concern was, of course, to establish a fictitious connection between Cherval and Marx so as to establish an artificial connection between the accused in Cologne and the Paris plot.

Whenever Stieber is required to go into details about the connections and correspondence of Cherval and his colleagues with Germany, he takes good care not even to mention Cologne and instead speaks complacently and at length of Heck in Brunswick, Laube in Berlin, Reininger in Mainz, Tietz in Hamburg, etc., etc., in short of the Willich-Schapper party. This party, says Stieber, had "the League's archive in its hands".—Through a misunderstanding it changed from their hands to his. In the archive he found *not one single* line written by Cherval to anyone in London, let alone to Marx in person, before September 15, 1850, *before the split* of the London Central Authority.

With the help of Schmidt-Fleury he swindled Frau Cherval out of her husband's papers. But again, he could not find a single line written by Marx to Cherval. To remedy this awkward state of affairs he makes Cherval write in his statement that

"he had fallen out with Marx because the latter had demanded that correspondence should *still* be sent to him even though the Central Authority was now situated in Cologne."

If Stieber found no Marx-Cherval correspondence *before* September 15, 1850, this must be due to the fact that Cherval ceased all correspondence with Marx *after* September 15, 1850. *Pends-toi, Figaro, tu n'aurais pas inventé cela!*[a]

The documents against the accused that had been laboriously brought together by the Prussian government and, in part, by Stieber himself during the year and a half that the investigation lasted refuted every suggestion of a connection between the accused and the Paris community or the Franco-German plot.

The Address from the London Central Authority of June 1850 proved that the Paris community was dissolved even before the split in the Central Authority. Six letters from the Dietz archive showed that after the Central Authority was transferred to Cologne the Paris communities were set up afresh by A. Majer, an emissary of the Willich-Schapper party. The letters of the leading district in Paris that were found in the archive proved that it was decidedly hostile towards the Cologne Central Authority. Finally, the French bill of indictment[b] proved that all the acts Cherval and his associates were accused of did not occur until the year 1851. In

---

[a] Hang yourself, Figaro, that's a thing you wouldn't have invented (Beaumarchais, *La folle journée, ou le mariage de Figaro*, Act V, Scene 8—paraphrased).— *Ed.*

[b] A resumé of it was published in *Le Moniteur universel*, No. 58, February 27, 1852.— *Ed.*

the sitting of November 8 Saedt, despite the Stieberian revelations, found himself therefore reduced to the bare supposition that it was surely not impossible that the Marx party had at some time somehow been involved in some plot or other in Paris but that nothing was known of this plot or the time when it took place other than the fact that Saedt, acting on official instructions, deemed it possible. How dull-witted the German press must be to go on inventing stories of Saedt's incisive intelligence!

De longue main[a] the Prussian police had sought to persuade the public that Marx and, through Marx, the accused in Cologne were involved in the Franco-German plot. During the Cherval trial Beckmann, the police spy, sent the following notice from Paris to the *Kölnische Zeitung* on February 25, 1852:

"Several of the accused have fled, among them a certain A. Majer, who is described as an agent of *Marx and Co.*"

Whereupon the *Kölnische Zeitung* printed a statement by Marx that "A. Majer is one of the most intimate friends of Herr Schapper and the former Prussian lieutenant Willich, and that he is a complete stranger to Marx".[b] Then, in his testimony of October 18, 1852, Stieber himself admitted:

"The members of the Central Authority expelled by the Marx party in London on September 15, 1850, sent A. Majer to France, etc."

and he even divulged the contents of the correspondence between A. Majer and Willich-Schapper.

In September 1851 during the police campaign against aliens in Paris a member of the "Marx party", *Konrad Schramm,* was arrested, together with 50 or 60 other people sitting in a café, and was detained for almost two months on the charge of being implicated in the plot instigated by the Irishman Cherval. On October 16 while still in the depot of the Prefecture of Police he received a visit from a German who addressed him as follows:

"I am a Prussian official. You are aware that all over Germany and especially in Cologne there have been many arrests following the discovery of a communist society. The mere mention of a person's name in a letter is enough to bring about his arrest. The government is somewhat embarrassed by the large number of prisoners of whom it is uncertain whether or not they are really implicated. *We know that you had no part in the* complot franco-allemand *but on the other hand you are very closely acquainted with Marx and Engels and are doubtless very well informed about all the details of the German communist connections.* We would be greatly indebted to you if you could help us in this respect and give us more detailed information as to

---

[a] For a long time.— *Ed.*
[b] See this volume, p. 223.— *Ed.*

who is guilty and who innocent. In this way you could bring about the release of a large number of people. If you wish we can draw up an official document about your statement. You will have nothing to fear from such a statement," etc., etc.

Schramm naturally showed this gentle Prussian official the door, protested to the French Ministry about such visits and was expelled from France at the end of October.

That Schramm was a member of the "Marx party" was known to the Prussian police from the official resignation found in the Dietz archive. That the "Marx party" had no connection with the Cherval plot, they themselves admitted to Schramm. If it was possible to establish a connection between the "Marx party" and the Cherval plot this could not be done in Cologne but only in Paris where a member of that party sat in gaol at the same time as Cherval. But the Prussian government feared nothing more than a confrontation of Cherval and Schramm, which was bound to nullify in advance the successful outcome they expected from the Paris trial with regard to the accused in Cologne. By his acquittal of Schramm the French examining magistrate ruled that the trial in Cologne was in no way connected with the Paris plot.

Stieber then made a last attempt:

"With reference to the above-mentioned leader of the French Communists, Cherval, we endeavoured, for a long time in vain, to discover Cherval's true identity. It finally became clear from a remark made in confidence to a police agent by Marx that he had escaped from gaol in Aachen in 1845, where he was serving a sentence for forgery of bills, that he was then granted admittance to the League by Marx during the troubles of 1848 and that he went as an emissary from there to Paris."

Just as Marx was unable to inform Stieber's *spiritus familiaris*,[a] the police agent, that he had admitted Cherval into the League in Cologne in 1848, for Schapper had admitted him into the League in London as early as 1846, or that he had induced him to live in London and at the same time to hawk propaganda around in Paris, so too, he was unable to inform Stieber's *alter ego*, the police agent as such, that Cherval served a sentence in Aachen in 1845 and that he had forged bills, facts that he learnt only from Stieber's testimony. Only a Stieber can allow himself such a *hysteron proteron*.[b] Antiquity has bequeathed to us its *dying warrior*[275]; the Prussian state will leave us its *swearing Stieber*.

Thus for a long, long time they had vainly endeavoured to

---

[a] Familiar spirit—a supernatural being which serves an individual.— *Ed.*

[b] Inversion of the natural order, figure of speech in which what should come last (*hysteron*) is put first (*proteron*).— *Ed.*

discover Cherval's true identity. On the evening of September 2 Stieber arrived in Paris. On the evening of the 4th Cherval was arrested, on the evening of the 5th he was taken from his cell to a dimly lit room. Stieber was there but in addition there was also a French police official present, an Alsatian who spoke broken German but understood it perfectly, had a policeman's memory and was not favourably impressed by the arrogantly servile Police Superintendent from Berlin. In the presence of this French official the following conversation took place:

> *Stieber* in German: "Now look here, Herr Cherval, we know what's at the bottom of this business with the French name and the Irish passport. We know who you are, you are a Rhenish Prussian. Your name is K. and it is entirely in your own hands to escape the consequences by making a full confession," etc., etc.
>
> Cherval denied this.
>
> *Stieber*: "Certain people who forged bills and escaped from Prussian gaols were extradited to Prussia by the French authorities. So I would again urge you to think carefully; the penalty is twelve years solitary confinement."
>
> *The French police official*: "We must give the man time to think it over in his cell."

Cherval was led back to his cell.

Naturally enough Stieber could not afford to blurt out the truth, he could not admit publicly that he was trying to force false admissions from Cherval by conjuring up the spectre of extradition and twelve years solitary imprisonment.

And even now Stieber had still not been able to discover Cherval's true identity. He still referred to him in front of the jury as Cherval and not as K. And that was not all. He did not know where Cherval really was. In the sitting of October 23 he had him still locked up in Paris. When in the sitting on October 27 Schneider II, counsel for the defence, pressed him to say "whether the afore-mentioned Cherval was at present in London?" Stieber answered that "he could not give any precise information on this point; and could only inform them of the rumour that Cherval had escaped in Paris".

The Prussian government suffered its customary fate of being duped. The French government had allowed it to pull the chestnuts of the Franco-German plot out of the fire but not to eat them. Cherval had managed to gain the sympathy of the French government and a few days after the Paris Assizes it let him and Gipperich flee to London. The Prussian government had hoped that in Cherval it would have a tool for the trial in Cologne, whereas in fact it only provided the French government with yet another agent.[276]

One day before Cherval's pretended flight he received a visit from a Prussian *faquin*[a] dressed in a black tail-coat and cuffs, with a bristling black moustache, and sparse grey hair cut short, in a word, a very pretty fellow who, he was told later, was Police Lieutenant Greif and who indeed afterwards introduced himself as Greif. Greif had obtained access to him by means of an entrance ticket he had obtained (having by-passed the prefect of police) directly from the Minister of Police. The Minister of Police thought it great fun to deceive the dear Prussians.

> *Greif*: "I am a Prussian official. I have been sent here to negotiate with you. You will never get out of here without our aid. I have a proposal to make to you. We need you as a witness in Cologne. If you submit a request to the French government to hand you over to Prussia they have agreed to grant permission. After you have fulfilled your obligations and the case is over we shall release you on your word of honour."
>
> *Cherval*: "I'll get out without your help."
>
> *Greif* (emphatically): "That is impossible!"

Greif also had Gipperich brought to him and proposed that he should spend five days in Hanover as a communist emissary. Likewise without success. The next day Cherval and Gipperich escaped. The French authorities smirked, the telegraph brought the bad news to Berlin and as late as October 23 Stieber swore in court that Cherval was locked up in Paris, and as late as October 27 he could not give any information and had merely heard the rumour that Cherval had escaped "in Paris". Meanwhile, Police Lieutenant Greif had visited Cherval in London three times during the Cologne proceedings in order to discover, among other things, Nette's address in Paris in the belief that he could be bribed to testify against the defendants in Cologne. This plan misfired.

Stieber had his reasons for casting a veil of obscurity over his relations with Cherval. K. therefore remained Cherval, the Prussian remained Irish and Stieber does not know to this day where Cherval is and what is "his true identity".*

* Even in the *Black Book*[277] Stieber still does not know who Cherval really is. It is written there, Part II, p. 38, under No. 111, Cherval: see Crämer; and under No. 116 Crämer: "as stated in No. 111, he has been very active in the Communist League under the name of Cherval. In the League he is also known as Frank. Under the name of Cherval he was sentenced to 8 years imprisonment by the Paris Assizes in February 1853" (this should read 1852) "but he soon escaped and fled to London." So ignorant is Stieber in Part II where he provides an alphabetical, numbered list of suspects with their particulars. He has already forgotten that in Part I, p. 81 he has let slip the admission: "Cherval is the son of a Rhenish official called Joseph Krämer who" (who? the father or the son?) "abused his craft of lithography to forge bills, and was arrested for this but escaped from prison in Cologne" (false, it was Aachen!) "in 1844 and fled

---

[a] Scoundrel.— *Ed.*

In Cherval's correspondence with Gipperich the trifolium Se-ckendorf-Saedt-Stieber had at last found what it was looking for:

Schinderhannes [a], Karlo Moor
Whom I took as model sure. [b]

In order that Cherval's letter to Gipperich might be deeply engraved upon the lethargic cerebral matter of the 300 top tax-payers whom the jury represented, it received the honour of being read aloud three times. Behind this harmless gipsy pathos no experienced person could fail to see the figure of the buffoon who tries to appear terrifying both to himself and others.

Cherval & Co., moreover, shared the general expectation of the democrats that the second [Sunday] of May 1852 [278] would work miracles and so they decided to join the revolution on that day. Schmidt-Fleury had helped to bestow upon this fixed idea the form of a plan and so the activities of Cherval and Co. now came within the legal definition of a plot. Thus through them proof was provided that the plot that had not been perpetrated by the accused in Cologne against the Prussian government had at any rate been perpetrated by the Cherval party against France.

With the help of Schmidt-Fleury the Prussian government had sought to fabricate the semblance of a connection between the plot in Paris and the accused in Cologne, a connection to the reality of which Stieber then swore on oath. This trinity of Stieber, Greif, Fleury played the chief role in the Cherval plot. We shall see them at work again.

Let us then sum up:

A is a republican, B also calls himself a republican. A and B are enemies. B is commissioned by the police to construct an infernal machine. Whereupon A is dragged before the courts. If B rather than A has built the machine this is due to the enmity between A and B. In order to find proof of A's guilt B is called as a witness against him. This was the comedy of the Cherval plot.

It will be readily understood that as far as the general public was concerned the logic of this was a flop. Stieber's "factual" revelations dissolved amidst malodorous vapours; the complaint of the indictment board that "there was no factual evidence of an indictable offence" was as valid as ever. New police miracles had become necessary.

to England and later to Paris."—Compare this with Stieber's evidence before the jury quoted above. The plain fact is that the police are absolutely incapable of telling the truth. [Note by Engels to the edition of 1885.]

---

[a] Jack the Skinner, a name given to Johann Bückler, a German robber.— Ed.
[b] Heinrich Heine, "Ich kam von meiner Herrin Haus" (Buch der Lieder).— Ed.

IV

THE ORIGINAL MINUTE-BOOK

During the sitting on October 23, the Presiding Judge[a] announced: "Police Superintendent Stieber has indicated to me that he has to make important new depositions" and for that purpose he called this witness back into the box. Up jumped Stieber and the performance began.

Hitherto Stieber had described the activities of the Willich-Schapper party, or more briefly, the Cherval party, activities that took place both *before* and *after* the arrest of the accused in Cologne. He said nothing about the accused themselves either *before* or *after* their arrest. The Cherval plot took place *after* their arrest and Stieber now declared:

"In my earlier testimony I described the development of the Communist League and the activities of its members only *up to the time* when the men now accused *were arrested.*"

Thus he admitted that the Cherval plot had nothing to do with "the development of the Communist League and the activities of its members". He confessed to the *nullity* of his previous testimony. Indeed, he was so complacent about his statements on October 18 that he regarded it as quite superfluous to continue to identify Cherval with the "Marx party".

"Firstly," he said, "the Willich group still exists and of its members hitherto only Cherval in Paris has been seized, etc."

Aha! So the ringleader Cherval is a leader of the Willich group.

But now Stieber wished to make some *most important* announcements, not merely the *very latest* announcements that is, but the *most important* ones. The very latest and most important ones! These most important announcements would lose some of their significance if the insignificance of his earlier announcements were not emphasised. Up to now, Stieber declared, I have not really said anything, but now the time has come. Pay attention! Hitherto I have talked about the Cherval party, which is hostile to the accused, and strictly speaking, none of that has been in place here. But now I shall discuss the "Marx party", and this trial is concerned exclusively with the Marx party. But Stieber could not put the matter as plainly as this. So he says:

"Up to now I have described the Communist League *before* the arrest of the accused; I shall now describe the League *after* their arrest."

___
[a] Göbel.— *Ed.*

With characteristic virtuosity he manages to convert even mere rhetorical phrases into perjury.

After the arrest of the accused in Cologne Marx formed a new central authority.

"This emerges from the statement of a police agent whom the late Chief of Police Schulz had managed to smuggle unrecognised into the London League and into the immediate proximity of Marx."

The new central authority kept a minute-book and this, the "*original minute-book*", was now in Stieber's possession. Horrifying machinations in the Rhine provinces, in Cologne and even in the courtroom itself, all this is proved by the original minute-book. It contains proof that the accused had maintained an uninterrupted correspondence with Marx through the very walls of the prison. In a word, if the Dietz archive was the Old Testament, the original minute-book is the New Testament. The Old Testament was wrapped in stout oil-cloth, but the New Testament is bound in a sinister red morocco leather. Now the red morocco is indeed a *demonstratio ad oculos*,[a] but people today are even more sceptical than in Thomas' time; they do not even believe what they see with their own eyes. Who still believes in Testaments, let them be Old or New, now that the religion of the Mormons[279] has been invented? But Stieber, who is not wholly unsympathetic to Mormonism, has foreseen even this.[b]

"It might be objected," Stieber the Mormon observed, "that these are nothing but the tales of contemptible police agents but," Stieber swore, "I have complete proofs of the veracity and reliability of their reports."

Just listen to that! Proofs of their veracity and proofs of their reliability! and complete proofs at that. *Complete* proofs! And what are these proofs?

Stieber had long known

"that a secret correspondence existed between Marx and the accused men in the gaol, but had been unable to track it down. Then on *the previous Sunday a special courier from London* arrived bringing me the news that we had finally managed to discover the secret address from which the correspondence had been conducted. It was the address of D. Kothes, a businessman in the Old Market here. The same courier brought me the original minute-book used by the London Central Authority which had been procured from a member of the League for money."

Stieber then communicated with Chief of Police Geiger and the postal authorities.

---

[a] Visual proof.— *Ed.*

[b] This sentence is omitted in the 1853 Basle edition; it occurs in the 1853 Boston edition and in the 1875 and 1885 editions.— *Ed.*

Karl Marx

"The necessary precautionary measures were taken and *after no more than two days* the evening post from London brought with it a letter addressed to Kothes. *On the instructions of the Chief Public Prosecutor* the letter was detained and opened and in it was found a seven-page-long briefing for Schneider II, the Counsel for the Defence, in Marx's own handwriting. It indicated the method of defence that Counsel should adopt.... On the reverse side of the letter there was a large Latin B. The letter was copied and an easily detachable piece of the original was retained together with the *original envelope.* The letter was then put into a new envelope, sealed and given to a police officer from another town with the order that he should go to Kothes, and introduce himself as an emissary from Marx," etc.

Stieber then narrated the rest of the disgusting farce enacted by the police, about how the police officer from another town had pretended to be an emissary from Marx, etc. Kothes was arrested on October 18 and after 24 hours he declared that the B on the inside of the letter stood for Bermbach. On October 19 Bermbach was arrested and his house searched. On October 21 Kothes and Bermbach were released.

Stieber gave this evidence on Saturday, October 23. "*The previous Sunday*", that is Sunday, October 17, was allegedly the day the special courier arrived with Kothes' address and the original minute-book and two days after the courier, the letter arrived for Kothes, that is on October 19. But Kothes had already been arrested on October 18 because of the letter the police officer from another town had brought him on October 17. The letter to Kothes, therefore, arrived two days before the courier with Kothes' address, that is Kothes was arrested on October 18 for a letter that he did not receive until October 19. A chronological miracle?

Later, having been worried by Counsel, Stieber declared that the courier with Kothes' address and the original minute-book arrived on October 10. Why on October 10? Because October 10 happened to be likewise a Sunday and on October 23 it too would be a "previous" Sunday and in this way the original statement about the previous Sunday could be sustained and to this extent the perjury could be concealed. In that event, however, the letter did not arrive two days but a whole week after the courier. The perjury now fell on the letter rather than on the courier. Stieber's oath is like Luther's peasant. If you help him to mount the horse from one side he falls down on the other.[a]

And finally during the sitting of November 3 Police Lieutenant Goldheim of Berlin declared that Police Lieutenant Greif of London had delivered the minute-book to Stieber on October 11,

---

[a] M. Luther, *Der Welt Bild (Tischreden).*— *Ed.*

that is to say on a Monday, in his presence and that of Chief of Police Wermuth. Goldheim's statement therefore makes Stieber guilty of perjury twice over.

As the original envelope with the London postmark shows, Marx posted the letter to Kothes on Thursday, October 14. So the letter should have arrived on Friday evening, October 15. For a courier to deliver Kothes' address and the original minute-book two days before the letter arrived, he must have come on Wednesday, October 13. He could not arrive on October 17th, nor on the 10th nor on the 11th.

Greif, in his role of courier, did indeed bring Stieber his original minute-book from London. Stieber was as well aware as his crony Greif of the real significance of this book. He hesitated therefore to produce it in court for this time it was not a matter of statements taken behind prison bars in Mazas.[280] Then came the letter from Marx. It was a godsend for Stieber. Kothes is a mere address, for the contents of the letter were not intended for Kothes but for the Latin B on the back of the enclosed sealed letter. Kothes is therefore nothing but an address. Let us suppose he is a *secret* address. Let us suppose further he is the secret address through which Marx communicates with the accused in Cologne. Let us suppose lastly that our London agents had sent by the same courier at the same time both the original minute-book and this secret address but that the letter arrived two days after the courier, the address and the minute-book. In this way we kill two birds with one stone. Firstly we have proof of the secret correspondence with Marx and secondly we prove that the original minute-book is authentic. The authenticity of the minute-book is shown by the correctness of the address, the correctness of the address is shown by the letter. The veracity and reliability of our agents is shown by the address and the letter, the authenticity of the minute-book is shown by the veracity and reliability of our agents. *Quod erat demonstrandum.* Then comes the merry comedy with the police official from another town and then come the mysterious arrests. Public, jurymen and even the accused, all stand thunderstruck.

But why did not Stieber let his *special courier* arrive on October 13, which would have been quite easy for him? Because in that case he would not have been special, because, as we have seen, chronology was not his strong point and the common calendar is beneath the dignity of a Prussian police superintendent. Moreover, he kept the original envelope; so who would be able to unravel the affair?

But giving his evidence, Stieber compromised himself from the outset by the omission of one fact. If his agents knew of Kothes' address they would also know to whom the mysterious B referred on the reverse of the inside letter. Stieber was so little initiated into the mysteries of the Latin B that on October 17 he had Becker searched in gaol in the hope of finding the letter from Marx on him. He only learnt from Kothes' statement that the B stood for Bermbach.

But how did Marx's letter fall into the hands of the Prussian government? Very simply. The Prussian government regularly opens the letters entrusted to its postal service and during the trial in Cologne it did this with particular assiduity. In Aachen and Frankfurt am Main they could tell some pretty stories about it. It was a pure chance whether a letter would slip through or not.

When the story about the original courier collapsed, the one about the original minute-book had to share its fate. Naturally, Stieber did not yet suspect this in the sitting on October 23 when he triumphantly revealed the contents of the New Testament, that is the red book. The immediate effect of his statement was the re-arrest of Bermbach, who was present at the trial as a witness.

Why was Bermbach re-arrested?

Because of the papers found on him? No, for after his house had been searched he was released again. He was arrested 24 hours after Kothes. Therefore if he had had incriminating documents they would certainly have disappeared by then. Why then was witness Bermbach arrested, when the witnesses Hentze, Hätzel, Steingens, who had been shown to be accomplices or members of the league, still sat unmolested on the witness bench?

Bermbach had received a letter from Marx which contained a mere criticism of the indictment and nothing else besides. This Stieber admitted since the letter was there for the jury to see. But he couched the admission in his hyperbolic policeman's manner thus: "Marx himself exercises an uninterrupted influence on the present case from London." And the jury might well ask themselves, as Guizot asked his voters: *Est-ce que vous vous sentez corrompus?*[a] What then was the reason for Bermbach's arrest? From the beginning of the inquiry the Prussian Government *as a matter of principle* strove *consistently* to deprive the accused of all means of defence. In direct contradiction to the law, defence counsel, as they announced in open court, were refused access to the accused even after presentation of the bill of indictment. On

---

[a] Do you feel you are corrupted?—*Ed.*

his own testimony Stieber had been in possession of the Dietz archive ever since August 5, 1851. But the Dietz archive was not appended to the indictment. Not until October 18, 1852, was it produced in the middle of a public hearing—and only so much of it was produced as Stieber thought politic. The jury, the accused and the public were all to be caught off their guard and taken by surprise; defence counsel were to stand by helplessly in the face of the surprise prepared by the police.

And even more so after the presentation of the original minute-book! The Prussian Government trembled at the thought of revelations. Bermbach however had received material for the defence from Marx and it could be foreseen that he would receive information about the minute-book. His arrest denoted the proclamation of a new crime, that of corresponding with Marx, and the punishment for this crime was imprisonment. That was intended to deter every Prussian citizen from permitting his address to be used. *À bon entendeur demi mot.*[a] Bermbach was *locked up* so that evidence for the defence might be *locked out.* And Bermbach remained in gaol for five weeks. For if they had released him immediately after the case was concluded the Prussian courts would have publicly proclaimed their docile subservience to the Prussian police. So Bermbach remained in gaol, *ad majorem gloriam*[b] of the Prussian judiciary.

Stieber swore on oath that

"after the arrest of the accused in Cologne, Marx joined together the ruins of his party in London and formed a new central authority with about eighteen people," etc.

The ruins had never come apart for they were so joined together that they had formed a private society[c] ever since September 1850. But at a word from Stieber they promptly vanished only to be revived by another command from Stieber after the arrest of the accused in Cologne and this time they appear in the form of a new central authority.

On Monday, October 25, the *Kölnische Zeitung* arrived in London with an account of Stieber's testimony of October 23.

The "Marx party" had neither formed a new central authority nor kept minutes of its meetings. They guessed at once who had

---

[a] A word is enough to the wise.— *Ed.*

[b] Paraphrase of a saying by Gregory I: *Ad majorem Dei gloriam*: for the greater glory of God, which later became the motto of the Society of Jesus.— *Ed.*

[c] Marx uses the English word.— *Ed.*

been the chief manufacturer of the New Testament—*Wilhelm Hirsch from Hamburg.*

Early in December 1851 Hirsch appeared at the "Marx society" saying he was a communist refugee. Simultaneously, letters arrived from Hamburg denouncing him as a spy. But it was decided to allow him to remain in the society for the time being and watch him with a view to procuring proof of his innocence or guilt. At the meeting on January 15, 1852, a letter from Cologne was read aloud in which a friend of Marx[a] referred to another postponement of the trial and to the difficulty experienced even by relatives in gaining access to the accused. On this occasion mention was made of Frau Dr. Daniels. People were struck by the fact that Hirsch was not seen again after this meeting either in anyone's "immediate proximity" or at a distance. On February 2, 1852, Marx was notified from Cologne that Frau Dr. Daniels' house had been searched as the result of a police denunciation which claimed that a letter from Frau Daniels to Marx had been read out in the communist society in London and that Marx had been instructed to write back to her telling her that he was busy reorganising the League in Germany, etc. This denunciation literally fills the first page of the original minute-book.

Marx replied by return of post that as Frau Daniels had never written to him he could not possibly have read out a letter from her; the whole denunciation had been invented by a certain Hirsch, a dissolute young man who had no objection to supplying the Prussian police with as many lies as they had a mind to pay for in cash.

Since January 15 Hirsch had disappeared from the meetings; he was now formally expelled from the society. At the same time it was resolved to change the time and place of the meetings. Hitherto, meetings had taken place on *Thursdays* on premises belonging to J. W. Masters, Markethouse, in Farringdon Street, City. From now on it was agreed that the society would meet on *Wednesdays* in the Rose and Crown Tavern, Crown Street, Soho. Hirsch, whom "Chief of Police Schulz had managed to smuggle unrecognised into the immediate proximity of Marx", despite his "proximity" was unaware even eight months later of the place and day of the meetings. Both before and after February he persisted in manufacturing his "*original minute-book*" on a Thursday and dating the meetings on Thursdays. If the *Kölnische Zeitung* is consulted the following can be found: Minutes of January 15

---

[a] Bermbach.— *Ed.*

(Thursday), likewise January 29 (Thursday), and March 4 (Thursday), and May 13 (Thursday), and May 20 (Thursday), and July 22 (Thursday), and July 29 (Thursday), and September 23 (Thursday), and September 30 (Thursday).

The landlord of the Rose and Crown Tavern made a declaration before the magistrate in Marlborough Street to the effect that "Dr. Marx's circle" had met in his tavern every Wednesday since February 1852. Liebknecht and Rings, whom Hirsch had named as the secretaries for his original minute-book, had their signatures witnessed by the same magistrate. And finally, the minutes Hirsch had kept in Stechan's Workers' Society[281] were obtained so that his handwriting might be compared with that in the original minute-book.

In this way the spurious nature of the original minute-book was demonstrated without it being necessary to embark upon a criticism of the contents which their own contradictions caused to disintegrate.

The real difficulty was how to send these documents to Counsel. The Prussian Post was merely an outpost, situated between the Prussian frontier and Cologne, and designed to frustrate the passage of munitions to the defence.

It was necessary to use roundabout ways and so the first documents, despatched on October 25, arrived in Cologne only on October 30.

Counsel were at first forced to make do with the very meagre resources that lay at hand in Cologne. The first blow against Stieber came from a direction he had not foreseen. Frau Dr. Daniels' father Müller, a King's Counsel and a man in high repute as a legal expert and well known for his conservative views, declared in the *Kölnische Zeitung* on October 26 that his daughter had never corresponded with Marx and that Stieber's original book was a piece of "mystification". The letter Marx had sent to Cologne on February 3, 1852, in which Hirsch was alluded to as a spy and a manufacturer of false police notices, was found by chance and put at the disposal of the defence. In the "Marx party's" notice of resignation from the Great Windmill Street Society[a] which was included in the Dietz archive, a genuine specimen of W. Liebknecht's handwriting was discovered. Lastly, Schneider II, Counsel for the Defence, obtained some genuine letters by Liebknecht from Birnbaum, the secretary of the Council for Poor-Relief in Cologne, and genuine letters by Rings from a private secretary called Schmitz. At the offices of the court

---

[a] See present edition, Vol. 10, p. 483.— *Ed.*

Counsel compared the minute-book with Liebknecht's handwriting in the notice of resignation and also with letters by Rings and Liebknecht.

Stieber, who was already alarmed by the declaration of Müller, King's Counsel, now heard of these ominous handwriting investigations. To forestall the imminent blow he again leaped up in court during the sitting on October 27, and declared that

"the fact that Liebknecht's signature in the minute-book differed greatly from a signature that already was in the dossier had seemed very suspicious to him.[a] He had therefore made further inquiries and had learnt that the signatory in the minute-book in question was **H.** Liebknecht whereas the name in the dossier was preceded by the initial **W.**"

When Counsel, Schneider II, asked him: "Who informed you that an H. Liebknecht also exists?", Stieber refused to answer. Schneider II then asked for further information about Rings and Ulmer who appear together with Liebknecht as secretaries in the minute-book. Stieber smelt a new trap. He ignored the question three times, and tried to conceal his embarrassment and to regain his composure by recounting three times and for no reason how the minute-book had come into his possession. At last he stammered: The names Rings and Ulmer are probably not real names at all but only "*League names*". Stieber explained the frequent mention in the minute-book of Frau Dr. Daniels as a correspondent of Marx by surmising that perhaps the young notary Bermbach was really *meant*, when the book *said* Frau Dr. Daniels. Counsel, von Hontheim, questioned him about Hirsch.

"*He did not know* this man Hirsch either," Stieber swore. "Contrary to rumour however it is obvious that he is not a Prussian agent if only because the Prussian police are on the lookout for him."

At a signal from Stieber Goldheim buzzed into view and said that

"in October 1851 he was sent to Hamburg in order to apprehend Hirsch".

We shall see how the very same Goldheim was sent to London on the following day to apprehend the very same Hirsch. So the very same Stieber who claimed that he had bought the Dietz archive and the original minute-book from refugees for cash, that same Stieber now asserts that Hirsch cannot be a Prussian agent because he is a refugee! You have only to be a refugee and Stieber will guarantee your absolute venality or absolute incorruptibility, just as it suits his book. And is not Fleury likewise a political refugee, the same Fleury

---

[a] The Basle edition of 1853 had (sic) after these words.— *Ed.*

whom Stieber denounced as a police agent in the sitting on November 3?

When the defences of his original minute-book had been breached on every side, Stieber summed up the situation on October 27 with a classical display of impudence, stating that

"his belief in the authenticity of the minute-book is firmer than ever".

At the sitting of October 29 an expert compared the letters of Liebknecht and Rings, which had been submitted by Birnbaum and Schmitz, with the minute-book and declared the signatures in the latter to be *false.*

The Chief Public Prosecutor, Seckendorf, said in his speech:

"The information contained in the minute-book coincides with facts derived from other sources. But the prosecution is quite unable to prove the book's authenticity."

The book is authentic, but its authenticity cannot be proved. The New Testament! Seckendorf continued:

"But the defence has itself shown that at least the book contains much that is true, for example it gives us information about the activities of Rings, who is mentioned there, activities about which no one knew anything before."

If no one knew anything about Rings' activities before, the minute-book does not provide any information about it either. Therefore the statements about Rings' activities could not confirm the truth of the minute-book's *contents* and as regards its form they demonstrated that the signature of a member of the "Marx party" was *in truth* false, and had been forged. They proved then, according to Seckendorf, that "at least the book contains much that is true"—i.e. *a true forgery.* The Chief Public Prosecutors (Saedt-Seckendorf) and the postal authorities had together with Stieber opened the letter to Kothes. Therefore they knew the date of its arrival. Therefore they knew that Stieber committed perjury when he caused the courier to arrive at first on October 17 and, later, on the 10th, and the letter first on October 19 and then on the 12th. They were his accomplices.

At the sitting on October 27 Stieber tried in vain to preserve a calm appearance. He feared that any day the incriminating documents might arrive from London. Stieber felt ill at ease and the Prussian state, incarnate in him, felt ill at ease too. The public exposure had reached a dangerous stage. So Police Lieutenant Goldheim was sent to London on October 28 to save the fatherland. What did Goldheim do in London? Aided by Greif and Fleury, he attempted to persuade Hirsch to go to Cologne and, under the name of *H. Liebknecht,* to swear to the authenticity of the minute-book. Hirsch was offered a real state pension, but Hirsch's policeman's instincts were as good as Goldheim's. Hirsch knew that he was neither Public Prosecutor nor Police Lieutenant, nor Police Superintendent, and therefore had not the privilege of committing perjury with impunity. His instincts told him that he would be dropped as soon as things began to go wrong. Hirsch did not want to become a goat,[a] and least of all a scapegoat. Hirsch flatly refused. But the Christian-Germanic government of Prussia won lasting fame for having attempted to bribe a man to bear false witness in the course of criminal proceedings in which the heads of its own citizens were at stake.

Goldheim thus returned to Cologne without having achieved his object.

In the sitting on November 3, when the prosecutor had concluded his address and before Counsel for the defence could commence his, Stieber, caught between the two, leaped once again into the breach swearing that

"he had now ordered further research into the minute-book. He had sent Police Lieutenant Goldheim from Cologne to London to pursue the inquiry there. Goldheim left on October 28 and returned on November 2. Here is Goldheim."

At a signal from his master Goldheim buzzed into view and swore that

"on arriving in London he went first to Police Lieutenant Greif who took him to police agent Fleury in the borough of Kensington for it was Fleury from whom Greif had obtained the book. Fleury admitted as much to him, the witness Goldheim, and asserted that he had really received the book from a member of the Marx party called H. Liebknecht. Fleury definitely recognised the receipt H. Liebknecht had given him for the money he had received for the book. Goldheim was not able to catch hold of Liebknecht himself in London because he was, according to Fleury, afraid to appear in public. During his stay in London witness became convinced that, a few errors apart, the content of the book was *entirely genuine*. Reliable agents who had been present at Marx's meetings had confirmed this to him. The book itself however was not the original minute-book but only a *notebook* on the proceedings at Marx's meetings. There are only two possible explanations for the admittedly still rather obscure origin of the book. Either, as the agent insists, it really emanates from Liebknecht, who has refused to give a specimen of his handwriting in order that there should be no proof of his treachery; or the agent Fleury obtained the notes for the book from Dronke and Imandt, two other émigré friends of Marx, and put them in the form of an original minute-book in order to increase the value of his commodity. Police Lieutenant Greif has officially stated that Dronke and Imandt frequently consorted with Fleury.... The witness Goldheim asserts his stay in London has convinced him that everything that had been said previously about secret meetings in Marx's home, about the contacts between London and Cologne and about the secret correspondence, etc., was true in every particular. As evidence of how well informed the Prussian agents in London were even today, he would inform the Court that a completely secret meeting took

---

[a] Marx plays on the name *Hirsch*, which means "stag".— *Ed.*

place in Marx's house on October 27 to discuss what steps should be taken to counteract the minute-book and above all the activities of Police Superintendent Stieber, who was a thorn in the side of the London Party. The relevant decisions and documents were sent in complete secrecy to the lawyer, Schneider II. In particular, among the papers sent to Schneider II was a private letter that Stieber himself wrote to Marx in Cologne in 1848 and that Marx had hitherto kept very secret in the hope that it might be used to compromise the witness Stieber."

Witness Stieber leaped up and declared that he had written to Marx about an infamous slander, and had threatened to sue him, etc.

"No one but Marx and he could know this and this was indeed the strongest proof of the accuracy of the information from London."

So according to Goldheim the original minute-book is "*entirely genuine*", apart from the false parts. What convinced him of its authenticity is in particular the circumstance that the original minute-book is no original minute-book but only a "*notebook*". And Stieber? Stieber was by no means thunderstruck; on the contrary a great weight had been lifted from his mind.[a] At the very last moment, when the sound of the prosecutor's last words had hardly faded away and before the first word of the defence had been uttered, Stieber managed with the aid of his Goldheim quickly to transform the original minute-book into a notebook. When two policemen accuse each other of lying, does that not prove that they are both addicted to telling the truth? Through Goldheim Stieber was able to cover his retreat.

Goldheim testified that "on arriving in London he went first to Police Lieutenant Greif, who took him to police agent Fleury in the borough of Kensington". Now who would not swear on oath that poor Goldheim and Police Lieutenant Greif must have worn themselves out walking or driving to Fleury's house in the remote borough of Kensington? But Police Lieutenant Greif lives in the same house as police agent Fleury, in fact he lives on the top floor of Fleury's house, so that in reality it was not Greif who took Goldheim to Fleury, but Fleury who took Goldheim to Greif.

"Police agent Fleury in the borough of Kensington!" What precision! Can you still doubt the truthfulness of a Prussian government that denounces its own spies, gives their name and address and every detail, body and soul? If the minute-book is false you can still rely on "police agent Fleury in Kensington". Yes, indeed. On private secretary Pierre in the 13th *arrondissement*. If you wish to specify a person you must give his Christian name

---

[a] A pun in the original: "*fällt* nicht aus den Wolken"—is not thunderstruck, and "ein Stein *fällt* ihm vom Herzen"—a weight is taken off his mind.— *Ed.*

as well as his surname. Not *Fleury* but *Charles* Fleury. And you must also name the profession that he practises in public, and not his clandestine activities. So it is *Charles Fleury, a businessman*, not Fleury, the police agent. And when you state his address you do not merely name a London borough, a town in itself, but you give the borough, the street and the number of the house. So it is not police agent Fleury in Kensington but *Charles Fleury, a businessman, 17 Victoria Road, Kensington.*

But *"Police Lieutenant Greif"*, that at any rate is frankly spoken! But when Police Lieutenant Greif attaches himself to the embassy in London and the Lieutenant turns into an attaché that of course is an attachment of no concern to the courts. The heart's desire is the voice of fate.[a]

So Police Lieutenant Goldheim asserts that police agent Fleury asserted that he had the book from a man who really asserted that he was **H.** Liebknecht and who had even given a receipt to Fleury. The only drawback is that Goldheim was unable "to catch hold of" the said H. Liebknecht in London. So Goldheim could have stayed quietly in Cologne for Police Superintendent Stieber's assertion does not look any healthier for the fact that it appears as an assertion of Police Lieutenant Goldheim's, which had been asserted by Police Lieutenant Greif, for whom in his turn police agent Fleury had done the favour of agreeing to assert his assertion.

Goldheim's London experiences were hardly encouraging but, undeterred and with the aid of his considerable faculty for convincing himself (which in his case must do duty for the faculty of reasoning), he convinced himself *"completely"* that *"everything"* that Stieber had affirmed on oath concerning the "Marx party", about its contacts in Cologne, etc., was *"all* true *in every particular"*. And now that Goldheim, his junior official, has issued him with a *testimonium paupertatis*,[b] surely Police Superintendent Stieber is fully covered now? Stieber's method of swearing has at least one achievement to its credit: he has turned the whole Prussian hierarchy upside down. You don't believe the Police Superintendent? Very well. He has compromised himself. But surely you will believe the Police Lieutenant? You don't believe him either? Better still. Then you have no other choice than to believe at least the police agent *alias mouchardus vulgaris*.[c] Such is the heretical conceptual confusion that our *swearing Stieber* has created.

---

[a] Schiller, *Die Piccolomini*, Act III, Scene 8.— *Ed.*
[b] Certificate of poverty.— *Ed.*
[c] An ordinary spy.— *Ed.*

Goldheim proved that in London he had established the non-existence of the original minute-book, and as for the existence of H. Liebknecht that he was unable "to catch hold" of it in London, and it was precisely this that convinced him that "*all*" Stieber's statements about the "Marx party" "were *true in every particular*". In addition to these negative proofs, which in Seckendorf's view contained "much that was true", he had in the end to produce the positive proof of "how well informed the Prussian agents in London were even today". As evidence of this he mentions that on October 27 there had been a "completely secret meeting in Marx's house". In this completely secret meeting steps were discussed to counteract the minute-book and Police Superintendent Stieber, that "thorn in their side". The relevant orders and decisions were "sent in complete secrecy to the lawyer, Schneider II".

Although the Prussian agents were present at these meetings the route taken by these letters remained so "completely secret" that all the efforts of the postal authorities to intercept them were in vain. Listen to the cricket chirping sadly from among the ageing and venerable ruins[a]: "The relevant letters and documents were sent in complete secrecy to the lawyer, Schneider II." Completely secret for Goldheim's secret agents.

The imaginary decisions about the minute-book cannot have been made at the completely secret meeting in Marx's house on October 27 for already on October 25 Marx had sent the chief reports about the spurious nature of the minute-book not indeed to Schneider II, but to Herr von Hontheim.

It was not merely the bad conscience of the police that gave them the idea that documents had been sent to Cologne. On October 29 Goldheim arrived in London. On October 30 Goldheim found a statement signed by Engels, Freiligrath, Marx and Wolff[b] in *The Morning Advertiser, The Spectator, The Examiner, The Leader* and *The People's Paper* in which the attention of the English public was drawn to the revelations that the defence would make of forgery, perjury, the falsification of documents,[c] in short of all the infamies perpetrated by the Prussian police. The sending of the documents was veiled in such "complete secrecy" that the "Marx party" openly informed the English public about this,

---

[a] A pun on the name *Goldheim* and the word *Heimchen* (cricket).— *Ed.*

[b] See this volume, pp. 378-79.— *Ed.*

[c] Marx and Engels use the English words "forgery, perjury, falsification of documents".— *Ed.*

though not until October 30 by which time Goldheim had arrived in London and the documents in Cologne.

However, on October 27 documents were also sent to Cologne. How did the omniscient Prussian police learn of this?

The Prussian police did not pursue their activities with quite such "complete secrecy" as the "Marx party". On the contrary, for weeks they had openly posted two of their spies in front of Marx's house and from the street they watched him *du soir jusqu'au matin* and *du matin jusqu'au soir*[a] and dogged his every step. Now the absolutely secret documents, containing the genuine specimens of Liebknecht's and Rings' handwriting together with the statement of the landlord of the Crown Tavern concerning the days of the society's meetings, these absolutely secret documents Marx had officially witnessed in the absolutely public police court in Marlborough Street in the presence of reporters from the English daily press on October 27. His Prussian guardian angels followed him from his house to Marlborough Street and from Marlborough Street back to his house and from his house to the post office. They did not in fact disappear until Marx had gone in absolute secrecy to the local magistrate in order to obtain a warrant for the arrest of his two "followers".

Moreover, yet another way lay open to the Prussian government. For Marx sent the documents that were dated October 27 and had been witnessed on October 27 directly to Cologne through the post in order to ensure that the talons of the Prussian eagle would not seize the *duplicates* that had been sent in *absolute secrecy*. Both postal authorities and the police in Cologne knew then that documents dated October 27 had been forwarded by Marx and there was no need for Goldheim to make the journey to London in order to unravel the mystery.

Goldheim felt that after all he ought "*in particular*" to reveal something "particular" that the "absolutely secret meeting on October 27" had resolved to send to Schneider II, he therefore *mentioned* the letter written by Stieber to Marx. Unfortunately Marx had sent this letter not on October 27 but on October 25 and it was sent not to Schneider II but to Herr von Hontheim. But how did the police know that Marx still had Stieber's letter in his possession and that he intended to send it to the defence? Let us however permit Stieber to leap up once more.

---

[a] From evening till morning and from morning till evening (Beaumarchais, *La folle journée, ou le mariage de Figaro*, Act I, Scene 1).— *Ed.*

Stieber hoped to forestall Schneider II and thus prevent him from reading aloud in court what was for him a very "unpleasant letter". Stieber calculated: If Goldheim says that Schneider II has my letter and that he has it thanks to his "criminal contact with Marx", then Schneider II will suppress the letter so as to prove that Goldheim's agents were misinformed and that he himself does not maintain any criminal contact with Marx. So Stieber leaped up, gave a false account of the content of the letter and concluded with the astonishing declaration that "no one but himself and Marx could know this and this was indeed the *strongest proof of the reliability* of the information from London".

Stieber has a strange method of keeping secret facts that he finds unpalatable. If he remains silent, the whole world must keep silence. Hence "no one can know" apart from him and a certain elderly lady that he once lived near Weimar as an *homme entretenu*.[a] But if Stieber had every reason to make sure that no one but Marx should know of the letter, Marx had every reason to let everyone apart from Stieber know about it. We now know the *strongest proof* of the information from London. What does Stieber's weakest proof look like?

But once again Stieber knowingly commits perjury when he says "no one but myself and Marx could know this". He knew that it was not Marx but another editor of the *Rheinische Zeitung* who had answered his letter.[282] So there had been at least "one man other than Marx and himself". In order that even more people may learn of it we print the letter here[b]:

"No. 177 of the *Neue Rheinische Zeitung* contains a news item from your correspondent in Frankfurt am Main dated December 21 in which a base lie is reported to the effect that being a police spy I went to Frankfurt to try, while pretending to hold democratic views, to discover the murderers of Prince Lichnowski and General Auerswald. I was in fact in Frankfurt on the 21st but stayed only one day and as you can see from the accompanying certificate I was engaged in purely private business on behalf of a lady from here, Frau von Schwezler. I have long since returned to Berlin and resumed my work as defence counsel. I would refer you moreover to the official correction in this matter that has already appeared in No. 338 of the *Frankfurter Oberpostamts-Zeitung* of December 21 and in No. 248 of the Berlin *National-Zeitung*. I believe that I may expect from your respect for the truth that you will print the enclosed correction in your paper without delay and that you will also give me the name of your slanderous informant in accordance with your legal obligations, for I cannot possibly permit such a libel to go unpunished, otherwise I shall regretfully be compelled to proceed against your editorial board.

---

[a] Kept man.— *Ed.*

[b] Stieber's letter was given in a footnote in the Basle and Boston editions of 1853 but in the 1875 and 1885 editions it was included in the main text.— *Ed.*

"I believe that in recent times democracy is indebted to no one more than *myself*. It was I who rescued hundreds of democrats who had been charged from the nets of the criminal courts. It was I who even while a state of siege was proclaimed here persistently and fearlessly challenged the authorities (and do so to this very day), while all the cowardly and contemptible fellows (the so-called democrats) had long since fled the field. When democratic organs treat me in this fashion it is scarcely an encouragement to me to make further efforts.

"The real joke, however, in the present case lies in the clumsiness of the organs of democracy. The rumour that I went to Frankfurt as a police agent was spread first by that notorious organ of reaction, the *Neue Preussische Zeitung,* in order to undermine my activities as defence counsel that gave that paper such offence. The other Berlin papers have long since corrected this report. But the democratic papers are so inept that they parrot this stupid lie. If I had wished to go to Frankfurt as a spy it would certainly not be announced beforehand in every newspaper. And how could Prussia send a police official to Frankfurt which has enough competent officials of its own? Stupidity has always been the failing of the democrats and their opponents' cunning has always brought them to victory.

"It is likewise a contemptible lie to say that years ago I was a police spy in Silesia. At that time I was openly employed as a police officer and as such I did my duty. Contemptible lies have been circulated about me. If anyone can prove that I insinuated my way into his favour let him come forth and do so. Anyone can make assertions and tell lies. I think of you as an honest, decent man and so I expect from you a satisfactory answer by return of post. The democratic papers are generally in disrepute here because of the many lies they publish. I hope that you are a man of a different stamp.

"Berlin, December 26, 1848
                                        Respectfully yours,

                                        Stieber, Doctor at Law, etc.,
                                        Berlin, Ritterstrasse 65."

How then did Stieber know that on October 27 Marx had sent this letter to Schneider II? But it was not sent on October 27 but on October 25, and it was not sent to Schneider II but to von Hontheim. Stieber therefore knew only that the letter still existed and he suspected that Marx would put it in the hands of some defence counsel or other. Whence this suspicion? When the *Kölnische Zeitung* brought Stieber's testimony on October 18 about Cherval, etc., to London, Marx sent a statement dated October 21 to the *Kölnische Zeitung*, the Berlin *National-Zeitung* and the *Frankfurter Journal* and at the end of this statement Stieber was threatened with his still existing letter. In order to keep this letter "completely secret" Marx himself announced it in the newspapers. He failed, because of the cowardice of the daily press in Germany, but the Prussian post was now informed and with the Prussian post, its—Stieber.

What then was the message Goldheim chirruped back from London?

That Hirsch has not committed perjury, that **H.** Liebknecht has no "tangible" existence, that the original minute-book is no original minute-book and that the all-knowing London agents know all that the "Marx party" has published in the London press. To save the honour of the Prussian agents Goldheim placed in their mouths the few titbits of information that Stieber discovered[a] in letters he had opened or purloined.

In the sitting on November 4 after Schneider II had annihilated Stieber and his minute-book and shown him to be guilty of forgery and perjury, Stieber leaped into the breach for the last time and gave vent to his moral indignation. They even dare, he cried out, his soul mortally wounded, they even dare to accuse Herr Wermuth, Chief of Police Wermuth, of perjury! Stieber thereby returned to the orthodox hierarchy, to the rising scale. Earlier he had moved on the heterodox, descending scale. If he, a police superintendent, could not be trusted, well then surely his police lieutenant could be; and if not the police lieutenant, then surely his police agent; and if not agent Fleury, then surely subagent Hirsch. But now it is in reverse. He, the *police superintendent*, can perhaps commit perjury, but Wermuth, a *Chief of Police*? Unbelievable! In his rage he praised Wermuth with mounting bitterness,[b] he served Wermuth up to the public neat, Wermuth as a human being, Wermuth as a lawyer, Wermuth as paterfamilias, Wermuth as a Chief of Police, Wermuth for ever.[c]

Even now, during the public hearing, Stieber did not stop trying to isolate the accused and to erect a barrier between the defence and the defence materials. He accused Schneider II of "criminal contact" with Marx. In attacking him Schneider was impugning the highest authorities of Prussia. Even Göbel, the Presiding Judge of the court, even a Göbel felt overwhelmed by Stieber's onslaught. He could not overlook it and even though in a timorous and servile way he did lash Stieber with a few rebukes. But Stieber was in the right for all that. It was not merely he as a person that stood exposed to public view: it was the prosecution, the courts, the postal authorities, the government, the police headquarters in Berlin, it was the ministries and the Prussian embassy in London, in short it was the whole Prussian state that stood in the pillory with him, original minute-book in hand.

---

[a] In the original a pun on Stieber: *aufstiebern* (*aufstöbern*) — to ferret out, to trace, to discover.— *Ed.*

[b] A pun on *Wermuth* (wormwood, vermouth, bitterness) and *Bitterkeit* (bitterness).— *Ed.*

[c] Marx uses the English phrase "for ever".— *Ed.*

Herr Stieber is herewith granted permission to print the answer the *Neue Rheinische Zeitung* returned to his letter.

Let us now return once more to London with Goldheim.

Just as Stieber is still ignorant of Cherval's whereabouts and true identity so too, according to Goldheim's testimony (in the sitting on November 3), the *origin* of the minute-book is an enigma that is still not fully resolved. To resolve it Goldheim put forward two hypotheses.

"There are only two possible explanations," he said, "for the still rather obscure origin of the book. Either, as the agent insists, it really emanates from Liebknecht, who has refused to give a specimen of his handwriting in order that there should be no proof of his treachery."

W. Liebknecht is well known as a member of the "Marx party". But it is no less well known that the signature in the minute-book does not belong to **W.** Liebknecht. In the sitting on October 27 Stieber therefore swore that the signature was not that of **W.** Liebknecht but of another Liebknecht, an **H.** Liebknecht. He had learnt of the existence of this double without being able however to disclose the source of his discovery. Goldheim swore: "Fleury asserted that he had really received the book from a member of the 'Marx party' called **H.** Liebknecht." Goldheim swore further: "I was not able to catch hold of the said **H.** Liebknecht in London." Up to now, therefore, what *signs of life* has the **H.** Liebknecht that Stieber has discovered given to the world in general and to Police Lieutenant Goldheim in particular? No sign of life other than his *handwriting* in the original minute-book; but now Goldheim declares: "Liebknecht has refused to give a specimen of his handwriting."

Up to the present **H.** Liebknecht existed only as a signature. Now nothing remains of **H.** Liebknecht at all, not even a signature, not even the dot on the i. How Goldheim could possibly know that **H.** Liebknecht's handwriting differs from the handwriting in the minute-book, when the handwriting in the minute-book is his only proof of **H.** Liebknecht's existence, that is Goldheim's secret. If Stieber has his miracles, why should not Goldheim have his miracles too?

Goldheim forgot that his superior, Stieber, had sworn to **H.** Liebknecht's existence before him, and that he too had just sworn to it. In the same breath in which he swears to **H.** Liebknecht he recollects that **H.** Liebknecht is nothing but a makeshift, invented by Stieber, a necessary fib and necessity knows no law. He remembers that there is but one genuine Liebknecht, **W.** Liebknecht, but that if

W. Liebknecht is genuine then the signature in the minute-book is a forgery. He cannot confess that Fleury's subagent Hirsch had manufactured the false signature along with the false minute-book. Accordingly he invents the hypothesis: "Liebknecht has refused to give a specimen signature." Let us likewise construct a hypothesis. Goldheim once forged banknotes. He is brought before the courts; it is proved that the signature on the banknote is not that of the bank director. Don't take offence, gentlemen, Goldheim will say, don't take offence. The banknote is genuine. It comes from the bank director himself. If his name appears signed by someone other than him what does that matter? "He merely refused to give a specimen of his handwriting."

Or, Goldheim continues, if the hypothesis with Liebknecht turns out to be false: "Or the agent Fleury obtained the notes for the book from Dronke and Imandt, two other émigré friends of Marx, and then put them in the form of an original minute-book in order to increase the value of his commodity. Police Lieutenant Greif has officially stated that Dronke and Imandt frequently consorted with Fleury."

Or? How so, or? If a book like the original minute-book is signed by three people, Liebknecht, Rings and Ulmer, no one will deduce that "it emanates either from Liebknecht"—or from Dronke and Imandt, but: It emanates either from Liebknecht or from Rings and from Ulmer. Should our unfortunate Goldheim, now that he has climbed to the dizzy heights of a disjunction—either—or—should he now repeat: "Rings and Ulmer have refused to give specimens of their handwriting"? Even Goldheim realises the need for new tactics.

If the original minute-book does not emanate from Liebknecht, as the agent Fleury claimed, then it must have been manufactured by Fleury himself, but the notes for it were provided by Dronke and Imandt of whom Police Lieutenant Greif has officially stated that they frequently consorted with Fleury.

"To increase the value of his commodity," says Goldheim, Fleury put the notes in the form of an original minute-book. He not only commits a fraud, he also forges signatures and all this to "increase the value of his commodity". So scrupulous a man as this Prussian agent, who for profit manufactures forged minutes and forged signatures, is obviously incapable of manufacturing *forged notes*. Such is Goldheim's inference.

Dronke and Imandt did not come to London until April 1852, after they had been expelled by the Swiss authorities. However, one-third of the original minute-book consists of entries for the months of January, February and March 1852. Fleury therefore manufactured one-third of the original minute-book *without* Dronke and Imandt although Goldheim had sworn that the minute-book was written either by Liebknecht—or else by Fleury, following, however, the notes of Dronke and Imandt. Goldheim swore to it, and Goldheim it is true is no Brutus[a] but he is Goldheim.

But the possibility still remains that Dronke and Imandt furnished Fleury with notes from April onwards for, Goldheim swore: "Police Lieutenant Greif has officially stated that Dronke and Imandt frequently consorted with Fleury."

Let us examine this association.

As we have noted above Fleury was known in London not as a Prussian police agent but as a businessman in the City, and indeed as a democratic businessman. Born in Altenburg he had come to London as a political refugee, had later married an English woman from a wealthy and respected family and apparently enjoyed a quiet life with his wife and his father-in-law, an old *Quaker* industrialist. On October 8 or 9 Imandt began to "consort frequently" with Fleury, in the capacity, that is, of tutor. But according to the improved version of Stieber's evidence the original minute-book arrived in Cologne on October 10—according to Goldheim's final statement on the 11th. By the time that Imandt, whom he had never set eyes on till then, had given him his first French lesson, Fleury had not only had the original minute-book bound in red morocco leather, he had already entrusted it to the special courier who brought it to Cologne. So heavily did Fleury rely on Imandt's notes when writing the original minute-book. As for Dronke, Fleury only saw him *once* and by chance with Imandt, and this was on October 30 by which time the original minute-book had long since dissolved into its original nothingness.

Thus the Christian-Germanic government is not content with breaking into desks, stealing papers, obtaining false testimony by underhand means, creating false plots, forging false documents, swearing false oaths, and attempting to suborn witnesses—all this to bring about the condemnation of the Cologne defendants. The government attempts also to cast suspicion on the London friends of the accused so as to conceal the activities of their Hirsch now

---

[a] Cf. Shakespeare's *Julius Caesar*, Act III, Scene 2, "Brutus is an honourable man".— *Ed.*

that Stieber has sworn that he does not know him and Goldheim has sworn that he is no spy.

On Friday, November 5, the *Kölnische Zeitung* arrived in London with the report of the court sitting on November 3 and Goldheim's evidence. Inquiries about Greif were made at once and the very same day it was learnt that he lived in Fleury's house. At the same time Dronke and Imandt paid Fleury a visit taking with them a copy of the *Kölnische Zeitung*. They gave him Goldheim's testimony to read. He went pale, tried to regain his composure, pretended to be utterly astonished and declared himself perfectly willing to make a statement against Goldheim before an English magistrate. But he said he must consult his solicitor first. They agreed to meet the following afternoon, Saturday, November 6. Fleury promised to have his statement officially witnessed and said he would bring it to the meeting. Of course, he did not appear. Imandt and Dronke then went to his house on Saturday evening and found there the following note addressed to Imandt:

"With the solicitor's help everything has been arranged; further steps can be taken as soon as the person in question has been found. The solicitor sent the relevant documents off today. Business commitments have made it imperative for me to go to the City. If you would like to visit me tomorrow I shall be at home the whole afternoon until 5 o'clock. *Fl.*"

On the other side of the note there was the following post-script:

"I have just arrived home but had to go out again with Herr Werner and my wife—*I can prove this to you* tomorrow. Leave me a note saying when you would like to come."

Imandt left the following reply:

"I am extremely surprised not to find you at home now, especially as you did not come to meet us this afternoon as arranged. I must confess that in the circumstances my opinion of you is already fixed. If you wish me to revise it you will visit me by tomorrow morning at the latest for I cannot guarantee that your activities as a Prussian police spy might not find their way into the English newspapers. *Imandt.*"

Fleury did not appear on Sunday morning either, so in the evening Dronke and Imandt went to his house once again in order to obtain his statement by making it appear as if their confidence in him had only at first been shaken. Finally, after all sorts of procrastinations and doubts the statement was formulated. Fleury hesitated most when it was pointed out to him that he must sign with his Christian name as well as his surname. The statement went literally as follows:

"To the editors of the *Kölnische Zeitung*

"The undersigned declares that he has known Herr Imandt for about a month during which time the latter gave him tuition in the French language and that he met Herr Dronke for the first time on Saturday, October 30 of this year.

"He declares further that neither of them gave him any information in connection with the minute-book mentioned in the Cologne trial.

"That he does not know of any person by the name of Liebknecht nor has he ever been in contact with anyone of that name.

"Kensington, London, November 8, 1852.   *Charles Fleury*"

Dronke and Imandt were, of course, quite sure that Fleury would instruct the *Kölnische Zeitung* not to print any statement signed by him. Accordingly they sent his statement not to the *Kölnische Zeitung* but to Schneider II, the lawyer, who however received it when the case was too far advanced for him to make use of it.

Fleury is not indeed the Fleur de Marie of the police prostitutes, but he is a flower[a] and he will bear blossom, albeit only *fleurs-de-lys*.*

But the story of the minute-book is not yet finished.

On Saturday, November 6, W. Hirsch of Hamburg made an affidavit before the magistrate at Bow Street, London, to the effect that under the direction of Greif and Fleury he himself had fabricated the original minute-book that figured in the Cologne communist trial.

Thus, it had at first been the original minute-book of the "Marx party"—after that it was the notebook of the police spy Fleury—and lastly it became the manufacture of the Prussian police, a simple police manufacture, a police manufacture *sans phrase*.

On the same day that Hirsch revealed the secret of the original minute-book to the English magistrate at Bow Street another representative of the Prussian state was busy packing at Fleury's house in Kensington, and this time the things he was packing in stout oil-cloth were neither stolen nor forged nor even documents at all, but his own personal belongings. And this bird was none other than Greif[b] whom we remember from Paris, the special courier to Cologne, the chief of the Prussian police agents in London, the official director of mystifications, the Police Lieutenant attached to the Prussian Embassy. Greif had received instructions from the

---

* *Fleurs-de-lys* [lilies] is the French colloquial name of the letters T. F. (*travaux forcés*, forced labour), the brand-mark of criminals. The accuracy of Marx's judgment is demonstrated in the Postscript (VIII, 1).[283] [*Note by Engels to the edition of 1885.*]

[a] A pun: Fleur de Marie—the heroine in Eugène Sue's novel *Les mystères de Paris, fleur*—a flower.— *Ed.*
[b] The word "Greif" means griffin.— *Ed.*

Prussian government to leave London at once. There was no time to be wasted.

Just as at the end of spectacular operas the rising amphitheatrical set in the background that had previously been obscured by curtains now suddenly flares up in a blaze of Bengal light dazzling all eyes, so too at the end of this Prussian police tragicomedy the hidden amphitheatrical workshop was revealed in which the original minute-book was forged. On the lowest level could be seen the wretched spy Hirsch working at piece rates; a little higher up was the respectably situated spy and agent provocateur, the City business-man Fleury; higher still the diplomatic Police Lieutenant Greif and highest of all the Prussian Embassy itself to which he was attached. For 6-8 months Hirsch had laboured week by week to forge the original minute-book in Fleury's study and under his watchful eyes. But one floor *above* Fleury dwelt the Prussian Police Lieutenant Greif, who supervised and inspired him. However, Greif himself regularly spent a part of his day in the Prussian Embassy, where he in his turn was supervised and inspired. Thus the Prussian Embassy was the real hothouse where the original minute-book grew and flowered.[a] Hence Greif had to disappear. He disappeared on November 6, 1852.

The authenticity of the original minute-book could not be sustained any longer, not even as a notebook. The Public Prosecutor, Saedt, buried it in the address he gave in reply to the concluding speeches by Counsel for the Defence.

The trial had now reached the point at which the Indictment Board of the Court of Appeal had begun when it ordered a new investigation because "*there was no factual evidence of an indictable offence*".

V

THE LETTER ACCOMPANYING THE *RED CATECHISM*

In his evidence during the sitting on October 27 Police Inspector *Junkermann* of Crefeld said that

"he confiscated a parcel containing copies of the *Red Catechism*[b]; it was addressed to the waiter in an inn in Crefeld and bore a Düsseldorf post mark. It contained also an accompanying letter which was unsigned. It has not been possible to identify the sender." "As the prosecution has pointed out, the accompanying letter appeared to *be written in Marx's hand*."

---

[a] The Basle edition of 1853 included this sentence: "The scandal that awaited him in London rebounded upon the Prussian Embassy." — *Ed.*

[b] [M. Hess,] *Rother Kathechismus für das deutsche Volk.—Ed.*

In the sitting on October 28 the expert (???) Renard discovered that the letter was in fact in Marx's handwriting. This accompanying letter said:

"Citizen! As we have complete confidence in you, we herewith present you with 50 copies of the *Red*. Your task is to push them under the doors of citizens—preferably workers—who are known to sympathise with the Revolution, on Saturday, June 5, at eleven o'clock at night. We are definitely counting on your civic virtues and accordingly expect you to carry out this instruction. The Revolution is closer than many people think. Long live the Revolution!

"Berlin, May 1852

With Fraternal Greetings.
The Revolutionary Committee"

Witness Junkermann declared further that "the parcels in question had been sent to the witness *Chianella*".

Chief Commissioner of Police *Hinckeldey* of Berlin was the Supreme Commander in charge of operations against the accused in Cologne during the preliminary investigations. The laurels won by Maupas prevented him from sleeping.

The actors in the proceedings include two Chiefs of Police, one alive and one dead, one superintendent (only one, but that one a Stieber), two police lieutenants one of whom was constantly en route from London to Cologne, the other constantly journeying from Cologne to London, myriads of police agents and subagents, named, anonymous, heteronymous, pseudonymous, with tails and without. Lastly an Inspector of Police.

No sooner had the *Kölnische Zeitung* arrived in London with the evidence heard on October 27 and 28 than Marx went to the magistrate in Marlborough Street, where he copied out from the newspaper the text of the accompanying letter and had the copy witnessed, and at the same time the following affidavit:

1. That he had not written the letter in question;
2. that he had only learnt of its existence from the *Kölnische Zeitung*;
3. that he had *never seen* the so-called *Red Catechism*;
4. that he had never helped in any way at all to distribute it.

It may be pointed out in passing that if such a declaration made before a magistrate is found to be false, then it counts as perjury in England with all the consequences attendant thereupon.

The above document was sent to Schneider II but it appeared simultaneously in the London *Morning Advertiser*[a] as the conviction had gained ground during the trial that as regards the observance of

---

[a] See this volume, pp. 380-81.— *Ed.*

the secrecy of correspondence the Prussian post seems to have the strange notion that letters entrusted to its care must be kept secret from the addressee. The prosecution objected to the submission of the document, even for purposes of *comparison*. For the prosecution was aware that a single glance from the original accompanying letter to the officially attested copy by Marx would reveal the deception, the deliberate imitation of his handwriting could not remain hidden even from such a sharpsighted jury as this. Therefore, in order to defend the morality of the Prussian state, the prosecution denounced any attempt at comparison.

Schneider II observed

"that Chianella, the addressee who had freely given information to the police about the supposed identity of the sender and who had even *offered to act as a spy*, had not in the remotest degree thought of Marx in this connection."

No one who has ever read a single line by Marx could possibly attribute to him the authorship of this melodramatic accompanying letter. The midnight dream hour in summer on June 5,[a] and the officiously graphic procedure of pushing the *Red* under the doors of the revolutionary philistines—that could perhaps point to Kinkel's turn of mind, just as the references to "civic virtues" and the way in which they are "definitely counting on" this military "instruction being carried out" seem to reflect the imagination of a Willich. But why should Kinkel-Willich write their prescriptions for revolution in Marx's hand?

If it is permissible to form a hypothesis about the "as yet somewhat obscure origins" of this accompanying letter written in an imitated hand: the police found the 50 *Reds* in Crefeld as well as the convenient, high sounding accompanying letter. In Cologne or in Berlin *qu'importe?* they had the text copied in Marx's handwriting. For what purpose? "So as to increase the value of their commodity."

However, even the Chief Public Prosecutor did not dare to revert to the accompanying letter in his catilinarian speech.[b] He let it drop. Hence it did not assist in ascertaining the still missing "*indictable offence*".

VI

THE WILLICH-SCHAPPER GROUP

With the defeat of the revolution of 1848-49 the party of the proletariat on the Continent lost use of the press, freedom of speech and the right to associate, i.e. the legal instruments of party

---

[a] Cf. Shakespeare, *A Midsummer Night's Dream.—Ed.*
[b] Marcus Tullius Cicero, *Orationes in Lucium Catilinam.—Ed.*

organisation, which it had enjoyed for once during that short interval. The social status of the classes they represented enabled both the bourgeois-liberal and the petty-bourgeois democratic parties to remain united in one form or another and to assert their common interests more or less effectively despite the reaction. After 1849 just as before 1848, only *one path* was open to the proletarian party—that of *secret association*. Consequently after 1849 a whole series of clandestine proletarian societies sprang up on the Continent, were discovered by the police, condemned by the courts, broken up by the gaols and continually resuscitated by the force of circumstances.

Some of these secret societies aimed directly at the overthrow of the existing state. This was fully justified in France where the proletariat had been defeated by the bourgeoisie and hence attacking the existing government and attacking the bourgeoisie were one and the same thing. Other secret societies aimed at organising the proletariat into a party, without concerning themselves with the existing governments. This was necessary in countries like Germany where both bourgeoisie and proletariat had succumbed to their semi-feudal governments and where in consequence a victorious assault on the existing governments, instead of breaking the power of the bourgeoisie or in any case of the so-called middle classes, would at first help them to gain power. There is no doubt that here too the members of the proletarian party would take part once again in a revolution against the *status quo*, but it was no part of their task to prepare this revolution, to agitate, conspire or to plot for it. They could leave this preparation to circumstances in general and to the classes directly involved. They had to leave it to them if they were not to abandon the position of their own party and the historic tasks that follow of themselves from the conditions governing the existence of the proletariat. For them the contemporary governments were but ephemeral phenomena, the *status quo* a brief stopping place and the task of toiling away at it could be left to the petty narrow-minded democrats.

The "*Communist League*", therefore, was no conspiratorial society, but a society which secretly strove to create an organised proletarian party because the German proletariat is publicly debarred, *igni et aqua*,[a] from writing, speaking and meeting. Such a society can only be said to conspire against the *status quo* in the sense that steam and electricity conspire against it.

---

[a] *Igni et aqua interdictus* (deprived of fire and water)—the formula of banishment in ancient Rome.— *Ed.*

Enthüllungen

über den

Kommunisten=Prozeß

zu

Köln.

~~~~~~

1853.

Title-page of the 1853 Boston edition
of Marx's *Revelations Concerning the Communist Trial in Cologne*

It is self-evident that a secret society of this kind which aims at forming not the *government party of the future* but the *opposition party of the future* could have but few attractions for individuals who on the one hand concealed their personal insignificance by strutting around in the theatrical cloak of the conspirator, and on the other wished to satisfy their narrow-minded ambition on the day of the next revolution, and who wished above all to seem important at the moment, to snatch their share of the proceeds of demagogy and to find a welcome among the quacks and charlatans of democracy.

Thus a group broke off from the Communist League, or if you like it was broken off, a group that demanded, if not real conspiracies, at any rate the *appearance* of conspiracies, and accordingly called for a direct alliance with the democratic heroes of the hour: this was the Willich-Schapper group. It was typical of them that Willich was, together with *Kinkel,* one of the entrepreneurs in the business of the German-American revolutionary loan.[a]

Such in short is the relation of this party to the majority of the Communist League, to which the Cologne defendants belonged. Bürgers and Röser defined it succinctly and exhaustively in the proceedings of the Cologne Assizes.

Let us pause before finally bringing our narrative to a close in order to take a glance at the behaviour of the Willich-Schapper group during the Cologne trial.

As was pointed out above, the data contained in the documents purloined from the group by Stieber make it plain that their documents contrived to find their way to the police even *after* Reuter's theft. To this day the group has failed to give an explanation of this phenomenon.

Schapper knew the facts about Cherval's past better than anyone. He knew that Cherval had entered the League on his nomination in 1846 and not on that of Marx in 1848, etc. By his silence he gives confirmation to Stieber's lies.

The group knew that Haacke, who was their member, had written the threatening letter to the witness, Haupt; but it allows the suspicion to remain on the heads of the party of the accused.

Moses Hess, a member of the group and the author of the *Red Catechism*[284]—that unfortunate parody of the *Manifesto of the Communist Party*—Moses Hess, who not only writes but also distributes his own works, knew exactly to whom he had delivered parcels of his *Red.* He knew that Marx had not deprived him of his profusion of *Reds* to the extent of even a single copy. But Moses

---

[a] See this volume, p. 325.— *Ed.*

calmly let suspicion fall on the accused, as if it were their party that had hawked his *Red*, together with its melodramatic accompanying letter, in the Rhine Province.

That the group made common cause with the Prussian police is apparent not only in their silence but also in their utterances: whenever they entered the trial it was not in the dock with the accused, but as *"witnesses for the Crown"*.

Hentze, Willich's friend and benefactor, who admitted that he knew about the activities of the League, spent a few weeks in London with Willich and then journeyed to Cologne where he falsely testified that Becker (against whom there was far less evidence than against himself) had been a member of the League in 1848.

Hätzel, as the Dietz archive reveals, was a member of the group and received financial support from it. He had already been put on trial in Berlin for his association with the League and now he appeared as a witness for the prosecution. His testimony was false for he invented a wholly fictitious connection between the Rules of the League and the exceptional arming of the Berlin proletariat during the revolution.

Steingens, whose own letters proved (in the sitting on October 18) that he was the group's chief agent in Brussels, appeared in Cologne not as a defendant, but as a witness.

Not long before the court action in Cologne Willich and Kinkel sent a journeyman tailor[a] as emissary to Germany. Kinkel is not indeed a member of the group but Willich was co-director of the German-American revolutionary loan.

Kinkel was at that time already threatened by the danger, which was later to become a reality, of seeing himself and Willich removed by the London guarantors from control of the loan moneys and seeing the money itself drift back to America despite the indignant protests of Willich and himself. Kinkel was just then in need of the pseudo-mission *to* Germany and a pseudo-correspondence *with* Germany, partly in order to demonstrate that an area still existed there for his revolutionary activities and the American dollars, and partly to provide a pretext for the enormous costs of the correspondence, postal expenses, etc., that he and Willich managed to charge to the account (see Count O. Reichenbach's lithographed circular). Kinkel knew he had no contacts either with the bourgeois liberals or with the petty-bourgeois democrats in Germany. As he could not afford to be particular he used an emissary of the group as the emissary of the German-American Revolutionary League.[285]

---

[a] August Gebert.— *Ed.*

This emissary's sole function was to promote antagonism among the workers towards the party of the accused in Cologne. It must be admitted that the moment was well chosen and it offered a new pretext in the nick of time to reopen the investigation. The Prussian police had been fully apprised of the emissary's identity, of the day of his departure and of his route. Who thus apprised them? We shall see. Their spies were present at the secret meetings he held in Magdeburg and they reported on the debates. The friends of the Cologne accused in Germany and in London trembled.

We have already narrated how on November 6 Hirsch went before the magistrate at Bow Street and admitted to having forged the original minute-book under the guidance of Greif and Fleury. It was Willich who induced him to take this step, and it was Willich and Schärttner the innkeeper who accompanied him to the magistrate. Three copies were made of Hirsch's confession and these were sent through the post to various addresses in Cologne.

It was of supreme importance to arrest Hirsch as soon as he left the court. With the aid of the officially witnessed statement in his possession it would have been possible for the case lost in Cologne to be won in London. If not for the accused, at any rate against the government. However, Willich did everything in his power to make such a step impossible. He observed the strictest silence not only towards the "Marx party", which was directly involved, but also towards his own people and even towards Schapper. Schärttner alone was taken into his confidence. Schärttner declared that he and Willich had accompanied Hirsch to the ship, for according to Willich's scheme Hirsch was to give evidence against himself in Cologne.

Willich informed Hirsch of the route by which the documents had been sent, Hirsch informed the Prussian Embassy, and the Prussian Embassy informed the post. The documents did not arrive at their destination; they disappeared. Some time after this, Hirsch, who had also vanished, re-appeared in London and declared at a public meeting of democrats that Willich was his accomplice.

Although it had been on a motion from Willich that Hirsch had been expelled as a spy from the Great Windmill Street Society in 1851, Willich admitted, when questioned, that he had resumed relations with Hirsch at the beginning of August 1852. For Hirsch had revealed to him that Fleury was a Prussian spy and had apprised him of all of Fleury's incoming and outgoing correspondence. He, Willich, made use of this to keep himself informed of the activities of the Prussian police.

It was notorious that Willich had been on terms of intimate

friendship with Fleury for about a year, and he had received assistance from him. But if Willich knew since August 1852 that he was a Prussian spy and if he was likewise familiar with his activities how was it possible that he should have remained ignorant of the original minute-book?

That he did not intervene until the Prussian government itself *disclosed* that Fleury was a spy?

That he intervened in a way which at best caused the removal of his ally Hirsch from England and of the officially witnessed proofs of Fleury's guilt from the hands of the "Marx party"?

That he continued to receive assistance from Fleury, who boasts that he has in his possession Willich's receipt for £15 sterling?

That Fleury continued to be actively engaged in the German-American revolutionary loan?

That he informed Fleury of the meeting place of his own secret society so that Prussian agents in the next room could make records of the debates?

That he revealed to Fleury the route of the above-mentioned emissary, the journeyman tailor, and that he even received money from Fleury towards the costs of this mission?

That, lastly, he told Fleury that he had instructed Hentze, who lived with him, how he should testify *against* Becker at the trial in Cologne?* It must be admitted— *que tout cela n'est pas bien clair.*[a]

VII
JUDGMENT[288]

As the police mysteries were gradually explained, public opinion declared itself increasingly in favour of the defendants. When it became apparent that the original minute-book was a fraud an acquittal was generally expected. The *Kölnische Zeitung* felt induced to defer to public opinion and to dissociate itself from the

---

* As to relations between Willich and Becker:

"Willich writes me the funniest letters; I do not reply, but this does not prevent him from describing his latest plans for a revolution. He has appointed me to revolutionise the Cologne garrison!!! The other day we laughed till the tears came. His idiocy will spell disaster for countless people yet; for a single letter would suffice to guarantee the salaries of a hundred Demagogue[286] judges for three years. As soon as I have completed the revolution in Cologne he would *have no objection* to assuming the leadership for all subsequent operations. Very kind of him!" (From a letter by Becker to Marx, January 27, 1851.) [*Note by Marx.*[287]]

[a] All that is not exactly clear (Beaumarchais, *La folle journée, ou le mariage de Figaro,* Act V, Scene 16).— *Ed.*

government. Little items favourable to the defendants and casting suspicion on Stieber suddenly found their way into columns that had earlier contained nothing but police insinuations. Even the Prussian government threw in the sponge. Its correspondents in *The Times* and *The Morning Chronicle* suddenly began to prepare public opinion abroad for an unfavourable outcome. Monstrous and destructive as the teachings of the defendants were, horrifying as were the documents found in their possession, conclusive evidence of a conspiracy was nevertheless wanting and a conviction was therefore unlikely. So low-spirited and discouraged did the Berlin correspondent of *The Times*[a] write, who obsequiously echoed the fears that were circulating in the upper circles of the city on the Spree. All the more extravagant then was the rejoicing of the Byzantine court and its eunuchs when the electric telegraph flashed its message of the jury's verdict of "Guilty" from Cologne to Berlin.

With the unmasking of the minute-book the case had advanced to a new stage. The jury was no longer free merely to find the defendants guilty or not guilty; they must either find the defendants guilty—or the government. To acquit the accused would mean condemning the government.

Replying to the summing-up for the defence, Public Prosecutor Saedt abandoned the original minute-book. He was unwilling to make use of a document on which such a slur had been cast, he himself thought that it was "unauthentic", it was an "unfortunate" book, it had resulted in much time being wasted, it added nothing factual to the case, Stieber's praiseworthy zeal had led in this instance to his being deceived, etc.

But the prosecution itself had maintained in its indictment that there was "much that was true" in the book. Far from declaring it spurious the prosecution had regretted only that it could not prove it to be authentic. But if the original minute-book was not authentic though Stieber had sworn to its authenticity, Cherval's statement in Paris was invalidated despite Stieber's sworn testimony, and to this statement Saedt had returned in his summing-up; indeed all the material evidence accumulated[b] by the most strenuous efforts of all the authorities of the Prussian state for $1^1/_2$ years was invalidated at one stroke. The court sitting set down for July 28 was postponed for three months. Why? Because Chief of Police Schulz had been taken ill. And who was Schulz? The original discoverer of the original

---

[a] The reference is to the item: "Prussia (From Our Own Correspondent)", Berlin, November 7, which was published in *The Times*, No. 21270, November 11, 1852.— *Ed.*

[b] A pun: instead of *aufgestöbert* (accumulated), Marx uses *aufgestiebert*—an allusion to *Stieber.— Ed.*

minute-book. Let us go back even further. In January and February 1852, Frau Dr. Daniels' house had been searched. On what grounds? On the grounds discovered in the *first few pages* of the original minute-book that Fleury had sent to Schulz, that Schulz had sent to the police authorities in Cologne, that the police authorities in Cologne had sent to the examining magistrate, that led the examining magistrate to the house of Frau Dr. Daniels.

In October 1851, despite the Cherval conspiracy, the Indictment Board was still unable to discover the missing indictable offence and on instructions from the Ministry it therefore ordered a new investigation. Who was in charge of this investigation? Chief of Police Schulz. It was therefore Schulz's task to discover the offence. What did Schulz discover? The original minute-book. The only new material he provided was limited to the loose leaves of the minute-book which on Stieber's orders were later completed and bound. Twelve months' solitary confinement for the accused simply to give the original minute-book the time necessary to be born and to grow. "Bagatelles!" Saedt exclaims and finds evidence of the guilt of the accused in the mere fact that it took them and their counsel eight days to clean out an Augean stable that all the authorities of the Prussian state had needed $1^1/_2$ years to fill while the accused had to remain $1^1/_2$ years in gaol. The original minute-book was no mere single item of evidence; it was the focal point where all the threads spun by the various Prussian governmental authorities met—embassy and police, ministry and magistracy, prosecution and postal authorities, London, Berlin and Cologne. The original minute-book meant so much to the case that it was invented in order that a case might be made out. Couriers, telegrams, the intercepting of letters, arrests, perjuries to support the original minute-book, forgeries to bring it into existence, attempted bribery to authenticate it. When the mystery of the original minute-book was revealed the mystery of the whole monster trial was revealed with it.

The miracles performed by the police were originally necessary to conceal the completely political nature of the trial. "The revelations you are about to witness, Gentlemen of the Jury," said Saedt when opening for the prosecution, "will prove to you that this trial is not a political trial." But now he emphasises its political character so that the police revelations should be forgotten. After the $1^1/_2$-year preliminary investigation the jury needed objective evidence in order to justify itself before public opinion. After the five-week-long police comedy they needed "politics *pure and simple*" to extricate themselves from the sheer mess. Saedt therefore did not only confine himself to the material that had led the Indictment Board to the conclusion that "there was no factual evidence of an indictable offence". He went even further. He attempted to prove that the law against conspiracy does not require any indictable action, but is simply a law with a political purpose, and the category of conspiracy is therefore merely a pretext for burning political heretics in a legal way. The success of his attempt promised to be all the greater because of the decision to apply the new Prussian Penal Code that had been promulgated after the accused had been arrested. On the pretext that this code contained extenuating provisions the servile court was able to permit its retroactive application.

But if it was simply a political trial why a preliminary investigation lasting $1^1/_2$ years? For political reasons.

As it is therefore a question of politics are we to engage in a fundamental discussion of politics with a Saedt-Stieber-Seckendorf, with a Göbel, with a Prussian government, with the 300 most highly taxed people in the district of Cologne, with the Royal Chamberlain von Münch-Bellinghausen and with the Freiherr von Fürstenberg? *Pas si bête.*[a]

Saedt admits (in the sitting on November 8) that

"when some few months ago, the Chief Public Prosecutor commissioned him to join him in representing the prosecution in this affair, and when, as a result, he began to read through the files he first hit upon the idea of making a somewhat more thorough study of communism and socialism. He felt impelled to impart the results of his studies to the jury, especially since he thought he might proceed on the assumption that many of them like himself may have not greatly concerned themselves with the subject hitherto."

So Saedt bought the well-known compendium by Stein.[b]

And what he has learnt today,
he'll teach to others tomorrow.[c]

But the prosecution was afflicted by a singular misfortune. It sought objective evidence for a case against Marx and found objective evidence for the case Cherval. It went in search of the communism propagated by the defendants and found the communism they combated. Various sorts of communism can indeed be found in Stein's compendium, but not the sort Saedt was seeking. Stein had not yet recorded German, critical communism. It is true that Saedt has in his possession a copy of the *Manifesto of the Communist Party* that the defendants recognise as the manifesto of their party. This *Manifesto* contains a chapter devoted to a criticism of the whole previous literature of socialism and communism, i.e. of

---

[a] We are not that stupid.— *Ed.*
[b] L. Stein, *Der Socialismus und Communismus des heutigen Frankreichs.*— *Ed.*
[c] Schiller, "Die Sonntagskinder" (paraphrased).— *Ed.*

the whole of the wisdom recorded in Stein. From this chapter the distinction between the kind of communism propounded by the defendants and all previous kinds must become apparent; that is to say the specific content and the *specific political tendency* of the theory against which Saedt seeks to act. But no Stein will help him over this stumbling-block.[a] Here understanding was essential, if only in order to prosecute. How did Saedt manage when Stein left him in the lurch? He claimed:

"The *Manifesto* consists of *three sections*. The first section contains a historical account of the social status of the various citizens (!) from the communist point of view" (very fine[b]). "...The second section expounds the communist point of view *vis-à-vis* the proletariat.... Lastly, the final section treats of the position of the Communists in different countries...." (!) (Sitting of November 6.)

Now in fact the *Manifesto* consists of four sections, not of three, but what the eye does not see the heart does not grieve over. Saedt claims therefore that there are three sections and not four. The section which for him does not exist is that same accursed section with the critique of communism as recorded by Stein, that is to say the section that contains the *specific brand* of communism advocated by the defendants. Poor Saedt! First he cannot find an *indictable offence*, and now he cannot find indictable *political views*.

But "grey, dear friend, is every theory".[c]

"In recent times," as Saedt observed, "competent and incompetent people have been concerned with the so-called social question and its solution."

Saedt at any rate belongs to the competent,[d] for three months ago the Chief Public Prosecutor, Seckendorf, officially authorised him to study socialism and communism. The Saedts of all times and all places have from time immemorial unanimously declared that Galileo was "incompetent" to explore the movements of the heavenly bodies, but that the inquisitor who accused him of heresy was "competent" to do so. *E pur si muove.**[e]

* Saedt was not only "competent". He was moreover—as a reward for his performance in this trial—appointed Chief Public Prosecutor for the Rhine Province and remained in this post until he was pensioned, and afterwards, provided with the holy sacraments, he passed on. [Note by Engels to the edition of 1885.]

---

[a] A pun on the name *Stein* and the phrase *Stein des Anstosses* (stumbling-block).— *Ed.*

[b] Marx uses the English words "very fine".— *Ed.*

[c] Goethe, *Faust*, Erster Teil, "Studierzimmer".— *Ed.*

[d] A pun on *berufen*—competent, authorised, appointed, called upon, and *unberufen*—incompetent, unauthorised, etc.— *Ed.*

[e] But it does move.— *Ed.*

The defendants, who represented the revolutionary proletariat, stood defenceless before the ruling classes who were represented by the jury; the defendants therefore were condemned because they stood before this jury. What could, for a moment, move the bourgeois conscience of the jury, just as it had deeply disturbed public opinion, was the unmasking of the intrigues of the government, the corruption of the Prussian government that had been laid bare before their eyes. But, the members of the jury reasoned, if the Prussian government could risk using such infamous and at the same time such foolhardy methods against the accused, if it could, as it were, stake its European reputation, then the accused must be damnably dangerous, however small their party, and their theories in any case must be a real power. The government has violated every law in the penal code in order to protect us from these monstrous criminals. Let us for our part sacrifice our little *point d'honneur* to save the government's honour. Let us be thankful and let us condemn.

With their verdict of *Guilty* the Rhenish nobility and the Rhenish bourgeoisie joined in the cry uttered by the French bourgeoisie after December 2: "Property can be saved only by theft, religion only by perjury, the family only by bastardy, order only by disorder!"

In France the whole political edifice has prostituted itself. And yet no institution prostituted itself so deeply as French courts of law and French juries. Let us surpass the French judges and jurymen, the judge and jury exclaimed in Cologne. In the Cherval case immediately after the coup d'état the Paris jury acquitted Nette though there was more evidence against him than against *any one* of the accused [in Cologne]. Let us surpass the jury of the coup d'état of December 2. Let us, in condemning Röser, Bürgers, etc., also condemn Nette retrospectively.

Thus the superstitious faith in the jury, still rampant in Rhenish Prussia, was broken. People realised that the jury was a court-martial of the privileged classes; it was created to bridge the gaps in the law with the broad bourgeois conscience.

Jena! [289] ...That is the final outcome of a government that requires such methods in order to survive and of a society that needs such a government for its protection. The word that should stand at the end of the communist trial in Cologne is ... **Jena!**

Karl Marx

PARLIAMENT.—VOTE OF NOVEMBER 26.—
DISRAELI'S BUDGET

London, Friday, December 10, 1852

My predictions on the eventful results of the renewed party struggle in Parliament have been realized.[a] At the opening of the session[b] the opposition commanded a negative majority against ministers; but the several conflicting fractions which composed that majority have, since then, mutually paralyzed each other. The House of Commons, on the 26th of November, when it adopted, instead of the "radical" free trade resolution of Mr. Villiers, the equivocal amendment of Lord Palmerston, offered the spectacle of universal and mutual cheating, of the general dissolution and dislocation of all the old parliamentary parties.

The resolution of Mr. Villiers, which designed the act of 1846[290] as "wise and just," was drawn up without the knowledge of Cobden and Bright, the free traders *par excellence*. The Whigs had resolved to act for the interests of the free traders, without conceding to them either the initiative or any share in the Government, after the presumed victory. Russell, the original author of the words "wise and just," so offensive to the ministry, gave his consent to the Graham amendment; the Peelites, joined by the Ministerialists, tendered a proposition which recognizes the expediency of free trade for the future, and denies it in the past, leaving the Tories at liberty to compensate for the losses sustained by the act of Sir Robert Peel; the same Peelites rejected the amendment of Disraeli, and reassuming their own proposition, prepared to support the original free trade resolution; the Whigs, on the very eve of triumph, routed by the appearance of

---

[a] See this volume, pp. 369-77.— Ed.
[b] On November 4, 1852.— Ed.

Palmerston, who took up the amendment of Graham, and thus, with the assistance of the Peelites, secured the victory to the Ministerialists; finally, the victory itself, won by a protectionist ministry, consisted in the recognition of free trade, and was opposed by none but the fifty-three most decided adherents of their own party. Such an imbroglio of false positions, party intrigues, Parliamentary maneuvers, mutual treasons, &c., is the *résumé* of the debate on the 26th, in which the policy of free trade was officially acknowledged, but interpreted by Protectionists, represented by Protectionists, and to be carried out by Protectionists.

In a former letter, written before the commencement of the session, I indicated already that Disraeli, after dropping himself, in his electioneering speeches, the restoration of the Corn Laws, intended to compensate the landlords in the shape of a tax reform, which would enable the farmers to continue to pay their old Protectionist rents.[a] By taking off the farmer's shoulders part of the present weight of taxation, and imposing it on the backs of the mass of the people, Disraeli flatters himself to have discovered a panacea for the suffering landlords far more available than the old precarious system of protection which speculated directly on the *stomachs* of the multitude. To speculate on their *pockets*—such is the ingenious plan of Mr. Disraeli, now revealed in his budget, which, on the 3d inst., he laid before the House of Commons, and the fate of which will probably be decided in this night's debate.

It is customary with German Governments and German philanthropists to talk of "measures for the elevation of the laboring classes." (Massregeln zur Hebung der arbeitenden Klassen.)[291] Now, Mr. Disraeli's budget might not improperly be called a series of "measures for the elevation of the idle classes." However, as in the case of our German Governments and philanthropists, such measures have regularly turned out mere shams, so also the plan at present contemplated by the English Chancellor of the Exchequer for the benefit of the idle classes is a plain humbug, intended to induce the farmers the more readily to pay their actual high rents, by holding out to them an apparent reduction of their burdens, a delusion which he can only practise upon them by some evident real defraudation of the town population.

Disraeli had, for a long time, mysteriously announced his

---

[a] See this volume, p. 364.— *Ed.*

budget; he had promised the world with no less than an eighth miracle. His budget was to

"put a term to the strife of interests; to end the internecine war between classes;" to "give satisfaction to all, without damaging any of them;" to "melt the different interests in one flourishing community;" to "create for the first time a harmony between our commercial and financial systems, by the establishment of new principles," *looming in the future*.[a]

Let us now examine his revelations which no longer loom in the future, but have already since a week been communicated to the English Parliament and the world at large. As it behoves such revelations of mysteries, Disraeli introduced them with the fitting ceremonial and important-looking behavior. Peel, in his financial statement of 1842, had spoken for two hours; Disraeli takes no less than full five hours.[b] One hour he dilated in showing that the "suffering" interests do not suffer; another one in what he did *not mean* to do for them, on which occasion he contradicted Walpole's, Packington's, Malmesbury's and his own former declarations; and the remainder of the five hours in the *exposé* of the budget, and sundry episodes on the condition of Ireland, the defense of the country, prospective reforms in the Administration, and other entertaining topics.

The principal features of the budget are as follows:

1. *The Shipping Interest.* A portion of the light dues is relaxed, amounting to about £100,000 per annum. This is a relief of less than sixpence per tun per annum, and cannot reach the shipping interest before the middle of the ensuing year. The charge for passing tolls is entirely to cease. Some of the powers of the Admiralty, which have given offense to the merchant navy, shall be done away with, viz.: the officers of the navy, if they enlist seamen of foreign stations, are not to require immediate payment of their wages—they are to furnish gratuitous assistance to vessels in distress—and in harbor they are not to drive peaceable craft out of the most eligible anchorage. Finally, a Committee of the

---

[a] Quoted from the following documents: Disraeli's address to the electors of the County of Buckingham, March 1, 1852, published in *The Times*, No. 21052, March 2, 1852, under the title "The New Chancellor of the Exchequer and His Constituences"; Disraeli's speech at a dinner arranged by the electors of the County of Buckingham, March 12, 1852 (*The Times*, No. 21062, March 13, 1852); Disraeli's speech in the House of Commons, November 11, 1852 (*The Times*, No. 21271, November 12, 1852).— *Ed.*

[b] Disraeli's speech in the House of Commons on December 3, 1852, published in *The Times*, No. 21290, December 4, 1852, under the title "The Financial Statement".— *Ed.*

House of Commons is to be appointed on the subject of pilotage and ballasting. So much for the shipping interest. Lest the free traders should boast of any positive concession made to them by these provisions, the remnant of the timber duties remains as it was.

2. *Colonial Interest.* Leave is granted to refine sugar in bond, so that henceforth duty will be payable upon the quantity of saleable refined sugar produced, instead of upon the raw produce itself. Besides this, the Chinese immigration to the West Indies is to be encouraged to supply the planters with a sufficient number of cheap labor. The differential duties on sugar shall not be abolished.

3. *Malt-Tax and Hop-Duties.* The malt-tax is to be reduced by one-half, which, according to Mr. Disraeli's statement, would engender a loss of revenue amounting to £2,500,000. The hop-duties are likewise to be reduced to one-half, which would create another loss of about £300,000. These reductions are to take place on and from the 10th of October, 1853. Instead of the existing prohibition of foreign malt, and the actual duty on foreign hop, foreign hop and malt will be admitted at a duty corresponding to the excise-duty charged there.

4. *Tea.* The present duty shall be reduced from 2s.2$^1/_2$ d. to ls. per lb. upon all qualities, but this reduction shall be effected gradually within six years, so that in 1853 there will be a reduction of 4$^1/_2$ d. and every following year of 2d. till the expiration of 1858. The reduction for the year 1853 would thereby amount to £400,000.

5. *Property-and Income-Tax.* This tax, which has only been voted until August 5, 1853, is to be renewed for three years, the amount remaining the same, but the distribution to be altered. There shall be a distinction between the charges on realized property and those on industrial income. Real properties and the funds continue to be charged at 7 pence the pound; while on industrial incomes (farmers, trades, professions, and salaries) an abatement on the charge from 3 per cent. upon 2 per cent. is projected. The latter are henceforth only to pay 5$^1/_4$d. in the pound. On the other hand the standard of exemption shall be lowered from £150 to £100 per annum, and upon property and funds to £50 a year. To prevent all losses to farmers by this projected change, they are to be charged at the rate of one-third of the rent, in place of one-half at present, so that the alteration will exempt all farmers renting less than £300 a year. As a boon to the Church, all parsons with an income of £100 a year shall

remain exempt from the tax. Finally, the income-tax is for the first time to be extended to Ireland, not by any means, to the landlords, but only as far as regards funds and salaries.

6. *House-Tax.*—This is to be extended to all occupiers of houses rented at £10 per annum, instead, as formerly, only to those occupiers of houses valued at £20 per annum. Besides, the rate of the house-tax shall be doubled, i.e., from sixpence in the pound on shops, and ninepence in the pound on dwelling-houses, to one shilling and one shilling sixpence respectively.

The *résumé* of this budget would be—

On one side: Extension of the income-tax in England to such classes of the town population as have hitherto been exempted from it, and introduction of the same into Ireland for fund-holders and public functionaries; extension of the house-tax to such classes of the town population as were hitherto exempted from it, and doubling of the rate of the tax. *On the other side:* Diminution of the agricultural malt-tax and hop-duty by £2,800,000; relief of the shipping interest by £100,000; reduction of the tea-duties by £400,000.

The town population is to receive an increase of taxation in the shape of a new income-tax, an extension of the house-tax, and a double rate of the same, in order to relieve the rural population of a tax-amount of £2,800,000. The small shopkeeper, the better-paid mechanic and the commercial clerk would thus find themselves contributors to the house-tax, and become for the first time subject to the income-tax. The land accordingly would have to pay sevenpence in the pound, while dwelling-houses would pay two shillings one penny. The reduction in the tea-duties does not affect this proportion, its amount being comparatively very small with regard to the increased direct taxation, and its advantages being alike accessible to the country and to the towns.

The exemption of Irish landlords from all income-tax, of English farmers and clergymen from the extended income-tax, is manifestly a favor bestowed on the country at the cost of the towns. But who is the gainer by the reduction of the malt-tax—the landlord, the farmer, or the consumer? A reduction of taxes is a reduction of the risks of production. According to the laws of political economy, a reduction in the costs of production would involve a reduction of prices, and consequently benefit neither the landlord nor the farmer, but only the consumer.

There are, however, two circumstances to be considered in this case. In the first place, the soil on which first-rate barley can be grown is monopoly land in England, and restricted to Nottinghamshire, Norfolk, etc., while the foreign supply of malt is limited by the nature of the commodity itself, neither barley nor malt being able to support long sea-voyages. Secondly, the large English brewers virtually possess a monopoly, chiefly supported by the present license system, so that even the abolition of the Corn Laws has effected no fall in the prices of porter and ale.

Thus, then, the gain on the reduction of the malt-tax would neither be in favor of the farmer nor the consumer, but only become divided between the landlords and the great brewers.—And as the odious interference of the excise with agriculture is to be maintained, the collecting of half the sum of the former taxes would continue to absorb the same amount of administrative costs as that of the whole did before. At present, the costs of collecting £14,400,000 of excise duties amount to £5 6s per cent. After the reduction of the tax by three millions, the rate would amount from £6 to £6 4s. Briefly, there would be so much less profit, and so much mischievous expense more.

The budget of Disraeli thus resumes itself into a compensation to landlords; "a compensation with a revenge."

But this budget has yet another no less interesting feature.

If you want to carry your commercial system of free trade, you have first of all to change your financial system. "You have to return from indirect taxation to direct taxation," says Disraeli, and Disraeli is right.

Direct taxation, as the most simple, is also the most ancient and first mode of taxation, contemporaneously with a state of society based on landed property. The towns afterward introduced the system of indirect taxation, but in the course of time, with the modern division of labor, the system of Great Industry, and the direct dependence of the home trade upon the foreign trade and the market of the world, the system of indirect taxation comes into a twofold conflict with the social wants. On the frontiers it becomes identical with protective duties, and disturbs or prevents the free intercourse with other countries. In the interior it is identical with fiscal interference in production—unsettles the relative value of commodities, and disturbs free competition and exchange. From both these reasons its abolition becomes a necessity. The system of direct taxation must be returned to. But direct taxation admits of no delusions, and every class perceives exactly what share it has in the contribution towards the public expenses. Nothing is therefore less popular in England than direct taxation, income-tax, property-tax, house tax, etc. Now the question is, how the industrial classes of England, forced by free trade to adopt the system of direct taxation will be able to introduce it without either incurring popular indignation or increasing their own burdens.

Only by three ways.

By attacking the public debt; but that would be a violation of public credit, confiscation, a revolutionary measure.

By chiefly taxing the rent of land; but that also would be an attack upon property, confiscation, a revolutionary measure.

By re-vindicating the Church estates; but that again is a further attack upon property, confiscation, revolutionary measure.

"By no means," says Cobden; "let us reduce the public expenses and we shall be able to reduce also our present taxation!"

This is Utopian. Firstly the international relations of England with the Continent require a perpetual increase of the national expenses; secondly, a victory of the industrial class, represented by Cobden, would have the same consequences, for the war between capital and labor would become only the more intense and the means of repression require to be increased—in other words, the budget admits of no reduction. Let me resume.

Free Trade drives towards the system of direct taxation; the system of direct taxation involves revolutionary measures against the Church, Landlords and Fund-holders; these revolutionary measures necessitate an alliance with the working classes; and this alliance deprives the English *bourgeoisie* of the principal results it expected from Free Trade, viz.: the illimited domination of capital over labor.

Written about December 10, 1852

First published in the *New-York Daily Tribune*, No. 3650, December 28, 1852, reprinted in the *Semi-Weekly Tribune*, No. 739, December 31, 1852

Signed: *Karl Marx*

Reproduced from the *New-York Daily Tribune*

Karl Marx

A REPLY TO KOSSUTH'S "SECRETARY"

TO THE EDITOR OF *THE N.-Y. TRIBUNE*

London, Tuesday, December 14, 1852

Sir: It is some time since I sent you an explanation[a] on my late correspondence respecting the movements of Kossuth and Mazzini,[b] which caused such a noisy outburst from the American press. This explanation—in which I stated, among other things, that Kossuth himself was a perfect stranger to the different articles called forth by my correspondence, and that my intention had been rather to give a warning, &c., than to make an attack on the parties alluded to—was all I considered necessary to say on the subject, until I received the latest American newspapers containing a sort of official refutation of my remarks from the pen of a pretended Secretary of Mr. Kossuth. With regard to this "document," I have to inform you that Kossuth, on being referred to, has assured me:

1. That, at the present time, he keeps no Secretary at all.

2. That the said "refutation" had not been written by his authorization.

3. That he had not even known of it before he received my communication.

After this "authorized" declaration I shall recur no more to the subject, leaving to the uncalled-for advocates to console themselves for their ill-applied zeal.

Your Private Correspondent

First published in the *New-York Daily Tribune*, No. 3656, January 4, 1853

Reproduced from the newspaper

---

[a] See this volume, pp. 382-83.— *Ed.*
[b] See this volume, pp. 354-56.— *Ed.*

Karl Marx

THE DEFEAT OF THE MINISTRY

London, Friday, December 17, 1852

I hasten to inform you of the result of last night's debate,[a] which is the defeat of the Ministry.

This general defeat of the Ministers was preceded by the disgraceful result of the single combat of their most audacious champion, Achilles-Beresford, the Secretary of War. The Committee on the Derby Elections have made their report. That report confirms all the different facts already denounced in the petition of the Liberals, and concludes that the evidence proves that a wholesale system of bribery was carried on during the elections at Derby. The Committee, however, have forborne to follow up the evidence, and instead of directly involving Mr. Beresford in a charge of attempted bribery, they contented themselves with a severe stricture on his "reckless indifference and disregard of consequences." It remains to be seen if Parliament will accede to the views of this honest Committee and allow Mr. Beresford to retain his seat. Should that be the case, it would itself grant its ratification to the memorable words of Mr. Secretary Beresford, that "the people of England are the vilest rabble he ever saw in the world." Be this as it may be, his seat as a Minister Mr. Beresford cannot retain.

After this short digression I return to my original subject.

The members of the House of Commons having debated during four consecutive nights and the greater part of the fifth, the question whether the question should be taken upon the whole budget, or on the whole resolution, on principles or on facts, upon

---

[a] The debate in the House of Commons on December 16, 1852.— Ed.

this or that point, the conclusion at which they arrived at last, was that the House had, at present, only to meddle with the increase of the house-tax, the extension of the area of *direct taxation.*

The House rejected this first proposition of Mr. Disraeli's budget, as follows:

Ayes.................................... 286   Noes 305

Majority against Ministers, 19. The House then adjourned till Monday next. The pressure of time forbids me to speak on the debate as extensively as I could wish. I shall, therefore, confine myself to discussing merely the most memorable passages of Mr. Disraeli's last speech, by far the most important of all.

Sir Charles Wood, the late Chancellor of the Exchequer, and Sir James Graham, had directed their chief attacks against his proposed appropriation of the Public Works Loan Fund (£400,000 per annum) to balance the effects of the reduction in the shipping dues. Sir James Graham, especially, had contended most strenuously for the beneficial working of that Fund. What does Mr. Disraeli answer?[a]

"I will show the Committee what flagrant misappropriation there has been of the funds of this country, and how immense an amount of money has been squandered away, virtually without the cognizance and control of Parliament, and entirely by the machinery of this Public Works Loan Fund."

And then follows a detailed description of the scandalous financial management of the Whig administration with regard to these funds. Disraeli then proceeds to explain the principles of his budget:

"There was a very important question to settle, before we could decide even as to the first step we should take, and that was the question how far we should prevail upon the country to fix upon that sum of direct taxation which was necessary for any Ministry that attempted to enter into a career of financial Reform. [Hear!] I have been accused by the member for Halifax (Sir Charles Wood) of making a proposition which recklessly increases the direct taxation of the country. [Hear! hear!] I have been accused by the member for Carlisle (Sir J. Graham) of pushing direct taxation to rash extremes. In the first place, the proposition I made on the part of the Government, instead of recklessly increasing the amount of direct taxation, would not, if it passed, occasion so great an amount of direct taxation as prevailed under the superintendence of the finances by the right honorable gentleman, the member for Halifax, when he enjoyed not only the income- and property-tax, but the window-tax, which, in the last year of its existence, brought him nearly two millions of pounds sterling. [Cheers.] The right honorable gentleman who says, you must not recklessly increase the amount of direct taxation, reduced the amount which he received in his last year from the

---

[a] Disraeli's speech in the House of Commons on December 16, 1852 is quoted from *The Times,* No. 21301, December 17, 1852.— *Ed.*

window-tax, and was content with the modest sum of seven hundred thousand pounds sterling by way of commutation for the window-tax. I cannot forget that the right honorable gentleman who recklessly charges me with increasing the amount of direct taxation proposed first a complete commutation which would have made his house-tax larger than the one I had proposed. [Loud cheers.] But is this all? Is this all that has been done by the right honorable gentleman who charges me with increasing recklessly the direct taxation of the country? Why, there is the Minister who with a property-tax you have now producing its full amount, with the window-tax that brought nearly two millions, came down to the House of Commons one day and proposed to a startled assembly to double nearly the property- and income-tax. [Great cheering.] I look on this conduct as indicating recklessness of consequences.... We hear of the duplication of the house-tax—an innocent amount; but if the right honorable gentleman had carried the duplication of the property- and income-tax, I think he might fairly have been charged with recklessly increasing the direct taxation of the country. [Loud cheers.] Talk of recklessness! Why, what in the history of finances is equal to the recklessness with which the right honorable gentleman acted? [Loud cheers.] And what was the ground on which he made this monstrous and enormous proposition; a proposition which only the safety of the State would have justified him in making? When he was beaten, baffled, humiliated, he came forward to say that he had sufficient revenue without resorting to that proposition. [Great and continued cheering.] The future historian will not be believed to be telling the truth when he says that the Minister came down to nearly double the income-tax, and the next day came down to say that the ways and means were ample." [Renewed cheering.]

Having thus retaliated upon Sir Charles Wood, he continues:

"We had to assert that there is a difference between property and income, a difference between precarious and certain income. We had next to vindicate a principle which we believed, and do believe, is a just one, and which, if not now, must ultimately be recognized and adopted—namely, that the *basis of direct taxation should be enlarged.* [Ministerial cheers.]... If it be sought to establish as a permanent feature of our social system that there shall be created classes who are to exercise political power by means of throwing an undue weight of direct taxation upon the wealthier portion of the community, and an undue weight of indirect taxation on the working classes, I cannot imagine a circumstance more fatal to this country, or one more pregnant with disastrous consequences. [Cheers.] But of this I feel convinced, that those who will first experience the disastrous consequences will be the privileged class."

Turning round upon the free traders Disraeli says:

"The great opponents of colonial imposts here we find them all arrayed in favor of high taxation for the producer, and here we find them, with taunts to us, using all the fallacies which we at least have had the courage honorably to give up. [Tremendous cheering.] Tell me protection is dead! Tell me, there is no Protectionist party! Why, 'tis rampant and 'tis there. [Pointing to the Opposition benches.] They have taken up our principles with our benches, and I believe they will be quite as unsuccessful." [Cheers.]

In conclusion, Disraeli replies to the benevolent suggestion of Sir Charles Wood to withdraw his budget, in the following words:

"I have been told to withdraw my budget. I was told that Mr. Pitt withdrew his budget, and that more recently other persons" (the Whigs and especially Sir Ch.

Wood) "had done so too. [Laughter.] Now, I do not aspire to the fame of Mr. Pitt, but I will not submit to the degradation of others. [Loud cheers.] No, Sir; I have seen the consequence of a government not being able to pass their measures—consequences not honorable to the government, not advantageous to the country, and not, in my opinion, conducive to the reputation of this House, which is most dear to me. [Loud cheers.] I remember a budget which was withdrawn, and re-withdrawn, and withdrawn again [laughter] in 1848. What was the consequence of the government existing upon sufferance? What was the consequence to the finances of this country? Why, that ignoble transaction respecting the commutation of the window and house duty, which now I am obliged to attempt to readjust. [Cheers.] The grievance is deeper than mere questions of party consideration.... Yes, I know what I have to face. I have to face a coalition. [Cheers.] This combination may be successful. A coalition has before this been successful. But coalitions, although successful, have always found this, that their triumph has been very brief. This I know, that England has not loved coalitions. [Cheers.] I appeal from the coalition to that public opinion which governs this country; to that public opinion whose wise and irresistible influence can control even the decrees of parliament, and without whose support the most august and ancient institutions are but the baseless fabric of a vision. [The Right Honorable gentleman resumed his seat amid deafening and prolonged cheering.]"

What now is the opinion of the daily press respecting the results of this ministerial defeat!

The Morning Chronicle (Peelite) and *The Morning Advertiser* (Radical) regard the retreat of the Ministry as a certainty. *The Times* is likewise of opinion that Ministers will retreat, doubting, however, the possibility of the Opposition of making as easily a new Administration as they have unmade the old one. *The Daily News* (Manchester School) assumes the possibility of a reconstitution of the fallen Ministry in combination with Lord Palmerston. *The Morning Post* (Palmerston) considers this recomposition as a matter of course. Lastly, *The Morning Herald* (Derby-Disraeli) declares that if Ministers tender their resignation to-day, the Queen[a] will be obliged to send for them again on the next day.

One thing is certain: Ministers have been defeated on the ground of a Free Trade resolution, the extension of direct taxation. At all events, they have this satisfaction, that, if they resisted successfully the first Parliamentary attack by denying their own principles, the Opposition have beaten them in the second battle only by the negation of theirs.

Thus, what I formerly said with regard to the position of the Parliamentary parties,[b] has been confirmed entirely in this debate. The coalesced Opposition possesses, compared with the compact-

---

[a] Victoria.— *Ed.*

[b] See this volume, pp. 369-72.— *Ed.*

ness of 286 Tories, only a majority of 19 votes. Let them form a new Government, and it will fall on the first opportunity. Should the Opposition Government dissolve the House of Commons, the new elections will return, under the old conditions, the same result, viz., another House of Commons, in which the different parties will again paralyse themselves, when the old game has to be recommenced, and England's politics are plunged once more in a *cercle vicieux*.

I, therefore, insist on the old dilemma: either *Continuation of the Tory Government*, or *Parliamentary Reform*.

Written on December 17, 1852   Reproduced from the newspaper

First published in the *New-York Daily Tribune*, No. 3659, January 6 (evening edition) and January 7 (morning edition), 1853

Signed: *Karl Marx*

Karl Marx

A SUPERANNUATED ADMINISTRATION.—
PROSPECTS OF THE COALITION MINISTRY, &c.

London, Tuesday, January 11, 1853

"We have now arrived at the commencement of the *political millennium* in which party spirit is to fly from the earth, and genius, experience, industry and patriotism are to be the sole qualifications for office. We have got a Ministry which seems to command the approval and support of men of every class of opinion. Its principles command universal assent and support."

Such are the words with which *The Times*, in their first excitement and enthusiasm, have ushered in the Aberdeen Administration.[a] From their tenor one would imagine that England is henceforth to be blessed with the spectacle of a Ministry composed entirely of new, young, and promising characters, and the world will certainly be not a little puzzled when it shall have learned that the new era in the history of Great Britain is to be inaugurated by all but used-up decrepit octogenarians. Aberdeen, an octogenarian; Lansdowne, with a foot already in the grave; Palmerston, Russell, fast approaching a similar state; Graham, the bureaucrat, who served under almost every Administration since the close of the last century; other members of the Cabinet—twice dead of age and exhaustion and only resuscitated into an artificial existence; on the whole a half score of centenarians, such is the stock of which, by a simple sum of addition, the new millennium appears to have been made up by the writer in *The Times*.

In this millennium then we are promised the total disappearance of party warfare, nay even of parties themselves. What is the meaning of *The Times*? Because certain portions of the Aristocracy

---

[a] The reference is to the leading article in *The Times*, No. 21316, January 4, 1853.— *Ed.*

have hitherto enjoyed the privilege of assuming the appearance of
national or parliamentary parties, and have now come to the
conclusion that the farce cannot be continued for the future,
because, on the ground of that conviction and in virtue of the
hard experiences lately undergone, these aristocratic côteries mean
now to give up their little quibbles and to combine into one
compact mass for the preservation of their common privileges—is
the existence of all parties to cease from this hour? Or is not the
very fact of such a "coalition" the most explicit indication that the
time has arrived when the actually grown-up and yet partially
unrepresented fundamental classes of modern society, the industrial bourgeoisie and the working class, are about to vindicate
to themselves the position of the only political parties in the
nation?

The Tories, under the Administration of Lord Derby, have once
for ever denegated their old Protectionist doctrine and professed
themselves Free Traders. The Earl of Derby, on announcing the
resignation of his Cabinet, said:

"I, My Lords, remember, and probably your Lordships will remember, that the
noble Earl (Aberdeen) has, upon more than one occasion, declared in this house
that, the question of Free Trade excepted, he knew of *none* upon which there was
any difference between himself and the present Government."[a]

Lord Aberdeen, in confirming this statement, goes still further
in his remarks: "He was ready to unite with the noble Earl (Derby)
in resisting the encroachments of Democracy, but he was at a loss
to see where this Democracy existed." On both sides it is granted
that there is no longer any difference between Peelites and Tories.
But this is not all. With regard to the foreign policy, the Earl of
Aberdeen observes:

"For thirty years, though there have been differences in execution, the principle of
the foreign policy of the country has never varied."[b]

Accordingly, the whole struggle between Aberdeen and Palmerston, from 1830 till 1850, when the former insisted on the alliance
with the Northern Powers, and the latter on the "entente
cordiale" with France, when the one was against and the other for
Louis Philippe, the one against and the other in favor of

---

[a] Speech in the House of Lords on December 20, 1852, *The Times*,
No. 21304, December 21, 1852.— *Ed.*

[b] Here and in what follows the quotations are from Aberdeen's speech in the
House of Lords on December 27, 1852, as published in *The Times*, No. 21310,
December 28, 1852.— *Ed.*

intervention; [292] all their quarrels and disputes, even their late common indignation at Lord Malmesbury's "disgraceful" conduct of the foreign affairs—all this is confessed to have been mere humbug. And yet, is there anything in the political relations of England that has undergone a more radical change than her foreign policy? Up to 1830—alliance with the Northern Powers; since 1830—union with France (quadruple alliance); [293] since 1848—complete isolation of England from the whole Continent.

Lord Derby having first assured us that there exists no difference between Tories and Peelites, the Earl of Aberdeen further assures us that there is also no difference between Peelites and Whigs, Conservatives and Liberals. In his opinion:

"The country is tired of distinctions without meaning, and which have no real effect on the conduct or principles of public men. No Government is possible except a Conservative Government, and it is equally true that none is possible except a Liberal Government."

"These terms have no very definite meaning. The country is sick of these distinctions without meaning."

The three factions of the Aristocracy, Tories, Peelites and Whigs, consequently agree, that they possess no real marks of distinction. But there is still another subject on which they agree. Disraeli had declared that it was his intention to carry out the principle of Free Trade. Lord Aberdeen says:

"The great object of the Queen's present ministers, and the great characteristic of their Government would be the maintenance and prudent extension of Free Trade. That was the mission with which they were peculiarly entrusted."

In a word, the entire Aristocracy agree, that the Government has to be conducted for the benefit, and according to the interests of the middle-class, but they are determined that the bourgeoisie are not to be themselves the governors of this affair; and for this object all that the old Oligarchy possess of talent, influence and authority are combined, in a last effort, into one Administration, which has for its task [to keep] the bourgeoisie, as long as possible, from the direct enjoyment of governing the nation. The coälized Aristocracy of England intend, with regard to the bourgeoisie, to act on the same principle upon which Napoleon I professed to act in reference to the people: "*Tout pour le peuple, rien par le peuple.*" [a]

---

[a] "Everything for the people, nothing through the people."—*Ed.*

"There must, however," as Ernest Jones observes in *The People's Paper*, "be some disguise to the evident object of excluding the middle-class, and this, they (the Ministers) hope, is afforded by an admixture in subordinate and uninfluential places of aristocratic Liberals, like Sir William Molesworth, Bernal Osborne, &c. But let them not imagine that this dandified Mayfair liberalism will satisfy the stern men of the Manchester School. They mean business, and nothing less. They mean pounds, shillings, pence—place, office, and the gigantic revenues of the largest empire of the world, placed with all its resources subservient to the disposal of their one class-interest."[a]

Indeed, a glance at *The Daily News, The Advertiser,* and more particularly *The Manchester Times,*[b] that direct organ of Mr. Bright, is sufficient to convince any one, that the men of the Manchester School, in provisionally promising their support to the Coalition Government, intend only to observe the same policy on which the Peelites and Whigs had acted in reference to the late Derby Cabinet; *i.e.* to give ministers a fair trial. What the meaning of a "fair trial" may be, Mr. Disraeli has recently had occasion to learn.

The defeat of the Tory Cabinet having been decided by the Irish Brigade,[294] the new Coalition Government, of course, considered it necessary to take steps for securing the Parliamentary support of that party. Mr. Sadleir, the broker of the brigade, was soon seduced by a Lordship of Treasury. Mr. Keogh had the offer of the Irish Solicitor-Generalship, while Mr. Monsell was made Clerk of Ordnance.

"And by these three purchases," says *The Morning Herald,* "the brigade is supposed to be gained."

However, there is ample reason for doubting the effectuality of these three purchases in securing the adhesion of the entire brigade, and in *The Irish Freeman's Journal*[c] we actually read:

"This is the critical moment for Tenant Right and Religious Liberty. The success or failure of these questions depend not now on Ministers, but on the Irish members. Nineteen votes have overthrown the Derby Administration. Ten men, by walking from one side to the other, would have altered the event. In this state of parties the Irish members are omnipotent."

At the conclusion of my last letter I had stated it as my opinion, that there was no other alternative but that of a Tory Government

---

[a] Ernest Jones, "The New Mixture", *The People's Paper*, No. 35, January 1, 1853.— *Ed.*

[b] The reference is to the *Examiner and Times.—Ed.*

[c] Of December 18, 1852.— *Ed.*

or a Parliamentary Reform.[a] It will interest your readers to become acquainted with 'Lord Aberdeen's views on the same subject. He says:

"The improvement of the condition of the people could not exclude (sic!) the amendment of the representative system; for unquestionably, the events of the last election had not been such as to render any man enamoured of it."

And at the elections consequent on their acceptance of office, Lord Aberdeen's colleagues declared unanimously, that reforms in the representative system were called for; but in every instance they gave their audiences to understand, that such reforms must be "moderate or rational reforms, and made not rashly, but deliberately and with caution." Consequently the more rotten the present representative system turns out and is acknowledged to be, the more desirable is it that it should be altered neither rashly nor radically.

On the occasion of the late re-elections of Ministers there has been made a first trial of a new invention for public men to preserve their character under all circumstances, whether *out* or *in.* The invention consists in a hitherto unpracticed application of the *"open question."* Osborne and Villiers had pledged themselves on former occasions upon the ballot. They now declare the ballot an open question. Molesworth had pledged himself to Colonial Reform—open question. Keogh, Sadleir, etc., were pledged on Tenant Right—open question. In a word, all the points which they had always treated as settled, in their quality of members, have become questionable to them as Ministers.

In conclusion I have to mention another curiosity, resulting from the coalition of Peelites, Whigs, Radicals and Irishmen. Each of their respective notabilities has been turned out of that department for which alone they were supposed to possess some talent or qualification, and they have been appointed to places wondrously ill-suiting them. Palmerston, the renowned Minister of Foreign Affairs, is appointed to the Home Department, from which Russell has been removed, although grown old in that office, to take the direction of Foreign Affairs. Gladstone, the Escobar of Puseyiteism,[295] is nominated Chancellor of the Exchequer. Molesworth, who possessed a certain reputation for his having copied or adopted Mr. Wakefield's[296] absurd colonization system, is appointed Commissioner of Public Works. Sir Charles Wood, who as a Minister of Finance, enjoyed the privilege of being upset either with a deficit or a surplus in the treasury, is

---

[a] See this volume, p. 500.— *Ed.*

entrusted with the Presidentship of the Board of Control of Indian Affairs. Monsell, who hardly knows how to distinguish a rifle from a musket, is made Clerk of Ordnance. The only personage who has found his proper place, is Sir James Graham, the same who, in the capacity of First Lord of the Admiralty, has already on a former occasion, gained much credit for having first introduced the rotten worm into the British Navy.

Written on January 11, 1853

First published in the *New-York Daily Tribune*, No. 3677, January 28, 1853; reprinted in the *Semi-Weekly Tribune*, No. 803, February 4, and the *New-York Weekly Tribune*, No. 595, February 5, 1853

Signed: *Karl Marx*

Reproduced from the *New-York Daily Tribune*

Karl Marx

POLITICAL PROSPECTS.—COMMERCIAL PROSPERITY.— CASE OF STARVATION

London, Friday, January 14, 1853

Lord John Russell, in receiving the diplomatic badge, at the Foreign Office, told them that he held the seals of that Department *ad interim* only, and that in no great length of time the Foreign Office would be transferred to the Earl of Clarendon. The fact is, that Russell has always been a perfect foreigner in the Foreign Department, in which he never made himself conspicuous, except by an insipid compilation on the history, I believe, of the treaties concluded since the time of the peace of Nymwegen,[a] a book which, to confess the truth, is at least as entertaining as the "tragedy" with which the same Russell once surprised the world.[b] Lord John will, in all probability, be entrusted with the leadership of the House of Commons, with a seat in the Cabinet, where his entire activity is likely to be absorbed in framing the new Reform Bill. Parliamentary Reform is Russell's traditionary field of action, since, by his measures in 1831, he proved such a masterly hand in dividing the rotten boroughs[297] between Tories and Whigs.

My predictions on the probable inefficiency of the three Irish purchases[c] made by the Ministry for securing the enlistment of the whole "Brigade" in the cause of the Coalition Government, have already been fulfilled to the very letter. The attitude of *The Freeman's Journal* and *The Tablet*—the tenor of the letters and declarations of Messrs. Lucas, Moore, and Duffy—lastly, the resolution adopted against Messrs. Sadleir and Keogh, at the last

---

[a] John Russell, *Memoirs of the Affairs of Europe from the "Peace of Utrecht".—Ed.*

[b] John Russell, *Don Carlos; or, Persecution.—Ed.*

[c] See this volume, p. 474.—*Ed.*

meeting of the Tenant-Right Association,[298] sufficiently indicate that the Aberdeen Administration will only dispose of a very small fraction of the Irish troops.

It is known that Lord Aberdeen, the Chief of the Cabinet, will take his seat in the House of Lords. Now, Mr. Bright, in a speech recently delivered at a banquet at Manchester to your new Ambassador, Mr. Ingersoll, has seized an opportunity to explain how the total suppression of the House of Lords is the *conditio sine qua non* for the "advancement" of the industrial middle-class.[a] This first official declaration of the Manchester school since the formation of the Coalition Ministry will do something toward enabling Lord Aberdeen in discovering where that Democracy, so much redoubted by Lord Derby, exists.

Thus the party warfare declared to have been abolished for ever, by a sanguine writer in *The Times,* has already burst forth, notwithstanding that the era of the "Millennium" had opened with the adjournment of Parliament until the 10th of February.

The continuation and increase of the commercial and industrial prosperity has been loudly and unanimously proclaimed at the beginning of the New-Year, and confirmed by the publication of the revenue accounts down to the 5th inst., by the returns of the Board of Trade for the month, and the 11 months ending Dec. 5, 1852,[b] by the reports of the Inspectors of Factories, and lastly by the annual trade circulars issued at the commencement of every New-Year, and giving a general survey of all the commercial transactions of the past year.

The Revenue Returns show a total increase on the year of £978,926, and on the quarter of £702,776. There is an increase in every item on the year with the exception of *Customs.* The total sum placed into the Exchequer amounted to £50,468,193.

The *Excise*, which is supposed to indicate the well-being of the people, amounted to £13,093,170 in the year ending Jan. 5, 1852. In the year ending Jan. 5, 1853, it amounted to 13,356,981.

---

[a] The speech was delivered on January 7, 1853. See *The Times*, No. 21321, January 10, 1853.— *Ed.*

[b] This refers to *The Revenue. An Abstract of the Net Produce of the Revenue of Great Britain in the Years and Quarters ended 5th Jan., 1852, and 5th of Jan., 1853,* as well as to *Exports of British and Irish Produce and Manufactures from the United Kingdom. An Account of the Exports of the Principal Articles of British and Irish Produce and Manufactures in the eleven months ended December 5, 1852;* the data cited below from these documents and from the factory inspectors' reports and trade bulletins are taken from *The Economist,* Nos. 489 and 490, January 8 and 15, 1853.— *Ed.*

The *Stamps*, which indicate the increase of commercial activity,

as in 1851-'52, yielded 5,933,549
Amounted in the years 1852-'53, to .... 6,287,261.

The *Property-Tax*, which indicates the increase of wealth of the upper classes,

amounting in 1851-'52, to 5,304,923
Yielded in the year 1852-'53. .... 5,509,637.

The Board of Trade Returns for the month and eleven months ending Dec. 5, 1852, show:

	1852	1851	1850
Value of exports for the month ending Dec. 5	£6,102,694	£5,138,216	£5,362,319
For the eleven months ending Dec. 5	65,349,798	63,314,272	60,400,525.

Consequently, there is an increase of nearly £1,000,000 on the month, and upward of £2,000,000 on the eleven months. Yet, in the absence of all value to the imports, we know not how far it is met or surpassed by the increased value of the latter.

Passing to the reports of the Inspectors of Factories, Mr. Horner, Inspector for the Lancashire District, in his report on the half year ending Oct. 31, 1852, which has just been published, writes as follows:

"In my district, very little change has taken place in the last year as regards woollen, worsted and silk factories, and flax mills remain as they were on the 1st of November, 1851. But the increase in cotton mills has been very large. After deducting those which are at present unoccupied (and many of them will, in all probability, be soon again at work, especially those from which the machinery has not been removed), there have been set to work in the last two years 129 new mills, with an aggregate of 4,023 horse power; and there have been 53 instances of additions to existing mills, with an aggregate of 2,090 horse power, so that there has been an increase of 6,113 horse power, which must have given employment to probably not fewer than 24,000 additional hands in the cotton trade. Nor is this all; for many new mills are at present being built. In the limited area which includes the towns of Ashton, Staleybridge, Oldham and Lees, there are eleven, which it is estimated will have an aggregate power of 620 horses. The machine-makers are said to be overwhelmed with orders; and a very intelligent and observing mill-owner told me lately that many of the buildings now going up would in all probability not be at work before 1854, from the impossibility to get machinery to them. But the above returns and those that will be given by my colleagues on the present occasion, however they may indicate a great increase, still they by no means give the whole; for there is a large and very fertile source of increase of productions of which it would be very difficult to obtain any account. I allude to the modern improvements in steam-engines, by which old engines and even new engines are made to do an amount of work far beyond their nominal horse power, and to an extent formerly believed to be impossible."

Mr. Horner then quotes a letter from the eminent civil-engineer, Mr. Nasmyth, of Birmingham, describing the gain of power by working the engines at greater speed, and by adapting to them the high pressure double cylinders of Woolf, the result of which is, that at least fifty per cent. more work is done by the identical engines still in use than was done before the improvement.

It appears from a summary of the reports of all the Inspectors, that in the year ending Oct. 31, 1852, the total number of new factories occupied was 229, with a steam power of 4,771 horses and a water-power of 586 horses, and the addition to existing factories amounted to 69, with a steam power of 1,532 horses, and a water-power of 28 horses, making a grand total of 6,917 horse power.

Passing next to the annual trade circulars, we find them all breathing the same enthusiastic style in which *The Times* predicted the political millennium, and having, at any rate, this advantage, that they are based on facts and not on mere expectations, as far as they refer to the past year.

The agricultural interest has no cause for complaint. On the opening of the year the weekly average price of wheat was 37/2; at the close of the year it has reached 45/11. The rise in the prices of grain has been accompanied by a rise in the price of cattle, meat, butter and cheese.

In August, 1851, an unprecedented fall in the prices of produce was known to have taken place, chiefly in the prices of sugar and coffee, and it did not cease with that year, for the panic in Mincing Lane[a] did not reach its height till the first month of the past year. The annual circulars indicate now a considerable advance in the prices of most articles of foreign production, especially of colonial produce, sugar, coffee, etc.

As to the movement in raw materials it will be seen from the following:

"The state of the wool trade" is described in Messrs. Hughes & Ronald's circular,

"as having been throughout the past year in the highest degree satisfactory.... The home demand for wool has been unusually large.... The export of woollen and worsted goods has been on a very extensive scale, even exceeding the year 1851,

---

[a] The centre of wholesale trade in colonial goods in London.— *Ed.*

the highest rate ever before attained.... Prices have been steadily looking up, but it is only during the last month, that any decided advance has taken place, and at present they may be quoted, on the average, about 15 to 20 per cent. above the corresponding period last year."

"The wood trade," say Messrs. Churchill & Sim, "has largely partaken in the commercial prosperity of the country during 1852.... The importation into London exceeded 1,200 cargoes during 1852—closely parallel to 1851. Both years were 50 per cent. in advance of those preceding, which average about 800 cargoes. While the quantity of hewn timber stands at the average of several years; the use of deals, battens, etc.; or the sawn wood, has taken an immense start during 1852, when 6,800,000 pieces replaced the previous average of 4,900,000 pieces."

With regard to leather, Messrs. Powell & Co. say:

"The year just concluded has doubtless been a favorable one for leather manufacturers in almost every department. Raw goods, at the commencement of the year, were at low rates, and circumstances have taken place which have given leather an increased value in a greater degree than for several past years."

The iron trade is particularly flourishing, the price of iron having risen from £5 per tun to £10 10/ per tun; and more recently to £12 per tun, with the probability of a rise to £15, and more furnaces continually coming into operation.

Of the shipping, Messrs. Offor & Gamman say:

"The year just closed has been of remarkable activity to British shipping, chiefly caused by the stimulus given to business by the gold discovery in Australia.... There has taken place a general rise in freights."

The same movement has taken place in the shipbuilding department. In reference to this branch, the circular of Messrs. Tonge, Currie & Co., of Liverpool, contains the following:

"On no occasion have we been able to report so favorably for the year past of the sale of ships at this port—both of the amount of tunnage sold, and the prices that have been obtained; prices of colonial ships having advanced fully 17 per cent., with a continuing tendency upward, while stocks have been reduced to 48 sail against 76 in 1852, and 82 in 1851, without any immediate supplies being expected.... The number of vessels that have come into Liverpool within the year and sold, is 120; equal to 50,000 tuns. The number of ships launched, and in course of construction, in our port this year, is 39, computed at 15,000 tuns, against 23, computed at 9,200 in 1851. The number of steamers built, and in the course of construction here, amounts to 13, equal to 4,050 tuns.... As regards iron-built sailing vessels, the most remarkable feature of our trade is the very increasing favor they are growing into, and which are now occupying the builders both here, in the Clyde, New-Castle and elsewhere, to an unprecedented extent."

As regards *railways,* Messrs. Woods & Stubbs write:

"The returns caused the most sanguine expectations, and far outstrip all previous calculations. The returns for last week show an increased mileage over 1851 of 348 miles, $5^1/_2$ per cent., and an increased traffic of £41,426, or 14 per cent."

Lastly, Messrs. Du Fay & Co.'s Circular (Manchester) records the transactions with India and China for the month of December, 1852, as extensive, and the abundance of money alluded to as having favored undertakings to distant markets, and as having enabled those interested in them to make up for losses sustained in the early part of the year on goods and produce.

"Various new land, and mining, and other schemes attract speculators and capitalists just now."

The prosperity of the manufacturing districts in general, and particularly of the cotton districts, has been shown from the reports of the Inspectors of Factories. In reference to the cotton manufacture, Messrs. John Wrigley & Son, of Liverpool, have the following:

"Viewed as a test of the general prosperity of the country, the progress of the cotton-trade, during the year now closed, affords results the most gratifying.... It has presented many striking features, but none more prominent and noteworthy than the extreme facility with which so unprecedentedly large a crop as upward of 3,000,000 of bales, the produce of the United States of America, has been disposed of.... Preparations are [in the] making in many districts for an extension of manufacturing powers, and we may expect a larger aggregate quantity of cotton to be worked up during the approaching year than any previous one."

Most other branches of industry are in the same position.

"We refer," say Messrs. McNair, Greenhow & Irving (of Manchester), "to Glasgow as connected with its cotton and iron manufacture: to Huddersfield, Leeds, Halifax, Bradford, Nottingham, Leicester, Sheffield, Birmingham, Wolverhampton, etc., as connected with their various productions—all seem in a high state of prosperity."

The only exceptions to the general prosperity are the silk-trade and the wool-combers in Yorkshire; and the general aspect of trade may be resumed in the words of a Manchester circular:

"*Our apprehensions are those of over-speculation,* rather than of inactivity and want of means."

In the midst of this universal prosperity, a step recently taken by the Bank of England has raised a general consternation among the commercial world. On the 22d of April, 1852, the Bank of England had lowered the rate of discount to 2 per cent. On the morning of January 6, 1853, notice was given that the discount would be raised from 2 to $2^1/_2$ per cent., an increase in the charges of 25 per cent. Attempts have been made to explain this increase by the large liabilities contracted lately by some extensive railway contractors, whose bills are known to be afloat in heavy amounts.

In other quarters it was believed, as for instance by *The London Sun*,[a] that the Bank of England intended, in their turn, to take advantage of the existing prosperity by increasing discounts. On the whole, the act has been reprobated as "uncalled for." In order to appreciate it in its true light, I subjoin the following statements from *The Economist*:[b]

BANK OF ENGLAND

1852	Bullion	Securities	Minimum rate of Discount
April 22	£19,587,670	£23,782,000	Reduced to 2 per ct.
July 24	22,065,349	24,013,728	2 per ct.
Dec. 18	21,165,224	26,765,724	2 per ct.
Dec. 24	20,794,190	27,545,640	2 per ct.
1853			
Jan'y 1	20,527,662	29,284,447	

$$\left\{ \begin{array}{l} \text{2 per ct., but} \\ \text{raised to } 2\tfrac{1}{2} \text{ per cent. Jan'y 6} \end{array} \right.$$

There is, accordingly, a million of gold more in the Bank than in April, 1852, when the rate of interest was reduced to 2 per cent., but the difference is very marked between the two periods; for it has changed in regard to the movements of gold from a flowing to an ebbing tide. The afflux is peculiarly powerful, from its overbearing all the imports from America and Australia of the last month. Besides, securities were five and a half millions less in April than at present. Consequently, in April, 1852, the supply of loanable capital was larger than the demand, while now the reverse is the case.

The emigration of bullion was accompanied by a marked decline in the foreign exchanges, a circumstance which must be accounted for, partly by the considerable advance in the prices of most articles of import, partly by the large speculations in imports. To this must be added the influence of the unfavorable autumn and winter on farmers, the consequent doubts and fears respecting the next harvest, and, as a result of the latter, immense operations in foreign grains and farinas. Lastly, English capitalists have very largely engaged in the formation of railway and other companies in France, Italy, Spain, Sweden, Norway, Denmark, Germany and

---

[a] The reference is to the item "Money and Commercial News" in *The Sun* for January 6, 1853.— *Ed.*

[b] "The Bank Rate of Interest", *The Economist*, No. 489, January 8, 1853.— *Ed.*

Belgium, and partake very much in the general swindle now going on at the Paris Bourse. Paper on London is therefore more abundant in all markets of Europe than at any former period, in consequence of which there has been a continued fall in the rate of Exchanges. On July 24th the Exchange on Paris was 25f. 30c. for the pound sterling; on the 1st of January it had fallen to 25 francs. Some transactions have even been made below 25 francs.

In so far as the demand for capital has increased in proportion to the supply, the late measure adopted by the Bank of England, appears to be perfectly justified. In so far as it was intended to put a check upon speculation and upon the emigration of capital, I venture to predict, that it will be thoroughly ineffectual.

Your readers having accompanied us to such a length, through all the testimonials of the growing prosperity of England, I request them to stop a moment and to follow a poor needle-maker, Henry Morgan, who started out from London, on his journey to Birmingham, in search of work. Lest I should be charged with exaggerating the case, I give the literal account of *The Northampton Journal*.[a]

"*Death from Destitution.— Cosgrove.—* About nine o'clock on the morning of Monday, two laboring men, while seeking shelter from the rain in a lone barn, occupied by Mr. T. Slade, in the parish of Cosgrove, were attracted by groans, which were found to come from a poor man, lying in a heap-hole, in a state of extreme exhaustion. They spoke to him, kindly offering him some of their breakfast, but without receiving any answer; and upon touching him, found his body almost cold. Having fetched Mr. Slade, who was near by, this gentleman, after some time had elapsed, sent him, by a boy, in a cart, with a bed and covering of straw, to the Yardley-Gobion union-house about a mile distant, where he arrived just before one o'clock, but expired a quarter of an hour afterward. The famished, filthy, and ill-clad condition of the poor creature presented a most frightful spectacle. It appears that this unhappy being, on the evening of Thursday, the 2d, obtained a vagrant's order for a night's lodging at the Yardley-house, from the relieving officer at Stoney-Stratford, and, having then walked to Yardley, a distance of three miles and upward, was accordingly admitted; he had food given him, which he eat heartily, and begged to be allowed to remain the next day and night, which was granted, and upon leaving on Saturday morning early, after his breakfast (most likely his last meal in this world), took the road back to Stratford. It is probable that, being weak and footsore, for he had a bad place on one heel, he was soon glad to seek the first friendly shelter he could find, which was an open shed, forming part of some outfarming-buildings, a quarter of a mile from the turnpike-road. Here he was found lying in the straw on Monday, the 6th, at noon, and, it not being wished that a stranger should remain on the premises, he was desired to go away. He asked leave to stay a little longer, and went off about four o'clock, once more to seek at nightfall the nearest place of rest and shelter, which was this lone barn, with its thatch partly off, with its door left open, and in the

---

[a] *Northampton Mercury*, December 18, 1852.— *Ed.*

coldest possible situation, into the heap-hole of which he crept, there to lie without food for *seven days* more, till discovered, as has been described above, on the morning of the 13th. This ill-fated man had given his name as Henry Morgan, a needle-maker, and appeared between thirty and forty years of age, and in person, a good-framed man."

It is hardly possible to conceive a more horrible case. A stalwart, strong-framed man, in the prime of life—his long pilgrimage of martyrdom from London to Stoney-Stratford—his wretched appeals for help to the "civilization" around him—his seven days fast—his brutal abandonment by his fellow men—his seeking shelter and being driven from resting-place to resting-place—the crowning inhumanity of the person named Slade and the patient, miserable death of the worn-out man—are a picture perfectly astonishing to contemplate.

No doubt he invaded the rights of property, when he sought shelter in the shed and in the lone barn!!!

Relate this starvation case in midst of prosperity, to a fat London City man, and he will answer you with the words of *The London Economist* of Jan. 8th:

"Delightful is it thus to see, under Free Trade, all classes flourishing; their energies are called forth by hope of reward; all improve their productions, and all and *each* are benefited."

Written on January 14, 1853

First published in the *New-York Daily Tribune*, No. 3681, February 2, 1853; reprinted in the *Semi-Weekly Tribune*, No. 803, February 4, and the *New-York Weekly Tribune*, No. 595, February 5, 1853

Reproduced from the *New-York Daily Tribune*

Karl Marx

ELECTIONS.—FINANCIAL CLOUDS.—
THE DUCHESS OF SUTHERLAND AND SLAVERY [299]

London, Friday, January 21, 1853

The re-elections consequent upon the new ministerial arrangements are finished. Ministers have suffered a defeat, Mr. Sadleir, one of the Lords of the Treasury, and hitherto considered the chief of the "Irish Brigade," having been beaten by Mr. Alexander, who was elected by a majority of six votes. Mr. Alexander owes his election to a coalition of the Orangemen [300] and the Catholics. On the other hand, Ministers were victorious at Oxford University, where the poll lasted fifteen days and the struggle was extremely animated. Gladstone carried the day by a majority of 124 against Dudley Perceval, the candidate of the High Church [301] Party. To amateurs of Hudibrasian[a] logic [302] we can recommend the leaders of the two contending journals in this struggle, *The Morning Chronicle* and *The Morning Herald.*

Yesterday, after a long debate, the Directors of the Bank of England again raised the minimum rate of discount from $2^1/_2$ to 3 per cent. This circumstance had an immediate effect upon the Paris Bourse, where all sorts of securities had to submit to another decline.—But if the Bank of England should succeed in checking speculation at Paris, there will remain open another outlet for the drain of bullion: the imports of corn. The last harvest both in England and on the Continent is estimated at one-third below the average. Besides, there exists some doubt as to the quantity of food available for consumption until next harvest, in consequence of the delay in sowing the seed caused by the wet state of the soil. Therefore, large imports of grain are arranged for, and will continue to keep the course of exchange unfavorable for England. The gold ships from Australia cannot keep pace with the sudden augmentation of grain imports.

In one of my late letters I mentioned the speculation going on in

---

[a] See Samuel Butler, *Hudibras, a Poem written in the Time of the Civil Wars.—Ed.*

iron.[a] The first raising of the rate of discount, by the Bank, from 2 to $2^1/_2$ per cent., had already had its effect upon this branch of trade. Scotch pigs, for the last fortnight selling at 78 shillings, on the nineteenth of this month dropped down to 61 shillings. The Railway Share market, too, will probably be depressed since the raising of the rate of interest, by forced sales of shares hitherto deposited as securities for loans, and the commencement of these operations has already taken place. My opinion, however, is that the drain of bullion is not caused by exportation of gold alone, but that the brisk home trade, especially in the manufacturing districts, has a full share in it.

During the present momentary slackness in political affairs, the address of the Stafford House Assembly of Ladies to their sisters in America upon the subject of Negro slavery,[b] and the "Affectionate and Christian address of many thousands of the women of the United States of America to their sisters, the women of England," upon white slavery, have proved a godsend to the press. Not one of the British papers was ever struck by the circumstance that the Stafford House Assembly took place at the palace and under the presidency of the Duchess of Sutherland, and yet the names of Stafford and Sutherland should have been sufficient to class the philanthropy of the British aristocracy—a philanthropy which chooses its objects as far distant from home as possible, and rather on that than on this side of the ocean.

The history of the wealth of the Sutherland family is the history of the ruin and of the expropriation of the Scotch-Gaelic population from its native soil. As far back as the tenth century, the Danes had landed in Scotland, conquered the plains of Caithness, and driven back the aborigines into the mountains. Mor-Fear Chattaibh,[c] as he was called in Gaelic, or the "Great Man of Sutherland," had always found his companions in arms ready to defend him at the risk of their lives against all his enemies, Danes or Scots, foreigners or natives. After the revolution which drove the Stuarts from Britain,[303] private feuds among the petty chieftains of Scotland became less and less frequent, and the British Kings, in order to keep up at least a semblance of dominion in those remote districts, encouraged the levying of family regiments among the chieftains, a system by which

---

[a] See this volume, p. 479.— Ed.

[b] "The Affectionate and Christian Address of Many Thousands of the Women of England to Their Sisters, the Women of the United States of America", The Times, No. 21268, November 9, 1852.— Ed.

[c] In the New-York Daily Tribune here and in what follows is "Mheor-Thair-Chattaibh".— Ed.

these *lairds* were enabled to combine modern military establishments
with the ancient *clan* system in such a manner as to support one by
the other.

Now, in order to distinctly appreciate the usurpation subsequently
carried out, we must first properly understand what the *clan* meant.
The *clan* belonged to a form of social existence which, in the scale of
historical development, stands a full degree below the feudal state;
viz., the *patriarchal* state of society. "*Klaen*" in Gaelic, means children.
Every one of the usages and traditions of the Scottish Gaels reposes
upon the supposition that the members of the *clan* belong to one and
the same family. The "great man," the chieftain of the clan, is on the
one hand quite as arbitrary, on the other quite as confined in his
power, by consanguinity, etc., as every father of a family. To the clan,
to the family, belonged the district where it had established itself,
exactly as, in Russia, the land occupied by a community of peasants
belongs, not to the individual peasants, but to the community. Thus
the district was the common property of the family. There could be
no more question, under this system, of private property, in the
modern sense of the word, than there could be of comparing the
social existence of the members of the clan to that of individuals
living in the midst of our modern society. The division and
subdivision of the land corresponded to the military functions of the
single members of the clan. According to their military abilities, the
chieftain entrusted to them the several allotments, cancelled or
enlarged according to his pleasure the tenures of the individual
officers, and these officers again distributed to their vassals and
under-vassals every separate plot of land. But the district at large
always remained the property of the clan, and, however the claims of
individuals might vary, the tenure remained the same; nor were the
contributions for the common defense, or the tribute for the laird,
who at once was leader in battle and chief magistrate in peace, ever
increased. Upon the whole, every plot of land was cultivated by the
same family, from generation to generation, under fixed imposts.
These imposts were insignificant, more a tribute by which the
supremacy of the "*great man*" and of his officers was acknowledged
than a rent of land in the modern sense, or a source of revenue. The
officers directly subordinate to the "*great man*" were called
"*Taksmen*," and the district entrusted to their care, "*Tak*." Under
them were placed inferior officers, at the head of every hamlet, and
under these stood the peasantry.

Thus you see, the *clan* is nothing but a family organized in a
military manner, quite as little defined by laws, just as closely
hemmed in by traditions, as any family. But the land is the *property of*

SUTHERLAND AND SLAVERY;
OR,
THE DUCHESS AT HOME.

By Dr. Charles Marx.

"How canst thou say to thy *sister*: Sister, let me take the mote out of thine eye, and perceivest not the beam in thine own eye."

[Under the sanctified hypocrisy of "Church and State" a system of oppression is carried on in this gloriously free country, that equals in kindred atrocity the slavery of the American South. We give as a fitting illustration, the following historical statement, showing how the Sutherland family got their wealth. The Duchess of Sutherland here alluded to, is the celebrated "Countess-Duchess" mother-in-law of the present Duchess. How the present Duke improved on the lessons of the Countess-Duchess, the reader may have occasion to see when we have done with the latter.]

The history of the wealth of the Sutherland family is the history of the ruin and of the expropriation of the Scotch Gaelic population from its native soil. As far back as the tenth century, the Danes had landed in Scotland, conquered the plains of Caithness, and driven back the aborigines into the mountains. Mheor-Thair-Chattaibh, as he was called, in Gaelic, or the "Great Man of Sutherland," had always found his companions in arms ready to defend him at the risk of their lives against all his enemies, Danes or Scots, foreigners or natives. After the revolution which drove the Stuarts from Britain, private feuds among the petty chieftains of Scotland became less and less frequent, and the British Kings, in order to keep up at least a semblance of dominion in these remote districts, encouraged the levying of family regiments among the chieftains, a system by which these *lairds* were enabled to combine modern military establishments with the ancient *clan* system in such a manner as to support one by the other.

Now, in order to distinctly appreciate the usurpation subsequently carried out, we must first properly understand what the Clan meant. The Clan belonged to a form of social existence which, in the scale of historical development, stands a full degree below the feudal state; viz., the *patriarchal* state of society. "*Kloan,*" in Gaelic, means children. Every one of the usages and traditions of the Scottish Gaels reposes upon the supposition that the members of the *clan* belong to one and the same family. The "great man," the chieftain of the Clan, is on one hand quite as arbitrary, on the other quite as confined in his power, by consanguinity, &c., as every father of a family. To the Clan, to the family, belonged the district where it had established itself, exactly as in Russia, the land occupied by a community of peasants belongs, not to the individual peasants, but to the community. Thus the district was the common property of the family. There could be no more question about this system, of private property, in the modern sense of the word, than there could be of comparing the social existence of the members of the Clan to that of individuals living in the midst of our modern society. The division and subdivision of the land corresponded to the military functions of the single members of the Clan. According to their military abilities, the chieftain entrusted to them the several allotments, cancelled or enlarged according to his pleasure the tenures of the individual officer, and these officers again distributed to their vassals and under-vassals every separate plot of land. But the district at large always remained the property of the clan, and, however the claims of individuals might vary, the tenure remained the same; nor were the contributions for the common defence, or the tribute for the Laird, who at once was leader in battle and chief magistrate in peace, ever increased. Upon the whole, every plot of land was cultivated by the same family, from generation to generation, under fixed imposts. These imposts were insignificant, more a tribute by which the supremacy of the "*great man*" and of his officers was acknowledged, than a rent of land in a modern sense, or a source of revenue. The officers directly subordinate to the "*great man*" were called "*Tahsmen,*" and the district entrusted to their care, "*Tak.*" Under them were placed inferior officers, at the head of every hamlet, and under these stood the peasantry.

Thus you see, the Clan is nothing but a family organised in a military manner, quite as little defined by laws, just as closely hemmed in by traditions, as any family. But the land is the *property of the family,* in the midst of which differences of rank, in spite of consanguinity, do prevail as well as in all the ancient Asiatic communities.

The first usurpation took place after the expulsion of the Stuarts, by the establishment of the family Regiments. From that moment, pay became the principal source of revenue of the *Great Man,* the Mhoir-Fhear-Chattaibh. Entangled in the dissipation of the Court of London, he tried to squeeze as much money as possible out of his officers, and they applied the same system to their inferiors. The ancient tribute was transformed into fixed money contracts. In one respect these of her generosity she allotted to the expelled natives about 6,000 acres, two acres per family. These 6,000 acres had been lying waste until then, and brought no revenue to the proprietors. The Countess was generous enough to sell the acre at 2s. 6d. on an average, to the clan-men who for centuries past had shed their blood for her family. The whole of the unrightfully appropriated clan-land she divided into twenty-nine large sheep farms, each of them inhabited by one single family, mostly English farm-labourers; and in 1821, the 15,000 Gaels had already been superseded by 131,000 sheep.

A portion of the aborigines had been thrown upon the sea-shore, and attempted to live by fishing. They became amphibious, and, as an English author says, lived half on land and half on water, and after all did not half live upon both.

Sismondi, in his "*Études Sociales,*" observes with regard to this expropriation of the Gaels from Sutherlandshire—an example, which, by-the-by, was imitated by the other "great men" of Scotland:—

"The large extent of seignorial domains is not a circumstance peculiar to Britain. In the whole empire of Charlemagne, in the whole accident, entire provinces were usurped by the warlike chiefs, who had then cultivated for their own account by the vanquished, and sometimes by their own companions in arms. During the ninth and tenth centuries the Counties of Maine, Anjou, Poitou, were for the Counts of these provinces rather three large estates than principalities. Switzerland which in so many respects resembles Scotland, was at that time divided among a small number of *Seigneurs*. If the Counts of Kyburg, of Lantzburg, of Hatsburg, of Gruyeres had been protected by British laws, they would have been in the same position as the Earls of Sutherland; some of them would perhaps have had the same taste for improvement as the Marchioness of Stafford, and more than one republic might have disappeared from the Alps in order to make room for flocks of sheep. Not the most despotic monarch in Germany would be allowed to attempt anything of the sort.''

Mr. Lock, in his defence of the Countess of Sutherland, (1820,) replies to the above as follows :—

"Why should there be made an exception to the rule adopted in every other case, just for this particular case? Why should the absolute authority of the landlord over his land be sacrificed to the public interest and to motives which concern the public only?"

And why then should the slaveholders in the Southern States of North America sacrifice their private interest to the philanthropic grimaces of her Grace, the Duchess of Sutherland?

The British aristocracy, who have everywhere superseded man by bullocks and sheep, will, in a future not very distant, be superseded in turn by those useful animals.

The process of *clearing estates,* which, in Scotland, we have just now described, was carried out in England in the sixteenth, seventeenth, and eighteenth centuries. Thomas Morus already complains of it in the sixteenth century. It was performed in Scotland in the beginning of the nineteenth, and in Ireland it is now in full progress. The noble Viscount Palmerston, too, some years ago cleared of men his property in Ireland, exactly in the manner described above.

If of any property it ever was true that it was *robbery,* it is literally true of the property of the British aristocracy. Robbery of the Church-property, robbery of commons, fraudulent transformation, accompanied by murder, of feudal and patriarchal property into private property—these are the titles of British aristocrats to their possessions. And what services in this latter process were performed by a servile class of lawyers you may see from an English lawyer of the last century, Dalrymple, who, in his "History of Feudal Property," very naively proves that every law or deed concerning property was interpreted by the lawyers, in England, when the middle class rose in wealth, in favour of the *middle class*—in Scotland, where the nobility enriched themselves, in favour of the *nobility*—in either case it was interpreted in a sense hostile to the *people.*

The above Turkish reform by the Countess of Sutherland was justifiable, at least, from a Malthusian point of view. Other Scottish noblemen went further. Having superseded human beings by sheep, they superseded sheep by game, and the pasture grounds by forests. At the head of these was the Duke of Athol. "After the conquest, the Norman Kings afforested large portions of the soil of England, in much the same way as the landlords here are now doing with the Highlands." (R. Somer's Letters on the Highlands, 1848.)

As for the large number of the human beings expelled to make room for the game of the Duke of Athol, and the sheep of the Countess of Sutherland, where did they fly to, where did they find a home?

In the United States of North America.

The enemy of British Wages Slavery has a right to condemn Negro-Slavery; a Duchess of Sutherland, a Duke of Athol, a Manchester Cotton-lord—never!

KARL MARX.

Part of a page from *The People's Paper* containing an abridged version of Marx's article "Elections.—Financial Clouds.—The Duchess of Sutherland and Slavery"

the family, in the midst of which differences of rank, in spite of consanguinity, do prevail as well as in all the ancient Asiatic family communities.

The first usurpation took place, after the expulsion of the Stuarts, by the establishment of the family regiments. From that moment, *pay* became the principal source of revenue of the "*Great Man*," the Mor-Fear-Chattaibh. Entangled in the dissipation of the Court of London, he tried to squeeze as much money as possible out of his officers, and they applied the same system to their inferiors. The ancient tribute was transformed into fixed money contracts. In one respect these contracts constituted a progress, by fixing the traditional imposts; in another respect they were a usurpation, inasmuch as the "great man" now took the position of landlord toward the "taksmen" who again took toward the peasantry that of farmers. And as the "great man" now required money no less than the "taksmen," a production not only for direct consumption but for export and exchange also became necessary; the system of national production had to be changed, the hands superseded by this change had to be got rid of. Population, therefore, decreased. But that it as yet was kept up in a certain manner, and that man, in the 18th century, was not yet openly sacrificed to net revenue, we see from a passage in Steuart, a Scotch political economist, whose work was published ten years before Adam Smith's where he says (Vol. 1, chap. 16):

"The rent of these lands is very trifling compared to their extent, but compared to the number of mouths which a farm maintains, it will perhaps be found that a plot of land in the highlands of Scotland feeds ten times more people than a farm of the same extent in the richest provinces.[a]

That even in the beginning of the 19th century the rental imposts were very small is shown by the work of Mr. Loch (1820), the steward of the Countess of Sutherland, who directed the improvements on her estates. He gives for instance the rental of the Kintradawell estate for 1811, from which it appears that up to then, every family was obliged to pay a yearly impost of a few shillings in money, a few fowls, and some days' work, at the highest.[b]

It was only after 1811 that the ultimate and real usurpation was enacted, the forcible transformation of *clan property* into the *private property*, in the modern sense, *of the chief*. The person who stood at the head of this economical revolution was a female Mehemet Ali,

---

[a] James Steuart, *An Inquiry into the Principles of Political Œconomy.*—*Ed.*

[b] James Loch, *An Account of the Improvements on the Estates of the Marquess of Stafford, in the Counties of Stafford and Salop, and on the Estate of Sutherland.*—*Ed.*

who had well digested her Malthus—the *Countess of Sutherland,* alias *Marchioness of Stafford.*

Let us first state that the ancestors of the Marchioness of Stafford were the "great men" of the most northern part of Scotland, of very near three-quarters of Sutherlandshire. This county is more extensive than many French *Départements* or small German Principalities. When the Countess of Sutherland inherited these estates, which she afterward brought to her husband, the Marquis of Stafford, afterward Duke of Sutherland, the population of them was already reduced to 15,000. My lady Countess resolved upon a radical economical reform, and determined upon transforming the whole tract of country into sheep-walks. From 1814 to 1820, these 15,000 inhabitants, about 3,000 families, were systematically expelled and exterminated. All their villages were demolished and burned down, and all their fields converted into pasturage. British soldiers were commanded for this execution, and came to blows with the natives. An old woman refusing to quit her hut was burned in the flames of it. Thus my lady Countess appropriated to herself *seven hundred and ninety-four thousand acres of land,* which from time immemorial had belonged to the clan. In the exuberance of her generosity she allotted to the expelled natives about 6,000 acres—2 acres per family. These 6,000 acres had been lying waste until then, and brought no revenue to the proprietors. The Countess was generous enough to sell the acre at 2s. 6d., on an average, to the clan-men who for centuries past had shed their blood for her family. The whole of the unrightfully appropriated clan-land she divided into 29 large sheep farms, each of them inhabited by one single family, mostly English farm-laborers; and in 1821 the 15,000 Gaels had already been superseded by 131,000 sheep.

A portion of the aborigines had been thrown upon the seashore, and attempted to live by fishing. They became amphibious, and, as an English author says, lived half on land and half on water, and after all did not half live upon both.

Sismondi, in his *Études Sociales,* observes with regard to this expropriation of the Gaels from Sutherlandshire—an example, which, by the by, was imitated by the other "great men" of Scotland:

"The large extent of seignorial domains is not a circumstance peculiar to Britain. In the whole Empire of Charlemagne, in the whole Occident, entire provinces were usurped by the warlike chiefs, who had them cultivated for their own account by the vanquished, and sometimes by their own companions in arms. During the 9th and 10th centuries the Counties of Maine, Anjou, Poitou were for the Counts of these provinces rather three large estates than principalities. Switzerland, which in so many respects resembles Scotland, was at that time divided among a small number of

Seigneurs. If the Counts of Kyburg, of Lenzburg, of Habsburg, of Gruyères had been protected by British laws, they would have been in the same position as the Earls of Sutherland; some of them would perhaps have had the same taste for improvement as the Marchioness of Stafford, and more than one republic might have disappeared from the Alps in order to make room for flocks of sheep. Not the most despotic monarch in Germany would be allowed to attempt anything of the sort."[a]

Mr. Loch, in his defense of the Countess of Sutherland (1820), replies to the above as follows:

"Why should there be made an exception to the rule adopted in every other case, just for this particular case? Why should the absolute authority of the landlord over his land be sacrificed to the public interest and to motives which concern the public only?"

And why, then, should the slave-holders in the Southern States of North America sacrifice their private interest to the philanthropic grimaces of her Grace, the Duchess of Sutherland?

The British aristocracy, who have everywhere superseded man by bullocks and sheep, will, in a future not very distant, be superseded, in turn, by these useful animals.

The process of *clearing estates* which, in Scotland, we have just now described, was carried out in England in the 16th, 17th, and 18th centuries. Thomas Morus already complains of it in the beginning of the 16th century.[b] It was performed in Scotland in the beginning of the 19th, and in Ireland it is now in full progress. The noble Viscount Palmerston, too, some years ago cleared of men his property in Ireland, exactly in the manner described above.

If of any property it ever was true that it was *robbery*,[c] it is literally true of the property of the British aristocracy. Robbery of Church property, robbery of commons, fraudulent transformation accompanied by murder, of feudal and patriarchal property into private property—these are the titles of British aristocrats to their possessions. And what services in this latter process were performed by a servile class of lawyers, you may see from an English lawyer of the last century, Dalrymple, who, in his "History of Feudal Property", very naively proves that every law or deed concerning property was interpreted by the lawyers, in England, when the middle class rose in wealth, in favor of the *middle class*—in Scotland, where the nobility enriched themselves, in favor of the *nobility*—in either case it was interpreted in a sense hostile to the *people.*

The above Turkish reform by the Countess of Sutherland was

---

[a] J.-C.-L. Simonde de Sismondi, *Études sur l'économie politique.—Ed.*

[b] Th. Morus, *Utopia,* Book 1.—*Ed.*

[c] An allusion to the description of property as robbery in Proudhon's book *Qu'est-ce que la propriété?—Ed.*

justifiable, at least, from a Malthusian point of view. Other Scottish noblemen went further. Having superseded human beings by sheep, they superseded sheep by game, and the pasture grounds by forests. At the head of these was the Duke of Atholl.

"After the conquest, the Norman Kings afforested large portions of the soil of England, in much the same way as the landlords here are now doing with the Highlands." (R. Somers, *Letters from the Highlands*, 1848.)

As for a large number of the human beings expelled to make room for the game of the Duke of Atholl, and the sheep of the Countess of Sutherland, where did they fly to, where did they find a home?

In the United States of North America.

The enemy of British Wages-Slavery has a right to condemn Negro-Slavery; a Duchess of Sutherland, a Duke of Atholl, a Manchester Cotton Lord—never!

Written on January 21, 1853

First published in the *New-York Daily Tribune*, No. 3687, February 8 (evening edition) and February 9 (morning edition), 1853; reprinted in the *Semi-Weekly Tribune*, No. 805, February 11, and in *The People's Paper* (without the first four paragraphs), No. 45, March 12, 1853

Signed: *Karl Marx*

Reproduced from the *New-York Daily Tribune* and checked with *The People's Paper*

Karl Marx

CAPITAL PUNISHMENT.—MR. COBDEN'S PAMPHLET.—REGULATIONS OF THE BANK OF ENGLAND [304]

London, Friday, January 28, 1853

The Times of Jan. 25 contains the following observations under the head of "Amateur Hanging":

"It has often been remarked that in this country a public execution is generally followed closely by instances of death by hanging, either suicidal or accidental, in consequence of the powerful effect which the execution of a noted criminal produces upon a morbid and unmatured mind."

Of the several cases which are alleged by *The Times* in illustration of this remark, one is that of a lunatic at Sheffield, who, after talking with other lunatics respecting the execution of Barbour, put an end to his existence by hanging himself. Another case is that of a boy of 14 years, who also hung himself.

The doctrine to which the enumeration of these facts was intended to give its support, is one which no reasonable man would be likely to guess, it being no less than a direct apotheosis of the hangman, while capital punishment is extolled as the *ultima ratio* of society. This is done in a leading article of the "leading journal."

The *Morning Advertiser*, in some very bitter but just strictures on the hanging predilections and bloody logic of *The Times*, has the following interesting data on 43 days of the year 1849[a]:

Executions of:		Murders and Suicides:	
Millan	March 20	Hannah Sandles	March 22
		M. G. Newton	March 22
Pulley	March 26	J. G. Gleeson—4 murders	
		at Liverpool	March 27

---

[a] The data are taken from the leading article in *The Morning Advertiser*, January 26, 1853.— *Ed.*

Smith	March 27	Murder and suicide at Leicester	April 2
Howe	March 31	Poisoning at Bath	April 7
		W. Bailey	April 8
Landick	April 9	J. Ward murders his mother	April 13
Sarah Thomas	April 13	Yardley	April 14
		Doxey, parricide	April 14
		J. Bailey kills his two children and himself	April 17
J. Griffiths	April 18	Charles Overton	April 18
J. Rush	April 21	Daniel Holmsden	May 2

This table, as *The Times* concedes, shows not only suicides, but also murders of the most atrocious kind, following closely upon the execution of criminals. It is astonishing that the article in question does not even produce a single argument or pretext for indulging in the savage theory therein propounded; and it would be very difficult, if not altogether impossible, to establish any principle upon which the justice or expediency of capital punishment could be founded, in a society glorying in its civilization. Punishment in general has been defended as a means either of ameliorating or of intimidating. Now what right have you to punish me for the amelioration or intimidation of others? And besides, there is history—there is such a thing as statistics—which prove with the most complete evidence that since Cain the world has neither been intimidated nor ameliorated by punishment. Quite the contrary. From the point of view of abstract right, there is only one theory of punishment which recognizes human dignity in the abstract, and that is the theory of Kant, especially in the more rigid formula given to it by Hegel. Hegel says:

"Punishment is the *right* of the criminal. It is an act of his own will. The violation of right has been proclaimed by the criminal as his own right. His crime is the negation of right. Punishment is the negation of this negation, and consequently an affirmation of right, solicited and forced upon the criminal by himself."[a]

There is no doubt something specious in this formula, inasmuch as Hegel, instead of looking upon the criminal as the mere object, the slave of justice, elevates him to the position of a free and self-determined being. Looking, however, more closely into the matter, we discover that German idealism here, as in most other instances, has but given a transcendental sanction to the rules of existing society. Is it not a delusion to substitute for the individual with his real motives, with multifarious social circumstances pressing

---

[a] G. W. F. Hegel, *Grundlinien der Philosophie des Rechts*, I. Theil, §§ 97-101.— *Ed.*

upon him, the abstraction of "free-will"—one among the many qualities of man for man himself! This theory, considering punishment as the result of the criminal's own will, is only a metaphysical expression for the old "jus talionis": [a] eye against eye, tooth against tooth, blood against blood. Plainly speaking, and dispensing with all paraphrases, punishment is nothing but a means of society to defend itself against the infraction of its vital conditions, whatever may be their character. Now, what a state of society is that, which knows of no better instrument for its own defense than the hangman, and which proclaims through the "leading journal of the world" its own brutality as eternal law?

Mr. A. Quételet, in his excellent and learned work, *l'Homme et ses Facultés,* says:

"There is a *budget* which we pay with frightful regularity—it is that of prisons, dungeons and scaffolds.... We might even predict how many individuals will stain their hands with the blood of their fellow men, how many will be forgers, how many will deal in poison, pretty nearly the same way as we may foretell the annual births and deaths."

And Mr. Quételet, in a calculation of the probabilities of crime published in 1829, actually predicted with astonishing certainty, not only the amount but all the different kinds of crimes committed in France in 1830. That it is not so much the particular political institutions of a country as the fundamental conditions of modern *bourgeois* society in general, which produce an average amount of crime in a given national fraction of society, may be seen from the following table, communicated by Quételet, for the years 1822-24. We find in a number of one hundred condemned criminals in America and France:

Age	Philadelphia	France
Under twenty-one years	19	19
Twenty-one to thirty	44	35
Thirty to forty	23	23
Above forty	14	23
Total	100	100

Now, if crimes observed on a great scale thus show, in their amount and their classification, the regularity of physical phenomena—if as Mr. Quételet remarks, "it would be difficult to decide in respect to which of the two" (the physical world and the social system) "the acting causes produce their effect with the utmost regularity"—is there not a necessity for deeply reflecting upon an alteration of the system that breeds these crimes, instead of

---

[a] "The right of retaliation by inflicting punishment of the same kind".— *Ed.*

glorifying the hangman who executes a lot of criminals to make room only for the supply of new ones?

One of the topics of the day is the publication of a pamphlet by Mr. Richard Cobden—"1793 and 1853, in Three Letters" (140 pages). The first part of this pamphlet, treating of the time of, and previous to, the revolution of 1793, has the merit of attacking openly and vigorously the old English prejudices respecting that epoch. Mr. Cobden shows that England was the aggressive party in the revolutionary war. But here he has no claim to originality, as he does but repeat, and in a much less brilliant manner, the statements once given by the greatest pamphleteer England has ever possessed, viz.: the late William Cobbett The other part of the pamphlet, although written from an economical point of view, is of a rather romantic character. Mr. Cobden labors to prove that the idea of Louis Napoleon's having any intention of invading England is a mere absurdity; that the noise about the defenseless state of the country has no material foundation, and is propagated only by persons interested in augmenting the public expenditure. By what arguments does he prove that Louis Napoleon has no hostile intentions toward England? Louis Napoleon, he contends, has no *rational* ground for quarreling with England. And how does he prove that a foreign invasion of this country is impossible? For 800 years, says Mr. Cobden, England has not been invaded. And what are his arguments to show that the cry about the defenseless state is a mere interested humbug? The highest military authorities have declared that they feel quite safe!

Louis Napoleon has never met, even in the Legislative Assembly, with a more credulous believer in his faith and peaceable intentions, than he finds now, rather unexpectedly, in Mr. Richard Cobden. *The Morning Herald* (in yesterday's number),[a] the habitual defender of Louis Napoleon, publishes a letter addressed to Mr. Cobden, and alleged to have been written under the immediate inspiration of Bonaparte himself, in which the prince-hero of Satory[b] assures us that he will only come over to England, if the Queen,[c] threatened by rising Democracy, should want some 200,000 of his *décembraillards* or bullies.[d] But this Democracy, according to *The Herald*, is nobody else than Messrs. Cobden & Co.

---

[a] Of January 27, 1853.—*Ed.*

[b] i.e. Louis Bonaparte. For the review of the troops in Satory see this volume, p. 151.—*Ed.*

[c] Victoria.—*Ed.*

[d] *Décembraillards* (*décembre*+ *braillards*)—literally "December bullies". An allusion to the members of the Bonapartist Society of December 10.—*Ed.*

We must confess that, having perused the pamphlet in question, we begin to feel an apprehension of something like an invasion of Great Britain. Mr. Cobden is no very happy prophet. After the repeal of the Corn Laws he made a trip to the Continent, visiting even Russia, and after his return stated that all things were right, that the times of violence had passed, that the nations deeply and eagerly involved in commercial and industrial pursuits, would now develop themselves in a quiet business-like manner, without political storms, without outbreaks and disturbances. His prophecy had scarcely reached the Continent, when the Revolution of 1848 burst forth over all Europe, and gave a somewhat ironical echo to Mr. Cobden's meek predictions. He talked peace, where there was no peace.

It would be a great mistake to suppose that the peace doctrine of the Manchester School has a deep philosophical bearing. It only means, that the feudal method of warfare shall be supplanted by the commercial one—cannons by capital. The Peace Society yesterday held a meeting at Manchester, where it was almost unanimously declared, that Louis Napoleon could not be supposed as intending anything against the safety of England, *if the press would but discontinue its odious censures on his Government, and become mute!* Now, with this statement, it appears very singular, that increased army and navy estimates have been voted in the House of Commons without opposition, none of the M. P.'s present at the Peace Conference [305] having had anything to say against the proposed addition to the military force.

During the political calm, produced by the adjournment of Parliament, there are two principal topics which occupy the press, viz.: The coming *Reform Bill,* and the last *Discount Regulations* of the Bank of England.

The Times of the 24th inst. informs the public that a new Reform Bill is on the stocks. What kind of a Reform Bill it will be, you may infer from Sir Charles Wood's election-speech at Halifax,[a] in which he declared against the principle of *equal electoral districts*; from Sir James Graham's at Carlisle,[b] where he rejected the *ballot*; and from the confidentially circulated statement, that even the small Reform pills prescribed in Feb. 1852 by Johnny Russell,[306] are considered as far too strong and dangerous. But there is something which looks yet more suspicious. The mouthpiece of the Coalition Ministry, *The Economist,* in the number of Jan. 22, states, not only:

"That the reform of our representative system stands not very early on the list of topics of pressing or immediate importance," but also, that "*we want the raw materials*

---

[a] On January 3, 1853, *The Times,* No. 21316, January 4, 1853.— *Ed.*
[b] On January 2, 1853, *The Times,* No. 21315, January 3, 1853.— *Ed.*

for legislative action. The extension, adjustment, purification, protection and re-distribution of the Franchise, are branches of the question, each of which demands profound reflection, and much inquiry.... It is not that several of our statesmen may not have a good deal of useful information on all or some of these points, but it is *picked up*, not *worked out*; it is miscellaneous, partial, and incomplete.... The obvious mode of remedying this, is by issuing a *Commission of Inquiry*, charged to investigate all points of fact directly or remotely connected with the subject." [a]

Thus the Methusalem Ministry will again begin their political studies, *coram publico.* The colleagues of Peel, the colleagues of Melbourne, the subaltern of Canning, the lieutenant of the elder Grey, men who served under Lord Liverpool, others who sat in the cabinet of Lord Grenville, all neophytes of half-a-century back, are unable, from want of experience, to propose to Parliament any decisive measure on Electoral Reform. Thus, the old proverb, that experience comes with age, appears to be refuted. "This coyness in a coalition of veteran partisans is something too comical to be easily described," exclaims *The Daily News*, asking: "Where is your Reform Bill?" [b] *The Morning Advertiser* replies:

"We should be inclined to the opinion that there will be no Reform Bill at all during the present session. There may be some attempt at legislating for the prevention and punishment of bribery at elections, and with regard to some other matters of minor importance; an effort may be made to remedy evils connected with the parliamentary representations of the country, but such legislation will not be deserving the name of a new Reform Bill." [c]

With regard to the late Discount Regulations of the Bank of England, the panic at first called forth by them, has now subsided, and businessmen alike with theorists, have assured themselves that the present prosperity will not be seriously interrupted or checked. But read the following extract from *The Economist*:

"This year, upon an immense extent of our wheat-land, there is no plant at all. On a very large proportion of our heavy soils, much of the land which should have been in wheat, remains unsown, and some of that which has been sown, is in no better plight, for the seed has either perished, or the plant has come up so thinly, or has been so destroyed by slugs, that the prospects of the occupiers are not better than those of the unsown lands. It has now become nearly impossible to plant all the wheat-land." [d]

Now the crisis, temporarily protracted by the opening of the Californian and Australian markets and mines, will unquestionably become due, in the event of a bad harvest. The Discount Regulations

---

[a] "The New Ministry and Parliamentary Reform", *The Economist*, No. 491, January 22, 1853.— *Ed.*

[b] Quoted from the leading article in *The Daily News*, January 27, 1853.— *Ed.*

[c] Quoted from the leading article in *The Morning Advertiser*, January 26, 1853.— *Ed.*

[d] "Agriculture. The Season", *The Economist*, No. 491, January 22, 1853.— *Ed.*

of the Bank are only the first forebodings. In 1847 the Bank of England altered its rate of discount 13 times. In 1853 there will be a full score of such measures. In conclusion, I wish to ask the English Economists, how it happens that modern Political Economy commenced its warfare against the mercantile system by demonstrating that the influx and efflux of gold in a country are indifferent, that products are only exchanged against products, and that gold is a product like all others, while the very same Economy, now at the end of its career, is most anxiously watching the efflux and influx of gold? "The real object to be accomplished by the operations of the Bank," says *The Economist*, "is *to prevent an exportation of capital.*" [a] Now, would *The Economist* prevent an exportation of capital in the shape of cotton, iron, woollen yarns and stuffs? And is gold not a *product like all other products*? Or has *The Economist* turned, in his old days, a Mercantilist? And after having set free the importation of foreign capital, does he aim at checking the exportation of British capital? After having freed himself from the civilized system of protection, will he recur to the Turkish one?

I am just concluding my letter, as I am informed, that a report is prevalent in political circles, that Mr. Gladstone is at variance with several of the leading members of the Aberdeen Ministry, on the subject of the *Income Tax*, and that the result of the misunderstanding will probably be the resignation of the Right Hon. gentleman. In that case, Sir Francis Baring, formerly Chancellor of the Exchequer under Lord Melbourne, will probably become his successor.

Written on January 28, 1853

First published in the *New-York Daily Tribune*, No. 3695, February 17 (evening edition) and February 18 (morning edition), and in the *Semi-Weekly Tribune*, No. 807, February 18, 1853; reprinted in the *New-York Weekly Tribune*, No. 598, February 26, 1853

Signed: *Karl Marx*

Reproduced from the *New-York Daily Tribune*

---

[a] "The Bank of England and the Rate of Discount", *The Economist*, No. 491, January 22, 1853.— *Ed.*

Karl Marx
DEFENSE.—FINANCES.—
DECREASE OF THE ARISTOCRACY.—POLITICS

London, Tuesday, February 8, 1853

The Daily News states that the establishment of a defensive coast-militia is under the serious consideration of the Government.

The Bank accounts show a further decrease of bullion to the amount of £362,084. There have been shipped, during the last fortnight, about £1,000,000 partly for the continent and partly in coin, for Australia. As the bullion in the Bank of France continues to also decrease, in spite of the large importation of gold from England, there has apparently sprung up a system of private hoarding, which strongly indicates the general distrust in the stability of Napoleonic government.

At present there is manifested a general demand for higher wages, on the part of working-men, especially shipwrights, colliers, factory-operatives and mechanics. This demand is owing to the prevailing prosperity and cannot be considered as a very particular event. A fact which deserves more notice, is a regular strike amongst agricultural laborers, a thing which has never taken place before. The laborers of South Wilts have struck for an advance of 2 shillings, their weekly wages amounting now only to 7s.

According to the quarterly returns of the registrar-general, emigration from Great Britain was going on through the past year, at the rate of 1,000 a-day, the increase of population being somewhat slower. Simultaneously there was a large increase of marriages.

The deaths of Viscount Melbourne and the Earl of Tyrconnel, with that of the Earl of Oxford, make no less than three peerages, that have become extinct within the last fortnight. If there be any class exempt from the Malthusian law of procreation in a geometrical progression, it is that of the hereditary aristocracy. Take, for instance, the peers and baronets of Great Britain. Few, if any, of the Norman nobility exist at this time and not much more of the original baronet families of King James I. The great majority of the House of Lords were created in 1760. The order of baronets commenced in 1611, under James I. There are at present only thirteen surviving out of the number of baronet families then created, and of those created in 1625 there remain but 39. The extraordinary decrease of the Venitian nobility affords another instance of the prevalence of the same law, notwithstanding that *all* the sons were ennobled by birth. *Amelot* counted in his time 2,500 nobles at Venice, possessing the right of voting in the council.[a] At the commencement of the 18th century there remained only 1,500, in spite of a later addition of several families. From 1583-1654, the sovereign council of Berne admitted into the hereditary patricia 487 families, of which 399 became extinct within the space of two centuries while in 1783 there survived only 108. To recur to remoter periods of history, Tacitus informs us that the Emperor Claudius created a new stock of patricians, "*exhaustis etiam quas dictator Caesar lege Cassia et princeps Augustus lege Saenia sublegere.*"[b] It is evident from these facts, that nature does not like hereditary aristocracy, and it may safely be asserted but that for a continual infusion of new blood, and an artificial system of propping up, the English House of Lords would ere this have died its natural death. Modern physiology has ascertained the fact, that fertility decreases among the higher animals, inversely with the development of the nervous system, especially with the growing bulk of the brain. But no one will venture to affirm that the extinction of the English aristocracy has anything to do with an exuberance of brain.

It appears that the "millennium" is already considered as broken down by the same parties who predicted and originated it, even before the House of Commons has taken place. *The Times*, in its number of Feb. 4, says:

"While Manchester has been fulminating her indignation against the Government of Lord Aberdeen, ... Irish Popery and *Socialism* (?) are bestowing their questionable praises on Lord Derby and Mr. Disraeli."

As to the *Irish Socialism* alluded to in *The Times*, this term applies, of course, to the Tenant-Right agitation. On a future occasion I intend to show that the theories of all modern English bourgeois economists are in perfect accordance with the principle of Tenant-Right.[307] How little the tenor of *The Times* article just quoted is shared in by other newspapers, may be seen from the following contained in *The Morning Advertiser*:

---

[a] Amelot de la Houssaye, *Histoire du gouvernement de Venise.*—*Ed.*

[b] "For even those had died out who had been added by the dictator Caesar under the law of Cassius and by the princeps Augustus under the law of Saenius", Publius Cornelius Tacitus, *Annales*, XI, 25.—*Ed.*

"We should despise the Irishmen, could we believe them capable of deserting the principle of Tenant-Right." [a]

The wrath of the Aberdeen organ is explained by the fact of the Millenarian Ministry being completely disappointed. Messrs. Sadleir and Keogh were the acknowledged leaders of the Brigade—the one in the Cabinet, the other in the field. Mr. Sadleir directed and managed, while Mr. Keogh made the speeches. It was supposed that the purchase of these two would bring over the whole lot. But the members of the Brigade were sent to Parliament pledged to stand in opposition to, and to remain independent of every Government that would not establish perfect religious equality, and realize the principle of Sharman Crawford's bill on the rights of the Irish tenants.[308] *The Times*, therefore, is indignated at these men being unwilling to break their faith. The immediate cause of the outbreak of this angry feeling was given by a meeting and banquet at Kells, County of Meath. The circular invited those to whom it was addressed, to express their indignation at "the recent desertion from the Irish Parliamentary party," and a resolution was passed in that sense.

This failure in the calculations of the Ministry with regard to the Brigade could have been anticipated; but a transformation is now going on in the character and position of Irish parties, of the deep bearing of which neither they nor the English press appear yet to be aware. The bishops and the mass of the clergy approve of the course taken by the Catholic members, who have joined the Administration. At Carlow, the clergy afforded their entire support to Mr. Sadleir, who would not have been defeated but for the efforts of the Tenant-Leaguers. In what light this schism is viewed by the true Catholic party, may be seen from an article in the French *Univers*, the European organ of Jesuitism. It says:

"The only reproach which can, with good foundation, be objected to Messrs. Keogh and Sadleir, is, that they suffered themselves to be thrown into connection with two Associations (the Tenant-League and the Religious Equality Association) which have no other object than to make patent the anarchy which consumes Ireland."

In its indignation, the *Univers* betrays its secret:

"We deeply regret to see the two Associations put themselves in open opposition to the bishops and clergy, in a country where the prelates and dignitaries of the Church have hitherto been the safest guides of popular and national organization."

We may infer that, should the Tenant-Leaguers happen to be in France, the *Univers* would cause them to be transported to Cayenne.

---

[a] Quoted from the leading article in *The Morning Advertiser*, February 5, 1853.— *Ed.*

The Repeal[309] agitation was a mere political movement, and therefore, it was possible for the Catholic clergy to make use of it, for extorting concessions from the English Government while the people were nothing but the tools of the priests. The Tenant-Right agitation is a deep-rooted social movement which, in its course, will produce a downright scission between the Church and the Irish Revolutionary party, and thus emancipate the people from that mental thraldom which has frustrated all their exertions, sacrifices, and struggles for centuries past.

I pass now to the "Reunion" of the leading reformers of the County of Lancaster and its representatives, which was held at Manchester on the 3d inst.[a] Mr. *George Wilson* was in the chair. He spoke only of the iniquitous representation of the commercial and industrial compared with the agricultural districts, upon which he expressed himself in the following terms:

"In the five Counties of Buckingham, Dorset, Wilts, Northampton, and Salop, 63 members were returned by 52,921 voters, while only the same number were returned by Lancashire and Yorkshire, with 89,669 county and 84,612 borough voters, making a total of 174,281. So that, if they returned members in proportion to voters alone, those five counties could only claim 19; while, if Lancashire took their proportion, it would be entitled to 207. There were twelve large cities or boroughs (taking London as a double borough) returning 24 members, with 192,000 voters, and a population of 3,268,218, and 383,000 inhabited houses. On the other side, 24 members were returned by Andover, Buckingham, Chippenham, Cockermouth, Totnes, Harwich, Honiton, Thetford, Lymington, Marlborough, Great Marlborough and Richmond; but they had only 3,569 voters, 67,434 inhabitants, and 1,373 inhabited houses.... The most timid reformer and most moderate man would hardly object to the disfranchisement of those boroughs which had a population less than 5,000, and to handing over the 20 members to those large constituencies."

Mr. Milner Gibson, M.P., took up the subject of National Education, and the Taxes on Knowledge. With regard to the Reform Bill, the only passage in his speech deserving notice, is his declaration on the point of equal electoral districts:

"It may be, if you please, a great *class-question.*"

Mr. Brotherton, another M.P., said:

"No Reform Bill would be satisfactory, at this time, which did not propose to equalize the distribution of the representation."

But by far the most memorable speech was that of Mr. Bright, M.P., the real man among the "Manchester men." He said:

---

[a] Speeches at a meeting of Parliamentary Reform supporters at Manchester on February 3, 1853 are quoted from the account of the meeting published in *The Times,* No. 21344, February 5, 1853, under the title "Social Soirée of Reformers at Manchester."—*Ed.*

"The Government is a coalition Government, composed of Whigs and Peelites.... There is no great cause for any throwing up of caps, as if we had in the Government men of new principles and of a new policy, who are about to take a great start, and who would not require to be urged on by all those who are favorable to Reform in every part of the country. [Hear.]"

In reference to Parliamentary Reform he said:

"If Louis Napoleon had started with a Representation like ours, in France; if he had given all the Members to the rural districts, where the Bonaparte family are so popular, and had not allowed Members to be returned from Paris, and Lyons, and Marseilles, all the Press of England would have denounced the sham Representation which he was establishing in that country. [Hear! hear!] ... We have one-eighth of the population of England here in Lancashire; we have one-tenth of its rateable property, and we have one-tenth of the whole number of houses.... We begin to know where we are now. [Loud cheers.]... There is another little difficulty, which is the difficulty of the ballot. [Hear! hear!] I read Lord John Russell's speech at his election, and really these London electors were in capital humor or they would not have allowed such an argument to pass without saying something against it. 'He was against secrecy everywhere'; and when I read the paragraph, I said to myself 'Very well; if I had been one of your supporters, I should have recommended you to take a reporter from *The Times* office to the next Cabinet-meeting with you.'" [Hear! laughter.] Now we come to Sir James Graham's argument: 'He did not think secret voting could be made compulsory.' Why can it not be made compulsory? Open voting is made compulsory, and secret voting could be made compulsory. It is compulsory, at any rate, in the State of Massachusetts, if not in the other States of North America; and Sir James Graham knows perfectly well that there was no force in what he was saying to 2,000 or 3,000 of the people of Carlisle, on a rainy day, when, I suppose, people did not weigh matters under their umbrellas very carefully.

"We must not forget," concluded Mr. Bright, "that everything the country has gained since the Revolution of 1688—and especially everything of late years—has been gained in a *manly contest of the industrial and commercial classes against the aristocratic and privileged classes of this country.* We must carry on the same conflict; there are great things yet to be done. [Hear! hear! and cheers.]"

The resolution unanimously agreed to was:

"That this meeting requests the Liberal Members connected with the County of Lancaster to consider themselves a committee for the purpose of aiding in any proceedings with reference to Parliamentary Reform, with a view to secure such additional representation for this County, as its population, industry, wealth and intelligence require."

The Manchester School have repeated at this meeting their battle cry: the industrial Bourgeoisie against the Aristocracy; but, on the other hand, they have also betrayed the secret of their policy, viz.: the exclusion of the people from the representation of the country, and the strict maintenance of their particular class-interest. All that was said with regard to the ballot, national education, taxes on knowledge, &c., is nothing but rhetorical flourishes; the only serious object being the *equalization of Electoral Districts*—at least the only one upon which a resolution was passed and a pledge taken by the members. Why this? With equal electoral districts the town interest would become the commander of the country interest—the bourgeoisie would become master of the House of Commons. If it were given to the Manchester men to obtain equal electoral districts, without a necessity of making serious concessions to the Chartists, the latter would find instead of two enemies, mutually trying to outbid each other in their appeals to them, one compact army of foes, who would concentrate all their forces to resist the people's demands. There would be, for a while, the unrestricted rule of capital, not only industrially but also politically.

A bad omen for the coalition Ministry may be found in the eulogiums bestowed at Kells and at Manchester on the fallen Administration. Mr. *Lucas*, M. P., said at Kells:

"There were no greater enemies to Tenant Right than the Marquis of Lansdowne, Lord Palmerston, Sidney Herbert, &c. ... Had they not had the Whig Ministry and the Grahamites nibbling at the Tenant question? They had on the other hand the Tory officials; and he would leave it to the conscience of any man, who read the propositions that emanated from the various parties, to say whether the treatment of the subject on the side of the Derby Government was not a thousand times more honest than that of the Whigs."

At the Manchester Reunion, *Milner Gibson* said:

"Although the Budget of the late Ministry, as a whole, was bad, still there were good indications of future policy in that budget.—[Hear! hear!] At least the late Chancellor of the Exchequer[a] has broken the ice. I mean with regard to the Tea Duties. I have heard from good authority that it was the intention of the late Government to repeal the Advertisement Duty."

Mr. *Bright* went still further in his eulogium:

"The late Government did a bold thing with regard to the Income Tax. For the country gentlemen of England, themselves the owners of a vast portion of the fixed landed property of the country, for them to come forward and support a proposition which made a distinction in the rate charged on fixed property, and that on income derived from trade and other precarious sources, was a step that we ought not to lose sight of, and that we, in this district, are bound to applaud. But there was another point to which Mr. Disraeli referred, and for which I must say I feel grateful to him. In the speech introducing his budget, and in the speech in which he contended for three hours with that mass of power opposed to him, on the night of his final defeat, he referred to the tax on successions, which is what we understand by the legacy and probate duties, and he admitted that it required to be adjusted. [Loud cheers.]"

Written on February 8, 1853

First published in the *New-York Daily Tribune*, No. 3699, February 23, and in the *Semi-Weekly Tribune*, No. 809, February 25, 1853
Signed: *Karl Marx*

Reproduced from the *New-York Daily Tribune*

---

[a] Disraeli.— *Ed.*

Karl Marx

THE ITALIAN INSURRECTION. —BRITISH POLITICS

London, Friday, February 11, 1853

The political torpor which, under the protection of nature's dullest fog, has for so long a time prevailed here, has been suddenly interrupted by the arrival of revolutionary news from Italy. Intelligence has been received by electric telegraph, that an insurrection took place at Milan on the 6th; that proclamations had been posted up, one by Mazzini,[a] the other by Kossuth,[b] exhorting the Hungarians in the Austrian army to join the revolutionists; that the insurrection had been at first suppressed, but had afterwards recommenced; that the Austrians stationed in the arsenal had been massacred, &c.; that the gates of Milan were shut up. The French Government papers, it is true, communicate two further dispatches, dated Berne the 9th, and Turin 8th, which report the definitive suppression of the outbreak on the 7th. But the non-arrival of any direct information at the English Foreign Office for two days, is regarded as a favorable symptom by the friends of Italy.

Rumors are current in Paris, that great excitement prevailed at Pisa, Lucca and in other towns.

At Turin the ministry met in haste, in consequence of a communication from the Austrian Consul, in order to deliberate on the aspect of affairs in Lombardy. The day, on which the first information reached London, was the 9th of February, which day, curiously enough, is also the anniversary of the proclamation of the Roman Republic in 1849,[310] of the decapitation of Charles I in 1649, and of the deposition of James II in 1689.

---

[a] G. Mazzini, A. Saffi, "Italian National Committee" (February 1853), *The Times,* No. 21350, February 12, 1853.— *Ed.*

[b] L. Kossuth, "In the Name of the Hungarian Nation.—To the Soldiers Quartered in Italy" (February 1853), *The Times,* No. 21348, February 10, 1853.— *Ed.*

As regards the chances of the present insurrection at Milan, there can be little hope of success, unless some of the Austrian regiments pass over to the revolutionary camp. Private letters from Turin, which I expect will shortly reach me, will probably enable me to furnish you a detailed account of the whole affair.

Several statements as to the character of the amnesty lately granted by Louis Napoleon, have been published on behalf of the French refugees. Victor Frondes (a former officer) declares in the *Nation*, a Brussels paper, that he was surprised to see his name in the list of the amnestied, he having already amnestied himself, five months ago, by making his escape from Algiers.

The *Moniteur*[a] announced at first, that 3,000 exiles were to be amnestied, and that only about 1,200 citizens would remain under the ban of proscription. A few days later the same authority stated, that 4,312 persons[b] had been pardoned, so that Louis Napoleon actually forgave 100 persons more than he had previously condemned. Paris and the Department of the Seine alone numbered about 4,000 exiles. Of these only 226 are included in the amnesty. The Department of the Hérault counted 2,611 exiles; 299 are amnestied. The Nièvre furnished 1,478 victims among whom there were 1,100 fathers of families averaging three children each; 180 have been amnestied. In the Department of the Var 687 out of 2,181 have been released. Among the 1,200 republicans transported to Cayenne, only a few have been pardoned, and precisely such as have escaped already from that penal settlement. The number of persons transported to Algeria and now released, is large, but still in no proportion to the immense mass of people that have been carried over to Africa, which is said to amount to 12,000. The refugees now living in England, Belgium, Switzerland and Spain, with very rare exceptions, are entirely excluded from the decree. On the other hand, the amnesty lists actually contain a large number of persons who have never quitted France, or who have long since been permitted to re-enter it; nay, more, there are names which figure in the list several times. But the most monstrous fact is, that the list is swelled with the names of a large number of persons well known to have been slaughtered during the sanguinary "*battues*" of December.

The new Parliamentary session commenced yesterday. As a worthy introduction to the future performances of the Millenarian Ministry, the following scene was produced in the House of Lords:

---

[a] Of January 31, 1853.—*Ed.*
[b] "Décret accordant la grâce à 4312 condamnés politiques, le 2 février 1853", *Le Moniteur universel*, No. 35, February 4, 1853.—*Ed.*

The Earl of Derby asked the Earl of Aberdeen what measures the Government proposed to submit to the consideration of Parliament; upon which the latter replied that he had already, on a former occasion, explained his principles, a repetition of which would be inconvenient; and that any further statement, before the communication to be made in the House of Commons, would be premature. And now ensued a most curious dialogue, in which the Earl of Derby spoke, and the Earl of Aberdeen only bowed significantly:[a]

The Earl of Derby—"He would ask the noble Lord what measures he intended to submit to their Lordships in the course of the Session?"

After a few seconds' pause, no noble Lord having risen—

The Earl of Derby—"Does silence mean no measures?" [A laugh.]

The Earl of Aberdeen—[Muttering some inaudible words.]

The Earl of Derby—"May I be permitted to ask what measures will be introduced in this House?"

No answer.

The question of adjournment being put by the Lord Chancellor,[b] their Lordships adjourned.

Passing from the House of Lords to "Her Majesty's liege Commons," we shall observe that the Earl of Aberdeen has expounded the programme of the Ministry much more strikingly by his silence than Lord John Russell by his long and grave speech last night. The short *resumé* of the latter was: "No Measures, but Men"; adjournment of all questions of Parliamentary importance for one year; and strict payment of the salaries of her Majesty's Ministers during that time. Lord John Russell stated the intention of the Government in nearly these words:

"With regard to the number of men to be voted for the Army, the Navy, and Ordnance, there will be no increase beyond the number voted before the Christmas holidays. With regard to the amounts in the various estimates, there will be found a considerable increase upon the estimates of last year.... A bill will be brought in to enable the Legislature of Canada to dispose of the Clergy Reserves in Canada.... The President of the Board of Trade[c] will move for the introduction of a Pilotage bill.... The disabilities of her Majesty's Jewish subjects will be removed.... Propositions will be made on the subject of Education. I am not prepared to say that I am about to introduce, on the part of her Majesty's Government, a very large plan on that subject. It will include educational measures for the poorer classes, and propositions with respect to the Universities of Oxford and Cambridge.... Transportation to Australia will cease.... There will be made a proposal with respect to the system of secondary punishments.... Immediately after the Easter recess, or as soon as possible after that period, the Chancellor of the Exchequer[d] will propose the financial statement for the

---

[a] Information about the debate in the House of Lords and Russell's speech in the House of Commons on February 10, 1853 are given according to the account of them in *The Times*, No. 21349, February 11, 1853.— *Ed.*

[b] Cranworth.— *Ed.*

[c] Cardwell.— *Ed.*

[d] Gladstone.— *Ed.*

year.... The Lord Chancellor will state in a few days what are the measures he proposes to bring in for the improvement of the law.... It is the intention of the Chief Secretary for Ireland,[a] in a few days, to move the appointment of a select Committee with regard to the law of Landlord and Tenant in Ireland.... Ministers would endeavor to effect a renewal of the Income Tax for the present year, without any observation or discussion whatever."

In reference to Parliamentary Reform, Lord John Russell declares that it may perhaps be taken into consideration in the next session. Accordingly, no Reform Bill at present. Nay more, Johnny was at great pains to disclaim the idea of ever having promised to give a more liberal measure of representative reform than his bill of last session.[311] He was even indignant that words to that effect should have been ascribed to him. He never said nor meant anything of the kind. Nor does he promise that his intended bill of next session will be as comprehensive as that of 1852. With respect to bribery and corruption, he said:

"I think it better to defer giving an opinion as to whether any further measures may be necessary to check bribery and corruption. I will only say that the subject is one of the highest importance."

It is impossible to describe the cool amazement with which this speech of Finality-John [312] was received by the House of Commons. It would be difficult to state, which was greater, the perplexity of his friends, or the hilarity of his foes. All seemed to regard his speech as a complete refutation of Lucretius's doctrine, that " *Nil de nihilo fit.* " [b] Lord John at least made something out of nothing; a dry, long and very tedious speech.

There were two subjects upon which Ministers were supposed to mean to stand or fall—a new assessment of the Income Tax and a new Reform Bill. Now, as to the Income Tax it is proposed to continue it for a year in its present form. As to a Reform Bill, even of Whig dimensions, it is declared that Ministers intend to introduce it only on the condition that they remain in office for a whole year. It is altogether the programme of the late Russell Administration, minus the Reform Bill. Even the financial statement is postponed till after the Easter recess, so that Ministers may be able, in any event, to touch their quarterly pay.

The particular reform propositions are nearly all of them borrowed from Mr. Disraeli's programme. Thus for instance, the law amendment, the abolition of transportation to Australia, the Pilotage bill, the Committee on the Tenant-Right question, etc. The

---

[a] John Young.— *Ed.*

[b] "Nothing comes out of nothing" (Lucretius Carus, *De rerum natura.* V).— *Ed.*

only points belonging properly to the present Ministry, are the proposed educational reform which Lord John assures us will be of no larger size than himself, and the removal of Baronet Lionel Rothschild's disabilities. It may be questioned, whether the English people will be very contented with this extension of the suffrage to a Jewish usurer, who was notoriously one of the accomplices of the Bonapartist coup d'état.

This impudence of a Ministry, composed of two parties that were completely beaten at the late general elections, it would be difficult to explain, were it not for the circumstance that any new Reform Bill would necessitate a dissolution of the present House of Commons, the majority of which stick to their dearly-bought seats, gained by narrow majorities.

Nothing is more delightful than the manner in which *The Times* attempts to comfort its readers:

> "Next session is not quite so uncertain an epoch as *to-morrow*; for to-morrow depends not only on the will, but even on the life of the procrastinator, while, if the world endures, next session will certainly arrive. Then put off to next session—the whole Parliamentary reform—give the Ministry a rest for one year!" [a]

I, for my part, am of opinion, that it is highly beneficial to the people, that no Reform Bill is to be *octroyed* by Ministers, in the present dull state of the public mind, and "under the cold shadow of an aristocratic Coalition Cabinet." It must not be forgotten that Lord Aberdeen was a member of the Tory Cabinet, which, in 1830, refused to agree to any measure of reform. National reforms must be won by National agitation, and not by the grace of my Lord Aberdeen.

In conclusion let me mention that, at a special meeting of the General Committee of the *National Association for the Protection of British Industry and Capital,* held in the South-Sea House, on Monday last, under the Presidency of the Duke of Richmond, this Society wisely resolved to dissolve itself. [313]

Written on February 11, 1853

First published in the *New-York Daily Tribune,* No. 3701, February 25, 1853; reprinted in the *Semi-Weekly Tribune,* No. 810, March 1, and the *New-York Weekly Tribune,* No. 599, March 5, 1853

Signed: *Karl Marx*

Reproduced from the *New-York Daily Tribune*

---

[a] Quoted from the leading article in *The Times,* No. 21349, February 11, 1853. — *Ed.*

Karl Marx

THE ATTACK ON FRANCIS JOSEPH.—
THE MILAN RIOT.—BRITISH POLITICS.—
DISRAELI'S SPEECH.—NAPOLEON'S WILL

London, Tuesday, February 22, 1853

The electric telegraph brings the following news from Stuhlweis-senburg[a]:

"On the 18th inst., at 1 o'clock, the Emperor of Austria, Francis Joseph, was walking on the ramparts of Vienna, when a Hungarian journeyman tailor named János Libényi, formerly a hussar from Vienna, rushed upon him in a moment and struck him with a poniard. The blow was warded off by an aid-de-camp, the Count O'Donnell. Francis Joseph was wounded below the occiput. The Hungarian, 21 years of age, was struck down by a blow of the aid-de-camp's sword and was arrested immediately."

According to other accounts, the weapon employed was a musket.

A very extensive conspiracy for the overthrow of the Austrian rule has just been discovered in Hungary.

The *Wiener Zeitung*[b] publishes several sentences passed by courts martial on thirty-nine individuals, accused principally of conspiracy with Kossuth and Ruszak, from Hamburg.

Immediately after the revolutionary outbreak in Milan had been crushed, Radetzky gave orders to intercept all communication with Piedmont and Switzerland. You will ere this have received the scanty information that has been allowed to find its way from Italy to England. I call your attention to one characteristic feature in the Milan affair.

Lieutenant-Marshal Count Strassoldo, in his first decree of the 7th inst., although imposing the severest state of siege upon Milan, plainly admits that the bulk of the population took no part whatever in the late insurrection. Radetzky, in his subsequent proclamation of

---

[a] The Hungarian name is Székesfehérvár.— *Ed.*
[b] Issue No. 35 of February 10, 1853.— *Ed.*

the 9th inst., dated from Verona, subverts the statement of his inferior, and takes advantage of the rebellion to obtain money under false pretenses. He subjects all persons not notoriously belonging to the Austrian party to fines of unlimited extent, for the benefit of the garrison. In his proclamation of the 11th inst. he declares "that the generality of the inhabitants, with a few praiseworthy exceptions,are unwilling to submit to the Imperial rule," and he instructs all judicial authorities, i.e. the courts martial, to sequestrate the property of all the accomplices, explaining this term in the following manner:

"*Che tale complicità consista semplicimente nella omissione della denuncia a cui ognuno è tenuto.*" [a]

He might as well have confiscated all Milan at once under the pretense that, the insurrection having broken out on the 6th, its inhabitants failed to denounce it on the 5th. Whoever will not become a spy and informer for the Hapsburg shall be liable to become the lawful prey of the Croat.[314] In a word, Radetzky proclaims a new system of wholesale plunder.

The Milan insurrection is significant as a symptom of the approaching revolutionary crisis on the whole European continent. As the heroic act of some few proletarians—the sons of Mammon were dancing, and singing, and feasting amid the blood and tears of their debased and crucified nation—proletarians who, armed only with knives, marched to attack the citadel of a garrison and surrounding army of forty thousand of the finest troops in Europe, it is admirable. But as the finale of Mazzini's eternal conspiracy, of his bombastic proclamations and his arrogant capucinades against the French people, it is a very poor result. Let us hope that henceforth there will be an end of *révolutions improvisées*, as the French call them. Has one ever heard of great improvisators being also great poets? They are the same in politics as in poetry. Revolutions are never made to order. After the terrible experience of '48 and '49, it needs something more than paper summonses from distant leaders to evoke national revolutions. Kossuth has seized the opportunity for publicly disavowing the insurrection in general, and the proclamation published in his name in particular.[b] It looks, however, rather suspicious that he claims for himself a post-factum superiority to his friend Mazzini as a politician. *The Leader* remarks on this subject:

---

[a] "And that complicity consists in the simple failure to denounce, to which everybody is obliged."—*Ed.*

[b] See this volume, p. 508.—*Ed.*

"We deem it necessary to caution our readers that the matter in question lies exclusively between Mr. Kossuth and Mr. Mazzini, the latter of whom is absent from England.[a]

Della Rocco, a friend of Mazzini, says in a letter addressed to *The Daily News*, with regard to Mr. Kossuth's and Mr. Agostini's disavowals:

"There are persons who will suspect that they were waiting the definitive news of the success or the failure of the insurrection, as ready to share the honor of the former as to repel the responsibility of the latter."[b]

B. Szemere, Ex-Minister of Hungary, protests in a letter addressed to the editor of *The Morning Chronicle*, "against the illegitimate usurpation of the name of Hungary by Kossuth." He says:

"Let those who are desirous of forming a judgment of him as a statesman, read attentively the history of the last Hungarian Revolution, or of learning his skill as a conspirator, cast a retrospective glance on the unhappy Hamburg expedition of last year."[315]

That the revolution is victorious even in its failures, one may see from the terrors the Milan *échauffourée*[c] has thrown in the very heart of continental potentates. Look only at the following letter published in the official *Frankfurter Oberpostamts-Zeitung*[d]:

"*Berlin*, Feb. 13.—The events at Milan have produced a deep impression here. The news reached the King[e] by telegraph on the 9th, just as the court was in the middle of a ball. The King immediately declared that the movement was connected with a deep conspiracy, which had its ramifications everywhere, and that it showed the necessity for the close union of Prussia and Austria in presence of these revolutionary movements.... A high functionary exclaimed: 'We may thus have to defend the Prussian crown on the banks of the Po.'"

So great was the alarm created in the first moment, that about twenty inhabitants of Berlin were arrested without any other cause than the "deep impression." The *Neue Preussische Zeitung*, the ultra Royalist paper, was confiscated for publishing the document purporting to be from Kossuth. On the 13th the Minister of Westphalia presented to the first chamber a hasty bill for empowering the Government to seize all papers or pamphlets published outside the frontiers of Prussia. Arrests and domiciliar

---

[a] "Kossuth and the Milan Revolt", *The Leader*, February 19, 1853.— *Ed.*
[b] Della Rocco, "Mazzini's Proclamation", *The Daily News*, February 21, 1853.— *Ed.*
[c] Affrays.— *Ed.*
[d] *Frankfurter Postzeitung* — *Fd*
[e] Frederick William IV.— *Ed.*

visits are the order of the day at Vienna. Negotiations immediately took place between Russia, Prussia and Austria, for a joint remonstrance to be addressed to the British Government on the subject of political refugees. So weak, so powerless are the so-called "powers." They feel the thrones of Europe vibrate to their foundations at the first forebodings of the revolutionary earthquake. In the midst of their armies, their gallows and their dungeons, they are trembling at what they call "the subversive attempts of a few paid miscreants."

"Quiet is restored." It is. The ominous and dreadful quiet that intervenes between the first burst of the tempest and its returning roar.

From the agitated scenes of the Continent I pass to quiet England. It would seem as if the spirit of little Finality-John[316] had obtained the whole of the official sphere for its dominion; as though the nation throughout had become as paralytic as the men who now govern it. Even *The Times* exclaims with despair:

"It may be the calm before a storm; it may be the smoke before the fire.... For the present it is dullness."[a]

Business has been resumed in Parliament, but till now the three times repeated bowing of Lord Aberdeen has been the most dramatic, and the only conspicuous act of the Coalition Ministry.[b] The impression Lord John's programme has made on his enemies has been best described by the professions of his friends:

"Lord John Russell," says *The Times*, "has made a speech with rather less spirit than an ordinary auctioneer would put into his preliminary remarks before a sale of old furniture, damaged goods, or shop fittings.... Lord John Russell creates mighty little enthusiasm."

You know that the new Reform Bill has been postponed under the presence of more urgent practical reforms calling upon the more immediate attention of legislators. Now an instance has already been given of what nature these reforms must turn out to be, while the instrument of reforming, viz., Parliament, remains itself unreformed.

On Feb. 14, Lord Cranworth laid his programme of legal reform before the House of Lords. By far the greater part of his prolix,

---

[a] This quotation and one that follows are from the leading article in *The Times*, No. 21350, February 12, 1853.— *Ed.*

[b] See this volume, p. 510.— *Ed.*

tedious, and indecisive speech consisted in the enumeration of the many things he was expected, but not at all prepared to do. He excused himself with being only seven weeks on the woolsack, but, as *The Times* observes, "Lord Cranworth has been 63 years in this world, and 37 at the Bar." [a] In the true spirit of Whiggery, he infers from the comparatively great results obtained by the small legal reforms hitherto made, that it would be an infraction of the laws of modesty to go on reforming in the same strain. In the true spirit of Aristocracy, he abstains from dealing with Ecclesiastical Law, as "It would interfere too much with vested interests." Interests vested in what? In public nuisances. The only measures of any importance prepared by Lord Cranworth are the following two: Firstly, a "Bill to facilitate the transfer of land," the principal features of which are, that it renders the transfer of land only more difficult, by increasing the expenses thereon, and augmenting the technical obstructions, without shortening the length, or diminishing the complexity of conveyances. Second, a proposition to form a commission for digesting the statute law,[317] the whole merit of which will be restricted to the compilation of an index for the 40 quarto volumes of statutes at large. Lord Cranworth certainly may defend his measures against the most inveterate opponents to law-reform with the same excuse which was offered by the poor girl to her Confessor, namely: that, though it was true that she had had a child, it was but a very little one.

Up to this day the only interesting debate in the House of Commons was that in which Mr. Disraeli, on the 18th inst., interpellated the Ministers on the relations of the country with France. Disraeli began with Poitiers and Azincourt,[318] and ended with the hustings at Carlisle, and the Cloth-Hall at Halifax, his object being to denounce Sir James Graham and Sir Charles Wood [b] for irreverent remarks made on the character of Napoleon III. Disraeli could not have rendered the utter decay of the old Tory party more evident, than by his throwing himself up as the apologist of the Bonapartes, the hereditary enemies of the very political class whose chief he himself is. He could not have opened his opposition career in a more inappropriate manner, than by this justification of the actual *regime* in France. The weakness of this part of his speech may be seen from a short analysis of it.

Attempting to explain the causes of the uneasiness felt by the

---

[a] Quoted from the leading article in *The Times*, No. 21352, February 15, 1853. — *Ed.*

[b] Graham was deputy from Carlisle and Wood from Halifax.— *Ed.*

public on the state of England's present relations with France, he was compelled to admit that the principal motive was just derived from the large armaments, which were commenced under his own administration. Nevertheless he endeavored to prove, that the increasing and completing of the defenses of Great Britain had their only reason in the great changes occasioned by the modern application of science to the art of war. Competent authorities, he says, had ere this recognized the necessity of such measures. In 1840, under the Ministry of M. Thiers, there had been made some efforts by the Government of Sir Robert Peel, at least to commence a new system with regard to the public defenses. But in vain. Again, at the outbreak of the Continental revolutions in 1848, an opportunity had been offered to the Government of the day to lead popular opinion in the direction which it desired, as far as the defense of the country was concerned. But again without result. The question of national defenses had not become ripe before he and his colleagues were placed at the head of the Government. The measures adopted by them were as follows:

I. A Militia was established.

II. The Artillery was placed in an efficient state.

III. Measures were introduced which will completely fortify the Arsenals of the country, and some important strong posts upon the coast.

IV. A proposition was made by which will be added to the Navy 5,000 sailors and 1,500 marines.

V. Arrangements were made for the establishment of the ancient force in the form of a Channel Fleet of 15 or 20 sail of the line with an adequate number of frigates and smaller ships.

Now, from all these statements, it is evident that Disraeli established exactly the contrary of what he wanted to prove. The Government was unable to effect an increase of armaments, when the Syrian and Tahitian questions menaced the *entente cordiale* with Louis Philippe[319]; it was equally unable to do so when Revolution spread all over the Continent and seemed to threaten British interests at their very root. Why, then, has it become possible to do so now, and why was it done by Mr. Disraeli's Government? Exactly because Napoleon III has raised more fears for the security of England than have existed at any time since 1815. And further, as Mr. Cobden justly observed:

"The proposed increase in the naval force was not an increase of steam machinery, but one of men, and the transition from the use of sailing vessels to that of steamers did not imply the necessity of a larger number of sailors, but quite the contrary."[a]

---

[a] Richard Cobden, Speech in the House of Commons on February 18, 1853, *The Times*, No. 21356, February 19, 1853.— *Ed.*

Disraeli said:[a]

"Another cause for the belief in an impending rupture with France is the existence in France of a military government. But when armies are anxious for conquests it is because their position at home is uneasy; and France is now governed by the army, not in consequence of the military ambition of the troops, but in consequence of the disquietude of the citizens."

Mr. Disraeli seems entirely to overlook that the question is just, how long the army will feel easy at home, and how long the entire Nation will bow, out of deference to the egotistical disquietude of a small class of citizens, to the actual terrors of a military despotism, which after all is but the instrument of exclusive class interests.

The third cause alleged by Mr. Disraeli was:

"The considerable prejudice in this country against the present ruler of France.... It is understood that in acceding to power he has terminated what we esteem a Parliamentary Constitution, and that he has abrogated the liberty of the press."

There is, however, but little which Mr. Disraeli knew of to oppose to that prejudice. He said "it was extremely difficult to form an opinion on French politics."

It is simply common sense which tells the English people, although less deeply initiated into the mysteries of French politics than Mr. Disraeli, that the reckless adventurer, being neither controlled by a Parliament nor a press, is the very man to make a piratical descent upon England, after his own exchequer has become exhausted by extravagance and dissipation.

Mr. Disraeli then records some instances, in which the cordial understanding between Bonaparte and the late Administration had greatly contributed toward the maintenance of peace, as in the case of an impending conflict between France and Switzerland, in the opening of the South America rivers, in the case of Prussia and Neuchâtel, in pressing upon the United States the Tripartite renunciation of Cuba, in the common action in the Levant with regard to the *Tanzimat* in Egypt, in the revision of the Greek Succession Treaty, in the cordial co-operation with regard to the Regency of Tunis, &c.[320] Now this reminds me of a certain member of the French party of order, who made a speech at the end of November, 1851, on the cordial understanding between Bonaparte and the majority of the Assembly which had enabled the latter so easily to dispose of the Suffrage, the Association, and the

---

[a] Here and below Disraeli's speech in the House of Commons on February 18, 1853 is quoted from *The Times*, No. 21356, February 19, 1853. His opponents' statements are also quoted from the same newspaper.— *Ed.*

Press questions. Two days later the coup d'état had been carried out.

Weak and inconsistent as was this part of Disraeli's speech, his attacks on the Coalition Ministry formed a brilliant conclusion:

"There is one other reason," he concluded, "why I am bound to pursue this inquiry at the present moment, and I find that reason in the present state of parties in this House. It is a peculiar state of things. We have at this moment a Conservative Ministry, and we have a Conservative Opposition. [Cheers.] Where are the great Liberal party is, I pretend not to know. [Cheers.] Where are the Whigs, with their great traditions? ...There is no one to answer. [Renewed cheering.] Where, I ask, are the youthful energies of Radicalism? Its buoyant expectations—its expanded hopes? Awakened, I fear, from the dreams of that ardent inexperience which attend sometimes the career of youth, it finds itself at the same moment used and discarded. [Cheers.] Used without compunction, and not discarded with too much decency. [Cheers.] Where are the Radicals? Is there a man in the House who declares himself to be a Radical? [Hear, hear!] No, not one. He would be afraid of being caught and turned into a Conservative Minister. [Roars of laughter.] Well, how has this curious state of things been brought about? Where is the machinery by which it has been effected, this portentous political calamity? I believe I must go to that inexhaustible magazine of political devices, the First Lord of the Admiralty (Graham), to explain the present state of affairs. The House may recollect that some two years ago the First Lord of the Admiralty afforded us, as is his wont, one of those political creeds in which his speeches abound. He said: 'I take my stand on progress.' Well, Sir, I thought at the time that progress was an odd thing to take one's stand upon. [Much laughter and cheering.] I thought at the time that this was a piece of oratorical slip-slop. But I apologize for the momentary suspicion. I find that it was a system perfectly matured, and now brought into action. For we have now a Ministry of progress, and every one stands still. [Cheers.] We never hear the word 'reform' now; it is no longer a Ministry of reform; it is a Ministry of progress, every member of which resolves to do nothing. All difficult questions are suspended. All questions which cannot be agreed upon are open questions."

The opponents of Disraeli had but little to say in reply to him, with the exception of that very "inexhaustible magazine of political devices," Sir James Graham, who, at least, conserved his dignity in not wholly retracting the offensive words against Louis Napoleon, of which he had been accused.

Lord John Russell charged Mr. Disraeli with making a party question of the country's foreign policy, and assured the Opposition:

"That after the contentions and struggles of last year the country would gladly see a short time at least of peaceable progress, without any of these great convulsive struggles of parties."

The result of the debate is, that the whole of the navy estimates will be voted by the House, but to the comfort of Louis Napoleon, not from a warlike but only a scientific view of the matter. *Suaviter in modo, fortiter in re.*[a] On Thursday morning last, the Queen's Advocate, appearing before Sir J. Dodson, in the Prerogative Court, requested, on behalf of the Secretary of Foreign Affairs, that the original will and codicil of Napoleon Bonaparte should be delivered up by the Register to the French Government; which desire was complied with. Should Louis Bonaparte proceed to open and endeavor to execute this testament, it might prove the modern box of Pandora.

Written on February 22, 1853

First published in the *New-York Daily Tribune*, No. 3710, March 7 (evening edition) and March 8 (morning edition), 1853
Signed: *Karl Marx*

Reproduced from the newspaper

---

[a] Literally: suavely in manner, strongly in matter; gently but firmly—an expression from the treatise *Industriae ad curandos animae morbos* by Claudio Acquaviva, General of the Society of Jesus.—*Ed.*

Karl Marx

PARLIAMENTARY DEBATES.— THE CLERGY AGAINST SOCIALISM.—STARVATION [321]

London, Friday, February 25, 1853

The Parliamentary debates of the week offer but little of interest. On the 22nd inst., Mr. Spooner moved, in the House of Commons, the repeal of the money grants for the Catholic College at Maynooth,[322] and Mr. Scholefield proposed the amendment "to repeal all enactments now in force whereby the revenue of the State is charged in aid of any ecclesiastical or religious purpose whatsoever." Mr. Spooner's motion was lost by 162 to 192 votes. Mr. Scholefield's amendment will not come under discussion before Wednesday next; it is, however, not improbable that the amendment will be withdrawn altogether. The only remarkable passage in the Maynooth debate is an observation that fell from Mr. Duffy (Irish Brigade):

"He did not think it wholly impossible that the President of the United States,[a] or the new Emperor of the French,[b] might be glad to renew the relations between those countries and the Irish Priesthood."

In the session of last night Lord John Russell brought before the House of Commons his motion for the "removal of some disabilities of Her Majesty's Jewish subjects." The motion was carried by a majority of 29. Thus the question is again settled in the House of Commons, but there is no doubt that it will be once more unsettled in the House of Lords.

The exclusion of Jews from the House of Commons, after the spirit of usury has so long presided in the British Parliament, is

---

[a] Frank Pierce.— *Ed.*
[b] Napoleon III.— *Ed.*

unquestionably an absurd anomaly, the more so as they have already become eligible to all the civil offices of the community. But it remains no less characteristic for the man and *for his times*, that instead of a Reform Bill which was promised to remove the disabilities of the mass of the English people, a bill is brought in by Finality-John for the exclusive removal of the disabilities of Baron Lionel de Rothschild. How utterly insignificant an interest is taken in this affair by the public at large, may be inferred from the fact that from not a single place in Great Britain a petition in favor of the admission of Jews has been forwarded to Parliament. The whole secret of this miserable reform farce was betrayed by the speech of the present Sir Robert Peel.[a]

"After all, the House were only considering the noble Lord's private affairs. [Loud cheers.] The noble Lord represented London with a Jew [cheers],and had made the pledge to bring forward annually a motion in favor of the Jews. [Hear!] No doubt Baron Rothschild was a very wealthy man, but this did not entitle him to any consideration, especially considering how his wealth had been amassed. [Loud cries of "hear, hear", and "Oh! Oh!" from the Ministerial benches.] Only yesterday he had read in the papers that the House of Rothschild had consented to grant a loan to Greece, on considerable guaranties, at 9%. [Hear!] No wonder, at this rate, that the house of Rothschild were wealthy. [Hear!] The President of the Board of Control[b] had been talking of gagging the Press. Why, no one had done so much to depress freedom in Europe as the house of Rothschild [Hear, hear!] by the loans with which they assisted the despotic powers. But even supposing the Baron to be as worthy a man as he was certainly rich, it was to have been expected that the noble Lord who represented in that House a government consisting of the leaders of all the political factions who had opposed the late Administration, would have proposed some measure of more importance than the present."

The proceedings on election-petitions have commenced. The elections for Canterbury and Lancaster have been declared null and void, under circumstances which proved the habitual venality on the part of a certain class of electors, but it is pretty sure that the majority of cases will be adjusted by way of compromise.

"The privileged classes," says *The Daily News*,[c] "who have successfully contrived to baffle the intentions of the Reform Bill and to recover their ascendancy in the existing representation are naturally alarmed at the idea of full and complete exposure."

On the 21st inst., Lord John Russell resigned the seals on the Foreign Office, and Lord Clarendon was sworn in as his successor. Lord John is the first Member of the House of Commons admitted to

---

[a] Delivered in the House of Commons on February 24, 1853. The account of speech in *The Times*, No. 21361, February 25, 1853.— *Ed.*

[b] Charles Wood.— *Ed.*

[c] February 23, 1853 (leading article).— *Ed.*

a seat in the Cabinet without any official appointment. He is now
only a favorite adviser, without a place—and without salary. Notice,
however, has already been given by Mr. Kelly of a proposition to
remedy the latter inconvenience of poor Johnny's situation. The
Secretaryship of Foreign Affairs is at the present juncture the more
important, as the Germanic Diet has bestirred itself to ask the
removal of all political refugees from Great Britain, as the Austrians
propose to pack us all up and transport us to some barren island in
the South Pacific.

Allusion has been made, in a former letter, to the probability of the
Irish Tenant-Right agitation becoming, in time, an anti-clerical
movement,[a] notwithstanding the views and intentions of its actual
leaders. I alleged the fact, that the higher Clergy was already
beginning to take a hostile attitude with regard to the League.
Another force has since stepped into the field which presses the
movement in the same direction. The landlords of the north of
Ireland endeavor to persuade their tenantry that the Tenant League
and the Catholic Defense Association are identical, and they labor to
get up an opposition to the former under the pretense of resisting
the progress of Popery.

While we thus see the Irish landlords appealing to their tenants
against the Catholic clergy we behold on the other hand the English
Protestant clergy appealing to the working classes against the
mill-lords. The industrial proletariat of England has renewed with
double vigor its old campaign for the Ten Hours Bill and against the
truck and shoppage system. As the demands of this kind shall be
brought before the House of Commons, to which numerous
petitions on the subject have already been presented, there will be an
opportunity for me to dwell in a future letter on the cruel and
infamous practices of the factory-despots, who are in the habit of
making the press and the tribune resound with their liberal
rhetorics. For the present it may suffice to recall to memory that
from 1802 there has been a continual strife on the part of the English
working people for legislative interference with the duration of
factory labor, until in 1847 the celebrated Ten Hours Act of John
Fielden[323] was passed, whereby young persons and females were
prohibited to work in any factory longer than ten hours a day. The
liberal mill-lords speedily found out that under this act factories
might be worked by shifts and relays. In 1849 an action of law was
brought before the Court of Exchequer, and the Judge decided that
to work the relay or shift-system, with two sets of children, the adults

---

[a] See this volume, p. 505.— *Ed.*

working the whole space of time during which the machinery was running, was legal. It therefore became necessary to go to Parliament again, and in 1850 the relay and shift-system was condemned there, but the Ten Hours Act was transformed into a Ten and a Half Hours Act.[a] Now, at this moment, the working classes demand a restitution *in integrum* of the original Ten Hours Bill; yet, in order to make it efficient, they add the demand of a restriction of the moving power of machinery.

Such is, in short, the exoteric history of the Ten Hours Act. Its secret history was as follows: The landed aristocracy having suffered a defeat from the bourgeoisie by the passing of the Reform Bill of 1831, and being assailed in "their most sacred interests" by the cry of the manufacturers for Free Trade and the abolition of the Corn Laws, resolved to resist the middle class by espousing the cause and claims of the working-men against their masters, and especially by rallying around their demands for the limitation of factory labor. So-called philanthropic Lords were then at the head of all Ten-Hours' meetings. Lord Ashley has even made a sort of "renommée" by his performances in this movement. The landed aristocracy, having received a deadly blow by the actual abolition of the Corn Laws in 1846, took their vengeance by forcing the Ten Hours Bill of 1847 upon Parliament. But the industrial bourgeoisie recovered by judiciary authority, what they had lost by Parliamentary legislation. In 1850, the wrath of the Landlords had gradually subsided, and they made a compromise with the Mill-lords, condemning the shift-system, but imposing, at the same time, as a penalty for the enforcement of the law, half an hour extra work *per diem* on the working classes. At the present juncture, however, as they feel the approach of their final struggle with the men of the Manchester School, they are again trying to get hold of the short-time movement; but, not daring to come forward themselves, they endeavor to undermine the Cotton-lords by directing the popular force against them through the medium of the *State Church Clergymen*. In what rude manner these holy men have taken the anti-industrial crusade into their hands, may be seen from the following few instances. At Crompton a Ten-Hours' meeting was held, the Rev. Dr. Brammell [of the State Church] in the chair. At this meeting, Rev. J. R. Stephens, Incumbent of Stalybridge, said:

"There had been ages in the world when the nations were governed by Theocracy.... That state of things is now no more.... Still the spirit of law was the same.... The laboring man should, first of all, be partaker of the fruits of the earth,

---

[a] "An Act to Amend the Acts Relating to Labour in Factories, 1850."—*Ed.*

which he was the means of producing. The factory law was so unblushingly violated that the Chief Inspector of that part of the factory district, Mr. Leonard Horner, had found himself necessitated to write to the Home Secretary, to say that he dared not, and would not send any of his Sub-Inspectors into certain districts until he had police protection.... And protection against whom? Against the factory-masters! Against the magistrates of the district, against the richest men in the district, against the most influential men in the district, against the men who hold her Majesty's Commission, against the men who sat in the Petty Sessions as the Representatives of Royalty.... *And did the masters suffer for their violation of the law?*... In his own district, it was a settled custom of the male, and to a great extent of the female workers in factories, to be in bed till 9, 10 or 11 o'clock on Sunday, because they were tired out by the labor of the week. Sunday was the only day on which they could rest their wearied frames.... It would generally be found that, the longer the time of work, the smaller the wages.... *He would rather be a slave in South Carolina, than a factory operative in England.*"

At the great Ten-Hours' meeting, at Burnley, Rev. E. A. Verity, Incumbent of Habbergham Eaves, told his audience among other things:

"Where was Mr. Cobden, where was Mr. Bright, where were the other members of the Manchester School, when the people of Lancashire were oppressed?... What was the end of the rich man's thinking? Why, he was scheming how he could defraud the working classes out of an hour or two.That was the scheming of what he called the Manchester School. That made them such *cunning hypocrites,* and such *crafty rascals.* As a minister of the Church of England, he protested against such work." [a]

The motive, that has so suddenly metamorphosed the gentlemen of the Established Church, into as many knights-errant of labor's rights, and so fervent knights too, has already been pointed out. They are not only laying in a stock of popularity for the rainy days of approaching Democracy, they are not only conscious that the Established Church is essentially an aristocratic institution, which must either stand or fall with the landed Oligarchy—there is something more. The men of the Manchester School are Anti-State Church men, they are Dissenters,[324] they are, above all, so highly enamored of the £13,000,000 annually abstracted from their pockets by the State Church in England and Wales alone, that they are resolved to bring about a separation between those profane millions and the holy orders, the better to qualify the latter for heaven. The reverend gentlemen, therefore, are struggling *pro aris et focis.*[b] The men of the Manchester School, however, may infer from this diversion, that they will be unable to abstract the political power from

---

[a] E. A. Verity, Speech at a Ten-Hours' meeting, at Burnley, on February 18, 1853, *The People's Paper,* No. 42, February 19, 1853.— *Ed.*

[b] For their alters and their firesides, i.e. for all that is sacred to them (M. T. Cicero, *De natura deorum,* Lib. 3, Cap. 40, 94).— *Ed.*

the hands of the Aristocracy, unless they consent, with whatever reluctance, to give the people also their full share in it.

On the Continent, hanging, shooting and transportation is the order of the day. But the executioners are themselves tangible and hangable beings, and their deeds are recorded in the conscience of the whole civilized world. At the same time there acts in England an invisible, intangible and silent despot, condemning individuals, in extreme cases, to the most cruel of deaths, and driving in its noiseless, every day working, whole races and whole classes of men from the soil of their forefathers, like the angel with the fiery sword who drove Adam from Paradise.[a] In the latter form the work of the unseen social despot calls itself *forced emigration*, in the former it is called *starvation.*

Some further cases of starvation have occurred in London during the present month. I remember only that of Mary Ann Sandry, aged 43 years, who died in Coal-lane, Shadwell, London. Mr. Thomas Peene, the surgeon, assisting the Coroner's inquest, said the deceased died from starvation and exposure to the cold. The deceased was lying on a small heap of straw, without the slightest covering. The room was completely destitute of furniture, firing and food. Five young children were sitting on the bare flooring, crying from hunger and cold by the side of the mother's dead body.

On the working of "*forced emigration*" in my next.

Written on February 25, 1853

First published in the *New-York Daily Tribune,* No. 3716, March 15, 1853

Signed: *Karl Marx*

Reproduced from the newspaper

---

[a] Cf. Genesis 3:24.—*Ed.*

Karl Marx

FORCED EMIGRATION. —KOSSUTH AND MAZZINI.— THE REFUGEE QUESTION.— ELECTION BRIBERY IN ENGLAND. —Mr. COBDEN [325]

London, Friday, March 4, 1853

From the accounts relating to trade and navigation for the years 1851 and 1852, published in Feb. last, we see that the total declared value of *exports* amounted to £68,531,601 in 1851, and to £71,429,548 in 1852; of the latter amount, £47,209,000 go to the export of cotton, wool, linen and silk manufactures. The quantity of *imports* for 1852 is below that for the year 1851. The proportion of imports entered for home consumption not having diminished, but rather increased, it follows that England has reexported, instead of the usual quantity of colonial produce, a certain amount of gold and silver.[a]

The Colonial Land Emigration Office gives the following return of the emigration from England, Scotland and Ireland to all parts of the world, from Jan. 1, 1847, to June 30, 1852:[b]

Year	English	Scotch	Irish	Total
1847	34,685	8,616	214,969	258,270
1848	58,865	11,505	177,719	248,089
1849	73,613	17,127	208,758	299,498
1850	57,843	15,154	207,852	280,849
1851	69,557	18,646	247,763	335,966
1852 (till June)	40,767	11,562	143,375	195,704
Total	335,330	82,610	1,200,436	1,618,376

---

[a] This paragraph is omitted in *The People's Paper.—Ed.*
[b] The returns are quoted from the article "Effects of Emigration on Production and Consumption" published in *The Economist*, No. 494, February 12, 1853 (the comments quoted below are from this article).— *Ed.*

"Nine-tenths", remarks the Office, "of the emigrants from Liverpool are assumed to be Irish. About three-fourths of the emigrants from Scotland are Celts, either from the Highlands, or from Ireland through Glasgow."

Nearly four-fifths of the whole emigration are, accordingly, to be regarded as belonging to the Celtic population of Ireland and of the Highlands and islands of Scotland. *The London Economist* says of this emigration:

"It is consequent on the breaking down of the system of society founded on small holdings and potato cultivation"; and adds: "The departure of the redundant part of the population of Ireland and the Highlands of Scotland is an indispensable preliminary to every kind of improvement.... The revenue of Ireland has not suffered in any degree from the famine of 1846-47, or from the emigration that has since taken place. On the contrary, her *net revenue* amounted in 1851 to £4,281,999, being about £184,000 greater than in 1843."

Begin with pauperizing the inhabitants of a country, and when there is no more profit to be ground out of them, when they have grown a burden to the revenue, drive them away, and sum up your Net Revenue! Such is the doctrine laid down by Ricardo, in his celebrated work, *The Principle of Political Economy.* The annual profits of a capitalist amounting to £2,000, what does it matter to him whether he employs 100 men or 1,000 men? "Is not," says Ricardo, "the real income of a nation similar?" The net real income of a nation, rents and profits, remaining the same, it is no subject of consideration whether it is derived from 10 millions of people or from 12 millions. Sismondi, in his *Nouveaux Principes d'Économie Politique,* answers that, according to this view of the matter, the English nation would not be interested at all in the disappearance of the whole population, the King[a] (at that time it was no Queen, but a King) remaining alone in the midst of the island, supposing only that automatic machinery enabled him to procure the amount of *Net Revenue* now produced by a population of 20 millions. Indeed, that grammatical entity "the national wealth" would in this case not be diminished.

In a former letter I have given an instance of the clearing of estates in the Highlands of Scotland.[b] That emigration continues to be forced upon Ireland by the same process, you may see from the following quotation from *The Galway Mercury:*

"The people are fast passing away from the land in the West of Ireland. The landlords of Connaught are tacitly combined to weed out all the smaller occupiers,

---

[a] The reference is to King George III.— *Ed.*
[b] See this volume, pp. 487-94.— *Ed.*

against whom a regular systematic war of extermination is being waged.... The most heart-rending cruelties are daily practiced in this province, of which the public are not at all aware." [a]

But it is not only the pauperized inhabitants of Green Erin and of the Highlands of Scotland that are swept away by agricultural improvements, and by the "breaking down of the antiquated system of society." It is not only the able-bodied agricultural laborers from England, Wales, and Lower Scotland whose passages are paid by the Emigration Commissioners. The wheel of "improvement" is now seizing another class, the most stationary class in England. A startling emigration movement has sprung up among the smaller English farmers, especially those holding heavy clay soils, who, with bad prospects for the coming harvest, and in want of sufficient capital to make the great improvements on their farms which would enable them to pay their old rents, have no other alternative but to cross the sea in search of a new country and of new lands. I am not speaking now of the emigration caused by the gold mania, but only of the compulsory emigration produced by landlordism, concentration of farms, application of machinery to the soil, and introduction of the modern system of agriculture on a great scale.

In the ancient states, in Greece and Rome, compulsory emigration, assuming the shape of the periodical establishment of colonies, formed a regular link in the structure of society. The whole system of those states was founded on certain limits to the numbers of the population, which could not be surpassed without endangering the condition of antique civilization itself. But why was it so? Because the application of science to material production was utterly unknown to them. To remain civilized they were forced to remain few. Otherwise they would have had to submit to the bodily drudgery which transformed the free citizen into a slave. The want of productive power made citizenship dependent on a certain proportion in numbers not to be disturbed. Forced emigration was the only remedy.

It was the same pressure of population on the powers of production that drove the barbarians from the high plains of Asia to invade the Old World. The same cause acted there, although under a different form. To remain barbarians they were forced to remain few. They were pastoral, hunting, war-waging tribes, whose manner of production required a large space for every individual, as is now the case with the Indian tribes in North America. By augmenting in numbers they curtailed each other's field of production. Thus the

---

[a] "State of the Country", *The Galway Mercury*, February 5, 1853. This quotation and the paragraph di ctly preceding it are omitted in *The People's Paper.—Ed.*

surplus population was forced to undertake those great adventurous migratory movements which laid the foundation of the peoples of ancient and modern Europe.

But with modern compulsory emigration the case stands quite opposite. Here it is not the want of productive power which creates a surplus population; it is the increase of productive power which demands a diminution of population, and drives away the surplus by famine or emigration. It is not population that presses on productive power; it is productive power that presses on population.

Now I share neither in the opinions of Ricardo, who regards "Net Revenue" as the Moloch to whom entire populations must be sacrificed, without even so much as complaint, nor in the opinion of Sismondi, who, in his hypochondriacal philanthropy, would forcibly retain the superannuated methods of agriculture and proscribe science from industry, as Plato expelled poets from his Republic.[a] Society is undergoing a silent revolution, which must be submitted to, and which takes no more notice of the human existences it breaks down than an earthquake regards the houses it subverts. The classes and the races, too weak to master the new conditions of life, must give way. But can there be anything more puerile, more shortsighted, than the views of those economists who believe in all earnest that this woeful transitory state means nothing but adapting society to the acquisitive propensities of capitalists, both landlords and money lords? In Great Britain the working of that process is most transparent. The application of modern science to production clears the land of its inhabitants, but it concentrates people in manufacturing towns.

"No manufacturing workmen," says *The Economist*, "have been assisted by the Emigration Commissioners, except a few Spitalfields and Paisley hand-loom weavers, and few or none have emigrated at their own expense."

The Economist knows very well that they could not emigrate at their own expense, and that the industrial middle class would not assist them in emigrating. Now, to what does this lead? The rural population, the most stationary and conservative element of modern society, disappears, while the industrial proletariat, by the very working of modern production, finds itself gathered in mighty centers, around the great productive forces, whose history of creation has hitherto been the martyrology of the laborers. Who will prevent them from going a step further and appropriating these forces, to which they have been appropriated before? Where will be

---

[a] Plato, *Politeia*. X.—*Ed.*

the power of resisting them? Nowhere! Then, it will be of no use to appeal to the "rights of property." The modern changes in the art of production have, according to the bourgeois economists themselves, broken down the antiquated system of society and its modes of appropriation. They have *expropriated* the Scotch clansman, the Irish cottier and tenant, the English yeoman, the hand-loom weaver, numberless handicrafts, whole generations of factory children and women; they will expropriate, in due time, the landlord and the cotton lord.

On the Continent heaven is fulminating, but in England the earth itself is trembling. England is the country where the real revulsion of modern society begins.[a]

In my letter of the 1st inst. I told you that Mazzini would remonstrate publicly with Kossuth.[326] On the 2d inst. there appeared actually in *The Morning Advertiser, Morning Post* and *Daily News* a letter from Mazzini. As Mazzini himself has now broken the ice, I may as well state that Kossuth disowned his own document under the pressure of his Paris friends.[b] In the past career of Kossuth we find many such symptoms of vacillating weakness, inextricable contradictions and duplicity. He possesses all the attractive virtues, but also all the feminine faults of the "artiste" character. He is a great artist "*en paroles.*" I recommend Mr. Szemere's lately published biographies of *Louis Batthyány, Arthur Görgey* and *Louis Kossuth* to those who, unwilling to bow to popular superstition, are anxious to form a matter-of-fact judgment.[c]

As to Lombardy, you may be sure that, if Mazzini has failed to draw the Italian middle classes into the movement, Radetzky will not fail therein. At this moment he is preparing to confiscate the property of all emigrants, even those who emigrated with Austrian permission, and have been naturalized in other countries, *unless they prove they are unconnected with the late rising.* The Austrian papers calculate the amount of confiscable property at £12,000,000.

Upon a question put by Lord Dudley Stuart, Lord Palmerston stated in the session of the House of Commons of March 1:

"That no application for the expulsion of the political refugees had been made by the Continental Powers, or that, if made, it would meet with a firm and decided refusal. *The British Government had never undertaken to provide for the internal security of other countries.*"

---

[a] The paragraph that follows is omitted in *The People's Paper.—Ed.*

[b] See this volume, p. 508.— *Ed.*

[c] B. Szemere, *Graf Ludwig Batthyány, Arthur Görgei, Ludwig Kossuth. Politische Charakterskizzen aus dem Ungarischen Freiheitskriege.—Ed.*

That such an application, however, was intended to be made, you may see from the stockjobbing *Moniteur* and the *Journal des Débats*, which, in one of its last numbers,[a] supposes England already bowing to the joint demands of Austria, Russia, Prussia and France. That journal adds:

> "If the Swiss Confederation should refuse to allow Austria to exercise a *surveillance* over the Cantons on her frontiers she will probably violate the Swiss territory and occupy the Canton of Tessin; in which case France, to preserve a political equilibrium would force her armies into the Swiss Cantons on her frontiers."

In substance, the *Journal des Débats* gives, with regard to Switzerland, that simple solution of the question jocosely proposed by Prince Henry of Prussia to the Empress Catherine in 1770, with regard to Poland.[327] In the meantime the venerable body called the German Diet[328] is gravely discussing on "the application about to be made to England," and expends as much breath on this solemn matter as would suffice to swell the sails of the whole German fleet.

In the session of the House of Commons of the 1st inst., there occurred a very characteristic incident. The representatives of Bridgenorth and Blackburn having been declared unduly elected on the ground of bribery, Sir J. Shelley moved that the evidence taken before their respective Committees should be laid upon the table of the House, and that the writs for reelection be suspended until the 4th of April. The Right Hon. Baronet Sir J. Trollope remarked with regard to this: "That 14 Committees had already been appointed to try boroughs for corrupt practices, and that about 50 more remained to be appointed," and he spoke of the difficulty in finding members enough in the House to constitute tribunals to judge the disputed elections, and at the same time to form Committees for the ordinary business of the House. Sifting a little deeper into its own foundation, a breaking down of the House must ensue, and the parliamentary machinery come to a deadlock.

In his recent pamphlet,[b] as well as in his *harangues*, at the Manchester Peace Congress,[329] and at various educational meetings, Mr. Cobden has amused himself with censuring the press. The whole press has retaliated upon him; but the most heavy blow strikes him from the hands of the "Englishman,"[c] whose letters on Louis Napoleon elicited such a sensation at the time of the *coup d'état*,[330] and who has since turned round upon the silken barons and cotton lords.

---

[a] Of March 1, 1853.— *Ed.*
[b] Richard Cobden, *1793 and 1853, in Three Letters.— Ed.*
[c] Alfred Bate Richards.— *Ed.*

He concludes a letter, addressed to Mr. Cobden, with the following epigrammatic characterization of the West-Riding oracle:

"Elated and *unbalanced* by one single triumph, he would compass a popular autocracy. The prophet of a *clique*, restlessly agitating, greedy of notoriety, chafed of opposition, crotchety, illogical, utopian, stubborn of purpose, arrogant of bearing, a quarrelsome peace preacher, and acrimonious proselyte of universal brotherhood, with liberty upon his lips, but despotism in his dogmas, he is exasperated with a press that will neither be bullied nor bamboozled—would geld its influence, intelligence, and independence, and would sink a profession of accomplished gentlemen to a gang of penny-a-liners, with himself for the only Leader." [a]

Written on March 4, 1853

First published in the *New-York Daily Tribune*, No. 3722, March 22, 1853; reprinted in the *Semi-Weekly Tribune*, No. 814, March 25, the *New-York Weekly Tribune*, No. 602, March 26, and in *The People's Paper*, No. 50, April 16, 1853 (in the form of two separate publications with certain omissions)

Signed: *Karl Marx*

Reproduced from the *New-York Daily Tribune* and checked with *The People's Paper*

---

[a] Quoted from Richards' letter to Cobden published in *The Morning Advertiser* on February 24, 1853.— *Ed.*

Karl Marx

[KOSSUTH AND MAZZINI.— INTRIGUES OF THE PRUSSIAN GOVERNMENT.— AUSTRO-PRUSSIAN COMMERCIAL TREATY.— THE TIMES AND THE REFUGEES][331]

London, Friday, March 18, 1853

Parliament will adjourn to-day, for the Easter recess, until April 4th.

In a former letter I reported, according to a generally accredited rumor, that Libényi's wife had been flogged by the Austrians at Pesth.[332] I have since ascertained that he was never married, and likewise that the story circulated in the English press, saying that he had attempted to revenge his father, who had been ill-treated by the Austrians, is wholly unfounded. He acted exclusively under the influence of political motives, and retained to the last hour a firm and heroic demeanor.

You will, ere this, have received with the English papers the reply of Kossuth to Mazzini's declaration.[a] For my part, I am of opinion that Kossuth has only made a bad case still worse. The contradictions in his first and his last declaration[b] are so palpable that I need not insist on urging them here. Besides, there is a repulsive heterogeneousness in the language of the two documents, the former being written in the Oriental hyperbolics of the Prophet, and the latter in the casuistic pleading-style of a lawyer.

---

[a] The reference is to Mazzini's letter to a number of English newspapers published on March 2, 1853 (see this volume, p. 508.). Kossuth's reply to this letter was given in his letter to Captain Mayne Reid (date unknown), excerpts from which were published in *The Leader*, No. 154, March 5, 1853.—*Ed.*

[b] The reference is to Kossuth's proclamation of February 1853 "In the Name of the Hungarian Nation.—To the Soldiers Quartered in Italy", published in *The Times*, No. 21348, February 10, 1853 (see this volume, p. 508), and to his letter to Captain Mayne Reid mentioned above.—*Ed.*

Mazzini's friends affirm now, to a man, that the Milanese insurrection was forced upon him and his associates by circumstances which it was beyond his power to control. But, on one side, it belongs to the very nature of conspiracies to be driven to a premature outbreak, either by treason or by accidents. On the other side, if you cry, during three years, *action, action, action*—if your entire revolutionary vocabulary be exhausted by the one word "Insurrection," you cannot expect to hold sufficient authority for dictating, at any given moment: *there shall be no insurrection*. Be this as it may, Austrian brutality has turned the Milanese failure into the real commencement of a national revolution. Hear, for instance, the well-informed organ of Lord Palmerston, *The Morning Post*, of to-day:

"The people of Naples wait for a movement which is sure to take place in the Austrian Empire. Then the whole of Italy, from the frontiers of Piedmont to Sicily, will be in revolt, and sad disasters will follow. The Italian troops will disband—the so-called Swiss soldiers, recruited from the revolution of 1848, will not save the sovereigns of Italy. An *impossible republic* awaits Italy. That will assuredly be the next act of the drama which began in 1848. Diplomacy has exhausted all its powers for the princes of Italy."[a]

Aurelio Saffi, who countersigned Mazzini's proclamation,[b] and who made a tour through Italy before the outbreak, avows, in a letter addressed to *The Daily News*, that "the *upper classes* were sunk in listless indifference or dispair," and that it was the "people of Milan," the proletarians, who,

"abandoned without direction to their own instincts, preserved their faith in the destiny of their country and, in the face of the despotism of Austrian Proconsuls and the judicial assassinations of military commissions, had unanimously made ready for vengeance."[c]

Now, it is a great progress of the Mazzini party to have at last convinced themselves that, even in the case of national insurrections against foreign despotism, there exists such a thing as class-distinctions, and that it is not the upper classes which must be looked to for a revolutionary movement in modern times. Perhaps they will go a step further and come to the understanding that they have to seriously occupy themselves with the material condition of the Italian country population, if they expect to find an echo to their "*Dio e popolo*." On a future occasion I intend to dwell on the material

---

[a] "Political Excitement in Sicily", *The Morning Post*, March 18, 1853.— *Ed.*
[b] See this volume, p. 508.— *Ed.*
[c] The reference is to Saffi's letter to *Italia e Popolo* which was reprinted in *The Daily News* on March 9, 1853.— *Ed.*

circumstances in which by far the greater portion of the rural inhabitants of that country are placed, and which have made them till now, if not reactionary, at least indifferent to the national struggle of Italy.

Two thousand copies of a pamphlet which I published some time ago at *Basle,* entitled "Revelations on the Trial of the Communists at Cologne" (*Enthülungen über den Kölner Kommunisten-Prozess*), have been seized at the Baden frontier and burned, on the request of the Prussian Government. According to the new Press Law imposed on the Swiss Bund by the Continental Powers, the publisher, Mr. Schabelitz, his son, and the printer[a] will be persecuted by the Basle Government, which has already confiscated a number of copies still in possession of the publisher. This will be the first trial of this kind in Switzerland, and the affair has become already a matter of controversy between the Radicals and the Conservative party. How anxious the Prussian Government is to conceal its infamies during the Cologne trial from publicity, you may infer from the fact that the Minister of the Exterior[b] has issued orders for the seizure (*Fahndebriefe*) of the pamphlet wherever it should appear, but does not even dare to call it by its title. In order to mislead the public, he gives as its name "*A Theory of Communism,*" while it contains nothing but revelations of the Prussian state mysteries.

The only "progress" made in official Germany since the year 1848, is the conclusion[c] of the Austro-Prussian Commercial Treaty — *et encore!* That Treaty is surrounded with so many *clausulae,* retrenched behind so many exceptions, and reserves so many chief questions to the future adjustment of yet unborn commissions, while the actual diminution in the tariffs is so small, that it amounts to a mere aspiration towards a real Commercial Union of Germany, and is, practically speaking, utterly insignificant. The most striking feature of the Treaty is the victory Austria has again won over Prussia. This perfidious, this base, this cowardly, this vacillating sham-power, has bowed again before its more brutal, but more straightforward rival. Not only has Austria forced a treaty on Prussia which the latter was most unwilling to accept, but Prussia has been compelled to renew the old *Zoll-Verein*[333] with the old tariff, or to promise not to change, for twelve years, anything in her Commercial policy without the unanimous consent of the minor *Zoll-Verein* States i.e. without the permission of Austria (the South-German

---

[a] Jakob Schabelitz and Chr. Krüsi.— *Ed.*
[b] Otto von Manteuffel.— *Ed.*
[c] On February 19, 1853.— *Ed.*

States being not only politically, but also commercially, the vassals of Austria, or the antagonists of Prussia). Since the restoration of "Divine Power," Prussia has marched from degradation to degradation. Her king,[a] "a wise man in his times," appears to think that his people may derive a comforting compensation in the infernal despotism they are subject to from the debasement their Government has to suffer abroad.

The refugee question is not settled yet. The semi-official *Oesterreichische Correspondenz* contradicts the statement, that Austria had addressed at this moment a fresh note to the English Government, because "recent events having shown that Lord Palmerston has recovered his influence, the Imperial Government could not expose its dignity to a certain check." I have written you before on Palmerston's declaration in the House of Commons.[b] From the English papers you know the philo-Austrian declaration of Aberdeen in the House of Lords,[c] that the English Government would make itself the spy and Attorney-General of Austria. Palmerston's journal[d] now remarks on the observation of his colleague:

"Even on the modified concession which Lord Aberdeen appears inclined to make, we cannot say that we look with much confidence to success.... No one will dare to propose to a British Government to attempt its conversion into an engine of foreign policy and a political man-trap."

You see what good understanding there is in the councils of the Methusalem ministry between "antiquated imbecility and liberal energy." In the whole London press there was a unanimous cry of indignation against Aberdeen and the House of Lords, *with one base exception,* that of *The Times* newspaper.

The Times, you will remember, commenced by denouncing the refugees and inviting the Foreign Powers to ask for their expulsion. Then, having ascertained that a renewal of the Alien Bill[334] would be refused with scorn to the Ministry in the House of Commons, it at once overflowed with rhetorically framed descriptions of the sacrifice it was ready to make—oh dear!—for the preservation of the right of asylum. Finally, after the amiable conversation between my Lords of the Upper House it revenged itself on its own highsounding civism, with the following angry explosion in its leading article of March 5th:

---

  [a] Frederick William IV.— *Ed.*
  [b] See this volume, p. 532.— *Ed.*
  [c] On March 4, 1853.— *Ed.*
  [d] *The Morning Post* (the quotation that follows is from its leading article of March 10, 1853).— *Ed.*

"It is believed in many parts of the Continent that we delight in this country in a menagerie of refugees—ferocious characters of all nations, and fit for all crimes.... Do these foreign writers who denounce the presence of their own outlawed countrymen in England suppose that the existence of a refugee in this country is an enviable fate? Let them be undeceived. *This wretched class of beings* live, for the most part, in squalid poverty, *eating the salt of the stranger,* when they can get it, sunk, as it were, beneath the turbid waves of this vast metropolis.... *Their punishment is exile in its harshest form.*"

As to the last point, *The Times* is right; England is a delightful country to live out of.

In the "heaven of Mars" Dante meets with his ancestor, Cacciaguida de Elisei, who predicts to him his approaching exile from Florence in these words:

> "Tu proverai si come sa di sale
> Lo pane altrui, e com'è duro calle
> Lo scendere, e'l salir per l'altrui scale."

> "Thou shalt prove how salt the savour is
> Of others' bread, how hard the passage,
> To descend and climb by others' stairs." [a]

Happy Dante, another "being of that wretched class called political refugees," whom his enemies could not threaten with the misery of a *Times*-leader! Happier " *Times*," that escaped a "reserved seat" in his " *Inferno!*"

If the refugees eat the salt of the stranger, as *The Times* says, getting it at strange prices, too, which it forgot to say, is *The Times* itself not feeding on the strangers' flesh and blood? How many leaders and how many pounds have its anonymous Pythias not made out of French revolutions, German insurrections, Italian outbreaks and Hungarian wars, of French "fusillades," of Austrian gallows, of confiscated heads and beheaded property? Unhappy *Times*, if there were no "ferocious characters" on the Continent, if it were to grow older day by day on the coarse food of Smithfield Market, London chimney smoke, dirt, *ferocious* cabmen, the six bridges of the Thames, intermural interments, pestilential churchyards, filthy drink-water, railway accidents, crippled pint and quart bottles, and other interesting topics, which form its regular stock-in-trade, in the intervals of continental dullness. *The Times* is unchanged since the epoch when it called upon the British Government to *murder* Napoleon I.

"Is it considered," it said, in its number of July 27, 1815, "what effect the knowledge of his being in existence must necessarily have on the disaffected in every

---

[a] Dante, *La Divina commedia*, "Il Paradiso", XVII.— Ed.

part of Europe? They will think, and think with truth, that the Allied Sovereigns are *afraid* to touch the life of a man who has so many adherents and admirers."

It is still the same paper which preached the crusade against the United States of America:

"No peace should be made with America, *until that mischievous example of successful democratic rebellion* has been done away."

In *The Times* editorial office there are no "ferocious" continental characters. Quite the contrary. There is, for example, a poor little man, a Prussian, named *Otto von Wenckstern*, once editor of a little German newspaper, afterward sunk in Switzerland, in squalid poverty, appealing to the pockets of *Freiligrath* and other refugees, and lastly finding himself at the same time in the service of the Prussian Ambassador in London—the far-famed *Bunsen*—and an integral member of the Printing-House-square[a] oracle. There are more such conciliatory continental characters in *The Times* Office, forming the connecting link between the Continental Police and the leading journal of England.

The liberty of the Press in England is exemplified by the following case: At the Bow-st. Police Office, in London, Mr. E. Truelove, of the Strand, appeared on an information laid at the instance of the Commissioners of Inland Revenue, under 6th and 7th William IV, cap. 76,[b] for having sold a newspaper, called *The Potteries Free Press*, and printed on paper not duly stamped. Four numbers of this paper had been published at Stoke-upon-Trent, the nominal proprietor being Collet Dobson Collet, Secretary of the *Society for the Abolition of Taxes on Knowledge*, who have issued it in "Conformity with the practice of the Stamp-Office, which permits records of current events, and comments thereon, to be published without a stamp in *The Athenaeum, Builder, Punch, Racing Times*, etc."; and with the avowed intention of inviting a Government prosecution, in order that a Jury might determine what description of news is to be entitled to exemption from the penny stamp. Mr. Henry, the magistrate, has reserved his decision. Much, however, will not depend on the decision, for the paper in question is not issued in defiance of the Stamp Law, but merely to avail itself of a still doubtful quibble in the law.

The English papers of to-day have a telegraphic dispatch from Constantinople, of March 6th, according to which, Fuad Effendi, the

---

[a] The address of *The Times.—Ed.*

[b] "An Act to reduce the Duties on Newspapers, and to amend the Laws relating to the Duties on Newspapers and Advertisments", 1836.—*Ed.*

Minister of Foreign Affairs, has been replaced by Rifaat Pasha. This concession has been extorted from the Porte by the Extraordinary Russian Envoy, Prince Menchikoff. The affair of the Holy Places[335] is not settled yet between Russia, France, and the Porte, as L. Napoleon, highly irritated at the intrigues of Russia and Austria for the prevention of his coronation by the Pope,[a] intends indemnifying himself at the expense of the Turk. In my next letter, I shall treat of this eternally-recurring Eastern question, the *pons asini*[b] of European Diplomacy.[336]

Written on March 18, 1853

First published in the *New-York Daily Tribune*, No. 3733, April 4, 1853, and in the *Semi-Weekly Tribune*, No. 820, April 5, 1853

Signed: *Karl Marx*

Reproduced from the *New-York Daily Tribune*

---

[a] Pius IX.— *Ed.*

[b] Stumbling-block; literally: asses' bridge (5th proposition of the 1st book of Euclid which the beginners found very difficult to understand).— *Ed.*

FROM THE PREPARATORY
MATERIALS

Frederick Engels

[CRITICAL REVIEW OF PROUDHON'S BOOK
IDÉE GÉNÉRALE DE LA RÉVOLUTION AU XIX-e SIÈCLE][337]

P. J. PROUDHON,
IDÉE GÉNÉRALE DE LA RÉVOLUTION AU XIX-e SIÈCLE
(*CHOIX D'ÉTUDES SUR LA PRATIQUE RÉVOLUTIONNAIRE ET INDUS-
TRIELLE*),
PARIS, GARNIER FRÈRES, 1851

1) *"To the bourgeoisie"*.
"You", bourgeois, "were always the most fearless and the most skilful revolutionaries...." Even before the invasion of the barbarians, it was you who by means of your municipal federations had laid the shroud over the Roman Empire in Gaul (p. I). From then on until now you were at the head of the revolution. Nothing that was attempted without you or against you met with success; everything that you attempted has been achieved, everything that you will attempt will be achieved.

The historical exposition of this theme in declamatory style.—

At the present moment the old political intriguers are again in the saddle and treat *you* as revolutionaries (p. V). Therefore, accept the title, be revolutionary!

2) *As to the subject matter*. There follow seven essays to develop the following three points of view:

a) the old regime, b) the parties at the time of the revolution, c) the solution, i.e. the revolution itself (pp. 1-2).

First Essay
"REACTIONS DETERMINE REVOLUTIONS"

A revolution cannot be prevented. The opinion of Droz, who believes that the first revolution[a] could have been prevented by concessions and skilful behaviour, is as absurd as that of Blanqui, who believes revolutions can be conjured up (pp. 3-4).
The French monarchy from Clovis to Richelieu was revolutionary, it became reactionary in 1614 at the time of the last *États généraux*[338]; the punishment: January

---

[a] The French Revolution.— *Ed.*

21, 1793.[a] The revolution can be guided, moderated, made to advance slowly, and this system of giving way step by step is the wisest (p. 5). But it cannot be curbed. Witness[b] the suppression of the conspiracies of 1822 and 1839,[339] and the revolutions of 1830 and 1848. But "established interests and governmental pride" always oppose the peaceful development of the revolution (p. 8). Reaction always creates revolution. So it was in 1789 et seq., so it was in 1848. In February[c] when the proletariat intervened in the conflict between the bourgeoisie and the Crown, it demanded only work. The Republicans promised it work and so it joined them (pp. 10-11). "Work and, by means of work, bread; that was what the working classes asked for in 1848, that was the unshakable foundation they gave to the Republic, that is the revolution." The Republic was the "act of a minority more or less ... usurpatory", "the revolutionary question of work" was something quite different. The Republic was merely the "pledge of the revolution" (p. 11).

The Provisional Government was serious in its promises of work, but it could not keep them, otherwise it would have had to "change course, to alter the economic system of society". But instead of dealing candidly with the difficulties, and turning to the journalists, it kept silent, became directly reactionary, declared itself against socialism, "the new name that the revolution was taking" (p. 13), drove the unemployed masses in Paris and Rouen into revolt, and tried to drown in blood the great idea of February and the protest action of the workers. Henceforth it was established that the Republic of 1848 and that of 1793 were two quite different things, and that socialism was the last word of the Republic of 1848.

Hence the present struggle between all the old revolutionary trends on the one side, and socialism on the other. And if at the outset one did not know what socialism was, the forces of reaction have taught us this since February; "it is by the reaction that the revolution will be determined" (p. 17).

A solemn description of reaction and repression gradually making the majority of the nation revolutionary, and the bourgeoisie itself, the "eternal friend of order", becoming suspect and therefore being punished, and consequently thrown into the arms of the revolution. This leads up to the new electoral law.[340]

Therefore, "the people having been mentally alienated", the sole remedy that remains is "force" (p. 26).

And this "force", for the crisis of 1852,[341] consists of a series of measures which is only completed by the restoration in full of the feudal *ancien régime*.

But that you cannot and dare not do (p. 31). Appeal to the Republicans now to become really revolutionary and give "the revolution pledges" and "plans of economic renovation" (pp. 33, 34).

---

[a] The day Louis XVI was executed after the Convention had sentenced him to death.— *Ed.*

[b] Engels uses the English word.— *Ed.*

[c] 1848.— *Ed.*

Second Essay
"IS THERE SUFFICIENT REASON FOR REVOLUTION
IN THE NINETEENTH CENTURY?"

1. "The Law Determining the Tendency of Society.
The Revolution of 1789 Accomplished Only Half Its Work"

"The motive for revolutions is not so much the unhappy state experienced by society at a given time as the continuation of this unhappy state which tends to nullify well-being and cause it to disappear" (p. 36). Hence it is the *tendency* of the society which is the cause of revolution. The people, being neither optimists nor pessimists, do not demand that society shall be perfect, but that it "should have a tendency towards well-being and virtue"; they revolt "when society has for them a tendency towards poverty and corruption" (p. 37).

What then is at present the tendency of society?

1789 merely overthrew things, but did not rebuild at all. Hence "the kind of impossibility of living to which French society has been a prey for the last sixty years".

(Therefore—the *actually existing* bourgeois social order is nothing positive, free competition is merely negative, consequently the *true* bourgeois order has yet to be found.)

The feudal organisation which was destroyed on August 4, 1789,[342] has not been replaced by a new "national economy and equilibrium of interests". "Since birth no longer determined the position the citizen occupied, for labour alone was all" (?!) "for even property depended on it ... it was evident that the problem of the revolution consisted ... in establishing everywhere ... **an egalitarian or industrial regime**" (p. 39).

(As if that did not exist as far as was possible!)

But that was not understood and people resorted merely to **politics**. The revolutionaries were led astray by "their lack of the rudiments of economics, their **idea of government**,[a] and their distrust of the proletariat" (p. 40). "In the minds of all, politics again took precedence over industry, **Rousseau and Montesquieu reigned to the exclusion of Quesnay and Adam Smith**." (!!!) Hence the new society remains always in an embryonic condition (p. 41).

2. "The Anarchy of Economic Forces.
The Tendency of Society Towards Poverty"

"I term *economic forces* certain principles of action such as *division of labour, competition, collective force, exchange, credit, property*, etc., which are to labour and wealth what class distinctions, the representative system, hereditary monarchy, centralised administration"

(a fine juxtaposition!)

---

[a] Engels has "l'idée gouvernementale", Proudhon "le préjugé gouvernemental"[343] (p. 40).— *Ed.*

"are to the state. If these forces are kept in equilibrium, subject to the laws appropriate to them, and which do not depend in any way on human arbitrariness, labour can be said to be well-organised and the well-being of all assured. If, on the other hand, they are left without guidance and without any counter-poise"

(against what??),[a]

"labour is in a state of complete anarchy; the useful effects of the economic forces are mixed with an equal amount of harmful effects, the deficiency outweighs the benefit, and society, insofar as it is the seat, agent, or subject of production, circulation and consumption, is in a state of increasing suffering" (pp. 42-43).

Up to now only two forms of social existence[b] are known, "the political form and the economic form, between which moreover there is an essential antipathy and contradiction".

"The anarchy of the economic forces, the struggle they wage against the system of government, which is the sole obstacle to their organisation,—such is the real, deep-seated cause of the malaise to which society in France is a prey."

(Thus Proudhon, like a true Frenchman, confuses the French bureaucratic government with the normal state of a bourgeoisie that rules both itself and the proletariat) (p. 43).

Examples: 1) "Division of labour".—The basic principle of modern industry and at the same time the chief cause of the workers' stupefaction and decreasing wages. In England, for instance, owing to division of labour and the use of machines, the workers in one workshop have been reduced to one-half, one-third or even one-sixth of the previous number, and "their wages have been seen to fall in the same proportion, from an *average of three francs down to 50 or 30 centimes*" (!!) (p. 46).

Apart from this remarkable information (p. 46), it is all very superficial and commonplace.

2) Competition.—"This is the very law of the market, the spice of commerce, the salt of labour." ·

(beautiful!)[c]

"Competition, however, lacking legal forms (!) and superior and regulative standards, is in its turn perverted." The workers are excluded from competition, except for competition among themselves to depress wages. It has become a monopoly and has created a new aristocracy.

Very superficial.

"Recently, when the Prefect of Police"

---

[a] A pun in the original: Proudhon has "contrepoids" (counterpoise), Engels has "contre quoi" (against what).— *Ed.*

[b] Proudhon has "l'ordre dans une société" (p. 43).— *Ed.*

[c] Engels uses the English word.— *Ed.*

(a compliment paid to Carlier),

"in response to the general wish, authorised the sale of meat by auction,[344] one saw what free competition can do for the well-being of the people and how illusory this guarantee[a] is still among us" (p. 48).

O crapaud![b] The bourgeois measures of Carlier are socialist! Free trade,[c] because it does not exist in France, is socialistic!

Next, credit. A monopoly of the Bank of France. According to Proudhon, this monopoly is to blame for the fact that "property has become progressively mortgaged to an amount of 12 milliard [francs], and the state to an amount of 6 milliard francs", that interest and other expenses in this connection amount to 1,200 million francs per annum

(still only 6²/₃ per cent),

and that in addition 700-800 million francs have to be paid annually in discount, "advances of money, payment of arrears, shares of joint-stock companies, dividends, obligations under private deed, judicial expenses, etc.", and that as a result house rents and land rents have become unbearably high, and that of 10 milliards of annual production, 6 milliards are swallowed up through parasitism[345] (pp. 51-52).

Further examples or quotations are intended to prove that the situation of the people is continually worsening, and their income continually decreasing, in arithmetic progression, a counterpart to that of Malthus, such as

65 centimes, 60, 55 ... 15, 10, 5, 0, -5, -10, -15 (p. 52),

so that a time comes when the worker, instead of being paid so and so many centimes for his work per day, must pay 5, 10, 15 centimes into the bargain! And what about the law of wages, and competition!!

Examples follow to prove that the situation of the people since the revolution has continually worsened.

Decrease in the consumption of wine, meat, etc. Reduction in "the height required for military service", and an increase in the number unfit for service—1830 to 1839 45¹/₂ per cent; 1839 to 1848 50¹/₂ per cent. Incompatibility of universal education with the present social state of affairs. Increase of crime:

1827—34,908	criminal cases,	47,443	accused persons
1846—80,891	„	„	101,433	„ „
1847—95,914	„	„	124,159	„ „

---

[a] Proudhon has said earlier: "la concurrence [doit] servir à garantir la sincérité du commerce" ("competition [must] serve as a guarantee of honesty in commerce").—*Ed.*

[b] Toad, contemptible person.—*Ed.*

[c] Here and below Engels uses the English term.—*Ed.*

and in the police courts:

        1829—108,390 cases, 159,740 accused persons
        1845—152,923   „   197,913   „   „
        1847—184,922   „   239,291   „   „

3. "Government Irregularities, Tendency to Tyranny and Corruption"

Prior to 1848, philanthropic concern for the workers, even on the part of the government. Since 1848 progress; people realise that only a revolution can achieve decisive results here and therefore leave matters alone.

Interest on the national debt amounted to 63 million in 1814, now it amounts to 271 million. In 1802 the budget was 589 million, in 1848 it was 1,692 million, an increase which cannot be explained by the stupidity and wickedness of the governments. Between 1830 and 1848 the total salaries of officials rose by 65 million. Ditto.

(In France there are 568,365 officials; taking this as the basis Proudhon calculates that every ninth man lives at the expense of the budget, that is to say that there are only 5,115,285 men in France, whereas over $6^{1}/_{2}$ million *voted* in 1848!) (p. 62).

This increase in the number of officials and in the size of the military budget is proof of the growing need to enhance the repressive power, and hence of the growing danger to the state from the proletariat.[a] This tendency of the state to maintain big landownership and capital leads directly to corruption, which is the direct consequence of all centralisation.

—Hence:

"there is sufficient reason for revolution in the nineteenth century".

This second essay contains among other things also the following gems:

1. "The system of taxation at present in force ... is conceived in such a way that the producer pays everything, the capitalist nothing. *In fact*, even when the latter is entered for a particular sum in the book of the tax collector, or when he pays the dues laid down by the Exchequer on articles of consumption, *it is clear* that his income, being derived exclusively from the prelibation of his capital and not from the exchange of his products, this income remains free from tax, *since only he who produces pays*" (p. 65).

This last "since" says the same as the first proposition which has to be proved, and this proposition is thus of course proved. *C'est là la logique tranchante de M. Proudhon.*[b] This is expounded further:

---

[a] Proudhon has: "des classes laborieuses" (p. 63).— *Ed.*
[b] Such is the trenchant logic of M. Proudhon.— *Ed.*

"There is *therefore* a pact between capital and the authorities for ensuring that taxes are paid exclusively by the worker, and the secret of this pact consists simply, as I have said, in *imposing taxes on products instead of on capital.* By means of this dissimulation, the capitalist property-owner *appears to be paying* for his lands, for his house, for his chattels, for the alterations he makes, for his travels, for his consumption, *like all the other citizens.* Moreover, he says that his income, which without the tax would be 3,000, 6,000, 10,000 or 20,000 francs, is, thanks to the tax, not more than 2,500, 4,500, 8,000 or 15,000 francs. And on top of that he protests more indignantly than his tenants against the size of the budget. Sheer equivocaton! *The capitalist does not pay anything, the government shares with him, that is all.*"

(It shares also with the producer when it takes part of his products from him, and the capitalist likewise, *dicitur potest,*[a] shares with the producer.)

"They make common cause."

(O Stirner!)

"What worker then would not regard himself as lucky to be written down in the public ledger for 2,000 francs of rent on the sole condition of parting with one quarter of it as amortisation?"!!! (pp. 65-66).

2) The register is drawn up "as if the purpose of the legislator[b] was to re-establish the inalienability of real estate—as if he continually wanted to remind the bondsman freed during the night of August 4 that his position was that of a serf, that it was not his lot to own the soil, that every cultivator was of right, except through a concession from the sovereign, a tenant by emphyteusis and in mortmain!" (p. 66).

O Stirner! As if the registration did not affect big real estate just as much as small, according to which Louis Philippe himself was a bondsman.

3) The theory of free trade and explanation of protective duties.

The duties yield 160 million to the state. Suppose the customs were abolished and foreign competition were strong in the French market; "suppose then the state makes the following proposal to the French industrialists: which do you prefer for safeguarding your interests: to pay me 160 million or to receive them? Do you think the industrialists would choose the first alternative? It is precisely this that the government imposes on *them.* To the ordinary expenses we have to pay on products from abroad and on those we send there, the state adds 160 million which serve it as a sort of premium; that is the meaning of customs" (pp. 68-69).

If considering the lunatic French tariff, such nonsense can be excused, it is still a bit steep that M. Proudhon measures protective tariffs in general by the French scale and makes out that they are a *tax on manufacturers.*

---

[a] One can say.— *Ed.*
[b] Proudhon has: "the legislator of 1789" (p. 66).— *Ed.*

4) pp. 73, 74. Proudhon quotes a speech by Royer-Collard in the Chamber of Deputies; the debate of January 19-24, 1822,[346] in which this lawyer expresses his regret at the disappearance of the independent Benches (parliaments)[347] and other "democratic institutions", "powerful assemblages of private rights, true republics in the monarchy"; they had set limits to sovereignty everywhere, whereas at present although the government is divided up it is unrestricted in its action.

This reactionary review of the old lawyer, who cannot conceal his hatred of the administrative system, M. Proudhon mistakenly regards as social-revolutionary;

"what Royer-Collard said about the monarchy of 1814 is true, what he says of the Republic of 1848 is still more so."

What leads M. Proudhon astray is the confused statement by Royer-Collard:

"The Charter,[348] therefore, at one and the same time has to provide the constitutional basis for *government and society*; no doubt society has not been forgotten or neglected, but postponed."

What Royer-Collard understands by society is evident from the fact that he says:

"It is only in establishing freedom of the press as a public right that the Charter has restored society to itself" (p. 75).

Hence "society"=the governed considered in their capability of resistance to the government.

Third Essay
"ON THE PRINCIPLE OF ASSOCIATION"

First of all, before we come to the solution, "it is advisable to estimate the value of the theories offered for public consumption, the compulsory baggage of all revolutions" (p. 79). But when we criticise their principle then we have disposed of all of them, the St. Simonists, Fourier, Owen, Cabet, Louis Blanc, etc. This principle of all systems is association.

Association is not an "equilibrium of economic forces", it is not even a "force", it is a "*dogma*" (p. 84). The further elaboration of the principle of association always leads to a *system* and the socialism based on it necessarily becomes a **religion** (p. 84).

Association is not an "economic force". **Commerce** is one, for "independently of the service performed by the material fact of transport it is by itself a direct stimulus to consumption, and consequently a cause of production, *a principle of the creation of values* (!) *the metaphysical act* of exchange, and just as much as labour, but in a different manner from labour, it produces real objects and wealth.... Moreover, the merchant enriched by speculative transactions divested of all stockjobbery (!!), deservedly enjoys the fortune he has acquired; this fortune is as legitimate as that produced by labour" (the bourgeois forgets here that without capital one can certainly work for another capitalist, but cannot carry on commerce without capital, otherwise this apologia for the merchant is very significant). Further ...

"exchange, this *purely moral* operation ... is also creation" (p. 85).

The "collective force",

which Proudhon flatters himself to have discovered in *Qu'est-ce que la propriété*,

is also an "economic force". Likewise competition, likewise division of labour, property, etc., etc.

What Proudhon calls "economic forces" are simply the modes of production and intercourse of the bourgeoisie, insofar as they serve his purpose, insofar as in his eyes they have either only a good side or, along with the bad side, have at least a very marked good side as well. Even general forms of intercourse and production, which when once discovered are everywhere applied in all succeeding generations, with appropriate modification, are as much at the disposal of society as the use of water power, knowledge of the spherical shape of the earth and the division of the latter into degrees of latitude and longitude, etc., etc., even these general forms Proudhon knows only in their bourgeois form. Exchange, for example, as we have just seen, is from the outset merged in commerce. If the collective force appears at least to be something eternal, it is on the other hand nothing but an attempt to convert the existence of society itself into an economic force. Without society, just as without a collective force, there is no relation between men, no intercourse. Exchange, division of labour, competition, credit are manifestations of the collective force. It takes at least two to produce a relationship, and where two collaborate to do something which cannot be done by one, there exists a collective force. However, it is ridiculous first of all to describe all the forms in which members of society carry on intercourse and produce as forces, and then finally trying to foist on us the existence of society, social production and social intercourse as a distinct economic force. Moreover, the primitive, crude form of collective force which Proudhon has in mind (mass labour in the construction of obelisks, pyramids, etc., etc.) has long ago been almost entirely replaced by the use of machines and horses, division of labour, etc., and converted into quite different forms.

If, however, commerce, competition, division of labour, etc., are economic forces, there is no reason why, for instance, the factory system, banking, paper money, the parcellation of landed property, big landownership, wage labour, capital, and rent, should not also be economic forces. On each of these it is easy to declaim a dithyrambic panegyric as Proudhon does for the former set of forces. But there's the rub.

It is strange that Proudhon, p. 88, calls these relationships *essentially non-material* forces, and makes this non-materiality the basis for hymns to the effect, for example, that

> the economists by their theory of industrial forces "have, without suspecting it, demonstrated the fundamental dogma of Christian theology, creation *de nihilo*",

(ex ??[a]) (p. 87), and earlier [he speaks] of

> the "***purely moral***" act of "commerce, which is also a ***creation***" (p. 86).

Next comes the following magnificent piece of sophistry on association:

> "Association is by its nature sterile, even harmful, since it impedes the freedom of the worker. The writers responsible for utopian fraternities ... have, without motives and without proofs, ascribed to the *social contract* [contrat de société] a virtue and an efficacy which belongs only to the collective force, to division of labour, or to exchange.... When an industrial or commercial society has as its aim either to put into operation one of the great economic forces, or to exploit a group of resources the nature of which demands that it remains undivided, one clientele, one monopoly, the society formed for this purpose can have a successful result; but this result is not created by virtue of its principle, but is due to its means. This is so true that whenever the same result can be achieved without association, people"

(i.e. the capitalists)

> "prefer not to associate" (pp. 88-89). People associate only when they must.
> Association—solidarity, "joint responsibility, fusion of rights and duties in relation to third parties".—"Equality of wages, the supreme law of association."—"One can say" therefore "that association is useful to the associate who is weak or lazy, and only to him."—"Solidarity of the unskilful and the unfit" (pp. 89, 90). Every prospering association "owes its prosperity to an objective cause which is foreign to it and is in no way bound up with its essence". Association is suitable only "in special conditions" (p. 91).

Furthermore, in all workers' associations at present piece-work[b] has been substituted for equality of wages—there is the least possible solidarity, the greatest possible independence when forces and capitals are combined,

that is to say, the least possible *association*, the greatest possible *means*.

> "Association established specially with a view to the family tie and the law of dedication, and apart from any external economic consideration and any preponderant interest, association for its own sake, in short, is purely an act of religion, a supernatural bond, devoid of positive value, a myth."

---

[a] Proudhon mistakenly has: "de nihilo"—"without ground", "without reason" (p. 87). Engels queries this and suggests "ex [nihilo]"—"out of nothing".— *Ed.*
[b] Engels uses the English term.— *Ed.*

As far as the Paris workers' associations are concerned, Proudhon gives the following cold-blooded classification:

"A fairly large number exist and can be expected to develop further; one knows why. Some of them are formed by the most skilled workers in their occupation; it is the monopoly of talent which helps them to succeed.... Others attract and keep their customers by cheapness; they live by competition.... In general, finally, in all these associations the workers ... have to work a little more and to content themselves with a smaller reward. There is nothing in that but what is quite usual in political economy and to obtain which ... there was no need of association" (pp. 96-97).

The associations of slaughtermen are not associations, "they are set up at joint expense by citizens of all estates to compete with the monopoly of the butchers. It is the application, such as it is, of a new principle, not to say"

(why not?)

"of a new *economic force, reciprocity*, which consists in the partners guaranteeing one another, irrevocably, their products at the cost of production."[349]

(Of course, M. Proudhon is the first inventor of "reciprocity", cf. *Organisation du crédit et de la circulation*, Garnier frères, 1848, and the *Banque du peuple*) (pp. 97, 98).[350]

Next come advertisements, M. Proudhon's witty remarks about Louis Blanc. *De chacun selon sa capacité, à chacun selon ses besoins*,[a] and then:

of 36 million Frenchmen, 24 million are peasants. "These you will never organise in associations. Agricultural work has no need of joint choreography, and the soul of the peasant rejects it."

Compare the rage of the peasants against the June insurgents, whom they believed to be communists. Moreover

of the remaining 12 million, at least half are "manufacturers, craftsmen, employees, for whom association is purposeless"; there remain 6 million who could perhaps be induced to join the associations, but the majority of whom would very soon break this yoke.

The existing workers' associations are not to be judged by their present results, but by their "secret tendency, which is to affirm the possibility of the social republic. Whether the workers know it or not, the importance of their work does not lie at all in the petty interests of the society ... later on ... the associations of workers, abandoning the production of fancy goods and toys, will have to turn to the major branches of industry which are their natural sphere" (p. 107).

Finally, he invites Louis Blanc,

---

[a] "From each according to his ability, to each according to his needs", L. Blanc, "Un homme et une doctrine", *Le Nouveau Monde*, No. 6, December 15, 1849.— *Ed.*

the "cicada of the revolution",[a] to "contribute his abstention and his silence as his obol to the cause of the proletariat, which on one day of mistakes fell into his feeble hands" (p. 108).

The point is: association *as such*, *in abstracto*, is of course just as much dependent on circumstances as any other social relationship. Where the prerequisites are absent, no economic force is of any avail. Competition presupposes the means for it just as much as association. Division of labour can be applied inopportunely just as much as association. One can carry out exchange badly, just as one can form associations badly. Viewed abstractly, every economic force is just as much a dogma as is association, it all depends on the existing conditions. And it is precisely in the investigation of existing conditions that Proudhon has contributed nothing at all; he has treated Parisian small-scale industry as the normal state of affairs, instead of seeing in the development of large-scale industry, machinery and division of labour, as it occurs in England, and the growing centralisation of capital bound up with it, a need for association which requires for its satisfaction a quite different type of amalgamation and centralisation of forces than the Parisian toy associations and the Proudhonist workers' companies.[351]

Fourth Essay
"ON THE PRINCIPLE OF AUTHORITY"

First of all a dithyramb on "anarchy", discovered by M. Proudhon.

1. *"The Traditional Negation of Government. Emergence of the Idea Which Succeeds It"* (p. 116)

All government has arisen from the patriarchal family. "The final stage of governmental evolution is democracy" (p. 119); the final stage of democracy is the direct government of Considérant, Rittinghausen, etc., etc. And this would logically lead directly to imperial tyranny, as in Greece and Rome (p. 121).

The "negation of government" dates from the Reformation. The principle of authority in the religious sphere supplanted by liberty of thought. Later carried over into the secular sphere as well, especially by Jurieu, who invented (?) the term social contract. The idea of contract, of "the reign of contract", applied in practice to social life, trade, etc., and not merely to politics, would have led beyond the whole government regime. But Rousseau, "who did not understand anything about the social contract", ruined everything.

---

[a] Proudhon has: "Louis Blanc considered himself the bee of the revolution, but was merely its cicada" ("Il s'est cru l'abeille de la révolution, il n'en a été que la cigale").— *Ed.*

The social contract must be freely discussed and accepted by every participant, otherwise it is invalid

—and other moral comments of a Stirner-like character (pp. 125-27).

But Rousseau's social contract 1) does not contain even the matters which should be the subject of contract; 2) it contains neither rights nor obligations, but merely punishments (p. 128).

Detailed proof that Rousseau, proceeding from the "broadest democratic basis",[a] abandons one aspect of it after another as being impracticable, and that having recognised the impossibility of maintaining equality and democratic government he "deduces the necessity of the proletariat, the subordinate position of the worker, dictatorship and the Inquisition", and simply puts forward "the code of capitalist and commercial tyranny" (pp. 131-33).

A furious attack on Rousseau in the highest style of Proudhonic declamation, but nevertheless sufficiently serious for people like L. Blanc and Co.

Saint-Simon was the first to envisage the end of the governmental system, the coming of the industrial system. He deduced the negation of the state "from historical observation and the education of mankind".

Proudhon deduces it

"from an analysis of economic functions, and from the theory of credit and exchange". The eighteenth century finally completed the reformation and replaced the idea of government by the idea of contract (of "liberty of thought" in the sphere of practice) (pp. 136-40).

2. "General Critique of the Idea of Authority" (p. 141)

1) *"Absolute authority"*

Trash.[b]

"Absolutism in its naive expression is repugnant to reason and liberty" (!),

and similar profound matters (pp. 142-46).

2) *"Laws"*

Infinity of cases, hence laws pass into bad infinity (pp. 147-50).

3) *"Constitutional monarchy"*

"A hybrid government." It is the **number**, the majority, that is decisive.

Verbose exposition of all the old abuse of the historical school[352] against majority, against counting heads, etc. (pp. 150-56).

---

[a] Engels' quotation marks.— *Ed.*

[b] Engels uses the English word.— *Ed.*

4) *"Universal suffrage"*

General platitudes about the moral justification of the February revolution.

What universal suffrage can do is shown by the two National Assemblies and the election of Louis Bonaparte.[353]

Universal suffrage is definitely discredited (pp. 156-62).

5) *"Direct legislation"*

It is at any rate consistently democratic and Robespierre and L. Blanc very wrongly (from their standpoint) oppose it.

Solemn discussion of direct government.

It is a question of ascertaining "the wish of all", as of a "collective being". But this is not possible. Hence a system of questions is necessary, questions which the representatives ask and to which the people have to answer yes or no. But that is nonsense, for no question can be formulated in such a way that all truth, fairness and justice are on one side and all unreason and injustice on the other.

There follows a mass of examples, mostly taken from Herr Rittinghausen himself. Among them is the following example of the *industrial* regime à la Proudhon:

Rittinghausen asks the people: "Should there be a railway from Lyons to Avignon?" and the people say yes. "This *yes*, however, can contain a serious mistake, in any case it is an infraction of the rights of the localities."
"There exists a navigable waterway from Châlon to Avignon which offers transport 70 per cent below all the railway rates (!). It can lower its charges (I know something about it) to 90 per cent (!!). Instead of constructing a railway which will cost 200 million and which will ruin the trade of four departments, why not **utilise**"

(what does this mean? is it not already utilised?)

"this waterway which would cost almost nothing? But that is not how matters are understood in the *Palais législatif*, where there is no freight commissioner, and since the French people, apart from those living along the Rhône and the Saône, do not know any more than their Ministers what takes place on the two rivers, they will pronounce, as can easily be foreseen, not according to their own thought, but according to the desire of their appointees. Eighty-two departments will decree the ruin (!!!) of four others; that is how direct legislation wants it to be" (p. 169).

Thus under the industrial system railways would never have been built if tug-boat navigation existed on the Rhine. This is already promising enough.

Then on p. 173 against Ledru and the Constitution of 1793,[354] and the system that the people should merely vote the laws, the general principles, but the deputies should make the decrees, i.e. the "executive part". Proof that then, with the help of the decrees, it is possible to reverse in detail that which the people have decided in general, in principle (pp. 174-76).

The final form: where the people themselves perform all governmental duties. But then they are unable to work, and they do not have slaves. Hence the "governmental idea" results in an absurdity.

As a practical example he considers the Constitution of 1793 and Robespierre. He says that Robespierre was a "juste milieu" man of 1791 and that he hated "direct government." By greater concentration of governmental power he wanted to abolish the Constitution of 1793. This was also the desire of the majority of the Convention, but this majority did not trust him, appropriated the same idea, removed him and subsequently carried out the idea. What the men of Thermidor did was what he wanted.

Proudhon writes that Robespierre was reactionary throughout the revolution and always preached tranquillity. Conclusion: a rhetorical characterisation of Robespierre.

Fifth Essay
"SOCIAL LIQUIDATION"

Recapitulation: the solution is said to lie in reciprocity and in the idea of contract, which is the juridical expression of reciprocity. According to this, three things have to be done: "1) to put a definite stop to the disorganising tendency bequeathed to us by the old revolution[a] and to proceed with the help of the new principle to the **liquidation of the vested interests**; 2) to organise with the help of the new principle the economic forces and give property its constitution; 3) to make the political or governmental system dissolve, merge and disappear in the economic system" (p. 196).

Assuming that the elections of 1852 turn out to be revolutionary, the following would have to be done:

1. "National Bank"

The citizens can agree on and if necessary contribute to any establishment which proves to be to the advantage of the participants—hence also to a discount bank, and in fact this can be founded without "either **association** or fraternity being necessary for it ... there need be nothing but a reciprocal promise of sale or exchange, in short, a simple contract" (p. 198).

The existing bank[355] endeavours to become a "public establishment" 1) because it makes use of capital that does not belong to it, 2) because it has the privilege of issuing paper money, and any privilege is a "public property", 3) because enjoyment of the interest on foreign capital and artificial increase of the price of the circulating medium are illegitimate, "hence the bank, owing to the illegitimacy of its profits, is condemned to become a public establishment" (p. 199). Hence the decree: "**The bank is declared to be not the property of the state but an establishment of public utility, and the liquidation of the company is ordered.**" As an "establishment of public utility having as capitalists its own clients" (!) it does not pay interest to anyone, since the public benefit requires that money shall be as cheap as possible. Once the interest accruing to the bank belongs to the public it can be so much reduced that it covers only the costs of administration, **i.e. to** $^1/_4$ **or** $^1/_2$ **per cent** (pp. 200-01). This is very different from the socialist State Bank, and from the "credit of the state", which is nothing but "the democratic and social consecration of the principle of plunder, the exploitation of the worker in the name of, on the model of and under the patronage of, the Republic" (pp. 201, 202). This, then, is what the National Assembly should decree.

---

[a] That of 1789-94.— *Ed.*

2. *"The National Debt"*

Six milliards, interest 270 million, and 74 million annually for redemption, hence 344 million annually, and 56 million for pensions and retirement payments.

With the bank revolutionised and the rate of interest reduced, the national debt can likewise be put on a lower rate of interest. Then it is paid off in annual instalments,[356] that is to say, from the 5 per cent paid $^1/_4$ per cent is reckoned as interest and $4^3/_4$ per cent as repayment of capital (pp. 204-05).

3. *"Mortgage Debts, Simple Bonds"*

Interest amounts to 1,200 million annually,

hence capital of about 24 milliards.

Decree: "Interest on all debts, mortgages, simple contract debts, joint-stock shares, is fixed at the same rate"

(as above, $^1/_2$ per cent[a]);

"repayment claims can be met only by annual instalments; the annual instalment for all sums below 2,000 fr. will be 10 per cent, for sums above 2,000 fr. 5 per cent. A section of the offices of the National Discount Bank will become a mortgage bank, the maximum of its advances will be 500 million per annum" (p. 213).

4. *"Buildings"*

If the rate of interest=O, house rent is also reduced to nil

(therefore profit and ground rent depend on the rate of interest) (p. 218).

Decree: "Every payment made in respect of rent shall be entered to the account of the property, reckoned as twenty times the rent"

(and what about repairs?).

"With every instalment of rent the tenant will acquire a proportional and joint share in the house he occupies and in the totality of all buildings let for rent and serving as dwellings for the citizens. Property thus paid for will pass by degrees into the hands of the communal administration (!), which by the fact of the payment"

(which it does not make at all!)

"takes over the mortgages and prerogatives in the name"

(and without the permission?)

"of the mass of tenants, and will guarantee"

(solidarity!!!)

"their domicile to all of them in perpetuity at the cost price of the building.—The communes[357] will be able to negotiate separate agreements with the owners for the immediate liquidation and repayment of the leased properties. In this case, and in

---

^{a} See this volume, p. 559.— *Ed.*

order that the present generation shall enjoy reduced rents, the said communes will be able immediately to reduce the rent of houses for which they have concluded agreements, in such a way that amortisation be completed only in thirty years.—For repairs, fittings and upkeep of the buildings, as in the case of new constructions, the communes will negotiate with the companies of masons or associations of building workers according to the principles and rules of the new social contract. The owners, sole occupiers of their own houses, will retain the property as long as they judge this advantageous to their interests" (pp. 221-22).

"5. Landed Property"

It will be revolutionised through the "mortgage bank". "The special character of the mortgage bank, in addition to the low price and facility of its credit, lies in *repayment by annual instalments*" (p. 223). For example, it has funds of 2 milliards and lends annually 400 million fr. with a 5 per cent annual repayment. In this way the peasants pay off their mortgage creditors and twenty years after taking up the loan they are free from debt. "At the end of five years the capital of 2 milliards would be exhausted; but because of the annual instalments it receives and the deductions it makes from credits (?!!) the bank will find that it has in hand a sum of approximately 400 million, which it will lend out afresh. The transactions therefore will continue in this way till at the end of twenty years the landed property will have repaid 4×2 milliards, i.e. 8 milliards of mortgages, and in 30 years it will be rid of usurers" (p. 224).

A fine calculation! 1) It is not possible to imagine that "the deductions made from credits" can be anything but acts of defraudation. 2) *No* annual instalment is recovered by the bank in the first year; at the end of the first year it gets 5 per cent of 400 million=20 million; at the end of the second year it gets 5 per cent of 800 million=40 million; at the end of the third year 60 million; of the fourth year 80 million; of the fifth year 100 million; it has therefore recovered 300 million, and not approximately 400 million. But supposing it could lend out 400 million in the sixth year, then at the end of this year it would receive only 120 million and therefore be unable to give out 400 million. Supposing the bank had been provided with a capital of 4 milliards instead of 2 milliards and could therefore lend 400 million per annum for ten years before having to resort to the money paid back, even then it would be broke in the 13th year and in this year could lend only 360 million instead of 400 million. With 4,400 million, that is with an original capital enabling it to pay out during 11 years, it would have reached bottom in the 17th year and could only expend 320 million. Finally, with 4,800 million it could give loans for 12 years from the original fund and afterwards from the repayments and at the end of the 20th year have 600 million over in addition to the periodically recurring repayments of 400 million annually, which fall due at that time.

Proof:

Up to the twelfth year payments are made from the capital.

Annual advances				Annual repayment		Excess		Total balance per year
lst-12th	year	4,800	mill.					1,320
13th	"	400	"	240	mill.	+(1320-400) 920		=1,160
14th	"	400	"	260	"	+	760	=1,020
15th	"	400	"	280	"	+	620	= 900
16th	"	400	"	300	"	+	500	= 800
17th	"	400	"	320	"	+	400	= 720
18th	"	400	"	340	"	+	320	= 660
19th	"	400	"	360	"	+	260	= 620
20th	"	400	"	380	"	+	220	= 600
21st	"	400	"	400	"	+	200	= 600
22nd	"	400	"	400	"	+	200	= 600 etc

never increasing.

That is how M. Proudhon lays the foundation for his National Mortgage Bank.

But the thing can be done even more speedily. One issues a decree stating:

"Every payment of rent for the use of a piece of real estate will make the farmer part-proprietor of it and will count as a mortgage payment by him. When the property has been entirely paid for it **will be immediately taken over by the commune, which will take the place of the former owner**"

(why does the new owner not immediately enter into his rights?)

"and will share with the farmer the ownership and the net product. The communes will be able to negotiate separate agreements with the owners who desire it for the redemption of the rents and the immediate repayment of the properties. In that case at the request of the communes steps shall be taken to instal (!?) the cultivators, and to delimit their properties, taking care that as far as possible the size of the area shall make up (!?) for the quality of the land, and that the rent"

(where did the annual instalments get to?)

"shall be proportional to the product. As soon as the property has been entirely paid for, all the communes of the Republic will have to reach agreement among themselves to equalise (!?) the differences in the quality of the strips of land, and also the contingencies of farming. The part of the rent due to them from the plots in their particular area will be used for this compensation and general insurance. Dating from the same period the old owners who worked themselves on their properties, will retain their title, and **will be treated in the same way as the new owners, will have to pay the same rent and will be granted the same rights**"

(what rights?)

"**in such a way that no one is favoured by the chance of location and inheritance and that the conditions of cultivation are equal for all** (!!!!). The land tax will be abolished"

(after a new one has been put in its place!).

"The functions of the rural police will devolve on the municipal councils" (p. 228).

Colossal nonsense.

Next he explains that

"the right to the increase in value", i.e. the right of the farmer to the improvements he makes to the soil, cannot be implemented, any more than "the right to work", however popular both of these are.

A very legal and moral point of view.

Sixth Essay
"ORGANISATION OF THE ECONOMIC FORCES"

Everything is done by way of contract. I make a contract about something with my neighbour—the contract expresses My will. I can equally well make a contract with all the inhabitants of my commune, and my commune with any other, with all the other communes of the country. "I could be sure that the law thus made throughout the Republic, derived from millions of different initiatives, would never be anything other than *My law*" (p. 236).

O Stirner!! Hence the regime of contract is something like the following:

1. "Credit"

This is already settled by the bank through the lowering of the rate of interest to $^1/_2$, $^1/_4$, $^1/_8$ per cent, and will be completed by the withdrawal of all gold and silver from circulation.

"As for *personal* credit"

(i.e. not based on security),

"it is not a matter that concerns the National Bank; it should be operated in the workers' companies and the industrial and agricultural societies" (pp. 237-38).

2. "Property"[a]

This is conceived by all socialists[358] either as property of the commune organised through association, where the peasant is an agricultural worker in an association, or as state property which is leased to peasants. The first form is "communistic", "utopian", "still-born"; if it should be seriously attempted "the peasant would be faced with the question of insurrection" (pp. 238-39). The second form, too, is inapplicable, "governmental", "feudal", "fiscal", etc. The reasons advanced in favour of it fall to the ground, for "the net product"

(i.e. the rent),

being the result of the unequal quality of the soil, belongs not to the state but to "the farmer who receives little; it is for this reason that in our plan for liquidation we have

---

[a] Proudhon deals with landed property here.— *Ed.*

stipulated that the rent should be proportionate to the type of land so as to form a fund in order to equalise the income of the farmers and to insure the products" (p. 240).

That means everything remains as it was before, the farmer pays the rent during the first 20-30 years to the old property-owner and then to the general assurance fund, which divides it among the owners of inferior land. Thus good and bad land will have exactly the same value, or rather the same lack of value, for it is inconceivable how land then can still have any capital value. In what way this differs from payment of rent to the state—especially as the communes will be at liberty to interfere in everything—is also inconceivable. And that is what Proudhon calls

"property separated from rent, liberated from its fetters and cured of its leprosy"

and believes that it has now become a pure medium of circulation (p. 242).

With the confiscation of landed property by the state, the value of the entire landed property in the country, worth 80 milliards, would be withdrawn from circulation and, as belonging to all, that is to say to no one would have to be struck from the inventory. "In any case, the *collective* wealth of the nation will undoubtedly neither lose nor gain; what does it matter to society whether the 80 milliards of real estate, which constitute individual fortunes, figure or do not figure in the total? But is it the same thing for the farmer in whose hands the mobilised soil once again becomes a value in circulation, money?" (p. 245).

With the system of tenure under the state, the peasant would very soon assert his right of ownership of the soil, which would be easy for him "since the peasants would always have the upper hand in France" (p. 246).

Quite correct, of course, if the lousy small-holding system, the only one that Proudhon knows, were to be retained. But then, too, in spite of Proudhon, mortgages and usury would just as quickly reappear.

"Given the facility of repayment by annual instalments, the value of a piece of real estate can be indefinitely divided, exchanged, and undergo any conceivable change, without the real estate being in the least affected. The rest is a matter of the police, and we do not have to concern ourselves with it" (pp. 246-47).

3. "Division of Labour, Collective Forces, Machinery. Companies of Workers"

"Agricultural labour is a kind of labour which least of all requires, or, better expressed, which rejects with the utmost vigour, the co-operative form; one has never seen peasants forming association for cultivating their fields; and one never will see it. The only relations of concord and solidarity which could exist between farmers, the only form of centralisation of which rural industry is capable ... is that which results from **the equalisation of the net product,** from mutual insurance and, above all, from **the abolition of rent**" (!!) (p. 247).

Last page of Engels' manuscript "Critical Review of Proudhon's Book
Idée générale de la Révolution au XIX-e siècle"

It is different with the railways, mines and manufactures. Here there is either wage labour under a capitalist, or association. "Every industry, mine or enterprise which by its nature requires the combined employment of a large number of workers with different skills is bound to become the basis for an association or company of workers" (p. 249).

As regards crafts, on the other hand, "unless for reasons of particular convenience, I cannot see that there is any reason for association". Moreover, the relation of master and worker is here quite different; "of the two men, one calls himself a boss, the other a worker, but basically they are perfectly equal, perfectly free" (!!). In these circumstances, "the only purpose" of assembling a number of workers in a single workshop "where all do more or less the same thing is to multiply the product, not to contribute to its essential character by means of their diverse abilities" (p. 251).

A wretched fellow, who knows only fancy goods and the petty Parisian handicraft industry without division of labour or machinery!

Contract between society and the companies of workers:

"Vis-à-vis society, which has created it and on which it depends, the workers' company undertakes to provide the products and services demanded from it at a price that is always as close as possible to the cost of production, and to enable the public to enjoy all the improvements and refinements that are desirable. To this end the workers' company does not enter any coalition, submits itself to competition,[a] puts its books and archives at the disposal of society, which retains in regard to it, as a sanction of its right of control, the **power to dissolve it**"

(who exercises this power?).

As to the members of the company itself:

"Every person working in the association ... possesses a joint right in the property of the company; he has the right to perform successively all duties, to occupy all posts proper to the sex, ability, age and seniority. His education, training and apprenticeship ought therefore to be conducted in such a way that, while he is made to take his share of disagreeable and arduous tasks, he will acquire experience in various sorts of work and fields of knowledge, so that when he reaches mature age he will have a wide range of qualifications and a sufficient income. Posts are subject to election and the rules are adopted by the members of the association. The size of the recompense depends on the nature of the work, the degree of the proficiency, and the amount of responsibility. Every member of the association shares both in the profits and in the expenses of the company in proportion to his services. Everyone is free to resign from the association whenever he wishes, and therefore to settle his accounts and renounce his rights; conversely the company is entitled to recruit new members at any time" (pp. 255-57).

"The application of these principles in an era of transition would cause **the bourgeois class to take the initiative and merge with the proletariat**, and this ... should **please every true revolutionary**" (p. 257). The proletariat is lacking in brains and the bourgeoisie will readily enter into association with it. "No bourgeois who is conversant with commerce and industry and their innumerable risks would not prefer

---

[a] Proudhon has: "se soumet à la loi de la concurrence" ("submits itself to the law of competition") (p. 256).— *Ed.*

a fixed salary and an honourable employment in a workers' company to all the anxiety connected with a private enterprise" (p. 258).

(*Vous les connaissez bien*, M. Proudhon.[a]

4. "The Determination of Value, the Establishment of a Cheap Market"

"The fair price",

the great desideratum,

consists of 1) the costs of production, 2) the **salary** of the merchant, or "the compensation for the advantages which the seller forgoes by parting with the article" (p. 262). In order to secure the fair price, one must ensure that the merchant will be able to sell his goods. The Provisional Government could have made commerce flourish at once if it had guaranteed 5 per cent interest to the first 10,000 industrialists to invest up to 100,000 francs each in their business

(where are these to be obtained from, even in the highest prosperity!).

One thousand million would have been invested in industry. "Ten thousand commercial and industrial establishments could not operate simultaneously without supporting one another; what one produces another consumes; work, that is the outlet."

(The landlubber only knows of home trade[b] and like the most shallow English Tory believes that he can make large-scale industry prosper by means of it!)

Thus the state would not have had to pay 50 million, it would not have had to pay 10 million, in order to meet this guarantee (pp. 266, 267).

Worse trash never was written not even by Proudhon himself.[c] Contracts therefore are made on the following basis:

"The state, on behalf of the interests which it temporarily represents, and the departments and communes on behalf of their respective inhabitants ... propose to guarantee that the entrepreneurs who offer the most advantageous conditions will receive either interest"

(after payment of interest has been abolished)

"on the capital and material invested in their enterprises, or a fixed salary, or in appropriate cases a sufficient quantity of orders. In return, the tendering parties will pledge themselves to meet all consumers' requests for the goods and services they have undertaken to supply. Apart from that, full scope is left for competition. They must state the component parts of their prices, the method of delivery, the duration of their commitments, and their means of fulfilment. The tenders submitted under seal within

---

[a] You know them very well, M. Proudhon.— *Ed.*

[b] Engels uses the English term.— *Ed.*

[c] Engels wrote this sentence in English.— *Ed.*

the periods prescribed will subsequently be opened and made public 8 days, 15 days[a] ... before the contracts are allocated. At the expiry of each contract, new tenders will be invited" (pp. 268, 269).

5. *"Foreign Trade, Balance of Exports and Imports"*

Inasmuch as the purpose of customs duties is to protect home industry, the reduction of the rate of interest, the liquidation of the national debt and private debts, the lowering of rents and leases, the determination of value, etc., will greatly decrease the costs of production of all articles and therefore make it possible to lower customs duties (p. 272).

Proudhon is in favour of abolishing customs duties as soon as the rate of interest is reduced to $^1/_2$ per cent or $^1/_4$ per cent.

"If tomorrow ... the Bank of France reduced its discount rate to $^1/_2$ per cent, interest and commission included, immediately all manufacturers and merchants of Paris and the provinces **who do not have credit at the Bank** would endeavour in their negotiations to obtain bills, **for it would cost only $^1/_2$ per cent** [to discount] **these bills received at par instead of 6, 7, 8 or 9 per cent, which money costs at the bankers**" (!!!!) "...Those abroad would also have recourse to this. French bills would cost only $^1/_2$ per cent, whereas those of other states would cost 10 or 12 times as much" (!!), "preference would be given to the former— **everybody would be interested in using this money in their payments**" (!!!) (p. 274). In order to have more French banknotes, the foreign producers would lower the prices of their commodities and our imports would rise. Since, however, foreign countries can neither buy French annuities with the exported banknotes, or lend them to us again, nor take up mortgages on our land, this import cannot harm us; "on the contrary, it is not we who would have to moderate our purchases, it would be up to the foreign countries to be cautious about their sales" (!!) (pp. 274-75).

Owing to the influx of these miraculous French banknotes foreign countries would be compelled to repeat the same economic revolution which Proudhon has achieved for France.

Finally, an appeal to the Republican lawyers, Crémieux, Marie, Ledru, Michel, etc., to take up these ideas. They, the representatives of the *idea of justice*, are called upon to pave the way here (pp. 275, 276).

Seventh Essay
"THE MERGING OF GOVERNMENT IN THE ECONOMIC ORGANISM"

1. *"Society without authority"*

Rhetoric.

---

[a] Proudhon has: "8 days, 15 days, one month, three months, depending on the importance of the contract" (p. 269).— *Ed.*

2. "*Elimination of governmental functions. Cults*"

Historical, religious philosophical fantasies. Result: this aspect of the voluntary system[a] that prevails in America amounts to the abolition of the state (pp. 293-95).

3. "*Justice*"

No one has the right to judge another unless the latter makes him his judge and freely consents to the law that he has transgressed ...

and other such profound observations.

Under the "regime of contract", everyone has given his consent to the law, and "in accordance with the democratic principle, the judge must be elected by those who are justifiable"

(this is the case in America).

In cases of common law the parties should choose arbitrators whose judgment has executive force in all cases. Thus the state is eliminated also from the judicature (pp. 301-02).

4. "*Administration, police*"

Where all stand in contractual relations to all, no police is necessary, "and the citizens and communes"

(hence also the departments and therefore also the nations)

"no longer need the intervention of the state to manage their property, to construct their bridges, etc., and to carry out all acts of inspection, preservation, and policing" (p. 311).

In other words, administration is not abolished but merely *decentralised.*

5. "*Public education, public works, agriculture, commerce, and finance*"

All these Ministries will be abolished. Fathers of families elect the teachers. The teachers elect the higher educational authorities right up to the supreme "Academic Council" (p. 317). Higher, theoretical education will be linked with vocational education; so long as it is divorced from apprenticeship it is aristocratic by nature, and serves to strengthen the ruling class and the power it wields over the oppressed (pp. 318-19).

On the whole, this, too, is very narrowly conceived and bound up with the division of labour, exactly as is apprenticeship in the workers' companies.

Incidentally, "I do not see any harm in the existence of a central research department, and a department of manufactures and arts in-the Republic".

---

[a] Engels uses the English term.— *Ed.*

Merely, the Ministries and the French system of centralisation have to be done away with (p. 319).

There must not be any Ministry of Public Works because it would preclude the initiative of the communes and departments, and of the workers' companies.

Therefore here, too, we have the Anglo-American system with social embellishments (pp. 320-21).

The Ministry of Agriculture and Trade is sheer parasitism and corruption. The proof: its budget (pp. 322-24).

The Ministry of Finance comes to an end of itself when there are no longer any finances that have to be administered (p. 324).

6. *"Foreign affairs, war, the navy"*

Foreign affairs will cease to exist in view of the inevitable universal character of the revolution. The nations will become decentralised, and their various sections will carry on intercourse with their neighbours as if they belonged to the same nation. Diplomacy and war will be at an end. If Russia wants to interfere, Russia will be revolutionised. If England is not willing to give in, then England will be revolutionised and there is an end of the difficulty. The revolutionised nations have the same interests because political economy, like geometry, is the same in all countries. "*There is no Russian, English, Austrian, Tartar or Hindu economics, any more than there is a Hungarian, German or American physics or geometry*" (p. 328).

"Epilogue"

Pure rhetoric. In between is the following point-blank shot which, rather amusingly, overthrows the whole edifice of anarchy.

In the economic regime, "reason aided by experience reveals to man the laws of nature and society, and then it tells him: These laws are those of necessity itself, no man has made them, no one imposes them on you.... Do you promise to respect the honour, the liberty and the well-being of your brothers? Do you promise never to appropriate the products or property of another, whether by violence or fraud, usury or stock-jobbing? Do you promise never to lie or deceive, whether in matters of law or commerce, or in any of your transactions? You are free to accept or refuse. *If you refuse, you belong to the society of savages; expelled from the community of the human race, you become a suspect; you have no protection. At the least insult, anyone can strike you without incurring any other charge than that of ill-treatment needlessly inflicted on a beast.* If, on the other hand, you swear adherence to the pact, you belong to the society of free men. All your brothers pledge themselves with you, promise you loyalty, friendship, assistance, service, exchange. In case of infringement, on their part or yours, by negligence, passion or malice, you are responsible to one another for the harm done, as also for the disgrace and insecurity of which you will have been the cause; this responsibility, taking into account the seriousness of perjury or repetition of the offence, can go as far as to incur excommunication *or death*" (pp. 342-43).

There follows the wording of the oath of the new alliance, sworn

"on one's conscience, before one's brothers, and before humanity".

570 Frederick Engels

Finally, reflections on the present state of affairs.

The peasant has no politics, the worker ditto, but both are revolutionary. Like them, the bourgeois minds his interests, and hardly worries about the form of government. He naively calls that "being conservative and not at all revolutionary". "The merchant, the industrialist, the manufacturer, the landowner ... these people want to live and to live well; they are revolutionary to their heart's core, only they seek the revolution under a false banner." Moreover, they have been frightened by the necessity that at the beginning the revolution had to take up a position corresponding to "the special point of view of the proletariat"; "today the question has been too clearly elucidated for such a split"

(between bourgeoisie and proletariat)

"to continue any longer" (p. 347). With credit and interest at $^1/_4$ per cent, the bourgeoisie will become revolutionary, this does not frighten them.

Final rhetoric addressed to Cavaignac and Ledru-Rollin:

When they say that "the republic stands above universal suffrage", that means: "the revolution stands above the republic".[359]

Written in August and October 1851

First published in Russian in *Marx-Engels Archives*, Vol. X, 1948

Printed according to the manuscript

Translated from the German and the French

Published in English for the first time

APPENDICES

Ernest Jones

A LETTER TO THE ADVOCATES
OF THE CO-OPERATIVE PRINCIPLE,
AND TO THE MEMBERS
OF CO-OPERATIVE SOCIETIES [360]

The co-operative principles!
The errors of the present movement.
The true basis of co-operation.

It is too much the custom to cry down the individual whose vision is not identical with our own—he who will not advocate a principle in the same way in which it is advocated by ourselves, is too often denounced as an enemy instead of being recognised as a friend, who thinks that better means may be adopted for the furtherance of the very principle itself.

The liberty of opinion is the most sacred of all liberties, for it is the basis of all, and claiming a right to the free expression of my views on a subject that I hold of vital importance to the interests of the people, I take this opportunity for offering a few remarks on the character and results of the co-operative movement.

In accordance with the prejudice above alluded to, some may say, indeed some *have* said, that I am opposed to co-operation: on the contrary, I am its sincere though humble advocate, and, from that very reason, feel bound to warn the people against what I conceive to be the suicidal tendency of our associative efforts as conducted now.

At the same time I feel bound to express my full conviction that the present leaders of the co-operative movement are honest, sincere, and well-meaning men, who, in their zeal for the furtherance of a good cause, have overlooked the fatal tendency of some of the details in their plan of action.

I contend that co-operation as now developed, must result in failure to the majority of those concerned, and that it is merely perpetuating the evils which it professes to remove.

I will divide the remarks I have to offer, under three heads:

1st, what are the means the present co-operative movement possesses, of defeating the system of monopoly and wages-slavery;

2nd, what would be its effects upon society if successful; 3rd, what is the only salutary basis for co-operative industry?

Before proceeding, however, to the consideration of these several points let us ask, what are the avowed objects of co-operation?

To put an end to profitmongering—to emancipate the working classes from wages-slavery, by enabling them to become their own masters; to destroy monopoly and to counteract the centralisation of wealth, by its equable and general diffusion. We now proceed to consider—

I. The means applied to effect these results.

For the above purposes the working classes are exhorted to subscribe their pence, under the conviction that, by so doing, they will soon be enabled to beat the monopolist out of the field, and become workers and shopkeepers for themselves.

They are told that the pence of the working-man are, collectively, more powerful than the sovereigns of the rich—that they can outbuy the money lords in their own markets—that they can outbuy the landlords on their own acres. The fallacy of this is proved by the fact, that out of the annual income of the empire, a by far *greater* portion is absorbed by the rich than by the working classes (a fact too well known to need statistics)—a fact most forcibly conveyed to us by the recollection, that during the last fifty years, while the savings of the working classes (a great portion of the same, however, belonging to the middle classes) have been £43,000,000, the rich classes have *increased* their capital by £2,414,827,575. It is, therefore, an error to say, that capital against capital—pence against pounds—the co-operation of the working classes can beat down the combination of the rich, *if their power of so doing is argued on the ground, that they possess more money collectively.*

But, it may be objected, "the facts you adduce prove the extent to which profitmongering has progressed, and still more forcibly point to the necessity for co-operation." — *Agreed.*— "Again," say they, "admitting that our capital is smaller than that of our masters, we do not merely intend to balance capital against capital as it stands, and there to stop, but so to employ whatever capital we possess, as to make it reproduce itself, while the effect of our success is to impoverish the great employer, and thus daily lessen the discrepancy in our relative resources."

It must, however, be recollected, that while the working classes are trying to do this with their little capital, the monied classes will be trying to do the same thing with their enormous riches; that the monied classes, further, have the advantage of being already far ahead in the race—that they wield all the national power—that they are, to a great extent, independent of home trade—that their cannonballs open new markets, of which they will take good care to maintain exclusive possession—that they control the entire monied and commercial system, and can, therefore, expand or contract the currency, raise or depreciate the various interests, glut or restrict the market, and create panic upon panic whenever their interest is enlisted in the measure. It may be said, that they would injure themselves by resorting to some of these means for crippling working class co-operation: granted. But, remember! they can *afford to lose*—you cannot! That which would but pinch their little finger would amputate your entire arm. Thus they would counteract the expansion of your capital by reproductive means. Again—never lose sight of this: they wield all the political power as well! If they should fail in other ways, they can destroy you by new laws—they can throw legal obstacles in the way of co-operation that would prove insurmountable: in this the middle class would support them, every shopkeeper, little or large, every profitmonger, down to the smallest, would be against you—for you *profess* to put an end to profitmonger-ing—you *profess* to supersede the shopocratic class.

It is amusing to remark, that many of those who advise a union with the middle classes are strenuous supporters of the present co-operative system; they seek the support of the middle class, and tell us to expect it—with the same breath shouting to the world, that their "co-operation" will destroy the shopkeepers! That destruction, however, proceeds but very slowly, co-operation on their plan has now been long tried—is widely developed, and they tell us it is locally successful—yet, never in the same period, has the monopolist reaped such profits, or extended his operations with such giant strides. Do we find Moses, or Hyam, waning before the tailors—Grissel, or Peto, shrinking before the builders—Clowes, or Odell, falling before the printers? Everywhere they are more successful than before!—Why! because the same briskness of trade that enables the co-operators to live, enables the monopolists, with their far greater powers, to luxuriate.

Thus much for the inequality of the contest—an inequality that might almost deter from the attempt. But that attempt may triumph, if those forces which we really *do* possess are but directed aright.

This brings me to the consideration of the co-operative plan by which you endeavour to effect the regeneration of society.

The co-operative power you have evoked can be applied to only three objects:

1. To the purchase of land;

2. To the purchase of machinery, for the purpose of manufacture;

3. To the establishment of stores, for the purposes of distribution.

1. *The Land.* Consider, firstly, the enormous amount you must subscribe for the purchase of land in sufficient quantity to relieve the labour market of its competitive surplus. Secondly, remember that the more an article is in demand, the more it rises in price. The more land you want, the dearer it will become, and the more unattainable it will be by your means. Thirdly, recollect that your wages have been falling for years, and that they will continue to fall; consequently, while the land is rising in price on the one hand, your means of purchase are diminishing on the other. Fourthly, two parties are required in every bargain—the purchaser and seller. If the rich class find that the poor are buying up the land, they won't sell it to them—we have had sufficient instances of this already. They have sagacity enough not to let it pass out of their hands, even by these means. Fifthly, never lose sight of this fact: only a restricted portion of the land ever *does* come into the market—the *laws of primogeniture, settlement, and entail* lock up the remainder; a *political* law intervenes, that *political power* alone can abrogate.

It may, however, be urged, in answer to the first objection, that the capital invested in the purchase of land would reproduce itself. I answer, reflect on how our forefathers lost the land—by unequal legislation. It was not taken from them by force of arms, but by force of laws—not by direct legal confiscation, but they were **taxed** *out* of it. The same causes will produce the same effects. If you re-purchase a portion of the land, you would re-commence precisely the same struggle fought by your ancestors of yore—you would wrestle for a time with adversity, growing poorer every year, till holding after holding was sold, and you reverted to your old condition. This can be obviated only by a re-adjustment of taxation—a measure that can be enforced by political power alone.

2. *Machinery and Manufacture.* The second object to which co-operation is directed, consists in the purchase of machinery for purposes of manufacture. It is argued, "we shall shut up the factories, and competing with the employer, deprive him of his workmen, who will flock to us to be partakers of the fruits of their own industry." It is impossible for you to shut up the factories, because the great manufacturer is not dependent on home-trade—he can live on foreign markets; and in all markets, both home and foreign, he can undersell you. His capital and resources, his command of machinery, enables him to do so. Is it not an undeniable fact, that the working-men's associations—the co-

operative tailors, printers, &c., are *dearer than their monopolising rivals?* And must they not remain so, if their labour is to have a fair remuneration? It is impossible to deprive the employer of workmen to such an extent as to ruin him—the labour surplus is too great; and were it even smaller, the constantly developed power of machinery, which he can always command the readiest, would more than balance the deficiency you caused.

If, then, we do not shut up the factories, we only increase the evil by still more overglutting the market. It is a market for that which *is* manufactured, far more than a deficiency of manufacture under which we labour. If we add to manufacture we cheapen prices; if we cheapen prices we cheapen wages (these generally sink disproportionately)—and thus add to the misery and poverty of the toiling population. "But," you may argue, "we shall *make* a market—create home-trade, by rendering the working classes prosperous " You fail a leverage: the prosperity of the working classes is necessary to enable your co-operation to succeed; and, according to your own argument, the success of your co-operation is necessary to make the working classes prosperous! Do you not see you are reasoning in a circle? You are beating the air. You want some third power to ensure success. In fine, you want political power to re-construct the bases of society. Under the present system, *on your present plan,* all your efforts must prove vain—have proved vain—towards the production of a *national* result.

3. *Co-operative Stores.*—By these you undertake to make the working-man his own shopkeeper, and to enable him to keep in his own pocket the profits which the shopkeeper formerly extracted from his custom.

These stores must be directed towards the distribution of manufactures or of food. If the former, you must either manufacture your goods yourselves, or else buy them of the rich manufacturer. If you manufacture them yourselves, the evil consequences, alluded to in the previous paragraph, meet you at the outset. If you buy them, the manufacturer can undersell you, because the first-hand can afford to sell cheaper than the second—and recollect the wholesale dealer is every year absorbing more and more the retailing channels of trade.

We then suppose your stores to be for the retailing of provisions. Under this aspect, their power, as a national remedy, is very limited. Food is wealth—money is but its representative; to increase the real prosperity of a country, you must increase its wealth, whereas these stores do not create additional food, but merely distribute that which is created already.

But the question is here raised: "If the working-man has to pay a less exorbitant price for the articles he wants, he will have so much more of his wages left to purchase land, and otherwise emancipate himself from wages' slavery. Therefore the co-operative stores are the very means for obviating one of the objections urged: they are the very means for counteracting the threatened fall of wages, and consequent diminution of subscriptions."

This observation brings me to the second division of the subject, as in that the answer is contained; and here again I admit that co-operation on a sound basis is salutary, and may be a powerful adjunct towards both social and political emancipation. The solution of this question, however, depends not only on the means at command, but also on the way in which those means are used—and I contend:

II. That the co-operative system, as at present practised, carries within it the germs of dissolution, would inflict a renewed evil on the masses of the people, and is essentially destructive of the real principles of co-operation. Instead of abrogating profitmongering, it re-creates it. Instead of counteracting competition, it re-establishes it. Instead of preventing centralisation, it renews it—merely transferring the rôle from one set of actors to another.

1. *It is to destroy profitmongering:* Here I refer you to the confessions at the recent meeting of Co-operative Delegates; it was the boast contained in every reported speech, that the society to which the speaker belonged had accumulated a large capital—some as high as £2,000 and £3,000 in a very short space of time—some having started with a capital as small as £25, others having borrowed large sums (in one instance as much as £9,000) from rich capitalists, a measure not much calculated to emancipate co-operation from the thraldom of the rich.

But to revert to the accumulated capital; how was this sum accumulated? By buying and selling. By selling at cost price? Oh no! By buying for little, and selling for more—it was accumulated by *profits,* and profits to such an extent, that in one case, 250 members accumulated a capital of £3,000 in a very short space of time! "Down with profitmongering!"

What is this but the very same thing as that practised by the denounced shopocracy? Only that it has not yet reached so frightful a stage. They are stepping in the footprints of the profitmongers, only they are beginning to do now what the others began some centuries ago.

2. *It is to put an end to competition,* but unfortunately it re-creates it. Each store or club stands as an isolated body, with individual

interests. Firstly, they have to compete with the shopkeeper—but, secondly, they are beginning to compete with each other. Two or more stores or co-operative associations are now frequently established in the same town, with no identity of interests. If they fail, there is an end of it, but if they succeed, they will spread till they touch, till rivalry turns to competition—then they will undermine each other—and be either mutually ruined, or the one will rise upon the ashes of its neighbour. I ask every candid reader—is not this already the case in several of our northern towns?

3. *It is to counteract the   ntralisation of wealth,* but it renews it. We proceed one step further—the fratricidal battle has been fought in the one town,—the one association has triumphed over the others, it absorbs the custom of its neighbours—the co-operative power falls out of many hands into few—*wealth centralises.* In the next town the same has been taking place—at last the two victor-associations dispute the prize with each other—they undersell each other—they cheapen labour—the same results attend on the same causes, and the working classes have been rearing up a strong, new juggernaut, to replace the worn out idol under which they bowed before.

Let us reflect, what are the great canal-companies, joint-stock companies, banking companies, railway companies, trading companies—what are they but co-operative associations in the hands of the rich? What have been their effects on the people? To centralise wealth, and to pauperise labour. Where is the essential difference between those and the present co-operative schemes? A few men club their means together. So did *they.* Whether the means are large or little, makes no difference in the working of the plan, otherwise than in the rapidity or slowness of its development. But many of our richest companies began with the smallest means. A few men start in trade, and accumulate profits. So did they. Profits grow on profits, capital accumulates on capital—always flowing into the pockets of those few men. The same with their rich prototypes. What kind of co-operation do you call this? It is the co-operation of Moses and Co., only a little less iniquitous—but, based on the same principle, who guarantees that it will not run to the same lengths? What benefit are the people to derive from this? What is it to us if you beggar the Moseses and the Rothschilds to-morrow, and create another Rothschild and Moses in their place? My idea of reform is not to ruin one man to enrich another—that is merely robbing Peter to pay Paul. As long as there are to be monied and landed monopolists in the world, it matters little to us, whether they bear the name of Lascelles or of Smith. Such is the present system of co-operation,—a system unstable in itself, and, if successful, injurious to the community. A system that makes a few new shopkeepers and capitalists to replace the old, and increases the great curse of the working classes, the aristocracy of labour.

III. Then what is the only salutary basis for co-operative industry? A **national** one. All co-operation should be founded, not on isolated efforts, absorbing, if successful, vast riches to themselves, but on a national union which should distribute the national wealth. To make these associations secure and beneficial, you must make it their interest to *assist* each other, instead of *competing* with each other—you must give them **unity of action, and identity of interest.**

To effect this, every local association should be the branch of a national one, and all profits, beyond a certain amount, should be paid into a national fund, for the purpose of opening fresh branches, and enabling the *poorest* to obtain land, establish stores, and otherwise apply their labour power, not only to their own advantage, but to that of the general body.

This is the vital point: *are the profits to accumulate in the hands of isolated clubs, or are they to be devoted to the elevation of the entire people? Is the wealth to gather around local centres, or is it to be diffused by a distributive agency?*

This alternative embraces the fortune of the future. From the one flows profitmongering, competition, monopoly, and ruin; from the other may emanate the regeneration of society.

Again—the land that is purchased, should be purchased in trust for the entire union—those located thereon being tenants, and not exclusive proprietors, of the farms they cultivate. Freehold land-societies,[361] companies, etc., but perpetuate the present system—they strengthen the power of landlordism. We have now 30,000 landlords—should we be better off if we had 300,000? We should be worse off—there are too many already! The land can be more easily and more rapidly nationalised, if held by merely 30,000 than if possessed by ten times that amount. And, again, the rent would increase the national fund—while the contributions of the freeholders would be but a chimerical treasure.

Such a union, based on such a plan of action, might hope for success. The present co-operative movement, I repeat, must perish as its kindred have done before it—and, if not, its success would be a new curse to the community. Why do the rich smile on it? Because they know it will prove in the long run harmless as regards them—because they know it has always failed, hitherto, to subvert their power. True the attempts often succeed in the beginning—and why? Because the new idea attracts many sympathisers—while it is too weak to draw down the opposition of the money lord. Thence the co-operators are enabled to pick up some of the crumbs that fall from the table of the rich. But what is the £3,000 of Rochdale[362] amid the proud treasures of its factory lords? Let the shock come among the mighty colossi of trade, and the pigmies will be crushed betw en them.

A national union, on the plan suggested, does not run these dangers. A national fund thus established, would, in all probability, be a large one—and place a great power in the hands of the association. Persecution would be far more difficult. Now each society stands isolated, and is attacked in detail by the combined forces of monopoly—then to touch one would be to touch all. The national centralisation of popular power and popular wealth (not its *local* centralisation), is the secret of success. Then restrictive political laws would be far more difficult, for they would encounter a gigantic union, instead of a disorganised body. Then the combination of the rich would be far less formidable—for, though superior in wealth, they would be far inferior in numbers. So they are now—but the numbers at present are without a connecting bond; nay, in but too many cases, essentially antagonistic.

I entreat the reader calmly and dispassionately to weigh the preceding arguments. They are written in a hostile spirit to no one at present concerned in co-operative movements—but from a sincere and earnest conviction that the opinions here expressed are founded upon truth. I have given the difficulties in the way of the co-operative movement—not with a view to discouragement—but that by seeing the dangers, we may learn how to avoid them. As it is we are falling from Scylla into Charybdis.

If, then, you would re-create society, if you would destroy profitmongering, if you would supplant competition by the genial influence of fraternity, and counteract the centralisation of wealth and all its concomitant evils,

NATIONALISE CO-OPERATION.

Written in late April and early May 1851   Reproduced   from   the   journal

Published in *Notes to the People*,
Vol. 1, No. 2, May 10, 1851

Signed: *Ernest Jones*

Ernest Jones

CO-OPERATION.
WHAT IT IS, AND WHAT IT OUGHT TO BE

Contents: — The errors of the present movement. Illustra-
tions: Padiham, Bradford, &c. A better spirit: Bingley,
Bury.— The true plan of co-operation.— A contrast
between the two.

The priest, if you inveigh against his priestcraft, says you are an
enemy of christianity itself. So does the co-operator, if you inveigh
against that kind of so-called co-operation, which, in reality, is
profitmongering, say you are an enemy of co-operation itself. But
the reverse is the case. As the true christian tries to rescue christianity
from priestcraft, so does the **real friend** of co-operation endeavour to
rescue that from the pernicious tendencies into which it is being
launched.

In No. 2 of this publication it has been shown how the present
erroneous system of co-operation leads, in reality, to competition,
and through that to monopoly. I will not recapitulate the arguments
here, to weary by repetition those readers who have already seen that
article — but most earnestly do I invite for it the attention of others.

On the present occasion, I will dwell on the actual working of some
of the co-operative efforts, on what they are, and then, on what, as it
appears to me, they ought to be.

The plan on which co-operative attempts are now conducted, is to
buy cheap in the wholesale market — and to sell *dearer.*

The sale takes place, in some few instances, only to the
shareholders themselves — in most, however, to the general public.

Where the sale takes place to the shareholders, the profit goes
partly to pay the working expenses, and the remainder of the profit
is divided among the shareholders at the end of the year. What is the
real meaning of this? — it means that the shareholders buy in the
wholesale market, that they then are charged so much more for the
retailing than they ought to be, and that, having lost the use of the
money for an entire year, they receive back that out of which they

have been robbed, at the end of twelve months. Can there be greater folly than this? People deliberately charge themselves too much, and pay themselves back at the end of the year, having lost the use of their money during all the intermediate time! The excuse for this is, that they must charge more than the wholesale price, to cover the working expenses, and that they cannot know beforehand what the working charges will be. In the first place, this might be known within a very narrow margin of allowance,—but the fact is this, that they want none, or scarcely any of these working charges. If twenty people club together to form a co-operative store, and then get the articles they want retailed to them at second hand by their own agents, they might just as well send one of their number to the wholesale market, buy at first-hand, and divide the goods in the proportionate shares required, among themselves, *without any* working charges, or any other expenses, except the one journey (if such were required) and the one transit of the goods. For instance, if twenty families agree together to buy their groceries wholesale, in the mass,—each says how much he wants,—he lays by so much per week, and keeps it at home, or pays it into the hands of any one who may be appointed to act as banker for the rest (instead of, as now, subscribing it to a store), and at given periods one or more of this little domestic league goes into the wholesale market, buys the groceries, divided there or afterwards into such portions as each of the members has given an order for,—the individual members receive their several shares as ordered—and there the transaction is complete. This is done every day by rich families of the middle-class. Two or three club together to get their coals or potatoes, &c., wholesale; one of them buys the lot,—they get them at the wholesale price—save all the retailing charges, and then divide the articles among themselves.

This could be done by twenty or thirty, as well as by two or three. Here you have all the advantages of a co-operative store, without any of its expenses and difficulties. You require no payment of rent, taxes and rates; no feeing of officers; no fittings and counters; no advertising and placarding; *no payments to lawyers*; **no registering, enrolling**, or **certifying**; no profitmongering whatever, under the plea of covering working charges;—the whole thing is merely a domestic arrangement of a few families among each other—and there you have all that is required: you keep your money in your own pockets; you do not clash with the law if unenrolled, or become slaves to it *if* enrolled—every member has the usual legal security against the other,—for the purposes of buying wholesale and selling to the shareholders, a co-operative store is utterly unnecessary—it is plundering yourselves—it is doing at second-hand that which you can do with a large saving of money at first-hand! Can anything be more comical, than men saying we'll buy at first-hand, but we won't take our goods home, we'll let them stop half way, we'll charge ourselves too much, we'll pay for an expensive machinery in order that we *may* be overcharged, and then, at the end of the year, we'll pay ourselves back a portion of what is left after payment of the working charges, that is, of the charges that are necessary for the process of enabling us to *cheat ourselves!*

Such is the real working of co-operative stores that profess to sell to the shareholders alone. But of such there are but few—for most profess to sell to the general public. The former are imperatively harmless, for a man may cheat himself, if he is fool enough to do so, without inflicting much injury on others.

But, if a man has a right to cheat himself, he has no right to cheat another. And this is done in the other modes of *so-called* co-operation, as existent at the present day.

The next order of co-operation is that in which the goods are sold not only to the shareholders, but to the public at large. In the former kind, we have seen that it is an absurd waste of time, trouble, and money, for an object that could be much better achieved without any co-operative store at all. But in the case now before us, the whole system of profitmongering, leading to competition and monopoly, is attempted over again, under the soothing name of co-operation itself.

Here the profit is taken direct from the purchaser, and no return made at all. The "co-operator" *buys in the cheapest market*, and he sells as dear as he can, coolly telling us that he is doing this with a view to the destruction of that horrid profitmongering of the shopocracy. The poor customer pays him the "profit"—and that he divides at the end of the year between himself and his brother co-operators. Then they boast, that they have made £2,000 net in one year! What did these £2,000 consist of? Of the difference between the wholesale price (the price at which they bought) and the retail price (the price at which they sold) *over and above the working charges.* Every farthing of this £2,000 is profitmongering of the most odious description, because it is done under the name of co-operation; every farthing of this £2,000 is as much direct plunder taken from the public.

Now, since during the last few months an exposure has been made of *this new system of profitmongering*, all the so-called "co-operators" have disclaimed violently against the charge, and have tried to slip unscathed through the imputation, by tacking some supposed "saving-clause" to their rules. For instance, the London tailors gravely tell us that they see the full force and justice of the resolution passed by the National Convention, for nationalising the tendency of co-operation, and therefore they intend to set five per cent of their net profits aside for a national fund. *Five per cent!* Then they are to pocket *ninety-five per cent* of clear profit! Every fraction of that 95 per cent is a deliberate robbery upon their customers! For, **no man has a right to take more from society than the value of what he gives to it.** All beyond that is robbery. The London tailors, therefore, have a right to a fair remuneration for their labour, and no more. A fair remuneration for labour is, supposing that the labourer gives his full strength to society, *as much as will enable that labourer to live in comfort.*

Therefore, every farthing of those net profits after the working charges are paid (a portion of the working charges being a fair remuneration for the work performed), is an imposition and a cheat upon society.

Some societies, however, try to evade the charge of profitmongering by a more roundabout, but equally transparent, trick. I will illustrate this by the *Bradford Co-operative Store.* This store professes to divide only **half** the *profits* among its members. Let us analyse the scheme.

Rule 1 says: The object of the Association is "to furnish its **members** with provision and clothing at **prime cost.**"

Rule 6 says: "All goods shall be sold at *reasonable* market prices, for ready money only, and the whole **surplus profits**, after deducting working expenses, and **five per cent interest on shares**, shall be *divided half-yearly among the members* according to the amount of purchases made by each; but no member to receive interest on part shares."

Now, in the first place, if the goods are to be sold at "prime cost," there could be no "surplus profits." But the "members" only get them at "prime cost," the "surplus profits" are to come from the public.

Pretty well this! In the first place, the *members* get their goods at *prime cost.* They are not even to bear their proportion of the working charges—the poor, good-natured "public" are to pay for this.

In the second place, the members are to receive "five per cent interest on their shares." Pretty well again!

Rule 3 provides that members may have *as many shares* as they like (though only one vote). A snug investment that! Five per cent! Elsewhere they could get only $3^1/_2$. Here they are to get five! Firstly, *they* get what they want at *prime cost*; secondly, they get five per cent on their investment. The poor, good-natured public are expected to pay for this too!

In the third place, "the *surplus profit* shall be divided half-yearly among the members, according to the amount of purchases made by each." Pretty well once more! So these lucky members are to get their goods at prime cost, to get five per cent. for their money, and besides all this, to get "*surplus profits*," and divide them every half-year among themselves. And the poor, good-natured public are expected to pay for all this as well!

Pretty well in the profitmongering line. This is worse *than the shopkeepers.* You catch us with a threefold gripe—and tell us all the while you are our benefactors.

In Rochdale and Padiham, "Co-operation" has assumed a form more injurious still to the best interests of humanity and progression. At the latter place, a "co-operative" factory has been built, by shares of £25 each payable in 5s. calls. This is a workingman's factory with a vengeance!—and here, as in almost all the co-operative attempts in England, all the profits are to be divided among the share-holders—the amount of profit to be extorted from the public, being left to the consciences of the profitmongers themselves.

Workingmen! Democrats! Can you for a moment tolerate or sanction such a system?

The least objectionable stores I know of, are those at Bingley and Bury.

So much of the true metal rings at these places, that they have not been as deeply tainted with the rust of profitmongering, as Padiham, Rochdale, Bradford, London, and most other places.

At Bingley they have raised, in two pound shares, a grocer's and draper's shop. In this, Rule 1 says—"One-half of the *clear profits* to be divided annually among its members, the other half to be given to the society, and never to be divided, but *to go to extend its operations* to other branches of business."

There is some recognition of principle in this, but, in reality, there is only a distinction without a difference. Though the members receive only half the profits direct, yet, as the other half goes to extend the business of the association, it, in reality, goes to extend their profits, or by enlarging the concern, it enlarges the "half" which they are to divide among themselves.

At Bury, if I understood them rightly, they adopt the rule, that any one of the general public, who chooses to deal at their store, and subscribe one penny weekly towards it, shall be entitled to a share of the profits proportionate to the amount of his purchase. This is a great advance on every attempt at "co-operation" that has hitherto been made.

Let us now glance at what co-operation ought to be. I believe the principle of co-operation is but very imperfectly understood in this country. People imagine if a few individuals co-operate together to start a trading concern and make as much money as they can, that this means co-operation in the real sense of emancipated and associated labour.

Nothing of the sort! If that were so, every railway, banking, or shipping company would realise the true principles of co-operation.

By co-operation, a very inadequate word, by the way, we mean the abolition of profitmongering and wages-slavery, by the development of independent and associated labour. But this can be established only on the basis of the following principle already laid down in this article:

No man has a right to take more from society, than the value of that which he confers upon it.

Consequently, associated labour has no right to take more from its customers, than will pay for the prime cost of production, and enable the man to live adequately, who devotes all his time to the production or the distribution of wealth.

To meet this position, associated labour has two alternatives: to charge merely thus much additional between the prime cost and the retail price, as will cover the expenses of retailing; or to charge more, but devote every fraction of that overcharge to a national purpose, such as the purchase of land, machinery, &c., whereon to set the present wages-slave at employment in self-remunerating labour.

Considering the present circumstances by which society is surrounded, I prefer the latter, as being the best calculated to further labour's emancipation.

Let us see how this would work. A co-operative association is formed; after payment of its working charges (including labour in production or distribution), it finds itself at the end of the year with a surplus in hand; instead of dividing this surplus among the members, it employs it to purchase land or machinery, which it lets out to other bodies of workingmen, on the associative principle. The rent paid for the land or the machinery, and the surplus of each concern beyond the working charges, is *again to be applied to the further purchase of machinery and land,* on the same terms, and under the same conditions; and so on, continually extending the power, strength, and resources of association. This is co-operation. It is co-operation, because it establishes a **community of interest**—the success of each "branch" furthers the success of every other, and of the whole collectively. There can be no conflicting interests—no rivalry—no *competition*—for the greater the success of each undertaking, the more the stability and permanency of the whole is ensured. It makes it the interest of each and of all to see co-operative associations spread and multiply. This, I repeat emphatically, **this is real co-operation.**

But what is the present isolated system? It is based on individual and antagonistic interests. It makes the vital interest of the "co-operator" to *prevent* others from co-operating—to hinder the spread of the associative principle. And it does it in this way: a co-operative trading concern is started on the present *isolated* plan; that is, the concern forming a "close borough,"—admitting no more within its pale—making what profits it can, and pocketing them among the same few individuals. What now becomes the interest of these individuals? To prevent another co-operative concern from being started in their immediate neighbourhood—to prevent another body of workingmen from deriving the advantages of co-operation. Because, if the original concern flourishes, it absorbs all the trade of the locality (if one don't, two or more do, it becomes merely a question of numbers—of how many customers there are in a place); if another independent concern is started, it must have a portion of that custom, or it cannot exist. Consequently it becomes a rival of the other association; it begins to compete; there not being customers enough for *all*, the one concern too many must try to draw away customers from those already established. To do this, it must undersell—it must buy still cheaper, and pay still cheaper for its labour, in order that it *may* undersell; the other concerns must do the same in self-defence; and there you have the old system of competition, with its *necessary consequences*, wages-slavery, plunder, ruin on the one hand, and monopoly on the other, added to that profitmongering on which the present plan, as already shown, is altogether based!

Therefore, the present plan is not true co-operation; it is essentially hostile to the spread of associated labour; instead of ending profitmongering, it renews it; instead of abolishing competition, it recreates it; instead of abrogating monopoly, it re-establishes it, and is the death-blow to the hopes of labour's emancipation.

Now, my friends, let me implore of you to weigh these remarks, and those previously given in this work, without prejudice or anger. I write with a sincere conviction of the truth, and of the paramount duty of combating a pernicious fallacy. I am not the *enemy* of co-operation, but its *friend*—its true friend—I do not oppose co-operation, but wish to rescue it from that course, in which it is digging its own grave. I trust those who have supported "co-operation" on its present plan, will not be offended by these

observations. They are made in all friendliness of spirit and sincerity
of heart. I believe the advocates of the present system to be generally
true, honest, and well-meaning—but may I escape the charge of
presumption if I also state my belief that they are quite blind as to the
nature and the consequences of what they are advocating with such
zeal? Believe me! you are digging the grave of co-operation, while
you think you are fashioning its cradle. Compare your plan with that
which I have here proposed—and judge dispassionately.

I know self-interest would dictate that I should write in favour of
the present movement, and not against it. I know this very article
may injure the circulation of these "Notes". But sooner write not at
all, *than be such a slave as not to dare write truth.* Then, sink or swim, the
truth **shall** be written. I launch this little article on the troubled tides
of controversy, and commend it to the good sense and honest feeling
of my readers.

Published in *Notes to the People,*   Reproduced   from   the   journal
Vol. 1, No. 21, September 20, 1851

Signed: *Ernest Jones*

[LIST OF DOCUMENTS DESPATCHED TO COLOGNE DURING THE COMMUNIST TRIAL][a] [363]

1) Brothers Braubach—Schneider (original) October 27, business friend.

2) J. A. Boecker—Schneider (copy) October 27, Michael Shawcross & Co.

3) I. D. Herstadt—Hontheim—to Marx—Fisher Brothers.

4) J. H. Stein—Esser I—to Marx—business friend.

5) Leonhard Sadée—Schneider II—to Marx—Smith (Wilson) Dryer & Co.

6) Düsseldorfer Haus—Schneider II—from London, October 25 (Marx on Cherval, theoretical explanation).[364]

7) Ebner—for von Hontheim—London, October 26 (triplicate of Marx's first letter to Schneider)—letters of Becker[b] and Daniels to Marx, new samples of Hirsch's handwriting—Cherval's statement in *The People's Paper*—original letter from Stieber to Marx.[365]

8) G. Jung—Schneider II. London, October 27? 1. Legally attested handwriting and affidavit. 2. Quadruple of the first letter to Schneider, together with samples of Hirsch's handwriting.[366] 3. Extract from Becker's letter to Marx on Willich. 4. Three letters from Bermbach to Marx. 5. Copy of Stieber's letter. 6. Instruction to Schneider together with information of the despatch of No. 9 and No. 10.

9) Schneider II, registered—Duplicate of the affidavit, October 28.

10) W. in Düsseldorf—Schneider II—Registration certificate on No. 9, October 28.

---

[a] This list was drawn up by Engels.— *Ed.*

[b] Hermann Heinrich Becker.— *Ed.*

Nos. 3, 4 or 5: one used for Schneider II. Explanation about Reuter, Stieber, Dietz,[367] October 29.

11) d. No. from B. & Co. von Hontheim—Extract from Marx's first letter to Schneider—Notification of the non-receipt of Schneider's letter.

12) G. Blank & Son.

13) Hasselmann Schults & Co.

Written about October 31, 1852

Printed according to the manuscript

Published in English for the first time

Georg Eccarius

A REVIEW OF THE LITERATURE
ON THE *COUP D'ÉTAT*[368]

[Preliminaries]

[*The People's Paper*, No. 21, September 25, 1852]

There is a subject with regard to this country which we have hitherto not been able to dwell upon but which we deem worthy of our most eager attention: namely, the utterly shortsighted and ignorant views on the change in the public destinies of France since the 2nd December, taken by nearly all the authors who have written on the character and consequences of the *coup d'état*. A short review of the publications that have appeared from different quarters on this subject will render the truth of this statement the more evident and the more important, as all these publications pretend more or less, to be the expressions and sentiments of the parties or classes to which their authors respectively belong.

On the 2nd December, in the face of the Bonapartist *coup*, it was but natural that all parties opposed to it should agree in their language—and so it was. The protest of the combined royalists and the proclamation of the Montagne, as dictated by the common interests of self-defence against a common foe, differed only in this, that the latter fraction had at least the courage to take up those arms to which the former merely made a cowardly appeal. Both had the name of the *constitution* in their mouth, of a constitution which had been as often attacked, violated, suspended and overthrown by the royalists, as it had been ridiculously and hopelessly defended by the republicans.

But, what have they done since? The legitimists have accepted, the Orleanists denounced, the republicans execrated, the *coup d'état*. Has any one explained, has any one understood its secret? With the legitimists the fault lies in the socialists; with the Orleanists in the Montagne; with the republicans in the *crime* of Bonaparte. To such casualties as the mistaken policy of a couple of representatives, or the frivolous ambition of an individual, the mighty changes in the condition of a people are ascribed by the political sages of the day, who still, by exempting themselves from all responsibility in past events, attempt to impose themselves on the public as the initiators of a future, when they, as well as their parties, are crushed for ever, and flung into nought long ago. What a poor argument for historical explanation! But what a rich source of pamphlets, of recriminations, and of all kinds of attacks on antagonistic personalities! We are certainly no partisans of Mr. Bonaparte; we do not mean to thank him as he did not mean to benefit us by it, for having replaced the tyranny of middle-class parliamentary rule by dictatorship of his own and of a military swell-mob; but we are glad at his success, we rejoice in his temporary triumph because it secures the triumph of *our* principles, the triumph of *our* class. His is the momentary glory, the revelry of an hour; but ours will be the final, the definitive victory. *The dictatorship of Bonaparte has prepared the sovereignty of the working-classes.* What are all these lamentations about the decay of French civilisation? What all these splendid comparisons with the fall of the Roman Empire in the mouth of the middle-class writers, but the elegiac confessions that the times of *their* glory are gone in France, never to return? What is it they understand by civilisation, but the government of landlords and capitalists with their append-age of priests and lawyers? Is it the ruin of the working-classes they deplore? Good Heavens! Let them be cheerful, their ruin depends not on the calamities of the middle class. It is just the political ruin of the latter, that prepares the advent of the working-classes, that guarantees their salvation, both political and social. How deeply those writers deplore, and almost weep over, the *decline and hopeless degeneration of France,* of that unhappy and blind nation which could sacrifice its public liberties (?) to the arbitrary pleasure of a tyrant! What are these liberties alleged to have been sacrificed? The Suffrage? You forget the law of the 31st of May.[a] The Press?—why you had gagged, fined, confiscated, and suppressed it. Associa-tion?—there never were such things as decrees of suspension, high tribunals, dungeons, or transportations for the leaders of the clubs! No—Blanqui never was in the pontoons of Belle Isle. You never provoked—you never laid an ambush for the people! You never slaughtered them at Rouen, nor massacred them at Lyons, nor shot them in the streets of Paris! To hear you, the people, before the 2nd of December, were as free and sovereign, as they were happy and

---

[a] This law adopted by the Legislative Assembly abolished universal suffrage.—*Ed.*

prosperous. You wonderful talkers and writers! Yes, decidedly; then it was madness and quite shameful on the part of the people to forsake such disinterested and loyal leaders, on the day when they proclaimed the liberties of the nation to be in danger. But, if it were otherwise—if the people really had nothing to lose—if it was only *your* liberties, *your* rule over the people, that were in danger—what do you say then? Never mind; for morality's sake the people ought to have resisted a man [a] who so openly broke his faith to them. To *them*? Why, he never swore *them* obedience or faithfulness! How preposterous to suppose a "vile and immoral multitude" to stand up for morality! Who accustomed the people to broken oaths? Not Thiers—not Berryer—not Molé—innocent, pure, and honest consciences! It was Bonaparte who invented the trade never known before. The world was so young, so harmless, and so perfect, that it knew almost no crimes before this ominous day of December, which put an end to the paradise of political innocence. The apple of perjury had never been eaten; but the spectacle of a drunken and infuriated army stabbing the peaceful (why were they peaceful, if their liberties were in danger?); violating the virgin, and demolishing the property of the citizen (this last was their worst crime):—should not that have animated the people to rise up in their defence? Why? They had no property; the rich leave them very few virgins; and if the killed had been peaceful, they remained so without being killed. The people allowed Bonaparte to revenge them on their enemies, awaiting the opportunity when they might take their revenge on both. They were right. But to suffer the dictator to enforce a constitution on them which is all but a mockery of the people's dearest principle, the Suffrage!—how disgraceful to a nation to be deluded and duped by the very appearances of unbounded liberty, which is still, in fact, an outrageous slavery! In the first place, they are neither duped nor deluded, because they know this as well as any liberal English newspaper. Then, how can they suffer it? They only take their time. The Orleanists and Republicans no doubt will find it rather long, wishing to return to their country. Now, the people do not have such a desire; they are, besides, in no hurry. Trade is doing well, as yet. And did not you always say, "the people ought to be quiet, and to mind nothing but their work?" Well, they will mind their work, as long as they have any, after which they will look out for themselves. For themselves? Yes, is not that frightful? To behold a people unwilling to hazard their lives for the restoration of a prince,

---

[a] Louis Bonaparte.— *Ed.*

or the revival of a middle-class parliament—a people who will only take up arms for murderers! Adieu! civilisation of France—the "Times" despairs of thee! No hopes in France but for the people. There is the terrible deluge, prophesied to the French people so often by every successive party in power. There it is coming, and no escape. O! sage Lord Maidstone! when will our English deluge begin?

In our next we shall commence giving a *résumé* of the works that have appeared on both sides of the Channel, on the subject of the French *coup d'état*, comprehending the "18th Brumaire of Louis Bonaparte," by Charles Marx; "The *coup d'état* of Louis Bonaparte," by Xavier Durrieu; "Napoleon the Little," by Victor Hugo; and "The Social Revolution," by Proudhon.

No. 1

[*The People's Paper*, No. 22, October 2, 1852]

The empire not having yet been proclaimed, and the new police farce of the infernal machine[369] offering little or no comment, I intend in this letter to criticise a series of works on the events of the 2nd December, enumerated in my last letter, which have as yet been not sufficiently circulated amongst the English public, and most superficially appreciated by the English press. The order in which I shall proceed differs from that in which I first placed the different works under notice; but it will be perceived how much better it suits the purposes of a gradually-progressing and yet all-exhausting criticism, to begin with that work which merely elucidates the data and facts of history, and next to take that which elevates itself to a contemplation of those same facts from the general point of view of current traditional ideas[a]; then to dispose of that work which, although advancing a step in the revolutionary direction, still affects to consider the whole change in the destinies of France, brought about by Bonaparte, as a proof of the truth or necessity of its author's doctrinary Socialist schemes[b]; and, finally, to conclude by reviewing that work which, as we may here at once point out, is the only one that has at once satisfied history, and the want of the present generation to understand the revolutionary movement in which it finds itself engaged.[c]

---

[a] An allusion to Victor Hugo's book.—*Ed.*
[b] The reference is to Proudhon's work.—*Ed.*
[c] This refers to Marx's *Eighteenth Brumaire of Louis Bonaparte.*—*Ed.*

I.—"THE *COUP D'ÉTAT* OF LOUIS BONAPARTE."
BY XAVIER DURRIEU, REPRESENTATIVE OF THE PEOPLE.[a]

The merits of this book consist in the great probability, or rather in the simple truth, of its narrative. As all the witnesses of the 2nd December, who have stood up to denounce the crimes and treachery of Louis Bonaparte, have been charged with gross exaggeration of the facts, by the "Moniteur" and other government organs, the author of this book has rendered a great service by his depositions, which certainly nobody will accuse of tending, by rhetorical or poetic licence, to impose on the public. And if Mr. Durrieu's talent as a writer may be doubted in England, where your penny-a-liners write such admirable articles, although he was a Paris journalist, his right of describing the horrible actions of which he was the spectator and victim at the same time, remains incontestable, and one can only applaud him for having had the courage to come before the public. Here you have a short account of the events he relates, and of the part he played in them.

He commences by a sketch of Louis Bonaparte, and of his principal accomplices in the perpetration of the *coup d'état*. We pass by that of the master, it being too inferior to the portrait which others, and Victor Hugo especially, have given us of that monster scoundrel; we will cast a glance only at those of his ministers.

General Magnan, the commander of the Boulevard-butchery, was accused in 1840 of having favoured Bonaparte's attempts at Strasburg, and Boulogne.[370] Called to appear at the bar of the Peers, he denied and betrayed his then unfortunate master, with so much coolness and contemptible egoism, that even the Peers—those veterans in the traffic of apostasy—felt disgusted. In 1848 he was charged by some Democratic paper with being in the pay of the Orleanists; he went himself to the office, and begged insertion of a protest, in which he denounced the Orleanists, and swore that, as a soldier of the old Republic, under the Convention, his sympathies had ever been attached to the Republican institutions. Three years afterwards he murdered that Republic for the payment of his debts.

General St. Arnaud, the Minister of War, was a simple captain in 1835, when, for certain services rendered at the Castle of Blaye, the prison of the unfortunate Duchess of Angoulême, he was suddenly promoted to the rank of a general. His debaucheries and dissipations would have brought him in contact with the criminal law, had not his

[a] Xavier Durrieu, *Le coup d'état de Louis Bonaparte*, Genève et New York, [1852].—*Ed.*

former crimes protected him. Louis Philippe sheltered him first—Louis Napoleon has sheltered him now.

M. Persigny, the Minister of the Interior of to-day, but who lacked the courage to become it on the 2nd December, raised himself from the station of a penny-a-liner to that of Louis Bonaparte's valet and confidant—the purveyor of his master's pleasures, in which he is even supposed to take a very close part, and the agent in his low intrigues and forgeries; the fellowship of crime is the secret of his present splendour.

M. de Morny, lastly, may be considered as the type of the higher swell-mob, that gang of gamblers, swindlers, and forgers, who always escape by some enormous crimes from the claws of the lower police. He was to be imprisoned on the 3rd; he imprisoned his creditors and accusers on the 2nd December. The portraits of these four men are as true as they are familiar to every Parisian.

I am sorry that I cannot delight you with their counterfeit—the work of Mr. Granier de Cassagnac,[a] a miserable but impudent Gascoign, who erected, almost on the smoking ruins of the December Insurrection, the statues of its murderers, elevating them to the rank of demi-gods, and idolising Bonaparte as the Saviour of society. By the way, it will amuse you to hear, that the *gendarmerie* and clergy of his department have received this new apostle under a triumphal arch, bearing the inscription—"To the defender of order and religion!" After this, may we not hope soon to see the downfall of the two pillars of class society?

Now to Mr. Durrieu. On the morning of the 2nd December, he hastened to the office of the "Révolution," a paper founded by Ledru-Rollin, and invested with that name, after its competitor, the real revolution, had been ruined by him in the struggle of June.[b] As is usual at Paris in times of excitement, the so-called revolutionary notabilities, which means a handful of petty ambitions, held a meeting at the newspaper-office. Durrieu was charged to draw up a proclamation. "Constitution—treason" were its two handles, the paltry weapons which alone were left to the Democrats, after their separation from the Revolution. The proclamation was placarded; so was that issuing from the office of the "Presse." Mr. Durrieu complains that they were so little responded to. But by whom were they signed, and to whom did they appeal? Was there any one of the people's leaders—of those the people acknowledged and cherished

---

[a] The reference is to a pamphlet by Granier de Cassagnac, *Récit populaire des événements de décembre 1851*, Paris, 1852.—*Ed.*

[b] The uprising of the Paris proletariat in June 1848.—*Ed.*

as their champions—amongst the names of the undersigned? They
were all known to be Montagnards, "liberal" writers, orators, drums
and trumpets of the tribune indeed, but whose greatness sprung
from the ruin of the proletarian party, whose eloquence had for
condition the silence of the people's defenders; in a word, who had
always preached submission and calm, when a combat had to be
fought, and who called to arms, when revolution had no interest in
the battle, but Mr. Durrieu himself has the naiveté to reveal the
reasons why his partisans had no influence on the masses, why their
alarm-cries were distrusted, like those of the shepherd-boy in
the fable.[371] They had raised their cry too often, when no wolf was to
be met; in fact, it was a thing used up. He tells us that, when the
surprised Republican Representatives were removed in prison vans
to Vincennes, on passing the Boulevards the people attempted to
break the file of their *escorte,* and actually offered to release the
prisoners. What did these heroes of the tribune reply? "For heaven's
sake, desist! Let us proceed to our prison, we know we are *innocent!*"
Such frightened, cowardly *innocents*—do they not deserve to be
laughed at by the people? These tame and timid souls—these
inviolable, but also non-violating personages—these knights of the
sorrowful figure, were offered to the people as their guides—nay,
their commanders. No, if the people had had the choice (but they
had not, nor did they want it then), they would have been right to
prefer Bonaparte, although a knave, a thief, an assassin, and
whatever else you may call him (for he deserves every one of these
titles), even when he struck them in the face, to that band of officious
mourners, who have buried Revolution to get the right of lamenting
over it. Their sermons have demoralised and torpified the people,
while Bonaparte's effrontery has awakened their senses. I say this in
respect of the Montagne, and the Democratic leaders as a body, I
don't mean to include in my invectives against that party every
individual belonging to it (French Democracy is not to be con-
founded with the English. In France, it represents the small
proprietors and tenants, but less their real wants than their
imaginary wishes. In England, Democracy applies directly to the
movement of the working class); such brave and generous men as the
heroic Charles Baudin, and the author of the present work himself,
regain as much estimation by their conduct as they may have lost by
their narrow principles and views. But these are exceptions, and no
hero or martyr ever deserves to have the people on his side, unless he
battles for the direct interest of the masses, instead of for the dead
letter of a class constitution, or the imaginary glory of some *abstract
truth.* But this latter point I will settle in my next, as Mr. Hugo still

affords me still better occasion for it. As for Mr. Durrieu, let me add that, after having issued his proclamation, he took his post on the barricades, where he fought until night, and whence, after all was lost, he escaped only to be taken prisoner, to be conducted to the prison of Mazas, thence to the casemates of Bicêtre and Ivry, the horrors of which he describes with much tact; transported thence on board the "Duguesclin," to be sent to Cayenne, and finally expelled by the Dictator from his country.

No. 2

[*The People's Paper*, No. 23, October 9, 1852]

Your readers will doubtlessly absolve me for another week from recording and commenting on those well-known despicable quack-performances composing the official history of the day—all the feasts, revelries, processions, demonstrations, conspiracies, triumphs, and final choruses, which make up the "*mise en scène*" of the Empire in France, and through which they hope to derive the power of producing an impression upon a public to whom the piece itself offers no other novelty, than that "the machinery is by electric telegraph." In fact, these are dull times, and men certainly want some leisure yet, before they will be able to come forth with "a new piece." And as good actors require to be critics first, so let the people become critics of their own revolutionary past, and let those who aspire to be their leaders, prove their vocation in guiding them through their studies, and the revolutionary drama of the future will be a hit, and no failure. I proceed with my review.

II. NAPOLEON THE LITTLE, BY VICTOR HUGO[a]

It would be difficult exactly to describe my feelings at the moment when I sit down to criticise a work of such generally acknowledged reputation, yet of so little solid or lasting merits as this last production of the most splendid of all French writers. What I cherish in it, what I could not omit expressing, without becoming guilty of ingratitude, is the pleasure it gave me on the first reading. And that pleasure will be shared by all people who do the same, particularly those who had it in the original language. Victor Hugo stands indeed unsurpassed in the ranks of French literature of the nineteenth century. He is a true genius. To compare, as some of his countrymen, or rather, his political enemies do, to compare Victor

---

[a] Victor Hugo, *Napoléon le petit*, Londres, 1852.— *Ed.*

Hugo with Lamartine as a poet, with Alexander Dumas as a dramatist, with Eugène Sue as a romance-writer, or with Odilon Barrot as an orator, would be comparing a Byron with a Wordsworth, a Shakespeare with a Bulwer, a Walter Scott with a James, or a Sheridan with an Osborne. Lamartine, that vainest of all authors, and that most hypocritical of all men, relates in his "Voyage in the Orient," [a] that in his youth he considered it the height of all human greatness for one man to unite in himself the poet's laurel, the orator's palm, and the politician's sceptre. He let us into the secret of his own ambition.

But how signally has that ambition failed! History will scarcely recognise him as an historian; but no doubt the Athenians would have given him the headmastership of a school of rhetoric. Ah! On your rival posterity will confer the honours that you have craved in vain. Yes! Victor Hugo's is the laurel! I cannot omit extracting the following poetic passage from his last work:—

"WILL MEN AWAKEN?"

"We are in Russia, the Neva is frozen over; houses are built on the ice, and heavy chariots roll over it. 'Tis no longer water, but rock. The people flock up and down this marble, which was once a river. A town is run up, streets are made, shops opened, people buy, sell, eat, drink, sleep, light fires on what once was water. You can do whatever you please there. Fear nothing. Laugh, dance; 'tis more solid than *terra firma.* Why, it sounds beneath the foot like granite. Hurrah for the winter! Hurrah for the ice! This will last till doomsday! And look up at the sky; is it day? is it night? what is it? A dull, wan light drags over the snow; why, the sun is dying!

"No, thou art not dying, O liberty! And these days, at the moment when thou art least expected, in the hour when they shall have most utterly forgotten thee, thou wilt rise dazzling! thy radiant face will suddenly be seen issuing from the earth, resplendent in the horizon! Over all that snow, over all that ice, over that hard, white plain, over that water become rock, over all that villainous winter, thou wilt cast thine arrow of gold, thine ardent and effulgent ray! Light, heat, life! and then, listen! hear you that murmuring sound! hear you that cracking noise wide-spread and so formidable! 'Tis the breaking up of the ice! 'tis the melting of the Neva! 'tis the river resuming its course! 'tis the water, living, joyous, and terrible, upraising the hideous, dead ice, and smashing it. 'T was granite, said you; see, it splinters like glass! 'tis the breaking up of the ice, I tell you: 'tis the truth returning, 'tis progress recommencing, 'tis humanity resuming its march, and uprooting, breaking to pieces, carrying off, and burying fathoms deep, and for ever, not merely the brand-new empire of Louis Bonaparte, but all the constructions and all the walls of the antique despotism. Look on these things as they are passing away; they will never return, you will never behold them again. That book, half submerged, is the old code of iniquity; that sinking stool is the throne; that other stool, standing upon it, is the scaffold!

"And for this immense engulfment, this supreme victory of life over death, what was needed? One of thy glories, O sun! one of thy rays, O liberty!" [b]

---

[a] A. Lamartine, *Voyage en Orient.—Ed.*

[b] Victor Hugo, *Napoléon le petit,* Book 1, Ch. IV.— *Ed.*

Yes, Victor Hugo's is the palm of eloquence! His is, also, what is more—the immortelle of the insurgent. He also fought on the barricades of December. But the sceptre of the politician: would that he never thought of aspiring to it; for that we must absolutely deny him, and withhold from his hands. His partisans might entrust him with the leadership of Democracy. Does he not behold the hopeless prostration of that party? His vanity might be flattered by the supposition of a talent which is not given to him. Does he not perceive how it endangers the glory of those talents which really are in his possession? Alas! is it then true that all human greatness—all the heroes and martyrs—all the stars and lumina—find a stone in their road, over which they will stumble! Revel, ye millions! you are rising in the scale; and that makes your great men go down.[a] Let them all break their necks over this stumbling stone of politics, let them be thrown into the sea, if they cannot devise the riddle of the modern Sphinx—the revolutionary solution of the war of classes. But I am forgetting Napoleon the Little. The title is well-chosen, if meant to humiliate Louis Bonaparte. Why, then, is it not carried through in the work itself? There was a Napoleon the Great; but Victor Hugo does not show us a little one. What if this is the work of one man: the dissolution of an assembly—the confiscation of the laws—the suppression of the public liberties—the imprisonment of the representatives—the slaughter of the Republicans—the transportation of thousands—the profanation of religion—the prostitution of justice—the proclamation of a new constitution—the sequestration of the national, and almost the private property—the submission of the proudest nation to his arbitrary pleasure—the restoration of a dynasty, of an Empire: if all this is the work of the one man, as you assert, Mr. Hugo, how can you call him "Little" in your work? But you do not. On the contrary, except in the title, you everywhere swell his personal dimensions to the most enormous bulk of a liar, a swindler, a perjurer, an assassin, it is true; but when you thus place him by the side of Nero, Attila, Jenghiz Khan, or King Bomba,[b] you cannot affirm, in the same breath, that he is the "Little." With all your brilliant parallels you do not obtain that object. Had you shown that for instance the Assembly was already

---

[a] Probably a paraphrase of the motto of the *Révolutions de Paris*, a revolutionary-democratic weekly which was published in Paris from July 1789 to February 1794. The motto was: "*Les grands ne nous paraissent grands que parce que nous sommes à genoux: levons-nous!*" ("The great only seem great to us because we are on our knees: Let us rise up!").— *Ed.*

[b] Ferdinand II, King of Naples.— *Ed.*

dead and decayed, when buried by Bonaparte; that the laws had ever been suspended and confiscated; that a systematic suppression of the public liberties had actually left little for the dictator to add; that your representatives were accustomed to imprisonment and transportation, by the same parties who had ever slaughtered your republicans; that religion had profaned itself on every occasion as an instrument of governmental oppression; that justice had proclaimed its prostitution in your High-Courts of May and your Courts-Martial of June,[372] in short, that your whole middle-class rule and bourgeois society was already rotten from top to bottom, smelling of bribery and corruption as much as the soldiery who kicked it from its pedestal, were smelling of brandy and sausages—then you might have justly called him "little" whose name only, not his person, was necessary at the head of a *coup d'état* effected by the last desperate exertions of the army, the priesthood, the functionaries and the mob, to save themselves from their inevitable destruction by the approaching revolution of the working-class, to which they felt themselves exposed by the weakness and incapacity of a parliamentary bourgeoisie. Then what remained for Bonaparte? To make himself the instrument of the situation. To command a situation is greatness. To obey one is littleness. There you would have reduced him to his proper dimensions. You would not have made such a noise of his oath—was he not as dependent, as "little," in breaking it, as he was in taking it? Then the title of your book would have indeed been to the purpose. Nevertheless, one admires your parallels.

"Peter the Cruel massacred, but he did not steal; Henry III assassinated, but he did not swindle; Timour Beg crushed children under horses' hoofs, much as M. Bonaparte exterminated women and old men on the Boulevard, but he did not tell lies."

No. 3

[*The People's Paper*, No. 24, October 16, 1852]

Having shown that the principal error of V. Hugo consists in ascribing the whole turn of events, before and after the 2nd of Dec., to the policy and conduct of an individual, L. Bonaparte, it becomes incumbent on me, further to develop the causes which necessarily led our author to such a fallacy. Reasoning from general principles—the general principles of society, laid down by the ruling classes and embodied in their very creeds, Victor Hugo judges from an erroneous point of view; he sees in the man the motive power, instead of seeking for it in class interests, class antagonism, and class revolution, while the man is the mere temporary exponent of the change—as the weathercock betokens the direction of the wind. Victor Hugo belongs to a class who thus look on the effect as the cause—on the instrument as the hand that uses it. In that class, certainly there are those who denounce the inequalities and horrors of the present system with a violence and a declamatory force often superior to the expressions of the very revolutionary class itself. To hear them one would believe that they are more socialist than the whole of the working class. And what are they in fact? They are reactionary. I shall not call them knaves; perhaps they are unconscious of the real tendency of their doctrines and actions, although in our present age illusions are hardly possible to men, who live in contact with the actual world. But most certainly are they the dupes of the class notions, instilled into their minds as the general principles of social life. Incapable of conceiving that such gregarious phrases as "Liberty of the individual," "Industry,""Prosperity," and "Humanity," proclaimed at the outset of our modern age, are just the promises under which all the results of middle-class society were necessarily brought about, they fancy those results to be all the faults of the moral degeneration of the governments, to whose care the development of the social principles had been trusted. And such is particularly the case with Victor Hugo. In his eyes the principles of present social government are right, and the men to be blamed. That is the opinion of all moralising middle-class reformers. Whatever there is wrong and perverted, pernicious and deleterious, it is the fault of the individuals—and the classes who support those individuals? Oh, they never think of classes. Far from them the misanthropical conception of a society composed of classes and ruled by class-interests. "Mend your morals, nations, and your governments will be perfect." Such is their motto. They always treat the people as a whole, address it as a whole, suppose them of the same creed, with one common conscience, with one universal opinion. Take that for granted, and those men would seem the greatest (would-be) benefactors of humanity, the initiators of a new era, the restorers of the paradise lost. Drive them from this ground, show the people that there is neither a community of morals, nor of conscience, nor of opinion ever possible between different classes with opposed interests, that the institutions of a class produce not only with necessity those facts over which our philanthropists lament, but also the men, whom they accuse of all the mischievous arrangements in the body politic—and from the dignity of demi-gods you reduce them to the nullity of sham-prophets. Deprive V. Hugo of these garments, which style, eloquence and poetry have spread over his work, all that remains is a moral sermon, full of vituperations of the Lord, and of reproach to the middle class, preached to poor peasants who are not a bit wiser for it, neither how it came that they fell into the hands of the former, nor how they will ever be able to escape the grasp of the latter.

No. 4

[*The People's Paper*, No. 25, October 23, 1852]

[III.] THE SOCIAL REVOLUTION.
AS PROVED BY THE *COUP D'ÉTAT*. BY J. P. PROUDHON.[a]

In suppressing the greater part of my last letter, you have, no doubt, followed such considerations of policy as, under existing circumstances, I can scarcely object to. I have now arrived, in the series of my critical remarks, at the last production of an author who has acquired a considerable reputation on the continent for the "boldness" of his opinions, and is sometimes considered by English middle-class writers as the very incarnation of the revolutionary Socialism in France, but whose only real merit consists, as I shall prove, in the severe, but true judgment which he has passed on all the hollow conceptions of plain Republicanism and of formal Democracy. The sarcasm with which he has attacked and exposed both the political leaders and literary notabilities of the said parties have merited for him the surname of the "Mephisto" of the French Democracy. As it is possible that the meaning of this epithet may not be generally understood by your readers, I think it expedient to give a short explanation of it. There exists an old German legend, long familiarised to the English by Marlowe,[b] but universally divulged in the matchless tragedy of Goethe,[c] in which the vague ideal aspirations of man towards an imaginary state of perfection, are ingeniously parodied by the materialist and practical suggestions of the spirit of the world (Mephisto), with whom the hero, Faust, has concluded an indissoluble treaty of union. Faust, a philosopher, or "black artist," as the medieval legend says, full of wild dreams, conceived in seclusion and ignorance of human society, calls upon the spirit who has the control of the material world, to assist him in

---

[a] P. J. Proudhon, *La révolution sociale démontrée par le coup d'état du 2 décembre*, Paris, 1852.— *Ed.*

[b] Ch. Marlowe, *The Tragical History of Doctor Faustus.—Ed.*

[c] Goethe, *Faust.—Ed.*

the realisation of his visionary schemes of perfection. Mephisto then acquaints him with the realities of life. But the more Faust becomes conversant with our common world, the more he believes to approach the accomplishment of his ardent desire of perfection by an accumulation of sensual pleasures, the more also does he lose recollection of his first proud conceptions, and the more he descends from the height of moral elevation; until, after a variety of adventures and experiences, in all of which he is attended by Mephisto, the witness and merciless scorner of his weaknesses and vacillations, our "noble, aspiring, and generous" Faust, turns out to be of the same low, degenerate, and egotistical nature of which he had thought himself to be the most competent reformer, and the most opposite example. Substitute for the "noble" Faust a "noble" Democracy, and you may not improperly call Proudhon its Mephisto, in so far as he has, indeed, not only recorded and urged all the manifold deceptions and weaknesses of the French Democracy, but treated with the severest scorn its hyperbolical pretensions and its ridiculous ambition. And that part he has performed ever since the Democrats in the Provisional Government had manifested their incapacity, and the Republicans in the National Assembly enacted their reactionary formalism in the Constitution of 1848. While arguing against the former, that raised upon the shoulders of Revolution, which, if it means anything at all, has for its invariable object "the displacement of the previously commanding interests of the substitution of a government for the benefit of the oppressed classes," they left all the enemies of progress in the undisturbed possession of the strongholds of society, such as the army, the administration, the church, the courts, and the police, and thus allowed them the means of organising their counter-revolutionary crusade. Proudhon crushes the Republican party by sarcastically demonstrating how their great formula of liberty—their "pure and sublime" Democracy obtained its practical realisation only by the slaughter of almost a whole class, and through the establishment of a military dictatorship, placed in the hands of General Cavaignac. But the best of his arguments he has spared for the refutation of the dogma of Universal Suffrage, and on this ground he has given the most deadly blow to the French sham Democracy. I recollect very well the attempts once made to persuade the people of England likewise, that Universal Suffrage alone was in itself the cure of all the social iniquities under which they are suffering, and that, at a certain time, it was held almost a sacrilege or a blasphemy to talk of Social Rights, or the Labour Question. Happily they have learnt that, far from being the definitive end of political development, it is only the first decisive step in the revolutionary direction, the piece of ground necessary for the organisation of their army, the open field in which the hitherto disguised war of classes can at last be fairly fought out, the means in a word, and not the end, of the people's emancipation. But how much are we indebted for this knowledge to the experiments which, for want of our own experience, the French nation has made on behalf of the whole world, and of which that nation itself could hardly be expected to reap the fruits, if it had not, on the denunciation of Blanqui and other revolutionary leaders, ceased at last to believe in the fatal delusion into which Democracy has led them by representing Universal Suffrage as the magic rod, that has only to be once applied, when the treasures of a new social paradise would be thrown open to the world.

It cannot be said that Proudhon was the first who discovered and exposed the insufficiency of the suffrage to effect the social enfranchisement of the people. As early as April, 1848, Blanqui, then at the head of the Paris proletarians, had the conviction that the result of the first general elections[a] would be the formation of a reactionary assembly, and he urged the Provisional Government to defer the time appointed for those elections, in order to gain the means of better influencing them by the organisation of revolutionary committees, the only condition as he then pointed out, under which the suffrage would be made a weapon in the hands of the people. Thus he indicated already, in opposition to the official Democracy, that he considered Universal Suffrage as a mere instrument of class-warfare which might be turned to advantage if used in the proper way, but which he declared might as well be employed for the purposes of any particular party in power. His views were confirmed by subsequent events, and as he was decided to carry the victory of Revolution in spite of all imposed sham legal decrees, he endeavoured to break up the very National Assembly, which was the first manifestation of Universal Suffrage. The 15th of May was a failure and Blanqui went to prison,[373] while Proudhon profited in safety by this lesson and restricted himself to protesting in the Press against the suffrage, as a political fiction. His peaceful remonstrance, however, did not save him from a similar fate, and he also went into prison for three years, whence he has now come forth, resuming with laudable vigour his former attacks. As it happens, that on this subject Proudhon, although still from a mere theoretical point of view, concurs in the arguments of the revolutionary party, I

---

[a] The elections to the French Constituent Assembly, held on April 23, 1848.—*Ed.*

give you the whole passage on the Suffrage, contained in his last work; observing that if the argumentation itself necessarily leads to extreme conclusions, his language will be found to lack that spirit and decision which would betray in every work, however disguised and moderate the author might have been obliged to be in his phraseology, from considerations of policy, the man of a determined principle—the man of Revolution.

Proudhon excuses himself, that writing as it were under the jealous eyes of a dictator, he could not allow himself to indulge in using such strong expressions as would expose him at once as the most terrible champion of Revolution. I think, however, that he has, nevertheless, said everything in this work as determinedly as he could have intended to do under any circumstances, seeing that those passages in which he endeavours, by an occasional flattering supposition, to captivate the indulgence of Louis Napoleon's censorship, have altogether nothing to do with, and interrupt in no wise, the strain of his observations. At any rate M. Proudhon could never make me believe him to be a decided champion of Revolution, when I remember him to have always been the loudest where nobody was in the field besides himself, and no immediate measure to be proposed to the people; and to have almost disappeared or entirely plunged himself into doctrinary expositions where a real revolutionary act was to be committed.

While Blanqui was leading the Proletarians onwards, to the direct destruction of the class obstacles that stood in the way of the people's enfranchisement, Proudhon went about preaching the wonderful blessings of petty co-operation; and when the terrible defeat of June had removed, with the best and bravest part of their army, the whole claims of the working class, Proudhon started up in the middle-class Assembly, and proposed the abolition of property. But of the nature of this proposition, and of the particular Socialist doctrine which makes up the chief contents of Proudhon's literary publications, I shall treat in my next letter. Here is the above-mentioned passages on Universal Suffrage[a]:

"It is just the republicans who, on the authority of the most suspicious traditions, have always repeated that the voice of the People is the voice of God. Then it is the voice of God that has elected Louis Napoleon! By the expression of the popular will he is your true and legitimate Sovereign. And to whom would you expect that the people should have given their votes? You have entertained them with 1789, with '92 and '93: the people have retained nothing but the legend of the Empire. In the memory of the people the Empire has wiped out the Republic. Do they remember

---

[a] The quotations that follow are taken from pp. 80-81 of Proudhon's book.—*Ed.*

Count Mirabeau, Robespierre, their 'Ami du Peuple,' Marat, or the Père Duchesne' (the journal of the Jacobins)? The people know only the good God and the Emperor, as they once knew but the good God and Charlemagne. It is in vain that you have preached the Rights of Man, or that you made a monarch swear to respect the Republic as above Universal Suffrage. The people only recognise the rights of force.

"And you are defeated in virtue of your own principles. You have been defeated because, relying on Rousseau and the most detestable orators of 1793, you would not acknowledge that monarchy is just the direct and inevitable product of popular spontaneity; because, after having abolished the government *by the Grace of God*, you have pretended to establish,by means of another fiction, a government *by the Grace of the People*; because, instead of making yourselves the educators of the multitude you have made yourselves its slaves. You, the same as the masses, required visible manifestations, palpable symbols, puppets in a word. Having chased a king from the throne you placed the mob in his stead, without conceiving that that was just the root from which, sooner or later, would spring up a new crown, the onion which would generate the 'lily.' [The lily is the emblem of Legitimate Monarchy in France.] Scarcely delivered of one idol you must already create a new one, resembling therein those soldiers of Titus who, after the taking of the Temple of Jerusalem, could not withhold their surprise at discovering in the Jewish sanctuary neither statues, nor oxen, nor asses, nor phalluses, nor wenches. They could not conceive an invisible Jehovah. Thus you could not conceive Liberty without chamberlains.

"May these severe remarks be pardoned to an author who has performed so often the part of Cassandra. [A high priestess of the Trojans who predicted the fall of their city.] I do not accuse Democracy as little as I mean to inveigh against the vote which has renewed the mandate of Louis Napoleon. But it is time that this sect of sham-revolutionary men should at once disappear who, speculating more on the agitation than on the instruction of the people, on handstrokes more than on ideas, have made themselves the courtiers of the multitude, and become the most dangerous blockers-up of the revolution.

"Who has named the Constituent Assembly, swarming with Legitimatist dynasties, nobles, generals, and prelates? Universal Suffrage. Who has made the 10th of December, 1848?[a] Universal Suffrage. Who has elected the Legislative Assembly? Universal Suffrage. And who has absolved Bonaparte of his *coup d'état*? Universal Suffrage.

"May it not be said also, that it was Universal Suffrage which commenced the reaction of the 16th of April,[374] which eclipsed itself behind the back of Barbès on the 15th of May, which remained deaf to the appeal of the 13th of June,[375] which allowed the passing of the law of the 31st of May,[b] which crossed arms on the 2nd of December.[c]

"In thus accusing the suffrage, I repeat that I do not intend to attack the established Constitution and the principle of the present government. I have myself defended the suffrage as a constitutional right, and the law of the state; and as it once exists, I do not demand its suppression; but let it be instructed and organised. To the philosopher, however, it must be permitted to argue, for the explanation of history and the information of the future, that Universal Suffrage given to a people of so neglected an education as ours, far from being the instrument of progress, is only the stumbling-block of liberty.

---

[a] On this day Louis Bonaparte was elected President of the Republic.—*Ed.*
[b] The law abolishing universal suffrage.—*Ed.*
[c] The reference is to Louis Bonaparte coup d'état.—*Ed.*

"Poor, inconsequent democrats! You made philippic speeches against tyranny, preached the respect of every nationality, the free exercise of the people's sovereignty; you were ready to take up arms to defend against everybody all those sublime and incontestable doctrines.—And with what right, if Universal Suffrage was your rule, did you suppose that the Russian nation felt the least uncomfortable under their Czar; that the Polish, Hungarian, Lombard, and Tuscan peasants were sobbing for their emancipation; that the Lazzaroni hated their King Bomba, and the Trasteverians[376] abhorred Monsignor Antonelli; that the Spaniards and Portuguese blushed for their Queens, Donna Maria and Isabella, when our own people, in spite of the appeal of their representatives, in spite of the written law of the Constitution, in spite of the bloodshed and the merciless proscription, from fear, ignorance, constraint or affection (you may choose), give 7,600,000 votes to the man the most detested by Democracy, whom it believed to have ruined, demolished and used up by a three-years exposure to ridicule, insults, and hatred, when the people make this man a dictator, and Emperor?"[a]

[No. 5]

[*The People's Paper*, No. 27, November 6, 1852]

While that Assembly of Bonapartist lackeys, called the Senate of France, is deliberating on the ceremonies by which the long expected Empire shall be ushered in at last, and the official world at Paris is all given up to conjectures about the manner of the coronation, the prince's marriage, the probable succession, &c., I shall take advantage of the leisure thus left to my pen, and, turning my back to those "important events" which furnish the gossiping middle-class papers with inexhaustible stuff for small talk, I continue to-day my review on Proudhon's last work. We have seen Proudhon criticising the actions and political systems of the different Republican parties in France; let us now become, in our turn, the critics of his own system. A few words only may be said before, on the career of an author who is yet so little known in England.

Proudhon is a native of Besançon, a town which is perspicuous for the number of eminent men it has sent forth, among whom the names of Victor Hugo and Béranger stand in the first rank. The son of a poor vine-grower, his means for obtaining a good education were but scanty; but thanks to the energy of his character, he had no

---

[a] At the end of this article the editors of *The People's Paper* added the following note in square brackets: "It is obvious that our correspondent does not attack Universal Suffrage, but the idea, that Universal Suffrage taken nakedly by itself, must necessarily emancipate a people. Here is another proof how necessary the *details* are to guard the suffrage—here is another proof how necessary is a knowledge of our *social rights*, to make the suffrage conducive to happiness and freedom. We trust our correspondent's strictures on a one-sided class-application of Universal Suffrage will not be misunderstood."—*Ed.*

sooner grown up, and secured a situation for himself as printer, than he began to make up the gaps in his knowledge by strenuously applying himself to the study of languages, of history, and of political economy. Proudhon is altogether an autodidact (self-taught),and as such he shares largely in that quality of tenaciously sticking to his first conceptions, so common to the whole of this class of people. It is curious to observe how regularly he relapses into those errors which his critics have so often exposed, and of which it would seem as if he had sometimes become conscious himself.

Napoleon, the uncle of course, has invented a term for such people which marvellously applies to M. Proudhon. He called them "ideologues"—an expression by which he meant to embrace all those speculative minds, philosophers and politicians, who standing aloof from the real movement of history, incapable or unwilling to take any active part therein, or to fill out any practical mission, still wanted to prescribe to the historical process the laws according to which it had to enact itself. Those philosophers, it must be said, deserved by no means the contempt in which they were held by Napoleon, who esteemed but two qualities in man: military genius and administrative talents. They are often superior observers of facts and admirable critics of past events; their weakness consists only in this: that they understand not to draw just conclusions such as correspond to the premises so well defined by them. In their proposed solutions they invariably substitute the arbitrary decrees of speculation to the force of circumstances, to the decisions of the combating elements, to the material power, from which in reality not only the motive force but also the direction can alone be derived. Materialists in their judgment of the past they fall back in the fathomless depths of idealism, of Utopianism, the moment they endeavour to indicate, or rather to fix the constitution of the future. And what is the cause of this error? Merely this: that our "ideologues," correct in their view of the past, by comparing the facts themselves with their representation in thought, neglect to secure for their conjectures on the future that same measure of comparison, which can exclusively guarantee the justice of human conceptions. And this comes because they either take their stand on the ground of a party or class which by its very conditions can have no future, or, what is more generally the case, because they pretend to keep themselves apart from all the actual parties, and to anticipate by speculation the solution of a problem which can only result from the co-operation or rather the conflict of those very parties. They conceive history as a mathematical problem, a sum of equations. Thus they conceive the possibility of calculating it on paper. The elements known are put in their respective order, a line is drawn, and the result is found without difficulty. But is it thus in reality? Are there any conflicts recorded by history which have proven their decision through the decree of a philosopher, the idea of an individual? Are they all decided by their mere force of an idea? They are decided by men, their solution is given by the triumph of a political class. That is what our "ideologues," including M. Proudhon, overlook.

Let us examine the "solution" offered by Proudhon. There is undoubtedly a conflict of antagonistic interest—a war of classes —existing in all European societies, consequently also in France. That conflict will lead to some final result; the war must end in the triumph of one or the other parties. Translate this into the language of Proudhon: "There is a problem,—hanging over modern society, a problem which must find its definitive solution. That solution is the social revolution of the 19th century." Ah, a revolutionary solution you will say. Then Proudhon is our man? Stop! stop! You think Proudhon would leave the solution of his "problem" to the action of a party, do you? He keeps that for himself; his is to remain the merit of having discovered the philosopher's stone. That solution is contained in the idea of the social revolution. And what is that idea? "The elements of the problem are given by our history." Let us resume them. What is the actual situation of France? In the first place the state is composed of:—[a]

"First, an organised clergy, numbering about 50,000 priests, and as many individuals of both sexes living in the various religious establishments; having at their disposition a capital of three hundred millions of francs, exclusive of the churches, the ecclesiastical estates, forming the private property of the priests, the produce of indulgences, the proceeds of collections, &c., an organ of public morality, presumed to be indispensable, and the more powerful, as its influence is secretly and privately exercised within the precincts of domestic life.

"Second, an army of 400,000 men, disciplined, stripped of all family ties, trained in the contempt of the National Guard, entirely at the command of the Executive, and alone considered to be able to defend so as to keep down the nation.

"Third, a centralised administration, ministers of the police, of public instruction, of the state-works, the taxes, the customs, the domains, numbering upwards of 500,000 functionaries in the salary of the state; holding in its dependence, directly or indirectly, every industry, arts, extending its power over all persons and things, governing and administrating everything, and leaving no other care to the taxpayers, but to produce and pay their rates.

"Fourth, a magistracy, hierarchically organised, and influencing by its inevitable arbitration every social relation, every private interest, Court of Cassation, Court of Appeal, Civil and Commercial Tribunals, Justice of the Peace, etc., all in

---

[a] There follow quotations from pp. 19-22 of Proudhon's book.—*Ed.*

perfect understanding with the Church, the Administration, the Police and the Army."

As to the nation, it is divided into

"First, the bourgeoisie—that class which comprehends all people living on the revenues of their capital, on their rents, official privileges, places and sinecures, more than on the fruits of their industry. The modern *bourgeoisie,*thus classified, forms a sort of aristocracy of capital and money, analogous to the ancient aristocracy of birth, by their riches as well as by the extent of their patronage; disposing of the bank, the railways, the mines, the insurances, the great industry, the wholesale commerce, and having for the basis of their operations a public and a hypotheticary debt of 1,000 millions of pounds.

"Second, *the small middle class,* composed of speculators, masters, shopkeepers, cultivators and professional men, etc., living much more on their personal produce than on their capital, privileges, or property, but distinguishing themselves from the proletarians by this, that they work for their own account and on their own risks, and enjoy for themselves the profits of their industry.

"Third, *the working class, or proletarians,* living on their wages, and having no economical or industrial initiative, thus fully deserving the name of a mercenary or salaried mass.

"The country has a population of thirty-six millions of inhabitants. Its annual produce is valued at 9,000 millions of francs, one-fourth of which goes off for the maintenance of the State, the Church and other unproductive or parasitic functions; another fourth falls under the title of interest, rent, agio, commission, etc., to the share of the bourgeoisie; which leaves for the working class, including the small middle class, an average revenue or salary of forty-one centimes ($3^1/_2$ d.) per head and per diem, but which in some extreme cases falls short of fifteen centimes ($1^1/_4$ d.) per day."

Here is a picture of the actual situation of France—which, for its exactitude and striking features, can scarcely be surpassed. Here Proudhon has collected all the elements that make up the groundwork, the foundation of the real social revolution. Now, what is the conclusion he draws from these premises?[a]

[No. 6]

[*The People's Paper,* No. 28, November 13, 1852]

"If the nation is thus divided into three natural categories (mark the expression!) one of which has for its formula: wealth and unproductive consumption; the other: industry, commerce and enterprise, free, but without guarantee; the third: absolute submission and progressive misery; the problem of the revolution is simply to dissolve the first and the third classes in the second, the extremes in the middle, and thereby to effect, that all, without exception, shall enjoy an equal proportion of capital, labour,

---

[a] Here the editors of *The People's Paper* added the following note in square brackets: "The valuable analysis which follows here we are compelled to leave out this week."—*Ed.*

exchange, liberty and well-being. In this consists the operation of the century, the objects, still so little understood, of Socialism."[a]

Here the "ideologue" becomes at once visible. The elements of the historical process are changed into the elements of an arithmetical sum; the classes become abstract "categories"—and the result, the conclusion is no longer dependent on the action of the principal and original elements, but on their arbitrary arrangement by the pencil of the calculator. The arithmetical means is substituted for the historical solution of the "problem" of reality. A stroke of his pencil is the touch of the new magic rod, by which Mr. Proudhon discovers at once the secret of the social revolution. The small middle class is henceforth the cardinal point of society! Decidedly every man must be made a shopkeeper! for this end. What has to be done? Why the political power must be entrusted to the shopkeepers; credit, the distribution of labour, the entire organisation of the community must be put into their hands—and they will give every man the means of placing himself in their class, the bourgeois as well as the proletarian. A nice solution that—on paper! If it could but be made accepted by the world? Let us see.

Will the bourgeois, the great mill owner, the banker, the 10,000 acres proprietor, the railway millionaire, the cotton growing slaveholder, the rich speculator, will these people accept Proudhon's theory, and modestly forswear their palace-like counting houses for the desk of a small shopkeeper? Will the proletarians, on the other hand, who have learned to appreciate the miraculous force of associated labour, in their great factories and workshops, will they renounce those immense means of production, and of their definitive emancipation, when once theirs, for the idyllic pictures of a ten acres freehold, or a £10 household? Suppose they would, Mr. Proudhon, is that the social solution of the nineteenth century? Why, man, you are behind your time; you are an anachronism. What you preach as a new theory, is an old worn-out fact—it is the solution attempted by the eighteenth century, executed in your own country. Did not 1789 give every peasant his ten acres of land?—were not your shopkeepers and burghers of the towns in possession of their £10 household?—was not liberty the great formula of 1793, the well-being of all the eternal phrases of your "Rights of man" constitutions? Whence, then, came the bourgeois and the proletarian? whence arose these extremes, but just from that middle, your small middle class, invested with the sovereign disposition of

---

[a] P. J. Proudhon, *La révolution sociale démontrée par le coup d'état du 2 décembre*, Paris, 1852.— *Ed.*

the national interests? And you propose to begin the same thing again! Because you have not learned your lesson, you would make the whole nation repeat their task. Strange philosopher, still stranger initiator of the social revolution of the nineteenth century. Like causes, like effects. Liberty of the individual to dispose over his capital and his labour—and concentration of wealth in the hands of the stranger and the more cunning or clever,— "Credit shall be given equally to all," very good. But can that be done at once? What is credit? The permission to use a portion of the accumulated labour, say the capital, of another man, or the state, if you like, for productive purposes, against the payment of interest, discount, &c.

Now, is the capital accumulated, even supposing it to be in the possession of individuals, of a class, is that capital sufficiently large to put every man on a shopkeeper's or small cultivator's footing, by dividing it into equal portions? That is the question,[a] sir, if you have any notions of credit, is it not? Then how will you proceed? You will give credit to as many as possible. Very well, they will get an advance on those that are provisionally left to look to their wages—labour for an existence. There is the proletarian. Ah, but afterwards, with the reflux of the first lent-out capital, you will afford the proletarians the same credit, and draw them from their slavery. Well, supposing that the population had not increased faster than the accumulation of capital, under your provisions, is it you that decides upon the question of extending the public credit, or is it the class into whose hands you have once, in the beginning, placed the capital? And do you think that class, once materially and economically constituted as such, would not keep the capital of the nation for itself, the more so as they are also entrusted by you with the political power? Acknowledge then, that the proletarians will get no credit; their social enfranchisement does not take place. There is one point. Now, it is obvious, that amongst the capital-holding class, cleverness, invention, ability, force, fraud, and competition, will in time mark out some palpable destructions; the one fraction will get the greater part of the capital into their hands, or the whole of the credit under their control. There is the bourgeoisie. There then you would have, after a similar lapse of time, perhaps at the beginning of the twentieth century, arrived again at the starting point of another "Social Revolution," and another Proudhon might again come forth and propose, for the third time, the same solution. The people, Mr. Proudhon, thank you for this prospect; they will even listen with pleasure to your stricture of other systems, but believe me they will never accept your own.

---

[a] Shakespeare, *Hamlet*, Act III, Scene 1.—*Ed.*

[No. 7]

[*The People's Paper,* No. 32, December 11, 1852]

4.—MR. LOUIS BONAPARTE'S EIGHTEENTH OF BRUMAIRE, BY CHARLES MARX.[a]

It is a very remarkable phenomenon that all the French authors, who have favoured the contemporary world with their accounts of the late *coup d'état,* and to whom not only the consequences but also the origin of that event might be supposed to be best known, have failed in the attempt to explain its real causes; while a German writer, who was himself but a distant observer of the progress of events in France, has given not merely the first, but the only competent version of the history of the Bonapartist Usurpation. This is a truly surprising fact. It might perhaps be thought, that the very circumstance of the author's absence from France had enabled him to take up a more impartial point of view, from which to judge of the character of the situation and the conduct of parties; but we are soon convinced, that such is not the case. No one has shown less of that objective impartiality, which is so wrongly supposed by many people to be the most important requisite in a historian. Such impartiality is simply a fiction, never to be met with in reality; and happily not—for to whom, except to the author himself, could it give satisfaction? Thus it is not his independence from party principles and party views, that has given the power to Mr. Marx of satisfactorily accounting for the causes and effects of the events he records, but rather the correctness of the method and the justice of the principles, which he has followed in his work. The secret of his success, to speak in plain terms, is his adhesion to a party, that was not immediately involved in the struggle, and yet, by its conditions, its growing and indestructible power, and by its future, must finally become the supreme arbiter of all the incidental quarrels and alternative defeats and triumphs of which the official history of the latter days in France is composed. The revolutionary party of the working class disappeared from the political stage with the insurrection of June, 1848. From that time they became the mere witnesses of the historical drama in which all other parties remained engaged: Legitimists, Orleanists, Bonapartists, Republicans, and Democratic Socialists. Consequently, they were the only independent judges of all the errors, faults, "crimes", &c., committed by each of the said fractions.

Let me now briefly state the argument, why it has not been possible to the representatives of any other party, than that of the

---

[a] See this volume, pp. 99-197.—*Ed.*

revolutionary proletariat, to pronounce a sound and true judgment on the character of the last historical epoch in France. Who are the Legitimists? The representatives of the great landed property, the aristocracy of the soil. And who are the Orleanists? The representatives of commerce, the aristocracy of money. Was it for either of them to confess: Our rule has been upset by the moneyed interest in 1830—and ours by the labour interests in 1848; having succeeded by the combination of our mutual power to grasp again on the political domination, the necessity of our class position, the contingencies of the social struggle compelled us so to strengthen and centralise the resources of the executive, placing it in the hands of a single individual, that it was but the natural and inevitable result of our exertions, if this individual has afterwards deprived us of our prerogative and made himself an absolute dictator and Emperor? Both Legitimists and Orleanists comprehended that, this being the only manner in which their defeat could have been accounted for, it would be better for them to hold their tongues. This they have done. Not so the Republicans, the Democrats, as well as the Democratic Socialists. But what expedient remained to them? History, the history of the human race, its development under the different social constitutions, is no less a physical process, a series of changes, dissolutions, formations, reformations, revolutions, as the history of our globe with its constantly changing and ever returning phenomena of revolution, change of matter, seasons, &c., &c. As there is not one of the manifestations of this permanent physical change which, even if it cannot be traced by our understanding to its immediate source, does not depend on some particular cause so also is there no event, no circumstance in the affairs of the body of a nation, without its necessary preceding impulse. Nowhere do we behold any miracles, nor casualties; nay, as the elements of the social phenomena are all known to us, open to investigation, subject to experience, they are just the very thing of which a full and circumstantial account can, in every instance, be given, unless prejudice or interest blind man's observation. This was the case with the Republicans, who tried everything in order to avoid arriving at conclusions which would have no longer permitted them to advocate interests without the conditions of vitality, and to profess principles of demonstrated importance. Rather than do so, they have preferred to misrepresent reality, to understate their actual defeat, to exaggerate the individual merits of their enemy, in short, to falsify history by the substitution of accidents, casualties and enormities to the simple laws of effects and causes, the law of necessity.

From the point of view of the revolutionary proletarians, no such deception was possible; no historical fraud could have been intended; and this being the stand, Mr. Marx has not only occupied in the present work, but which he has filled so eminently in all his critical labours: he, the representative of the revolutionary theory of the working-class movements, the literary pilot of the most advanced fraction of European Democracy, he has also shown himself the best historian of the Presidency, Dictature, and Empire of Louis Bonaparte.

[No. 8] [377]

[The People's Paper, No. 33, December 18, 1852]

The first chapter of this book, which may be considered as its programme, begins with contrasting the character of the revolution of 1789 with that of 1848. The former was the work of the middle class, the latter announced itself as the revolution of the working class; the former was victorious through the energies and conscience of their objects possessed by its originators; the latter turned out a failure, through the indecision and ignorance of its leaders as well as of the masses. A social revolution was to be made. Nobody knew how. What else could be possible but that people looked back for guidance to the pages of past history? So they tried alternately a National Assembly, declared a Republic, established a Dictature, received the Convention, created another Napoleon. They had only drawn up so many caricatures of a dead epoch, the spirit of which was gone. But have these experiments been useless, or what lesson, yet indispensable towards the completion of their education, have the working classes learned by them?

The social revolution of the nineteenth century cannot draw its poetry from the past, but only from the future. It cannot begin by itself, until stripped of all superstitious veneration of the past. Former revolutions needed the recollections of history, in order to deceive themselves as to their object. The revolution of the nineteenth century must let the dead bury their dead,[a] in order to arrive at a clear perception of its own ends and purposes. There the phrase overstepped the object, here the object far oversteps the phrase.

The Revolution of February, 1848, was a surprise of the governmental stronghold of existing society, and the people proclaimed this unhoped-for *coup-de-main* as a first-rate historical event by which a new epoch was to be opened. On the 2nd of

---

[a] Matthew 8 : 22.— *Ed.*

December the revolution of February is lost by the *volte* of a political cheat at cards; and society, instead of having conquered the basis for a new stage of historical development, *seems* only to have restored the state in its most obsolete form, the simple and impudent rule of sword and priest-gown.

Time, however, has not passed away without fruit. French society, during the years 1848-51, has made up—following an abridging because revolutionary method, for those studies and experiences which, in the ordinary and regular course of things, ought to have preceded the revolution of February, if that revolution was to have been something more than a mere superficial shock. Society seems now to have stepped back beyond its point of departure: but, in reality, it had first to create the revolutionary point of issue, the situation, the circumstances, and the conditions in which alone modern Revolution becomes serious.

Middle-class revolutions, like those of the eighteenth century, rapidly storm from conquest to conquest; their dramatic efforts surpass each other; men and things appear as if surrounded by a halo of radiating fire; ecstasy is the spirit of every day. But they are short-living—they soon reach their zenith: and a long apathy seizes upon society before it soberly learns to appropriate the results of the heroic intoxication of its youthful epoch. Proletarian revolutions, like that of the nineteenth century, on the contrary, continually interrupt their own course, sceptically criticise their own performances, return periodically to what they appear to have already completed, in order to do it over again; they rail at the inconsistencies, frailties, contemptibilities of their own first experiments with the merciless superiority of gained experience; they seem to prostrate their antagonist only that he may draw, Antaeus-like, new strength from the earth, and rise again the more gigantically before them; every moment they recoil before the indefinite, monstrous grandeur of their own objects, till that situation has arrived where retreat is no longer possible; and circumstances themselves impose their

> "Hic Rhodus! hic salta!
> Here is Rhodus! come and dance!"[a][378]

I regret that want of space, and the necessity of putting a term to my reflections on the general literature on the *coup d'état*, prevent us from dwelling at greater length on the review of Mr. Marx's particular work, which contains, besides its historical pages, such a picture on the actual condition of the different classes in France,

---

[a] Marx translates this line as "Here is the rose, here dance!" — *Ed.*

chiefly of the peasantry, as I have not met with in any other place.

I have already said, that the Insurrection of June was the turning point of the tide of Revolution in 1848. Consequently that event must contain in its germs the original and last explanation of all subsequent history, including the *coup d'état* and the proclamation of another Empire. Let us see if our author has successfully argued this idea. I again extract his own words, touching the changed aspect of a class-struggle, after the defeat of the working class.

"After this defeat, the proletarians attempt, indeed, to step forward, every time that the movement appears to take a fresh start; but their efforts become gradually weaker, and the results more insignificant. As soon as one of the higher strata of society passes into revolutionary fermentation, they combine with it, and thus share all the defeats suffered in succession by the respective parties. But these subsequent blows become less severe the more they extend over the whole surface of society. The more prominent leaders of the working class in the assembly and in the press fall, each in its turn, the victims of the courts of law, and more and more equivocal individuals appear at their head. A portion of them throw themselves into doctrinary experiments, such as labour exchange, banks and co-operative associations,[a] and thus engage in a new movement where they renounce the attempt to overthrow the whole world by appropriating and putting in movement its own great resources, labouring instead to effect their emancipation privately and clandestinely behind the back, so to say, of society, and within the narrow limits prescribed by their actual condition. In this they, of course, are defeated. They seem neither to recover from their own energies, their past revolutionary grandeur, nor do they appear likely to gain new energy from their alliance with other classes, until all those classes against which they fought in June, be prostrate aside of them. They, however, do not fall without the honours of the grand historical battle; not only France—all Europe trembles under the earthquake of June, while the subsequent victories over the higher classes[b] are so cheaply bought, as to require the most impudent exaggeration on the part of the conqueror, in order to pass as anything like events, and turn out the more ignominiously the more remote the vanquished class stands from the proletariat.[c]

"All classes and all parties[d] had fused themselves into the one

---

[a] Marx has here "exchange banks and workers' associations".—*Ed.*

[b] Marx has here "while the ensuing defeats of the upper classes".—*Ed.*

[c] The next paragraph from Chapter I of *The Eighteenth Brumaire of Louis Bonaparte* is omitted by Eccarius.—*Ed.*

[d] Marx has here "During the June days all classes and parties".—*Ed.*

Party of Order, in opposition to the proletariat, the party of Anarchy, of Socialism, and of Communism. They had saved society from 'the enemies of society'. They had given out the watchwords of *bourgeois* society: 'Property, Family, Religion, and Order,' to the army, and encouraged the counter-revolutionary crusade by the sacramental words: '*In hoc signo vinces!*'[a]

"From this moment, as often as any one of the numerous parties that had ranged themselves under this sign against the insurgents of June, ventures to contest the revolutionary battle-field on the grounds of its own separate class interests it succumbs to the cry of 'Property, Family, Religion, and Order.' Society is saved as often as the number of its rulers is diminished by the victory of a more exclusive interest over wider and more general interests. Every demand of simple, middle-class financial reform, of ordinary liberalism—of mere Republican formalism and etiquette—of common-place Democracy, is at once branded as an 'attack upon society', and stigmatised as 'Socialism'. And, finally, the high priests of the religion of order[b] themselves are kicked from their Pythian stools, carried away from their beds in the depth of night, thrown into prison vans, incarcerated, and exiled; their temple levelled to the ground—their mouths gagged—their pens broken—their laws torn to pieces—in the name of 'Religion, of Order, of Property, and of Family.'[c] 'Respectable' capitalists, themselves fanatics of order,[d] are shot down from their balconies by a drunken soldiery—the sanctity of their families profanated—their houses bombarded for pastime, in the name of 'Religion, of Family, of Order, and of Property.'[e] The lowest caste of all society[f] in the end, forms the sacred phalanx of order; and the hero, Crapulinski,* triumphantly enters the Tuileries as the 'saviour of society'."

Published in *The People's Paper*, Nos. 21, 22, 23, 24, 25, 27, 28, 32 and 33, September 25, October 2, 9, 16, 23, November 6, 13, December 11 and 18, 1852

Reproduced from the newspaper

* See Heine's *Romanzero*, Hamburg, 1851. [*Note by Eccarius*. The reference is to the poem "Zwei Ritter".]

---

[a] "By this sign thou shalt conquer!"—*Ed.*
[b] See this volume, p. 112.—*Ed.*
[c] Marx has here "in the name of religion, of property, of the family, of order".—*Ed.*
[d] Marx has here "Bourgeois fanatics for order".—*Ed.*
[e] Marx has here "in the name of property, of the family, of religion and of order".—*Ed.*
[f] Marx has here "the scum of bourgeois society".—*Ed.*

[APPEAL FOR SUPPORT
OF THE MEN SENTENCED IN COLOGNE][379]

We have received the following letter together with the appended appeal. We are publishing the communication in accordance with its authors' wishes.

For the *California Staats-Zeitung*
Washington, January 14, 1853

TO THE GERMAN-AMERICAN PUBLIC![380]

With the monster trial in Cologne, the workers' movement in Germany has entered a new phase. It has cast off the fetters which the small compass of a fanatical sectarian movement imposed upon it and has stepped out openly into the political arena. Statesmen of the proletariat confronted the public prosecutors of the bureaucratic police state; the aristocrats and members of the bourgeoisie from the Rhineland who formed the jury set themselves up as a court martial and pronounced their verdict "guilty" on labour's opposition to their privileges. This being the situation, it is an agreeable duty for us to publicise the appended appeal, which members of our association have received from the signatories for distribution in the United States, and at the same time we offer our services to transmit to London any small sums remitted, against statement of account.

Whatever title your organisations bear, in these times when your members are enjoying many a frolicsome evening of conviviality, give heart to our active friends back home by stretching out a helping hand to those struck down in the struggle by donating the money raised at such gatherings. Contributions should be sent to the following address: Relief Fund, care of Adolf Cluss, Adams Express, Iron Building, Washington D.C.

Washington, January 10, 1853

J. Gerhardt, President
Ad. Cluss, Secretary

APPEAL

The workers' party has a duty to alleviate the plight of those in the vanguard of the struggle who were sentenced in Cologne and in particular to take care of their families who are bereft of support. We expect that the German workers in the United States will also wish to be associated with this debt the party owes. The treasurer appointed to receive the sums intended for the prisoners and their families is: Ferdinand Freiligrath, 3 Sutton Place, Hackney, London.

London, December 7, 1852

Johann Baer	*Ernest Jones*	*L. W. Rings*
E. Dronke	*G. Lochner*	*E. Rumpf*
J. G. Eccarius	*K. Marx*	*J. Ulmer*
J. F. Eccarius	*W. Liebknecht*	*Ferd. Wolff*
Fr. Engels	*F. Münks*	*W. Wolff*
F. Freiligrath	*K. Pfänder*	*Münks II*
Imandt	*W. Pieper*	

The German-American press is urged to copy.

Published in the *California Staats-Zeitung*, January 1853

Printed according to the newspaper

Published in English for the first time

APPEAL FOR SUPPORT OF THE REPRESENTATIVES OF THE PROLETARIAT SENTENCED IN COLOGNE, AND THEIR FAMILIES

Among the obligations which political parties implicitly assume towards themselves and their members is above all that of support for those who fall into the hands of the enemy while occupying outposts which they have defended with the utmost courage and tenacity.—For the proletarian or workers' party, those sentenced in Cologne in Germany fall into this category; they were not sentenced on account of the crime of which they stood accused—ridiculous revolutionary machinations—but because they had helped to organise the workers' party, and they were sentenced by judges who were members of the moneyed and feudal aristocracy, whose verdict was for that reason bound to be unjust, and to cap it all the Prussian government resorted to the basest forgeries to eliminate any possible stirrings of scrupulousness in these judges.

As workers and writers having no private resources, who had earned their daily bread by their hands and their writing, the convicted men have by their imprisonment been robbed of any means of further supporting their families, and as a result of the sufferings and deprivations to which they are subject in prison they themselves risk losing that freshness and elasticity of mind which previously gave them their pre-eminent positions in the party, unless every effort is made to alleviate their situation and relieve them of the burden of anxiety about the maintenance of their families.

A committee was immediately set up in London which elected Ferd. Freiligrath, the poet of the proletariat, to be its treasurer and includes the leader of the English Chartists, Ernest Jones, among its members. It has addressed the following appeal to the German workers in America, to which we have hastened to respond:

"The workers' party has a duty to alleviate the plight of those in the vanguard of the struggle who were sentenced in Cologne and in particular to take care of their families who are bereft of support. We expect that the workers of the United States will also wish to be associated with this debt the party owes."

The treasurer appointed to receive the sums intended for the prisoners and their families is: *Ferdinand Freiligrath*, No. 3 Sutton Place, Hackney, London.

> Signed: *Joh. Baer, E. Dronke, Joh. Georg Eccarius, Joh. Fried. Eccarius, Fr. Engels, F. Freiligrath, Imandt, Ernest Jones, W. Liebknecht, G. Lochner, F. Münks, Münks II, K. Marx, K. Pfänder, W. Pieper, W. Rings, E. Rumpf, J. Ulmer, Ferd. Wolff, Wilh. Wolff*

The Socialist Gymnastic Association has requested its administrative council to organise this support; the undersigned are members of the latter who have constituted a special committee and now request all Germans in New York who still have feelings for the cause of freedom and for those who espouse it back in the home country to send their contributions to them; the Gymnastic Association will in due course render a full account of their use.—We take it for granted that associations of like persuasion will gladly and enthusiastically take up this opportunity for offering support.

An appeal has already been sent out by the Executive Committee to all gymnastic societies in the United States.

In conclusion we would further mention that it has been decided the socialist gymnastic societies are to hold a general lottery on the first Monday in March, and we are convinced it will prove highly productive thanks to the generosity which the German women young and old have frequently demonstrated on similar occasions, as an expression of their sympathy for liberty and those in the vanguard of the struggle for it.

Lists for the subscription of contributions, whether they consist of money or other gifts, bear the seal of the Socialist Gymnastic Association and are to be found at the latter's premises, No. 38 Canal Street; at the house of Reicherzer and Hein, No. 12 North William Street; and with V. Keck, at the house of Jos. Müller, No. 24 Allen Street.

New York, January 16, 1853

The administrative council
of the Socialist Gymnastic Society,
in the name of the latter:
the Relief Committee:
*K. Reicherzer, J. L. Schuler, B. Becker,
V. Keck, E. Reistle*

Published in the *New-Yorker Criminal-Zeitung,* January 1853

Printed according to the newspaper

Published in English for the first time

NOTES
AND
INDEXES

NOTES

[1] *Revolution and Counter-Revolution in Germany* was written after Charles Dana, one of the editors of the *New-York Daily Tribune,* had suggested to Marx, early in 1851, that he contribute to the newspaper. Being engaged in economic research, Marx asked Engels, on August 14, 1851, to write "a series of articles about Germany, from 1848 onwards". Engels agreed, and in the course of thirteen months he wrote 19 articles about the German revolution of 1848-49. He intended to write one more, concluding article, but it did not appear in the *Tribune* and most probably was not written at all. Engels used as the main source of reference a file of the *Neue Rheinische Zeitung,* apart from some additional material given him by Marx, whom he constantly consulted and who read every article before mailing it.

The series of articles, *Revolution and Counter-Revolution in Germany,* was printed in the *New-York Daily Tribune* over the signature of Karl Marx, the paper's official correspondent. It was only in 1913, when the correspondence between Marx and Engels was published, that it became known that the articles had in fact been written by Engels. During Marx's and Engels' lifetime the work was never republished, apart from the first two articles, which were reprinted in the *New-Yorker Abendzeitung,* a newspaper of the German refugees in the United States, at the end of October 1851. The first separate edition of this work in English was prepared in 1896 by Marx's daughter, Eleanor Marx-Aveling; the same year a German translation appeared. In this and a number of later editions Marx was given as the author.

In the *New-York Daily Tribune* the articles were printed under the general heading: *Germany: Revolution and Counter-Revolution,* and numbered in Roman figures. In the 1896 English edition Eleanor Marx Aveling provided subheadings which are preserved in this edition. p. 3

[2] The *Tribune* is short for the *New-York Daily Tribune.* Marx's work in this progressive newspaper continued from August 1851 to March 1862, but a large number of the articles he dispatched were written at his request by Engels. Marx began to send his own articles to New York in August 1852, the first being "The Elections in England.— Tories and Whigs" (see this volume, pp. 327-32). Initially, he wrote them in German, and his friends, most often Engels, translated them into English. But by January 1853 he had sufficiently mastered the English language to write his contributions in English. Marx's first

English-language article was "Capital Punishment.—Mr. Cobden's Pamphlet.—
Regulations of the Bank of England" (see this volume, pp. 495-501).

Marx's and Engels' articles in the *New-York Daily Tribune* dealt in the main with
major questions of foreign and home policy, the working-class movement, the
economic development of European countries, colonial expansion, the national
liberation movement in oppressed and dependent countries. The articles at once
attracted attention by the amount of information they conveyed, their acute
political assessments and brilliant literary style. The editors of the *Tribune* publicly
acknowledged their outstanding quality. Thus, in a leading article on April 7,
1853, they saw fit "to pay a tribute to the remarkable ability of the
correspondent". They went on to say: "Mr. Marx has very decided opinions of his
own, with some of which we are far from agreeing; but those who do not read his
letters neglect one of the most instructive sources of information on the great
questions of current European politics." In a letter to Mrs. Marx of July 1, 1853,
Charles Dana, one of the editors, wrote that her husband's articles were highly
thought of by the *Tribune* owners and the reading public.

Many of the articles by Marx and Engels were reprinted in the *Tribune's* special
editions, the *New-York Weekly Tribune* and the *Semi-Weekly Tribune*, and were
quoted by other American newspapers, in particular by the *New-York Times*. The
articles also reached England. Some were reprinted in the Chartist *People's Paper*,
and in his speech in the House of Commons on July 1, 1853, John Bright, the
Free-Trade leader, specially mentioned Marx's *Tribune* article on Gladstone's
budget.

The editors of the *New-York Daily Tribune* arbitrarily printed some of Marx's
and Engels' articles without the author's signature as editorial leading articles, and
occasionally made insertions and additions to the text which were sometimes
contrary to their content. Marx repeatedly protested against this. In the autumn of
1857, in view of the economic crisis in the USA, which had also affected the
newspaper's finances, Marx had to reduce the number of his contributions. His
final break with the newspaper occurred during the Civil War in the United States.
It was largely due to the fact that its editorial policies increasingly supported
compromise with the slave-owning states and to its general falling away from
progressive views.   p. 7

[3] Serfdom was abolished in the territories along the left bank of the Rhine annexed
to France during the French Revolution and the Napoleonic wars, as were the
privileges of the nobility and the clergy, and the church estates.   p. 7

[4] The *Continental System*, or the *Continental Blockade*, proclaimed by Napoleon I in
1806, forbade the countries of the European Continent to trade with Great
Britain.   p. 8

[5] The *Protective Tariff of 1818* (*Schutzzolltarif*) abolished internal duties throughout
the territory of Prussia and created the conditions for the formation of the
Customs Union (*Zollverein*).

The *Zollverein*, a union of German states, which established a common customs
frontier, was set up in 1834 under the aegis of Prussia. Brought into being by the
need to create an all-German market, the Customs Union subsequently embraced
all the German states except Austria and a few of the smaller states.   p. 8

[6] The reference is to the uprising of the Silesian weavers on June 4-6, 1844, the first
big class battle between the proletariat and the bourgeoisie in Germany, and to the

uprising of the Bohemian workers in the second half of June 1844. The workers' movement, which was accompanied by factory and machine wrecking, was brutally suppressed by government troops.   p. 11

[7] The *German Confederation* (*der Deutsche Bund*)—an ephemeral confederation of German states founded in 1815 by decision of the Congress of Vienna.

The *Federal Diet* (*Bundestag*)—the central body of the German Confederation, which consisted of representatives of the German states and held its sessions in Frankfurt am Main. Having no actual power, it nevertheless served as an instrument of monarchist feudal reaction. After the March 1848 revolution in Germany, Right-wing circles tried to revive the Diet, but in the summer of 1848 it had to cede its functions to the Imperial Regent elected by the Frankfurt National Assembly and to the Imperial Government which the Assembly set up. The Diet's powers were restored in March 1851. The formation in 1866 of the North-German Confederation under Prussia's hegemony put an end to the German Confederation and the Diet.   p. 12

[8] The *Customs Union* (*Steuerverein*) was formed in May 1834; it included the German states of Hanover, Brunswick, Oldenburg and Schaumburg-Lippe, which were interested in commerce with Great Britain. In 1854 this separatist union disintegrated and its participants joined the *Zollverein* (see Note 5).   p. 12

[9] The *Congress of Vienna* of European monarchs and their ministers (September 1814-June 1815) established a system of all-European treaties after the Napoleonic wars. The Congress decisions helped to restore the feudal system and a number of old dynasties in states that had been subjugated by Napoleon and to preserve the political dismemberment of Germany and Italy, sanctioned the annexation of Belgium to Holland and the partition of Poland, and planned measures to combat the revolutionary movement.   p. 13

[10] The July 1830 revolution in France was followed by a revolution in Belgium, and a revival of the revolutionary movement and uprisings in Poland, Germany and Italy.   p. 14

[11] "*Young Germany*" (*Junges Deutschland*)—a literary group that emerged in Germany in the 1830s and fell under the influence of Heinrich Heine and Lüdwig Börne. The members of this group (Gutzkow, Wienbarg, Mundt, Laube, Jung and others) engaged in both fiction-writing and journalism, through which they advocated freedom of conscience and the press, the introduction of a Constitution, the emancipation of women, and other reforms. Their political views were, however, vague and inconsistent, and many of them soon became indistinguishable from ordinary liberals.   p. 14

[12] The *Holy Alliance*—an association of European monarchs founded in September 1815, on the initiative of the Russian Tsar Alexander I and the Austrian Chancellor Metternich to suppress revolutionary movements and preserve feudal monarchies in European countries.   p. 16

[13] The *Historical School of Law*—a trend in German historiography and jurisprudence which emerged in the late eighteenth century. The representatives of this

school—Gustav Hugo, Friedrich Karl Savigny and others—sought to justify feudal institutions and the privileges of the nobility on the grounds of the inviolability of historical tradition.

For a criticism of this trend see Marx's works: *The Philosophical Manifesto of the Historical School of Law* and *Contribution to the Critique of Hegel's Philosophy of Law. Introduction* (present edition, Vols. 1 and 3).

Legitimists—supporters of the Bourbon dynasty, which represented the interests of the big hereditary landowners. By the "first generation of French Legitimists" Engels means royalist writers and politicians who were vehemently hostile to the French Revolution, being particularly outraged when, in 1792, the monarchy was overthrown. After the restoration of the Bourbons, in 1815-30, the Legitimists formed a Right-wing political party which continued to be active even after 1830, when the dynasty was overthrown a second time. p. 16

14 The question of introducing a Constitution in Prussia was raised by moderate reformers after the defeat of the Prussian feudal state in the war with Napoleonic France in 1806-07. As early as October 1810, under pressure from the reformers, Frederick William III promised in very vague terms (in his "Edikt über die Finanzen des Staats und die neuen Einrichtungen wegen der Abgaben") to grant "representation both in the provinces and in the entire country". Illusions about the King's intention to introduce a representative system were encouraged by the Prussian ruling circles during the upsurge of patriotism connected with Prussia's entry, in 1813, into the war of liberation waged by the European peoples against Napoleonic rule. However, practical steps were postponed until the end of the war. Article 13 of the Act setting up a German Confederation, adopted by the Congress of Vienna in June 1815, provided for the introduction in the German states of constitutions based on the estate principle. But this provision was not carried out in the majority of states, including Prussia, despite the King's promises to set up representative institutions made by him in a number of patents and manifestos, in particular in a special decree of May 22, 1815 ("Verordnung über die zu bildende Repräsentation des Volkes").

According to the "Verordnung wegen der künftigen Behandlung des gesammten Staatsschulden-Wesens" (Decree on the future handling of all state debts) issued in Prussia on January 17, 1820, new loans and state debts had to be guaranteed by the forthcoming Prussian assembly of the estates as well as by the government. p. 18

15 The reference is to the *Ständische Ausschüsse*—committees of the estates of the provincial assemblies set up in Prussia in June 1842. They were elected by the provincial assemblies from among their members (on the estate principle) and formed a single advisory body—the United Committees (*Vereinigte Ausschüsse*), which were a sham representative assembly. The session of the United Committees mentioned by Engels below took place from October 18 to November 10, 1842.

Marx refers rather derisively to this body and to the attempts made by the ruling circles and the conservative newspapers to give it the appearance of a constitutional organ in his article "The Supplement to Nos. 335 and 336 of the Augsburg *Allgemeine Zeitung* on the Commissions of the Estates in Prussia" (present edition, Vol. 1, pp. 292-306). p. 18

16 The reference is to the *Preussische Seehandlungsgesellschaft* (Prussian Maritime Trading Company)—a commercial and banking company founded in 1772 and

enjoying a number of important state privileges. It advanced big loans to the
government and in fact became its banker and broker.   p. 19

[17] On February 3 and 8, 1847, Frederick William IV issued an order setting up the
United Diet and a patent on its convocation ("Verordnung über die Bildung des
Vereinigten Landtages" and "Patent wegen Einberufung des Vereinigten
Landtages"). The session of the United Diet opened on April 11 and continued
until June 26, 1847.   p. 19

[18] In his speech from the throne at the opening of the first United Diet on April 11,
1847, Frederick William IV declared that he would never let the "natural relations
between the monarch and the people" turn into "conditioned, constitutional"
relations and a "written sheet of paper" become a substitute for "genuine sacred
loyalty" (see *Der erste Vereinigte Landtag in Berlin 1847*. Erster Theil).   p. 20

[19] The reference is to German or "true socialism" which was widespread in Germany
in the 1840s, mostly among petty-bourgeois intellectuals. The "true socialists"—
Karl Grün, Moses Hess, Hermann Kriege—substituted the sentimental preaching
of love and brotherhood for the ideas of socialism and denied the need for a
bourgeois-democratic revolution in Germany. Marx and Engels criticised this
trend in the following works: *The German Ideology* (see present edition, Vol. 5),
Circular Against Kriege, German Socialism in Verse and Prose and *Manifesto of the
Communist Party* (Vol. 6).   p. 20

[20] In April and May 1847, bread riots broke out in many parts of Germany (primarily in Berlin) and other European countries. They were caused by the general rise
in food prices due to the crop failure in 1846, and to the effects of the economic
crisis which had gripped the whole of Europe.   p. 21

[21] On June 26, 1849 the liberal deputies of the Frankfurt National Assembly, who
had walked out after the Prussian King's refusal to accept the Imperial Crown,
met in Gotha for a three-day conference which resulted in the formation of the
so-called *Gotha party*. It expressed the interests of the pro-Prussian German
bourgeoisie and supported the policy of the Prussian ruling circles aimed at
uniting Germany under the hegemony of Hohenzollern Prussia.   p. 22

[22] *German Catholicism*—a religious movement which arose in a number of German
states in 1844 and affected considerable sections of the middle and petty
bourgeoisie. The "German Catholics" did not recognise the supremacy of the
Pope, rejected many dogmas and rites of the Roman Catholic Church and sought
to adapt Catholicism to the needs of the German bourgeoisie.
     Free Congregationalism—a movement that took shape in 1846 among
Protestant communities which sought to free themselves from the official
Lutheran Church. It developed under the influence of the *Friends of Light*
(*Lichtfreunde*)—a religious trend that arose in 1841 and was directed against the
pietism predominant in the Lutheran Church and distinguished by extreme
mysticism and bigotry. This religious opposition expressed the German
bourgeoisie's discontent with the reactionary system in Germany in the 1840s. The
"free congregations" broke away from the official Lutheran Church and on
March 30, 1847 received the right to conduct their own religious services.
     In 1859 Free Congregationalism merged with "German Catholicism". p. 23

23 The *Unitarians* (or *Anti-Trinitarians*) reject the dogma of the "Holy Trinity". The Unitarian Church first appeared in England and America in the seventeenth century, and its teachings have always emphasised the moral and ethical side of the Christian religion in contrast to its external ritualistic aspect.   p. 24

24 Napoleon's victories in Germany in 1806 led to the dissolution of the Holy Roman Empire of the German Nation which was founded in 962. At different periods it included German, Italian, Austrian, Hungarian and Bohemian territories, Switzerland and the Netherlands, forming a motley conglomeration of feudal kingdoms and principalities, church lands and free towns with different political structures, legal standards and customs. In August 1806 the Austrian Emperor Francis I renounced the title of Emperor of the Holy Roman Empire.   p. 24

25 Marx, Engels and their followers advocated a single German republic before the 1848 revolution (see present edition, Vol. 6, p. 335). The same slogan was put forward as the first point in the "Demands of the Communist Party in Germany" (Vol. 7, pp. 3-7) — the political programme of the Communist League in the German revolution formulated by Marx and Engels in March 1848.   p. 25

26 The reference is to the First Opium War (1839-42) — an aggressive war waged by Britain against China which started China's transformation into a semi-colony. One of the clauses of the Nanking Treaty imposed on China provided for the opening of five Chinese ports to foreign trade.   p. 26

27 In February-March 1846, simultaneously with the national liberation insurrection in the free city of Cracow, which had been under the joint control of Austria, Prussia and Russia since 1815, a big peasant uprising flared up in Galicia. Taking advantage of class contradictions, the Austrian authorities provoked clashes between the insurgent Galician peasants and the Polish nobility who were trying to come to the support of Cracow. After putting down the insurgent movement of the nobility, the Austrian Government also suppressed the peasant uprising in Galicia.   p. 26

28 The reference is to the *Academic Legion*, a para-military student organisation set up in March 1848 in Vienna. It also included university lecturers and other intellectuals, mostly radical democrats. The Legion played a significant part in the Austrian revolutionary movement in 1848. After the suppression of the October uprising in Vienna, it was disbanded.   p. 33

29 The reference is to the national liberation war waged by the Italian people against Austrian domination in 1848-49. The war began in March 1848, following a victorious popular uprising in Lombardy and the Venice region, which were under Austrian rule. Under pressure from the masses, the Italian monarchist states, headed by Piedmont, also entered the war. But the treachery of the Italian ruling classes, who feared a revolutionary unification of Italy, led to the defeat of the struggle against Austria.

The first stage of the war resulted in a defeat for the Piedmontese troops at Custozza on July 25, 1848, and the conclusion of an Austro-Piedmont armistice on August 9. In view of the new revolutionary upsurge in Italy, the King of Piedmont had to resume fighting on March 20, 1849, but already on March 21-23 the Piedmontese army was routed at Mortara and Novara. The military rout of Piedmont and the capitulation of its ruling circles enabled the Austrians to suppress the centres of popular resistance and restore their rule in Northern Italy.

p. 34

[30] The reference is to the resolution of the Austrian Imperial Diet abolishing feudal servitude which was passed on August 31, 1848 and which, following its approval by the Emperor, became law on September 9 ("Gesetz über die Aufhebung des Unterthänigkeitsbandes und die Entlastung des bäuerlichen Besitzes."). p. 34

[31] *Penates*—household gods of the ancient Romans. p. 35

[32] The session of the second United Diet, which adopted a law on elections to the Prussian National Assembly ("Wahlgesetz für die zur Vereinbarung der Preussischen Staatsverfassung zu berufende Versammlung. Vom 8. April 1848"), was held from April 2 to 10, 1848. p. 37

[33] In the spring of 1848, Mainz (Mayence) was the scene of bloody clashes between the civic militia and Prussian soldiers. These clashes had repercussions throughout Germany and were discussed in the Frankfurt National Assembly; the latter was content to appoint a committee which submitted its report only after the Mainz civic militia had already been disarmed by Prussian soldiers. p. 41

[34] This apparently refers to the statement by the Frankfurt National Assembly on May 27, 1848, which said that all clauses in the constitutions of individual German states must coincide with those of the all-German Constitution to be drawn up by the Assembly.

Archduke John of Austria was elected Regent of Germany on June 29, 1848, whereupon a provisional Imperial Government, consisting of Right-wing and moderate deputies of the Assembly, was set up under him. It possessed no real power, but nevertheless the Regent and his Ministers were officially vested with the functions of a German Central Authority. p. 41

[35] The reference is to the armistice concluded on August 26, 1848 in the Swedish town of Malmö between Denmark and Prussia for a term of seven months. Under the impact of the March 1848 revolution a national liberation uprising had flared up in the duchies of Schleswig and Holstein, which were subject to the King of Denmark but populated mainly by Germans. The uprising was widely supported by the advocates of German unification. The ruling circles of Prussia, which was at war with Denmark over Schleswig and Holstein, fearing a popular outbreak and an intensification of the revolution, sought an agreement with the Danish monarchy to the detriment of overall German interests, which also had a negative effect on the military operations of the Prussian army. The armistice virtually preserved Danish rule in Schleswig and Holstein, provided for the replacement of the provisional authorities in Schleswig by a new government (in which placemen of the Danish monarchy were preponderant), the separation of the Schleswig and Holstein troops, and other terms unfavourable to the national

liberation movement in the duchies. The revolutionary-democratic changes that had been introduced there were virtually nullified. (The attitude of the Frankfurt National Assembly to the armistice of Malmö is described in detail by Engels in Article X of this series; see this volume, p. 53.)

In March 1849, however, the ruling circles of Prussia, hoping to raise the prestige of the Prussian monarchy by taking part in this popular war and to realise their aggressive plans, resumed hostilities, which proceeded with varying success. However, under pressure from Britain and Russia, which supported Denmark, Prussia signed a peace treaty with Denmark on July 2, 1850, temporarily relinquishing its claims to Schleswig and Holstein and withdrew its military support in the war waged by the duchies. The Schleswig-Holstein troops were defeated and ceased all resistance. As a result, the two duchies remained part of the Kingdom of Denmark.   p. 42

[36] On Engels' views on the historical destiny of the Slav peoples incorporated into the Austrian Empire see the Preface to this volume (pp. XV-XVI).   p. 43

[37] The first partition of Poland by Prussia, Austria and Tsarist Russia took place in 1772. Russia appropriated mainly the Byelorussian lands which had been earlier annexed by the Kingdom of Poland. As a result of the second and third partitions, by Russia and Prussia in 1793 and by Russia, Prussia and Austria in 1795, Poland ceased to exist as an independent state.   p. 44

[38] The March revolution of 1848 provided an impetus for an insurrection of the Poles in the Duchy of Posen for liberation from the Prussian yoke. Polish peasants and artisans took an active part in the insurrection together with members of the lesser nobility. The Prussian Government was forced to promise that a committee would be set up to carry out a reorganisation in Posen: creation of a Polish army, admission of Poles to administrative and other posts, recognition of Polish as an official language, etc. Similar promises were contained in the Convention of April 11, 1848, signed by the Posen Committee and the Prussian Commissioner. However, the Prussian troops broke the Convention and brutally suppressed the insurrection. The reorganisation promised to the Poles was never carried out.
                                                                         p. 45

[39] The *wars of the Hussites*, named after the Czech patriot and reformer Jan Huss, who was burnt at the stake in 1415, began with a popular uprising in Prague on July 30, 1419. The revolutionary wars of the Czech people against feudal exploitation, the Catholic Church and national enslavement continued until 1437 and ended in the defeat of the Hussites.   p. 46

[40] The *Slavonic Congress*—the congress of representatives of the Slav lands forming part of the Austrian Empire met in Prague on June 2, 1848. The Right, moderate liberal wing, to which Palacký and Šafařik, the leaders of the Congress, belonged, tried to solve the national question through autonomy of the Slav lands within the framework of the Habsburg monarchy. The Left, radical wing (Sabina, Frič, Libelt and others) wanted joint revolutionary action with the democratic movement in Germany and Hungary. The radical delegates took an active part in the popular uprising in Prague on June 12-17, 1848 against the arbitrary rule of the Austrian authorities, and were subjected to cruel reprisals. On June 16 the moderate liberal delegates declared the Congress adjourned for an indefinite period.   p. 47

[41] The mass demonstration in London, called by the Chartists for April 10, 1848, was to present a petition to Parliament for the adoption of the People's Charter. The Government prohibited the demonstration, and troops and police were brought to London to prevent it. The Chartist leaders, many of whom vacillated, called off the demonstration and persuaded the masses to disperse. The failure of the demonstration was used by the Government for an attack on the workers and repressions against the Chartists.   p. 50

[42] On April 16, 1848 a peaceful procession of Paris workers marched towards the Town Hall to present a petition to the Provisional Government for "organisation of labour" and "abolition of the exploitation of man by man". The workers encountered battalions of the bourgeois national guard and were forced to retreat.

On May 15, 1848 Paris workers led by Blanqui, Barbès and others took revolutionary action against the anti-labour and anti-democratic policy of the bourgeois Constituent Assembly which had opened on May 4. The participants in the mass demonstration forced their way into the Assembly, demanded the formation of a Ministry of Labour and presented a number of other demands. An attempt was made to form a revolutionary government. National guards from the bourgeois quarters and regular troops succeeded, however, in restoring the power of the Constituent Assembly. The leaders of the movement were arrested and put on trial.   p. 50

[43] On May 15, 1848 Ferdinand II, King of Naples, subsequently nicknamed "King Bomba" for the bombardment of Messina in September 1848, suppressed a national uprising in Naples, disbanded the National Guard, dissolved Parliament and abrogated the reforms introduced under pressure from the masses in February 1848.   p. 50

[44] Seeing that the war with Denmark over Schleswig and Holstein was waged by the whole of Germany, during the armistice talks in Malmö (see Note 35) the Prussian representatives formally based themselves on the sanction of the Central Imperial Government and the latter's draft agreement. But actually they ignored this draft and changed many of its important points. Nevertheless, the imperial Ministers, fearing that a rupture with Prussia would strengthen the democratic circles, consented to Prussia's terms, and an armistice agreement was concluded on August 26, 1848. When it was rejected by the Frankfurt Parliament on September 5, 1848, the Ministers resigned. An attempt to form a more liberal cabinet failed, and a new government was set up, of almost the same composition as the former one. On September 16 the National Assembly cancelled its earlier decision and ratified the armistice. This evoked a popular uprising on September 18, which was suppressed by Prussian and Austrian troops summoned to Frankfurt by the Imperial Government.   p. 53

[45] The temporary press regulations ("Provisorische Vorschrift über die Presse") of March 31, 1848 provided for the payment of high caution deposits by newspaper publishers, preserved censorship and made persons guilty of "misuse of the press" liable to trial at police courts and not by jury.

The Constitutional Act of the Austrian Empire ("Verfassungs-Urkunde des Oesterreichischen Kaiserstaates") of April 25, 1848 provided for the establishment of two Chambers—a Chamber of Deputies and a Senate—and the preservation of provincial representative institutions based on the estate principle. It vested executive power and command of the armed forces in the Emperor and granted him the right to reject laws adopted by the Chambers.

The Provisional Election Regulations to the Constitutional Act of April 25, 1848 ("Provisorische Wahlordnung zur Verfassungs-Urkunde vom 25. April 1848") adopted on May 9, 1848, deprived the majority of the population of the right to vote. They stipulated that "workers receiving pay by the day or by the week, servants, and persons receiving benefits from public charities cannot act as electors". Some senators were appointed by the Emperor, others were elected by the big landowners from among their own ranks.   p. 54

[46] The reference is to the battle at the village of Pákozd, near Székesfehérvár (Stuhlweissenburg), on September 29, 1848, in which the Hungarian revolutionary troops defeated the army of the Croatian Ban Jellachich, who had invaded Hungary on September 11 on the secret instigation of the Austrian ruling circles. Pursuing the enemy, the Hungarians reached the Austrian frontier on October 10.

The victory of September 29, 1848 was a landmark in the national liberation war of the Hungarian people. Beginning with the popular uprising in Pest on March 15, 1848 the revolution in Hungary developed along an ascending line. Already in March the country was proclaimed independent in financial and military matters (connection with the Empire continued in the form of Hungary's recognition of a common monarch of the Habsburg dynasty), a national government was set up, and a number of progressive reforms carried out (abolition of serfdom, etc.). In July the National Assembly was convened which adopted a decision on the formation of a national army (its soldiers were called "Honveds"—"defenders of the homeland"). Though at first the Austrian ruling circles had to tolerate these changes, they were secretly preparing a blow against revolutionary Hungary. They did their utmost to fan the conflict caused by the Hungarian Government's refusal to satisfy the national demands of the Croats, the Voivodina Serbs and other national minorities which, according to the then existing administrative division, belonged to the Kingdom of Hungary, and incited the Right-wing landowners and bourgeoisie in the national movements of these peoples to start a war against the Hungarians. All this resulted in Jellachich's invasion which, contrary to the Habsburgs' expectations, evoked a new revolutionary upsurge in the country. On September 22, 1848 a Defence Council headed by Lajos Kossuth was set up, to which power was soon transferred; the moderate elements in the National Assembly and the government apparatus were forced into the background. But advocates of compromise with the Habsburgs continued to sabotage resolute revolutionary actions.   p. 57

[47] The Hungarian command's delay in taking offensive action in support of the Vienna insurgents—due mainly to the opposition of the advocates of a compromise with the Habsburgs (including the influential General Görgey)—had unfavourable consequences for Hungary too. Having defeated the Hungarians at Schwechat, on the approaches to Vienna, on October 30, 1848, having captured this town and suppressed the Vienna insurrection, Windischgrätz and Austrian counter-revolutionary forces began to concentrate forces for a campaign against Hungary. In December the Austrian army under Windischgrätz invaded Hungary, captured Pest and occupied a considerable part of the country up to the Theiss. The Hungarian National Assembly and the Defence Council were forced to move to Debrecen. But the Hungarian revolutionary army reinforced its

ranks, mobilised all available resources and, supported by the local population and guerrillas in the enemy's rear, began a counter-offensive in early April 1849, delivered a number of crushing blows on the Austrians and drove them out of Hungary (see Engels' articles on the revolutionary war in Hungary for the *Neue Rheinische Zeitung* in Vols. 8 and 9). The Austrian Emperor Francis Joseph had to ask the Russian Tsar Nicholas I for help. By the autumn of 1849 the Hungarian revolution had been suppressed by the joint forces of Habsburg Austria and Tsarist Russia.   p. 61

[48] On August 13, 1849, at Világos, the Hungarian army commanded by Görgey surrendered to the Tsarist troops sent to help the Habsburgs to suppress the revolution in Hungary.   p. 63

[49] *Lancastrian schools*—primary schools for children of non-propertied parents, in which a system of mutual instruction was employed. For lack of teachers, senior and more capable pupils helped to teach the rest of the pupils. Named after Joseph Lancaster (1778-1838), an English pedagogue, these schools were widespread in England and a number of other countries in the first half of the nineteenth century.   p. 64

[50] In the new Prussian Government, formed on November 8, 1849, Count von Brandenburg held the post of Prime Minister, and Manteuffel, the most influential member of the Cabinet, assumed the post of Minister of the Interior (in 1850 he became Prime Minister). The royal decree transferring the Prussian National Assembly from Berlin to Brandenburg ("Botschaft an die zur Vereinbarung der Verfassung berufene Versammlung") was also dated November 8 and announced to the Assembly on the following day.   p. 67

[51] In 1637 John Hampden, member of Parliament and later a prominent figure in the English revolution, refused to pay the royal tax collectors the "ship money" tax which had not been approved by the House of Commons. His refusal resulted in a trial which stimulated the growth of opposition to the Stuart monarchy.

The movement in America against the taxes and customs duties introduced by the British Government in the colonies was the prelude to the American War of Independence (1775-83). In 1766 the British Parliament was compelled to cancel the stamp-duty introduced in the preceding year, and later the Americans declared a boycott of English goods subject to indirect taxation. In 1773 an attempt forcibly to bring into America tea on which high duties were imposed, resulted in the destruction of a cargo in the port of Boston, Massachusetts. All this led to further conflicts and culminated in the rebellion of the American colonies against Britain.   p. 67

[52] The reference is to a resolution passed by the Prussian National Assembly on November 15, 1848, at a sitting held in a Berlin hotel. It declared the levying of taxes illegal until the Assembly was in a position to continue its sittings in Berlin unhindered. However, it did not call on the people to resist the collection of taxes.

The sitting of November 15 was the last one which the deputies held in Berlin. Early in December some of them, mostly Right-wing deputies, assembled in Brandenburg. But on December 5, 1848 royal decrees were issued dissolving the National Assembly and introducing a Constitution imposed by the King. This completed the Prussian counter-revolutionary coup d'état.   p. 67

[53] On March 4, 1849 the counter-revolutionary Austrian Government promulgated a Constitution imposed by the Emperor without waiting for the end of the discussion of constitutional drafts in the Constituent Imperial Diet. Despite the promises of autonomy to the lands inhabited by non-Austrians, the imposed Constitution was conceived in an anti-democratic spirit of centralised bureaucracy and anti-democratic government (the Emperor and his Ministers were to enjoy full powers). In reply to the deputies' protests, the Imperial Diet was dissolved on March 7. The Constitution of March 4 was a step towards restoring absolutism in Austria (it was finally restored by the imperial patent of December 31, 1851, which abolished constitutional rule).   p. 70

[54] *Vendée*—a department in Western France; during the French Revolution of 1789-94 a centre of a royalist revolt in which the mass of the local peasantry took part. The name "Vendée" came to denote counter-revolutionary activity. p. 72

[55] Under the Constitution imposed by Frederick William IV on December 5, 1848, a two-Chamber parliament was introduced in Prussia. By the imposition of age and property qualifications the First Chamber was made a privileged chamber of the gentry. The two Chambers met on February 26, 1849. However, the government, displeased with the position of the Left-wing deputies of the Second Chamber, though their opposition was rather moderate, dissolved it on April 27. The pretext for the dissolution was the approval by the Second Chamber of the Imperial Constitution drawn up by the Frankfurt National Assembly. Subsequently, the imposed Constitution was repeatedly revised, on the initiative of the Right-wing ruling circles of Prussia, in a still more anti-democratic spirit.   p. 72

[56] The *Fundamental Rights of the German People* ("Die Grundrechte des deutschen Volkes")—a document adopted by the Frankfurt National Assembly as a Declaration of Rights and published as early as December 1848 was incorporated into the text of the Imperial Constitution ("Verfassung des deutschen Reiches") as a separate, sixth, chapter. At its sitting on March 27, 1849, the National Assembly adopted the Imperial Electoral Law ("Reichsgesetz über die Wahlen der Abgeordneten zum Volkshause") along with the Constitution, which was published on March 28. Also on March 28 the Assembly elected the King of Prussia "Emperor of the Germans".   p. 76

[57] On March 21, 1848, on the initiative of Prussian bourgeois ministers who sought to bolster the King's prestige, a royal pageant was staged in Berlin accompanied by demonstrations in favour of German unification. Frederick William IV drove along the streets of Berlin wearing a black-red-and-gold armband—the symbol of united Germany—and delivered pseudo-patriotic speeches, posing as an advocate of "German freedom and unity".   p. 80

[58] The reference is to the conference of representatives of Prussia, Saxony, Hanover and Württemberg which met in Berlin on March 17, 1849 to revise the so-called Imperial Constitution drawn up by the Frankfurt National Assembly. It resulted in an agreement concluded on May 26, 1849, between the kings of Prussia, Saxony and Hanover (the "Three-King-League") based on the Prussian project for reorganising the German Confederation, which was aimed at establishing Prussia's hegemony in Germany. By trying to make other German princes join this League (known as the Prussian Union), Prussia's ruling circles hoped to unify the German

states, without Austria, under Prussian rule. However, under pressure from
Austria, supported by Russia, the Prussian Government was forced to give up its
plans in 1850.   p. 83

59 At the elections to the Frankfurt National Assembly in May 1848, the Silesian
district of Striegau (Strzegom) elected Wilhelm Wolff to deputise when necessary
for the liberal deputy Stenzel, who obtained a majority vote. When Stenzel and a
group of other liberal deputies walked out of the Assembly in May 1849, his seat
went to Wolff. It was on May 26, 1849, during the Assembly's discussion of an
appeal to the German people couched in very moderate terms, that Wolff made
the speech referred to, demanding that the Imperial Regent and his Ministers
should be outlawed.   p. 87

60 The battle at Waghäusel (Baden) between the Baden-Palatinate insurgent army
and the Prussian punitive force took place on June 21, 1849.
   Under the walls of Rastatt fortress the Prussian and other punitive forces
defeated the Baden-Palatinate army on June 29-30. The latter had to retreat to the
south and on July 11-12 crossed over into Switzerland. On July 23 the insurgent
garrison of Rastatt capitulated after a severe siege.   p. 91

61 The Imperial Regent and his Ministers were declared deposed and a new
executive body—a Regency of five—was formed in their place at the sitting of the
National Assembly on June 6, 1849, after its "rump" had moved from Frankfurt
to Stuttgart. The Regency consisted of the moderate democrats Raveaux, Vogt,
Simon, Schüler and Becher. Their attempts to implement the Imperial
Constitution by parliamentary means ended in complete failure.   p. 93

62 The last article in the series Revolution and Counter-Revolution in Germany did not
appear in the New-York Daily Tribune. The English edition of 1896 and a number
of later editions included as the last article Engels' "The Late Trial at Cologne"
(see this volume, pp. 388-93), which did not belong to this series.   p. 96

63 This statement was written in connection with the arrest of Bürgers, Röser,
Daniels and other members of the Communist League by the Prussian police in
Cologne in May 1851, following the arrest of Nothjung, an emissary of the
League, by the Saxon authorities in Leipzig, and in view of the rumours spread by
the reactionary press of a communist plot, the threads of which allegedly led to
Marx in London.
   Marx's statement was not published in the Augsburg Allgemeine Zeitung but was
printed in the Kölnische Zeitung on October 9, 1851. On October 13, Marx wrote to
Engels: "You'll have seen in the Kölnische Zeitung that I've made a statement
refuting the Augsburg Allgemeine Zeitung's nonsense. The tittle-tattle was
becoming altogether too wild. The ruffians' intention, in launching the recent
series of prolonged attacks on me in all the German newspapers, was, I am quite
sure, to place me on the horns of a dilemma. Either I must publicly disown the
conspiracy and hence our party friends, or I must publicly acknowledge them,
thus committing an act of treason 'in law'. However, these gentlemen are too
clumsy to catch us out" (see present edition, Vol. 38).   p. 97

64 The Eighteenth Brumaire of Louis Bonaparte (Der achtzehnte Brumaire des Louis
Bonaparte) was written by Marx from December 1851 to March 1852,
immediately following the coup d'état in France engineered by the French

President, who called himself "Louis Napoleon". In the course of his work on the book Marx constantly exchanged views with Engels concerning these events. Thus, in this book Marx developed some of the ideas contained in Engels' letter of December 3, 1851, in particular the ironical comparison of the Bonapartist coup d'état of December 2, 1851 with the coup of November 9, 1799 (the 18th Brumaire according to the republican calendar), as a result of which the Directory was overthrown and a dictatorship set up under General Napoleon Bonaparte, who was proclaimed First Consul and later, in 1804, Emperor of the French. Besides periodicals and official documents, Marx also used private letters from Paris as his sources.

The Eighteenth Brumaire of Louis Bonaparte was originally intended as a series of articles in the weekly Die Revolution, which was being prepared for publication by Joseph Weydemeyer, a friend of Marx and Engels and a member of the Communist League in the United States. But Weydemeyer managed to put out only two issues (January 1852), following which publication ceased for lack of funds. Marx's articles arrived too late for inclusion. On Marx's advice, Weydemeyer published this work in May 1852 as the first issue of the "non-periodic journal" Die Revolution, and provided it with a short preface. In giving it the title The Eighteenth Brumaire of Louis Napoleon, Weydemeyer failed to take into account that throughout the book Marx referred to the chief initiator of the coup d'état as Louis Bonaparte, which he did deliberately (see his letter to Jenny Marx of June 11, 1852). Being in financial straits, Weydemeyer could not buy up the bulk of the impression from the print-shop, and only a small number of copies reached Europe. All attempts to publish the book in Germany or England (in an English translation) were unsuccessful.

The second edition of the book, this time under the title The Eighteenth Brumaire of Louis Bonaparte, appeared only in 1869. For this edition Marx revised the text, corrected a large number of misprints, mainly in accordance with the list appended to the 1852 edition, eliminated repetitions, abridged certain passages, and wrote a preface dated June 23, 1869, in which he described the editorial work he had done as follows: "A revision of the present work would have robbed it of its peculiar colouring. Accordingly I have confined myself to mere correction of printer's errors and to striking out allusions now no longer intelligible." This 1869 edition is the one translated here, but since the passages omitted by Marx are of great interest because they show how he revised the book and, in a number of cases (especially the abridgments in Chapter VII) because of their theoretical content, they are reproduced in this volume as footnotes.

The third edition came out in 1885 under the editorship of Engels and with his preface. The text in the main coincided with that of the 1869 edition. Passages from The Eighteenth Brumaire of Louis Bonaparte were published in Der Sozialdemokrat, an illegal organ of the German Social-Democratic Party, on March 18, 1887 (No. 12) and on March 16, 1889 (No. 11). During Engels' lifetime two translations were made from the 1885 edition: a French translation (published in Le Socialiste, organ of the Workers' Party of France, from January to November 1891, and in a separate pamphlet that appeared in Lille the same year) and a Russian translation (appeared as a pamphlet in Geneva in 1894).

In English, excerpts from this work were first published in "A Review of the Literature on the Coup d'État" by Georg Eccarius, a Communist League member, which was printed in the Chartist People's Paper from September to December 1852. In the last section of this review, printed on December 18,

1852, Eccarius quoted long passages from Chapter I of *The Eighteenth Brumaire of Louis Bonaparte* (see this volume, pp. 617-20). In English this work was first published in full in *The People*, the weekly of the Socialist Labour Party of the United States, in September-November 1897. It was published in book form in New York in 1898.   p. 99

[65] Hegel expressed this idea in his work *Vorlesungen über die Philosophie der Geschichte* (its first edition came out in Berlin in 1837). In the third part of this work, at the end of Section 2, entitled "Rom vom zweiten punischen Krieg bis zum Kaiserthum", Hegel wrote in particular that "A coup d'état is sanctioned as it were in the opinion of people if it is repeated. Thus, Napoleon was defeated twice and twice the Bourbons were driven out. Through repetition, what at the beginning seemed to be merely accidental and possible becomes real and established." Hegel also repeatedly expressed the idea that in the process of dialectical development there is bound to be a transition from the stage of formation and efflorescence to that of disintegration and ruin (see, in particular, G. W. F. Hegel, *Grundlinien der Philosophie des Rechts*, Th. 3, Abt. 3, §347). Developing this thought and Hegel's idea about the recurrence of historical phenomena Marx wrote in his *Contribution to the Critique of Hegel's Philosophy of Law. Introduction* (end of 1843-beginning of 1844): "History is thorough and goes through many phases when carrying an old form to the grave. The last phase of a world-historical form is its *comedy*" (see present edition, Vol. 3, p. 179). A similar interpretation of Hegel's idea, albeit in the form of a vague hint, can be found in Marx's article "The Deeds of the Hohenzollern Dynasty" written in 1849 (see present edition, Vol. 9, p. 421).
                                                           p. 103

[66] *Montagne* (the Mountain)—representatives in the Constituent and subsequently in the Legislative Assembly of a bloc of democrats and petty-bourgeois socialists grouped round the newspaper *La Réforme*. They called themselves Montagnards or the Mountain by analogy with the Montagnards in the Convention of 1792-94.   p. 103

[67] An allusion to the fact that, while in emigration in England, Louis Bonaparte volunteered for the special constabulary (a police reserve consisting of civilians) which helped the regular police disperse the Chartist demonstration on April 10, 1848.

The *"Little Corporal"*—a nickname of General Bonaparte (later Emperor Napoleon I) popular among the French army.   p. 103

[68] At *Marengo* (North Italy) Napoleon Bonaparte's army, which had crossed the Alps at the St. Bernard Pass, defeated the army of the Austrian General Melas on June 14, 1800.

"*A company of gendarmes to be sent across the Jura*"—Marx refers here to the conflict between France and Switzerland in December 1851-January 1852 over Louis Bonaparte's demand for the deportation of French republican refugees from Switzerland. The Jura—a mountain range on the French-Swiss border.

Order of St. Andrew—the highest order of the Russian Empire. Marx apparently refers to the need for Louis Bonaparte to be recognised by the Russian Tsar Nicholas I.   p. 103

[69] On December 10, 1848 Louis Bonaparte was elected President of the French Republic by a majority vote.   p. 105

[70] As the Bible has it (Exodus 16 : 3), during the exodus of the Jews from Egypt the faint-hearted among them, depressed by the difficulties of the journey and by hunger, began to sigh for the days spent in captivity when they at least had something to eat. The expression "to sigh for the fleshpots of Egypt" became a proverb.   p. 105

[71] *Hic Rhodus, hic salta!* ("Here is Rhodes, leap here!"—meaning: here is the main point, now show us what you can do!)—words addressed to a swaggerer (in a fable by Aesop, "The Boasting Traveller") who claimed that he had made tremendous leaps in Rhodes.

Here is the rose, here dance!—a paraphrase of the preceding quotation (in Greek Rhodes, the name of an island, also means "rose") used by Hegel in the preface to his work *Grundlinien der Philosophie des Rechts.*   p. 107

[72] In May 1852 Louis Bonaparte's term of office as President expired. Under the French Constitution of 1848, presidential elections were to be held every four years on the second Sunday in May, and the outgoing President could not stand for re-election.   p. 107

[73] *Chiliasts* (from the Greek word *chilias,* a thousand)—preachers of a mystical religious doctrine that Christ would come to earth a second time and usher in a "millennium" of universal equality, justice and well-being. Chiliastic beliefs sprang up in the period of early Christianity and were continuously revived in the doctrines of the various medieval sects which voiced the sentiments of the peasants and the urban poor.   p. 107

[74] The *dynastic parties*—the Legitimists (see Note 13) and the Orleanists. The latter supported the House of Orleans, which was overthrown by the February revolution of 1848. They represented the interests of the finance aristocracy and the big bourgeoisie.

The *blue republicans*—bourgeois republicans; *red republicans*—democrats and socialists of various trends.

The *heroes of Africa*—Generals Cavaignac, Lamoricière and Bedeau, who took an active part in the colonial wars in Algeria.   p. 107

[75] The *dynastic opposition*—an opposition group in the French Chamber of Deputies during the July monarchy (1830-48). The group, headed by Odilon Barrot, expressed the views of the liberal industrial and commercial bourgeoisie and favoured a moderate electoral reform, which they regarded as a means of preventing a revolution and preserving the Orleans dynasty.   p. 108

[76] On the events of May 15, 1848 see Note 42.   p. 110

[77] The *Mobile Guard* was set up by a decree of the Provisional Government on February 25, 1848 with the secret aim of fighting the revolutionary masses. Its armed units consisted mainly of lumpenproletarians and were used to crush the June uprising of the Paris workers. Subsequently, it was disbanded on the insistence of the Bonapartists, who feared that in the event of a conflict between President Bonaparte and the republicans the Mobile Guard would side with the latter.

For Marx's description of the Mobile Guard see his work *The Class Struggles in France, 1848 to 1850* (present edition, Vol. 10, pp. 62-63).   p. 110

[78] An allusion to a legend according to which the Roman Emperor Constantine (274-337) on the eve of a battle against his rival Maxentius in 312 saw in the sky the sign of the Cross and over it the words: "By this sign thou shalt conquer!" With this legend the Church links Constantine's "conversion" from the persecution of Christianity to its protection.   p. 111

[79] The *Vienna treaties*—the treaties and agreements concluded at the Congress of Vienna held by European monarchs and their Ministers in 1814-15. They established the borders and status of European states after the victory over Napoleonic France and sanctioned, contrary to the national interests and will of the peoples, the reshaping of Europe's political map and the restoration of the "legitimate" dynasties overthrown as a result of the French Revolution and the Napoleonic wars. The Vienna treaties confirmed France's territory within the borders of 1790 and the restoration of the Bourbons in France.
                                                               p. 113

[80] On February 24, 1848 Louis Philippe abdicated in favour of his grandson, the Count of Paris. In view of the latter's minority, his mother, the Duchess of Orleans, was to assume the regency. But the King's abdication failed to halt the development of the revolution. Under pressure from the insurgent masses a Provisional Government was set up which proclaimed a republic the next day.
                                                               p. 113

[81] The *Executive Commission* (*Commission du pouvoir exécutif*)—the Government of the French Republic set up by the Constituent Assembly on May 10, 1848 to replace the Provisional Government, which had resigned. It existed until June 24, 1848, when Cavaignac's dictatorship was established during the June proletarian uprising. Composed mostly of moderate republicans, the commission included Ledru-Rollin as a representative of the Left.   p. 113

[82] The text of the *Constitution of the French Republic* was originally published in *Le Moniteur universel*, No. 312, November 7, 1848, and the same year it appeared as a pamphlet. Marx examined this document in 1851 in a special article entitled "The Constitution of the French Republic" (see present edition, Vol. 10, pp. 567-80). In *The Eighteenth Brumaire of Louis Bonaparte* Marx often designates articles of this Constitution as paragraphs (§§).

The *constitutional Charter*, adopted after the bourgeois revolution of 1830, was the fundamental law of the July monarchy. Nominally the Charter proclaimed the sovereign rights of the nation and restricted somewhat the king's power. But the bureaucratic and police apparatus remained intact, as did the severe laws against the working-class and democratic movement.   p. 114

[83] "*Frère, il faut mourir!*" ("Brother, one must die!")—this is how Trappists, monks of a Catholic order, greeted each other. The order was founded in 1664 and was noted for its strict rules and the ascetic life of its members.   p. 116

[84] *Clichy*—a debtors' prison in Paris from 1826 to 1867.   p. 116

[85] This refers to the Cavaignac Government's attitude towards the new revolutionary upsurge in Italy that began in the autumn of 1848. Though Cavaignac declared a policy of non-interference, he actually rendered diplomatic aid to the ruling circles of the Kingdom of Naples and Austria in their struggle against the Italian

national liberation movement. When Pius IX fled to the Neapolitan fortress of Gaeta after the popular uprising in Rome on November 16, which started a series of events that resulted in the proclamation of the Roman Republic on February 9, 1849, Cavaignac offered him asylum in France. Incited by the French Government, Pius IX called on all Catholic states on December 4, 1848 to intervene against the Roman revolutionaries, and Naples and Austria immediately responded to this call. By his policy Cavaignac in effect prepared for the dispatch of a French expeditionary corps against the Roman Republic undertaken later by President Louis Bonaparte. p. 119

[86] In 1832 Louis Bonaparte became a Swiss citizen in the canton of Thurgau; on his joining the special constabulary in England, see Note 67. p. 119

[87] An ironical allusion to Louis Bonaparte's book *Des Idées napoléoniennes*, which he wrote in England and published in Paris and Brussels in 1839. p. 123

[88] The French Government managed to get allocations from the Constituent Assembly for the dispatch to Italy of an expeditionary corps under General Oudinot in April 1849 on the pretext of defending Piedmont in its struggle against Austria, and of protecting the Roman Republic. The true aim of the expedition was intervention against the Roman Republic and restoration of the Pope's temporal power. (On this subject see also Marx's *The Class Struggles in France, 1848 to 1850*, present edition, Vol. 10, pp. 91-94). p. 123

[89] The reference is to the Bill introduced on November 6, 1851 by the royalists Le Flô, Baze and Panat, questors of the Legislative Assembly (deputies of the Assembly charged with economic and financial matters and safeguarding its security). It was rejected on November 17 after a heated debate, in which Thiers supported the Bill and the Bonapartist Saint-Arnaud opposed it. When the vote was taken, the Montagne supported the Bonapartists because it saw the main danger in the royalists. p. 123

[90] On the events of April 16 and May 15, 1848 see Note 42. p. 124

[91] The *Fronde*—a movement in France against the absolutist regime and its prop, the government of Cardinal Mazarin. It was active from 1648 to 1653 and involved various social sections, which in many cases pursued opposite aims, from radical peasant and plebeian elements and oppositional bourgeoisie, to high-ranking officials who sought to maintain their privileges, and aristocrats seeking lucrative posts, pensions and allowances. The defeat of the Fronde led to the strengthening of absolutism. p. 125

[92] The ruling Bonapartist circles and the counter-revolutionary press, preparing the coup d'état of December 2, 1851, did everything they could to scare all timid and law-abiding citizens by the prospect of anarchy, revolutionary plots, a new Jacquerie and encroachments on property during the presidential elections scheduled for May 1852. A special role in this campaign was played by the pamphlet *Le spectre rouge de 1852* (Brussels, 1851) by A. Romieu, a former prefect of police. p. 125

[93] *Ems*—a health resort in Germany where a Legitimist conference was held in August 1849; it was attended by the Count de Chambord, pretender to the French throne under the name of Henry V.

Claremont—a house near London, residence of Louis Philippe after his flight from France.   p. 128

[94] Marx uses the term "*Haupt- und Staatsaktionen*" ("principal and spectacular actions"), which has several meanings. In the seventeenth and the first half of the eighteenth century, it denoted plays performed by German touring companies. The plays, which were rather formless, presented tragic historical events in a bombastic and at the same time coarse and farcical way.

Secondly, this term can denote major political events. It was used in this sense by a trend in German historical science known as "objective historiography". Leopold Ranke was one of its chief representatives. He regarded *Haupt- und Staatsaktionen* as the main subject-matter of history.   p. 128

[95] The expeditionary corps under General Oudinot, sent to Italy by decision of President Louis Bonaparte and the French Government, was driven back from Rome by the troops of the Roman Republic on April 30, 1849. But, in violation of the terms of the armistice signed by the French, Oudinot launched a new offensive on June 3. Throughout the siege of Rome until the fall of the Republic on July 3, 1849 the city was repeatedly subjected to heavy bombardment.

Article V belongs to the introductory part of the French Constitution of 1848; the articles of the main part of the Constitution are numbered in Arabic numerals.   p. 131

[96] On August 10, 1849 the Legislative Assembly adopted a law under which "instigators and supporters of the conspiracy and the attempt of June 13" were liable to trial by the High Court. Thirty-four deputies of the Montagne (Alexandre Ledru-Rollin, Félix Pyat and Victor Considérant among them) were deprived of their mandates and put on trial (those who had emigrated were tried by default).

On June 13 the editorial offices of democratic and socialist newspapers were raided and many of these papers were banned.   p. 132

[97] The events in Paris sparked off an armed uprising of Lyons workers and artisans on June 15, 1849. The insurgents occupied the Croix-Rousse district and erected barricades there, but were overcome by troops after several hours of stubborn fighting.   p. 132

[98] An ironical allusion to the plans of Louis Napoleon, who expected to receive the French Crown from the hands of Pius IX, whose temporal power he helped restore. According to the Bible, David was anointed king by the prophet Samuel in oppositon to the Hebrew king Saul (1 Samuel 16 : 13).   p. 135

[99] The *battle of Austerlitz* between the Russo-Austrian and the French armies on December 2, 1805 ended in victory for the French commanded by Napoleon I.
                                                                p. 136

[100] See Note 87.   p. 140

[101] The *wine tax*, abolished as of January 1, 1850 by decision of the Constituent Assembly, was re-introduced by a law of the Legislative Assembly on December 20-21, 1849.

The *education law*, which virtually placed the schools under the control of the clergy, was adopted by the Legislative Assembly on March 15-27, 1850. For an assessment of these laws see Karl Marx, *The Class Struggles in France, 1848 to 1850* (present edition, Vol. 10, pp. 119-20).   p. 140

[102] The reference is to the commission of 17 Orleanists and Legitimists—deputies of the Legislative Assembly—appointed by the Minister of the Interior on May 1, 1850 to draft a new electoral law. Its members were nicknamed *burgraves*, a name borrowed from the title of a historical drama by Victor Hugo, as an allusion to their unwarranted claims to power and their reactionary aspirations. The drama is set in medieval Germany, where the Burggraf was governor, appointed by the emperor, of a *Burg* (city) or district.   p. 144

[103] From March 7 to April 3, 1849 the leaders of the Paris workers' uprising of May 15, 1848 were tried at Bourges on a charge of conspiring against the government. Barbès and Albert were sentenced to exile, Blanqui to ten years solitary confinement and the rest of the accused to various terms of imprisonment or exile.

On the events of May 15, 1848 see Note 42.   p. 144

[104] The press law passed by the Legislative Assembly in July 1850 ("Loi sur le cautionnement des journaux et le timbre des écrits périodiques et non périodiques. 16-23 juillet 1850") considerably increased the caution money which newspaper publishers had to deposit, and introduced a stamp-duty, which applied also to pamphlets. This new law was a continuation of reactionary measures which virtually led to the abolition of freedom of the press in France (see also Karl Marx, *The Class Struggles in France, 1848 to 1850*, present edition, Vol. 10, pp. 137-38).   p. 145

[105] *Lazzaroni*—a contemptuous name for declassed proletarians, primarily in the Kingdom of Naples. These people were repeatedly used by reactionary governments against liberal and democratic movements.   p. 149

[106] The reference is to French Guiana where political prisoners were sent for penal servitude.   p. 149

[107] This refers to Louis Bonaparte's attempts during the July monarchy to stage a coup d'état by means of a military mutiny. On October 30, 1836 he succeeded, with the help of several Bonapartist officers, in inciting two artillery regiments of the Strasbourg garrison to mutiny, but they were disarmed within a few hours. Louis Bonaparte was arrested and deported to America. On August 6, 1840, taking advantage of a partial revival of Bonapartist sentiments in France, he landed in Boulogne with a handful of conspirators and attempted to raise a mutiny among the troops of the local garrison. This attempt likewise proved a failure. He was sentenced to life imprisonment, but escaped to England in 1846.   p. 149

[108] The *national ateliers* (workshops) were instituted by the Provisional Government immediately after the February revolution of 1848. By this means the Government sought to discredit Louis Blanc's ideas on "the organisation of labour" in the eyes of the workers and, at the same time, to utilise those employed in the national workshops, organised on military lines, against the revolutionary

proletariat. Revolutionary ideas, however, continued to gain ground in the national workshops. The Government took steps to reduce the number of workers employed in them, to send a large number off to public works in the provinces and finally to liquidate the workshops. This precipitated a proletarian uprising in Paris in June 1848. After its suppression, the Cavaignac Government issued a decree on July 3, disbanding the national workshops.

For an assessment of the national workshops see Karl Marx, *The Class Struggles in France, 1848 to 1850* (present edition, Vol. 10, p. 63).   p. 150

[109] The *parliaments in France*—judicial institutions that came into being in the Middle Ages. The Paris parliament was the highest court of appeal and also performed important administrative and political functions, such as the registration of royal decrees, without which they had no legal force. The parliaments enjoyed the right to remonstrate against government decrees. In the seventeenth and eighteenth centuries they consisted of officials of high birth called the "nobility of the mantle". The parliaments ultimately became the bulwark of Right-wing opposition to absolutism and impeded the implementation of even moderate reforms, and were abolished during the French Revolution, in 1790.   p. 159

[110] *Belle Isle*—an island in the Bay of Biscay, a place of detention of political prisoners in 1849-57; among others, workers who took part in the Paris uprising in June 1848 were detained there.   p. 162

[111] Here Marx is drawing a parallel with a story told by the Greek writer Athenaeus (2nd-3rd cent. A.D.) in his book *Deipnosophistae* (Dinner-Table Philosophers). The Egyptian Pharaoh Tachos, alluding to the small stature of the Spartan King Agesilaus, who had come with his troops to the Pharaoh's help, said: "The mountain was in labour. Zeus was afraid. But the mountain has brought forth a mouse." Agesilaus replied: "I seem to you now only a mouse, but the time will come when I will appear to you like a lion."   p. 163

[112] In the 1850s, the Count of Chambord, the Legitimist pretender to the French throne, lived in Venice.

Claremont—see Note 93.   p. 166

[113] The reference is to tactical disagreements in the Legitimist camp during the Restoration period. Louis XVIII and Villèle favoured a more cautious introduction of reactionary measures while the Count d'Artois (King Charles X from 1824) and Polignac ignored the actual situation in France and advocated the complete restoration of the pre-revolutionary regime.

The *Tuileries Palace* in Paris was Louis XVIII's residence.

The *Pavillon Marsan*, one of the wings of the Palace, was the residence of the Count d'Artois during the Restoration.   p. 168

[114] General Magnan directed the suppression of the armed uprising of workers and artisans in Lyons on June 15, 1849 (see Note 97).   p. 169

[115] The *Great Exhibition in London*, from May to October 1851, was the first world trade and industrial exhibition.   p. 174

[116] On December 4, 1851 government troops commanded by Bonapartist generals suppressed a republican uprising directed against the coup d'état in Paris. The

uprising was led by a group of Left-wing deputies of the Legislative Assembly and leaders of workers' corporations and secret societies. Employing cannon, the government troops destroyed the barricades erected by the defenders of the Republi . While fighting the insurgents, drunken soldiers and officers fired at passers-by, at customers in cafés and at spectators at windows and balconies. Several bourgeois mansions were also damaged in this Bonapartist terror.

p. 179

[117] This refers to the participation of peasants in the republican uprisings in France in late 1851 in protest against the Bonapartist coup d'état. These uprisings, involving mainly artisans and workers of small towns and settlements, local peasants, tradesmen and intellectuals, embraced nearly twenty departments in south-east, south-west and central France. Lacking unity and centralisation they were fairly quickly suppressed by police and troops.

p. 188

[118] Here Marx compares the Bonapartist authorities' reprisals against the participants in the republican movement, including peasants, with the persecution of the so-called demagogues in Germany in the 1820s and 1830s.

Demagogues in Germany were participants in the opposition movement of intellectuals. The name became current after the Karlsbad Conference of Ministers of the German States in August 1819, which adopted a special decision against the intrigues of "demagogues".

p. 188

[119] *Cévennes*—a mountain region in the Languedoc Province of France where an uprising of peasants, known as the uprising of "Camisards" (*camise* in old French means shirt) took place between 1702 and 1705. The uprising, which began in protest against the persecution of Protestants, assumed an openly anti-feudal character.

Vendée—see Note 54.

p. 188

[120] This refers to a speech by Montalembert, leader of the Legitimists, in the Legislative Assembly on May 22, 1850, in which he urged them to "wage a serious war against socialism".

p. 192

[121] The *Council of Constance* (1414-18) was convened to strengthen the weakened position of the Catholic Church at that period. The Council condemned the teachings of John Wycliffe and Jan Huss, and put an end to the split in the Catholic Church by electing a new Pope instead of the three pretenders competing for the papacy.

p. 194

[122] On the "true socialists" see Note 19.

p. 194

[123] This witticism of Countess Lehon and the caustic remark of Madame de Girardin on the Bonapartist regime, which Marx quotes at the end of the paragraph, were forwarded to him, together with many other items used in *The Eighteenth Brumaire*, by Richard Reinhardt, a German refugee in Paris, Heinrich Heine's secretary. In his letter to Ferdinand Lassalle of February 23, 1852 Marx quotes a letter to him from Reinhardt, in particular the following passage: "As for de Morny, the minister who resigned with Dupin, he was known as the *escroc* [swindler] of his mistress' (Countess Lehon's) husband, a circumstance which caused Émile de Girardin's wife to say that while it was not unprecedented for governments to be in the hands of men who were governed by their wives, none

had ever been known to be in the hands of *hommes entretenus* [kept men]. Well, this same Countess Lehon holds a salon where she is one of Bonaparte's most vociferous opponents and it was she who, on the occasion of the confiscation of the Orleans' estates let fall '*C'est le premier vol de l'aigle*'. [A pun: "It is the first flight of the eagle" and "It is the first theft of the eagle".] Thanks to this remark of his wife's, Emile de Girardin was expelled" (see present edition, Vol. 39).   p. 196

[124] The reference is to the Regency of Philippe of Orléans in France from 1715 to 1723 during the minority of Louis XV.   p. 196

[125] The *Holy Coat of Trier*—a relic exhibited in the Catholic Cathedral at Trier, allegedly a garment of Christ of which he was stripped at his crucifixion. Generations of pilgrims came to venerate it.   p. 197

[126] The *Vendôme Column* was erected in Paris between 1806 and 1810 in tribute to the military victories of Napoleon I. It was made of bronze from captured enemy guns and crowned by a statue of Napoleon; the statue was removed during the Restoration but re-erected in 1833. In the spring of 1871, by order of the Paris Commune, the Vendôme Column was destroyed as a symbol of militarism.

p. 197

[127] Engels' articles on England were intended for *Die Revolution*, a New York weekly published by Joseph Weydemeyer. Of the four articles written by Engels in December 1851 and January 1852, only two reached Weydemeyer, the other two having been lost on the way. But even the articles which reached Weydemeyer were not published in *Die Revolution*, since the journal had ceased publication. The first of these articles was published in an abridged form (without the first four paragraphs and the last one) in the *Turn-Zeitung* (No. 15, November 15, 1852), a newspaper published in New York of which Weydemeyer was an editor. The second article was used by Weydemeyer in a number of his own writings for the press.

In the manuscript the title "England" is written by Engels over each of the two extant articles. This title was crossed out above the second article, apparently by Weydemeyer, and it was probably he who numbered the articles with Roman numerals.   p. 198

[128] Palmerston, Foreign Secretary in the Whig Ministry of Russell, was dismissed because in a conversation with the French ambassador he had expressed his approval of the Bonapartist coup d'état in France on December 2, 1851, without consulting the other members of the Ministry. The dismissal occurred on December 19, 1851, and in February 1852 Russell's Ministry was replaced by the Tory Ministry of Derby.   p. 198

[129] At the battle of Waterloo (June 18, 1815) Napoleon's army was defeated by British and Prussian forces commanded by the Duke of Wellington and Blücher.   p. 198

[130] From 1850 to 1853 Britain waged one of its Kaffir wars against the Xhosan tribe in Africa. In the first years of the war the local population defeated the British troops several times, but under the Peace Treaty of 1853 the Xhosas had to cede part of their lands to Britain.

   In 1851 the British made an attempt to seize the Slave Coast (West Africa),
for which purpose they intervened in an internecine war of the local Yoruba
tribes. Despite their bombardment of the town of Lagos in December 1851, the
British failed to subjugate the local population and had to content themselves
with installing a henchman of theirs in power. It was not until they had
"purchased" Lagos in 1861 that the British consolidated themselves on the
Slave Coast and laid the foundations of their colony, Nigeria.   p. 198

[131] This refers to the French colonial troops who took part in the conquest of
Algeria.   p. 199

[132] In his song *Les mirmidons ou les funérailles d'Achille*, Béranger allegorically
portrayed the base and worthless rulers of France under the Restoration.
There is a pun in the title: *mirmidons* (myrmidons) is the name of a legendary
tribe in South Thessaly whose warriors fought in the Trojan War under
Achilles' command; it also means dwarfs and, figuratively, base, worthless
people.   p. 200

[133] On the defeat of the Chartists on April 10, 1848 see Note 41.   p. 200

[134] Here and below the reference is to the Punic Wars (264-241, 218-201 and
149-146 B.C.) which were waged between the two major slave-owning states of
antiquity, Rome and Carthage, for supremacy in the Western Mediterranean,
for the conquest of new territories and for slaves. They ended in the defeat of
Carthage.   p. 201

[135] During the war against the first anti-French coalition (1792-97), Napoleon's
army fighting the Austrian forces occupied the neutral Venetian Republic in
May-June 1797. Under the Franco-Austrian treaty concluded in Campoformio
in October 1797, part of the republic's territory, including Venice, was given to
Austria in exchange for concessions the latter made on the frontier along the
Rhine; the other part went to the Cisalpine Republic formed by Napoleon out
of lands he had captured in Northern Italy; the Ionian Islands and the
Venetian Republic's possessions on the Albanian coast were annexed to France.
                                                                           p. 201

[136] The reference is to the British fleet in Portugal, stationed in Tagus estuary,
which was used by the British Mediterranean fleet as an intermediate base in
the nineteenth century.   p. 202

[137] An allusion to the camp at Boulogne established by Napoleon I in 1803-05 for
the invasion of England across the Channel. Concentrated here were nearly
2,500 small transport ships and a 120,000-strong army of invasion. The defeat
of the French fleet at Trafalgar by Admiral Lord Nelson and the formation in
Europe of a new anti-French coalition including Russia and Austria compelled
Napoleon to abandon his plan.   p. 203

[138] The reference is to an operation in the Schleswig-Holstein war (see Note 35),
when, on April 5, 1849, a Danish squadron of ten ships attacked from the sea
the Schleswig town of Eckernförde, situated on the shore of a bay, with a view
to landing troops there. The ships were destroyed by cross-fire from coastal
batteries.   p. 204

[139] The *Peace Society*—a pacifist organisation founded by the Quakers in London in 1816. The society was actively supported by the Free Traders, who thought that in conditions of peace free trade would enable England to make full use of her industrial superiority and thus gain economic and political supremacy.
p. 205

[140] Here the following editorial note was added, apparently by Weydemeyer: "The letter discussing Palmerston's dismissal has not reached us, it has probably been lost on the way from England."   p. 205

[141] The *People's Charter*, which contained the demands of the Chartists, was published on May 8, 1838, in the form of a Bill to be submitted to Parliament. It consisted of six points: universal suffrage (for men of 21 years of age), annual elections to Parliament, secret ballot, equal constituencies, abolition of property qualifications for candidates to Parliament, and salaries for M.P.s. In 1839 and 1842 petitions for the Charter were rejected by Parliament. p. 206

[142] As a result of the Union of 1707 England and Scotland were united into a single state, the Kingdom of Great Britain. The Act of Union abolished the Scottish Parliament and Scotland was given several dozen seats in the London Parliament. But the autonomous rights of the Scottish (Presbyterian) Church were preserved.   p. 207

[143] Later, in a series of articles "Lord John Russell", written in the summer of 1855 (see present edition, Vol. 14), Marx characterised Russell's Reform Bill introduced in early 1852 and gave the reasons for its failure.   p. 208

[144] This letter was written by Engels on the initiative of Marx (see his letter to Engels of January 24, 1852) and sent by the latter to the editor of *The Times*. At Marx's request Engels prepared a similar letter for *The Daily News*. But the letters were not published because of the openly hostile attitude of these newspapers towards the Communist League leaders. In this volume the letter is published according to the draft written on the back of Engels' letter to Marx of January 28, 1852. The signature "A Prussian" is in Marx's hand.   p. 210

[145] The *Grand Jury*—until 1933 a body of from 12 to 23 jurors appointed by the sheriff from among "good and loyal persons" to make a preliminary examination of cases before the accused were brought to trial.   p. 211

[146] This series was written by Engels for *Notes to the People*, the weekly organ of the revolutionary wing of the Chartists edited by Ernest Jones. After their temporary break with George Julian Harney, who became associated with the petty-bourgeois democrats and the separatist Willich-Schapper group responsible for the split in the Communist League, Marx and Engels strengthened their ties with Jones, who remained true to the Chartist revolutionary traditions. They supported his agitation and organising work and actively helped him in publishing periodicals. In the summer of 1851, Marx published his article "The Constitution of the French Republic" (present edition, Vol. 10, pp. 567-80) in *Notes to the People* and helped Jones write a number of articles on co-operation

(published in this journal), of which Marx was virtually a co-author (see this volume, pp. 571-89).

This series of articles by Engels was printed anonymously in three issues of *Notes to the People* under the editors' headings: "The Continental Correspondent of the 'Notes'", "Letter of Our Foreign Correspondent" and "Our Foreign Correspondent's Letter". Only the first article was provided with a title. Judging by the concluding paragraph of the third article, the published articles did not exhaust the author's plans. However, the continuation of the series did not appear in this weekly, which ceased publication on April 24, 1852. It is not known whether Engels had written the rest of the series.   p. 212

[147] The reference is to the attempts at armed resistance to the Bonapartist coup d'état in Paris and to the republican uprisings in a number of French departments (see notes 116 and 117).

Having suppressed these actions in defence of the republic, the Bonapartists staged a "plebiscite" in an atmosphere of fierce police terror, on December 20-21, 1851, thus giving the coup d'état the semblance of popular approval. On January 14, 1852 a new constitution was introduced which conferred all state power upon the President, elected for ten years; the composition and legislative functions of the Council of State, the Legislative Corps and the Senate—the supreme state institutions modelled on the corresponding bodies of Napoleon I—were placed under his direct control. This constitution in fact restored the regime of the Empire in France. On December 2, 1852 the Second Republic was abolished and the Prince-President was formally proclaimed Emperor of the French under the name of Napoleon III.   p. 212

[148] This refers to a number of press laws passed by the Constituent and Legislative Assemblies—"Décret relatif aux cautionnement des journaux et écrits périodiques du 9-12 août 1848"; "Décret relatif à la répression des crimes et délits commis par la voie de la presse du 11-12 août 1848"; "Loi sur la presse du 27-29 juillet 1849"; "Loi sur le cautionnement des journaux et le timbre des écrits périodiques et non périodiques du 16-23 juillet 1850." These laws introduced high caution deposits for the publication of newspapers, a stamp-duty on newspapers and pamphlets and severe punishment for attacks on "the principle of property and family right" and for "incitement to civil war". These laws virtually abolished freedom of the press and freedom of speech in France.

Engels called these press laws "gagging laws" by analogy with the six English acts adopted by the British Parliament in 1819, which abolished inviolability of the person and freedom of the press and assembly.   p. 213

[149] As Engels foresaw, in late 1853 and in 1854 there were signs of economic crisis in the major capitalist countries. Gluts in the market, above all in America and Australia, resulted in production cutbacks in the English textile and iron industries. Similar processes took place in France. The US industry also experienced serious difficulties. But a world economic crisis did not occur until 1857.   p. 221

[150] *Belgrave Square*—a fashionable residential district in London's West End.
                      p. 221

[151] The reference is to the confiscation of the property of the House of Orleans decreed by Louis Bonaparte on January 22, 1852.   p. 221

[152] In September 1851 arrests were made in France among members of local communities belonging to the Willich-Schapper group, which was responsible for the split in the Communist League in September 1850. The petty-bourgeois conspiratorial tactics of this group, ignoring realities and aiming at an immediate uprising, enabled the French and Prussian police, with the help of the agent-provocateur Cherval, who headed one of these local communities in Paris, to fabricate the case of the so-called Franco-German conspiracy. In February 1852 the accused were sentenced on a charge of plotting a coup d'état. Cherval was allowed to escape from prison. The attempts of the Prussian police to incriminate the Communist League led by Marx and Engels failed. Conrad Schramm, a League member, arrested in Paris in September 1851, was soon released for lack of evidence. Nevertheless, the Prussian Police Superintendent Stieber, one of the organisers of the Cologne Communist trial in 1852, repeated the false police accusation. His perjury was exposed by Marx (see this volume, pp. 404-38).   p. 223

[153] In September 1849 Marx was elected to the Committee of Support for German Refugees formed by the German Workers' Educational Society in London. With a view to counteract the attempts of petty-bourgeois refugee democrats to influence the proletarian refugees, the Committee was reorganised into the Social-Democratic Refugee Committee, as suggested by Marx and other Communist League leaders. Engels was among the leaders of the new Committee. In mid-September 1850 Marx and Engels withdrew from the Refugee Committee because the majority of its members were under the influence of the Willich-Schapper group.   p. 223

[154] These are Marx's introductory and concluding remarks on the "Political Programme" of General Klapka, who took part in the 1848-49 revolution in Hungary. Marx may have received this document from Bertalan Szemere, Gustav Zerffi or some other Hungarian émigré among his acquaintances. His interest in it, judging by his letter to Engels of May 6, 1852, was aroused by the preparations for armed actions in Hungary and Italy against Austrian rule being made by the followers of Kossuth and Mazzini. Klapka was to be one of the military leaders. In conditions of the temporary triumph of reaction everywhere, Marx regarded these actions as adventurism which could only play into the hands of the counter-revolutionaries. He saw as particularly dangerous the tendency of certain Hungarian and Italian leaders to seek support for their liberation struggle from Louis Bonaparte and his entourage, who were coquetting with the national movements in an attempt to raise the prestige of the Bonapartist regime and further its foreign policy aims. Later, Marx wrote special articles for the *New-York Daily Tribune* warning of the danger of this tendency (see "Movements of Mazzini and Kossuth.—League with Louis Napoleon.—Palmerston", "Kossuth, Mazzini, and Louis Napoleon" and other articles in this volume). Klapka's "Programme" apparently attracted Marx's attention also because of the author's criticism, though timid and half-hearted, of Kossuth's activity and because of his attempt—in opposition to Kossuth—to propose a more democratic course, that of recognising the rights of national minorities from the outset. As can be seen from Marx's letter to Cluss, dated

May 10, 1852, he intended to publish his remarks on the "Programme" as an article in the *New-York Daily Tribune*. In this volume, they are published according to the copy made by Mrs. Marx.   p. 224

155 *The Great Men of the Exile* (*Die grossen Männer des Exils*) is a satirical *exposé* of the leaders of the petty-bourgeois emigration and of the separatist Willich-Schapper group which caused a split in the Communist League in the autumn of 1850. In conditions of the offensive of reaction throughout the European Continent, Marx and Engels attached great importance to exposing these circles, whose adventurist, conspiratorial and pseudo-revolutionary activities were accompanied by internal strife and squabbles, provided opportunities for police provocations, and diverted the attention of the proletarian and democratic forces from the truly revolutionary tasks.

It was in early 1851 that Marx and Engels conceived the idea of publishing a satirical *exposé* of the leaders of the emigration who were only playing at revolution. As can be seen from Engels' letters to Marx of January 25 and February 5 and from their joint declaration against Ruge of January 27, 1851 (see present edition, Vols. 10 and 38), Engels already then wanted to publish a series of articles about "continental democracy" in Harney's Chartist weekly *Friend of the People*. However, Harney's association with petty-bourgeois émigrés and the Willich-Schapper group, which resulted in a temporary break with him, made Engels interrupt this work and prompted him and Marx to look for other possibilities for a public criticism of the petty-bourgeois émigré groups. This is testified by Marx's letters to the Frankfurt journalist Hermann Ebner, written in August and on December 2, 1851, containing factual material against Arnold Ruge, Gottfried Kinkel, August Willich and others which is textually close to the corresponding pages of the future *exposé*. It was apparently at that time too that the title of the pamphlet was conceived: in his letter to Ebner written in August 1851 Marx called the people he was unmasking "the great men of the future". Engels, too, returned to this theme. In the autumn of 1851 he began writing a satirical article about Karl Schapper, one of those responsible for the split in the Communist League. He hoped to publish it in the USA with the help of Joseph Weydemeyer. But soon Schapper showed signs of disillusionment with sectarian tactics, as a result of which Marx and Engels presumably decided not to include him among the main characters of their pamphlet. For some time they thought it possible to publish it in Weydemeyer's weekly *Die Revolution*, but this soon ceased publication. Nevertheless, Marx provided Weydemeyer and Cluss, another of his followers in the USA, with information about the habits and intrigues of the émigrés, which they used in their writings in the American labour and democratic press.

By the spring of 1852 the plan had crystallised. The pamphlet was written in May and June 1852, partly in London and partly at Engels' home in Manchester, where Marx arrived at the end of May. The authors used their previous notes and also a wealth of new factual material collected with the help of their friends: articles and pamphlets by the émigré leaders themselves, the latter's biographies compiled by their admirers, various émigré publications, documents, memoirs, the German, French and English press, including periodicals printed by German émigrés in the USA (unfortunately, some of these periodicals were not available to the compiler of this volume), and so on. Apart from Mrs. Marx, Ernst Dronke, a Communist League member, also took part in selecting the material and preparing the manuscript for the press. Early in July Marx passed on the manuscript to the Hungarian émigré Bangya,

who offered to publish it in Germany. Later, it turned out that Bangya was a
police spy, who had sold the manuscript to the Prussian police. The actions of
Bangya, who managed to win even Marx's confidence for a time, were
unmasked by the latter in the article "Hirsch's Confessions" written in April
1853 and published in the American newspaper *Belletristisches Journal und
New-Yorker Criminal-Zeitung* on May 5, 1853 (see present edition, Vol. 12).

The *Great Men of the Exile* was not printed during the lifetime of Marx and
Engels. The preliminary copy of the manuscript (the first pages are in Dronke's
hand and the remainder in Engels' with Marx's additions) was preserved by
Marx and later fell into the hands of Eduard Bernstein who, far from taking
steps to have it printed, omitted all passages about Marx's talks with Bangya
concerning *The Great Men of the Exile* when publishing the Marx-Engels
correspondence in 1913. It was not until 1924 that the MS was handed over by
Bernstein to the archives of the German Social-Democratic Party, which was
custodian of Marx's and Engels' papers. The pamphlet was first published in
1930 in Russian translation in Book 5 of *Marx-Engels Archives* by the
Institute of Marxism-Leninism of the CC CPSU and was not printed in the
original German until its inclusion in Marx/Engels, *Werke* in 1960 (Vol. 8).

In English this work was first published in 1971 in the book: Karl Marx and
Frederick Engels, *The Cologne Communist Trial*, Lawrence & Wishart, London.

In this volume editorial corrections made by Marx and Engels have been
taken into account. Passages deleted by the authors in the manuscript are not
reproduced, except for two which sum up, as it were, the preceding text. These
are given in footnotes (see pp. 231, 273).   p. 227

[156] Marx and Engels refer here to the sentimental trend in German literature
typified by Johann Martin Miller's novel *Siegwart, Eine Klostergeschichte* (1776),
which was popular in the late eighteenth century.   p. 229

[157] *Rationalists*—representatives of a trend in German Protestant theology which
enjoyed a considerable following in the eighteenth and the early nineteenth
century. As distinct from the pietists, another trend in the Lutheran Church
which was distinguished by extreme mysticism, the rationalists sought to
combine theology with philosophy and prove that "divine revelation" could be
explained by reason.   p. 234

[158] In E.T.A. Hoffmann's story *Meister Johannes Wacht*, the carpenter Johannes
Wacht, overwhelmed by grief over the recent loss of his wife and son, finds
consolation in artistic work and designs an original building.   p. 238

[159] The *Hainbund* (Grove Union)—a circle of young poets including Johann
Heinrich Voss, Ludwig Heinrich Hölty, Johann Martin Miller and Johann
Friedrich Hahn. It was founded in Göttingen University in 1772 and belonged
to a trend which soon became known as the *Sturm und Drang* and expressed the
discontent of the German burghers with the existing system in Germany. The
Union's ideological inspirer was Friedrich Gottlieb Klopstock. Characteristic of
the *Hainbund* was lyric poetry in which protest was interwoven with sentimental
praise of the philistine way of life of German burghers. The Union
disintegrated in 1774.   p. 244

[160] Marx and Engels refer here to the utopian programmes for restoring guilds
put forward by artisans' congresses in different towns of Germany in 1848.
They nicknamed them *Winkelblechiads* after the German economist K. G. Win-

kelblech, who called for a return to the guild system. On July 15, 1848 an All-German Artisans' Congress met in Frankfurt am Main to work out a common programme. As apprentices were not admitted to the congress by the master-workmen, they convened their own congress and invited representatives of the workers from South German towns. But the programme of this congress was likewise drawn up in the spirit of the utopian ideas of Winkelblech, who took part in both congresses.

p. 249

161 The *Lower Chamber* of the Prussian Diet (*Landtag*) was convened on February 26, 1849, on the basis of the Constitution imposed by Frederick William IV on December 5, 1848 following the coup d'état in Prussia (see Note 52). Despite the fact that in many provinces the elections to it were held in conditions of a virtual state of siege, and notwithstanding the undemocratic electoral law of December 6, 1848, a strong opposition was formed in the Chamber. It was made up of the majority of Left- and Right-Centre deputies of the dissolved Berlin National Assembly. Though the Left wing took a rather moderate stand, the Lower Chamber was dissolved by the government on April 27, 1849.

p. 252

162 See Note 60.

p. 253

163 Kinkel's speech before the military tribunal in Rastatt (he was tried for his part in the campaign for the Imperial Constitution), published in the Berlin *Abend-Post* on April 5 and 6, 1850, was sharply criticised by Marx and Engels in their article "Gottfried Kinkel" which appeared in the fourth issue of the *Neue Rheinische Zeitung. Politisch-ökonomische Revue* (see present edition, Vol. 10). In this article Marx and Engels also quoted this passage from Kinkel's speech, describing it as a cowardly renunciation of his revolutionary comrades and unprincipled adaptation to the reaction. Later, this speech of Kinkel's and his speech on May 2, 1850 at the Cologne trial, where he was charged with taking part in the insurgent movement in the Rhine Province in the spring of 1849 (passages from this speech are quoted further in the text), were reproduced in Schrodtmann's book *Gottfried Kinkel. Wahrheit ohne Dichtung*, Vol. 2, Hamburg, 1851.

p. 254

164 According to a thirteenth-century romance, the English King Richard Lionheart, imprisoned by Duke Leopold I of Austria when returning from the third Crusade (1189-92), was freed by the French troubadour Blondel, Richard's court poet, who made his presence known by singing a song known only to the King and himself.

p. 257

165 The *Crystal Palace* was built of metal and glass for the first world trade and industrial exhibition in London in 1851.

p. 258

166 The article "Kinkel's Lectures", which was published in the weekly *Der Kosmos* in 1851, was quoted by Marx in his letter to Engels on May 28, 1851 (see present edition, Vol. 38).

p. 258

167 Under the Constitution, presidential elections were to be held in France on the second Sunday in May 1852. The petty-bourgeois democrats, and in particular the émigrés, hoped this day would bring the democratic parties to power.

p. 259

[168] The reference is to the campaign for the Imperial Constitution which was adopted by the Frankfurt National Assembly on March 28, 1849, but rejected by the governments of the majority of German states. In May and June uprisings flared up in Saxony, Rhenish Prussia, Baden and the Palatinate in support of the Constitution, but the movement, led by petty-bourgeois democrats, was largely local and was defeated in July 1849. Engels assessed it in his works *The Campaign for the German Imperial Constitution* (present edition, Vol. 10) and *Revolution and Counter-Revolution in Germany* (this volume, pp. 69-87).   p. 259

[169] This refers to an attempt by Gustav Struve and other German democrats to set up an émigré organisation, a *Democratic Association*. In April 1850 they distributed in England and Germany a circular announcing the formation of a single émigré leading body—the Central Bureau of the United German Emigration. But their plans for unification proved ephemeral. The efforts of the petty-bourgeois and bourgeois democrats were directed largely against the Social-Democratic Refugee Committee (see Note 153), headed at the time by Marx and Engels, and were aimed at bringing the proletarian refugees under the petty-bourgeois influence. Marx and Engels subjected these actions to criticism in the June 1850 "Address of the Central Authority to the League" (see present edition, Vol. 10, p. 373).   p. 260

[170] The *Club of Resolute Progress*, founded in Karlsruhe on June 5, 1849, was the more radical wing of the petty-bourgeois democratic republicans (Struve, Tzschirner, Heinzen and others) discontented with the capitulatory policy of the Baden Provisional Government headed by Brentano, and the growth of Rightist elements within it. The Club suggested that Brentano should extend the revolution beyond Baden and the Palatinate and introduce radicals into his government. Brentano refused, so the Club tried, on June 6, to force the government to comply by threatening an armed demonstration. But the government, supported by the civic militia and other armed units, proved the stronger party in the conflict. The Club of Resolute Progress was disbanded.
                                                                          p. 261

[171] See Note 7.   p. 261

[172] See Note 22.   p. 262

[173] The four faculties usual in German universities were: theological, law, medical and philosophical.   p. 262

[174] The first of these uprisings in the Grand Duchy of Baden occurred in April 1848. Led by the petty-bourgeois democrats Friedrich Hecker and Gustav Struve, it started with republican detachments invading Baden from the Swiss border. But this poorly organised uprising was crushed by the end of April.

On September 21, 1848 German refugees led by Struve invaded Baden from Swiss territory. Supported by the local republicans, Struve proclaimed a German Republic in the frontier town of Lörrach and formed a provisional government. The insurgent detachments were soon dispersed by troops, and Struve, Blind and other leaders of the uprising were imprisoned by decision of a court-martial. They were released during the third republican uprising in Baden in May 1849, which occurred in connection with the spread of the campaign in defence of the Imperial Constitution (see Note 168).   p. 262

[175] On the *demagogues* see Note 118.   p. 265

[176] The *Palais-Royal* in Paris was the residence of Louis XIV from 1643; in 1692 it became the property of the Orleans branch of the Bourbons. In the 1830s and 1840s its grounds and galleries were places of amusement.   p. 269

[177] An allusion to the order of the French authorities of January 16, 1845, expelling from France Karl Marx, Heinrich Bürgers, Michael Bakunin and other contributors to the German-language newspaper *Vorwärts!*, published in Paris, for their sharp criticism of the absolutist system in Prussia and other German states and for spreading revolutionary ideas.   p. 269

[178] The *Wahl-Manifest der radicalen Reformpartei für Deutschland*, written by Ruge and published in *Die Reform* (Berlin), No. 16, April 16, 1848, proclaimed "the editing of the *rationale* of events" as the main task of the German National Assembly.   p. 270

[179] The reference is to the *Second Democratic Congress* of representatives of democratic and workers' organisations of various German towns which was held in Berlin from October 26 to 30, 1848. It discussed the question of constitutional principles, adopted the "Declaration of the Rights of Man" and elected a new Central Committee of German democrats (d'Ester, Reichenbach, Hexamer). Several points of the "Demands of the Communist Party in Germany" written by Marx and Engels were made the basis of the practical proposals on the social question submitted by the Congress for discussion to all democratic associations. The report at the Congress was made by Beust, a delegate from the Cologne Workers' Association. The motley composition of the Congress led to discord and differences on the main political issues. Instead of adopting resolute measures to mobilise the masses for struggle against counter-revolution, the Congress confined itself to sterile and contradictory decisions. Thus, a manifesto adopted on Ruge's proposal on October 29 was couched in bombastic terms and contained nothing but an appeal to secure aid for revolutionary Vienna from the governments of the German states, which were manifestly hostile to it. Marx sharply criticised this document in the *Neue Rheinische Zeitung*, in the article "Appeal of the Democratic Congress to the German People" (see present edition, Vol. 7, pp. 490-92).   p. 272

[180] The reference is to the tactics of passive resistance to the Prussian coup d'état in October-November 1848 (see this volume, pp. 66-70) adopted by the Prussian and German liberals and moderate democrats, including deputies to the Prussian National Assembly (see Note 52).   p. 272

[181] Arnold Winkelried was a semi-legendary popular hero of the Swiss war of liberation against the Austrian yoke. According to tradition, during the battle of the Swiss against the forces of Prince Leopold III of Austria at Sempach (Lucerne canton) on June 9, 1386, Winkelried opened the attack with the cry "Der Freiheit eine Gasse!" ("Path to Freedom!") and at the cost of his own life decided the outcome of the battle in favour of the Swiss.   p. 274

[182] *Sophiens Reise von Memel nach Sachsen*—a moralising and sentimental novel by Johann Timotheus Hermes, popular in Germany at the end of the eighteenth and the beginning of the nineteenth centuries.   p. 275

[183] The *March Association* (thus named after the March 1848 revolution in Germany) had branches in various towns of Germany. It was founded in Frankfurt am Main at the end of November 1848 by the Left-wing deputies of the Frankfurt National Assembly. Fröbel, Simon, Ruge, Vogt and other petty-bourgeois democratic leaders of the March associations confined themselves to revolutionary phrase-mongering and showed indecision and inconsistency in the struggle against the counter-revolutionaries, for which Marx and Engels sharply criticised them.   p. 275

[184] The French judicial system was introduced in Germany in 1811 in the regions conquered by the French. In the Rhine Province it remained in force even after the province was incorporated in Prussia in 1815, and was superseded by the Prussian system only gradually.   p. 277

[185] *Quakers* (or *Society of Friends*)—a religious sect founded in England during the seventeenth-century revolution and later widespread in North America. They rejected the Established Church with its rites and preached pacifist ideas. The "wet" Quakers, so called in opposition to the Orthodox or "dry" Quakers, were a trend which emerged in the 1820s and sought to renew the Quaker doctrines.   p. 281

[186] The *European Central Committee* (*Central Committee of European Democracy*) was set up in London in June 1850 on the initiative of Giuseppe Mazzini and united bourgeois and petty-bourgeois refugees from various countries. Extremely heterogeneous in composition and ideological principles, the Central Committee of European Democracy had actually disintegrated by March 1852 because of the strained relations between the Italian and French democratic refugees. Its Inaugural Manifesto, "Aux peuples!", of July 3, 1850, was criticised by Marx and Engels in their international review (May to October) published in the autumn of 1850 in the *Neue Rheinische Zeitung. Politisch-ökonomische Revue* (see present edition, Vol. 10, pp. 528-32).   p. 281

[187] *Wasserpolacken*—originally a name given to ferrymen on the Oder who were mainly natives of Upper Silesia; subsequently it became widespread in Germany as a nickname for Silesian Poles.   p. 282

[188] *Bronzell* (in the electorate of Hesse-Cassel or Kurhessen) was the site of an unimportant skirmish between Prussian and Austrian detachments on November 8, 1850. Prussia and Austria, contending for hegemony in Germany, claimed to have the sole right to intervene in the internal affairs of Hesse-Cassel in order to crush the growing movement for a constitution there against the Elector Frederick William I and his reactionary Ministers. Austria received diplomatic support from Nicholas I, Emperor of Russia, and Prussia had to yield and allow Austria to undertake a punitive mission in Hesse-Cassel.   p. 282

[189] This refers to the international congress of pacifists in Frankfurt am Main in August 1850 attended by such prominent figures as the American philanthropist, Elihu Burritt, the leader of the English Free Traders, Richard Cobden, and the former head of the liberal government in Hesse, Heinrich Jaup. Representatives of the Quaker religious sect were also among the delegates.   p. 283

662   Notes

190 On the demagogues see Note 118.   p. 284

191 A national liberation movement flared up in Greece in the spring of 1821 and
after a long struggle led to the country's independence. As a result of Russia's
victory in the Russo-Turkish War of 1828-29, Turkey had to recognise the
independence of Greece. However, the ruling circles of the European powers who were compelled, under pressure from public opinion, to render
military aid to Greece, imposed a monarchy on the newly liberated country.

                                                                      p. 285

192 This refers to the Polish national liberation uprising of November 1830-
October 1831. Its participants belonged mostly to the revolutionary gentry and
its leaders were mainly from aristocratic circles. It was crushed by Tsarist
Russia aided by Prussia and Austria, the states which had taken part in the
partition of Poland at the end of the eighteenth century.   p. 285

193 The *Hambach Festival* was a political demonstration by South-German liberal
and radical bourgeoisie at the castle of Hambach (in the Bavarian Palatinate)
on May 27, 1832. Its participants called on all the Germans to unite against the
German princes in the struggle for bourgeois freedoms and constitutional
reforms. The Federal Diet and the governments of German states replied by
fresh police measures against the opposition movement.   p. 285

194 In early April 1833, in response to the police measures undertaken by the
Federal Diet after the Hambach Festival, a group of conspirators, mainly
students, attempted to seize Frankfurt am Main, overthrow the Diet and
proclaim a republic. But the conspirators only managed to take possession of
the guard-house for a short time, following which they were dispersed by
troops.   p. 286

195 The reference is to the march of revolutionary emigrants organised by Mazzini
in 1834 with a view to inciting a republican uprising in Piedmont. A
detachment of insurgent emigrants of various nationalities under the command
of Ramorino invaded Savoy from Switzerland but was defeated by Piedmontese
troops.
    The *Brimstone Gang* (*Schwefelbande*)—the name of a students' association in
Jena University in the 1770s whose members were notorious for their brawls;
subsequently the expression "Brimstone Gang" became widespread.   p. 286

196 *"Young Europe"*—an international association of revolutionary political emigrants which was founded on Mazzini's initiative in Switzerland in 1834 and
existed until 1836. It included "Young Italy", "Young Poland", "Young
Germany" and other national organisations and aimed at establishing a
republican system in European states.   p. 287

197 *"Young Germany"* was a secret revolutionary organisation of German émigrés in
Switzerland in the 1830s and 1840s (not to be confused with the literary group
also known as "Young Germany"—see Note 11). Initially it comprised mainly
petty-bourgeois intellectuals, whose object was to set up a democratic republic
in Germany, but it soon came more under the influence of the workers'

associations and socialist clubs. In the mid-1830s, the Swiss Government, under pressure from Austria and Prussia, deported the German revolutionaries; the workers' associations were closed. "Young Germany" virtually ceased to exist, though several groups of its followers still remained in the cantons of Geneva and Vaud. In the 1840s "Young Germany" was revived, when, under the influence of Ludwig Feuerbach's ideas, its members carried on mainly atheistic propaganda among the German émigrés, vigorously opposing the communist trends, especially that of Weitling, although some of the members of "Young Germany" were more and more attracted by social questions. In 1845 "Young Germany" was again crushed. p. 288

[198] In June 1844 the Bandiera brothers, who were members of a conspiratorial organisation, landed on the Calabrian coast at the head of a small detachment of Italian patriots with the intention of sparking off an insurrection against the Bourbons of Naples and the Austrian rule. But the participants in the expedition were betrayed by one of their number and taken prisoner; the Bandiera brothers were shot. p. 288

[199] The reference is to the supporters of the German Augustenburg dynasty, which disputed the claims of the Danish kings to Schleswig-Holstein. p. 289

[200] The text of this manifesto is cited by Marx in his letter to Engels written on December 2, 1850 (see present edition, Vol. 38). Apart from the leaders of the separatist Willich-Schapper group, it was signed by French émigrés, followers of Blanqui (including Adam, Barthélemy, Fanon, Gouté, Caperon), and by several Polish and Hungarian émigrés. p. 293

[201] On October 28, 1850 there was a meeting in Warsaw between the Russian Emperor Nicholas I, the Austrian Emperor Francis Joseph and the head of the Prussian Government, the Count of Brandenburg, during which Nicholas I resolutely took the side of Austria in the Austro-Prussian conflict and brought pressure to bear upon the Prussian Prime Minister, demanding that Prussia should abandon all plans to unite Germany under her hegemony. p. 294

[202] The reference is to the former members of the *Labour Commission* that met at the Luxembourg Palace under the chairmanship of Louis Blanc. It was set up on February 28, 1848 by the Provisional Government under pressure from the workers, who demanded a Ministry of Labour. The Commission, on which both workers and employers were represented, acted as mediator in labour conflicts, often taking the side of the employers. The revolutionary action of Paris workers on May 15, 1848 (see Note 42) led to the end of the Luxembourg Commission, which was disbanded by the government the next day. p. 295

[203] The toast which Blanqui sent to London from the Belle-Isle prison and which the organisers of the meeting of February 24, 1851 ("banquet of the equal") deliberately concealed from its participants, was published in a number of French newspapers. In *La Patrie* it appeared on February 27 ("Toaste envoyé par le citoyen L.-A. Blanqui à la commission près les réfugiés de Londres pour le banquet anniversaire du 24 février. Prison de Belle-Isle-en-Mer, 10 février

1851"). In March 1851 Marx and Engels translated it into German and English and provided it with an introduction (see present edition, Vol. 10, pp. 537-39). The German translation was published in 30,000 copies and was circulated in Germany and Austria.   p. 295

[204] The reference is to the all-German National Assembly which met in Frankfurt am Main in 1848 and 1849.

The *Pre-parliament*, which met in Frankfurt am Main from March 31 to April 4, 1848, consisted of representatives from the German states, most of the delegates being constitutional monarchists. The Pre-parliament passed a resolution to convoke an all-German National Assembly and produced a draft of the "Fundamental Rights and Demands of the German People". Although this document proclaimed certain rights and liberties, including the right of all-German citizenship for the residents of any German state, it did not touch the basis of the semi-feudal absolutist system prevalent in Germany at the time.
                                                                        p. 298

[205] See Note 125.   p. 299

[206] See Note 48.   p. 300

[207] See Note 95.   p. 300

[208] This refers to the events of June 6, 1849 in Karlsruhe, capital of Baden, when the radical wing of the democrats—founders of the Club of Resolute Progress—attempted to bring pressure to bear upon the Brentano Provisional Government (see Note 170).   p. 301

[209] See Note 121.   p. 309

[210] The *Holy Grail*—according to a medieval legend, a miraculous cup in which Joseph of Arimathea had received the blood of Christ.   p. 311

[211] The reference is to Willisen's views as set out in his book *Theorie des grossen Krieges angewendet auf den russisch-polnischen Feldzug von 1831* (Berlin, 1840) in which he based the science of war on abstract philosophical propositions instead of observable facts.   p. 313

[212] The reference is to a unit which was formed by Willich in November 1848 out of German émigré workers and artisans in Besançon (France). Its members received allowances from the French Government but at the beginning of 1849 the latter stopped paying them. Later the unit was incorporated in the Willich detachment which took part in the Baden-Palatinate uprising in May-June 1849.   p. 314

[213] The reference is to one of the best-known paintings by Wilhelm von Kaulbach, the *Battle of the Huns* (*Hunnenschlacht*), which shows the ghosts of fallen warriors fighting in the air over the battlefield.   p. 322

[214] The reference is to the former members of the Imperial Regency appointed by the German National Assembly on June 6, 1849 (see Note 61).   p. 325

215 Marx's contribution to the *New-York Daily Tribune* (see Note 2) actually begins with the article "The Elections in England.—Tories and Whigs". Up to that time he had sent to the newspaper only articles from the series *Revolution and Counter-Revolution in Germany* written by Engels. This article and the one that follows it, "The Chartists", were written by Marx in German as a single article and sent by him on August 2, 1852 to Engels in Manchester to be translated into English. Marx's subsequent articles until the end of January 1853 were also, as a rule, translated by Engels. Later Marx mastered the English language sufficiently to be able to write his contributions in English. In making the English translations, Engels sometimes divided a long article into two parts, which were then sent by Marx to the newspaper as independent articles. In this case Engels thus divided the article which Marx had sent to him into two: "The Elections in England.—Tories and Whigs" and "The Chartists". The dates of this and many other articles given in the *New-York Daily Tribune* do not coincide with the actual dates of their writing. The editors frequently published the articles under the date given by Marx when sending the translated articles to New York, or dated them at their discretion.

In October 1852 the two articles mentioned above, together with the articles "Corruption at Elections" and "Result of the Elections" (see this volume, pp. 342-47 and 348-53), were reprinted in several issues of the Chartist *People's Paper* (which began to appear in May 1852) as a single series under the heading "General Election in Great Britain". The name of the author was followed by an acknowledgement that the articles were reprinted from the *New-York Daily Tribune*. The first article was prefaced with the following brief editorial note in square brackets: "We point our readers' attention to the following valuable papers by Dr. Marx, which have appeared in the *New-York Daily Tribune*, a paper which enjoys the largest circulation of any in the United States, and certainly is the ablest journal in the union. Dr. Marx's view of parties in England is the more valuable, as emanating from one beyond the vortex of party interest, and whose antecedents vouch for his Democracy, and his discriminating judgment." The article "The Chartists" was published in *The People's Paper* with abridgements, some details which Marx had borrowed from this paper being omitted. Later, besides reprints of Marx's and Engels' most important articles from the *New-York Daily Tribune*, *The People's Paper* published a number of articles specially written for it by Marx and Engels.

As a rule, Marx's articles from the *Tribune* were reprinted in *The People's Paper* without any changes, but sometimes they were abridged. The editors of *The People's Paper* frequently altered the paragraphing and made stylistic improvements. In the present edition some of these changes are preserved where there are misprints in the *New-York Daily Tribune*. In very important cases divergent readings from the texts of these two newspapers are given in footnotes.

p. 327

The *Manchester School*—a trend in economic thinking which reflected the interests of the industrial bourgeoisie. Its supporters, known as Free Traders, advocated freedom of trade and non-interference by government in economic life. The centre of the Free Traders' agitation was Manchester, where the movement was headed by two textile manufacturers, Richard Cobden and John Bright, founders of the Anti-Corn Law League in 1838. In the 1840s and 1850s the Free Traders formed a separate political group which later formed the Left wing of the Liberal Party.   p. 327

[217] The *High Church*—a trend in the Anglican Church which found support chiefly among landowners. It preserved traditional rites and stressed its continuity with Catholicism. The *Low Church*—another trend in the Anglican Church—was supported mainly by the bourgeoisie and the lower clergy and was evangelical in tendency.   p. 327

[218] The Bill repealing the Corn Laws was passed in June 1846. The English Corn Laws imposed high import duties on agricultural products in the interests of landowners, in order to maintain high prices for them on the home market. Their repeal marked a victory for the industrial bourgeoisie who opposed them under the slogan of free trade.   p. 327

[219] *Dissenters* were members of Protestant sects and trends in England which to some extent rejected the dogmas and rituals of the official Anglican Church.
                                                                                                        p. 328

[220] *American Whigs* were members of a political party in the USA mainly representing the interests of the industrial and financial bourgeoisie and supported by some of the plantation owners. The American Whig Party existed from 1838 to 1854, when the intensification of the struggle over slavery gave rise to splits and regroupings in the political parties of the country. In 1854 the majority of the Whigs, together with a section of the Democratic Party and the farmers' party (Free-Soilers), formed the Republican Party, which opposed slavery. The Right Whigs joined with the Democratic Party, which defended the interests of the slave-owning planters.   p. 329

[221] An allusion to the nickname "Finality-John" which was given by the radicals to John Russell, the leader of the Whig Party in England, after his speech in 1837 in which he characterised the Parliamentary Reform of 1832 as the final point of constitutional development in England.   p. 330

[222] The reference is to the revolution of 1688 (the overthrow of the Stuart dynasty and the enthronement of William III of Orange), after which constitutional monarchy was consolidated in England on the basis of a compromise between the landed aristocracy and the bourgeoisie.   p. 330

[223] The *Reform Bill* of 1831 was finally passed by the British Parliament in June 1832. The reform of 1832 was directed against the political monopoly of the landed and finance aristocracy and enabled the industrial bourgeoisie to enjoy its due representation in Parliament. The proletariat and the petty bourgeoisie, the main forces in the struggle for the reform, remained disfranchised.   p. 330

[224] "The Chartists" was the first of Marx's and Engels' articles which were published not only in the main edition of the *New-York Daily Tribune* but were also reprinted in the paper's special editions, the *Semi-Weekly Tribune* and the *New-York Weekly Tribune.* Known cases of such reprinting are given in the present edition at the end of articles.
      Concerning this article see also Note 215.   p. 333

[225] *Court of Chancery* or *Court of Equity*—one of the high courts of England, which after the judicial reform of 1873 became a division of the High Court of Justice.

The jurisdiction of the court, presided over by the Lord Chancellor, covered matters concerning inheritance, contractual obligations, joint-stock companies, etc. In a number of cases the powers of this court overlapped those of other high courts. In counterbalance to the English common law accepted in other courts, the legal proceedings in the Court of Chancery were conducted on the basis of the so-called law of equity.   p. 334

[226] *Freeholders*—a category of English small landowners dating from feudal times.
                                                                                                        p. 336

[227] In February 1852 Russell made a preliminary statement of his intention to introduce a franchise Bill, but it was not discussed in Parliament. For Engels' analysis of this Bill see this volume, pp. 205-09.   p. 338

[228] This refers to the subsidies granted by the British Parliament in 1846 for the construction of a new building for the Catholic College in Maynooth (Ireland) founded in 1795, and to allocations for its maintenance. These measures of the English ruling classes were aimed at winning over the Irish Catholic clergy to their side and thus weakening the national liberation movement in Ireland.
On the *dissenters* see Note 219.   p. 340

[229] Originally, this and the next article, "Result of the Elections", were written by Marx in German as a single article which he sent to Manchester, about August 16, to be translated into English by Engels. Engels divided it into two; when Marx sent these articles to New York, he dated the first article August 20, 1852 and the second August 27, 1852.   p. 342

[230] The *Thirty-Nine Articles*, which enunciated the compulsory articles of faith of the Church of England, were promulgated in 1571.   p. 342

[231] On June 29 and 30, 1852 a fanatical crowd of English Protestants attacked the Irish population of the town of Stockport (Cheshire). They acted with the connivance of the local authorities and police, who had been inflaming Anglo-Irish national differences. The houses of the Irish Catholics, who made up nearly a third of the town's population, were severely damaged; many Irishmen were badly wounded and one of them was killed. At the same time the police took into custody over a hundred innocent Irishmen, supposedly for participating in the disturbances.   p. 344

[232] According to Greek mythology, the Curetes guarded the infant Zeus (Jupiter in Roman mythology) on the Island of Crete, where he had been hidden by his mother, the Goddess Rhea, from his father, the Titan Cronos, who devoured his children because he feared that they would deprive him of his power. The Curetes drowned the cries of the newly born Zeus by beating on their shields with swords.   p. 346

[233] On the details about the writing and publication of this article see Note 229.
                                                                                                        p. 348

[234] In accordance with the procedure adopted in the British Parliament, the House of Commons, when discussing certain important questions, declares itself the Committee of the Whole House. The functions of the Chairman of the

Committee at such sittings are fulfilled by one of the list of chairmen specially
appointed by the Speaker to conduct this sitting.   p. 350

[235] *Navigation Laws*—a series of acts passed in England to protect English shipping
against foreign competition. The best known was that of 1651, directed mainly
against the Dutch, who controlled most of the sea trade. It prohibited the
importation of any goods not carried by English ships or the ships of the
country where the goods were produced, and laid down that British coasting
trade and commerce with the colonies were to be carried on only by English
ships. The Navigation Laws were modified in the early nineteenth century and
repealed in 1849 except for a reservation regarding coasting trade, which was
revoked in 1854.   p. 350

[236] The *Irish Brigade*—the Irish faction in the British Parliament in the 1830s-1850s.
Until 1847 it was led by Daniel O'Connell, who adopted in the main the tactics of
parliamentary manoeuvre to secure concessions for the big Irish bourgeoisie from
the British Government. Early in the 1850s, a number of deputies belonging to
this faction entered into an alliance with the radical Irish Tenant-Right League
and formed in the House of Commons an Independent Opposition. However,
the leaders of the Irish Brigade soon came to terms with the British ruling
circles and refused to support the League's demands, which led to the demorali-
sation and final dissolution of the Independent Opposition in 1859.   p. 352

[237] The editors of the *New-York Daily Tribune* prefaced this anonymous article with
the following note in square brackets: "In giving place to the following letter
from a private correspondent, the Editors of *The Tribune* do not vouch for the
exactness of its statements, but only for the extensive means of information
possessed by the writer. We give his communication as a matter of interesting
news whose correctness or incorrectness time will show."   p. 354

[238] The *Centralisation*, the leading executive organ of the Polish Democratic
Society, was set up in 1836. The Democratic Society was an organisation of the
Left wing of the Polish emigration which united representatives of the small
nobility (*szlachta*) and the bourgeoisie. Its programme envisaged the abolition of
feudal obligations and of inequality of social estates, the transfer of land
allotments to the peasants without payment, and a number of other progressive
measures. The Democratic Society took an active part in preparing the national
liberation uprising in Cracow in 1846. In the summer of 1849, following the
prohibition of the Polish Democratic Society by the French authorities, London
became the seat of the Centralisation though the majority of its members still
remained in France. The 1850s were marked by discord in the Democratic
Society. In 1862, when the Central National Committee for Preparing the
Uprising was formed in Poland, the Society decided to dissolve itself.   p. 355

[239] Originally Marx wrote this article and "Political Consequences of the
Commercial Excitement" in German as a single article, which he sent to Engels
in Manchester on October 12 to be translated into English. Engels divided the
text into two independent articles. When sending the translated articles to New
York, Marx dated the first article October 15, 1852, and the second October
19, 1852. In this volume some figures have been verified on the basis of the
sources used by the author.   p. 357

[240] The *Poor Law of 1834*—"An Act for the Amendment and Better Administration of the Laws Relating to the Poor in England and Wales"—provided for only one form of relief for the able-bodied poor: workhouses with a prison-like regime in which the workers were engaged in unproductive, monotonous and exhausting labour. The people called these workhouses "Bastilles for the poor".   p. 358

[241] In 1845-47 a grievous famine blighted Ireland due to the ruin of farms and the pauperisation of the peasants. Although the potato crop, the principal diet of the Irish peasants, had been largely destroyed by blight, the English landlords continued to export grain and livestock-products from the country, condemning the poorest sections of the population to starvation. About a million people starved to death and the new wave of emigration caused by famine carried away another million. As a result large districts of Ireland were depopulated and the abandoned land was turned into pasture by the Irish and English landlords.   p. 358

[242] For the details about the writing of this article see Note 239.   p. 364

[243] See Note 139.   p. 366

[244] The *Court of Queen's Bench* is one of the high courts in England; in the nineteenth century (up to 1873) it was an independent supreme court for criminal and civil cases, competent to review the decisions of lower judicial bodies.   p. 366

[245] The *Court of Common Pleas*, the court for trial of civil cases, was one of the high courts of England based on English Common Law (after the reform of 1873 it became a division of the High Court of Justice). Among other matters it examined appeals against decisions of lawyers who were responsible for revising the voters' lists. In accordance with English Common Law only questions of law, i.e. questions concerning the violation of legal and judicial procedure, came within the competence of a court of appeal, while questions of fact, i.e. questions concerning the factual circumstances of a case, were examined by jury.   p. 367

[246] Originally, this article and "Attempts to Form a New Opposition Party" formed a single article written in German and sent by Marx to Engels in Manchester on October 16, 1852 to be translated into English. Engels divided the material into two articles. When Marx sent them to New York he dated the first article November 2, 1852, and the second November 9, 1852.   p. 369

[247] The *Cinque ports*—a confederation of five maritime towns (Hastings, Sandwich, Dover, Romney and Hythe) in south-east England formed in the Middle Ages. They enjoyed privileges in sea trade and fishing but had to supply the king with warships and equipment. The Lord Warden of the Cinque Ports possessed wide administrative and judicial powers. With the formation of a standing royal fleet his office gradually became one of the major sinecures of the British monarchy.   p. 370

[248] For the details concerning the writing of this article see Note 246. In the *New-York Daily Tribune* it was published without a title in the section "England".   p. 373

[249] See Note 141.   p. 374

[250] This is a reference to the representatives of a radical political trend among the Free Traders who founded the National Parliamentary and Financial Reform Association in 1849. The Association campaigned for the so-called Little Charter, a reform Bill repeatedly introduced in Parliament by the bourgeois-radical leader Joseph Hume from 1849 to 1851. As distinct from the Chartist People's Charter, the Little Charter consisted of three points containing demands for household suffrage, three-yearly elections to Parliament and voting by ballot. By opposing their programme to that of the Chartists and at the same time borrowing some of their demands from them, though in a rather curtailed form, the bourgeois radicals hoped to influence the workers during the decline of the Chartist movement. But the majority of the politically active English workers did not support the Little Charter, except for the reformist elements in the Chartist movement including Feargus O'Connor's followers who had degenerated into a reformist sect. The Association ceased to exist in 1855.   p. 375

[251] The reference is to the Executive Committee, the leading body of the *National Charter Association* founded in July 1840. This Association was the first mass workers' party in the history of the working-class movement, numbering up to 50,000 members at its peak. The Executive Committee was elected at congresses and conferences of delegates. After the defeat of the Chartists in 1848 and the ensuing split in their ranks the Association lost its mass character. However, under the leadership of Ernest Jones and other revolutionary Chartists it fought in 1851-52 for the revival of Chartism on a revolutionary basis, for the adoption of the People's Charter, and for the socialist principles proclaimed by the Chartist Convention in 1851. It ceased its activities in 1858.
                                                                       p. 376

[252] This statement, as well as other newspaper items by Marx and Engels, was written in connection with the Cologne trial of members of the Communist League arrested in the spring of 1851, which started on October 4, 1852 and continued until November 12. During the trial the Prussian police authorities who had organised it resorted to forged documents and false evidence in order not only to convict the accused but also to defame their London friends and the entire proletarian organisation. Official government and bourgeois newspapers, including in England the conservative newspaper *The Times* and the liberal *Daily News* (see, in particular, *The Times*, No. 21245, October 13, 1852), conducted a concerted anti-Communist campaign. In response to the police provocations and slanders, Marx and Engels sent to the counsel for the defence in Cologne material exposing the false accusations and printed refutations in newspapers.

As can be seen from Marx's letter to Engels of October 28, 1852, this statement was written mainly by Marx but it also contained material from Engels' letter to Marx of October 27, 1852. Marx sent the statement to a number of London weeklies and dailies. On December 7 he wrote to Adolf Cluss: "What particularly annoyed the Prussian Embassy was that this public denunciation of the Prussian Government was published in the *most distinguished* and *most respectable* London weeklies *The Spectator* and *The Examiner.*" The statement was published simultaneously by five newspapers on October 30, 1852 (under different titles): *The People's Paper* ("The Cologne Trials"), *The*

Spectator ("The Cologne Prisoners"), *The Examiner* ("The Communist Trials in Prussia"), *The Morning Advertiser* ("The Prussian Press Contrasts with Two London Journals"), and *The Leader* ("The Trials of Cologne"). In the last two papers the text differs slightly from that of the first three. All these newspapers reproduced the signatures (*The Spectator* with a misprint: *K. Alarx* instead of K. Marx).

As is evident from a letter of Mrs. Marx to Adolf Cluss of October 28, 1852, the statement was also sent to the USA to be published in the *New-York Daily Tribune* and German workers' papers. A German translation was printed in the *Republik der Arbeiter*, a newspaper published in New York by Wilhelm Weitling, No. 49, December 4, 1852.   p. 378

253 In his letter to Adolf Cluss dated December 7, 1852, Marx informed him of the motives which prompted him to write this statement: it was the clamour raised by a number of German-American democratic newspapers over Marx's warning concerning the danger of a tie-up between the followers of Mazzini and Kossuth and Bonapartist circles.   p. 382

254 A draft of this declaration was drawn up by Marx shortly after the Cologne trial (the sentence was passed on November 12 and published in the German newspapers the next day). On November 16 Marx informed Engels of his intention to discuss the declaration with his London comrades, and then to send his variant to Engels for editing. The final text was sent to *The Morning Advertiser* on November 20 and also to some other newspapers.

This declaration was published in German in the USA by the *New Yorker Criminal-Zeitung*, No. 39, December 10, 1852.   p. 384

255 See Note 115.   p. 385

256 See Note 152.   p. 385

257 Under the sentence passed by the court in Cologne on November 12, 1852, Heinrich Bürgers, Peter Nothjung and Peter Röser were each condemned to six years' imprisonment in a fortress; Hermann Heinrich Becker, Karl Otto and Wilhelm Reiff to five years; and Friedrich Lessner to three years. Four of the accused—Roland Daniels, Johann Jacob Klein, Johann Erhard and Abraham Jacobi—were acquitted. Roland Daniels died a few years later of tuberculosis contracted during the 18 months he had been imprisoned awaiting trial. Ferdinand Freiligrath evaded arrest and trial by emigrating to London.
                                                                              p. 386

258 See Note 139.   p. 386

259 This article was written by Engels at Marx's request for the *New-York Daily Tribune* (see Marx's letter to Engels of October 16, 1852). Later it was included in the separate edition of the series of articles *Revolution and Counter-Revolution in Germany* (1896), prepared for publication by Eleanor Marx-Aveling, in place of the last article of the series which Engels had promised to write but which did not appear in the newspaper.   p. 388

260 The reference is to the *Communist League*, the first German and international communist organisation of the proletariat formed under the leadership of Marx and Engels in London early in June 1847, as a result of the reorganisation of the League of the Just (a secret association of workers and artisans that appeared in

672 Notes

the 1830s and had communities in Germany, France, Switzerland and England). The programme and organisational principles of the Communist League were drawn up with the direct participation of Marx and Engels. The League's members took an active part in the bourgeois-democratic revolution in Germany in 1848-49. Though the defeat of the revolution dealt a blow to the League, in 1849-50 it was reorganised and continued its activities. In the summer of 1850 disagreements arose in the League between the supporters of Marx and Engels and the sectarian Willich-Schapper group which tried to impose on the League its adventurist tactics of immediately unleashing a revolution without taking into account the actual situation and the practical possibilities. The discord resulted in a split within the League. Owing to police persecutions and arrests of League members in May 1851, the activities of the Communist League as an organisation practically ceased in Germany. On November 17, 1852, on a motion by Marx, the London District announced the dissolution of the League.

The Communist League played an important historical role as the first proletarian party based on the principles of scientific communism, as a school of proletarian revolutionaries, and as the historical forerunner of the International Working Men's Association. p. 389

261 See Note 152. p. 390

262 See Note 257. p. 393

263 *Revelations Concerning the Communist Trial in Cologne* is a militant work in which Marx exposed the unseemly methods used by the Prussian police state against the communist movement. On October 27, 1852 Marx wrote to Engels: "My pamphlet is not intended to defend any principles but to brand the Prussian Government on the basis of an account of the facts and the course of the trial." Marx began writing the pamphlet at the end of October 1852, when the trial of the Communists was still in progress in Cologne (see Note 252), and completed it by early December despite his material difficulties and the fact that he was very busy collecting evidence for the defence counsel in Cologne to discredit the prosecution. His main sources of information were the documents of the trial, in particular the official minutes published in the *Kölnische Zeitung* from October 5 to November 13, 1852 (*Assisen-Procedur gegen D. Herm. Becker und Genossen. Anklage wegen hochverrätherischen Complottes*), newspaper reports, and the material collected by himself and his friends, Engels included. On December 6 a copy of the MS was sent to the publisher Schabelitz Junior, in Switzerland, and on the following day a second copy was despatched to Adolf Cluss, a member of the Communist League in the USA, to be published there. In his covering letter to Cluss Marx wrote: "You will appreciate the humour of the pamphlet when you realise that its author is practically interned through his lack of adequate covering for his posterior and feet and moreover at any moment expects to see *really horrid misery overwhelming his family*. The trial is to blame for this as well, because I have had to spend five weeks working for the Party against the machinations of the government instead of working for my daily bread."

The pamphlet was published in Basle in January 1853, but in March almost the whole edition (2,000 copies) was confiscated by the police in the Baden frontier village of Weill on the way to Germany. In the USA the work was at first published in instalments (on March 6 and April 2 and 28, 1853) in the democratic Boston newspaper *Neue-England-Zeitung* and at the end of April 1853 it was printed as a separate pamphlet by the same publishing house. However, the Boston edition was circulated at the time mostly among the German refugees in North America.

In 1874 this work was reprinted in 13 instalments in the *Volksstaat* (Leipzig), organ of the Social-Democratic Workers' Party (from October 28 to December 18, 1874), and Marx was named as its author for the first time. On January 20 and 22, 1875, the *Volksstaat* published, as a supplement to the *Revelations*, Marx's Appendix 4 ("The Communist Trial in Cologne") to his pamphlet *Herr Vogt* written in 1860, and on January 27 it published his special postscript to the *Revelations* dated January 8, 1875. The *Revelations* appeared as a book in Leipzig in 1875, reproducing the text from the *Volksstaat*.

The third edition came out in Hottingen-Zürich in 1885 under the editorship of Engels, with notes and an introductory article by Engels: "On the History of the Communist League". Engels included in this edition Marx's Postscript of 1875, Appendix 4 to *Herr Vogt* and the March and June 1850 Addresses of the Central Authority to the Communist League (see present edition, Vol. 10).

The editions of the *Revelations* printed during Marx's lifetime, and the 1885 edition prepared for publication by Engels after Marx's death, differ only in minor respects, such as discrepancies in separate words, the spelling of some proper names and the use of italics. In the 1875 and 1885 editions some misprints of the first edition are corrected and certain factual and stylistic improvements made, sometimes on the basis of the Boston (1853) edition. In the present edition these improvements of the text, as well as those made in the 1885 edition as compared with the last authorised edition of 1875, are taken into account.

In English the *Revelations* were first published in 1971 in the book: Karl Marx and Frederick Engels, *The Cologne Communist Trial*, Lawrence and Wishart, London.   p. 395

264 The *Code pénal*, adopted in France in 1810 and introduced in the regions of West and South-West Germany conquered by the French, remained in force in the Rhine Province, along with the *Code civil*, even after its incorporation into Prussia in 1815.   p. 400

265 The reference here is to the Willich-Schapper group, which Marx and Engels called the Sonderbund—perhaps an allusion to the separatist union of the seven economically backward Catholic cantons of Switzerland formed in the 1840s to resist progressive bourgeois reforms. This sectarian-adventurist group split away from the Communist League after September 15, 1850, and formed an independent organisation with its own Central Authority. In view of the factionalists' refusal to abide by the decision to transfer the Central Authority to Cologne and because of their disorganising activities, on November 11, 1850 the London District proposed to the Cologne Central Authority to expel the members of the Sonderbund from the League (see present edition, Vol. 10, p. 633). The Central Authority endorsed the proposal and gave notification of this in its Address of December 1. By their activities the members of the Willich-Schapper group helped the Prussian police to discover the League's illegal communities in Germany and frame a case in Cologne in 1852 against prominent members of the League.   p. 402

266 See Note 186.   p. 402

267 See Note 115.   p. 405

268 Van Diemen's Land—the name initially given by Europeans to the island of Tasmania, which was a British penal colony up to 1853.   p. 406

269 The reference is to the German Workers' Educational Society in London which was founded in February 1840 by Karl Schapper, Joseph Moll and other members of the League of the Just (an organisation of German artisans and workers and also of emigrant workers of other nationalities). After the reorganisation of the League of the Just in the summer of 1847 and the founding of the Communist League, the League's local communities played the leading role in the Society. During various periods of its activity, the Society had branches in working-class districts in London. In 1847 and 1849-50 Marx and Engels took an active part in the Society's work, but on September 17, 1850 Marx, Engels and a number of their followers withdrew because the Willich-Schapper sectarian and adventurist faction had temporarily increased its influence in the Society, causing a split in the Communist League. In the late 1850s Marx and Engels resumed their work in the Educational Society, which existed up to 1918, when it was closed down by the British Government.   p. 406

270 See Note 153.   p. 407

271 See Note 152.   p. 407

272 An allusion to the following episode from the period of the Fronde (see Note 91). In September 1650 the Duke de La Rochefoucauld and two of his associates travelled in the coach of their powerful adversary, Cardinal Mazarin, and when the latter jokingly noted that a week ago nobody would even have thought such a situation possible, the Duke said: "Anything can happen in France" ("Tout arrive en France").   p. 409

273 This is an expression used by the Prussian Minister of the Interior von Rochow. In his letter of January 15, 1838 to the citizens of Elbing, who had expressed their dissatisfaction at the expulsion of seven oppositional professors from the Göttingen University, Rochow wrote: "It behoves a loyal subject to exhibit due obedience to his king and sovereign...; it does not behove him to apply the measure of his limited understanding to the actions of the head of the state."
                                                                                      p. 412

274 Marx emphasises the fact that Cherval was admitted into the League of the Just prior to its reorganisation into the Communist League in June 1847. Though Marx and Engels were not members of the League of the Just, founded in 1836, they were in touch with its leaders. They agreed to join the League and take part in its reorganisation provided it became transformed from a conspiratorial society into an association built on democratic principles, and provided it adopted the principles of scientific communism as its programme.   p. 413

275 The Dying Warrior is the well-known statue The Dying Gaul (Pergamum School, 3d cent. B.C.).   p. 416

276 Marx adduced fresh data exposing Cherval as a spy and an agent provocateur in his work Herr Vogt, in the appendices to it, and in the Postscript to the 1875 edition of his Revelations Concerning the Communist Trial in Cologne. According to these data, Cherval, whose real name was Joseph Crämer, was an agent of the

Prussian envoy in Paris and a French spy. He escaped from prison with the connivance of the French and Prussian police. On his arrival in London in May 1852 he was admitted into the German Workers' Educational Society led by Schapper but was soon expelled from it because of his role of provocateur in the case of the so-called German-French plot. p. 417

277 The reference is to the book *Die Communisten-Verschwörungen des neunzehnten Jahrhunderts* (Berlin, Part One 1853, Part Two 1854) by the police officials Wermuth and Stieber. In his article "On the History of the Communist League" (1885), Engels describes it as a "crude compilation, which bristles with deliberate falsifications, fabricated by two of the most contemptible police scoundrels of our century". The appendices to the first part, which purported to tell the history of the workers' movement for the information of police agents, reproduced some of the League's documents that had fallen into the hands of the police. The second part contained a "black list" and biographical particulars of people connected with the workers' and democratic movement. p. 418

278 See Note 167. p. 419

279 *Mormons*—members of a religious sect founded in the United States in 1830 by Joseph Smith (1805-1844) who wrote the *Book of Mormon* (1830) on the basis of alleged divine revelations. In the name of the prophet Mormon this book tells of the migration of the Israelite tribes into America which, it claims, took place in antiquity. p. 421

280 *Mazas*—a prison in Paris. Marx refers to statements made by people imprisoned in connection with the so-called Franco-German plot. p. 423

281 This refers to the workers' society founded in London in January 1852 with Marx's support, its president being a Hanoverian refugee, the joiner Gottlieb Stechan. It included workers who broke away from the German Workers' Educational Society, which had come under the influence of the Willich-Schapper group. Georg Lochner, a worker close to Marx and Engels and member of the Communist League, also took an active part in organising this society. Later, many of its members, including Stechan himself, became influenced by the Willich-Schapper group and joined the earlier organisation. p. 427

282 Among Marx's manuscripts is preserved a draft in Marx's own hand of a reply to Stieber which contains a sharp accusation of him as a police spy (see present edition, Vol. 38). The letter refutes Stieber's attempts to dispute the revelations concerning his activities as a spy, in particular in Silesia before the revolution of 1848-49, made in a report from Frankfurt am Main which was published in issue No. 177 of the *Neue Rheinische Zeitung* on December 24, 1848 under the title "Dr. Stieber". Concerning Stieber's attempts to depict himself as a more consistent democrat than representatives of the democratic trends and his attacks against the latter, Marx limited himself to this remark: "We excuse the lectures on democracy and democratic organs contained in your letter on the grounds of novelty." At the same time the editors of the newspaper thought fit to publish, in a supplement to issue No. 182, December 30, an official correction to the passage of the above-mentioned report which said that Stieber went to Frankfurt in connection with the popular uprising in September 1848, and pointed out that he went there to arrange personal matters.

The reply to Stieber drafted by Marx was in all probability sent over the signature of another editor of the *Neue Rheinische Zeitung*, most likely Wilhelm Wolff, who may have been well aware of Stieber's activity in Silesia.   p. 435

283 Engels refers to the first supplement to the 1875 and 1885 editions of the *Revelations Concerning the Communist Trial in Cologne*, which reproduced without the title Appendix 4 ("The Communist Trial in Cologne") to Marx's pamphlet *Herr Vogt* (1860) (see present edition, Vol. 17). It said that soon after the Cologne trial Fleury was charged with forgery and sentenced to several years' penal servitude.   p. 442

284 In the Postscript to the 1875 edition of his work Marx pointed out that the Red Catechism had been written not by Moses Hess but by a certain Levy. However, it turned out later that Marx had been right in affirming that the *Red Catechism* had in fact been written by Hess. This can be proved in particular by a letter of Hess to Weydemeyer of July 21, 1850, which Marx did not know about.   p. 449

285 The reference is apparently to the *German-American Revolutionary Association*—an organisation of German emigrants in the USA founded in January 1852 by the petty-bourgeois democrats Goegg and Fickler who went to the USA to place the so-called German-American revolutionary loan.   p. 450

286 See Note 118.
                        p. 452

287 Criticism of the behaviour of the leader of the sectarian group and some of his followers during the Cologne Communist trial evoked a mordant reaction on the part of Willich. On October 28 and November 4, 1853 he published his article "Doctor Karl Marx und seine 'Enthüllungen'" (*Belletristisches Journal und New-Yorker Criminal-Zeitung*, Nos. 33 and 34) violently attacking Marx and his work *Revelations Concerning the Communist Trial in Cologne*. Marx replied with his pamphlet *Knight of Noble Consciousness* published with the help of Adolf Cluss and Joseph Weydemeyer in New York in January 1854 (see present edition, Vol. 12).
                        p. 452

288 See Note 257.   p. 452

289 An allusion to the defeat of Prussia by Napoleonic France at Jena on October 14, 1806. The defeat led to Prussia's capitulation and revealed the instability of the social and political system of the Hohenzollern feudal monarchy.   p. 457

290 This refers to the repeal of the Corn Laws (see Note 218).   p. 458

291 The reference is to the demagogic attempts made by some representatives of ruling circles in the German states, above all in Prussia, to present the monarchy as the guardian of the working people's welfare (Marx exposed this idea of "social monarchy" even before the 1848-49 revolution in Germany in his article "The Communism of the *Rheinischer Beobachter*", see present edition, Vol. 6, pp. 220-34), and to the philanthropic measures proposed by the German liberal bourgeoisie as a means to solve the social question. Thus in 1844-45 in a number of Prussian towns, associations for the improvement of the condition of the working classes were formed on the initiative of the liberal bourgeoisie, who were alarmed by the uprising of the Silesian weavers in the

summer of 1844. They hoped to divert the attention of the German workers
from the struggle for their class interests.   p. 459

292 This refers to Palmerston's attitude to the Belgian question in connection with
the revolution in Belgium in August 1830 and its separation from the Kingdom
of the Netherlands in which it had been incorporated in 1815 by decision of
the Vienna Congress. The northern states (Russia, Prussia and Austria)
insisted on Belgium's return under the rule of the King of the Netherlands.
The ruling circles of the July monarchy in France supported the Belgians while
secretly planning to incorporate Belgium in France. To counterbalance certain
conservative elements in Britain, Palmerston acted in alliance with the French
diplomats (the Belgian question was a pretext for a temporary Anglo-French
rapprochement in the sphere of foreign policy known in history as *entente
cordiale*), but at the same time he resolutely opposed their plans to annex
Belgium to France. The efforts of Britain and France were successful: in 1831
the European powers concluded in London a treaty on the independence and
neutrality of the Kingdom of Belgium, and the King of the Netherlands'
refusal to recognise this treaty and to withdraw the Netherlands garrison from
Antwerp led in 1832 to Anglo-French armed intervention in the war. French
troops entered Belgium and besieged Antwerp by land, and the English ships
by sea, forcing the Dutch to capitulate. In 1833 the King of the Netherlands
was compelled to recognise Belgium's independence.   p. 473

293 The relations established between Great Britain and France after the July
revolution of 1830 and known in history as *entente cordiale* were confirmed by
treaty only in April 1834, when the so-called Quadruple Alliance was concluded
between Great Britain, France, Spain and Portugal. But when this treaty was
being concluded contradictions between Britain and France became apparent
and they subsequently led to the aggravation of relations between the two
countries. Formally directed against the absolutist "northern states" (Russia,
Prussia and Austria), the treaty in fact allowed Britain to strengthen her
position in Spain and Portugal under the pretext of rendering armed assistance
to both governments in their struggle against the pretenders to the throne
(Don Carlos in Spain and Dom Miguel in Portugal).   p. 473

294 See Note 236.   p. 474

295 *Puseyism*—a trend in the Anglican Church from the 1830s to the 1860s, named
after one of its founders, Edward Pusey, an Oxford University theologian. He
advocated the restoration of Catholic rites and dogma in the Anglican Church.
Many of the Puseyites were converted to Catholicism.   p. 475

296 A criticism of Wakefield's theory of colonisation was later given by Marx in
Volume I of *Capital* (see present edition, Vol. 31).   p. 475

297 *Rotten boroughs*—sparsely populated or depopulated small towns and villages in
England which enjoyed the right to send representatives to Parliament since
the Middle Ages. These representatives were in fact appointed by the landed
aristocracy, who controlled the handful of "free voters" who nominally elected
them. The "rotten boroughs" were disfranchised by the electoral reforms of
1832, 1867 and 1884.   p. 477

[298] The *Tenant-Right League* was founded in August 1850. One of its chief organisers was Charles Gavan Duffy, formerly a leader of the radical "Young Ireland" group. The League aimed at liquidating, by constitutional means, the semi-feudal methods of exploitation of the Irish peasantry which hampered the development of capitalism in Ireland. Despite its moderate leadership, the League reflected the interests of the Irish tenants fighting against the landlords and speculators in land. Its programme included the following demands: prohibition of arbitrary lease cancellation by landlords and compensation of the tenants for land-reclamation work in case of termination of lease, establishment of a fair rent, and recognition of tenants' right to transfer the lease by means of free sale.

During the general elections to Parliament in 1852 the League's demands were supported by the mass of Irish tenants, both Catholic and Protestant. At the re-elections in January 1853 the League campaigned against the Right-wing leaders of the Irish Brigade—Irish M.P.s who, despite their former promises to secure an agrarian reform, conducted a policy of agreement and entered the coalition government. The landlords, together with the Irish Catholic and Protestant higher clergy who feared the rise of the democratic movement in the country, opposed the League. The League had ceased its activities by the end of the 1850s.

p. 478

[299] The greater part of this article, beginning with the words "The history of the wealth of the Sutherland family" (see this volume, p. 487) to the end, was reprinted in *The People's Paper* on March 12, 1853, as an independent publication signed by Marx and headed "Sutherland and Slavery; or, the Duchess at Home". It had as an epigraph a paraphrase of Luke 6:42: "How canst thou say to thy *sister*: *Sister*, let me take the mote out of thine eye, and perceivest not the beam in thine own eye." After this epigraph, came a short editorial introductory note in square brackets: "Under the sanctified hypocrisy of 'Church and State' a system of oppression is carried on in this gloriously free country, that equals in kindred atrocity the slavery of the American South. We give as a fitting illustration, the following historical statement, showing how the Sutherland family got their wealth. The Duchess of Sutherland here alluded to, is the celebrated 'Countess-Duchess', mother-in-law of the present Duchess. How the present Duke improved on the lessons of the Countess-Duchess, the reader may have occasion to see when we have done with the latter." Marx's article followed.

The text in *The People's Paper* makes more frequent use of italics and has several insignificant omissions of words as compared with that in the *New-York Daily Tribune*. In the quotation from Sismondi's book *The People's Paper* corrected some misprints.

The material on the expropriation of the land of the Celtic population of the Scottish highlands by the Sutherland family, quoted in this article, was subsequently used by Marx in Volume I of *Capital*, in the chapter on the so-called primitive accumulation. In a footnote to the relevant passage Marx wrote: "When the present Duchess of Sutherland entertained Mrs. Beecher Stow, authoress of *Uncle Tom's Cabin*, with great magnificence in London to show her sympathy for the Negro slaves of the American republic—a sympathy that she prudently forgot, with her fellow-aristocrats, during the civil war, in which every 'noble' English heart beat for the slave-owner—I gave in the *New-York Daily Tribune* the facts about the Sutherland slaves. (Epitomised in part by Carey in *The Slave Trade*, Philadelphia, 1853, pp. 203, 204.) My article was reprinted in a Scottish newspaper, and led to a pretty polemic between the latter and the sycophants of the Sutherlands."   p. 486

300 *Orangemen*—members of the *Orange Society* (Order), a Protestant terrorist organisation founded in Ireland in 1795 and employed by the authorities, Protestant landlords and the clergy against the Irish national liberation movement. The name was derived from William III, Prince of Orange, who suppressed the Irish uprising of 1689-91 for restoration of the Stuart dynasty. The Order had especially strong influence in Ulster, Northern Ireland, with a mainly Protestant population. Contrary to the will of the landlords and both Catholic and Protestant higher clergy, when the Tenant-Right League (see Note 298) was active in Ireland, there were cases of *rapprochement* between rank-and-file Protestant Orangemen and Catholics on the basis of their common support for the League's agrarian demands.   p. 486

301 See Note 217.   p. 486

302 *Hudibras*—the title character of a satirical poem by the English poet Samuel Butler written in 1663-78. Hudibras was distinguished for his inclination to absurd reasoning and disputes and for his ability to prove the most absurd propositions by means of syllogisms. The poem was directed against the hypocrisy and religious bigotry of the English bourgeoisie.   p. 486

303 This refers to the revolution of 1688 (see Note 222).   p. 487

304 This was the first article written by Marx in English (see Note 215). On January 29, 1853 he wrote to Engels: "Yesterday I risked for the first time to write an article for Dana in *English.*" Until then Marx wrote his articles for the *New-York Daily Tribune* in German; then they were translated into English, mostly by Engels, but sometimes by Wilhelm Pieper, a German political refugee, philologist and journalist.   p. 495

305 This is a reference to the international Peace Congress convened by the Peace Society (see Note 139) at the end of January 1853 in Manchester. Free Traders were especially active at it. The Peace Congress adopted a number of resolutions of no practical importance, against anti-French military propaganda in England and against the growth of armaments.   p. 499

306 See Note 227.   p. 499

307 On the Tenant-Right League see Note 298. Marx soon carried out his intention by writing the article "The Indian Question.—The Irish Tenant Right" in June 1853 (see present edition, Vol. 12).   p. 503

308 This Bill of the Irish radical Sharman Crawford, providing for compensation of tenants for land improvements when the lease was terminated, was first introduced in the House of Commons in 1835 and was rejected in 1836. Reintroduced in 1847, 1852 and 1856, it was each time rejected.
     On the *Irish Brigade* see Note 236.   p. 504

309 The reference is to the *Repealers*, supporters of the repeal of the Anglo-Irish Union of January 1, 1801, which abolished the autonomy of the Irish Parliament and made Ireland still more dependent on England. In the

1820s, the demand for the repeal of the Union became the most popular slogan of the Irish national liberation movement. In 1840 a Repeal Association was founded whose leader, Daniel O'Connell, stood for a compromise with the English ruling circles and practically reduced the programme of the movement to the demand for autonomy and other political concessions. In January 1847 its radical elements broke away from the Association and formed an Irish Confederation; representatives of the latter's Left revolutionary wing stood at the head of the national liberation movement and in 1848 were subjected to severe repression. Later the Repeal Association finally ceased to exist.

p. 505

[310] On February 9, 1849 the Constituent Assembly in Rome, elected by universal suffrage, abolished the secular power of the Pope and proclaimed a republic. The Roman Republic had to repulse attacks of the counter-revolutionary Neapolitan and Austrian troops and the French expeditionary corps sent to Italy in April 1849 by decision of President Louis Bonaparte to restore the Papal power. The republic lasted only until July 3, 1849, the main blow having been dealt to it by the French interventionists.

p. 508

[311] See Note 227.

p. 511

[312] See Note 221.

p. 511

[313] The reference is to the *Association for the Protection of Agriculture and British Industry* which originally was named the Association for the Protection of Agriculture. Founded in 1845 to fight the Free Traders it expressed the interests of the big landowners and opposed the repeal of the Corn Laws (see Note 218).

The *South Sea Company*, in the former premises of which the above-mentioned meeting was held, was founded in England about 1712, officially to trade with South America and the islands of the Pacific Ocean. Its true aim was to speculate in state securities, which led to the bankruptcy of the Company in 1720.

p. 512

[314] The reference is to the Croatian border regiments stationed in the Military Border Area, a special militarily organised region of the Austrian Empire along the frontier with Turkey. They were used by the Austrian command to suppress the national liberation movements in the provinces, in Northern Italy in particular.

p. 514

[315] In November 1851 Kossuth sent his emissary Mihály Pataki Piringer from London to Hungary via Hamburg, where he established contact with the Hungarian émigré Ignác Ruscsák who was in touch with the Hungarian soldiers of the Austrian regiments stationed in Holstein. The soldiers spread Kossuth's appeals and manifestos. In Hamburg both Piringer and Ruscsák were arrested, and arrests among the soldiers followed. Piringer and Ruscsák were sentenced to death. Piringer was executed on February 5, 1852, but Ruscsák's death sentence was commuted to 18-year hard labour; the arrested soldiers were sentenced to hard labour (from three to eight years) or imprisonment in a fortress. The sentences were published in the *Wiener Zeitung*, No. 35, February 10, 1853.

p. 515

[316] See Note 221.

p. 516

[317] The *Statute Law*—English law based on Acts of Parliament.   p. 517

[318] This refers to two major battles in the Hundred Years' War (1337-1453) between England and France: in 1358 at Poitiers and in 1415 at Azincourt (Agincourt) the English bowmen routed the French knights' cavalry. p. 517

[319] The Turko-Egyptian conflict over Syria, which was occupied by the Egyptian troops in 1833, recommenced in 1839. French aid to the Egyptian Pasha Muhammed Ali aggravated Anglo-French relations in the Middle East at the time. In an effort to prevent France from spreading its influence in this important region on the approaches to its Asian colonies, Britain rendered military assistance to Turkey against Egypt and, supported by Russia, Austria and Turkey, brought diplomatic pressure to bear upon France, forcing it to refuse aid to Egypt.

In 1844 a new aggravation of Anglo-French relations occurred in connection with the expulsion in March of a British agent from Tahiti, which shortly before had been proclaimed a French protectorate. The Tahiti incident resulted from increased Anglo-French rivalry in the Pacific.   p. 518

[320] On the conflict between France and Switzerland see Note 68.

During the 1841 war with Uruguay, Argentina closed the Parana and Uruguay rivers. Demanding the opening of these rivers to their merchant ships, Britain and France brought diplomatic and military pressure to bear upon the Argentine Government and in 1845 they declared war on Argentina. As a result of a long blockade of the coast by the British and French navies, Argentina had to yield and in 1853 signed a treaty opening the above-mentioned rivers to foreign ships.

Neuchâtel, a Swiss canton, was at the same time in vassalage to Prussia. In February 1848 a bourgeois revolution in Neuchâtel put an end to Prussian rule and a republic was proclaimed there. Diplomatic interference by the European powers, including Britain and France, prevented Prussia from using force. It was not until 1857 that Prussia finally relinquished her claims to Neuchâtel.

In 1852 the British and French governments suggested to the US Government that they sign a tripartite convention renouncing any claim to Cuba, as they feared that the United States might seize this island belonging to Spain. The convention was not signed because the United States refused.

In 1851, under the pretext of spreading the *Tanzimat* to Egypt (*Tanzimat*—a reform policy carried out in Turkey from 1839 to strengthen the monarchy by a compromise with the nascent bourgeoisie), Turkey suggested that Egypt's governor should carry out a number of "reforms" which would bring Egypt back under Turkish rule. Under pressure from Britain and France, Egypt was forced to accept some of the Turkish demands.

In November 1852 a protocol was signed in London between Britain, France, Russia, Bavaria and Greece under which Adalbert of Bavaria was appointed heir to his childless elder brother King Otto of Greece instead of another prince of Bavaria who had refused to adopt the Orthodox faith.

In the 1840s and 1850s Britain and France raising obstacles to Tunisia's independence interfered in its foreign policy and helped Turkey in its claim to rule in Tunisia.   p. 519

[321] This article was published in many editions under the editorial heading: "Parliamentary Debates.— The Clergy and the Struggle for the Ten-Hour

Day.—Starvation". The word "socialism" given in the heading by the *New-York Daily Tribune* should be understood ironically, in the same sense in which Marx spoke of *The Times* attempting to declare the Free Trade principles of the bourgeois Tenant-Right League "Irish socialism". See his article "Defense.—Finances.—Decrease of the Aristocracy.—Politics" (this volume, p. 502). p. 522

322 See Note 228.   p. 522

323 This Act was examined by Engels in his articles "The Ten Hours' Question" and "The English Ten Hours' Bill" (see present edition, Vol. 10, pp. 271-76 and 288-300). However, these articles show that Marxist political economy had not yet been fully developed, as reflected in a certain underestimation of the positive consequences of legal limitation of the working day. Marx and Engels gave an exhaustive assessment of this Act in their later works, particularly Marx's "Inaugural Address of the International Working Men's Association" and *Capital* (Vol. I, Chapter X, Sections 5-7).   p. 524

324 See Note 219.   p. 526

325 The text of this article was reprinted, somewhat abridged, on April 16 in *The People's Paper* as two separate items: as a correspondent's report under the general heading "The American Press and the European Movement", containing the concluding sections of the original text, from "On the Continent heaven is fulminating" to the end, and an article entitled "Forced Emigration". The article was published giving the name of the author, "Dr. Marx", while the correspondent's report was published unsigned but with the editors' note: "From the *New-York Daily Tribune*". In a number of cases the use of italics does not coincide in the two newspapers; passages omitted in *The People's Paper* are indicated in footnotes in this volume. There are no other textual discrepancies.   p. 528

326 The article mentioned by Marx was not published in the *New-York Daily Tribune* and the manuscript is not extant.   p. 532

327 This refers to the plan to partition Poland proposed by Henry of Prussia when he visited St. Petersburg in 1770. Striving to preserve its influence over the whole of Poland, the tsarist government at first opposed this plan but the *rapprochement* between Prussia and Austria prompted Catherine II in 1772 to conclude a convention with them sharing part of the Polish territory between the three powers (first partition of Poland).   p. 533

328 See Note 7.   p. 533

329 See Note 305   p. 533

330 The reference is to articles by an English journalist, Alfred Bate Richards, published from December 1851 to November 1852 in *The Times* under the pen-name "Englishman".   p. 533

331 This article was published in the *New-York Daily Tribune* without a heading.
                                                                                    p. 535

332 The facts which Marx refers to were probably cited in his report of March 1, 1853, which he mentions in his article "Forced Emigration.—Kossuth and Mazzini.—

Refugee Question.—Election Bribery in England.—Mr. Cobden". This report is
not extant (see Note 326).   p. 535

[333] See Note 5.   p. 537

[334] The *Alien Bill*, enacted by the British Parliament in 1793, was renewed in 1802,
1803, 1816, 1818 and, finally, in 1848 in connection with revolutionary events
on the Continent and the Chartist demonstration on April 10. Enacted for one
year, this law authorised the deportation of aliens from England at any time by
decision of the government. In 1850 public opinion prevented the renewal of
this Bill despite Conservative efforts, which were repeated also in the following
years.   p. 538

[335] The long-standing quarrel between the Greek Orthodox Church and the Roman
Church over rights to the Christian Holy Places in Palestine was resumed in 1850
on Louis Bonaparte's initiative, with a view to strengthening France's positions in
the Middle East. It grew into a serious diplomatic conflict which served as a
pretext for the Crimean War.   p. 541

[336] By this time Marx and Engels had prepared an article, "British Policy.—
Disraeli.—Emigrants.—Mazzini in London.—Turkey", which was published on
April 7, 1853 in the *New-York Daily Tribune* and was the first of their articles
on the Eastern Question in this newspaper (see present edition, Vol. 12).
                                                                    p. 541

[337] This review of Proudhon's book, *Idée générale de la Révolution au XIX-e siècle*
(1851), containing many critical remarks, was written by Engels at the request
of Marx who had decided to write a polemical work against Proudhon. In
August 1851 Marx and Engels discussed Proudhon's book in many of their
letters. In his letter to Engels of August 8 Marx gave a detailed account of its
contents, citing large excerpts, and in mid-August he sent the book to Engels in
Manchester asking him for a detailed opinion on it. Engels worked on the review
in August (from about August 16 to 21) and from mid-October, and returned it to
Marx at the end of October. On November 24, 1851 Marx wrote to Engels: "I
have been through your critique again. It's a pity *qu'il n'y a pas moyen* [that there's
no means] of getting it printed. Otherwise—and if my own twaddle were added to
it—we could bring it out under both our names, provided this didn't upset your
firm in any way" (see present edition, Vol. 38).
   When Marx learned that Joseph Weydemeyer (who had emigrated to the
United States in the autumn of 1851) was going to publish the weekly *Die
Revolution* in New York beginning in January 1852, he decided to publish the
critique of Proudhon in that journal. On December 19, 1851 he asked
Weydemeyer to publish in his weekly an announcement of the forthcoming
publication of the *Neuste Offenbarungen des Sozialismus oder "Idée générale de la
Révolution au XIX-e siècle, par P. J. Proudhon."* *Kritik von K. M.* in the form of a
series of articles. In January 1852 the notice was published in the first issue of
Die Revolution, but the plan did not materialise. Until April 1852 Marx was
engrossed in writing *The Eighteenth Brumaire of Louis Bonaparte.* By that time
Die Revolution had already ceased to exist as a periodical due to the editor's lack
of funds.
   In this volume excerpts from Proudhon's book are printed in small
type, literal quotations being given in quotes while Engels' expositions of
Proudhon's text in German are not. Engels' own text is in ordinary type and

the emphasised words are italicised. The French quotations and the German text are translated into English; the French words and expressions used by Engels in his own text are reproduced in the original and supplied, whenever necessary, with translations in footnotes. Editorial insertions in square brackets are made only when there are obvious omissions in the text or when it is advisable to give Proudhon's terms in French besides their English translations. In the small-type text the words in ordinary italics are ones emphasised by Proudhon, those in heavy italics by Engels.

p. 545

338 *États généraux* (States-General)—in feudal France the supreme consultative body composed of representatives of the various estates. From 1614 they did not meet until 1789, when they proclaimed themselves the National Assembly.

p. 545

339 Proudhon here refers to a series of trials in 1822 of members of republican societies (including *carbonari*) who tried to foment anti-monarchist uprisings in Belfort, La Rochelle and Saumur, and to an uprising on May 12, 1839 in Paris. The May uprising, in which revolutionary workers played the leading part, was prepared by the secret republican-socialist Society of the Seasons led by Auguste Blanqui and Armand Barbès; it was suppressed by troops and the National Guard.

p. 546

340 The new electoral law which in fact abolished universal suffrage in France was adopted by the Legislative Assembly on May 31, 1850 (see this volume, p. 145, where Marx characterises this law).

p. 546

341 See Note 72.

p. 546

342 During the night of August 3, 1789 the French Constituent Assembly, under pressure from the growing peasant movement, announced the abrogation of a number of feudal obligations which had already been abolished by the insurgent peasants.

p. 547

343 Here and below Proudhon uses the terms *le préjugé gouvernemental, le système gouvernemental* and *l'évolution gouvernementale* to denote different aspects of the political system of government to which he counterposes the economic system, organisation of economic forces, invented and proposed by himself. p. 547

344 According to a medieval tradition which even the French Revolution was unable to do away with, the sale of meat in Paris was in the hands of a butchers' corporation that maintained low prices on livestock and high prices on meat. When speaking of "the sale of meat by auction" (*le vente de la viande à la criée*), Proudhon had in mind a series of measures carried out by the government from 1848 to liquidate the monopoly of the butchers' corporation (authorisation of daily trade in meat by people who did not belong to the corporation, etc.).

p. 549

345 Proudhon further discloses the meaning of the term "parasitism": "Parasitism is finance, abusive property, the budget and all that accompanies it" (pp. 51-52).

p. 549

346 Royer-Collard made this speech on January 22, 1822, when an anti-press bill was being debated in the Chamber of Deputies.

p. 552

347 On the French parliaments see Note 109.

p. 552

[348] The reference is to the *Charte octroyée* granted in 1814 by Louis XVIII. It was the fundamental law of the Bourbons, introducing a regime of moderate constitutional monarchy with wide powers for the king and high electoral qualifications ensuring above all political privileges for the landed aristocracy.
p. 552

[349] Proudhon goes on explaining his idea: "...This principle which is of all importance in the so-called butchers' associations has so little in common with the essence of the association that in many of these slaughter-houses the work is done by hired workers under the guidance of the director who represents the depositors."
p. 555

[350] Engels refers to the following footnote by Proudhon on pp. 97 and 98 of the book in question: "Reciprocity is not identical with exchange; meanwhile it increasingly tends to become the law of exchange and to mix up with it. A scientific analysis of this law was first given in a pamphlet, *Organisation du crédit et de la circulation* (Paris, 1848, Garnier frères), and the first attempt to apply it was made by the *People's Bank*."

The *People's Bank* (*La Banque du Peuple*) was founded by Proudhon in 1849 to implement the reforms he suggested in the sphere of credit and circulation which he saw as a means of solving the social question and establishing class harmony. By means of these reforms Proudhon hoped to liquidate loan-interest and to organise exchange without money while preserving private property in the means of production and the wages system. According to Proudhon, this peaceful process was to transform capitalism into a system of equality under which every member of society could become a free producer and exchange equal quantities of labour with others. The short-lived People's Bank only showed how groundless were Proudhon's projects both in theory and in practice.
p. 555

[351] Engels refers here to workers' associations permissible in Proudhon's system. While stressing the need for a reform in the sphere of credit and money circulation and for the maintenance of individual property in the means of production, Proudhon also admitted the need for the transfer of a number of big factories, railways, mines, etc., to associations of workers employed in them. Accordingly, Proudhon's term *compagnies ouvrières* is further translated as "workers' associations".
p. 556

[352] See Note 13.
p. 557

[353] The reference is to the Constituent National Assembly which held its sessions from May 4, 1848, and to the Legislative National Assembly which replaced it on May 28, 1849. Louis Bonaparte was elected President of the French Republic by universal suffrage on May 10, 1848.
p. 558

[354] The Jacobin Constitution, adopted by the Convention on June 24, 1793, proclaimed the freedom of person, religion, legislative initiative and the press, freedom to present petitions, and the right to work, to education, and to resist oppression while leaving private property intact. The difficult situation in the republic caused by foreign intervention and counter-revolutionary revolts made the Jacobins postpone the implementation of the constitution and temporarily introduce a democratic-revolutionary dictatorship. After the counter-

revolutionary coup d'état of the ninth Thermidor (July 27-28), 1794, the Constitution of 1793 was replaced in 1795 by a new qualification and anti-democratic constitution.
                                                                    p. 558

355 The reference is to the Bank of France founded in 1800 by a shareholders' company under Bonaparte's protection. It enjoyed a number of state privileges while remaining the property of the company. In 1848 this bank was granted the monopoly right to issue banknotes of small denomination; its monopoly position was also consolidated by the fact that provincial banks were deprived of the right to issue money.
                                                                    p. 559

356 In his letter to Engels on August 8, 1851, Marx wrote concerning this passage in Proudhon's book: "Instead of interest the state pays annuities, i.e. it repays in yearly quotas the capital it has been loaned" (see present edition, Vol. 38).
                                                                    p. 560

357 In accordance with the Constituent Assembly's decrees of January 15 and February 16 and 26, 1790, a new administrative division was introduced in France: the country was divided into 83 departments which, in their turn, were subdivided into cantons and the latter into communes.
                                                                    p. 560

358 Among the socialists Proudhon names Saint-Simon, Fourier, Owen, Cabet, Louis Blanc, and the Chartists.
                                                                    p. 563

359 The beginning of Chapter One of Pushkin's novel in verse *Yevgeny Onegin* is reproduced on the last page of Engels' manuscript. It corresponds to the Russian original though it is written in Latin letters. This is apparently connected with Engels' study of the Russian language which he began in Manchester in 1851 (see illustration between pages 564 and 565 in this volume).
                                                                    p. 570

360 In 1851 the Chartist weekly *Notes to the People* published two articles by Ernest Jones, the editor, on co-operation: "A Letter to the Advocates of the Co-operative Principle, and to the Members of Co-operative Societies" (No. 2, May 10, 1851), and "Co-operation. What It Is, and What It Ought to Be" (No. 21, September 20, 1851). They were written at a time when especially close, friendly relations had been established between Marx and Engels on the one hand and Ernest Jones, the Left-wing Chartist leader on the other. Marx and Engels constantly helped Jones in his fight for the revival of Chartism on a socialist basis, in his propaganda campaign and his work as publisher and editor of the Chartist papers, *Notes to the People* and, later, *The People's Paper*, by publicising these periodicals in their articles and contributing to them. Marx also helped Jones to write his articles, particularly on economics. On November 4, 1864 Marx wrote to Engels the following: "I happened to come across several numbers of E. Jones' *Notes to the People* (1851, 1852) which, as far as economic articles are concerned, had been written in the main points under my direction and in part even with my close participation. Well! What do I find there? That then we conducted the same polemic—only in a better way—against the co-operative movement, since in its present narrow-minded form it claimed to be the *latest word*, as ten to twelve years later Lassalle conducted in Germany against Schulze-Delitzsch."

The publication of Jones' articles on co-operation met with a response from Edward Vansittart Neale, a Christian socialist and prominent bourgeois co-operator. On October 11, 1851 the weekly published (issue No. 24) Neale's first letter and Jones' reply to it. Neale's second letter was published on November 15, 1851 (No. 29) and Jones' reply on November 22 (No. 30).

These two letters by Neale and Jones' replies to them show clearly the difference between the viewpoints of the Christian socialist and the proletarian revolutionary. The former saw the aim of the co-operative movement in distracting the workers from the class struggle and called for the collaboration of hostile classes and the reconciliation of their interests. Jones, supported by Marx, emphasised that from the viewpoint of the workers' liberation struggle peaceful co-operation had no prospect and that under capitalism workers' co-operative societies could not exist for long; they would not withstand competition on the part of big capital and would go bankrupt, or else they would turn into purely capitalist enterprises deriving profit from exploiting workers. The decisive condition, Jones said, for the workers' co-operative societies to be really of use to the working class was that the latter win political power in order to reorganise the existing system in the interest of the working people.

Of Jones' many articles on co-operation the two mentioned at the beginning of this note are included in this volume because they most vividly reflect the influence of Marx's views on Jones and show clearly that Marx in fact took part in writing them.   p. 573

361 See Note 226.   p. 580

362 The reference is to the funds of the Equitable Pioneers of Rochdale, a consumers' retail co-operative society founded by Rochdale workers in 1844. It was the embryo of the co-operative movement in England and other countries.
                                                          p. 581

363 This list of documents shows the efforts made by Marx and Engels to help the accused Communists in Cologne and their defence counsel to prove how unfounded were the charges fabricated against them by means of perjury, juggling with facts and forged material. The documents enumerated in the list were to provide the defence with material exposing the provocative actions of the police and judicial authorities. As addressees the list often mentions businessmen and trading houses which Marx and Engels used for safe dispatch of the documents to the defence counsels Schneider II, Esser I and Hontheim. Most of these conspiratorial addresses were supplied by Engels, making use of his commercial ties.

The calendar for July-October 1852 (in Engels' handwriting) at the end of the manuscript is not reproduced in this volume.   p. 590

364 In points 3 to 5 Engels lists the envelopes with commercial addresses which he sent to Marx in London on October 28 to be delivered to Hontheim, Esser I, Schneider II (see Engels' letter to Marx of October 28, 1852).

Point 6 refers to a letter from Marx which was sent via Düsseldorf to Schneider II at the address of a German merchant, an acquaintance of Freiligrath. The letter is not extant. On its contents see Marx's letter to Engels dated October 28, 1852.   p. 590

365 The following documents are listed:

1) Marx's letter of October 26, 1852 to the lawyer Schneider II which, in view of its importance, was sent to Cologne in four copies through different hands, including Weerth from Manchester (see Marx's letter to Engels of October 26, 1852); two other copies, besides the third spoken of in this point,

are mentioned by Engels in the list under No. 1 and No. 8; the letter has not been found.

2) A letter from Hermann Becker, one of the main accused at the trial, to Marx dated January 27, 1851 (see this volume, p. 452; it is also mentioned in point 8 of this document), and letters from Roland Daniels to Marx, written between February and May 1851, concerning his book *Mikrokosmos. Entwurf einer physiologischen Anthropologie*. The letters in question were written by Becker and Daniels prior to their arrest.

3) Cherval's statement, printed in *The People's Paper* after his escape to England arranged by the French police (see this volume, p. 418).

4) A letter from Stieber to Marx of December 26, 1848, quoted by Marx in his *Revelations Concerning the Communist Trial in Cologne* (see this volume, pp. 435-36); this letter is also mentioned in point 8.   p. 590

366 The reference is to the documents which Marx sent to Schneider II (through Hermann Jung living in Frankfurt am Main) proving that the "original minute-book" was a forgery and that Hirsch participated in its fabrication, and exposing Stieber's perjury (see this volume, pp. 426-35, and Marx's letter to Engels of October 28, 1852).   p. 590

367 This refers to the theft of the so-called Dietz archive (Dietz was secretary of the sectarian Willich-Schapper group that broke away from the Communist League) by Max Reuter, a Prussian police agent in London (see this volume, pp. 403-07).
                                    p. 591

368 This work was published in instalments in nine issues of the Chartist *People's Paper*, from the end of September 1852 until the end of the year. The articles were published unsigned under the editorial heading "Our Paris Correspondence". Their author was Georg Eccarius—a tailor from London, a close associate of Marx and an active member of the Communist League—which can be seen from Marx's letter to Adolf Cluss written in November 1853. This letter also shows that it was Marx who helped to get Eccarius to contribute to the Chartist paper and, most probably, looked through his writings in manuscript before Eccarius sent them to Jones. Marx and Engels rated highly Eccarius' intelligence and theoretical ability (see, for example, their opinion of Eccarius' article "Tailoring in London or the Struggle Between Big and Small Capital" in Volume 10 of the present edition, p. 485). Marx encouraged and assisted his literary activities in every possible way. There is no doubt that Marx also helped Eccarius to write this review, especially in examining the writings of different authors on the coup d'état of December 2, 1851. It is noteworthy that in assessing Victor Hugo's book on this subject Eccarius expresses ideas close to those which Marx himself expressed on the same subject later, in 1869, in the Preface to the second edition of *The Eighteenth Brumaire of Louis Bonaparte* (see present edition, Vol. 21). Eccarius' criticism of Proudhon's social projects in this review coincides with their assessment in the works of Marx and Engels (see, in particular, this volume, pp. 557-68).

The first, introductory, article of the series was printed in *The People's Paper* without the general heading, "A Review of the Literature on the *Coup d'État*", under which the ensuing articles were published. Four articles immediately following the introductory one were marked No. 1, No. 2, etc., while the remaining articles were not numbered. But the general heading and the editors' "to be continued" given in some cases show that the series was not only written but also published as a single work, of which the separate articles seemed to be chapters. Accordingly, in this volume the missing numbers (5-8) are added in square brackets. In the eighth and ninth articles Eccarius assesses Marx's *Eighteenth Brumaire of Louis Bonaparte.* (As distinct from the erroneous title of the first edition, *The Eighteenth Brumaire of Louis Napoleon,* he uses the right one which indicates that Marx took part in writing the "Review".) These articles, containing the most important excerpts from Chapter I of *The Eighteenth Brumaire,* acquainted the English reader with this outstanding work for the first time. Later, in his "Statement to the Editorial Boards of the Newspapers *Reform, Volkszeitung* and *Allgemeine Zeitung*" (November 7, 1859), Marx pointed out that his work *The Eighteenth Brumaire of Louis Bonaparte* "appeared in excerpts in the then London organ of the Chartists" (i.e. *The People's Paper*) (see present edition, Vol. 17).   p. 592

369 At the end of September 1852 the French police declared that an infernal machine had been discovered in Marseilles with which the conspirators wanted to kill Louis Bonaparte, who at the time was touring the South of France. The public regarded this communication as a crude farce providing an additional pretext for proclaiming Louis Bonaparte emperor.   p. 595

370 See Note 107.   p. 596

371 The reference is to Aesop's fable "The Shepherd Boy and the Wolf" in which the shepherd boy repeatedly raised false alarms by shouting that wolves were attacking the herd. After a number of such episodes, nobody responded to his cries for help when wolves really did attack the herd.   p. 598

372 This refers to the High Court in Bourges which passed severe sentences on the participants in the revolutionary events of May 15, 1848 (see Note 103), and to the courts-martial which dealt with the participants in the June uprising in Paris in 1848.   p. 602

373 See Note 42.   p. 606

374 See Note 42.   p. 608

375 On June 13, 1849 the Montagne organised a peaceful demonstration in Paris in protest against a violation of the Constitution—the dispatch of French troops against the Roman Republic. The demonstration was dispersed by troops.
                                                                               p. 608

376 On the *lazzaroni* see Note 105.
      Trasteverians—inhabitants of a district of Rome situated on the right bank of the Tiber.   p. 609

377 In this article Eccarius sets forth the contents of Chapter I of Marx's *The Eighteenth Brumaire of Louis Bonaparte,* in some places almost literally. Further he cites a long quotation in his own translation, embracing, except for one paragraph, the concluding part of this chapter (see this volume, pp. 106-12). Eccarius' translation differs from that accepted in modern English publications and from the translation in this volume. The use of italics in the passage quoted by Eccarius does not coincide with that in the original.   p. 617

378 See Note 71.   p. 618

[379] This and the following document include an appeal to the German workers in America written by Marx in the name of a committee founded by him in London for aid to the Communists sentenced in Cologne. On December 7, 1852 Marx wrote to Adolf Cluss in Washington: "Herewith also an appeal for money for the Cologne prisoners and their families. See that it appears in various papers. It might also be a good idea for you too to form committees over there. Here it is being done as a party demonstration. You will observe that Ernest Jones actually appears as a party member. In an introductory note, signed by you both, you might specially emphasise that this is not a case of raising revolutionary funds Kinkel-fashion, etc., but rather of a *definite* party aim whose fulfilment is demanded by the honour of a workers' party" (see present edition, Vol. 39).   p. 621

[380] The letter accompanying the appeal was written in the name of the Washington branch of the Socialist Gymnastic Association (*Sozialistischer Turnverein*), an organisation of the German democratic emigrants in the USA founded at a congress of German gymnastic societies in Philadelphia on October 5, 1850. In the early stage of its activity the Association maintained contacts with the German labour movement in America. Joseph Weydemeyer and Adolf Cluss contributed to its periodical, *Turnzeitung*. During the American Civil War it took an active part in the struggle against the slave-owning states. In 1865 it was renamed North-American Gymnastic Association.   p. 621

NAME INDEX

A

Aberdeen, George Hamilton, Earl of (1784-1860)—British statesman, Tory, from 1850 leader of the Peelites, Foreign Secretary (1828-30, 1841-46) and Prime Minister of the coalition cabinet (1852-55).—471-75, 478, 501, 503-04, 510, 512, 516, 538

Abraham a Sancta Clara (real name *Ulrich Megerle*) (1644-1709)—Austrian Catholic preacher and popular humorous writer.—317, 319-20

Acquaviva, Claudio (1543-1615)—General of the Society of Jesus (1581-1615).—521

Aesop (6th cent. B.C.)—semi-legendary Greek author of fables.—107

Agesilaus (c. 442-c. 360 B.C.)—King of Sparta (c. 398-c. 360 B.C.), brother of Agis II.—163

Agis II—King of Sparta (c. 427-c. 400 B.C.), elder brother of Agesilaus.—163

Agostini, Cesare (1803-1855)—Italian revolutionary, follower of Mazzini; participant in the 1848-49 revolution in Italy; refugee in England; subsequently departed from Mazzini.—515

Ailly, Pierre d' (1350-1420)—French cardinal, played an important role at the Council of Constance.—194

Alexander of Macedon (Alexander the Great) (362-323 B.C.)—military leader and statesman; King of Macedon (336-323 B.C.).—151

Alexander, John—Irish politician, M.P. (1853).—486

Allais, Louis Pierre Constant (born c. 1821)—French police agent.—150, 154

Amelot de la Houssaye, Abraham Nicolas (1634-1706)—French writer, author of *Histoire du gouvernement de Venise.*—503

Anglas—see *Boissy d'Anglas*

Angoulême, Marie Thérèse Charlotte, duchesse d' (1778-1851)—daughter of Louis XVI.—596

Anneke, Friedrich (1818-1872)—Prussian artillery officer, discharged from the army for his political views; member of the Communist League; one of the founders of the Cologne Workers' Association in 1848; editor of the *Neue Kölnische Zeitung*; member of the Rhenish District Committee of Democrats.—252

Antoine, Gustav—French émigré in London in the early 1850s; son-in-law of Auguste Blanqui.—296
Antonelli, Giacomo (1806-1876)—Italian cardinal, adviser to Pius IX; virtually

Hungarian revolutionary army (1848-49); after the defeat of the revolution emigrated to Turkey.—60, 300

Benoist (Benoît) d'Azy, Denis, comte (1796-1880)—French politician, financier and industrialist; Vice-President of the Legislative Assembly (1849-51); Legitimist.—162, 166

Béranger, Pierre Jean de (1780-1857)—French poet, wrote many satirical songs on political subjects; democrat.—200, 609

Beresford, William (b. 1798)—English politician, Tory, M.P., Secretary of War (March-December 1852).—337, 343, 466

Berkeley, Francis Henry Fitzhardinge (1794-1870)—English liberal politician, M.P. (1837).—340

Bermbach, Adolph (1821-1875)—Cologne lawyer, democrat, deputy to the Frankfurt National Assembly; witness for the defence in the Cologne Communist trial (1852); corresponded with Marx.—422, 424, 425, 426, 428, 590

Bernal Osborne, Ralph (1808-1882)—British liberal politician, M.P., Secretary of the Admiralty (1852-58).—473, 475, 600

Bernal, Ralph (d. 1854)—British politician, Whig, M.P., Chairman of Committees of the House of Commons (1830s-1850s).—350

Bernard—French colonel, headed military commissions meting out reprisals against the participants in the June 1848 uprising in Paris; after the coup d'état on December 2, 1851 took part in organising trials of republicans.—118-19

Berryer, Pierre Antoine (1790-1868)—French lawyer and politician, deputy to the Constituent and Legislative Assemblies during the Second Republic, Legitimist.—129, 144, 160, 166, 168, 170, 173, 594

Bettina—see Arnim, Bettina (Elisabeth) von

Bianca, von—Cologne patrician; juryman in the Cologne Communist trial (1852).—400

Billault, Augustin Adolphe Marie (1805-1863)—French politician, moderate monarchist, in later years a Bonapartist.—162

Birnbaum, Wilhelm—secretary of the organisation for the relief of the poor in Cologne, witness for the defence in the Cologne Communist trial (1852).—427, 429

Blanc, Jean Joseph Louis (1811-1882)—French socialist, historian; member of the Provisional Government and President of the Luxembourg Commission in 1848; pursued a policy of conciliation with the bourgeoisie; emigrated to England in August 1848 and became one of the leaders of the petty-bourgeois emigration in London.—6, 103, 295-97, 552, 555-58

Blanqui, Louis Auguste (1805-1881)—French revolutionary, utopian Communist; organised a number of secret societies and plots; adhered to the extreme Left of the democratic and proletarian movement during the 1848 revolution.—110, 183, 295, 296, 545, 593, 606, 607

Bleek, Friedrich (1793-1859)—German Protestant theologian, professor of Bonn University.—229

Blind, Karl (1826-1907)—German democratic journalist, active in the revolutionary movement in Baden in 1848-49; one of the leaders of the German petty-bourgeois emigration in London in the 1850s; became a national-liberal in the 1860s.—272

Blondel de Néelle—French troubadour at the end of the twelfth and the beginning of the thirteenth century; according to tradition, Richard the Lionheart's court poet, who freed the King from Austrian captivity.—257

Blum, Robert (1807-1848)—German democrat, journalist, leader of the Left in the Frankfurt National Assem-

man robber nicknamed *Schinderhannes* (Hans the Flayer).—419

Buhl, Ludwig Heinrich Franz (1814-c. 1882)—German writer, Young Hegelian, author of pamphlets in the *Patriot* series.—306

Bulwer—see *Lytton, Edward George*

Bunsen, Christian Karl Josias, Baron von (1791-1860)—Prussian diplomat, writer and theologian; Ambassador to London (1842-54).—540

Bürgers, Heinrich (1820-1878)—German journalist, contributor to the *Rheinische Zeitung* (1842-43), member of the Cologne community of the Communist League (1848), one of the editors of the *Neue Rheinische Zeitung.*—210, 211, 399, 400, 402, 449, 457

Buridan, Jean (1300-1358)—French philosopher.—178, 245

Burritt, Elihu (1810-1879)—American linguist, philanthropist and pacifist, organiser of several international pacifist congresses.—283

Butler, Samuel (1612-1680)—English satirical poet, author of the poem *Hudibras.*—486

Byron, George Gordon Noel, Lord (1788-1824)—English romantic poet.—600

C

Cabet, Étienne (1788-1856)—French writer, utopian Communist, author of *Voyage en Icarie.*—295, 552

Caesar, Gaius Julius (c. 100-44 B.C.)—Roman general and statesman.—104, 262, 284, 321, 412, 503

Caligula, Gaius Caesar (A.D. 12-41)—Roman Emperor (37-41); was enthroned by the praetorian guard.—122

Cambridge, George William Frederick Charles. Duke of (1819-1904)—British general, commander-in-chief of the British army (1856-95).—340

Camphausen, Ludolf (1803-1890)—German banker, a leader of the Rhenish liberal bourgeoisie, Prime Minister of Prussia from March to June 1848.—36, 39, 45-46, 66, 260

Canning, George (1770-1827)—British statesman, Tory, Foreign Secretary (1807-09, 1822-27), Prime Minister (1827).—200, 500

Caperon, Paulin—French émigré, member of the Committee of the French society of Blanquist emigrants in London in the early 1850s.—294

Cardwell, Edward Cardwell, Viscount (1813-1886)—British statesman; a Peelite leader, later a Liberal; President of the Board of Trade (1852-55), Chief Secretary for Ireland (1859-61), Secretary for the Colonies (1864-66) and Secretary for War (1868-74).—332, 350, 510

Carlier, Pierre Charles Joseph (1799-1858)—Prefect of the Paris police (1849-51), Bonapartist.—140, 150, 156, 177, 407-09, 412, 549

Carnot, Lazare Hippolyte (1801-1888)—French writer and politician.—144

Cassius, Gaius (d. 42 B.C.)—Roman politician, people's tribune.—503

Catherine II (1729-1796)—Russian Empress (1762-96).—533

Catiline, (Lucius Sergius Catilina) (c. 108-62 B.C.)—Roman politician, organiser of a conspiracy against the aristocratic republic.—375, 445

Cato, Marcus Porcius (Cato the Elder) (234-149 B.C.)—Roman statesman and writer, upheld aristocratic privileges; in 184 B.C. was elected censor, the strictness of his censorship became proverbial.—197, 318

Caussidière, Marc (1808-1861)—French democrat, took part in the Lyons uprising of 1834; Prefect of the Paris police after the February revolution of 1848; deputy to the Constituent Assembly; emigrated to England in June 1848.—103

INDEX OF LITERARY AND MYTHOLOGICAL NAMES

Figaro—the main character in Beaumarchais' comedy *La folle journée, ou le mariage de Figaro.*—414

Fleur de Marie—heroine in Eugène Sue's novel *Les Mystères de Paris,* a girl who grew up among criminals but preserved her purity and noble-mindedness; Sue gave her the name of lily, a flower which grows in dirty swamps but has snow-white petals.—442

Habakkuk (Bib.)—a prophet.—105

Hecuba (Gr. *Hekabe*)—wife of the Trojan King Priam, mother of Hector and Paris.—235

Hudibras—the title character in Samuel Butler's satirical poem, a man inclined to meaningless arguments and debates and capable of proving the most absurd propositions with the help of syllogisms.—486

Israel (Bib.).—231, 232

Janus (Rom. myth.)—god represented with two faces looking in opposite directions.—309

Jehovah (Bib.).—608

Jeremiah (Bib.)—a prophet who in his Lamentations mourns the destruction of Jerusalem.—297

Jesus—see *Christ, Jesus*

Jobs—hero of Karl Arnold Kortum's *Die Jobsiade. Ein komisches Heldengedicht,* a satirical poem popular in the late eighteenth and early nineteenth centuries.—283

John Bull—the title character in John Arbuthnot's book *The History of John Bull* (18th cent.). His name is often used to personify England.—198

Jonah (Bib.).—412

Judas (Bib.)—the apostle who betrayed Christ for thirty silver coins.—303

Jupiter (*Jove*)—supreme god of. the Romans, corresponding to the Greek god Zeus.—235

Krapülinski (*Crapulinski*)—one of the main characters in Heine's poem *Zwei Ritter,* a spendthrift Polish nobleman (the name comes from the French word *crapule* meaning gluttony, hard drinking as well as base scoundrel, idler).—112, 620

Lorelei—heroine of a popular legend which was widely used by German poets; a synonym of baneful, indifferent beauty.—245

Mahadeva (*Mahadö*)—"great god", the nickname of Shiva, one of the chief Indian gods.—235

Mammon—wealth or the idol of wealth among some ancient peoples.—514

Mary (Bib.).—232, 237

Matthew (Bib.)—one of the four evangelists.—106, 141, 196, 406

Mephistopheles—a character in Goethe's tragedy *Faust* and Marlowe's play *The Tragical History of Doctor Faustus.*—230, 604-05

Methuselah—a Biblical patriarch who is stated to have lived 969 years; his name is a synonym of longevity.—500, 538

Moor, Karl—hero of Schiller's drama *Die Räuber.*—419

Moses (Bib.).—171, 449, 575

Narcissus (Gr. myth.)—a handsome youth who fell in love with his own reflection in the water; figuratively: a man absorbed in his own personal perfections.—233

Nestor (Gr. myth.)—the oldest and wisest of the Greek heroes who took part in the Trojan War.—372

Noah (Bib.).—230, 232

Odysseus—the title character in Homer's poem.—64, 258

Ofterdingen, Heinrich von—the title character in Novalis' unfinished novel, a romantic poet who spent his life in

INDEX OF QUOTED
AND MENTIONED LITERATURE

WORKS BY KARL MARX AND FREDERICK ENGELS

Marx, Karl

The Class Struggles in France, 1848 to 1850 (present edition, Vol. 10)
— Die Klassenkämpfe in Frankreich 1848 bis 1850 (published in 1850 under the title "1848 bis 1849"). In: *Neue Rheinische Zeitung. Politisch-ökonomische Revue,* No. 1, January 1850; No. 2, February 1850; No. 3, March 1850; No. 5-6, May to October 1850.—119

Contribution to the Critique of Hegel's Philosophy of Law. Introduction (present edition, Vol. 3)
— Zur Kritik der Hegelschen Rechtsphilosophie. Einleitung. In: *Deutsch-Französische Jahrbücher,* hrsg. von A. Ruge und K. Marx, 1-ste und 2-te Lieferung, Paris, 1844.—269

Corruption at Elections (this volume). In: *New-York Daily Tribune,* No. 3552, September 4, 1852.—348

The Defeat of the Ministry (this volume). In: *New-York Daily Tribune,* No. 3659, January 7, 1853.—474

Defense.—Finances.—Decrease of the Aristocracy.—Politics (this volume). In: *New-York Daily Tribune,* No. 3699, February 23, 1853.—524

The Eighteenth Brumaire of Louis Bonaparte (this volume)
— Der achtzehnte Brumaire des Louis Bonaparte. In: *Die Revolution,* Erstes Heft, New York, 1852.—595, 615

Elections.—Financial Clouds.—The Duchess of Sutherland and Slavery (this volume). In: *New-York Daily Tribune,* No. 3687, February 9, 1853.—529

Kossuth, Mazzini, and Louis Napoleon (this volume). In: *New-York Daily Tribune,* No. 3627, December 1, 1852.—465

Movements of Mazzini and Kossuth.—League with Louis Napoleon.—Palmerston (this volume). In: *New-York Daily Tribune,* No. 3590, October 19, 1852.—382, 465

On the Jewish Question (present edition, Vol. 3)
— Zur Judenfrage. In: *Deutsch-Französische Jahrbücher,* hrsg. von A. Ruge und K. Marx, 1-ste und 2-te Lieferung, Paris, 1844.—269

Political Consequences of the Commercial Excitement (this volume). In: *New-York Daily Tribune,* No. 3602, November 2, 1852.—459

[*Public Statement to the Editors of the English Press.*] London, October 28, 1852 (this volume). In: *The Morning Advertiser,* October 30, 1852.—380

Statement on Resignation from the German Workers' Educational Society in London, London, September 17, 1850 (present edition, Vol. 10)
— Erklärung über den Austritt aus dem Deutschen Bildungsverein für Arbeiter in London, London, 17. September 1850. Manuscript.—427

WORKS BY DIFFERENT AUTHORS

Aberdeen, G. [Speech in the House of Lords on December 27, 1852.] In: *The Times,* No. 21310, December 28, 1852.—472, 475

Acquaviva, Claudio. *Industriae ad curandos animae morbos,* Florentiae, 1600.—521

Amelot de la Houssaye. *Histoire du gouvernement de Venise,* Paris, 1676.—503

Antoine, G. À. M. *le rédacteur du journal "La Patrie"* [le 6 mars 1851]. In: *La Patrie,* No. 66, March 7, 1851.—296

Ariosto, L. *L'Orlando furioso.*—274, 315

Athenaeus Deipnosophistai. Ex Recensione Guilielmo Dindorfii, Lipsiae, 1827.—163

Balzac, H. *Cousine Bette.*—196

Barthélemy, E. *Au rédacteur en chef du journal "La Patrie"* [le 8 mars 1851]. In: *La Patrie,* No. 71, March 12, 1851.—295

Batrachomyomachia, die blutige und mutige Schlacht der Mäuse und Frösche, mit Fleiss beschrieben, lustig und lieblich zu lesen von I. H. Wolterstorf, Hamburg, 1784.—311

Beaumarchais, P.A.C. de. *La folle journée, ou le mariage de Figaro.*—414, 434, 452

Beckmann. [Notice sent from Paris on February 25, 1852.] In: *Kölnische Zeitung,* No. 51, February 28, 1852.—415

Béranger, P. J. de. *Les Mirmidons, ou les funérailles d'Achille.*—200

Bible

  The Old Testament
    Genesis.—527
    Exodus.—105
    Joshua.—132
    The Wisdom of Solomon.—46
    Ezekiel.—193
    Jonah.—412

  The New Testament
    Matthew.—106, 141, 305, 617
    Apocalypse. The Revelations of St. John.—421

Blanc, L. *To the Editor of "The Times",* London, March 3. In: *The Times,* No. 20741, March 5, 1851.—295
— *Un homme et une doctrine.* In: *Le Nouveau Monde,* No. 6, December 15, 1849.—555

[Blanqui, L.-A.] *Toste envoyé par le citoyen L.-A. Blanqui à la commission près les réfugiés de Londres, pour le banquet anniversaire du 24 février.* In: *La Patrie,* No. 58, February 27, 1851.—295

Boiardo, M.M. *Orlando innamorato.*—274, 310, 326

Bonaparte, N.-L. *Des idées napoléoniennes,* Paris, 1839.—140, 190, 191, 192

Brentano, C. *Gockel, Hinkel und Gackeleia. Ein Mährchen.* In: *Clemens Brentano's Gesammelte Schriften,* hrsg. von Ch. Brentano, Bd. 5, Frankfurt a. M., 1852.—243

Bright, J. [Speech at a banquet in Belfast on October 4, 1852.] In: *The Times,* No. 21240, October 7, 1852.—372
— [Speech at a banquet in Manchester of January 7, 1853.] In: *The Times.* No. 21321, January 10, 1853.—478

Butler, S. *Hudibras, a Poem written in the Time of the Civil Wars,* Vols. 1-3, London, 1757.—486

Cicero, M. T. *De divinatione et de fato.*—318
— *De natura deorum,* Lib. 3.—526
— *Orationes in Lucium Catilinam.*—445

Cobden, R. [Speech in the House of Commons on February 18, 1853.] In: *The Times,* No. 21356, February 19, 1853.—518
— *1793 and 1853, in Three Letters,* London, 1853.—497, 498, 533

Cooke, G. W. *The History of Party; from the Rise of the Whig and Tory Factions, in the Reign of Charles II, to the Passing of the Reform Bill,* Vols. 1-3, London, 1836-1837.—329

Cranworth, R. [Speech in the House of Lords on February 14, 1853.] In: *The Times,* No. 21352, February 15, 1853.—517

Dalrymple, J. *An Essay towards a General History of Feudal Property in Great Britain...* (second edition), London, 1758.—493

Dante, Alighieri. *La Divina commedia.*—539

Danton, J. [Speech in the Legislative Assembly on September 2, 1792.] In: *Gazette nationale, ou le Moniteur universel,* No. 248, September 4, 1792.—86

Della Rocco. *Mazzini's Proclamation* (To the Editor of *The Daily News*). In: *The Daily News,* February 21, 1853.—515

Derby, E. [Speeches in the House of Lords:]
— March 15, 1852. In: *The Times,* No. 21064, March 16, 1852.—374
— May 24, 1852. In: *The Times,* No. 21124, May 25, 1852.—349
— December 20, 1852. In: *The Times,* No. 21304, December 21, 1852.—472

Dickens, Ch. *Gottfried Kinkel; A Life in Three Pictures.* In: *Household Words,* No. 32, November 2, 1850.—258

Diderot, D. *Rameau's Neffe.* In: *Goethe's Werke,* Bd. 1-20, Stuttgart und Tübingen, 1815-1819, Bd. 20.—260

Disraeli, B. [Address to the electors of the County of Buckingham, March 1, 1852.] In: *The Times,* No. 21052, March 2, 1852: "The New Chancellor of the Exchequer and His Constituencies".—460
— [Speech at a dinner arranged by the electors of the County of Buckingham on March 12, 1852.] In: *The Times,* No. 21062, March 13, 1852.—460
— [Address to the electors of the County of Buckingham, June 2, 1852.] In: *The Times,* No. 21135, June 7, 1852.—349, 364

— [Speech at a dinner arranged by the electors of the County of Buckingham on July 14, 1852.] In: *The Times*, No. 21168, July 15, 1852.—349, 364
— [Speeches in the House of Commons:]
— November 11, 1852. In: *The Times*, No. 21271, November 12, 1852.—460
— December 3, 1852. In: *The Times*, No. 21290, December 4, 1852: "The Financial Statement".—460
— December 16, 1852. In: *The Times*, No. 21301, December 17, 1852.—467
— February 18, 1853. In: *The Times*, No. 21356, February 19, 1853.—519

Dupont. *Chronique de l'Intérieur*, Londres, le 10 décembre, 1850. In: *La Voix du Proscrit*, No. 8, December 15, 1850.—196

Durrieu, X. *Le coup d'état de Louis Bonaparte*, Genève et New York [1852].—595, 596

Gammage, R. G. *Respectable Democracy*. In: *The People's Paper*, No. 23, October 9, 1852.—376

[Goegg, Amand.] *Rückblick auf die Badische Revolution unter Hinweisung auf die gegenwärtige Lage Teutschlands*. Von einem Mitgliede der Badischen constituirenden Versammlung, Paris, 1851.—263, 308-10

Goethe, J.W. von. *Anmerkungen über Personen und Gegenstände, deren in dem Dialog Rameau's Neffe erwähnt wird.*—306
— *Elegien.*—237, 238
— *Erlkönig.*—122
— *Faust. Der Tragödie, Erster Teil.*—108, 230, 316, 456, 604
— *Der Gott und die Bajadere.*—235
— *Die Leiden des jungen Werthers.*—256
— *Die Wahlverwandtschaften.*—245
— *Wilhelm Meisters Lehrjahre.*—230
— *Zahme Xenien.*—237

Graham, J. [Speech at a meeting of electors of the Carlisle Constituency on January 2, 1853.] In: *The Times*, No. 21315, January 3, 1853.—499

Granier de Cassagnac. *Récit populaire des evénements de décembre 1851*, Paris, 1852.—597

Grimm, Jacob and Wilhelm. *Tischlein deck dich, Esel streck dich, Knüppel aus dem Sack.*—277

[Hansemann, D.] [*Rede in der Sitzung der ersten Vereinigten Landtages am 8. Juni 1847.*] In: *Der Erste Vereinigte Landtag in Berlin 1847*, Th. 3.—294

Harring, Harro. *Blutstropfen*. Deutsche Gedichte, Strassburg, 1832.—285
— *Historisches Fragment über die Entstehung der Arbeiter-Vereine und ihren Verfall in Communistische Speculationen*, London, 1852.—284-89
— *Die Monarchie, oder die Geschichte vom König Saul*, Strassburg, 1832.—285
— *Männer-Stimmen, zu Deutschlands Einheit*. Deutsche Gedichte, Strassburg, 1832.—285
— *Poesie eines Scandinaven*, Rio de Janeiro, Montevideo, 1843.—285, 286, 288, 289
— *Sendschreiben an die "Schleswig-Holsteiner"*, 29. November 1850.—289
— *Sendschreiben an die Scandinaven und an die Deutschen*, 3. Februar 1851.—289
— *Das Volk*. Dramatische Szenen, Th. 1, Strassburg, 1832.—286
— *Die Völker*. Ein dramatisches Gedicht, Strassburg, 1832.—285
— *Worte eines Menschen*. Dem Gläubigen von La Mennais gewidmet, Strassburg, 1834.—286

— *The Reign of the Tories.* In: *The People's Paper*, No. 15, August 14, 1852.—343

Kinkel, G. [*Der Brief an die Bürger von St. Louis.*] In: *Bremer Tages-Chronik*, No. 507, February 25, 1851.—304
— *Gedichte*, Stuttgart and Tübingen, 1843.—238, 248
— *Handwerk, errette Dich! oder Was soll der deutsche Handwerker fordern und thun, um seinen Stand zu bessern?*, Bonn, 1848.—249
— *Mein Vermächtnis.* In: Strodtmann, A. *Gottfried Kinkel. Wahrheit ohne Dichtung,* Bd. 2, Hamburg, 1851.—254
— *Eine Rede Kinkel's* [13. März 1851]. In: *Bremer Tages-Chronik,* No. 531, March 25, 1851.—297
  Vertheidigungsrede des Dr. G. Kinkel vor dem preussischen Kriegsgericht zu Rastatt am 4. August 1849. In: *Abend-Post*, Nos. 78 and 79, April 5 and 6, 1850; Strodtmann, A. *Gottfried Kinkel. Wahrheit ohne Dichtung,* Bd. 2, Hamburg, 1851.—254
— [*Vertheidigungsrede vor dem Geschworenengerichte zu Köln am 2. Mai 1850.*] In: Strodtmann, A. *Gottfried Kinkel. Wahrheit ohne Dichtung,* Bd. 2, Hamburg, 1851.—256

Kinkel, J. [*Auszug aus dem Brief.*] In: *Kölnische Zeitung,* No. 114, May 13, 1851.—302
— *Lebenslauf eines Johannisfünkchens.* In: *Erzählungen* von Gottfried und Johanna Kinkel, Stuttgart and Tübingen, 1849.—256

Klopstock, F. G. *Der Messias,* Bd. 1-4.—229

Kock, P. de. *L'amant de la lune,* Paris, s.a.—269

Kortum, K. A. *Die Jobsiade.* Ein komisches Heldengedicht.—283

Kossuth, L. *In the Name of the Hungarian Nation.— To the Soldiers Quartered in Italy.* In: *The Times,* No. 21348, February 10, 1853.—508, 535
— [Letter to Captain Mayne Reid, early March 1853.] In: *The Leader,* No. 154, March 5, 1853: "Mazzini and Kossuth; the Authenticity of the Proclamation".—535

Kotzebue, A. von. *Menschenhass und Reue.* Schauspiel in fünf Aufzügen.—239

Lamartine, A. de. *Voyage en Orient, 1832-1833,* Paris, 1841.—600

Las Cases. *Mémorial de Sainte-Hélène, ou journal où se trouve consigné, jour par jour, ce qu'a dit et fait Napoléon durant dix-huit mois,* Paris, 1823-1824.—182

Ledru-Rollin, A. [Speech in the Legislative Assembly on June 11, 1849.] In: *Le Moniteur universel,* No. 163, June 12, 1849.—131

Loch, J. *An Account of the Improvements on the Estates of the Marquess of Stafford, in the Counties of Stafford and Salop, and on the Estate of Sutherland.* With remarks, London, 1820.—491

Lucretius, C. T. *De rerum natura,* Lipsiae, 1801.—511

Luther, M. *Der Welt Bild.* In: Luther, M. *Tischreden oder Colloquia. Anhang.*—422

Marlowe, Ch. *The Tragical History of Doctor Faustus.*—604

Mazzini, G. [Letter to the editors of the English newspapers] (n.d.), published on March 2, 1853 in *The Morning Advertiser, The Morning Post* and *The Daily News.* In: *The Morning Advertiser,* March 2, 1853: "Mazzini and Kossuth.—The Recent Proclamation".—532, 535

Mazzini, G., Saffi, A. *Italian National Committee.* In: *The Times,* No. 21350, February 12, 1853.—508

Miller, J. M. *Siegwart.* Eine Klostergeschichte.—229

Molinari, G. de. *Un nouveau manifeste rouge.* In: *La Patrie,* No. 332, November 28, 1850.—294

Montalembert, Ch. [Speech in the Legislative Assembly on May 22, 1850.] In: *Compte rendu des séances de l'Assemblée nationale législative,* T. 8, Paris, 1850.—192

Morus, Th. *De optimo statu rei publicae deque nova insula Utopia,* Louvanii, 1516. The first English translation was published in 1551.—493

Peel, R. [Speech in the House of Commons on February 24, 1853.] In: *The Times,* No. 21361, February 25, 1853.—523

Plato. *Politeia.*—531

Proudhon, P.-J. *Aux citoyens Ledru-Rollin, Charles Delescluze, Martin Bernard, et consorts, Rédacteurs du "Proscrit", à Londres,* 20 juillet 1850. In: *Le Peuple de 1850,* No. 2, July 1850.—134

— *Banque du peuple, suivie du rapport de la commission des délégués du Luxembourg...,* Paris, 1849.—555
— *Idée générale de la Révolution au XIXe siècle* (Choix d'études sur la pratique révolutionnaire et industrielle), Paris, 1851.—545-70
— *Organisation du crédit et de la circulation et solution du problème social...,* Paris, 1849.—555
— *Qu'est-ce que la propriété? Ou recherches sur le principe du droit et du gouvernement,* Paris, 1841.—493, 553-55
— *La révolution sociale démontrée par le coup d'état du 2 décembre,* Paris, 1852.—595, 604, 607-09, 611, 613

Prutz, R. E. *Gedichte,* Leipzig, 1841.—268

Quételet, A. *Sur l'homme et le développement de ses facultés, ou Essai de physique sociale,* T. 1-2, Paris, 1835.—496, 497

Ricardo, D. *On the Principles of Political Economy, and Taxation,* s.l., 1817.—529

[Richards, A. B.] [Letter of A. B. Richards to Cobden, signed "*Englishman*".] In: *The Morning Advertiser,* February 24, 1853.—533

Romieu, A. *Le spectre rouge de 1852,* Bruxelles, 1851.—125

Rotteck, C. von. *Allgemeine Weltgeschichte für alle Stände, von den frühesten Zeiten bis zum Jahre 1831, mit Zugrundelegung seines grösseren Werkes,* Bd. 1-4, Stuttgart, 1832-1833.—262, 263, 301

Rotteck, C. von, und Welcker, C. *Das Staats-Lexikon. Encyklopaedie der sämmtlichen Staatswissenschaften für alle Stände,* Bd. 1-12, Altona, 1845-1848.—262, 281

Ruge, A. (anon.) *An das deutsche Volk!* In: *Die Preussische Revolution seit dem siebenten September und die Contrerevolution seit dem zehnten November,* Leipzig, 1848.—272
— (anon.) *The German Democratic Party.* 1. The Origin and Elements of the Party. 2. The Revolution and the Present Condition of Parties and of the Nation. In: *The Leader,* Nos. 39 and 40, December 21 and 28, 1850.—273

— *Gesammelte Schriften,* Bd. 1-2, Th. 3-4, Mannheim, 1848.—267, 270, 273
— *A letter from Dr. Arnold Ruge, member for Breslau in the German Parliament, at Frankfort.* Presented by the Delegates from Brighton to the Peace Congress assembled at Frankfort, August, 1850.—283
— *Motivirtes Manifest der radical-demokratischen Partei in der constituirenden National-versammlung zu Frankfurt am Main.* In: *Die Reform,* No. 66, June 7, 1848.—271
— *Die Religion unsrer Zeit,* Leipzig, 1849.—273
— *Unsre letzten zehn Jahre Ueber die neueste deutsche Philosophie an einen Franzosen.* In: *Arnold Ruge's sämmtliche Werke.* 2 Aufl., Bd. 6, Mannheim, 1848.—267, 270
— *Wahl-Manifest der radicalen Reformpartei für Deutschland.* In: *Die Reform,* No. 16, April 16, 1848.—270

Russell, J. [Speech at a banquet in Perth on September 24, 1852.] In: *The Times,* No. 21231, September 27, 1852.—371, 373
— [Speech in the House of Commons on February 10, 1853.] In *The Times,* No. 21349, February 11, 1853.—510-11
— *Don Carlos; or, Persecution.* A tragedy in five acts (and in verse), London, 1822.—477
— *Memoirs of the Affairs of Europe from the "Peace of Utrecht",* Vols. 1-2, London, 1824-1829.—477

Saffi, A. [Letter of February 1853 to *Italia e Popolo.*] In: *The Daily News,* March 9, 1853.—536

Saint-Arnaud, A. de. [Speech in the Legislative Assembly on November 17, 1851.] In: *Le Moniteur universel,* November 18, 1851.—123

Schiller, F. von. *An die Freude.*—156
— *Die Bürgschaft.* Ballade.—163, 264, 307
— *Kabale und Liebe.* Ein bürgerliches Trauerspiel.—239
— *Lied von der Glocke.*—252
— *Die Piccolomini.*—432
— *Die Räuber.* Ein Schauspiel.—150
— *Die Sonntagskinder.*—455

Schramm, R. *Der Standpunkt der Demokratie in und zur octroyirten zweiten Kammer,* Berlin, 1849.—261

Schramm, R., Struve, G. *Entwurf eines Rundschreibens an deutsche Demokraten, als Manuscript gedruckt.* Begleitschreiben an die Führer [London, 1850].—260

Shakespeare, W. *Hamlet.*—185, 614
— *As You Like It.*—159
— *Julius Caesar.*—440
— *King Richard III.*—165
— *A Midsummer Night's Dream.*—149, 445

Sismondi, J.-C.-L. Simonde de. *Études sur l'économie politique,* T. 1-2, Paris, 1837-1838.—493
— *Nouveaux principes d'économie politique ou de la richesse dans ses rapports avec la population.* Seconde édition, Paris, 1827.—529

Smith, A. *An Inquiry into the Nature and Causes of the Wealth of Nations,* Vols. 1-2, London, 1776.—491

Somers, R. *Letters from the Highlands; or, the Famine of 1847,* London, 1848.—494

Stein, L. von. *Der Socialismus und Communismus des heutigen Frankreichs.* Ein Beitrag zur Zeitgeschichte, Leipzig, 1842.—270, 455

Steuart, J. *An Inquiry into the Principles of Political Œconomy: being an Essay on the Science of Domestic Policy in Free Nations*, Vols. 1-2, London, 1767.—491

Stirner, M. *Der Einzige und sein Eigenthum*, Leipzig, 1845.—270

Strauss, D. F. *Das Leben Jesu*, Tübingen, 1835-1836.—247

Strodtmann, A. *Gottfried Kinkel. Wahrheit ohne Dichtung. Biographisches Skizzenbuch*, Bd. 1-2, Hamburg, 1850-1851.—229-242, 244-247, 256

Struve, A. *Erinnerungen aus den badischen Freiheitskämpfen*, Hamburg, 1850.—263

Struve, G. von. *Abschiedsbrief Struve's Havre, 7. Oktober 1849.* In: *Deutsche Londoner Zeitung*, No. 238 (supplement), October 26, 1849.—264

— *Erster Versuch auf dem Felde des deutschen Bundesrechts, betreffend die verfassungsmässige Erledigung der Streitigkeiten zwischen deutschen Bundesgliedern*, Bremen, 1830.—261

— *Geschichte der drei Volkserhebungen in Baden*, Bern, 1849.—262

— *Die Grundrechte des deutschen Volkes*, Birsfelden bei Basel, 1848.—262

— *Grundzüge der Staatswissenschaft*, Bd. 1-4, Mannheim, Frankfurt a. M., 1847-1848.—280

— *Die neue Zeit. Ein Volkskalender auf das Jahr 1.* (Vom 21. März 1850 bis 20. März 1851 der alten Zeit.) Herisau, 1849.—264

— *Weltgeschichte in 9 Büchern.* 7. bis auf die neueste Zeit fortgeführte Ausg. in 6 Bdn., Coburg, 1864.—262, 263

Sue, E. *Les mystères de Paris.*—442

Szemere, B. *Graf Ludwig Batthyány, Arthur Görgei, Ludwig Kossuth. Politische Charakterskizzen aus dem Ungarischen Freiheitskriege*, Hamburg, 1853.—532

— [Letter to the editor of *The Morning Chronicle.*] In: *The Morning Chronicle*, February 21, 1853.—515

Tacitus, C. *Annales*, Lipsiae, 1834.—503

Tausenau, K. *The German Agitation Union of London.* In: *The Leader*, No. 73, August 16, 1851.—320

Tausend und eine Nacht. Arabische Erzählungen. Deutsch von Alexander König. Neue, verb. Aufl., durchges. von Fr. Herring. Bd. 1, Brandenburg (n.d.).—410

Thiers, L. A. [Speech in the Legislative Assembly on May 24, 1850.] In: *Le Moniteur universel*, No. 145, May 25, 1850.—189

— [Speech in the Legislative Assembly on January 17, 1851.] In: *Le Moniteur universel*, No. 18, January 18, 1851.—129, 134

— [Speech in the Legislative Assembly on November 17, 1851.] In: *Le Moniteur universel*, No. 322, November 18, 1851.—123

Tooke, Th. *A History of Prices, and of the State of the Circulation, from 1793 to 1837;* preceded by a Brief Sketch of the State of the Corn Trade in the last two Centuries, Vols. 1-2, London, 1838.—362

— *A History of Prices, and of the State of the Circulation, in 1838 and 1839*, London, 1840.—362

— *A History of Prices, and of the State of the Circulation, from 1839 to 1847 Inclusive*, London, 1848.—362

Venedey, J. *Preussen und Preussenthum*, Mannheim, 1839.—277

Verity, E. A. [Speech at a Ten-Hours' meeting, at Burnley, on February 18, 1853.] In: *The People's Paper*, No. 42, February 19, 1853.—526

[Vidil, J.]. [*Au rédacteur du journal "La Patrie", le 8 mars 1851.*] In: *La Patrie*, No. 69, March 10, 1851.—296

Voltaire, F.M.A. *L'enfant prodigue.*—307

Wermuth, Stieber, W. *Die Communisten-Verschwörungen des neunzehnten Jahrhunderts.* Im amtlichen Auftrage zur Benutzung der Polizei-Behörden der sämmtlichen deutschen Bundesstaaten auf Grund der betreffenden gerichtlichen und polizeilichen Acten dargestellt, Th. 1-2, Berlin, 1853-1854.—417, 418

Willisen, K.W. von. *Theorie des grossen Krieges, angewendet auf den russisch-polnischen Feldzug von 1831*, 2 Th., Berlin, 1840.—313

Wood, Ch. [Speech at an election meeting in Halifax on July 6, 1852.] In: *The People's Paper*, No. 12, July 24, 1852.—338
— [Election speech in the Halifax District on January 3, 1853.] In: *The Times*, No. 21316, January 4, 1853.—499

DOCUMENTS

Accounts Relating to Trade and Navigation. For the Eight Months Ended September 5, 1852. In: *The Economist*, No. 476, October 9, 1852.—362

An Act for the Amendment and Better Administration of the Laws Relating to the Poor in England and Wales (1834).—358

An Act to Amend the Acts Relating to Labour in Factories (1850).—525

An Act to Authorize for One Year, and to the End of the Then Next Session of Parliament, the Removal of Aliens from the Realm (1848).—538

An Act to Limit the Hours of Labour of Young Persons and Females in Factories (1847).—524

An Act to Provide for More Effectual Inquiry into the Existence of Corrupt Practices at Elections for Members to Serve in Parliament (1852).—342

An Act to Reduce the Duties on Newspapers and to Amend the Laws Relating to the Duties on Newspapers and Advertisements (1836).—540

The Affectionate and Christian Address of Many Thousands of the Women of England to Their Sisters, the Women of the United States of America. In: *The Times*, No. 21268, November 9, 1852.—487

The Affectionate and Christian Address of Many Thousands of the Women of the United States of America to Their Sisters, the Women of England. In: *The Times*, No. 21324, January 13, 1853.—487

Allerhöchster Erlass vom 8. November 1848, betreffend die Bildung eines neuen Staatsministeriums und die Ernennung des General-lieutenants Grafen v. Brandenburg zum Präsidenten desselben. In: *Gesetz-Sammlung für die Königlichen Preussischen Staaten*, Berlin, No. 51, 1848.—67

Allgemeines Gesetz wegen Anordnung der Provinzialstände. Vom 5ten Juni 1823. In: *Gesetz-Sammlung für die Königlichen Preussischen Staaten*, No. 13, 1823.—18

[An Appeal of the Committee for German Affairs to the Germans.] Published in the article "Die Flüchtlinge in England". In: *Bremer Tages-Chronik*, No. 534, March 28, 1851.—297, 298

Assisen-Procedur gegen D. Herm. Becker und Genossen. Anklage wegen hochverrätherischen Complottes. In: *Kölnische Zeitung*, October 5-November 13, 1852.—380, 386, 405-57

[A Bill of Indictment on the Franco-German Conspiracy. An exposition.] In: *Le Moniteur universel*, No. 58, February 27, 1852.—414

Bonaparte, L.-N. [*Le président de la République au peuple français.*] Paris, le 13 juin 1849. In: *Le Moniteur universel*, No. 165, June 14, 1849.—135
— *Lettre adressée par le président de la République au lieutenant-colonel Edgar Ney, son officier d'ordonnance, à Rome, le 18 août 1849.* In: *Le Moniteur universel*, No. 250, September 7, 1849.—138
— *Message du président de la République française à l'Assemblée législative* [*le 31 Octobre 1849*]. In: *Le Moniteur universel*, No. 305, November 1, 1849.—137, 140
— *Message du président de la République* [*à l'Assemblée législative*], *le 12 novembre 1850.* In: *Le Moniteur universel*, No. 317, November 13, 1850.—152, 170
— *Réponse* [*au discours du maire de Dijon au banquet offert par la ville à M. le Président de la République, le 1 juin 1851*]. In: *Le Moniteur universel*, No. 154, June 3, 1851.—171
— *Message du président de la République* [*à l'Assemblée législative*], *le 4 novembre 1851.* In: *Le Moniteur universel*, No. 309, November 5, 1851.—177
— [Speech at the ceremony of giving prize medals for the London Industrial Exhibition delivered on November 25, 1851.] In: *Journal des Débats*, November 26, 1851.—179

— *Proclamation du président de la République, le 2 décembre 1851.* In: *Le Moniteur universel*, No. 336, December 2, 1851 (Supplément extraordinaire) and No. 337, December 3, 1851.—180
— [Decree on the procedure of the plebiscite issued on December 2, 1851.] In: *Le Moniteur universel*, No. 338, December 4, 1851.—184
— [Notification on the organisation of a consultative commission.] In: *Le Moniteur universel*, No. 337, December 3, 1851.—180
— [Decree amending the procedure of the plebiscite issued on December 4, 1851.] In: *Le Moniteur universel*, No. 339, December 5, 1851.—184

Botschaft an die zur Vereinbarung der Verfassung berufene Versammlung vom 8. November 1848. In: *Verhandlungen der constituirenden Versammlung für Preussen*, 1848, VIII, Berlin, 1848.—67

Code Napoléon, Paris und Leipzig, 1808.—188, 190, 211

Code pénal, ou code des délits et des peines, Cologne, 1810.—157, 400, 404

Le Comité Central démocratique européen, aux allemands. In: *La voix du proscrit*, No. 4, November 17, 1850.—283

Constitution de 1848, Paris, 1848.—76, 114-19, 131

[Decision of the Prussian Constituent Assembly of November 15, 1848, declaring the exaction of taxes illegal until it is in a position to continue its sessions in Berlin unhindered.] In: *Verhandlungen der constituirenden Versammlung für Preussen*, 1848, IX (Supplement Band), vom 9. November bis zur Steuerverweigerung, Leipzig, 1849.—67

[*La déclaration de la commission du Banquet des Egaux du 1 mars 1851.*] In: *La Patrie*, March 7, 1851.—296

Déclaration de la Montagne au peuple français, Paris, 12 juin [1849]. In: *Le Peuple,* No. 206, June 13, 1849.—131

[Decree of the Baden Provisional Government reducing customs duties, September 22, 1848.] In: *Republikanisches Regierungs-Blatt,* No. 1, September 22, 1848.—263

Décret accordant la grâce à 4312 condamnés politiques [le 2 février 1853]. In: *Le Moniteur universel,* No. 35,. February 4, 1853.—509

Décret relatif aux cautionnements des journaux et écrits périodiques, 9-12 août 1848. In: *Collection complète des lois, décrets, ordonnances, règlemens et avis du Conseil d'État....* Par J. B. Duvergier. T. 48, Paris, 1848.—213

Décret relatif à la repression des crimes et délits commis par la voie de la presse du 11-12 août 1848. In: *Collection complète des lois, décrets, ordonnances, règlemens et avis du Conseil d'État....* Par J. B. Duvergier. T. 48, Paris, 1848.—213

Edikt über die Finanzen des Staats und die neuen Einrichtungen wegen der Abgaben u.s.w. Vom 27sten Oktober 1810. In: *Gesetz-Sammlung für die Königlichen Preussischen Staaten,* Berlin, No. 2, 1810.—18

[*Erklärung betreffend den Einfluss der Beschlüsse der constituirenden Nationalversammlung auf die Verfassungen der einzelnen deutschen Staaten vom 27. Mai 1848.*] In: *Stenographischer Bericht über die Verhandlungen der deutschen constituirenden National-versammlung zu Frankfurt a. M.,* Bd. 1, Frankfurt am Main, 1848.—41

Exports of British and Irish Produce and Manufactures from the United Kingdom. An Account of the Exports of the Principal Articles of British and Irish Produce and Manufactures in the eleven months ended December 5, 1852. In: *The Economist,* No. 490, January 15, 1853.—478

Frankfurter Protokolle—see *Verhandlungen der deutschen verfassunggebenden Reichsver-sammlung zu Frankfurt am Main*

Friedrich Wilhelm IV. *Thronrede Sr. Majestät des Königs am 11. April 1847.* In: *Der erste Vereinigte Landtag in Berlin 1847,* Th. 1, Berlin, 1847.—20

Gesetz, betreffend die Dienstvergehen der Richter und die unfreiwillige Versetzung derselben auf eine andere Stelle oder in den Ruhestand. Vom 7. Mai 1851. In: *Gesetz-Sammlung für die Königlichen Preussischen Staaten,* 1851, No. 13.—210, 400

Gesetz, betreffend die Grundrechte des deutschen Volkes [vom 21. Dezember 1848]. In: *Die Grundrechte des deutschen Volkes, mit dem dazu gehörigen Einführungs-Gesetze,* Leipzig, 1849.—76

Gesetz über die Aufhebung des Unterthänigkeitsbandes und die Entlastung des bäuerlichen Besitzes [vom 9. September 1848]. In: *Wiener Zeitung,* No. 246, September 10, 1848.—34

Gesetz vom 16. Juni 1849 über die Bildung der Volkswehr. In: *Stenographischer Bericht über die Verhandlungen der deutschen constituirenden Nationalversammlung zu Frankfurt am Main,* Bd. 9, Frankfurt am Main, 1849.—93

Gesetz wegen Anordnung der Provinzialstände für das Königreich Preussen. Vom 1sten Juli 1823. In: *Gesetz-Sammlung für die Königlichen Preussischen Staaten,* Berlin, 1823, No. 13.—17

Handels- und Zoll-Vertrag zwischen Seiner Majestät dem Könige von Preussen und Seiner Majestät dem Kaiser von Oesterreich. Vom 19. Februar 1853. In: *Gesetz-Sammlung für die Königlichen Preussischen Staaten,* Berlin, 1853, No. 28.—537

Königliches Rescript [dissolving the Hungarian Diet and appointing the Croatian Ban Jellachich Civic and Military Governor of Hungary, October 3, 1848]. In: *Wiener Zeitung,* No. 275, October 5, 1848.—56

Loi qui modifie la loi électorale du 15 mars 1849, 31 mai-3 juin 1850. In: *Collection complète des lois, décrets, ordonnances, règlemens et avis du Conseil d'État....* Par J. B. Duvergier. T. 50, Paris, 1850.—145, 213

Loi sur le cautionnement des journaux et le timbre des écrits périodiques et non périodiques du 16-23 juillet 1850. In: *Collection complète des lois, décrets, ordonnances, règlemens et avis du Conseil d'État....* Par J. B. Duvergier. T. 50, Paris, 1850.—145, 213

Loi sur l'enseignement du 15-27 mars 1850. In: *Collection complète des lois, décrets, ordonnances, règlemens et avis du Conseil d'État....* Par J. B. Duvergier. T. 50, Paris, 1850.—140

Loi sur la presse du 27-29 juillet 1849. In: *Collection complète des lois, décrets, ordonnances, règlemens et avis du Conseil d'État....* Par J. B. Duvergier. T. 49, Paris, 1849.—213

Loi sur les boissons du 20-21 décembre 1849. In: *Collection complète des lois, décrets, ordonnances, règlemens et avis du Conseil d'État....* Par J. B. Duvergier. T. 49, Paris, 1849.—140

[Manifesto of the Central Committee of European Democracy, November 13, 1850.] In: *La voix du proscrit,* No. 4, November 17, 1850.—283

[Manifesto of the European Committee of the Democratic Émigrés, November 10, 1850.] In: *Le Constitutionnel,* November 18, 1850.—293

[Motion for a revision of the Constitution, tabled at the sitting of the Legislative Assembly in France on June 2, 1851.] In: *Le Moniteur universel,* No. 154, June 3, 1851.—168

Parliamentary Intelligence. House of Lords, Thursday, February 10. In: *The Times,* No. 21349, February 11, 1853.—510

Patent wegen Einberufung des Vereinigten Landtages. Vom 8. Februar 1847. In: *Der Erste Vereinigte Landtag in Berlin 1847,* Th. 1, Berlin, 1847.—19

[*Provisorische Vorschrift über die Presse vom 31. März 1848.*] In: *Amtsblatt zur Wiener Zeitung,* No. 92, April 1, 1848.—54

[*Provisorische Wahlordnung zur Verfassungs-Urkunde vom 25. April 1848* vom 9. Mai 1848.] In: *Besondere Beilage zur Wiener Zeitung,* No. 131, May 11, 1848.—54

Reichsgesetz über die Wahlen der Abgeordneten zum Volkshause. [Vom 27. März 1849.] In: *Reichsgesetz über die Wahlen der Abgeordneten zum Volkshause,* Frankfurt a.M., 1849.—76

Reichs-Verfassung für das Kaiserthum Oesterreich. Vom 4. März 1849. In: *Wiener Zeitung,* No. 57, March 8, 1849.—74

[Resolution of the Constituent Assembly of France on the Roman expedition, adopted on May 7, 1849.] In: *Le Moniteur universel,* No. 128, May 8, 1849.—123

The Revenue. An Abstract of the Net Produce of the Revenue of Great Britain in the Years and Quarters ended 5th January, 1852, and 5th of January, 1853, showing the Increase or Decrease thereof. In: *The Economist*, No. 489, January 8, 1853.—478

Statuten des Kommunistischen Bundes (1. Dezember 1850).—399

Verfassung des deutschen Reiches vom 28. März 1849. In: *Verhandlungen der deutschen verfassunggebenden Reichsversammlung zu Frankfurt am Main*, Bd. 4, Frankfurt am Main, 1849.—76

Verfassung-Urkunde des Oesterreichischen Kaiserstaates [vom 25. April 1848]. In: *Wiener Zeitung*, No. 115, April 25, 1848.—54

Verfassungs-Urkunde für den preussischen Staat. [Vom 5. Dezember 1848.] In: *Preussischer Staats-Anzeiger*, No. 216, December 6, 1848.—67, 69

Verhandlungen der deutschen verfassunggebenden Reichsversammlung zu Frankfurt am Main. Hrsg. auf Beschluss der Nationalversammlung durch die Redactions-Commission und in deren Auftrag von dem Abgeordneten, Prof. Dr. K. D. Hassler, Bd. 1-4, Frankfurt am Main, 1849.—65

Verordnung, betreffend die Auflösung der zur Vereinbarung der Verfassung berufenen Versammlung. Vom 5. Dezember 1848. In: *Gesetz-Sammlung für die Königlichen Preussischen Staaten*, No. 55, Berlin, 1848.—67, 69

Verordnung über die zu bildende Repräsentation des Volks. Vom 22sten Mai 1815. In: *Gesetz-Sammlung für die Königlichen Preussischen Staaten*, No. 9, 1815.—18

Verordnung über die Bildung eines Ausschusses der Stände des Königreichs Preussen. Vom 21. Juni 1842. In: *Gesetz-Sammlung für die Königlichen Preussischen Staaten*, No. 20, Berlin, 1842.—18

Verordnung über die Bildung des Vereinigten Landtages. Vom 3. Februar 1847. In: *Der Erste Vereinigte Landtag in Berlin 1847*, Th. 1, Berlin, 1847.—19

Verordnung wegen der künftigen Behandlung des gesammten Staatsschulden-Wesens. Vom 17ten Januar 1820. In: *Gesetz-Sammlung für die Königlichen Preussischen Staaten*, No. 2, 1820.—17, 18, 19

Victoria, R. *A Proclamation [against Roman Catholic Processions]*, June 15, 1852. In: *The Times*, No. 21143, June 16, 1852.—344

Wahlgesetz für die zur Vereinbarung der Preussischen Staatsverfassung zu berufende Versammlung. Vom 8. April 1848. In: *Gesetz-Sammlung für die Königlichen Preussischen Staaten*, No. 12, Berlin, 1848.—37

ANONYMOUS ARTICLES AND REPORTS
PUBLISHED IN PERIODIC EDITIONS

Allgemeine Zeitung, No. 70, March 10, 1844: *Frankreich. Die ersten Proben der deutsch-französischen Jahrbücher.*—269
— No. 273. September 30, 1851, Beilage: *Köln, 26. September.*—97

The Daily News, October 12, 1852 (leader).—370, 371

— January 27, 1853 (leader).—500
— February 23, 1853 (leader).—523

The Economist, No. 388, February 1, 1851: *France.—The Triumph of the President.*—170
— No. 431, November 29, 1851: *France.—The Political Dissensions.*—170, 173
— No. 435, December 27, 1851: *Louis-Napoleon's Policy.*—173
— No. 437, January 10, 1852: *The Spirit of the Annual Trade Circulars. The Year That Is Past.*—175
— No. 463, July 10, 1852: *The Elections.*—350
— No. 465, July 24, 1852: *The Results of the Elections.*—352
— No. 467, August 7, 1852: *The Cost of a New Parliament.*—343, 344
— No. 475, October 2, 1852: *Lord John Russell and the Democracy.*—365
— No. 475, October 2, 1852: *Mr. Henley and Pauperism.*—357
— No. 489, January 8, 1853: *Business in 1852.*—478, 480, 481, 482
— No. 489, January 8, 1853: *The Bank Rate of Interest.*—483
— No. 489, January 8, 1853: *Spirit of the Trade Circulars.*—481, 482
— No. 491, January 22, 1853: *Agriculture. The Season.*—500
— No. 491, January 22, 1853: *The Bank of England and the Rate of Discount.*—501
— No. 491, January 22, 1853: *The New Ministry and Parliamentary Reform.*—499
— No. 494, February 12, 1853: *Effects of Emigration on Production and Consumption.*—528, 531

Frankfurter Postzeitung, No. 39 (Beilage), February 15, 1853: *Report from Berlin, February 13, 1853.*—515

The Galway Mercury, February 5, 1853: *State of the Country.*—529

The Globe, September 28, 1852 (leader).—371

The Guardian, No. 357, October 6, 1852: *The Week.*—369

Kölnische Zeitung, No. 51, February 28, 1852: *Report from Paris*, February 25, 1852.—223, 415

The Leader, February 19, 1853: *Kossuth and the Milan Revolt.*—515

Lloyd's Weekly Newspaper, No. 516, October 10, 1852: *Mr. Hume's "Rope of Sand".*—365

The Morning Advertiser, January 26, 1853 (leader).—500
— February 5, 1853 (leader).—504

The Morning Chronicle, October 5, 1852 (leader).—371

The Morning Post, October 7, 1852 (leader).—370
— March 10, 1853 (leader).—538
— March 18, 1853: *Political Excitement in Sicily.*—536

Neue Preussische Zeitung, Nos. 165, 166, July 20, 21, 1850: [Report on the suppression of the *Abend-Post*].—307

Northampton Mercury, December 18, 1852: *Death from Destitution.—Cosgrove.*—484-85

The People's Paper, No. 23, October 9, 1852: *Lord Derby and the People.*—366, 367
— No. 12, July 24, 1852: *The Halifax Election.*—338-40

The Sun, January 6, 1853: *Money and Commercial News.*—483

The Times, No. 21160, July 6, 1852: *Election Bribery and Corruption.*—342
— No. 21227, September 22, 1852: *Cotton Manufactures.*—360
— No. 21245, October 13, 1852: *Prussia (from Our Own Correspondent)*, Berlin, October 9.—378

— No. 21270, November 11, 1852: *Prussia (from Our Own Correspondent). Berlin, November 7.*—453
— No. 21316, January 4, 1853 (leader).—471
— No. 21334, January 25, 1853: *Amateur Hanging.*—495
— No. 21343, February 4, 1853 (leader).—504
— No. 21344, February 5, 1853: *Social Soirée of Reformers at Manchester.*—505-07
— No. 21349, February 11, 1853 (leader).—512
— No. 21350, February 12, 1853 (leader).—516
— No. 21352, February 15, 1853 (leader).—516
— No. 21368, March 5, 1853 (leader).—538-39

INDEX OF PERIODICALS

Christoterpe. Ein Taschenbuch für christliche Leser—a literary journal of pietist orientation published in Tübingen in 1833-53 by Albert Knapp.—235

Le Constitutionnel—a daily published in Paris from 1815 to 1817 and from 1819 to 1870; in the 1840s it spoke for the moderate Orleanists, during the 1848 revolution for the monarchist bourgeoisie (the Thiers party), and after the 1851 coup d'état for the Bonapartists.—196, 293

Correspondent—see *Der Deutsche Correspondent*

The Daily News—an English liberal newspaper, organ of the industrial bourgeoisie; appeared under this title in London from 1846 to 1930.—206, 207, 353, 368, 370, 371, 378, 379, 469, 474, 500, 502, 515, 523, 532, 536

La Démocratie pacifique—a Fourierist daily edited by Victor Considérant and published in Paris from 1843 to 1851.—132

Der Deutsche Correspondent—a German-language newspaper published in Baltimore.—311, 325

Deutsche Jahrbücher für Wissenschaft und Kunst—a Young Hegelian literary and philosophical journal published in Leipzig from July 1841 under the editorship of Arnold Ruge. Earlier (1838-41) it appeared under the title *Hallische Jahrbücher für deutsche Wissenschaft und Kunst* (q.v.). In January 1843 the journal was closed down by the Saxon Government and prohibited throughout Germany by order of the Federal Diet.—265, 266, 268

Deutsche Londoner Zeitung. Blätter für Politik, Literatur und Kunst—a literary and political weekly published by German refugees in London from April 1845 to February 1851. It was edited by the petty-bourgeois democrat Ludwig Bamberger and supported financially by the deposed Duke Charles of Brunswick. Ferdinand Freiligrath was a member of the editorial board from 1847 to 1851. The newspaper carried a number of works by Marx and Engels.—264, 276, 279, 301

Deutsche Schnellpost für Europäische Zustände, öffentliches und sociales Leben Deutschlands—organ of the German moderate democratic émigrés in the USA published twice weekly in New York from 1843 to 1851. In 1848 and 1851 its editor was Karl Heinzen; in 1851 Arnold Ruge was also on its editorial board.—278, 290, 293, 301, 302, 303, 311, 316, 323, 325

Deutscher Musenalmanach—a literary journal published in Leipzig from 1832 to 1838 by Adelbert von Chamisso and Gustav Schwab.—235

Deutscher Zuschauer—a radical weekly published by the petty-bourgeois democrat Gustav Struve from December 1846 to April 1848 in Mannheim and from July to September 1848 in Basle.—262, 263, 264, 281, 294, 298, 301

Deutscher Zuschauer. Neue Folge—a newspaper published in Mannheim by the petty-bourgeois democrat Florian Mördes. As distinct from the above weekly, it bore the subtitle *Neue Folge* (New Series), and had its own numbering.—262

Deutsch-Französische Jahrbücher—a German-language yearly published in Paris under the editorship of Karl Marx and Arnold Ruge; only the first issue, a double one, appeared in February 1844. It carried a number of works by Marx and Engels.—269

Deutschland—a democratic newspaper published twice weekly under the editorship of Harro Harring in Strasbourg from December 1831 to March 1832.—285

SUBJECT INDEX

Holy Roman Empire of the German Nation (962-1806)—18, 24, 76

Hungary—26, 28-29, 31, 41, 46-49, 51, 56, 60-63, 71-72, 355, 513
   See also *Emigration* (Hungarian); *National liberation war of 1848-49 in Hungary; Revolution of 1848-49 in Hungary*

I

Idealism—402, 496
   See also *Hegel*
Interests
   — material—8, 130, 131, 139, 173, 328, 364
   — class—8, 15, 31-32, 89, 95, 111, 130, 133, 146, 160, 165-66, 172-73, 213, 216, 218, 221, 328, 330, 337, 346, 364, 389, 506, 519, 603
   — material interests as the basis of class struggle—216
   — and the state—139, 165, 171, 186, 334
   — their expression in ideology and theory—128, 130, 143
   — opposing interests and struggle between them—12, 128, 133, 164, 166, 168, 187, 191, 216, 221

Ireland—201, 349, 352, 357, 366, 462, 474-75, 477, 486, 493, 503-04, 524, 528-30

Italy—26-27, 50, 287, 354-56, 508, 513-15, 532, 536-37
   See also *Bourgeoisie, Italian; Emigration* (Italian); *Literature* (Italian); *Revolution of 1848-49 in Italian states; Working class in Italy; "Young Italy"*

J

Jesuits—121, 141
Jews—30, 44, 257, 512, 522-23
June insurrection of the Paris proletariat in 1848—51, 53, 68, 110, 111, 113, 118, 120, 124, 134, 136, 180, 213, 214

L

Lancashire—208
Landed property—7, 11-12, 26, 104, 128, 166, 190, 192, 195, 216, 488-94
Landowner—7, 26, 128, 165, 213, 328, 525

Land rent—26, 128, 327-28
Legislation, bourgeois—115, 185, 346, 493
   See also *Power, legislative and executive*
Liberalism—9-10, 20, 39, 96, 112, 142-43, 388, 446
Liberal Party (England)
   — its foundation—349, 351-52, 373-74, 376, 464, 499, 500
Literature—14, 28, 30
   — French—196, 260, 269
   — German—14, 229-30, 237-39, 240-41, 243-45, 256, 266
   — Italian—274, 310, 315, 326, 539
   See also *Poetry*
London—8, 12, 208
Lumpenproletariat—110, 143, 149, 155, 182, 193-95, 217, 313

M

Machines, machine production—29, 200, 360-61, 365, 479-80, 525, 529
Manchester School, the—327, 333-34, 367, 372, 375, 379, 474, 478, 499, 506, 525, 526
Material conditions of the life of society—6, 10-11, 29, 128, 187, 189, 200-01, 446, 496
Materialism
   — its opposition to idealism—402
Migration of peoples—531
Monarchy—5, 9-10, 166, 185
   — absolute—15, 16, 18, 23-24, 26-27, 35, 39, 127, 134, 166, 185
   — constitutional (bourgeois)—13, 14, 82, 110, 127, 129, 134, 166-67, 186, 278
Mortgage
   — as form of capitalist exploitation of small peasants—141, 190, 195, 216, 564

N

Nation—6, 12, 27, 42, 46, 51, 71, 88, 109, 185, 200, 215, 334, 337, 389, 403, 514
National liberation movement—45, 536
National liberation war of 1848-49 in Hungary—48-49, 56, 59, 61-64, 70, 83, 85, 90, 300
National question—26, 44-45, 49-50, 536
Nineteenth century—10
Nobility (aristocracy), German—7, 13, 44, 331, 400, 457